WAY BEYOND COMPARE

WAY BEYOND COMPARE

Volume One: 1957–1965

THE BEATLES' RECORDED LEGACY

JOHN C. WINN

THREE RIVERS PRESS
NEW YORK

Published in the United States by Three Rivers Press, an imprint of the Crown Publishing Group, a division of Random House, Inc., New York.
www.crownpublishing.com

Three Rivers Press and the Tugboat design are registered trademarks of Random House, Inc.

Originally published in slightly different form by Multiplus Books, Sharon, VT, in 2003.

Library of Congress Cataloging-in-Publication Data

Winn, John C.
Way beyond compare / John C. Winn.—1st ed.
p. cm.
Includes bibliographical references and discography.
1. Beatles—Discography. 2. Beatles—History—Chronology. I. Title.
ML156.7.B4W55 2008
782.42166092'2—dc22 2008034072

ISBN 978-0-307-45157-6

Printed in the United States of America

Design by Nancy Beth Field

10 9 8 7 6 5 4 3 2 1

First Three Rivers Press Edition

This book is dedicated to my father.
I apologize for all the times I made fun of you
for taking so long to write a book.
Now I know.

CONTENTS

FOREWORD

I've been in the business of Beatles research for thirty years. I don't often broadcast this because those who hear it usually react with the same question: "They were together for only ten—how can it take so long to find out what they did?"

There are a number of reasons, but primary among them is that the Beatles left behind a diverse and intricately woven collection of material, and it's never been possible to say "we have it all" (let alone the oh-so-foolish "we know it all") because new discoveries are unearthed on a regular basis. Since the Beatles scarcely went a day without being recorded some way or another, there's a vast amount of information to assess and slot into the chronological framework in which it will best make sense.

A quest for knowledge accompanied the Beatles' rise and, I've come to realize, goes right back to their beginning. It wasn't just from the moment they first scorched through the music scene in 1963–64 that fans wanted to find out all they could about them. It was also true in 1961 and 1962, when the Beatles were a rock-and-roll group whose appeal hadn't yet broken out beyond Liverpool and Hamburg. The earliest fans set the tone, and, if you know where to look, there exist documents, photos, lists, and letters setting out much about the Beatles' performing and private lives from before anyone else knew them. It could have been the trousers that invoked this reaction, but more likely it was the Beatles' thrilling talent, their personalities, their charisma. In other words, it's who they were that raised—and still raises—the unending questions.

Back in 1987–88, I wrote *The Beatles Recording Sessions,* a book that took readers inside the previously closed archive at Abbey Road and revealed what went on each time the Beatles set foot inside that special North London studio. For the first time, details about the Beatles' great body of recorded work became known: when songs were recorded, how long they took to complete, how they were put together. For some, the book answered every question; for others—John C. Winn certainly among them—it merely created a new set of questions: How did this data marry to the considerable collection of officially unissued recordings that somehow or other had emerged from the archives? And what new knowledge and appreciation could be gleaned from combining the recordings and the facts?

In *Way Beyond Compare* and its companion volume, *That Magic Feeling,* Mr. Winn draws upon every conceivable source to paint an indispensable and absorbing chronicle of the Beatles and their work. And this goes way beyond their extraordinary albums and singles. With astounding speed, once they became nationally and internationally popular, a mountain of audio material began to accumulate—broadcasts, interviews with journalists, concert tapes, private home recordings, press conferences, and more, material that has circulated among fans for decades, usually with little accompanying information. With the home-video age, the 1980s, an immense amount of TV, film, and newsreel footage was added to the pile, for the Beatles were also being followed by cameras much of the time.

It takes a rare and special kind of mind to sift through it all, to research and inquire, catalog and chronicle, assess and contrast, identify and label, and to fit all the myriad pieces into the vast jigsaw puzzle that is the Beatles' career. John C. Winn is that person, and he's done it with a rare skill and intelligence. That vast mountain of once-unidentified audio and video material now makes sense, and it has been set down in a style that is perfectly readable, written with character and refreshing consistency. Winn has also scrutinized every interview and every press conference—no task for the halfhearted, I can assure you—and reported the essence of everything that was said. For the music, Winn has earned his stripes by carefully analyzing recordings, noting the variations in a song's performance, and assessing its musical progression.

The net result is a significantly important contribution to the knowledge and understanding of the Beatles, of inestimable value to me in my daily work—I keep it right on the desk—and nothing less than essential for anyone, now and in the future, who seeks to know more about the Beatles, to learn what audio and visual material was captured, what survives (thankfully, most of it does), and where to find it.

The Beatles were not only the best, they consistently brought out the best in the people around them. John C. Winn's remarkable work is proof that their potent force continues absolutely undiminished.

Mark Lewisohn
London

Mark Lewisohn is the author of *The Beatles Recording Sessions, The Complete Beatles Chronicle,* and other books, and coauthor of *The Beatles' London.* He is presently researching and writing a comprehensive narrative history of the Beatles and their times, to be published in three volumes by Crown.

INTRODUCTION

Why?

"Many people ask what are Beatles? Why Beatles?" If you're reading this book, the first answer should be clear, but the second is a fair question. Some people want to fill the world with Beatle volumes. If I turn my chair slightly, I can see about seventy-five from where I'm sitting.

And what's wrong with that? Think of the recent *1* collection of the Beatles' number 1 hits. All the marketing in the world wouldn't push a CD of thirty-five-year-old songs to the top of the charts around the world, and keep it there for weeks, if the music wasn't durable. New generations are interested in hearing these recordings, collecting them, and examining the circumstances surrounding them.

As far as John, Paul, George, and Ringo were concerned, their music was made to be enjoyed, not scrutinized, and it's a testament to the quality of their work that "She Loves You" still gives me a rush after hearing it sung and played forty different ways. If the music is all you're interested in, you'll find plenty about that in these pages. But most books stop there and only examine the nonmusical elements of the Beatles' career in strictly sociological terms.

Imagine, if you will, a newly uncovered film clip of Tchaikovsky conducting his *Pathétique* Symphony; a tape of an interview with Beethoven explaining the composition of one of his piano sonatas; a recording of Mozart holding a press conference. Isn't it likely that the Beatle equivalents of these will be a lot more instructive and valuable in two hundred years' time than, for instance, a slightly alternate mix of "I Call Your Name"? Spoken words and film/video are two woefully underexplored areas of Beatle recordings, and this book is a first step toward rectifying that imbalance.

I tried to make this book detailed enough for hardcore collectors but with a narrative flow that more casual fans would find engrossing. I found that the recordings themselves ended up telling the Beatles' story for me, once I arranged them chronologically and set them in the context of the group's career. The tapes and films chart the group's progress from naive amateurs to cynical professionals, from exuberant imitators to self-assured innovators.

Reading about these recordings is one thing, but nothing compares to hearing and seeing them for yourself; to this end, I've done all the preliminary looking and listening for you, so you'll know where to find the material and what to take note of when you acquire it and can inspect it firsthand.

What?

The purpose of this work in simplest terms is to identify, compile, catalog, delineate, describe, and compare all available Beatles recordings.

"Available" means a recording officially released on LP, CD, audio or videotape, or any other medium with an audio or moving visual component; or any recording on the above media either semiavailable to the public (promotional discs or videos) or broadcast on radio or TV and simultaneously captured for posterity; or any recording never meant for public consumption but sold or traded in bootleg form, including privately traded video or audio tapes widely available in collectors circles. In purely practical terms, what this means is everything I could get my hands on, but I believe I've had access to 99 percent of all recordings not locked away in a vault or in someone's high-level collection. If I haven't personally heard or viewed it, I declined to include it unless provided strong evidence that it was indeed in circulation.

Beatles means John Lennon, Paul McCartney, George Harrison, and Ringo Starr, as a group, individually, or any combination thereof. "All recordings" means every recording prior to and including April 1, 1970, which includes new sound added by one or more of the Beatles either instrumentally or vocally (sung or spoken), or which captures the image of one or more Beatle on film or videotape.

Probably the largest omission is the lack of any footage, dialogue, and non-lip-synced music from the group's feature films, namely *A Hard Day's Night* and *Help!* The reasons are twofold. First, unlike their music and spontaneous interview remarks, there is little to be gained by examining footage of the group reading lines written for them by others.

The second reason for the no-film rule was that most of the dates for filming of particular scenes are not known precisely enough (particularly the non-location shoots) to warrant their inclusion in a work attempting to show chronological development of the group as artists and individuals. Never mind the fact that we don't know which lines of dialogue were overdubbed during postproduction!

Another realm of recordings not included is songs written or produced by a Beatle for another artist, unless they actually contribute vocally or instrumentally as well. These just don't fall under the definition of "all recordings" (see above).

Partially thanks to the pioneering of the Beatles themselves, the messy issues of remixing and recording variations rear their ugly heads when compiling a work such as this. Basically the question is: To what degree should these different soundscapes arranged from the exact same pieces of physical tape be separated and scrutinized as individual entities? How important is it that one mix of a Beatles song has two extra handclaps? Well, it became increasingly important later in their career when they became personally involved in the remix process and their personal tastes dictated the mixing differences. Unfortunately, it also became more complicated in the later period as more tracks were added to the tape machines and experimentation flourished; the result was a sharp increase in the number of variables to be changed from mix to mix.

All alternate mixes done from the original multitrack tapes for official releases (records or videos) are given individual subentries. No variations in soundscape done accidentally at the mastering or pressing stage in any country are included as discrete subentries, nor are those done purposely outside of EMI, Apple, or the original studio of the recording and without the group's knowledge and/or approval. The best example of the latter is the echo added to many early tracks by Capitol U.S.A. These oddities and anomalies are occasionally mentioned in the body of the text, however. Fake, simulated, or "rechanneled" stereo tracks, even those done at EMI, are avoided wherever possible, unless it is either the only source of a recording or of extra importance for some reason.

How?

As a collector, I've tried to write the kind of book I've always wanted to see, so while the format may be intuitive for like-minded readers, others may be scratching their heads upon first glance. The more you examine the book, the more familiar you will become with its characteristics and quirks, and the easier it will become to use.

Let's break down a typical entry:

6. Studio session P, G

The header contains a number (sequential within each chapter—this would be the sixth entry for that year), followed by a categorical designation for the entry. When fewer than all four Beatles participate in a recording, I've also included the capital letters of their first names (Paul and George in this instance). For this purpose, Pete Best and Jimmy Nicol count as official members, and all studio sessions for Beatle product are exempt from the rule (thus the entry for "Yesterday" is not labeled with a "P," even though Paul is the only Beatle to sing or play).

Here are some definitions of the categories I've used:

Studio session: Audio recordings (musical or spoken) made in a professional location for the purpose of record release.

Location recordings: Audio recordings (musical or spoken) made in a nonprofessional location for the purpose of record release.

Composing tape: Songwriting or rehearsal sessions recorded in a nonstudio location for personal reference.

Home demo: Finished musical performances in nonstudio locations made for personal reference or for other artists/listeners.

Concert: Any live performance before an audience, not specifically for a TV or radio show, captured on audio or film/videotape.

TV/radio performance: Usually denotes musical performance, but can include acting or other creative contributions. Any appearance exclusively for a series or documentary in either medium that does not consist solely of an interview.

Documentary footage: Film or videotape recorded professionally for inclusion in an official production.

Amateur footage: Home movies and any other film recorded for noncommercial purposes.

Newsreel footage: Catchall term for film recordings, often in a raw or unedited/unproduced state, not specifically for broadcast in a particular TV show or documentary. This can include film screened in cinemas as legitimate newsreels, or offcuts and full reports from local television stations.

TV feature: A program or segment comprised of various clips such as interviews, concerts, and newsreel/documentary footage.

TV/radio coverage: On-the-spot reporting from a live event other than a performance or press conference/interview.

Promo clip: Forerunners of today's music videos, these are fully produced and edited film or videotape performances of individual songs usually not made for exclusive broadcast on any single program.

Interview: Conversation recorded on audio or film/videotape; further defined as a TV interview or a radio interview if it was broadcast exclusively or primarily in either medium.

Open-end interview: Conversation recorded on audio in which only the answers are retained, leaving space for a generic DJ or reporter to overdub questions in his own voice.

Press conference: Audio or visual recording of one or more Beatles taking questions from a number of journalists at once, as opposed to a one-on-one interview.

Speech: Any spoken-word audio recording that doesn't otherwise fall under any of the aforementioned categories.

Obviously, some of these may overlap; for instance, a concert may also have been filmed for newsreels.

Date:
Time:
Location:
Producer:
Host:
Interviewer:
Broadcast:
Length:

These are all fairly straightforward, but note that the date of an entry is the *final* date new sound was added to a recording. For instance, most of the song "Slow Down" was recorded June 1, 1964, but it wasn't completed until George Martin's piano overdub three days later; thus it falls under June 4. Under **Location,** "EMI Studio 2" should be taken to read Abbey Road Studio 2, London; similar shortcuts are used for John's ("Kenwood"), George's ("Kinfauns"), and Ringo's ("Sunny Heights") London homes.

[A.] Zip Your Zucchini—takes 2–6 (stereo) (3:55)
[B.] Zip Your Zucchini—take 17 (mono) (2:19)
[C.] Zip Your Zucchini—RM8 (2:14)
Mixed: 30 January 1964

Studio session subentries are generally grouped into blocks of raw sessions followed by finished mixes. For the hypothetical song above, we have a continuous stereo recording of five takes, a mono recording of a later take, and a finished mono mix created January 30, 1964. (RM stands for remix mono; RS for remix stereo.) For concert recordings and TV/radio performances, the songs are listed in the likely order of performance. "Intro" and "outro" can consist of stage patter or merely audience screaming between songs. All timings in this book are meant to be approximate, not definitive; when faced with different lengths on various sources, I always went with the recording closest to the presumed correct pitch.

RELEASE HISTORY

1964: **C** was released on a single and is available on a CD single of the same title.

1976: **A** and **B** surfaced on the vinyl bootleg *Beatles Tut-Tut Album* in very good quality.

The release history is an attempt to show the genealogy of each recording. It always includes the first appearance, whether on a legitimate or bootleg source, any subsequent upgrades in sound quality or length, and the currently available commercial issues. Sound quality assessments are obviously subjective and are meant for comparative purposes only.

If you come across any unfamiliar terms or jargon, a glossary is included at the end of the book. Reading an entry for an interview or video and not sure if it's the same one in your collection? The following online resources may help:

Beatles Spoken Word Transcriptions
(http://members.aol.com/dinsdalep/interdex.html)

Beatles on Video
(http://mapage.noos.fr/beatlesonvideos/index.htm)

Any questions, corrections, comments, or additions? Drop me a line at DinsdaleP@aol.com—I'm always glad to talk Beatle.

ACKNOWLEDGMENTS

Although I had to do all the dirty work myself, such as transcribing press conferences, this book would simply not exist without the support and help of a lot of other people.

First and foremost are Scott Raile and John McEwen. Scott has given me invaluable feedback on the majority of the manuscript, and he has always been there to nitpick over the finer points of arcane Beatle trivia over the last six years. Were it not for John McEwen, you'd be reading a guide to audio recordings only—his expertise in the field of Beatles video and generosity in sharing the material are unparalleled.

Other fellow Beatle fans and authors who provided encouragement, recordings, and facts include Mark Ashworth, Chazz Avery, Andrea Bucchieri, Jay Donnelly, Harald Gernhardt, Don Giller, Ted Greenwald, Randy Hall, Chris Hanzl, Walt Janeck, Mike Johnson, LRE King, Katz Kisaki, Tim Kocher, Allan Kozinn, Jason Kruppa, Mark Lewisohn, Chip Madinger, Warren Raab, Tim Riley, Bamiyan Shiff, Doug Sulpy, Dirk Van Damme, and Michael White.

Special thanks to Mark Lewisohn for his munificent foreword, and to my agent, Matthew Elblonk, for his persistence in getting this revised edition published.

A tip of the hat to Andrew Croft for helping to launch my writing career in the pages of his *Beatlology* magazine. Thanks to all my friends who have talked Beatles with me over the years: Oliver Graham, Chris Mirski, Dominic Robillard, Karyn O'Bryant, and especially Abby Dees. Lots of love to my parents, grandparents, and Aunt Cathy and Uncle Jim for helping to raise a fine Beatlemaniac.

Finally, eternal gratitude to my best friend, Janis—for believing in me, and giving me the confidence to have faith in myself and my abilities.

1957–1962: WHO WAS TO KNOW?

1. Concert J

Date: 6 July 1957
Time: 8:45–10:30 p.m.
Location: St. Peter's Church Hall, Woolton, Liverpool
Producer: Bob Molyneux

[A.] Puttin' on the Style (1:40)
[B.] Baby Let's Play House (0:28)

What are the odds? Not that a sixteen-year-old John Lennon and a fifteen-year-old Paul McCartney would meet at a church fête and go on to conquer the music world, but that someone would be there to record Lennon's band, the Quarry Men, that very day. After all, of the dozens of shows the Quarry Men played from 1957–1959, this is the only one for which a tape has surfaced. Not only that, there are no other known recordings of a Beatle performing in front of an audience prior to 1962!

Without knowing the rich history behind it, the recording itself (or what we have of it) is distinctly underwhelming: the distant *thumpa-thumpa* of Colin Hanton's drums and Len Garry's tea-chest bass, with a higher-pitched but unmistakably nasal John Lennon vocal cutting through the murk. His and Eric Griffiths' guitars, Pete Shotton's washboard, and Rod Davis' banjo are essentially inaudible, but judging by John's vocal pitch, they performed both songs in the key of G major.

"Puttin' On the Style" was a skiffle standard popularized by Lonnie Donegan, whose other numbers featured heavily in the Quarry Men's repertoire ("John Henry," "Railroad Bill," "Diggin' My Potatoes," "Lost John," "Cumberland Gap," "Midnight Special," and of course "Rock Island Line"). They also played a few rock numbers that day; John recalled singing Gene Vincent's "Be-Bop-A-Lula," while Paul has said he heard John sing the Del-Vikings' "Come Go with Me," substituting his own words for the lyrics he hadn't deciphered.

Maybe that explains why Paul was able to impress John by playing a word-perfect rendition of Eddie Cochran's "Twenty Flight Rock" backstage between the Quarry Men's two sets that day. In the afternoon, they had played outdoors, but moved inside the church hall for the grand dance that evening. Also attending the dance was amateur recording enthusiast Bob Molyneux, whose mother owned a shop in Woolton. He switched on his portable Grundig TK8 reel-to-reel machine and pointed the handheld microphone in the direction of the stage.

The tape captured performances by the George Edwards Band as well as their support act, the Quarry Men Skiffle Group. In the months afterward, Molyneux copied portions of the recordings to a separate 3-inch reel and erased the original tapes. By 1963, the Beatles were making a splash across Great Britain, and Molyneux checked the recordings to discover that two songs from the Quarry Men's set had been preserved—"Puttin' On the Style" and a rendition of Elvis Presley's "Baby Let's Play House." He apparently tried to contact John (via Ringo) to see if he was interested in the tape, but never received a reply, so the tape went into storage for the next thirty years.

All three verses of "Puttin' On the Style" have surfaced over the years, beginning with the second verse in 1994, in which John sings lyrics updated by Donegan to change the "pair of horses" and "whip" to a "hot-rod car" and "yellow gloves." In 2007, on the fiftieth anniversary of the performance, BBC Radio aired the song's first verse (played at a slower tempo), along with 28 seconds of "Baby Let's Play House." The final verse of "Puttin' On the Style" appeared shortly thereafter, from an offline recording apparently taped at an EMI exhibit.

RELEASE HISTORY

1994: The Bob Molyneux tape, along with the Grundig reel-to-reel recorder used to tape it, was auctioned by Sotheby's on September 15. EMI acquired the lot for £78,500, but neglected to release it as part of the *Anthology* CD or video projects. A poor-quality 27-second excerpt of **A** stems from a sample tape circulated to the media, which took a surprisingly long time to reach bootleg. It finally appeared on the 1998 bootleg CD *Puttin' On the Style.*

2007: **B** and a further 29 seconds of **A** were broadcast on BBC Radio 2's documentary *The Day John Met Paul.* The remaining 44 seconds of **A** surfaced online the same year, in truly dismal quality. Both songs appear on the CD-R *Strong Before Our Birth.*

2. Studio session

Date: spring–early summer 1958
Time: afternoon
Location: P. F. Phillips Studio, Liverpool
Producer: Percy Phillips

[A.] That'll Be the Day (2:06)
[B.] In Spite of All the Danger (2:43)

Over the winter of 1957–58, various Quarry Men dropped out, while new guitarist Paul McCartney inducted his schoolmate George Harrison, the youngest but most musically dedicated band member. With Colin Hanton on drums and John "Duff" Lowe on piano, the core lineup of John, Paul, and George gathered outside the Hippodrome Cinema on a cold, wet morning midway through 1958.

Their destination was the nearby home of Percy Phillips, who had professional recording equipment installed in his drawing room, which he would operate for a small fee. The Quarry Men scraped together the necessary seventeen shillings and sixpence needed to cut a 78 rpm single. For one pound, they could have gone to tape first, which would have allowed for editing, but they opted for the budget method of recording directly onto a 10-inch shellac disc via an MSS disc-cutting machine.

For the A-side, they chose the first big hit from their idol Buddy Holly, "That'll Be the Day," with John singing lead, Paul harmonizing, and George playing the guitar solo (spurred on by a shout of "honky tonk!" from an unidentified Quarry Man). The B-side was an original composition: Paul's "In Spite of All the Danger," a ballad fashioned after Elvis Presley's "Trying to Get to You." It's a charming performance, with John continually missing his vocal entrance cues, Paul adding "wah-wah" backing vocals, and George playing another solo (enough to garner him co-composer credit on Paul's handwritten disc label).

The song actually ran on for 3:25, long enough to cause Mr. Phillips to signal the boys frantically that the disc was running out of room, but for release on *Anthology 1,* it's been edited by 42 seconds (the edit removes a repeated verse and chorus). "Day" is performed in the key of A major, while "Danger" is in E, including the elusive B7 chord the Quarry Men had ridden clear across town to obtain.

When the disc was finished, they paid Phillips (though he later claimed they had only 15 shillings with them and had to pay the balance later) and secured the sole copy of the disc. John kept it first, and it passed from band member to band member, even getting broadcast over the PA at a local factory, before ending up in John Lowe's linen drawer.

In July 1981, Lowe made noises about auctioning the disc but was served with an injunction by Paul to keep him from selling it until he could make an offer of his own. Lowe eventually accepted a generous amount, and Paul took possession, having copies made so the songs could be played without further degrading the valuable original. He played a segment of **A** on a TV documentary in 1985 (see release history), but it wasn't until 1995 that the world would hear the full A-side and edited B-side. Portions played in the *Anthology* documentary do not suffer from the heavy noise reduction heard on the *Anthology 1* CD.

RELEASE HISTORY

1985: On September 12, BBC TV's *Arena* broadcast a documentary about Buddy Holly, coproduced by McCartney Productions, Ltd. Paul appeared on the show talking about his love for Holly and played a 70-second excerpt of **A,** strumming along on acoustic guitar. This source was copied the following year on the bootleg LP *That'll Be the Day: The Music That Inspired the Beatles.*

1995: **A** and **B** were released on *Anthology 1.* The CD-R *The Beatles Complete • July 6, 1957, to April–May 1960* (part 1) uses composites of both songs from this source and the versions on the *Anthology* soundtrack that haven't been subjected to noise reduction.

3. Home demo

Date: ca. April 1960
Location: 20 Forthlin Road, Liverpool

[A.] Instrumental #1 (7:45)
[B.] Instrumental #2 (11:10)
[C.] Instrumental #3 (aka "Turn the Switches Off") (4:58)
[D.] Cayenne (2:27)
[E.] Come On People (aka "That's an Important Number") (7:49)
[F.] I Don't Need No Cigarette Boy (5:56)
[G.] Well Darling (5:03)
[H.] I Don't Know (5:54)

The so-called Quarry Men rehearsal tapes have a long and confusing history. In late January 1960, John's art college chum Stuart Sutcliffe was persuaded to buy a bass guitar and join the (now drummerless) group, newly dubbed the Beatals. This reel of extremely rough recordings probably preserves some of the earliest rehearsals with Stu, whose rudimentary bass skills are in evidence throughout.

Stu gave a copy of this reel (**A–H**) to his fiancée, Astrid Kirchherr, and it remained in her possession until 1994, when she returned it to George. In the late 1970s, German musician Frank Dostal went into Teldec Studio in Hamburg with this Kirchherr tape and the Braun tape (see following entry) and compiled the two onto a third reel, adding a "simulated stereo" effect. It's most likely via this compilation that the material began to appear on bootlegs in the 1980s.

On November 3, 1994, in an interview with Mark Lewisohn released on the *Anthology* CD, Paul recalled: "Sometimes I'd borrow a tape recorder, a Grundig with a little green eye, and we'd sort of go 'round to my house and try and record little things . . . but those were very much home demos. Very bad quality. But I think a couple of those still exist." Coincidentally, that very month back in Liverpool, Reginald Hodgson came across the very Grundig his brother Charles had loaned to Paul in 1960, complete with a reel of tape.

The Hodgson tape is actually a compilation made by Paul back in 1960 as a gesture of thanks; it reportedly includes three songs from the Kirchherr tape (**C, D,** and **G**), eleven from the Braun tape (see below), and three songs unavailable elsewhere: "When I'm Sixty-four," the instrumental "Winston's Walk," and a surprisingly early version of "Ask Me Why." Reginald's son Peter Hodgson traveled to Sussex on March 27, 1995, to deliver his copy of the tape to Paul, with the result that a 1:13 edit of "Cayenne" appeared on *Anthology 1* later that year.

Paul recalled that the songs were probably taped in the bathroom of his home in Allerton during Easter vacation 1960. He also thinks that his brother Mike plays the occasional percussion that can be heard. With Stuart still learning the ropes, no cover versions were attempted, merely rambling twelve-bar instrumentals, often with John and Paul interjecting lyrics off the top of their heads.

"Cayenne" is apparently not improvised, but rather a very early McCartney instrumental composition. "Well Darling," which has some nice harmonizing from John and Paul, may also be a real attempt at writing a song, although they clearly didn't sweat over the words ("Meanwhile, what do you think?/I think you stink like a sink").

As for the instrumentals, they're not much fun to listen to, compounded by the fact that bootleggers have seen fit for some unfathomable reason to extend nearly all of them by means of editing. The timings above represent the length as heard on bootleg: **A** should last only 5:33 (the edit is at 5:07); **B** is really 6:38 (edit is at 5:24); **C** is actually 3:00 (edit at 2:47). Also note that most of these songs seem to be sped up to run about a half step too high in pitch, although it's doubtful the Beatals' guitars were tuned to exact concert pitch.

RELEASE HISTORY

1987: The vinyl bootleg *Liverpool, May 1960* included **A–C, E, F,** and **H** in fair quality. The same year, **D** and an incomplete version of **G** appeared in similar quality on the bootleg LP *The Quarrymen at Home.*

1995: An incomplete copy of **D** was released on *Anthology 1.*

1996: Slight upgrades of **A–H** appeared from tape source on the bootleg CD *Wildcat!*

2002: A complete version of **G** surfaced on the CD-R *The Braun-Kirchherr Tapes.*

2007: The best-quality tapes of **A–H** appeared on the CD-R *Strong Before Our Birth,* speed-corrected and unlooped.

4. Home demo

Date: ca. July 1960
Location: 20 Forthlin Road, Liverpool

[A.] Hallelujah I Love Her So (2:34)
[B.] One After 909—take 1 (2:24)
[C.] Movin' and Groovin'/Ramrod (3:43)
[D.] Instrumental #1 (11:50)
[E.] You'll Be Mine (1:42)
[F.] unknown/Matchbox (0:58)
[G.] I Will Always Be in Love with You (2:19)
[H.] The World Is Waiting for the Sunrise (2:40)
[I.] That's When Your Heartaches Begin (1:15)
[J.] Instrumental #2 (17:50)
[K.] Wildcat—take 1 (2:32)
[L.] One After 909—take 2 (1:27)
[M.] Some Days (1:38)
[N.] You Must Write Every Day (2:30)
[O.] I'll Follow the Sun (1:46)
[P.] Hello Little Girl (1:53)
[Q.] Wildcat—take 2 (1:23)

In May 1960, the newly christened Silver Beetles (John, Paul "Ramon," "Carl" Harrison, Stuart "DeStael," and drummer Tommy Moore) went on their first semiprofessional tour, backing singer Johnny Gentle in Scotland and performing an opening set of their own. Back in Liverpool in June, they dropped the "Silver," becoming the Beatles at last, and lost their drummer.

During this drummerless period, they recorded another batch of songs on the Grundig at Paul's house. Given the obvious improvement in playing ability, these probably stem from after the tour, and given the louder guitar sound, may have been taped after Paul's June 30 purchase of a Rosetti Solid 7 electric guitar. A copy of this reel was given to Hamburg pal Hans-Walther "Icke" Braun in the spring of 1961. Braun was filmed playing a portion of "I'll Follow the Sun" for German TV in 1966, and he contributed his reel to the aforementioned Dostal compilation, but has held on to his original copy. In addition, the Hodgson tape includes **A, B, E–I, K,** and **N–P** from this reel (**A** and **E** appear on *Anthology 1* from this source).

This is generally a much more professional and entertaining group of songs than the Kirchherr tape, although it does have a pair of second-rate instrumentals: **D,** stretched from 7:15 by bootleggers via an edit at 5:48, and **J,** which ought to last 10:07 but has an edit at 8:24 extending the length beyond the limits of human tolerance. We do get a glimpse into the Silver Beetles' stage repertoire via competent covers of Eddie Cochran (**A**), Duane Eddy (**C**), Carl Perkins (**F**), Fats Domino (**G**), Les Paul/Mary Ford (**H**), Elvis Presley (**I**), and Gene Vincent (**K**).

Most intriguing are another handful of early Lennon/McCartney originals, including two takes of "One after 909," and quite different arrangements of "I'll Follow the Sun" and "Hello Little Girl" (both sounding very much like Buddy Holly). "You'll Be Mine" is an over-the-top parody ballad, while "Some Days" and "You Must Write Every Day" vanished into the mists of time along with other originals from the era such as "Won't You Please Say Goodbye," "Too Bad About Sorrows," "Keep Looking That Way," "Thinking of Linking," "I Fancy Me Chances," "Years Roll Along," "Wake Up in the Morning," "Just Fun," "If Tomorrow Ever Comes," and "Looking Glass."

With the August addition of drummer Pete Best, the Beatles showed enough promise to take up residency in Hamburg, West Germany, *maching shau* for upward of six hours a night until deportations and other intrigues forced them to return home to Liverpool in December.

RELEASE HISTORY

1967: An excerpt of **O,** played directly from Hans-Walther Braun's tape, was aired January 6 on the German TV special *Damals In Hamburg,* which circulates on video.

1987: The vinyl bootleg *Liverpool, May 1960* included **A–D, J, O,** and **Q** in fair quality. The same year **E–G, I, K–N,** and **P** appeared in similar quality on the bootleg LP *The Quarrymen at Home.*

1989: After circulating on tape, **H** surfaced on the 7-inch EP *1989 Beatleg News Christmas Record.*

1995: Incomplete copies of **A** and **E** were released on *Anthology 1.*

1996: Slight upgrades of **A–Q** appeared from tape source on the bootleg CD *Wildcat!*

1997: The bootleg CD *Anthology Plus* included minor upgrades of **G, L, O,** and **P;** these were copied on Black Dog's CD *Puttin' On the Style* the following year.

2002: Slightly longer versions of **A, I, K, L,** and **P** surfaced on the CD-R *The Braun-Kirchherr Tapes.*

2007: The best-quality assembly of **A–H,** including a few previously unbootlegged fragments, appeared on the CD-R *Strong Before Our Birth,* speed-corrected and unlooped.

5. Studio session

Date: 22–23 June 1961
Location: Friedrich Ebert Halle, Hamburg
Producer: Bert Kaempfert

[A.] My Bonnie (Mein Herz Ist Bei Dir Nur) (stereo) (2:39)
[B.] My Bonnie—w/English intro (stereo) (2:38)
[C.] The Saints (When the Saints Go Marching In) (stereo) (3:17)
[D.] Why (Can't You Love Me Again) (stereo) (2:57)
[E.] Cry for a Shadow (stereo) (2:21)

In April of 1961, John, Paul, George, and Pete returned to Hamburg to play at Peter Eckhorn's Top Ten Club, where they occasionally backed British singer and guitarist Tony Sheridan. The move paid off early in May when German bandleader and record producer Bert Kaempfert visited the club and liked what he heard enough to sign Sheridan to a record contract—and hire the Beatles as his backing band. The terms of the Beatles' contract were for a flat fee of 300 DM per man over the period of a year, with no future royalties.

But who cared about the future at that point? Getting signed by a real label was exciting enough, even if it was as an anonymous support group (they would be billed as the Beat Brothers on most releases). Although Stuart Sutcliffe was still occasionally joining the group onstage to play bass, he didn't sign the contract, leaving the bass duties squarely in Paul's hands.

The sessions took place over a period of three days, the first two on the stage of a concert hall, with engineer Karl Hinze manning the portable twin-track stereo recording equipment. The main task was to tape a single, and the traditional song "My Bonnie (Lies over the Ocean)" was chosen for the A-side, in Tony Sheridan's rock/twist arrangement, inspired by Gene Vincent.

The song itself was probably taped first, with George playing the lead guitar apart from Tony's solo (which itself seems to be spliced in from a different take), and very audible screaming from Paul in places. Two edit pieces were then taped as introductions, each being a slow-tempo verse crooned by Tony with wordless vocals from John, Paul, and George. This was done at least twice, in English (**B**) and a German translation (**A**) prepared by Bernd Bertie.

For the B-side, they recorded Tony's arrangement of another standard, "When the Saints Go Marching In," which also happened to be the first number Paul had learned on trumpet. Kaempfert then let them try out some original material, first a Sheridan/Crompton ballad, "Why (Can't You Love Me Again)," often sung in Liverpool by Gerry Marsden. But more importantly, the Beatles were allowed to record an instrumental John and George had written, which they played from time to time in their act.

The song (**E**) had evolved out of John's "messing around" with the vibrato arm (whammy bar) on his Rickenbacker guitar, with George tossing in some ersatz Shadows licks for the main melody. For the session, Tony lent John his Gibson ES-175 to use as a rhythm guitar. A coin toss apparently decided the tune's final name, with "Beatles Bop" losing out to the tongue-in-cheek "Cry for a Shadow." On June 28, John and George signed a contract with Alfred Schacht of Aberbach Music to have the song published under that title (this may also be the date all four Beatles signed the record contract with Bert Kaempfert, which went into effect July 1).

The "My Bonnie"/"The Saints" single was issued in West Germany in October, briefly entering the charts there. More importantly, the release provided the impetus for fans back in Liverpool to order imported copies via Brian Epstein's NEMS record store. By November 6, Polydor had apparently gotten enough orders to make the decision to release the single in the UK, which they did in January 1962 (with version **B** of "My Bonnie" substituted for its German-intro equivalent). On November 9, Brian would visit the Cavern to see what all the fuss was about, and by December 3 he would informally agree to manage them.

The "My Bonnie" single even received an extremely limited release by Decca in the United States in April 1962. Polydor also planned to issue a German single of "Why"/"Cry for a Shadow" in March 1962, but for some reason it was canceled and the songs ended up on a French EP in April.

RELEASE HISTORY

1961: Mono mixes of **A** and **C** were released as a single in Germany, marking the Beatles' debut on commercial vinyl.

1962: Mono mixes of **B** and **C** appeared on a single in the UK; stereo mixes of both were included a few months later on the German LP *My Bonnie.* The same year, mono mixes of **D** and **E** were released on a French EP, *Mister Twist.*

1964: The French 10-inch LP *Les Beatles* included **A** in stereo. The same year, stereo mixes of **D** and **E** were included on the German compilation LP *Let's Do the Twist, Hully Gully, Slop, Surf, Locomotion, Monkey.*

2001: The CD *Beatles Bop—Hamburg Days* contained all the aforementioned mixes, as well as other edits and overdubbed variations.

6. Studio session

Date: 24 June 1961
Location: Studio Rahlstedt, Hamburg
Producer: Bert Kaempfert

[A.] Ain't She Sweet (stereo) (2:09)
[B.] Take Out Some Insurance on Me Baby (stereo) (2:51)
[C.] Nobody's Child (stereo) (3:54)

The Sheridan/Kaempfert sessions apparently moved to a more professional studio for their third day, producing at least three more finished songs, all of which would remain in the vaults until 1964 (see the January 3, 1964, entry for details).

The most important of these was John's rough but superb lead vocal performance on the oldie "Ain't She Sweet." They had been performing Gene Vincent's rock arrangement in the clubs, but the Hamburg audiences spurred them on to create this harder-edged rendition. Tony also sang a Jimmy Reed blues number, "Take Out Some Insurance on Me Baby," sometimes released under the title "If You Love Me Baby."

A third song most likely from the Rahlstedt sessions is the old Hank Snow country ballad "Nobody's Child," a number that future Beatle Ringo Starr would sing as a child to make his mom weep. Although the original documentation has vanished, I place this here rather than with the Ebert Halle sessions because of the louder and deeper bass sound, common to **A** and **B** (and that some have erroneously identified as an upright acoustic bass).

RELEASE HISTORY

1964: **A–C** appeared in mono on the French EP *Ain't She Sweet.* The same year, the French 10-inch LP *Les Beatles* included **A–C** in stereo.

2001: The CD *Beatles Bop—Hamburg Days* contained all the aforementioned mixes, as well as other edits and overdubbed variations.

7. Studio session

Date: 1 January 1962
Time: 11:00 a.m.–noon
Location: Decca Studios, London
Producer: Mike Smith

[A.] **Like Dreamers Do (mono)** (2:34)
[B.] **Money (That's What I Want) (mono)** (2:22)
[C.] **Till There Was You (mono)** (2:58)
[D.] **The Sheik of Araby (mono)** (1:40)
[E.] **To Know Her Is to Love Her (mono)** (2:35)
[F.] **Take Good Care of My Baby (mono)** (2:26)
[G.] **Memphis, Tennessee (mono)** (2:20)
[H.] **Sure to Fall (In Love with You) (mono)** (2:01)
[I.] **Hello Little Girl (mono)** (1:38)
[J.] **Three Cool Cats (mono)** (2:23)
[K.] **Crying, Waiting, Hoping (mono)** (2:01)
[L.] **Love of the Loved (mono)** (1:50)
[M.] **September in the Rain (mono)** (1:54)
[N.] **Besame Mucho (mono)** (2:38)
[O.] **Searchin' (mono)** (3:04)

Even before the Beatles informally accepted his management terms on December 10, 1961, Brian Epstein had been working on their behalf, using his position as a record-store manager as leverage. Early in the month, he brought a copy of the "My Bonnie" single to a meeting with EMI's marketing manager Ron White and played it for him, asking him to ignore Tony Sheridan's vocal and pay attention to the backing group. White politely accepted the disc and said he would pass it on to the A&R men for review.

In the meantime, Brian played the single to Tony Barrow, a music columnist for the *Liverpool Echo* who often wrote sleeve notes for the Decca label. Barrow contacted Decca's A&R chief, Dick Rowe, who agreed to have one of his subordinate producers, Mike Smith, give the Beatles a look at the Cavern Club on December 13. Brian tried to play both sides of the fence, writing to EMI on the eighth to inform them of Decca's possible interest, but Ron White deflated his hopes with a rejection letter on the eighteenth.

Smith, however, liked what he saw enough to arrange for an audition at Decca's London studio on New Year's Day 1962, and the Beatles excitedly rehearsed a suitable repertoire, chosen from among their rock-and-roll favorites and a few novelty- or cabaret-type numbers probably suggested by Brian. The audition lasted about an hour, producing two reels of tape containing fifteen songs. Although the sequence of recording is unknown, the order listed above does jibe with the order of four songs (**A, C, G, I**) performed during their BBC audition a month later.

The performances are best described in John Lennon's own words, which also give further clues to the running order: "I remember when we made our first recording. We didn't sound natural. Paul sang 'Till There Was You,' and he sounded like a woman. I sang 'Money,' and I sounded like a madman. By the time we made our demos of 'Hello Little Girl' and 'Love of the Loved' we were okay, I think."

Paul's quavering vocals on "Like Dreamers Do" and "Till There Was You" did the group no favors, nor did Pete Best's dull drumming on "Money." John does a bit better, although his singing lacks the power familiar from later versions of these songs (he never did figure out Chuck Berry's lyric in "Memphis," though: "'cause my uncle" somehow became the mysterious "smallco"). George is the only one who acquits himself admirably here, with assured vocals and lively playing.

When it was all over, whether due to overoptimism or encouragement from Smith, the Beatles felt sure they'd passed and waited to hear back from Decca. In the meantime, they happily signed a management contract with Brian on January 24, effective February 1 and running five years. It seemed a good sign when Tony Barrow's Disker column ran this bulletin on January 27: "Commenting upon the outfit's recent recording test, Decca disc producer Mike Smith tells me that he thinks The Beatles are great. He has a continuous tape of their audition performance which runs for over 30 minutes and he is convinced that his label will be able to put The Beatles to good use."

RELEASE HISTORY

1973: An extended edit of **L** first surfaced in poor quality on the vinyl bootleg *LS Bumblebee.* An unedited upgrade appeared on a bootleg single two years later.

1977: Fourteen of the Decca audition tracks appeared as bootleg singles on the Deccagone label, issued by a fan club.

1979: The singles were collected with the fifteenth song (**F**) on the bootleg LP *The Decca Tapes.* All were semi-legitimately released over the next few years by various labels, although it's never been clear who owned the rights to release them; the Beatles were under contract to Bert Kaempfert Productions at the time the recordings were made, and Decca apparently relinquished or waived their rights when they handed over the physical tapes to Brian Epstein.

1991: All these songs (**A–O**) appeared from an excellent-quality tape source on the bootleg CD *The Original Decca Tapes & Cavern Club Rehearsals 1962.* As with all previous issues, this ran a half step too slow, but was speed-corrected for Yellow Dog's later issue on *The Ultimate Collection, Volume 1: The Early Years, 1962.* The speed-corrected versions are also on Vigotone's CD bootleg *March 5, 1963, plus the Decca Tape,* with the sound improved slightly, but a tape glitch marring **O.**

1995: Apple released five of these songs (**A, D, I, J,** and **O**) on *Anthology 1,* with the intro to **O** looped and obscured by dialogue.

8. Amateur footage

Date: 10 February 1962 (?)
Location: St. Paul's Church Hall, Birkenhead (?)
Length: 0:30

While waiting for Decca's response, the Beatles had a typically grueling schedule of gigs to keep them occupied. On February 2, half of their twenty-two-song set list at Manchester's Oasis Club consisted of songs from their audition. Three days later, with Pete Best ill, his place at the kit was temporarily filled by a twenty-one-year-old drummer from the Dingle district. John, Paul, and George were already mightily impressed by Ringo Starr's talents playing with Rory Storm and the Hurricanes and had befriended him during their long nights in Hamburg.

One Beatles performance from this era was apparently filmed by an audience member (on color film, no less) and only rediscovered twelve years later. It was auctioned by Sotheby's in September 1996. Judging from the instrumentation and a St. Valentine's heart visible, this was filmed around mid-February 1962. There's a possibility this was filmed February 20 at Floral Hall in Southport.

RELEASE HISTORY

1996: Brief extracts from this silent color footage were aired on ITN News in the UK on May 15 and on *Extra* in the United States May 22.

2004: The complete footage was released on the DVD *Best of the Beatles.*

9. Radio performance

Date: 7 March 1962
Time: 8:00–8:45 p.m.
Location: Playhouse Theatre, Manchester
Producer: Peter Pilbeam
Host: Ray Peters
Broadcast: 8 March 1962, 5:00–5:29 p.m.
BBC Light Programme
Teenager's Turn—Here We Go

[A.] intro (0:07)
[B.] Dream Baby (How Long Must I Dream?) (1:48)
[C.] intro (0:08)
[D.] Memphis, Tennessee (2:13)
[E.] outro (0:01)
[F.] intro (0:11)
[G.] Please Mr. Postman (1:59)
[H.] outro (0:07)

Another sign of Brian Epstein's take-charge management approach was his filing of an application for a BBC Radio audition on January 10. The test took place on February 12 in Manchester, where staff producer Peter Pilbeam listened to four songs and made his infamous pronouncement on the Beatles' vocal capabilities: "Paul McCartney: NO; John Lennon: YES."

His assessment was positive enough to have a contract drawn up February 20 booking the Beatles on a pop show called *Teenager's Turn—Here We Go.* On January 29, the group had been measured for custom-tailored stage suits—leathers and sweatshirts wouldn't do any longer, especially for professional organizations such as the BBC. They wore the new suits for the first time this evening, performing the above three songs to an enthusiastic audience.

Host Ray Peters launched an unforeseeably fruitful Beatles/BBC partnership with the following words: ". . . 'Dream Baby,' which seems to be doing very well for Roy Orbison in the American charts. With Paul McCartney on vocal lead, it's the Beatles!" John took the lead vocal on the group's other two numbers: Chuck Berry's "Memphis, Tennessee" (once again starring "Smallco") and "the record which is doing so much at present for the Marvelettes," one of Motown's earliest successes, "Please Mr. Postman."

RELEASE HISTORY

1982: Incomplete, fair-quality versions of **A** and **B** were broadcast in the radio special *The Beatles at the Beeb.* They were booted the same year on the LP *Wonderful Picture of You,* along with an incomplete copy of **D,** in similar quality.

1988: The complete show (**A–H**) first appeared on the vinyl bootlegs *Meet the Beeb* and *The Beatles at the Beeb w/Pete Best,* still in mediocre quality. The tape source booted on Great Dane's boxed CD set *The Complete BBC Sessions* sounds similar and runs too slow. These sources are missing the first word of **A** and the very end of **H.**

1998: The CD-R *Attack of the Filler Beebs!, Episode 1* contained a rather muffled copy of this show (**A–H**); more complete than elsewhere.

2001: A minor upgrade of the entire show (**A–H**) was included on the CD-R *The Complete BBC Sessions—Upgrade.* It's at the right speed and sounds a lot brighter than any previous release. However, **C** and **H** are both clipped slightly compared to the versions on *Attack of the Filler Beebs!, Episode 1.*

10. Studio session

Date: 6 June 1962
Time: 7:00–10:00 p.m.
Location: EMI Studio 2
Producers: Ron Richards, George Martin

[A.] Besame Mucho (mono) (2:29)
[B.] Love Me Do (mono) (2:30)

On February 6, the other shoe dropped during Brian Epstein's trip to London. Over lunch, Decca's Dick Rowe told him that "guitar groups are on their way out." Rowe tried to smooth things over by hooking Brian up with Tony Meehan, the ex–Shadows drummer and now a record producer, but during their meeting the next morning, the insulting offer became plain: Pay a fee and we'll record your group, but finding someone to release and market it will be up to you.

Desperate, Brian went across town with his copy of the Decca audition tapes and had them transferred to vinyl at EMI's HMV disc-cutting shop, figuring it'd be an easier way to present his clients than playing a Tony Sheridan single. Brian and the Beatles finally caught a break when the disc-transfer engineer, Jim Foy, suggested having the three original Lennon/McCartney compositions published by Ardmore & Beechwood, whose offices just happened to be upstairs in the HMV building.

A disc was cut of the two most promising compositions, "Hello Little Girl" and "Like Dreamers Do," which Brian played for Sid Colman, who in turn agreed not only to consider handling the song publishing, but to arrange a meeting with an EMI A&R man, Parlophone's George Martin. Colman met Martin on February 9 to discuss Epstein's overture, and the next day, buoyed by this turn of events, Brian sent off a terse letter to Dick Rowe at Decca, declining the offer of Tony Meehan's producer-for-hire services and claiming that "the Group have received an offer of a recording Contract from another Company." Nothing like the power of positive thinking!

On February 13, Brian returned to London and met with George Martin. Martin heard something in the recordings that nobody else had—potential, even though his main concern was deciding whether John, Paul, or George would be the "star singer." He agreed to hear them play at Abbey Road Studios, and so Brian wrote to Bert Kaempfert on February 20, asking to extricate the Beatles from their current recording contract.

Here the waters become murky—Martin claims that he first met the Beatles during an audition in March at EMI's Studio 3 (others on the staff confirm the location). However, all written documentation (session fees and recording sheets) point to June 6 as the earliest date the Beatles set foot inside Abbey Road. But as the Decca audition proved, there was no reason an "artiste test" would produce written documentation, and there would be no reason for EMI to foot the bill for so much as a reel of recording tape.

If such an audition did occur, it would have been on February 22, March 27, or April 3, the only free days in the Beatles' schedule for the period in question. By April 11, they were off to Hamburg without a new record contract, only to be met with the horrendous news of Stuart Sutcliffe's death. Brian met with George Martin again on May 9, and whether on the strength of an in-person inspection or a hunch based on hearing recordings, Martin offered Brian a one-year contract. Epstein ran off to send triumphant telegrams to the boys at the Star-Club in Hamburg, and to the *Mersey Beat* paper in Liverpool.

On May 18, Martin submitted an application for a standard, if paltry, contract (with royalties of 1 penny per disc sold), which was approved on the twenty-fourth, and signed by Brian on his clients' behalf June 4. By that time, the Beatles were back in Liverpool, rehearsing at the Cavern Club and determined not to make the same mistakes they had with Decca. Their first proper EMI session took place in Abbey Road's Studio 2 on the evening of June 6.

The recording protocol, written up June 4, specified a three-hour session to record "4 titles—to be determined." Brian had typed up a list of thirty-three suggested candidates, from which three originals and a cover version were selected. "Besame Mucho" was taped first (**A**), the lone holdout from the Decca audition, performed in a slightly different arrangement, less frenetic and with no backing vocals. Paul sounds a lot calmer here as well, but he'd be thrown a curveball on the next song.

Although Martin's assistant, Ron Richards, took charge of the session's start, when he heard "Love Me Do," a simple and catchy song John and Paul had written years earlier, he called his boss into the studio. "Love Me Do" (**B**) had always featured John singing the title refrain alone, but after realizing that the harmonica overlapped with that line, Martin insisted Paul step in and take the role. His shaky singing isn't the only problem with this take, though; John's harmonica playing is a bit stilted, and Pete Best sounds completely lost when switching to a different drum pattern for the middle eight.

The session concluded with "P.S. I Love You" and "Ask Me Why," two more originals completed by John and Paul during their recent Hamburg trip. All four songs were cut onto 7-inch acetates after the session, but only the first two have turned up (the session tape itself is long gone). George Martin was less than thrilled with the material and more importantly, the drumming. On June 26, Ron White sent a letter of apology to Brian for his earlier rebuff. It contained the following passage: "George Martin tells me that he has been suitably impressed with them and has made certain suggestions to you which in his view may improve them still further." These "certain suggestions" would spell an ominous fate for Pete Best.

RELEASE HISTORY

1985: **A** first appeared in excellent quality on the bootleg LP *Sessions,* reportedly from a "private reel" discovered in 1983, not an acetate. It's available on Spank's CD of that title as well as the CD *Ultra Rare Trax, Volume One.*

1995: **A** and **B** were both released on *Anthology 1.* **B** came from an acetate discovered by George Martin's wife in 1994 while cleaning out his closet! The version of **A** prepared by Geoff Emerick for *Sessions* (and released on *Anthology*) has the final line looped to repeat during the fade-out, but an earlier version of *Sessions* circulates that includes the song's true ending (this has yet to be bootlegged).

11. Studio session

Date: 7 June 1962
Location: Studio Rahlstedt
Producer: Bert Kaempfert

[A.] Sweet Georgia Brown (stereo) (2:02)

One potential roadblock to securing the Beatles a record deal was the fact that until June 30, they were still under contract to Bert Kaempfert Productions. Brian worked through the winter and spring to release them from this obligation, which Kaempfert agreed to if they would consent to some final sessions during their next visit to Hamburg. Brian arrived on April 9, a few days ahead of his group, to arrange the details with Kaempfert. Sessions were penciled in for May 28 and 29 in the hopes of accumulating twelve titles for an LP, but these were changed ahead of time to a single May 24 date.

Tony Sheridan was unable to make the session, which began at 6 p.m. with Günther Sörensen engineering. Although Tony wasn't present, the Beatles were joined by pianist Roy Young, who had been playing alongside them during their current Star-Club stint. The backings for at least two numbers were cut by this lineup: "Sweet Georgia Brown" (arranged by Paul) and "Swanee River." The day after this session, the Beatles and Kaempfert signed an agreement terminating their contract.

On June 7, Tony was in the studio to record some German-language songs with the Bert Kaempfert Orchestra, and he used the date to add his vocals on the May 24 backings, probably as twin-track tape-to-tape copies with live overdubs. He apparently assumed it was Paul playing the piano on "Sweet Georgia Brown" (**A**), judging from his exclamation of "Tell it to 'em, Paul!" during the keyboard solo.

This recording was used as filler on an EP before vanishing into obscurity in favor of a newly cut vocal (see the January 3, 1964, entry). "Swanee River" was never released, and the master tapes are probably no longer in existence. However, an earlier recording (December 21, 1961) of Tony and a different Beat Brothers lineup performing "Swanee River" has been released.

RELEASE HISTORY

1962: A mono mix of **A** was released on the German EP *Ya Ya.*

1997: **A** made its stereo debut on the EP *Hamburg Twist,* included in copies of the book *From Cavern to Star-Club.*

2001: The CD *Beatles Bop—Hamburg Days* contained both mixes of **A.**

12. Radio performance

Date: 11 June 1962
Time: 8:45–9:30 p.m.
Location: Playhouse Theatre, Manchester
Producer: Peter Pilbeam
Host: Ray Peters
Broadcast: 15 June 1962, 5:00–5:29 p.m.
BBC Light Programme
Teenager's Turn—Here We Go

[A.] intro (0:06)
[B.] Ask Me Why (2:16)
[C.] outro (0:03)
[D.] intro (0:08)
[E.] Besame Mucho (2:25)
[F.] outro/intro (0:16)
[G.] A Picture of You (2:13)
[H.] outro (0:05)

For their second BBC Radio performance, the Beatles were cheered on by a coachload of fans who had ordered tickets via the Beatles Fan Club. The fans were picked up outside NEMS Records at 6 p.m. and returned at 10:30, paying 10 shillings and sixpence each for the inclusive package. Their enthusiasm is evident on this off-air recording, particularly the clapping along and screaming during George's first BBC vocal, a cover of Joe Brown's hit single at the time, "A Picture of You."

"Ask Me Why" and "Besame Mucho" had just been recorded at EMI; perhaps the Beatles already knew the other two numbers ("Love Me Do" and "P.S. I Love You") were being favored as candidates for release and didn't want to tip their hand before the single was available.

July and early August continued as normal for the Beatles, who performed daily alongside such established artists as Gene Vincent, Acker Bilk, Joe Brown, and Johnny Kidd and the Pirates. But matters came to a head when George Martin informed Brian Epstein that he would definitely be replacing the Beatles' drummer for studio purposes on future sessions. John, Paul, and George reached a mutual decision to replace Pete Best entirely, handing over the onerous task to Brian on August 15, making sure to secure Ringo's services beforehand.

It was an unpopular decision around Merseyside when word spread, particularly among Pete's female admirers. In a letter to a fan dated August 24, George made his predilection clear. "Ringo is a much better drummer, and he can smile, which is a bit more than Pete could do. It will seem different for a few weeks . . . but I think that the majority of our fans will soon be taking Ringo for granted."

RELEASE HISTORY

1982: An incomplete, fair-quality version of **G** was booted on the LP *Wonderful Picture of You.*

1984: **D** and an incomplete copy of **E** surfaced in fair quality on the vinyl bootleg *Directly from Santa Claus.*

1988: The complete show (**A–H**) first appeared on the vinyl bootlegs *Meet the Beeb* and *The Beatles at the Beeb w/Pete Best* in mediocre quality.

1994: Great Dane's boxed CD bootleg *The Complete BBC Sessions* included the entire show from a tape source, but most of it (**D–H**) was "speed-miscorrected" to run a half step too low in pitch.

1998: The CD-R *Attack of the Filler Beebs!, Episode 1* contained a rather muffled copy of this show (**A–H**) at the correct speed.

2001: A minor upgrade of the entire show (**A–H**) was included on the CD-R *The Complete BBC Sessions—Upgrade.* It's at the right speed and sounds a lot brighter than any previous release.

1962: THE TWIST

TIMELINE

August 18 Following an evening rehearsal, John, Paul, George, and Ringo take the stage at Hulme Hall in Birkenhead. The Beatles as the world would know them are born.

August 22 During the group's lunchtime Cavern Club set, camera crews from Granada TV capture the five-day-old Beatles lineup performing a couple of songs specifically for broadcast. One song is eventually aired, but not until November 6, 1963.

August 23 John weds Cynthia Powell at the Mount Pleasant Register Office; Paul is present as a witness, and Brian Epstein and George also attend. The wedding party follows with a celebratory luncheon at Reece's, a Liverpool restaurant (Brian's treat).

September 4 The Beatles' first EMI recording session with Ringo.

September 5 Granada TV sound crews return to the Cavern Club to record new Beatles performances for dubbing onto the poor-quality soundtrack of the film shot August 22.

September 11 The Beatles finish recording their first single for EMI.

October 1 The Beatles sign a five-year management contract with Brian Epstein.

October 5 UK release of "Love Me Do"/"P.S. I Love You" single.

October 6 The Beatles sign copies of their debut single at Dawson's Music Shop in Widnes.

October 9 The Beatles spend their day off in London schmoozing with various journalists.

October 12 Concert at the Tower Ballroom, New Brighton, where the Beatles meet top-billed Little Richard.

October 17 In a performance sadly lost to the ages, The Beatles make their first television appearance, singing "Some Other Guy" and "Love Me Do." The show, Granada TV's *People and Places,* is broadcast live locally from Manchester's Granada TV Centre Studio 4.

October 21 The Beatles attend Billy Fury's concert at the Empire Theatre in Liverpool.

October 26 "Love Me Do" becomes the Beatles' first Top 40 chart entry, at number 27 in the *New Musical Express.*

October 28 Concert at Liverpool's Empire Theatre with Little Richard.

October 30 The Beatles fly from London to Hamburg for a fortnight's stint with Little Richard at the Star-Club.

November 15 The Beatles fly from Hamburg to London.

November 16 The Beatles are interviewed for *Disc* magazine at their Fleet Street offices.

November 23 The Beatles fail a ten-minute audition for BBC TV at Saint James's Church Hall.

November 26 Taping "Please Please Me" and "Ask Me Why" at EMI for their second single.

November 27 Brian signs the Beatles to a music publishing contract with Dick James at James' Charing Cross Road office.

December 2 Concert at Peterborough's Embassy Cinema, backing Frank Ifield.

December 4 The Beatles' first appearance on TV in the London area, lip-syncing both sides of their debut single on ITV's *Tuesday Rendezvous,* broadcast live from Wembley Studio 4.

December 18 The Beatles fly to Germany to begin a two-week engagement at Hamburg's Star-Club, playing every night through the end of the year except Christmas Day. Several sets of the Beatles' performances are taped on amateur equipment.

1. TV performance

Date: 22 August 1962
Time: afternoon
Location: Cavern Club, Liverpool
Broadcast: 6 November 1963, 6:30–7:00 p.m.
Granada TV
Scene at 6:30

[A.] Some Other Guy (2:06)

After Granada TV producers attended the Beatles performances on July 26 and August 1, they decided to film a few minutes of the group's stage show for potential inclusion in a locally broadcast magazine series, *Know the North*. Apparently, nothing was set in stone, no contracts were signed, and even a newspaper ad from August 21 states only vaguely that "The show will be filmed by Granada T.V. cameras with a view to future transmission." Probably due to the poor filming conditions in the Cavern (they did attempt to improve the sound by rerecording the audio portions—see entry for September 5), and the Beatles' lack of a record release, the footage wasn't aired at the time—but luckily it was preserved.

Cavern DJ Bob Wooler's introduction opens the proceedings: "It's the Beatles!" The entire performance of "Some Other Guy" was filmed from the back of the hall and opens with a wide shot of the entire stage before zooming in on Paul and John in turn. The group wears white shirts with identical dark vests and ties; John and Paul share lead vocals. Just after the performance, amid the applause and cheers, a lone wiseguy in the crowd shouts, "We want Pete!," which must have thrilled Ringo to no end.

Following this, the film crew set up at the side of the stage to capture various reverse-angle shots and close-ups of each Beatle to use as coverage, also getting several shots of the audience. During this footage, the Beatles are performing "Money (That's What I Want)," among other songs. Two minutes and fifty seconds of these silent cutaways have recently surfaced from Granada's archive, and they include at least seventy-one individual shots, some split into as many as five pieces.

Close examination of this footage proves that two complete takes of "Some Other Guy" were filmed this day, although only the audio to (presumably) take 2 survives on the soundtrack, as does an alternate intro from Bob Wooler ("At this midday session at the Cavern, we proudly present . . . the Beatles!"). The edit used in *Anthology* has three portions of take 1 inserted: the first 37 seconds, the segment from 1:08–1:12, and the final 23 seconds. Pieces of take 1 can also be seen in the 1969 TV special *Man of the Decade* and the 1971 *Guinness Book* special, *The Record Makers*. The otherwise continuous footage of take 2 used in Granada's *The Early Beatles* has seven insert pieces from 0:32 to 0:45, the last of which is from take 1.

RELEASE HISTORY

Realizing what they had in their archive, Granada finally aired "Some Other Guy" on November 6, 1963, in the show *Scene at 6:30*. The bootleg DVD *The Early Beatles* includes the most complete edit of this performance, as well as the silent cutaways, but the *Anthology* edit does contain unique material.

There is a distinct tape stretch in the soundtrack right at the end of verse 1 that is present on all versions. It must be on the original reel, as even the cleaned-up version in *Anthology* includes the glitch. The best place to find the soundtrack is Silent Sea's CD-R *The Beatles Complete • January 1 to September 5, 1962,* which sonically "irons out" the stretch.

2. Studio session

Date: 4 September 1962
Time: 7:00–11:15 p.m.
Location: EMI Studio 2
Producer: George Martin

[A.] How Do You Do It—RM from take 2 (1:55)
[B.] Love Me Do—RM from unknown take (2:21)
Mixed: 4 September 1962

The story of just how, when, and why the Beatles came to record "How Do You Do It" has evolved over the last thirty years or so. The latest scenario shapes up as follows: The Beatles' first EMI recording session on June 6 convinced producer George Martin of two things. First, drummer Pete Best was unsuitable for studio purposes (the group took care of that by replacing him with Ringo). Second, none of the material offered by the group, original compositions or covers, was strong enough for a debut single. Martin took this problem into his own hands by searching for a promising new song from London's talent pool of songwriters.

Meanwhile, across town, composer Mitch Murray watched as his new song, "How Do You Do It," was demoed by Barry Mason (with instrumental accompaniment from the Dave Clark Five), offered to singer Adam Faith, and turned down. Murray and Mason next brought the demo acetate to EMI's resident rock producer, Ron Richards, who convinced publisher Dick James to purchase the rights to the tune. The acetate sat in Richards' office until sometime after the Beatles' June 6 session, which Richards and Martin coproduced. Both producers agreed the song might be suitable for the Beatles' style and mailed a copy to Liverpool so the band could learn the song in time for a planned September session.

Thus the Beatles were put in the ironic position of having to rearrange a song performed by future chart rivals the Dave Clark Five, and there is evidence that they tried out their new arrangement during July and August performances at the Cavern. The response must not have been overwhelming enough to fill them with confidence, based on the recorded performance they ultimately put in. And they clearly wanted to make it on their own terms, rather than become known for parroting "professional" songwriters' corny fare. However, with no great original songs to draw from, and frightened at the prospect of upsetting the big-time producers who presumably knew what made a hit (which was what they wanted more than anything), they finalized an arrangement of the song with new drummer Ringo in the last weeks of August.

The first three hours of the session, held in Studio 3, comprised rehearsals of six songs, ostensibly to take stock of the candidates for the single release, but in truth more of an audition (embarrassingly enough) for Ringo, who passed for the moment. George Martin emphasized his superiority in the producer/artist relationship, first by letting Richards oversee the rehearsals in his absence, then by buying the group an Italian dinner. Finally, at 7 p.m., Martin was ready to get to work recording the Beatles in Studio 2. Presumably they nailed "How Do You Do It" on the first take, since the handclaps were an overdub, which would have been called take 2.

Having satisfied their producer for the time being, the Beatles more enthusiastically tackled their own composition "Love Me Do" (**B**) next. Legend has it they needed at least fifteen takes just to nail down the rhythm track to Martin's satisfaction, and more than anything it was probably this struggle that caused him to have second thoughts about Ringo's drumming. Engineer Norman Smith recalled that the basic track was edited together from several takes prior to overdubbing, though there is no written evidence and only flimsy aural evidence to support this.

Ringo's performance was an obvious improvement over Best's more mechanical style, helped along by the new arrangement. The rhythm pattern during the instrumental bridge was now smoothed out, and John threw in some harmonica triplets during the song's intro. Handclaps were also overdubbed alongside the harmonica solo to add a bit more texture. The final result, while clearly better than the June 6 recording, left something to be desired in Martin's mind.

Holding off any final decisions, Martin mixed both songs into mono and cut an acetate, mulling it over for a week or so. On September 5, Brian Epstein got a first listen to the results, and on September 7, Mitch Murray did likewise. By September 11, Martin declared "Love Me Do" more suitable to the Beatles' style, and (to his credit) being aware of the Beatles' uneasiness at recording force-fed material, consigned the sole mono mix of "How Do You Do It" (**A**) to the vaults.

It rested there untouched for almost fifteen years, long after the session tapes were scrapped. The composition itself was offered to another Epstein-managed/James-published Liverpool group, Gerry and the Pacemakers, who had no qualms about recording "How Do You Do It" (using basically the Beatles' arrangement, minus harmonies) and taking it to number 1 in the UK charts. Once he decided to chuck "How Do You Do It" and focus on "Love Me Do," Martin ordered up a remake for one week hence, being careful to hire a professional session drummer in the interim, and even more careful not to inform the Beatles of this fact.

RELEASE HISTORY

1962: **B** was released on a single, although later pressings substituted the September 11 remake. As the session and mix tapes were both scrapped, this song has appeared on CD only from vinyl; it's on *Past Masters, Volume One.*

1976: **A** first appeared on a bootleg single in excellent quality.

1983: A 42-second excerpt of **A** was used in the *Beatles at Abbey Road* presentation; it appears from this source on the bootleg CD *Abbey Road Video Show.*

1985: Geoff Emerick's edit of **A** created for *Sessions* began to appear on vinyl bootlegs; it can be heard on Spank's CD of that title. This replaces the line "wish I knew how you do it to me, I'd do it to you" in the final chorus with the line "wish I knew how you do it to me, but I haven't a clue" from the second chorus.

1988: **A** appeared from tape source, in excellent quality, on the bootleg CD *Ultra Rare Trax, Volume One.* It's also on *Unsurpassed Masters, Vol. 1,* running too slow.

1995: Geoff Emerick's edit of **A** was released on *Anthology 1.*

3. Concert

Date: 5 September 1962
Time: evening
Location: Cavern Club, Liverpool
Producer: Gordon Butler

[A.] Some Other Guy (2:14)
[B.] Kansas City/Hey Hey Hey Hey! (1:01)

After reviewing the footage shot August 22, Granada TV decided to return to the Cavern to enhance the soundtrack by retaping it (this time using three microphones rather than one). These recordings could then be dubbed onto the film in order to improve the sonic clarity. Sound engineer Gordon Butler captured two songs on a reel-to-reel at 15 inches per second, then had a 12-inch reference acetate and five 7-inch two-sided acetates pressed. Two of the latter were given to Cavern Club compere/DJ Bob Wooler, who played them to promote the TV appearance that never occurred. Brian Epstein likewise had the bright idea to have a batch of discs manufactured (also double-sided, but with "Some Other Guy" on both sides) and sold exclusively from his NEMS record shop.

This version of "Some Other Guy" (**A**) begins with Wooler's introduction: "[O]kay, this is it, the Beatles sing 'Some Other Guy'!" followed by a count-in from Paul. It is distinguishable from the August 22 recording by Paul's "Yeah!" during the opening bars, as well as the soon-to-be traditional Beatles shouts leading into the guitar solo. There is also no tape stretch at the end of the first verse. As it ends, John laments, "We'll probably have to do it again."

"Kansas City/Hey Hey Hey Hey!" (**B**) opens with Paul's stage announcement ("Had a couple of requests to do a tune called 'Kansas City,' so we'd like to do 'Kansas City'"), followed by the familiar Beatles arrangement of the song itself. Only a portion of this is circulating, from a copy of the acetate auctioned by Christie's in 1993 and purchased by Apple.

NOTE

On September 12 (a Wednesday, the same as August 22 and September 5), the Beatles backed a young female singer, Simone Jackson, at the Cavern. According to a contemporary report in *Mersey Beat,* "the Granada TV Unit were at the Cavern again on the night she appeared." Could this mean more audio or visual recordings of the Beatles at the Cavern are out there waiting to be discovered? Or did the unit merely comprise producers doing advance scouting?

RELEASE HISTORY

1984: The radio special *Sgt. Pepper's Lonely Hearts Club Band: A History of the Beatle Years 1962–1970* included **A,** partially obscured by narration. This version comes from a good-quality acetate auctioned by Sotheby's in September 1983; it has plenty of surface noise and runs too slow. It was copied from this source on the vinyl bootleg *The Stereo Walk.*

1994: The bootleg boxed CD set *The Ultimate Collection, Volume 1: The Early Years, 1962* included a nearly complete version of **A**, with Bob Wooler's introduction (and severe noise reduction), but missing John's final comment.

1995: The truncated **B** first appeared in the *Anthology* documentary (a portion on the TV broadcast, and even more on the home video the following year), a half step too low in pitch. It appears from this source on the CD-R *The Beatles Complete • January 1 to September 5, 1962.*

1998: The bootleg CD *Puttin' On the Style* contained a version of **A** with John's final comment intact but most of Wooler's introduction absent.

2005: The CD-R *Can You Hear Me?* included the most complete edit yet of **A.**

4. Studio session

Date: 11 September 1962
Time: 5:00–6:45 p.m.
Location: EMI Studio 2
Producer: Ron Richards

[A.] P.S. I Love You—RM from take 10 (2:01)
[B.] Love Me Do—RM from take 18 (2:18)
[C.] Please Please Me—RM from unknown take (1:57)
Mixed: 11 September 1962

[D.] Love Me Do—RS from take 18 (fake stereo) (2:18)
[E.] P.S. I Love You—RS from take 10 (fake stereo) (2:01)
Mixed: 25 February 1963

Difficult as it is to believe (and fuzzy as Ringo's and George Martin's memories are on the whole subject), it appears certain that the Beatles' drummer of one month was sandbagged in only his second session. The occasion was a retaping of "Love Me Do" and its flip side, and Ringo arrived fully expecting to play drums. Not only was a professional session drummer waiting when the group walked in, Martin wasn't even present, again handing down production chores to Ron Richards.

After minimal rehearsal with session man Andy White on drums, they began recording "P.S. I Love You" (**A**), a song composed mainly by Paul during their May 1962 Hamburg stint. It had also been taped during the June 6 EMI session, and it's unfortunate that the earlier tape no longer exists; it would be interesting to hear whether they had improved the arrangement or whether Martin simply had a change of heart about the song.

Martin even briefly toyed with the notion of making "P.S. I Love You" the A-side of the single (apparently "Love Me Do" would have been B-side to "How Do You Do It"). Richards supposedly nixed this idea because another song with the same title had already been published. More likely, the Beatles preferred to have a more bluesy, less soppy song played on the radio.

Ringo made sure he was somewhere on the recording, grabbing his maracas and shaking them alongside White's tepid "One-two-cha-cha-cha" drum pattern. Lyrically and musically, the song was decidedly non-groundbreaking; only the vocal arrangement showed some imagination. During the first three choruses, John and George sing key words ("treasure," "words," "home") in backing Paul—however, they sing all the words for the final chorus. Similarly, on the intro, they sing along in unison with Paul, switching to harmony for the phrase "be in love with you." The next two times, the entire verse is backed with harmony. Clearly, however embryonic their songwriting skills were, the Beatles excelled at vocal arrangement from the start.

With George Martin still absent, Ron Richards then presided over the third and final EMI recording session of "Love Me Do" (**B**). Ringo was handed a tambourine, which he duly tapped throughout while Andy White remained behind the drums (photos from the September 4 session show maracas and a tambourine sitting on Ringo's drum kit, so at least we can assume he was using his own instruments). Apart from dropping the idea of handclaps during the solo, this arrangement was identical to the September 4 recording.

Perhaps feeling guilty for belittling Ringo, Martin decided to release the earlier take on the single, changing his mind by the time of their first album release, for which he used this September 11 recording (even mixing a fake "rechanneled" version (**D**) for the stereo pressing).

George Martin finally showed up around the time the session was wrapping up with the Beatles' first attempt to record a new John Lennon composition. "Please Please Me" was originally envisioned at a slower tempo, with dramatic crescendos, à la Roy Orbison. At the September 4 session, the Beatles played this song during their six-song rehearsal/warm-up. At the time, Martin hated the arrangement and told them to pep things up and add some harmonies.

With White still playing drums, an attempt to tape this new arrangement (**C**) concluded the September 11 session. Martin liked what he heard, but thought there was more room for improvement, though not enough time on the clock to work out the problems. It was held over for their second single, taped November 26.

The most obvious difference in this earlier take is the lack of harmonica, but it's impossible to say whether they hadn't yet added this to the arrangement or just didn't bother to overdub it onto what was a rejected recording. The drumming is notably different to Ringo's, lacking the flurries underneath "in my heart" and adding a halfhearted fill bridging "come on" and the title phrase. Paul and George's answer vocals in the middle eight are also absent, replaced by another tame drum fill.

RELEASE HISTORY

1962: **A** was released on the "Love Me Do" single; later pressings also included **B.**

1963: **A** and **B** were released on mono copies of the LP *Please Please Me;* both are available on EMI's CD of that title. **D** and **E** were released on stereo copies of the *Please Please Me* LP.

1995: **C** was released on the CD *Anthology 1,* possibly taken from an acetate auctioned by Sotheby's in 1994.

5. Rehearsal

Date: ca. October 1962
Location: Cavern Club, Liverpool

[A.] I Saw Her Standing There (3:10)
[B.] One After 909—take 1 (3:12)
[C.] One After 909—take 2 (3:17)
[D.] Catswalk—take 1 (1:24)
[E.] Catswalk—take 2 (1:24)

This fascinating rehearsal tape dating from the fall of 1962 features run-throughs of three original group compositions in early versions. The tape is said to have been recorded in the Cavern Club, and the ambiance isn't that far removed from the August and September Cavern recordings (although no audience is present here). Author Mark Lewisohn reports that a jazz musician who played at the club was responsible for unearthing this tape. A check of the Beatles' fall 1962 concert schedule has them playing alongside at least two jazz bands at the Cavern: the Saints Jazz Band (September 23) and the Red River Jazzmen (September 30 and October 7). Note that these are all Sunday night dates; perhaps this was a regular jazz/beat night at the club. Thus it may not be going too far to assume that this entire session was taped one Sunday afternoon before the Cavern had opened for the evening.

Narrowing down the exact date is trickier. Certainly Ringo is the drummer (not only has he confirmed this after hearing the tape, but his voice is audible), so the tape dates from at least mid-August 1962. A famous photograph of John and Paul running through "I Saw Her Standing There" was taken by Paul's brother Michael and dated (by the photographer) September 1962. In front of them is a notebook with the lyrics and chord changes—indicating that they still needed to read along as they played. They seem very familiar with the song on this tape, though the arrangement isn't as polished as on the December 1962 Star-Club recordings. Thus we have a likely range of mid-September through December 18 (the day they left for Hamburg).

"I Saw Her Standing There" is finalized lyrically and structurally at this point. John plays harmonica throughout, rather than guitar, and some have suggested that his "sloppy playing" indicates that he was just learning the instrument. This would mean the tape was recorded prior to June 1962 and "Love Me Do." Actually, I think he simply didn't have a harmonica in the right key! The song is played in E, a key that requires four sharps (F-sharp, G-sharp, C-sharp, and D-sharp). Although he tries to limit his playing to suitable notes (the root, E; the fifth, B; and the bluesy flatted seventh, D), John slips a few times and plays C-natural and F-natural. Not once does he play a sharp or flat, suggesting he was using a C-major harmonica. His relative unfamiliarity with the song probably contributed to his inability to cover up this problem smoothly.

Since John is otherwise occupied, George provides the rhythm guitar, throwing in an occasional lead lick (i.e., following verse 2). When the big moment comes for a guitar solo, it's clear that this is one of George's first attempts, and his playing hangs together by a thread. One subtle difference in the arrangement: During the solo, the chords follow the form of the chorus exactly (E, A, C, E, B, E); on the released version, the leap to C major is omitted for the solo. Paul makes a conspicuous mistake in the second bridge—rather than singing, "Well, my heart went boom," he begins to sing the final verse (John, oblivious as ever, sings along with him). It takes Paul a second to realize that the lyrics don't quite scan ("Well, we danced all night/ And I held her tight"), and he laughs at his error.

Take 1 of "One after 909" follows, and this time it's John's turn to make a howling blunder. In the first middle eight, he sings the second line first, then repeats it again (stumbling over the words and mumbling an aside when he realizes what he's done). The guitar solo follows the same sixteen-bar form as the verses, but lacks the pauses where "move over once" and "twice" would occur. Take 2 of "One after 909" begins with John asking, "Got that beginning still?" before counting in.

Two takes of a McCartney instrumental complete the rehearsal tape. "Catswalk" was later retitled "Catcall" and donated to the Chris Barber Band (Paul contributed to their recording of the song—see the entry for July 20, 1967). Though they had a hit in 1959 as the Chris Barber Jazz Band, I could turn up no evidence that they ever played at the Cavern Club, which would seem to eliminate them as suspects for having unearthed this tape.

"Catswalk" has a surprisingly sophisticated chord structure for such an early tune—in fact, much of the melody is derived from the changes, which come fast and furious (almost one chord change per bar and several modulations of key). The tune begins in Gm and runs through E♭, B♭, D, Cm, C, Fm, A♭, B♭m, and A before it finishes. Since the whole pattern repeats itself once, and the song lasts only 80 seconds, that's an average of just 4 seconds per chord!

As take 1 winds down, Ringo stops playing two bars before everyone else, coming back in briefly when he discovers his error. Just before the tape cuts off, Ringo can be heard commenting, "I finished early." Perhaps they rehearsed the ending again for Ringo's benefit, since Paul can be heard saying, "Well, try a verse," and counting in; unfortunately, the tape was shut off at that point. It starts up again with another count-in, followed by take 2 of "Catswalk." This take is decidedly inferior to the first, particularly George's guitar playing. Paul's bass is almost inaudible through much of take 2.

RELEASE HISTORY

1984: The radio special *Sgt. Pepper's Lonely Hearts Club Band: A History of the Beatle Years 1962–1970* included **C** and **D,** both partially obscured by narration. They were copied from this source on the bootleg LP *Not For Sale.*

1990: The full tape (**A–E**) first surfaced on the bootleg CD *The Cavern Tapes Circa 1962,* which remains the most complete issue. A cleaned-up version on *The Ultimate Collection, Volume 1: The Early Years, 1962* has slightly early fades on a couple of tracks.

6. Radio performance

Date: 25 October 1962
Time: 8:00–8:45 p.m.
Location: Playhouse Theatre, Manchester
Producer: Peter Pilbeam
Host: Ray Peters
Broadcast: 26 October 1962, 5:00–5:29 p.m.
BBC Light Programme
Here We Go

[A.] A Taste of Honey (0:47)

Despite being fragmentary, this poor-quality tape is historically important for being the earliest BBC Radio session to include Ringo. The excerpt of "A Taste of Honey" begins with the second verse and continues to the end; note the audience screaming during the pause following Paul's final "for the HONEY." Since the first recording of "A Taste of Honey" with vocals was released by Lenny Welch on September 17, 1962, the Beatles must have finalized their arrangement quickly and satisfactorily—this version (what we have of it) is very similar to the take issued on *Please Please Me.*

Note that this tape has been previously identified as coming from the episode of *People and Places* that aired October 29, but I've discovered at least two reasons to relabel it. First, at least one electric guitar can be heard in this performance, but Mark Lewisohn implies that John and George are both playing acoustic guitars on that TV broadcast (*The Complete Beatles Chronicle,* p. 83).

Second, Lewisohn confirms that this BBC session was performed in front of a live audience (evident on this tape). He is less clear about whether *People and Places* was taped in front of an audience, but in a radio interview taped two days later (see next entry), Paul comments on their first TV appearance (October 17, also on *People and Places*) and specifically mentions the lack of an audience. It's possible but unlikely that an audience was present for the October 29 taping, done for the same TV show in the same TV studio.

RELEASE HISTORY

1989: **A** first appeared in poor quality (with the last note cut off) on the 7-inch EP *1989 Beatleg News Christmas Record.* Its first CD appearance was on the bootleg *Artifacts;* it also appears on the boxed CD set *Mythology, Volume 1.*

7. Radio interview

Date: 27 October 1962
Time: 8:45 p.m.
Location: Hulme Hall, Port Sunlight, Birkenhead
Interviewers: Monty Lister, Malcolm Threadgill, Peter Smethurst
Broadcast: 28 October 1962
Cleaver and Clatterbridge Hospitals
Sunday Spin
Length: 7:18

Over and above its historical value, this earliest-surviving taped interview with the Beatles is also noteworthy because they hadn't quite perfected their PR game, and some of their earnestly candid answers are charming compared to their future blasé posturing and eventual disgust with talking to the press.

The location was backstage at Hulme Hall just before taking the stage as bill-toppers for a Recreations Association dance; supporting acts can be heard playing in the background throughout the recording. The conversation was recorded for the radio program *Sunday Spin,* limited to closed-circuit broadcasting in Cleaver and Clatterbridge, two local hospitals, and was first broadcast October 28. The interview tag-team consisted of Monty Lister, Malcolm Threadgill, and Peter Smethurst. (The latter two adolescents were brought along to cover "the teenage angle.")

The revelations begin immediately as each Beatle identifies himself and the instruments he plays. When George proclaims himself lead guitarist, Lister asks if that makes him the leader of the group. Paul quickly steps in and states, "John is in fact the leader of the group." The imbalance is made clear when the new boy, Ringo, head still spinning at being thrust into the limelight, says he's been in the group "nine weeks now" (in fact it was ten weeks to the day). Asked if he appears on the Beatles' first single, Ringo confirms, "Yes, I'm on the record," his voice unable to mask the disgust with the way he was almost elbowed from the session completely.

Discussion of an imminent trip to Germany leads Paul to mention their first manager, Allan Williams, offhandedly describing him as "an old agent" (which draws laughter from John and George). Malcolm Threadgill asks a few questions about their brief recording career, inquiring about the Tony Sheridan sessions. Paul describes how the "My Bonnie" single reached number 5 in the German charts and goes on to mention "an EP released in France" by Tony Sheridan.

Paul concludes that he and John have written over one hundred songs together, dismissing half of them as below par, which is saying something considering that the mediocre "Love Me Do" was par for the course to date. Asked about unused compositions, John says they did record another number, but "it wasn't finished enough," and that they plan to take it back next time they go into the studio ("Please Please Me," taped September 11 and remade November 26).

Peter Smethurst asks for the Beatles' impressions of their first TV performance (October 17), and Paul says it was nerve-wracking having two million people watching, even if none of them were physically present in the TV studio. Finally, Lister announces that "Love Me Do" has been requested by patients at Cleaver Hospital, and the Beatles introduce it, sneaking in some last-minute plugs for the single. (John: "Parlophone R4949"; Ringo: "Buy it, folks!")

RELEASE HISTORY

1986: The interview, carefully preserved on a reel-to-reel, was remixed by DJ Roger Scott and pressed onto a flexi-disc sold with copies of Mark Lewisohn's first book, *The Beatles Live!* It's been copied on numerous bootleg CDs.

1995: A small bit of this interview was released on the CD *Anthology 1.*

8. Studio session

Date: 26 November 1962
Time: 6:00–9:45 p.m.
Location: EMI Studio 2
Producer: George Martin

[A.] Please Please Me—RM from edit of unknown takes (1:59)
[B.] Ask Me Why—RM from take 6 (2:23)
Mixed: 30 November 1962

[C.] Ask Me Why—RS from take 6 (2:23)
[D.] Please Please Me—RS from takes 16–18 (1:58)
Mixed: 25 February 1963

At the end of the Beatles' previous studio session, they had attempted to record a newly sped-up arrangement of "Please Please Me." John later explained, "We were getting very tired, though, and we just couldn't seem to get it right."

Two months later, they were back at Abbey Road to record their second single, observed by journalist Alan Smith. The session began at 6 p.m., an hour earlier than booked, with rehearsals of the potential material. They ran through "Tip of My Tongue," a dreadful new composition by Paul that George Martin politely described as "a great number, but we'll have to spend a bit of time giving it a new arrangement." Brian Epstein would later foist the song on a singer in his stable, Tommy Quickly.

The two songs chosen for the single had already been heard by Martin: "Ask Me Why" during the June audition with Pete Best on drums and "Please Please Me" in September. By now, they had polished the latter to a radiant sheen and it became a unanimous choice for the new A-side. It was taped first, beginning just after 8 p.m. Although the original session tapes and sheets are gone, close examination of the mono and stereo mixes, along with knowledge of the procedures used to record "From Me to You," allow for a reasonable reconstruction of events.

The song was taped with instruments (guitars, bass, and drums) on one track of the tape and vocals from John, Paul, and George on the second. Once a suitable rhythm track was perfected, John overdubbed his harmonica phrases via tape-to-tape copying. Including the overdub attempts, the song was completed by take 15. A twin-track master was edited together from at least two takes (the edit at 1:45 is obvious on the *Please Please Me* CD single, but was cleaned up a bit for a new digital master used on *The Beatles' Hits* CD-EP and *The Beatles 1962–1966* CD).

This edited master was mixed into mono (**A**) for single release four days later. Sometime between then and February 1963, the edited twin-track master tape must have been scrapped or damaged. Apparently, this master contained not only second-generation harmonica edit pieces but bits of the "best" rhythm track take as well. So how to produce a stereo mix (**D**) for the *Please Please Me* LP?

George Martin went back to the session tape and found a complete but inferior take of the song. The most obvious error on this take is John's vocal goof on the last verse: "Why do I never even try, girl," but Paul also blows that line the first time around, singing, "Why do you never even try, girl." The bass is also sloppy, missing notes during the "come on" sections, coming in late on the bridge, and dropping out for a moment in the coda.

As this take was lacking harmonica, Martin did a tape-to-tape copy, adding in the harmonica phrases directly from the mono mix and feeding the new sound to the vocal track. Since the two basic takes were performed at slightly different tempos, they would get out of sync quickly, requiring the job to be done in pieces. Take 16 covers the first harmonica piece and ends at 0:31. Take 17 continues through the second and third pieces, but the third is already starting to get delayed (it was also faded down late, so Ringo's drum fill that follows can be heard in both channels, once from each basic take). At 1:16, take 18 begins, carrying us through the fourth and fifth harmonica sections. The last one sounds very strange as it's not only out of sync, but contains the different vocals from the mono mix on top of the vocal track from the alternate take.

Luckily, no such trickery was required for the single's B-side, "Ask Me Why," which was recorded in six takes following a tea break. The song features John singing lead, with Paul and George harmonizing; at the start of each middle eight, John and Paul sing one of those eerily synchronized duets that give the impression of John singing double-tracked. With no overdubs or editing required, stereo mixing (**C**) was a simple matter of copying the twin-track master of the best take. Mark Lewisohn's *The Beatles Recording Sessions* seems to indicate that a new mono mix was done for the *Please Please Me* LP, but I can think of no reason why the mono single mix (**B**) wouldn't have sufficed, nor has anyone detected any difference between the single and mono LP mixes.

George Martin's bold prediction during the November 26 session—"Congratulations, gentlemen, you've just recorded your first number-one single!"—would come true in three short months.

RELEASE HISTORY

1963: **A** and **B** were released on a single and on mono copies of the LP *Please Please Me;* both are available on EMI's CD of that title. **C** and **D** were released on stereo copies of the *Please Please Me* LP.

9. Concert

Date: 28 December 1962 (?)
Time: 3:00–4:00 a.m.
Location: Star-Club, Hamburg

[A.] **Nothin' Shakin' (but the Leaves on the Trees)** (1:14)
[B.] **intro** (1:13)
[C.] **I Saw Her Standing There** (2:46)
[D.] **intro** (0:48)
[E.] **To Know Her Is to Love Her** (3:06)
[F.] **intro** (0:37)
[G.] **Everybody's Trying to Be My Baby** (2:28)
[H.] **intro** (0:50)
[I.] **Till There Was You** (2:02)
[J.] **intro** (0:41)
[K.] **Where Have You Been All My Life?** (2:16)
[L.] **intro** (1:10)
[M.] **Lend Me Your Comb** (1:46)
[N.] **intro** (0:39)
[O.] **Your Feet's Too Big** (2:19)
[P.] **intro** (0:11)
[Q.] **I'm Talking About You** (1:54)

[R.] intro (1:03)
[S.] A Taste of Honey (1:48)
[T.] intro (1:17)
[U.] Matchbox (2:34)
[V.] intro (0:47)
[W.] Little Queenie (3:56)
[X.] intro (1:01)
[Y.] Roll Over Beethoven (2:33)

Accounts and histories of the Star-Club recordings are numerous, confusing, and often contradictory. To make a long story medium-size, toward the final days of their last stint in Hamburg, several of the Beatles' sets were taped, seemingly by chance, alongside performances by the Dominoes and Cliff Bennett and the Rebel Rousers.

Star-Club sound man (and Big Three guitarist) Adrian Barber was working on improving the venue's PA system, and he used a mono recorder (made by Philips, Grundig, or Telefunken, depending on whose account you believe) to record about four hours of material between Christmas and New Year's. The fidelity was extremely limited, due to the use of a single microphone suspended from the ceiling, as well as the slow recording speed, which allowed for more material to be squeezed onto the tape.

The tape(s) ended up with Ted "Kingsize" Taylor, lead singer of the Dominoes, who would later claim that John Lennon accepted payment of a round of drinks in exchange for the right to record the Beatles' performances. George would dispute this claim in court thirty-five years later, but as the group was under contract to EMI at the time, Taylor wouldn't have been able to release them. He tried unsuccessfully to sell the tapes to Brian Epstein the following year, brought them to a Liverpool studio in 1967 or 1968 to look into cleaning up the sound quality, and then left them behind.

In 1972, Taylor retrieved the tapes from the now-unused studio with the assistance of the early Beatles manager Allan Williams. The pair spent the better part of four years hawking the material around to record labels (George and Ringo turned them down on behalf of Apple) and fan conventions before raising interest. In 1976, the mono tapes were copied to a sixteen-track tape in New York, equalized, filtered, and processed into a vaguely "stereo" ambiance for release in 1977.

Much of the material has since surfaced from untampered tapes; although the quality isn't always as good as the officially released portions, hearing the original songs without the distractions of edits, looping, and noise reduction is enlightening and entertaining.

This particular set was probably recorded December 28 (there is a reference on the tape to "Friday"). A running joke in the stage banter has John and Paul wondering whether the German audience knows what they are saying, with John taunting the crowd at one point (**L**): "I don't know whether you can understand me or not . . . but piss off! You got that? Christmas or not." The tape opens with George singing "Nothin' Shakin'," which has a truncated intro, apparently recorded "already in progress."

This version of "I Saw Her Standing There" (**C**) was released with the guitar solo chopped out, probably due to a dropout in the tape source. "To Know Her Is to Love Her" is dedicated to fellow musician Lee Curtis, and "Till There Was You" to Beatles pal Hans-Walther "Icke" Braun, whose girlfriend requested it. Paul's "cha-cha" request announcement (**H**) is falsely edited in front of "Besame Mucho" on the commercial release. John heckles Paul throughout the number. ("He never saw them at all. *Wonderful* roses!")

John takes the lead vocal for "Where Have You Been All My Life" (extended for official release by repeating the solo), a composition by Lennon hero Arthur Alexander. The dedications continue, with "Your Feet's Too Big" going out to barmaid Bettina Derlien, and "A Taste of Honey" to a Scottish lady in the audience.

The main staples are Berry and Perkins, with John, Paul, and George spotlighted for a number each from Chuck ("I'm Talking About You," "Little Queenie," and "Roll Over Beethoven," respectively) and Carl ("Matchbox," "Lend Me Your Comb," and "Everybody's Trying to Be My Baby"). "Roll Over Beethoven" suffers from an amusing false start where George tries to play the opening riff in the key of F major before correcting himself and lowering it to D.

RELEASE HISTORY

1977: Many of these songs were released on the LP *Live! at the Star-Club in Hamburg, Germany, 1962.* The UK version included **A, C** (partial), **E, G, M, O, S, U,** and **W.** The U.S. version dropped **C** and added **I** and **K.**

1985: The vinyl bootleg *Mach Shau!* included much of this show (all but **C** and most of **S**) in good quality.

2008: The Purple Chick CD-R *Star Club* contained the entire concert assembled from the best possible sources.

10. Concert

Date: 25–31 December 1962
Time: evening
Location: Star-Club, Hamburg

- [A.] **intro** (0:04)
- [B.] **Be-Bop-A-Lula** (2:03)
- [C.] **intro** (0:26)
- [D.] **I Saw Her Standing There** (2:55)
- [E.] **intro** (0:40)
- [F.] **Hallelujah I Love Her So** (2:09)
- [G.] **intro** (0:28)
- [H.] **Red Hot** (1:03)

- [I.] **Sheila** (1:58)
- [J.] **intro** (0:42)
- [K.] **Kansas City/Hey Hey Hey Hey!** (2:09)
- [L.] **intro** (0:19)
- [M.] **Shimmy Like Kate** (2:17)
- [N.] **intro** (0:58)
- [O.] **Reminiscing** (1:41)
- [P.] **intro** (0:55)
- [Q.] **Red Sails in the Sunset** (2:20)
- [R.] **intro** (0:13)
- [S.] **Sweet Little Sixteen** (2:48)
- [T.] **intro** (1:11)
- [U.] **Roll Over Beethoven** (2:15)
- [V.] **intro** (0:40)
- [W.] **A Taste of Honey** (1:59)

- [X.] **Ask Me Why** (2:36)
- [Y.] **Long Tall Sally** (1:50)
- [Z.] **Besame Mucho** (2:34)
- [AA.] **I'm Gonna Sit Right Down and Cry (Over You)** (1:42)
- [BB.] **Twist and Shout** (1:26)
- [CC.] **Mr. Moonlight** (2:13)
- [DD.] **Falling in Love Again (Can't Help It)** (2:13)
- [EE.] **I'm Talking About You** (2:01)
- [FF.] **I Remember You** (1:32)

The twenty-one songs listed in this entry comprise one or two further sets from the Beatles' Star-Club stint. As no full source tapes have surfaced, it becomes difficult to determine which songs are from which set, let alone their original recording dates. The most that can be said is that the first four songs (**A–H**) fall in sequence on one set, according to information first published in *Melody Maker* in August 1973.

Allan Williams played the raw tapes to reporter Mike Evans, who described the first few songs he heard in some detail, along with most of the other titles. He wrote that the tapes contained two versions of "Roll Over Beethoven" (both of which have surfaced) and two of "To Know Her Is to Love Her" (only one has surfaced). As there are also dual versions of "A Taste of Honey," "I Saw Her Standing There," and "I'm Talking about You," it makes sense to ascribe one version each to the Christmas and New Year periods alluded to by Ted Taylor.

Hans Olof Gottfridsson's excellent book *From Cavern to Star-Club* assigns the material in this entry to Christmas 1962, and claims they had Christmas Eve off (Mark Lewisohn contradicts this, stating that the twenty-fifth was their sole day off). The book offers no evidence other than Paul's proclamation that "only the Beatles would be playing for you tonight," which could equally apply to December 31. Many sources mention that the Dominoes and the Beatles shared the bill for only a "three-night stand," and Star-Club employee Horst Fascher has stated that only on New Year's Eve did he and brother Fred (a waiter) join the groups onstage to sing.

That's the case with the first number here (**B**), a version of Gene Vincent's "Be-Bop-A-Lula" enthusiastically sung by Fred ("Let's rock again!"). While they wait for Horst to return from the toilet, the Beatles launch into "I Saw Her Standing There" (**D**), ending with Paul's wishing the crowd a happy New Year, and wild cheering for Horst's arrival. The Beatles back Horst on a rendition of Eddie Cochran's version of "Hallelujah I Love Her So" (**F**) and continue their set with George and John trading vocals on an exciting performance of "Red Hot" (**H**), complete with organ solo, unfortunately truncated on the surviving tape.

Paul dubs "Kansas City" (**K**) "a Bach fugue in B minor," and George sings Buddy Holly's posthumous single "Reminiscing" (**O**) for "Mary." Paul announces "the one you've all come for" in dedicating "Red Sails in the Sunset" (**Q**) to Bettina Derlien. "A Taste of Honey" (**W**) is dedicated to Bettina and Horst; midway through, John yells at the clientele to "shut up talking!" It's performed with an extra verse compared to the familiar *Please Please Me* LP rendition, but the ending is cut off on the tape source.

John delights in tinkering with the lyrics, altering "knees" to "nose" in "Mr. Moonlight" and interjecting plenty of "shitty's" in "Shimmy Like Kate." Prior to the latter number, Paul sings a snatch of "South of the Border," and after "Sweet Little Sixteen," someone shouts out a request for the Pat Boone single "Speedy Gonzales," which John surprisingly plays and sings a bit of.

The beginning of "Twist and Shout" (**BB**) is missing entirely. It was extended to 2:04 for release by starting with the solo, jumping back from the last rave-up to the previous one and repeating the end of the song. Similarly, the end of "I'm Gonna Sit Right

Down and Cry (Over You)" and beginning of "I Remember You" weren't captured. The former merely had an unrelated chord tacked on to create a false ending, but major surgery extended "I Remember You" to 1:58 by looping a verse, chorus, and bridge to repeat.

RELEASE HISTORY

1977: Most of these songs were released on the LP *Live! at the Star-Club in Hamburg, Germany, 1962.* The UK version included **B, F, K, M, O, Q, S, U, X–Z,** and **BB–FF.** The U.S. version dropped **BB,** adding **I** and **AA.** See above for details on editing.

1979: An excerpt of **H,** taken from a broadcast on Earth Radio News, was bootlegged on the LP *The Beatles vs. Don Ho.*

1985: The vinyl bootleg *Mach Shau!* included **W** (edited to the ending of **S** in the previous entry) in good quality.

1989: **D** first appeared in good quality on the 7-inch EP *1989 Beatleg News Christmas Record.*

1996: An even longer excerpt of **H** was included on the soundtrack of the *Anthology* home video documentary.

2008: The Purple Chick CD-R *Star Club* contained the entire concert assembled from the best possible sources.

11. Concert

Date: 31 December 1962 (?)
Time: evening
Location: Star-Club, Hamburg

[A.] Road Runner (1:52)
[B.] intro (0:10)
[C.] The Hippy Hippy Shake (1:43)
[D.] outro (0:05)

[E.] intro (0:37)
[F.] A Taste of Honey (1:49)
[G.] intro (0:19)
[H.] Money (That's What I Want) (3:38)
[I.] outro (0:02)

These songs are grouped together as being from the same New Year's Eve set in the book *From Cavern to Star-Club.* As the Beatles take the stage (**A**), John interrupts Paul's attempted stage announcement by repeatedly playing riffs from Bo Diddley's "Road Runner." Manfred Weissleder introduces the group and announces the time as five minutes to midnight. Bits of these riffs and announcements have been released.

Paul orders a round of whiskey for "Tony 'My Bonnie' Sheridan" prior to this rendition of "A Taste of Honey" (**F**), which has the alternate lyric "I dream of your *sweet* kiss." The Beatles then back an unknown singer on "Money (That's What I Want)"; upon hearing the tape, Tony Sheridan ruled himself out as the vocalist and suggested it may be Bobby Thompson of the Dominoes.

Several of the Dominoes' numbers from these tapes have surfaced, with four songs appearing on the bootleg CD *Road Runner* ("Sparkling Brown Eyes," "Lovesick Blues," "First Taste of Love," and "Dizzy Miss Lizzy"). Another song, "Hully Gully" by Cliff Bennett and the Rebel Rousers, even received official release under the Beatles' own name on a few labels.

RELEASE HISTORY

1977: **C** and a fragment of **A** were released on the LP *Live! at the Star-Club in Hamburg, Germany, 1962.*

1998: **A** and **H** surfaced from a fair-quality tape source on the bootleg CD *Road Runner.*

2008: The Purple Chick CD-R *Star Club* contained the entire concert, including the numbers from the Dominoes and Cliff Bennett and the Rebel Rousers, assembled from the best possible sources.

1963: HOLD THAT LINE!

TIMELINE

January 1	The Beatles fly from Hamburg to London.
January 2	The Beatles fly from London to Aberdeen; their evening concert at Keith is canceled due to snowstorms, so John flies to Liverpool to visit relatives overnight, returning to Scotland the next morning.
January 11	UK release of "Please Please Me"/"Ask Me Why" single.
	Snowstorms conspire to cancel a second evening concert at the Ritz Ballroom in Birmingham.
January 13	The Beatles are videotaped performing "Please Please Me" for ABC's *Thank Your Lucky Stars* at Alpha Television Studios in Birmingham (aired January 19).
January 21	While at EMI House, the Beatles pose for pictures to promote "Please Please Me," peeking around a wall in George Martin's office. They also sign a contract with American record label Vee-Jay, who end up releasing sixteen of their songs.
January 22	The Beatles tape their debut appearance on BBC Radio's *Saturday Club* at the Playhouse Theatre.
January 24	PR appearance to promote "Please Please Me" at NEMS Records' Whitechapel store.
January 26	Backstage at a concert in Stoke, John and Paul begin to compose "Misery."
February 2	Concert at Gaumont Cinema in Bradford; the opening night of a tour headlined by Helen Shapiro.
February 4	Concert at Cavern Club; the group's last lunchtime performance there.
February 7	U.S. release of "Please Please Me"/"Ask Me Why" single.
February 8	The Beatles are thrown out of a golf club dance at the Crown and Mitre Hotel in Carlisle for wearing leather jackets.
February 10	Cyrus Andrews conducts a photo shoot with the Beatles at various locations around Sloane Square.
February 11	Taping eleven songs at EMI Studios for their first LP, *Please Please Me.*
February 19	Concert at Cavern Club. Onstage, it is announced that "Please Please Me" will be the Beatles' first number 1 single in next week's *NME* chart.
February 22	Formation of Northern Songs, a company set up exclusively to publish Lennon/McCartney songs, and cochaired by Dick James and Brian Epstein/NEMS.
February 28	En route to the evening's show at Shrewsbury, John and Paul compose their next single, "From Me to You," on the tour bus.
March 5	Taping their third single at EMI Studio 2.
March 12	A flu-stricken John misses concerts on this and the following two nights.
March 22	UK release of *Please Please Me* LP (mono version).
March 25	Dezo Hoffmann photographs and films the Beatles on their day off at various Liverpool locations.
April 4	Photo shoot outside the BBC's Paris Studio in London and elsewhere. A Dezo Hoffmann shot from this session is used on the cover of *Live at the BBC* thirty-one years later. Color film shot of the Beatles walking past the studio entrance is used to promote the "Baby It's You" single in 1995.
	Concert at Stowe School's Roxburgh Hall. Afterward, the Beatles dine with the headmaster's family.
April 5	The Beatles are presented with their first silver disc, for the single "Please Please Me," in a ceremony at EMI House. They also perform a brief set for the assembled journalists and EMI bigwigs.
April 8	John and Cynthia's first son, John Charles Julian, is born at Sefton General Hospital.

April 11 UK release of "From Me to You"/"Thank You Girl" single.

The Beatles hire a new press agent, Tony Barrow.

April 13 Taping three songs for their BBC TV debut on *The 625 Show* at Lime Grove Studio E (aired April 16).

The Beatles meet Cliff Richard while attending a party at the home of Shadows' guitarist Bruce Welch.

April 14 The Beatles meet the Rolling Stones after watching the Stones perform at the Crawdaddy Club. Following the show, both groups convene at Mick Jagger and Brian Jones' squalid Edith Grove flat to discuss and listen to music.

April 18 Backstage following a show at the Royal Albert Hall, Paul meets future fiancée Jane Asher.

April 22 Classic photo shoot at Dezo Hoffmann's studio showing off the Beatles' brand-new collarless stage suits. Paul is seen smoking throughout the session, in which the group poses around chairs and a stool, using a stuffed animal and a ski as props. Capitol uses these pictures the following year on the sleeves of several singles and the back cover of the *Meet the Beatles!* LP.

April 26 UK release of *Please Please Me* LP (stereo version).

April 28 John and Brian Epstein fly to Spain for a two-week holiday. The rest of the group vacations in Santa Cruz, Tenerife, in the Canary Islands.

May 4 *Please Please Me* becomes the Beatles' first number 1 LP, topping this week's *Melody Maker* chart. It remains at number 1 for seven months, replaced by the Beatles' own follow-up album.

May 6 U.S. release of "From Me to You"/"Thank You Girl" single.

May 9 The Beatles and Brian Epstein return to London from their respective holidays.

May 10 While judging the finals of a local beat group contest, George Harrison recommends an up-and-coming London group, the Rolling Stones, to fellow panelist and Decca Records' executive Dick Rowe. Some fifteen months earlier, Rowe had turned down another up-and-coming group, the Beatles, commenting that "guitar groups are on their way out." This time, he does not miss the bus.

May 18 *Disc* magazine presents the Beatles with a silver record for sales of "From Me to You."

Opening night for the Beatles' tour with Roy Orbison.

May 24 Taping seven songs (including the title theme) for the first episode of *Pop Go the Beatles,* their own BBC Radio show, at Aeolian Hall Studio 2.

June 18 Paul's twenty-first birthday celebration, at his auntie Gin's house, turns sour when a drunken John pummels DJ Bob Wooler for making a wisecrack about John and Brian's recent trip to Spain.

June 20 Dezo Hoffmann photographs a series of portraits of John, Paul, and Ringo at his Soho studio.

June 22 John videotapes an appearance on the panel of BBC TV's *Juke Box Jury* at Television Theatre; immediately after the taping, John flies in a rented helicopter from Battersea Heliport to the Beatles' gig in Wales.

June 26 John and Paul compose "She Loves You" in their hotel room after a concert in Newcastle.

June 27 John and Paul attend the Billy J Kramer with the Dakotas' recording session for two Lennon/McCartney numbers, "Bad to Me" and "I Call Your Name."

July 1 Taping "She Loves You"/"I'll Get You" single at EMI Studio 2.

July 4 The Beatles and Peter Asher attend the Rolling Stones' show at the Scene Club in London.

July 12 UK release of *Twist and Shout* EP.

UK release of *My Bonnie* EP.

July 18 First session for *With the Beatles,* their second LP, at EMI studios.

July 27 The Beatles are filmed and photographed by Dezo Hoffmann by the seaside and on a go-kart track in Somerset.

July 29 The Beatles pose for *Radio Times* photographer Don Smith at the Washington Hotel.

August 3 Concert at Cavern Club; the Beatles' final appearance at the venue that launched their career.

August 11 Mal Evans begins his road-managerial career when he meets the Beatles' plane (from the Channel Islands) at Manchester Airport.

August 23 UK release of "She Loves You"/"I'll Get You" single.

August 27 Filming commences for BBC TV's documentary *The Mersey Sound.*

September 6 UK release of *The Beatles' Hits* EP.

September 9 The Beatles are interviewed by Donald Zec of the *Daily Mirror* at his Lancaster Terrace flat. The article is published the following day.

September 10 The Beatles attend an awards luncheon at the Savoy Hotel, thrown by the Variety Club of Great Britain. "From Me to You" wins best vocal record.

John and Paul attend the Rolling Stones' rehearsal at the Ken Colyer Jazz Club, and after polishing off "I Wanna Be Your Man," donate it to the Stones.

September 13 Paul sits in on the judging panel of the Imperial Miss 1963 contest, held at the Imperial Ballroom in Nelson.

September 14 The Beatles hold press interviews at NEMS offices in Liverpool.

September 16 The Beatles take off in three directions for a fortnight's vacation: Paul and Ringo travel to Greece; John and Cynthia fly to Paris; and George becomes the first Beatle to visit the United States, staying with his sister, Louise, in Illinois.

U.S. release of "She Loves You"/"I'll Get You" single.

October 2 Paul and Ringo return to London from Greece, and John flies back from Paris.

October 3 George arrives in London from his American vacation too late to participate in the morning EMI recording session.

Ringo attends a Rolling Stones/Bo Diddley/Everly Brothers triple-bill package concert at the Southend Odeon Cinema.

October 8 The Beatles attend Roland Kirk's performance at the Ronnie Scott Jazz Club in London.

October 12 At NEMS' London offices, the Beatles rehearse in the evening for their important TV performance the following day.

October 13 A major night in the Beatles' rise to the top—the coveted closing spot on ATV's *Sunday Night at the London Palladium,* broadcast live to 15 million viewers. The Beatles perform four songs and celebrate afterward at the Grosvenor House Hotel.

October 14 The Beatles use a rare day off to travel by train to Liverpool.

John attends a Billy J Kramer with the Dakotas' recording session. Among the songs recorded are two Lennon/McCartney numbers: "I'll Keep You Satisfied" and "I'm in Love."

October 15 The Beatles pose on a staircase at their Green Street apartment for *The Beatles Book* photographer Leslie Bryce.

October 16 While rehearsing at the Playhouse Theatre, the Beatles meet Richard Lester for the first time.

October 17 The Beatles have lunch with four *Boyfriend* magazine contest winners at the Old Vienna restaurant.

Taping their fifth single and first annual Christmas fan club record at EMI Studio 2.

October 23 The Beatles fly from London to Sweden after their morning EMI session.

October 28 Record-signing session at Waidele record shop in Borås.

October 31 Dame Fortune once again smiles on the Beatles as the mob scene of their London Airport arrival from Sweden is witnessed by Ed Sullivan, killing time at the airport due to flight delays. Ed declares, "Book me those boys!" when he discovers they are a musical act. He does just that eleven days later when Brian meets him in New York.

George attends the Rolling Stones/Bo Diddley/Everly Brothers/Little Richard package show at the Odeon Cinema.

November 1 UK release of *The Beatles (No. 1)* EP.

Opening night of The Beatles' Autumn Tour.

November 4 The Beatles perform at the Royal Variety Performance, in the Prince of Wales Theatre. BBC TV and Radio both document the event for later transmission.

November 6 Granada TV's *Scene at 6:30* finally gets around to broadcasting footage of the Beatles performing "Some Other Guy," shot August 22, 1962, at the Cavern.

November 7 The Beatles arrive at Dublin Airport for their sole concerts in Ireland.

November 9 The Beatles attend a party at the London home of "washing-machine tycoon" John Bloom.

November 12 Paul has the flu, causing the evening's concerts in Portsmouth to be postponed until December 3.

November 16 Two concerts at Bournemouth's Winter Gardens, covered (for the first time) by American TV; in fact, all three networks have reporters and camera crews on hand.

November 18 The Beatles attend a ceremony and luncheon at EMI House, where they are presented with several silver discs.

November 22 UK release of *With the Beatles* LP.

November 29 UK release of "I Want to Hold Your Hand"/"This Boy" single.

December 4 Ringo flies to Liverpool to visit his family.

December 5 John, Paul, and George return to Liverpool for a brief break from touring.

December 6 UK release of *The Beatles' 1963 Christmas Record,* the Beatles' first annual Christmas flexi-disc for fan club members.

December 24 Opening night concert of The Beatles' Christmas show, which runs semiregularly through January 11, 1964, at the Astoria Cinema, Finsbury Park, London.

The Beatles return home to spend Christmas Eve and day with their families in Liverpool.

December 26 U.S. rush release of "I Want to Hold Your Hand"/"I Saw Her Standing There" single.

December 27 The *London Times* prints an article by music critic William Mann acclaiming and overanalyzing the Beatles' compositions in terms, such as "pandiatonic clusters" and "Aeolian cadence," unrecognizable to laymen like John and Paul.

1. Radio performance

Date: 16 January 1963
Time: 8:45–9:30 p.m.
Location: Playhouse Theatre, Manchester
Producer: Peter Pilbeam
Host: Ray Peters
Broadcast: 25 January 1963, 5:00–5:29 p.m.
BBC Light Programme
Here We Go

[A.] **Chains** (1:36)
[B.] **Please Please Me** (1:36)
[C.] **Ask Me Why** (2:11)

The Beatles' first BBC Radio performance of 1963 has surfaced recently, although their unaired rendition of "Three Cool Cats" from this date is still missing. In front of an enthusiastic audience, the group played both sides of their new single, as well as "Chains" (incomplete on the circulating tape), the Goffin/King number they would soon cover on their debut LP.

RELEASE HISTORY

2003: Fair-quality copies of all three songs were bootlegged on the CD boxed set *The Beatles at the Beeb.*

1a. Radio performance

Date: 22 January 1963
Time: 4:00–5:00 p.m.
Location: Playhouse Theatre, London
Producer: Jimmy Grant
Host: Brian Matthew
Broadcast: 26 January 1963, 10:00 a.m.–noon
BBC Light Programme
Saturday Club #225

[A.] Some Other Guy (2:01)
[B.] intro (0:18)
[C.] Love Me Do (1:29)
[D.] Please Please Me (0:32)
[E.] Keep Your Hands off My Baby (2:28)
[F.] Beautiful Dreamer (1:51)

On New Year's Eve 1962, as the Beatles prepared to play their final set at the Star-Club in Hamburg, Brian Epstein was busy securing a contract with the BBC for their first appearance on *Saturday Club.* The series was BBC Radio's premiere showcase for rock and pop talent (it had begun in 1958 as a skiffle program), with an average weekly listening audience of over 10 million. This booking and a timely appearance on *Thank Your Lucky Stars* January 19 (their first nationally screened TV broadcast) helped push their second single, "Please Please Me," to the top of the charts by mid-February.

But *Saturday Club* host Brian Matthew could not have known how prescient his intro (**B**) for "Love Me Do" would prove to be: "At the moment, the majority of the Beatles' fans are in their hometown of Liverpool, and I have a very strong suspicion it won't be long before they're all over the country." The circulating copy of "Please Please Me" (performed sans harmonica) is fragmented, containing only three short segments of the number.

In addition to their first two single A-sides, the group performed three cover versions. The first of these, "Some Other Guy," was already a staple of their Cavern set list, and the other two would be featured on their first national tour headlined by Helen Shapiro the following month. John does an outstanding job tackling the Goffin-King composition "Keep Your Hands off My Baby," Little Eva's recent follow-up to her number 1 hit "The Loco-Motion."

Reaching back a hundred years or so, the Beatles closed their set with Paul singing Stephen Foster's "Beautiful Dreamer," probably based on Tony Orlando's 1961 rocked-up arrangement.

RELEASE HISTORY

1982: **A, E,** and **F** first appeared on the bootleg LP *Beautiful Dreamer* in fair sound quality. **A** was also partially included in the radio special *The Beatles at the Beeb.*

1988: These same three songs then appeared in slight upgrades (now including Brian Matthew's spoken intro during **F**) on the vinyl bootlegs *Meet the Beeb* and *The Beatles at the Beeb w/Pete Best.* They are also on Great Dane's *The Complete BBC Sessions,* with the hiss reduced at the expense of the bass frequency.

1994: **E** was officially released on Apple's *Live at the BBC,* but with a new intro manufactured by digital editing to repeat and extend a brief drum phrase.

1999: **B** and **C** surfaced, from a very good-quality tape, on the bootleg boxed CD set *Mythology, Volume 1.*

2000: A slight upgrade of **B** and **C** appeared on the CD boot *The Beatles Broadcast Collection, Trailer 1.*

2001: Minor upgrades of **A, E,** and **F** were included on the CD-R *The Complete BBC Sessions—Upgrade.*

2004: **D** appeared from a good-quality source tape on the CD-R *The Complete BBC Sessions—Upgraded for 2004.*

1b. Radio performance

Date: 22 January 1963
Time: 7:00–8:00 p.m.
Location: BBC Paris Studio, London
Producer: Brian Willey
Host: Gary Marshal
Broadcast: 29 January 1963, 5:00–5:29 p.m.
BBC Light Programme
The Talent Spot

[A.] **intro** (0:03)
[B.] **Ask Me Why** (2:11)
[C.] **outro** (0:04)

Introduced by John as the B-side of their new single, this low-fidelity recording of "Ask Me Why" is all that has survived from the Beatles' two appearances on *The Talent Spot*. On this occasion, they also sang "Please Please Me" and "Some Other Guy."

RELEASE HISTORY

2003: A fair-quality copy of this performance was bootlegged on the CD boxed set *The Beatles at the Beeb*.

2. Studio session

Date: 11 February 1963
Time: 10:00 a.m.–1:00 p.m.
Location: EMI Studio 2
Producer: George Martin

[A.] **There's A Place—take 1 (stereo)** (2:03)
[B.] **There's A Place—take 2 (stereo)** (1:59)
[C.] **There's A Place—takes 3–4 (stereo)** (2:05)
[D.] **There's A Place—takes 5–6 (stereo)** (2:15)
[E.] **There's A Place—takes 7–8 (stereo)** (2:35)
[F.] **There's A Place—take 9 (stereo)** (2:00)
[G.] **There's A Place—take 10 (stereo)** (1:56)
[H.] **I Saw Her Standing There—take 1 (stereo)** (2:58)
[I.] **I Saw Her Standing There—take 2 (stereo)** (3:04)
[J.] **I Saw Her Standing There—take 3 (stereo)** (0:28)
[K.] **I Saw Her Standing There—take 4 (stereo)** (0:43)
[L.] **I Saw Her Standing There—take 5 (stereo)** (0:54)
[M.] **I Saw Her Standing There—takes 6–9 (stereo)** (4:51)

[N.] **I Saw Her Standing There—RS from take 9** (2:49)

February 11, 1963, was easily the most industrious day the Beatles were to spend in the studio, as the remaining ten songs for their debut LP were wrapped up in just under ten hours. Some of the master tapes of this session have been erased or scrapped, but thanks to bootleggers, we have been able to study all those that have survived.

The only songs that required a large number of takes were the five original compositions (including "Hold Me Tight," which didn't make the cut and would be remade on the next album). The other six songs, requiring a minimal number of attempts, were cover versions of songs the group had performed hundreds of times, and they were able to infuse these recordings with an assured excitement that comes with practice and confidence in the material. Also common throughout all of the February 11 session tapes is the sniffling and coughing from Paul and John in particular, both suffering from seasonal colds.

Paul seems to cop to this when the beginning of the first reel of tape catches him in mid-cough and he exclaims, "It's so hard," before counting in for take 1 of "There's a Place." The first take (**A**) is fairly similar to all the takes in structure and tempo, and it's hard to say for certain why this take was rejected. Perhaps the vocals are a bit lacking in energy and the lead guitar stumbles around looking for the best phrases and fills, but they were just warming up.

The second take (**B**) sounds much like the first, but it's easier to detect why they didn't use it (though it is complete). During the bridge, John's "In my mind, there's no sorrow" should be answered by "Doncha know that it's so" in the backing vocals. Paul gets it right, but George sings "Doncha know that it's true." Another minor flaw occurs going into the coda, just after the last full stop by the band, when Ringo hesitates slightly before coming back in.

Engineer Norman Smith announces "Take three" (**C**) and Paul, trying to raise his own energy level, counts in a bit more enthusiastically: "One, two, three, four, hey!" But it's all for naught as the rhythm isn't quite together for the first three bars, so during the pause, George Martin calmly interrupts over the talkback: "And again." John and Paul stop singing in mid-title before Smith calls take 4. This attempt runs smoothly until the first chorus, when John sings correctly, "And it's my mind" against Paul's "And in my mind." But it's almost undetectable, and they press on. Paul goes on to blow a line in the second verse, mumbling through "the things you've said."

The tape begins again in mid-discussion (**D**) as John and Paul try and work out the problems with their vocals. As George plays a riff from "Please Please Me" in the background, Paul tests out the first word of the song, singing it several times. John says, "Do that bit you do," to make sure Paul has the phrasing right. After John sneezes and sniffs, Paul asks him, "Y'ready?" But John has some more words of advice for Paul: "If you count, if you go [taps the rhythm on his guitar] 'The-ee-ere . . .' it works better if you do it on the beat somehow, y'know, think the beat in your head." Alas, take 5 is halted by Paul only three seconds in. George and John ask why, and Paul admits, "It was bad, that beginning." Take 6 is complete and without major flaws, but there's still room for improvement.

As Paul continues to cough (**E**), Norman Smith announces, "Seven. Take seven." Ringo can be heard very faintly in the left channel presumably discussing the microphone setup: "That boom's no different." All is well until George gets sticky fingers playing the guitar phrase just before the second verse, and Martin calls a halt to take 7: "And again. From the top." Take 8 is also botched by George, who drops out for a few beats during the final chorus.

So they press on for a ninth take (**F**), but this time Paul sabotages things during the last verse, beneath the line "When I feel low, when I feel blue." He plays an E followed by an A, rather than by a C-sharp (very noticeable against a C#m chord), and though they finish up the take, it's evident they'll have to try again. Clearly the Beatles are getting annoyed at this point, for when Norman Smith announces take 10 (**G**), Paul mutters sarcastically under his breath, "Take fifteen." Happily, they get it right, performing an energetic backing track with lively harmonized vocals.

They move on to "I Saw Her Standing There," and as Norman Smith presses the talkback, George Martin is caught prophetically telling someone, "I think we'll probably have a different title"—which Smith announces as " 'Seventeen,' take one." Following a tentative count-in from Paul, the Beatles swing into a high-energy take (**H**) that is amazing in its initiatory perfection. The only hint of error is a minor clash of words in the third chorus: Paul sings "Since I saw her . . ." while John opts for "When I saw her . . ." However, the exuberant screaming after this chorus inspires George to lay down a solo for the ages—not technically brilliant or wildly abandoned but with each note falling just where it should. Despite eight more tries, no way could they improve on this as a backing track, so it ended up as the lead-off to their first album.

As the tape rolls again for take 2 (**I**), John notices the red light that signals that tape is rolling and notifies the others: "Okay, go on." But first he makes a last-minute check with Paul about how to kick things off: "I go—one, two, three, four [plays intro riff]." Paul concurs and counts in for the second complete take, one riddled with imperfections. John and Paul continue to sing different words at the same time in the choruses. Thus in chorus 2, Paul's "She wouldn't dance" is countered by John's (incorrect) "I didn't dance . . ." Even worse, in the third chorus, John incorrectly sings, "She wouldn't dance" and Paul, starting correctly, changes in mid-lyric to match John: "Now I—she wouldn't dance . . ." George's solo is ineffective and sloppy, and Paul's bass line simply quits for almost two bars soon afterward, perhaps indicating that he's given up on this take. Though they play on through the song's end, John's comment as the last chord dies away sums up take 2: "Dreadful."

Presumably to assist the ailing take 2, the Beatles turn momentarily to taping short sections for editing into the main track. Take 3 (**J**) consists of the last three lines of the song and the final chord. Take 4 (**K**) is an attempt to improve the "dreadful" guitar solo from take 2. Paul is busy figuring out how to launch in to the edit piece when John interrupts him, noticing the red light: "Okay, it's on . . ." Unfortunately, this solo isn't much better, so they'll have to do it again. Norman Smith: "Another edit piece, take—same edit piece, rather, take five." Paul is again goofing around as the tape rolls (**L**) and John nudges him impatiently: "Come on." This time George's solo is all over the place, much livelier than previous attempts if a bit unkempt. As take 5 ends, Paul croons dementedly: "Held her hand in my-EEEEEEN!"

It is decided to take the whole song from the top, and the tape begins again (**M**) with Norman Smith noting the start of another full take: "[Com]plete one, uh . . . take six." Meanwhile, Paul runs through the first line of each chorus to make sure he and John don't clash anymore: "How could I dance, she'll ne—she wouldn't dance, I'll never dance. Okay. Where's the tempo?" John, anxious as ever to record, shushes him, but again Paul asks about the tempo. Apparently he has forgotten they are starting anew rather than trying to match a previous take, as George Martin reminds him: "We're doing the whole lot. So you don't need to worry about that. Okay?" Paul replies, "Oh, of course, no," but John shushes him again and double-checks the intro, as he had on take 2.

Clearly John should have been worrying about the lyrics instead, since he blows them again in the second verse. And just like on take 2, Paul tries to jump horses in mid-stream to match John's flub: "She—I wouldn't dance." This is way too obvious, though, and Martin whistles for them to stop. Paul complains, "Too fast," and Martin interjects, "No, you had a wrong word, didn't you. 'She—I' " Paul agrees but contends the take was too fast anyway. Despite practicing the count-in twice, take 7 lasts only a few bars before Paul halts it: "No, that's too fast! And again. And again, I'm sorry, you know . . ." Paul rehearses the tempo again, and John, fed up, says, "Go on." After a promising start, take 8 gets as far as the second line when Ringo unexpectedly drops out for a brief moment. They stop again, and John inquires obliviously, "What 'appened?"

The silver lining appears when the tensions and mistakes cause Paul to count take 9 in with a forceful mandate to reign rhythmically: "One, two, three, FAH!" The performance is flawless vocally, but just not as exciting as take 1. It appears in a narrow stereo mix (**N**) on the "Free as a Bird" CD single. Opting for the best of both worlds, they ultimately joined the count-in from take 9 to the song proper from take 1, launching their LP career in grand style.

NOTE

Unlike previous takes, for takes 6 through 9 both guitars are in the left channel, but during the take 9 guitar solo, George's guitar suddenly appears in the right channel. This was probably done live from the control booth in order to isolate the solo from the rest of the backing track. Such a quick-pan technique would make it easier to replace the solo with an edit piece later on should George screw it up.

RELEASE HISTORY

1983: The announcement for **H** plus a portion of **M** were included in the *Beatles at Abbey Road* presentation, now booted in excellent sound on the CD *Abbey Road Video Show.*

1984: Excerpts of dialogue from this session were heard in the radio special *Sgt. Pepper's Lonely Hearts Club Band: A History of the Beatle Years 1962–1970.*

1988: **I** and **C** appeared in excellent quality and at the correct speed on the bootleg CDs *Ultra Rare Trax, Volume One* and *Volume Two* respectively. **A** was included on the LP *Ultra Rare Trax, Volume 3 & 4.*

1989: **D** and **M** (complete for the first time) surfaced on *Unsurpassed Masters, Volume 1,* running too slow but with excellent sound.

1991: **J** was included on the bootleg CD *Unsurpassed Masters, Volume 6.*

1994: *The Ultimate Collection, Volume 2: Studio Sessions, February 11, 1963* contained the best-sounding tapes yet of this entire session (**A–M,** excepting the announcement for **H**). Unfortunately, the whole thing ran too slow, as do most of the studio outtakes released on the Yellow Dog label.

1995: Apple's "Free as a Bird" CD single treated us to **N,** a new remix of take 9 with very narrow stereo separation and echo added.

3. Studio session

Date: 11 February 1963
Time: 2:30–6:00 p.m.
Location: EMI Studio 2
Producer: George Martin

[A.] **Do You Want to Know a Secret—take 7 (mono)** (2:01)
[B.] **Do You Want to Know a Secret—take 8 (mono)** (2:35)
[C.] **A Taste of Honey—take 6 (mono)** (2:08)
[D.] **A Taste of Honey—take 7 (mono)** (2:09)
[E.] **There's a Place—take 11 (mono)** (2:01)
[F.] **There's a Place—takes 12–13 (mono)** (2:21)
[G.] **I Saw Her Standing There—take 10 (mono)** (2:55)
[H.] **I Saw Her Standing There—takes 11–12 (mono)** (3:33)
[I.] **Misery—take 1 (mono)** (1:50)
[J.] **Misery—takes 2–6 (mono)** (4:48)
[K.] **Misery—take 7 (mono)** (1:50)
[L.] **Misery—take 8 (mono)** (0:23)

[M.] **Do You Want to Know a Secret—RM from take 8** (1:54)
[N.] **There's a Place—RM from take 13** (1:47)
[O.] **I Saw Her Standing There—RM from edit of takes 10 and 12** (2:51)
[P.] **A Taste of Honey—RM from take 7** (2:00)
[Q.] **Do You Want to Know a Secret—RS from take 8** (1:54)
[R.] **There's a Place—RS from take 13** (1:48)
[S.] **I Saw Her Standing There—RS from edit of takes 10 and 12** (2:51)
[T.] **A Taste of Honey—RS from take 7** (2:01)
Mixed: 25 February 1963

Following a lunch break, during which the Beatles opted to dine in the studio and continue rehearsing, the session's first cover version was taped, as Paul crooned "A Taste of Honey" in five takes, accompanied by Ringo's softly brushed drum work and John's acoustic guitar. With this done, George's first EMI lead vocal was recorded in six takes. John had written "Do You Want to Know a Secret" based around the opening lines of "I'm Wishing," a song from Walt Disney's *Snow White and the Seven Dwarfs* that his mother used to sing.

Having perfected the song's backing track, the Beatles now turned to adding backing vocals and percussion as a tape-to-tape overdub. The unused take 7 (**A**) has several interesting differences: The backing "doo-dah-doo" vocals are present throughout all three verses, handclaps supply the percussion during the middle eight, and there is what sounds like an aborted attempt to sing "aah" behind the word "hear" at the end of verse 1. The song also comes to a complete ending, following which John complains, "I can't get off that . . ."

The session tape for take 8 (**B**) captures some interesting discussion about the arrangement. George wonders about the "doo-dah-doo" vocals and asks nobody in particular, "We're not doing it the first verse, are we?" John checks with the control booth: "Shall we just do it on the second verse, like we said?" Paul agrees, but nobody is paying attention in the booth, so John calls, "Hello?" Martin, oblivious, instructs, "Okay, here we go." John asks again, and Martin concurs: "Yes, the second verse." John: "Okay, so we wait."

Ringo, drumsticks in hand, asks for clarification: "So I don't do it the first time?" This throws everyone into confusion as John, Paul, and George all respond at once: George tells Ringo just to tap the sticks on the middle eight (in place of the handclap percussion from take 7). Paul, still thinking of the vocals, elucidates: "Well, we keep doing that from the second verse." In other words, the second and third verses will both have backing vocals. Finally, John makes sure they all know when not to sing: "And none on the 'hear'—just 'doo-dah-doo' all the time." Take 8 was satisfactory and duly added to the LP's lineup.

Overdubs continued with Paul's doubling his lead vocal for "A Taste of Honey" in two places; during the first refrain ("I will return . . .") and then from the final refrain through the ending. The tape begins (**C**) with yet another control-booth announcement, behind which a female voice is discernible over the talkback. George then mumbles something about the song's title and is shushed by Paul.

The tape of take 5 is rolled, on which the tail of Paul's waltz-tempo count-in (only the "three") can be heard prior to the song. All goes well until the next-to-last word, when Paul cannot sync up "and you" following the dramatic pause. Knowing that he blew it, Paul stops singing, and the tape is switched off before the last chord has faded in order to be rewound for another pass. Take 7 (**D**) finds Paul in almost-perfect sync with his original vocal (only the second "I will return" is slightly off) and so becomes the master take.

The next task was for John to overdub harmonica onto take 10 of "There's a Place." The first attempt, take 11 (**E**), has no major flaws but is rejected. Take 12 (**F**) is a false start of the harmonica overdub lasting for the opening four bars. Either John's not close enough to the mic, or the engineer is asleep at the switch, as the harmonica begins too quietly then suddenly increases in volume. Take 13 is splendid and would be remixed into mono and stereo for the LP.

"I Saw Her Standing There" was next on the agenda. The written session sheets are extremely sketchy about what take 10 (**G**) really is. What it seems to be is a straight tape-to-tape copy of take 9 from which the count-in and pick-up note were physically edited out (both elements are missing from the tape heard on bootlegs), to be spliced onto a copy of take 12.

For the next two takes, they definitely *are* adding handclaps to take 1. Paul makes some remark about "echoed claps" that causes giggling just prior to take 11 (**H**). This is a false start as the rhythm is a bit out of sync; as take 1 is shut off, the clapping continues for a few seconds, dwindling into applause and laughter. Paul continues to clown around, but George reminds him they're still rolling: "Shh. We're on." Take 12 is complete and was joined to the count-in from take 10 at the mixing stage. Both released mixes (**O, S**) cut off rather abruptly during the decay of the song's final note.

Despite all the work and takes recorded so far, the Beatles were only halfway through completing their first album. Next up was "Misery," a song written by John and Paul for Helen Shapiro (they were currently touring with her), who rejected it. Take 1 (**I**) is complete but had to be scrapped when they realized they had left out some lyrics. Rather than singing a new set of lyrics for the second middle eight, they accidentally repeat the same lines both times.

An amusing piece of tape follows (**J**) that captures the group's frustrating attempts to perform "Misery" correctly. As the tape starts, George is practicing the descending riff from the middle eight while Paul asks George Martin something about acoustics (or acoustic guitars). Suddenly George realizes the light is on, and they begin take 2. Martin whistles them to a stop during the second verse, though, because he thinks George has changed guitars. When this is denied, Martin explains, "I'm getting a thicker noise from him somehow." George admits, "I probably changed the tone," and Martin asks him to thin it up and turn down his volume. Meanwhile John rehearses the Am to G intro chord change (saying, "I must remember that"). George then asks about how a certain riff goes, but John and Paul tell him to leave it out entirely.

Take 3 is ruined when John gets tangled up in his strings, playing a C rather than changing to F in the first verse. After a quick announcement of "take four" there is a pause. John asks if they should start again and Paul responds, "Yeah, why not?" This time the lyrics trip them up; in the second verse, "I won't see her no more" (sung correctly by Paul) comes out of John's mouth as "She won't come back no more." They stop again, and John bitches, "It's these damn words . . ."

Take 5 doesn't get far; in the second verse, Paul plays an F against a C major and they halt again. (Martin points out helpfully, "Wrong bass notes.") John makes sure he knows the words—"I won't see her no more"—and after a momentary false start (the opening guitar strum), they are off again. Take 6 is complete and has some interesting differences from other takes. George throws in extra guitar riffs at the end of each bridge, and Ringo adds drum fills during the bridge and the fade-out. Both ideas were dropped by the next take.

It's hard to say why take 7 (**K**) was rejected—it is complete and sounds flawless to me. More conversation is captured following the announcement for take 8 (**L**): Paul seems to be telling George to play during a part when he shouldn't: "Come in on the 'The w— . . . I'm the kind of'—first verse. Okay, go on." John ridicules him: "He's not coming in on that bit!," and Paul sheepishly agrees. But Paul has his revenge as they begin take 8. John makes the same mistake (singing) that Paul had (talking): "The w— . . . I'm the kind of guy." Paul gleefully proclaims, "Stop it, he said the wrong word." As the tape cuts off, John chuckles, "I just looked . . ." By the eleventh take, "Misery" was perfected, but it wouldn't be complete until George Martin overdubbed piano nine days later.

RELEASE HISTORY

1963: **M–T** were released on the mono and stereo pressings of Parlophone's *Please Please Me* LP, and the mono mixes are currently available on the CD of that title.

1983: A portion of **H** was included in *The Beatles at Abbey Road* presentation, now booted in excellent sound on the CD *Abbey Road Video Show.*

1984: **A** and various segments of dialogue from this session were heard in the radio special *Sgt. Pepper's Lonely Hearts Club Band.* **A** was soon copied onto *Back-Track* and the CD version of *Not For Sale.*

1988: **I** appeared in excellent quality and at the correct speed on *Ultra Rare Trax, Volume 2.* **B, D, E, G,** and **J** were included on the LP *Ultra Rare Trax, Volume 3 & 4.*

1989: **B, F,** and **H** (now complete) surfaced on *Unsurpassed Masters, Volume 1* running too slow but with excellent sound.

1991: **A** was included on *Unsurpassed Masters, Volume 7* in a slightly longer form than usual but slowed down a half step.

1994: *The Ultimate Collection, Volume 2: Studio Sessions, February 11, 1963* contained the best-sounding (but still slow) tapes yet of this entire session (**A–L**). The opening chord to **A** and the last second of **B** are missing from this release, however.

4. Studio session

Date: 11 February 1963
Time: 7:30–10:45 p.m.
Location: EMI Studio 2
Producer: George Martin

[A.] Anna (Go to Him)—RM from take 3 (2:53)
[B.] Boys—RM from take 1 (2:23)
[C.] Chains—RM from take 1 (2:22)
[D.] Twist and Shout—RM from take 1 (2:32)
[E.] Anna (Go to Him)—RS from take 3 (2:54)
[F.] Boys—RS from take 1 (2:24)
[G.] Chains—RS from take 1 (2:22)
[H.] Twist and Shout—RS from take 1 (2:32)
Mixed: 25 February 1963

The morning and afternoon sessions had yielded five usable songs; together with the four previously recorded single tracks, that left five to fill the LP's quota. After a dinner break, the Beatles attempted to cut another original composition, "Hold Me Tight," but after nine takes and four edit pieces, they realized it wasn't working and left it for another day.

With the clock running out, they opted for familiar cover versions the rest of the way. As they were all staples of their concert set lists, none required more than two full takes to perfect. John sang Arthur Alexander's "Anna (Go to Him)," Ringo romped through the

Shirelles' "Boys" (the only twin-track recording with drums on the vocal track), and George sang the Cookies' "Chains," supported by John's wailing harmonica and John and Paul's girl-group harmonies. Another Shirelles number, "Baby It's You," was sung beautifully by John with "sha-la-la" assistance from Paul and George; like "Misery," it would be completed later with a George Martin keyboard overdub.

That left one slot on the album to be filled. Reports that a version of "Keep Your Hands off My Baby" was recorded at this session seem to be sadly unfounded (although it may have been rehearsed). Instead, the Beatles, George Martin, Norman Smith, and *New Musical Express* reporter Alan Smith went down to the Abbey Road canteen to have a late-night snack and a brainstorming session. Smith had heard their rendition of the Isley Brothers' "Twist and Shout" a few months earlier on BBC Radio's *The Talent Spot* and suggested it to George.

The others agreed and returned to Studio 2. Tape operator Richard Langham cued up a fresh reel of tape. John fortified his throat with another lozenge and some milk to ward off the effects of his cold and the long day of singing. And they went for it. Two and a half minutes later, with a final sputtering croak from John, it was done.

George Martin was impressed: "I don't know how they do it . . . the longer we go on, the better they get!" They attempted a second take, but John's throat couldn't hold out anymore. It scarcely matters that the session tape containing take 2 is long gone, because take 1 is perfection. It's also the only cover version on the album that blows the original entirely out of the water.

RELEASE HISTORY

1963: All of these songs were released on the mono and stereo pressings of *Please Please Me,* and the mono mixes are on the current CD of that album.

5. Studio session

Date: 20 February 1963
Time: 10:30 a.m.–1:00 p.m.
Location: EMI Studio 1
Producer: George Martin

[A.] Misery—RM from take 16 (1:46)
[B.] Baby It's You—RS from take 5 (2:37)
[C.] Baby It's You—RM from take 5 (2:33)
[D.] Misery—RS from take 16 (1:46)
Mixed: 25 February 1963

George Martin's original idea for the Beatles' first LP was to simply record their live stage act at the Cavern Club (possibly during their January 31 lunchtime show, a date scratched out on the group's EMI session fee sheets and replaced with February 11). One visit to the cramped, dank, and gloomy cellar dissuaded him from that idea, but with the exception of a handful of vocal, handclap, and harmonica overdubs, the entire album was basically live.

Martin decided that the lead guitar in two songs needed a bit of strengthening, so he added keyboard parts to both in a session this morning at Abbey Road Studio 1. For "Misery," piano was added to the vocal channel, doubling the arpeggiated intro and the descending riff during the bridges. The song's opening note is cut short on the mono mix (**A**).

On "Baby It's You," Martin experimented with the celesta for take 5 and piano for take 6, eventually preferring the former. The celesta overdub went onto the instrumental channel, doubling George's guitar solo. The stereo mix (**B**) of this song lasts a few seconds longer during the fade than its mono counterpart. This overdub session marked tape operator Geoff Emerick's first work on a Beatles recording. From 1966 on, he would become their regular engineer.

RELEASE HISTORY

1963: All of these songs were released on the mono and stereo pressings of *Please Please Me,* and the mono mixes are on the current CD of that album.

6. Studio session

Date: 5 March 1963
Time: 2:30–9:00 p.m.
Location: EMI Studio 2
Producer: George Martin

[A.] From Me to You—takes 1–2 (stereo) (3:26)
[B.] From Me to You—take 3 (stereo) (1:53)
[C.] From Me to You—take 4 (stereo) (1:50)
[D.] From Me to You—take 5 (stereo) (2:12)
[E.] From Me to You—takes 6–7 (stereo) (2:14)
[F.] From Me to You—take 8 announcement (stereo) (0:06)
[G.] From Me to You—master edit from takes 12, 8, 9, and 10 (stereo) (2:03)
[H.] From Me to You—take 8 remnant (stereo) (0:16)
[I.] From Me to You—take 9 remnant (stereo) (0:27)
[J.] From Me to You—take 10 remnant (stereo) (0:11)
[K.] From Me to You—take 11 (stereo) (0:20)
[L.] From Me to You—take 12 remnant (stereo) (0:08)
[M.] From Me to You—take 13 (stereo) (0:18)
[N.] Thank You Girl—take 1 (stereo) (2:07)
[O.] Thank You Girl—takes 2–4 (stereo) (2:31)
[P.] Thank You Girl—take 5 (stereo) (2:03)
[Q.] Thank You Girl—take 6 (stereo) (2:15)
[R.] Thank You Girl—takes 7–8 (stereo) (0:40)
[S.] Thank You Girl—take 9 (stereo) (0:24)
[T.] Thank You Girl—takes 10–12 (stereo) (2:11)
[U.] Thank You Girl—take 13 (stereo) (0:28)
[V.] One after 909—take 1 (stereo) (1:21)
[W.] One after 909—take 2 (stereo) (2:54)
[X.] One after 909—take 3 (stereo) (1:45)
[Y.] One after 909—take 4 (stereo) (2:30)
[Z.] One after 909—take 5 (stereo) (1:11)

[AA.] From Me to You—RM from master edit synced with take 8 (1:55)
[BB.] From Me to You—RS from master edit (1:55)
Mixed: 14 March 1963

[CC.] One after 909—edit #1 of takes 4–5 (mono) (2:54)
Mixed: 21 April 1976

[DD.] From Me to You—edit of takes 8–10 (stereo) (1:55)
[EE.] One after 909—edit #2 of takes 4–5 (fake stereo) (2:53)
[FF.] One after 909—edit #3 of takes 4–5 (mono) (2:53)

The Beatles entered the studio during a break in their tour schedule to record the important follow-up single to "Please Please Me." They began with a catchy five-day-old composition, "From Me to You," of which the group initially thought so little that it was planned to be the B-side to "Thank You Girl." The sides were reversed when George Martin came up with some invaluable suggestions (as he had for "Please Please Me") to improve the song's arrangement. For example, the initial takes lacked the call-and-response verse before the second bridge; Martin also had the idea to add harmonica (probably so that people would identify the song with the group's first two singles). Apparently, John hadn't brought his harmonica to the session, as he borrowed one from Abbey Road's disc-cutter Malcolm Davies.

Take 1 (**A**) gets as far as the third verse before a squeaking noise (sounding like George scraping his guitar strings) brings things to a halt. Paul, sounding baffled, asks, "Wha' happened?" Martin responds from the control booth: "You tell *me*. What happened?" Paul, John, and (ironically) George all respond that they heard Martin whistling for them to stop playing. Martin denies this, and the mystery goes unsolved. Take 2 is rough around the edges but complete; Ringo forgets to play the drum fills during the ending, hitting only the final one. Paul teases him, "Ah ha ha, you missed the ending, bay-BEE!"

Following Norman Smith's "take three" announcement, John mutters, "No, that speed's all right." Apparently Paul is worried about the tempo, and despite what John says, take 3 (**B**) ends up at a sluggish pace, with sloppy vocals. Ringo again misses the first drum fill over the coda, as John points out, "He didn't get the ending." The tape rolls again as John says, "We can't get any . . . much closer, y'know." Take 4 (**C**) is complete and sounds much like the previous two takes, though Ringo manages to play all the drum fills. Between takes (not captured on tape), George Martin suggested lengthening the song by adding an extra verse of guitar/vocal call-and-response.

Presumably the group took a few minutes to practice the new arrangement, but there is some confusion as the tape begins (**D**). John is instructing George: "Yeah, do the first bit, but not the second bit, he said." Martin is ready to record, the red light is on, and he asks, "Are you with us?" But they need to clarify things first. John asks Martin if George should play the "first bit of instrumental"—meaning the call of the call-and-response. George begins to protest just as the tape is shut off. When it starts up again, they have decided to overdub the calls later in the session and sing the responses live. Paul is worried that the new arrangement will trip him up and that he'll forget to harmonize on the second bridge. John says: "Well, keep right in with your harmony bits." But sure enough, Paul goofs, not harmonizing until ". . . long to hold you."

Take 6 (**E**) only gets as far as the intro, which is too ragged for Martin's taste. He whistles the group to a halt immediately. Paul mutters, "I thought that was great," and tries to tap out the beat before counting in take 7. As he does so, he whispers, "Yeah, I wanna swing," in a faux-hipster voice. John, who clearly thinks Paul has gone mad, impatiently says, "Go on!" Take 7 is complete and flawless and would form the basis for further overdubs.

The overdubs were fed equally into both channels of a second-generation tape, placing them squarely centered in the stereo image. Take 8 had John add harmonica to the intro and call-and-response, joined on the latter by Paul's bass and George's guitar. Take 9 was a better attempt at the call-and-response overdub, but it broke down due to John's confusion about whether to play on the coda. Take 10 was a successful harmonica overdub for the coda.

Some experimental overdubs for the intro followed; take 11 (**K**) had John and Paul humming the opening phrase (in a neat parallel, Paul says, "Go on!" just before the playback starts—with John on take 7 telling Paul to "Go on!"). Take 12 was the familiar "da-da-da da-da-dun-dun-da" intro, while take 13 (**M**) was a blessedly rejected idea: screeching the same intro at a ludicrously high pitch, sounding more like Muppets than mop-tops.

A master take (**G**) was assembled as follows, with each edit piece physically removed from the session tape:

> 0:00–0:07—take 12 (the intro overdub of "dun-dun-da" vocals)
> 0:07–1:03—take 8 (no overdub, but second-generation tape used to assure uniform sound)
> 1:03–1:44—take 9 (the call-and-response overdub of harmonica, bass, and guitar)
> 1:44–end—take 10 (the coda overdub of harmonica)

This reflects the contents of the released stereo mix (**BB**) which may be the mix done in 1963 or a straight twin-track copy of the master take. For the mono single mix (**AA**), George Martin wanted to include a harmonica intro as well as the "dun-dun-da" vocal, so he synced that portion of take 8 with the master take. In 1982, engineer John Barrett created a new stereo variation (**DD**) by splicing the harmonica intro from take 8 to the master take.

The session reel as heard on bootleg reflects all this editing. At the end of the reel, after all the takes of "Thank You Girl," the overdub tape was tacked on, with the master take (**G**) inserted between the announcement (**F**) and unused bits (**H**) of take 8. The remnants that follow (**I, J,** and **L**) are what remained after George Martin chopped out portions to assemble the master take (my thanks to Trevor Hilton and Rohan Byrnes for solving this mystery).

With "From Me to You" completed, the Beatles move on to its flip side; as Norman Smith announces, the working title for this song is "Thank You Little Girl" (though this phrase is nowhere to be found in the lyrics). When the tape begins (**N**), George Martin seems to be instructing John and Paul how to sing the "oh, oh's," which they practice a few times. Following a last-minute reminder from Paul ("Same as we did"), they are off. Take 1 has several minor differences in arrangement from the released take. Lyrically, John and Paul can't seem to decide whether to sing "All I wanna do" or "gotta do" during the choruses. A two-bar guitar vamp (similar to the song's intro) is missing right after the third chorus. The song also fades out with a repeated "oh, oh" rather than coming to a musical conclusion.

After a smooth start, the Beatles hit a few roadblocks in taping the next few takes of "Thank You Girl." The tape begins (**O**) with several attempts to arrange the ending. John tells Ringo, "Just fill it how you can," for which Ringo facetiously thanks him. John and Paul practice the coda; while Paul alternates between playing D and G, John simply strums a D chord, before realizing, "Oh, it's the same as before, that's right." Paul wants to make sure they're all on the same wavelength and begins to ask, "Are we keeping—" before the tape cuts off.

He's still talking as the tape begins again: "After we do the 'oh' again, okay." Take 2 begins and lasts about two seconds before Paul stops it: "Hang on. You were out . . ." (it's not clear who he's talking about). Take 3 is similarly short, as John forgets to repeat the first two bars, jumping ahead to D too soon. He comes perilously close to swearing out loud, and they stop again. Take 4 is very messy: John and Paul clash on "wanna do"/"gotta do" in the first chorus; Paul forgets to sing the response vocal "way that you do"; there's another clash in the bridge between "seems too good"/ "is too good"; and Paul begins to sing too early following the last chorus. The two-bar guitar vamp after the third chorus is present on this take. The song still fades out, with Ringo doing his best to add drum fills.

Take 5 (**P**) is a great improvement from previous takes for the most part; by now, John and Paul seem to have agreed to sing "all I gotta do," and there are no vocal clashes. But during the fourth chorus, Paul suddenly fancies himself a jazz vocalist, wandering from the melody. This causes John to stop momentarily (and probably glare at him). Paul again comes in too soon with the final "oh" vocals, and Ringo's first drum fill during the coda is truly horrid. The song fades out as in previous takes.

Ringo asks for more assistance prior to the next take (**Q**): "Tell me when the last ones are." As nobody responds verbally, perhaps they gave him a visual cue when the time came. Paul mocks Norman Smith's take announcement ("take five, take six") and George counts in. Take 6 was used as the basic track for the released version, despite some vocal mistakes. Having sorted out the chorus lyrics, John and Paul now diverge during the second verse, as John sings, "Would doubt our love," and Paul counters, "Could doubt our love." Likewise, they can't decide whether it "seems" or "is" too good to be true. The song comes to a complete ending without fading out, with some drum flurries from Ringo and screaming from Paul.

Dissatisfied with the ending of take 6, the Beatles make several attempts to record an edit piece to replace the final 15 seconds. Take 7 (**R**) is preceded by John's reminder: "Three times, remember?" But Paul stays on A rather than switching to a G, and they stop. (John demands, "What've you done?") Take 8 is seen through to completion and error-free.

Take 9 (**S**) is another attempt to record an edit piece of the song's ending, but regrettably, Ringo blows his first drum fill. Clearly, further discussion is necessary to help Ringo out. John says, "I've thought of a way we could do it, if we play what he's doin' to keep him on the beat." Nobody seems interested, so they begin take 10 (**T**). By the second fill, Ringo has gotten out of sync, and the take breaks down. John tries again to offer his suggestion of playing along during the drum fills. George says, "Just on D?" and John agrees. Ringo seems to think just the bass should accompany him. John tells Ringo the drums will be loud enough to drown out the bass by itself. Before the take starts, Paul clarifies: "Staying . . . not going to G, in other words?" John concurs, but George goes ahead and plays D-G-D-G during take 11.

The take breaks down, and John blames George for this fact: "You shouldn't have gone [plays D-G-D-G]. Just go [plays D], it's . . . even that's hard." But George Martin interrupts: "I think Ringo just has to keep that himself, I don't think it'll help him at all, John." John reluctantly agrees, and George offers that "the first one was okay" (meaning Ringo's first fill). Paul tells Ringo, "Just keep the beat yourself." George asks which chords to play, and John says, "Do the G one now" (alternating D and G as before). Take 12 is a complete edit piece, but Ringo's last fill isn't quite up to par.

John comments, "No, they're all right, the breaks" as the tape rolls again for take 13 (**U**). Finally, Ringo plays the drum fills to everyone's satisfaction, and the song is ready for future overdubbing (this would occur eight days later).

With some time left on the studio clock, and both sides of the single in the can, the Beatles attempted to tackle one of the earliest Lennon/McCartney compositions, "One after 909." The studio tape opens (**V**) with George practicing some train-whistle imitation guitar licks for the song's intro. John tells him to "just throw 'em in somewhere," and they're off.

Take 1 breaks down in the second chorus when Ringo plays straight through what the rest of the band obviously considers a break. John is clearly annoyed and he turns on Ringo: "What're you doing? You're out of yer mind? Do the 'boom, boom, boom, boom'!" (A listen to the earlier tapes from this session will reveal John's temper steadily rising). Ringo points the finger at Paul: "He said, keep going!" Paul explains, "I know, but I meant the *bass* drum!"

Take 2 (**W**) follows a break in the tape, so any more of the argument is missing. This take is complete, and it features one of the worst guitar solos on record from George. As the take ends, John gripes, "What kinda solo was that?" Unlike the October 1962 rehearsals, the solo lasts twelve bars during this take—this matter will cause some confusion in a few minutes. The second middle eight has also been dropped from the arrangement, though careful listening reveals that someone forgets this fact, momentarily playing the wrong chord.

Featuring a count-in from George, take 3 (**X**) runs smoothly until the middle eight, when Paul has trouble keeping up his bass line. As they stumble to a halt, John, sounding completely fed up, demands to know what Paul thinks he's doing. Paul responds that he can't keep up with the others, and George asks why Paul isn't using a plectrum (pick). Paul says, "I haven't got one! Fuckin' hell, 'Where's your plec?' . . . I've been trying to cadge one all day." John lectures him: "Well, your clothes have been brought hours ago." Paul shifts the blame to road manager Neil Aspinall, saying his guitar cases haven't been brought in, but Neil will have no part in this: "I said to you before, Paul, I didn't get your plec because I didn't want to go through your clothes . . . I said, 'Do you want me to bring your case in?,' and you just walked away!" Paul sputters in protest, "I didn't say . . . I thought you said I didn't think you want . . ." as the tape is mercifully cut off by the engineer.

Take 4 (**Y**) makes it through the guitar solo, which George and Paul have suddenly decided to lengthen from twelve to sixteen bars (probably through force of habit rather than planning). Nobody has informed John, in any case, and he duly begins singing the last verse after twelve bars of solo. He explodes, "Oh bloody hell, I told ya!" Paul gleefully gets back at John: "It's you! It's you . . . comin' in at the wrong—halfway through the solo!" John is confused, thinking first that the problem was the dropped second middle eight. But they hadn't made it that far. John then asks, "What, was it twelve-bar?" George Martin chimes in, "Yeah, you had four bars left to go."

In a last-ditch attempt to save this song (and this session, which was rapidly deteriorating into squabbling), the Beatles taped an edit piece (**Z**) consisting of the solo, last verse, and final chorus. This is George's best solo so far, though still nothing to write home about.

There is no documentation to suggest that a complete take was ever assembled in 1963, and this version of "One after 909" remained unreleased for the remainder of the group's career. In April 1976, a trial edit (**CC**) of takes 4 and 5 was made (the edit occurs right at the beginning of the guitar solo) and mixed into mono, presumably for a possible rarities album.

In 1984, Geoff Emerick prepared a new edit of "One after 909" for the aborted *Sessions* album (**EE**). This was mixed in pseudostereo and used takes 4 and 5, but this time the edit didn't occur until the ninth bar of the guitar solo. Yet another mono mix (**FF**), released on *Anthology 1,* has the same edit point as the 1976 trial edit.

RELEASE HISTORY

1963: **AA** was released on a single; this mix is available on the CD *Past Masters, Volume 1.*

1965: **BB** finally surfaced on the German LP *The Beatles Greatest* and was used a year later on *A Collection of Beatles Oldies* in the UK. It didn't appear in the United States until *The Beatles 1962–1966* LP was released in 1973; however, the CD of this title uses **AA.**

1983: An incomplete mono recording of **Y** appeared in the show *The Beatles at Abbey Road* and can be found on the bootleg CD *Abbey Road Video Show.*

1984: The count-in from take 1 (**A**) was included in the radio special *Sgt. Pepper's Lonely Hearts Club Band: A History of the Beatle Years 1962–1970.* The same year, **CC** was included on the bootleg LP *File Under: Beatles.* It later appeared on the CD *Unsurpassed Masters, Volume 7.*

1985: **EE,** prepared by Geoff Emerick for *Sessions,* began to appear on vinyl bootlegs; it can be heard on Spank's CD of that title.

1988: **W** was bootlegged on the CD *Ultra Rare Trax, Volume 1,* with **A** appearing on *Ultra Rare Trax, Volume 2.* Both releases are excellent-sounding and at the correct speed.

1989: The bootleg CD *Unsurpassed Masters, Volume 1* included very good copies of **F–M, O,** and **R–W.** Unfortunately, these all have channels reversed and run too slow.

1991: The bootleg CD *Unsurpassed Masters, Volume 6* treated us to **E** and **N,** again at the wrong speed.

1994: *The Ultimate Collection, Volume 2: Studio Sessions, March 5 and September 11, 1963* contained the best-sounding (but slow) tapes yet of this entire session (**A–Z**).

1995: Apple's *Anthology 1* included portions of **X–Z,** as well as **FF,** which has the same edit point as **CC** but is probably a newly created mix.

1996: The remastered version (matrix VT-123) of Vigotone's *March 5, 1963, plus the Decca Tape* included speed-corrected versions of **A–Z.**

1999: **DD,** created around 1982, surfaced from John Barrett's personal tapes, along with a copy of **G.** Both can be found on the bootleg CD *Turn Me On Dead Man: The John Barrett Tapes.*

2000: A slightly upgraded (but still slow!) tape of **V–Z** came out on *Studio Sessions.* This was free of the tape defects that marred all previous bootlegs of **V.**

7. Radio performance

Date: 6 March 1963
Time: 8:00–8:45 p.m.
Location: Playhouse Theatre, Manchester
Producer: Peter Pilbeam
Host: Ray Peters
Broadcast: 12 March 1963, 5:00–5:29 p.m.
BBC Light Programme
Here We Go

William Tell (the Trad Lads)
[A.] **intro** (0:22)
[B.] **Misery** (1:50)
[C.] **outro/intro** (0:16)
[D.] **Do You Want to Know a Secret** (1:54)
[E.] **outro/intro** (0:24)
[F.] **Please Please Me** (1:55)
[G.] **outro** (0:08)
Warmed-over Kisses (Ben Richmond)
Waltz in Jazz Time (Northern Dance Orchestra)
Peoria (the Trad Lads)

Making their fifth and last appearance on the show in just under a year, the Beatles are introduced by Ray Peters as "one of the regular *Here We Go* groups." Over that period, they had evolved from an unsigned and unknown Liverpool band to "one of the most dynamic groups in the country today."

Two original compositions make their broadcast debuts here, both of which were offered to other artists as well as appearing on the upcoming *Please Please Me* LP. These are the only circulating live Beatles recordings of "Misery" (released March 22 by Kenny Lynch) and "Do You Want to Know a Secret" (recorded by Billy J Kramer March 21 for a single that would top the charts by June).

The Beatles' own "Please Please Me" was topping the *Melody Maker* chart the day of this session, and Peters congratulates them on returning to the show with a number 1 hit. As with all live versions of the song, this performance lacks John's harmonica contribution.

RELEASE HISTORY

1994: This is the earliest Beatles BBC broadcast to survive in excellent quality. One of the acts on the show, Ben Richmond, recorded nearly fourteen minutes of the original broadcast on reel-to-reel back in 1963. Some thirty years later, he had the recording transferred to cassette. Soon after Great Dane's *The Complete BBC Sessions* boxed set was issued, its producers were contacted by the party who did the conversion, and Great Dane issued the complete tape as a supplementary CD titled *Here We Go.* The Beatles' portion has been reissued on the CD-R *Attack of the Filler Beebs!, Episode 1.*

8. Studio session

Date: 13 March 1963
Time: 10:00 a.m.–1:00 p.m.
Location: EMI Studio 2
Producer: George Martin

[A.] Thank You Girl—RM from edit of unknown takes (2:00)
[B.] Thank You Girl—RS from take 30 (2:00)
Mixed: 13 March 1963

[C.] Thank You Girl—edit of takes 14 and 30 (stereo) (2:11)
[D.] Thank You Girl—take 30 (stereo) (2:01)

Between stops on the Chris Montez/Tommy Roe package tour, the Beatles dropped by Abbey Road Studios to finish off their new single. The strain of freezing weather and a grueling schedule had finally caught up with John's voice, and he'd missed the previous evening's concert. He was well enough to play harmonica, though, and added a mouth organ overdub to the vocal track of the "Thank You Girl" master (an edit of takes 6 and 13) this morning. The overdubs were done in short sections as takes 14–28. Harmonica was added at five points in the song: the intro, the middle eight, a pair of two-bar vamps before and after the last verse, and a quick burst on the ending.

A new master was edited together from various takes and called take 30 (**D**). This includes harmonica at all five spots and would form the basis of the stereo mix (**B**) used by Capitol. They released it on the LP *The Beatles' Second Album,* boosting the bass frequencies, adding echo, and combining the channels slightly for a murky-sounding mix. Despite many opportunities (their *Rarities* LP, the *Beatles Box,* the *Past Masters* CD), EMI has yet to release this song in true stereo in the UK.

The original mono mix (**A**) is edited together from different takes than take 30. The body (0:03–1:02) seems to be from the basic master before overdubbing and thus is lacking the middle eight harmonica. The intro (0:00–0:03) and first two-bar vamp (1:02–1:13) come from the same takes used in stereo. A different harmonica overdub take (1:13–1:40) is used for the last vamp, while the ending (1:40–2:01) is from the basic master again, lacking the final harmonica overdub. It's not clear which takes were used on which mixes; Mark Lewisohn indicates that both mixes use a combination of overdub takes 17, 20, 21, and 23.

One further variation (**C**) has escaped thanks to a new edit prepared by engineer John Barrett. It's mostly from the first overdub attempt, take 14 (complete with Norman Smith's take announcement), and has otherwise unavailable performances of the first, third, and fourth harmonica overdubs (there's no attempt at the middle eight). The last 6 seconds are from the end of take 30, and thus include the same final harmonica overdub used in the released stereo mix.

RELEASE HISTORY

1963: **A** was released on a single. It's now available on the CD *Past Masters, Volume 1.*

1964: **B** was released on all copies of *The Beatles' Second Album,* with mono copies having both stereo channels combined.

1999: **C** (slightly incomplete) and **D,** prepared around 1982 by engineer John Barrett, were bootlegged on the CD *Turn Me On Dead Man: The John Barrett Tapes* in excellent quality. The same year, **C** and **D** appeared on the CD *More Masters* in slightly lesser quality, but with greater stereo separation; **C** now included Norman Smith's take announcement.

9. Radio performance

Date: 16 March 1963
Time: 10:00 a.m.–noon
Location: Studio 3A, Broadcasting Place, London
Producer: Jimmy Grant, Bernie Andrews
Host: Brian Matthew
Broadcast: live
BBC Light Programme
Saturday Club #232

[A.] I Saw Her Standing There (2:36)
[B.] outro/intro (0:45)
[C.] Misery (1:45)
[D.] Too Much Monkey Business (1:50)
[E.] I'm Talking About You (1:51)
[F.] intro (0:51)
[G.] Please Please Me (1:53)
[H.] The Hippy Hippy Shake (1:39)

An attempted March 11 recording session for *Saturday Club* at the Playhouse Theatre in London was abandoned when it was clear John's sore throat would be a problem. Instead, it was decided to let them perform during the live broadcast on Saturday morning, from a small studio at Broadcasting House. On the strength of their chart-topping single, the Beatles were given time to perform six numbers, as well as chatting with host Brian Matthew between songs.

The first song, "I Saw Her Standing There," is the earliest example of the shortened arrangement wherein the second middle eight is dropped entirely. Perhaps it was due to time restraints in what was a live broadcast; perhaps they were already getting tired of the song. They returned to performing a full version for the next few broadcasts, but adopted this shorter arrangement for good by July.

John discusses the sore throat that caused him to miss three recent concert dates and stresses that he's recovered: "I joined 'em last night [in Bristol]." Matthew asks if it's true that John and Paul write songs, and John responds coyly, "Oh, is that what we do?" John then discusses giving "Misery" away to Kenny Lynch and throws in a plug for the *Please Please Me* album ("out next week," as Matthew reminds everyone).

A pair of Chuck Berry covers, both sung by John, once again demonstrate his difficulty understanding Berry's lyrics. In "Too Much Monkey Business," the line "for me to be involved in" becomes "for me to imbibe again." John throws in a hometown shout-out during "I'm Talking About You" with an interjected "up the 'Pool!"

Further chat with Brian Matthew follows, as he plugs the Beatles' upcoming Albert Hall concert (April 18), which would be partially simulcast by BBC Radio. Paul then attempts to read requests from fans while John mocks him; one card is from fans who had attended their March 3 show in Hanley. The show closes with an energetic rendition of "The Hippy Hippy Shake," with Paul screaming to spur on George's guitar solo.

RELEASE HISTORY

1982: **E** was the first track to surface from this broadcast, on the LP *Beautiful Dreamer.*

1988: A nearly complete tape was booted on *The Beatles at the Beeb w/Pete Best.* Missing from this release were the beginnings of **A, C, D,** and **H,** part of **F,** and all of **B.**

1993: A secondary source tape for this program had been circulating for some time which was more complete (missing only **D**). Unfortunately, this recording was plagued by bursts of static and other glitches throughout. Still, Great Dane used this tape on *The Complete BBC Sessions,* splicing in **D** (the first seven words of which have yet to turn up) from the earlier release.

2000: The static-free version of **E** was included on the CD-R *Deflating the Mythology.*

10. Amateur footage

Date: 25 March 1963
Location: Allerton Golf Course, Liverpool
Length: 1:32

Czechoslovakian-born photographer Dezo Hoffmann was an early favorite of the Beatles, and he was present at most of the major events in their career from Ringo's first recording session through their first American tour.

After covering their March 24 Liverpool Empire concert for *Record Mirror,* Dezo joined them the next day for a series of photo shoots at various locations in their hometown. They visited Paul's house in Allerton, the Cavern Club, and a barbershop where the others pretended to "cut" Paul's hair. A stop at a nearby golf course provided the famous "jumping Beatles" photo that would inspire the cover of their *Twist and Shout* EP.

Dezo had also brought his 8 mm movie camera, and the group took turns commandeering it as they romped through the grounds, producing the earliest surviving color footage of the Beatles with Ringo. They are seen leapfrogging over Dezo, dancing and running toward the camera, and popping up from behind a car. John also does his hunchback impression. Footage shot inside Dezo's car shows Paul at the wheel, pointing out various sights, and Ringo beside him in the passenger seat.

RELEASE HISTORY

This silent color footage circulates on video. Excerpts were first aired in the UK December 3, 1982, during a profile of Dezo Hoffmann on Channel 4's *The Tube.* A bit of this footage was used in the *Anthology* documentary during a sequence set to "It Won't Be Long."

11. Radio performance

Date: 1 April 1963
Time: 2:30–5:30* and 6:30–10:30 p.m.
Location: Studio 1, BBC Piccadilly Studios, London
Producer: Bryant Marriott
Host: John Dunn
Broadcast: 13 May 1963, 5:00–5:29 p.m.
BBC Light Programme
Side by Side

[A.] Side by Side (0:10)*
[B.] Long Tall Sally (1:45)
[C.] intro (0:22)
[D.] A Taste of Honey (2:01)
[E.] Chains (2:21)
[F.] intro (0:22)
[G.] Thank You Girl (1:58)
[H.] intro (0:12)
[I.] Boys (1:50)

The Beatles recorded two appearances on BBC Radio's *Side by Side* in a single session, including the show's theme song. The gimmick of the program was to feature the house band, the Karl Denver Trio, alternating tunes with a guest artist each week. None of the April 22 broadcast has turned up, but a very clean tape of this May 13 edition is widely available. "From Me to You" was included in both broadcasts, but (presumably) recorded only once.

The theme song, "Side by Side," is performed and sung by the Karl Denver Trio with John, Paul, and George merely singing along. Different takes (at least vocally; the backing is probably the same) were taped at the April 1 and fourth sessions (see entry below). Each broadcast of the theme song also had a unique voice-over introduction by host John Dunn.

"Long Tall Sally" is followed by some chat with John Dunn, who has evidently just asked about the Beatles' name as the tape begins. John gives his standard goonish answer about seeing a man on a flaming pie, after which Paul introduces "A Taste of Honey" as a "great favorite of me auntie Gin's."

"Thank You Girl" is also prefaced by some chat, as the Beatles jokingly answer Dunn's questions by talking simultaneously, all four attempting to hog the spotlight. Dialogue between Dunn and Ringo introduces "Boys," which fades out abruptly during the last chorus.

RELEASE HISTORY

1984: This abbreviated (fair-quality) version of **A** was the first track to surface, on the vinyl picture disc *Directly from Santa Claus.* It remained uncollected for a long time, but was copied on the 1999 CD-R compilation *Vinyl to the Core.*

1987: An excellent-sounding tape of the rest of this show (**B–I**) was released on vinyl copies of *The Beatles at the Beeb, Volume 2.* The Pyramid CD of this title and the boxed set *The Complete BBC Sessions* are missing portions of **C** and **F** and all of **H.** The latter is found on the CD-R *Attack of the Filler Beebs!, Episode 1.*

12. Radio performance

Date: 3 April 1963
Time: 8:30–9:45 p.m.
Location: Playhouse Theatre, London
Producer: Ron Belchier
Host: Brian Matthew
Broadcast: 7 April 1963, 10:31–11:30 a.m.
BBC Light Programme
Easy Beat

[A.] **intro** (0:40)
[B.] **From Me to You** (1:52)

The Beatles debuted their upcoming single, "From Me to You," in front of a live audience for this broadcast. As with most live versions of this song, John's harmonica is missing from the arrangement.

A humorous introduction from host Brian Matthew and Gerry Marsden (of Gerry and the Pacemakers) precedes the song. Gerry quips, "All I can say is, er—'How Do You Do It'?" This draws an enormous laugh from John, no doubt recalling his own dislike for that song, which the Beatles had rejected seven months earlier. Matthew asks Gerry if he thinks "From Me to You" will be a number 1 hit, as "How Do You Do It" had been for the Pacemakers. Though he's rather coy about it, Gerry says he hopes so ("From Me to You" would reach number 1, of course).

RELEASE HISTORY

1988: This recording circulated among tape traders briefly before surfacing on the bootleg LPs *Meet the Beeb* and *The Beatles at the Beeb w/Pete Best* in mediocre sound. It has been treated with noise reduction on *The Complete BBC Sessions.*

13. Radio performance

Date: 4 April 1963
Time: 11:00 a.m.–2:00 p.m.
Location: BBC Paris Studio, London
Producer: Bryant Marriott
Host: John Dunn
Broadcast: 24 June 1963, 5:00–5:29 p.m.
BBC Light Programme
Side by Side

[A.] **Side by Side** (0:52)
[B.] **intro** (0:04)
[C.] **Too Much Monkey Business** (2:04)
[D.] **outro** (0:02)
[E.] **intro** (0:14)
[F.] **Boys** (2:30)
When Day Is Done (the Karl Denver Trio)
[G.] **intro** (0:40)
[H.] **I'll Be on My Way** (1:59)
[I.] **outro** (0:04)
[J.] **From Me to You** (1:56)
[K.] **outro** (0:01)

The Beatles' third and final appearance on *Side by Side* was taped during the morning. A fourth session, penciled in for 2 p.m., was canceled when the group accepted an invitation to play at Stowe School in the late afternoon.

A short burst of indecipherable speech after "Too Much Monkey Business" is present on the source tape; perhaps this is what's left of the intro for "Love Me Do," the missing number from this broadcast. "Boys" is introduced with some typically wacky ad-libs from John and Karl Denver. This take of "Boys" is distinguishable from the April 1 version, because here Ringo repeats the first verse in place of the third verse.

The next song is introduced by way of poking fun at George, who has a sore throat. As George hoarsely rasps his way through a bit of "From Me to You," John Dunn laughs at him before reminding the audience that the show is prerecorded and that by the time it airs, George should be healed.

"I'll Be on My Way" sounds like a very early McCartney composition; the lyrics are painfully amateurish (particularly the "June light/Moonlight" rhyme), and the obvious inspiration of Buddy Holly permeates the tune, as with many Quarry Men–era songs. The guitar fills and solo from George are particularly reminiscent of "Crying, Waiting, Hoping." Why the Beatles performed "I'll Be on My Way" at this point in their career is puzzling; Billy J Kramer had recently recorded it (though his version hadn't been released yet), and perhaps Paul just wanted the Beatles' version available for posterity.

RELEASE HISTORY

1973: A rare and mysterious one-sided bootleg single contained a fair-quality tape of **H,** the most intriguing song from this program. It was copied the following year on the LP *Soldier of Love* and reissued many times, usually at the wrong speed and incomplete, on bootlegs such as *Happy Birthday* and *The Beatles vs. Don Ho*.

1980: A slight upgrade of **H** appeared on the LP *Rough Notes*.

1982: The same murky copy of **H,** taken from some bootleg or other, was included in the radio special *The Beatles at the Beeb,* which itself was widely bootlegged.

1984: A fair-quality (and off-speed) copy of **F,** along with the most complete version yet of **H,** surfaced on the picture LP bootleg *Directly from Santa Claus*.

1986: One of the more exciting releases in Beatleg history was the LP *The Beatles at the Beeb, Volume 1,* particularly since it contained a truly excellent tape of this entire program (**A–K**). Unfortunately, the Pyramid CD of this title has a botched edit of **A,** which tried to clean up a gap in the source tape but ended up chopping out some of the song. The full version is on the CD-R compilation *Vinyl to the Core*. The Pyramid disc also omits **K** (no big loss; it's merely John Dunn saying, "The Beatles"), and the boxed set *The Complete BBC Sessions* duplicates the Pyramid release.

1994: Apple's *Live at the BBC* saw the long-awaited release of **H** in excellent sound, but fading out a second too early compared to the best bootleg sources!

2003: The entire show, including the Karl Denver Trio number, was bootlegged on the CD boxed set *The Beatles at the Beeb*.

14. Amateur footage

Date: 4 April 1963
Time: afternoon
Location: BBC Paris Studio, London
Length: 0:54

As the Beatles left the BBC's studio to head for their gig in Stowe, the Karl Denver Trio's guitarist Kevin Neill, perhaps using Dezo Hoffmann's 8 mm camera, filmed their departure. It's quite similar to the earlier home movies from Liverpool (see the March 25 entry), as the Beatles wave and do silly dances; John even reprises his hunchback impression.

The silent color footage, slowed down and even played backwards at one point, finally surfaced in the promo clip for the 1995 single "Baby It's You." It includes glimpses of Neil Aspinall, BBC producer Bryant Marriott, and host John Dunn, and ends with the Beatles' van (registration # 6934 KD) pulling away into traffic.

RELEASE HISTORY

1995: Since no film footage of the Beatles recording in BBC studios seems to have survived (if any was ever shot), this home movie from outside the studio was used to promote Apple's *Live at the BBC* release, specifically in three different edits of the video for "Baby It's You" (the third of which was part of an *Anthology* electronic press kit).

15. Radio interview

Date: 18 April 1963
Location: Dressing room 5A, Royal Albert Hall, London
Interviewer: Roger Henning
Broadcast: 3DB, Melbourne
Length: 0:32

Roger Henning was an Australian-born broadcaster working out of London who had first interviewed the Beatles around late January. He sent the tape to radio station 3DB in Melbourne, but it was met with indifference. A couple of months later, the group was getting some airplay down under, and Henning went backstage during the Beatles' Albert Hall appearance to try again.

3DB's disc jockey Barry Ferber had been one of the first to play their records, so Paul sends him a greeting in between the Fabs' off-key renditions of "Waltzing Matilda," accompanied by harmonica and ukelele.

RELEASE HISTORY

1981: This brief interview was released on the LP *The Beatles Talk Downunder* and was usually identified as being either a recording from EMI Studio 2, September 12, 1963, or from the train location of *A Hard Day's Night,* March 2–6, 1964 (see entries for more information on those actual recordings). This recording has been reissued on numerous CDs such as *Inside Interviews: Talk Downunder: Australia Beatlemania, Beatles Tapes II: Early Beatlemania 1963–1964,* and *Talk Downunder, Volume 1*.

16. Concert/Radio performance

Date: 18 April 1963
Time: 10:02 p.m.
Location: Royal Albert Hall, London
Producers: Terry Henebery, Ron Belchier
Hosts: George Melly, Rolf Harris
Broadcast: live
BBC Light Programme
Swinging Sound '63

[A.] Twist and Shout (2:07)
[B.] intro (0:02)
[C.] From Me to You (1:56)
[D.] outro (0:22)

This recording captures a unique Beatles performance: a concert appearance simulcast live via BBC Radio throughout the UK. The first half of the concert was neither taped nor broadcast; it concluded with the Beatles playing "Please Please Me" and "Misery." A twenty-minute intermission followed before the concert continued, being transmitted live over the airwaves this time. Again, the Beatles closed the second half by playing two songs.

Interestingly, they had planned to play "Thank You Girl," performing it at that morning's rehearsal. During the live show, they substituted the raucous "Twist and Shout" in its place without telling the BBC's producers. One can only imagine the havoc this caused in the control booth. But the Beatles had another trick up their sleeve: They performed a shortened version of "Twist and Shout," omitting half of the third verse, so it would roughly equal the length of "Thank You Girl" (which ran 2:01 on disc as compared to "Twist and Shout" at 2:32). Thirty seconds may not seem like much time, but consider the circumstances: a live radio simulcast nearing the finale, with other programming scheduled to begin in ten minutes. It seems the Beatles didn't want to get into too much trouble.

It must have been a good choice to close the proceedings, as the tape ends with compere Rolf Harris' description of people "twisting all over the Albert Hall!"

RELEASE HISTORY

1986: There seems to be only one (fair-quality and sped-up) source tape for this broadcast, and it was first issued on the vinyl bootleg *The Beatles at the Beeb, Volume 1.* The Pyramid CD of this title (copied on *The Complete BBC Sessions* box) omits the last few seconds of **D.**

17. Home demo J, P

Date: ca. May 1963

[A.] Bad to Me (1:32)

John wrote this song while he was in Spain with Brian Epstein between April 28 and May 9, 1963. Brian had requested that John write a song for Billy J Kramer, who went on to record "Bad to Me" with the Dakotas at Abbey Road on June 27 and took it to number 1 in the UK (it was knocked from the top spot by "She Loves You"). This demo is very simple, just John and Paul singing in unison (until the harmonized ending) and playing acoustic guitars. It was possibly taped during a spare minute in their tour with Roy Orbison (May 18–June 9), either backstage or in a hotel room.

The tape reached our ears through a rather circuitous route; as with many original compositions, an acetate of this demo was pressed by Dick James, the group's music publisher. A copy of this acetate wound up in the hands of Brian Epstein's assistant, Alistair Taylor, who auctioned it off at Sotheby's on December 22, 1981. It sold in a lot with an acetate demo of "Goodbye" for £308 to an unknown bidder.

The demo was probably recorded for copyright purposes, and not to demonstrate the song to Billy. According to Dakotas drummer Tony Mansfield, John and Paul "came down to Abbey Road with the lyrics scrawled on the back of a Senior Service cigarette pack." He makes no mention of a demo tape, and Kramer remembers the song being played for him by all four Beatles. John and Paul did attend the June 27 session, but this demo seems to be a more primitive arrangement than Kramer's recorded version (particularly the middle eight), suggesting the demo was taped earlier.

RELEASE HISTORY

1984: It didn't take long for the acetate to make it to bootleg LP, and it first appeared on *File Under: Beatles,* as well as *Not For Sale* the following year. It was also included in the radio series *Sgt. Pepper's*

Lonely Hearts Club Band: A History of the Beatle Years 1962–1970, but with the intro cut off and narration over the ending.

1991: The song was also copied on the CD *Acetates,* with noise reduction to remove scratches, but sounding muffled and slightly incomplete at each end.

1999: The *Not For Sale* version was copied directly onto the CD-R compilation *Vinyl to the Core.*

17a. TV performance

Date: 16 May 1963
Time: 5:00–5:30 p.m.
Location: Television Theatre, London
Producer: Peter Whitmore
Broadcast: live
BBC TV
Pops and Lenny

[A.] From Me to You (0:40)

Although the original footage is missing, a brief off-air recording of the Beatles' second nationwide TV performance does exist. *Pops and Lenny* was a kids show starring a puppet named Lenny the Lion who introduced and interacted with guests from the pop music world. In addition to their new single, the Beatles performed a truncated "Please Please Me," and reportedly sang along with the day's other guests to the closing number, "After You've Gone" (later covered by Paul in a mid-1970s home demo).This is the earliest recording to feature Ringo playing his new Ludwig drum kit, acquired May 12; around this date, George also obtained his first Gretsch Country Gentleman electric guitar.

RELEASE HISTORY

2007: This fair-quality recording appeared on the Lazy Tortoise CD-R *April to August 1963.* It first surfaced in a BBC4 documentary, *When the Stranglers Met Roland Rat,* which aired June 1.

18. Radio performance

Date: 21 May 1963
Time: 5:30–6:30 p.m.
Location: Playhouse Theatre, London
Producers: Jimmy Grant, Bernie Andrews
Host: Brian Matthew
Broadcast: 25 May 1963, 10:00 a.m.–noon
BBC Light Programme
Saturday Club #242

[A.] intro (0:04)
[B.] I Saw Her Standing There (2:54)
[C.] intro (0:23)
[D.] Do You Want to Know a Secret (1:46)
[E.] Boys (2:25)
[F.] intro (0:17)
[G.] Long Tall Sally (1:46)
[H.] intro (0:11)
[I.] From Me to You (1:51)
[J.] Money (That's What I Want) (2:11)

This BBC session, the first of two taped in a single day, is one of the earliest for which a musically complete, excellent-sounding tape exists. The performances have very similar arrangements to their released counterparts. "I Saw Her Standing There" contains both middle eights, and "From Me to You" has overdubbed harmonica. "Do You Want to Know a Secret" and "Boys" each have full endings rather than fading out. "Money (That's What I Want)" is missing the first three notes on the source tape and is performed with only one chorus at the end (the final chorus is repeated on *With the Beatles*).

The Beatles are top-billed on *Saturday Club* for the first time, and George, John, and Ringo each get to read requests from fans (including some from Egypt and Germany), though there is none of the humorous give-and-take that would become common between the group and host Brian Matthew.

RELEASE HISTORY

1986: An excellent-quality tape of this entire broadcast was included on the bootleg LP *The Beatles at the Beeb, Volume 1.* The Pyramid CD of this title (also used on *The Complete BBC Sessions* box) is missing bits and pieces of **A, F,** and **H.** The full show is reconstructed on the CD-R *The Complete BBC Sessions—Upgraded.*

19. Radio performance

Date: 21 May 1963
Time: 10:00–11:15 p.m.
Location: Playhouse Theatre, London
Producer: Terry Henebery
Host: Diz Disley
Broadcast: 3 June 1963, 10:31–11:30 a.m.
BBC Light Programme
Steppin' Out

[A.] **intro** (0:03)
[B.] **Please Please Me** (1:52)
[C.] **intro** (0:02)
[D.] **I Saw Her Standing There** (2:52)
[E.] **outro** (0:05)

Recordings of "Roll Over Beethoven," "Thank You Girl," and "From Me to You" from this show, performed in front of an audience, have yet to surface. "Twist and Shout" was also taped, but not included in the broadcast.

The performances are standard live run-throughs for the era; "Please Please Me" lacks harmonica and "I Saw Her Standing There" is performed with both middle eights intact. There is quite a bit of distortion during the louder parts of both songs. Mark Lewisohn, writing in *The Complete Beatles Chronicle,* seems to imply that a longer version of this tape may exist, as he transcribes the full introduction from host Diz Disley; however, in an interview, Lewisohn revealed that many of the BBC Radio hosts' introductions were scripted and that the BBC still retained written copies of these. Only the final word of this intro, "Beatles," is included on bootlegs.

RELEASE HISTORY

1986: All that exists is a mediocre-quality copy of less than half of the Beatles' appearance. It debuted on vinyl copies of *The Beatles at the Beeb, Volume 1.* The Pyramid CD of this title (used on *The Complete BBC Sessions* box) is speed-corrected, but chops off about a second at either end (**A** and **E**).

20. Radio performance

Date: 24 May 1963
Time: 2:00–6:00 p.m.
Location: Studio 2, Aeolian Hall, London
Producer: Terry Henebery
Host: Lee Peters
Broadcast: 4 June 1963, 5:00–5:29 p.m.
BBC Light Programme
Pop Go the Beatles #1

[A.] **Pop Go the Beatles—opening edit** (0:19)
[B.] **intro** (0:05)
[C.] **Everybody's Trying to Be My Baby** (2:02)
[D.] **intro** (0:19)
[E.] **Do You Want to Know a Secret** (1:47)
[F.] **outro/intro** (0:24)
[G.] **You Really Got a Hold on Me** (2:51)
[H.] **outro** (0:02)
[I.] **Misery** (1:42)
[J.] **intro** (0:19)
[K.] **The Hippy Hippy Shake** (1:41)
[L.] **Pop Go the Beatles—closing edit** (1:09)

In an astonishing decision, the BBC decided to give the Beatles their own weekly radio series. Astonishing because they had achieved only small success to this point (two top 10 singles), and dedicating a half hour a week to a single pop group was nearly unheard of for the BBC, even on the more entertainment-oriented Light Programme. It's possible that the BBC simply wanted to strike while the iron was hot, before the Beatles' "inevitable" fade into obscurity. At any rate, it took only twenty-five days for the project to grow from conception to this first taping date. After the initial four episodes proved wildly successful, eleven more were ordered up; finding time in the Beatles' increasingly hectic schedule to tape all these appearances would prove troublesome as the summer ground on.

Thankfully, the Beatles eschewed playing just the "hits" or familiar material and exhausted most of their six-year repertoire of cover versions, everything from Elvis' "That's All Right (Mama)" (1954) through recent hits like the Crickets' "Don't Ever Change" (1962). Even more thankfully for us, 95 percent of the material from this entire series has survived on tape, mostly in very good quality.

Once the program's title, *Pop Go the Beatles,* had been decided upon, the next task was taping a title theme song to open and close each week's edition. Predictably, it was a rock-instrumental version of "Pop Goes the Weasel," punctuated by what sounds like host Lee Peters announcing the title, and some screaming from Paul in the background. It's unclear who is playing which instruments here; clearly the harmonica is played by John, and the drumming sounds like Ringo. Mark Lewisohn also reports that members of the Lorne Gibson Trio (the premiere week's guest artists) "aided" the Beatles with the recording. L.R.E. King quotes Gibson as saying that the guitarist and bassist of his trio played on this recording, along with Diz Disley (another BBC announcer), so perhaps it's Disley's voice announcing the title, rather than Lee Peters.

Whoever plays on the theme song, two edits were made from the same basic recording. The shorter one (**A**), used to open each week's program, runs for about 15 seconds before cutting to a final chord. The longer closing version (**B**) faded out at different points, depending on how long the show ran that week.

Unfortunately, the very first song from this series, "From Me to You," is currently unavailable, and the rest of this premiere episode is only in mediocre sound quality, with most of the chat missing.

RELEASE HISTORY

1972: Among the first BBC songs to be booted were **E, G, I,** and **K,** all of which appeared on the vinyl bootleg *Outtakes 1* (aka *Studio Sessions, Volume 1*). These were recycled on dozens of bootlegs over the next decade, despite being mediocre quality and at the wrong speed.

1974: A fair-quality tape of the *Pop Go the Beatles* theme song (from an unknown episode) was included on the vinyl boot *Rare Beatles* (aka *Happy Birthday*).

1980: A very good-quality (incomplete) copy of **L** was booted on the LP *Broadcasts.*

1982: The radio special *The Beatles at the Beeb* included a nice copy of **L,** cross-faded with narration, and probably dubbed directly from *Broadcasts.*

1984: The vinyl picture disc *Directly from Santa Claus* contained both **C** and **I,** in good quality.

1987: A new tape containing **B–G** was bootlegged on the LP *The Beatles at the Beeb, Volume 2.* Unfortunately, it ran too slow and didn't sound much better than previous releases. The Pyramid CD of this title is missing parts of **C** and **F.** Excellent tapes of **A** and **L** (the latter in most complete form to date) surfaced on the LP *The Beatles at the Beeb, Volume 3.*

1993: Great Dane's CD box, *The Complete BBC Sessions,* reconstructed this session from various sources—**A** sounds fine, but **B–G** come from the Pyramid CD and are missing bits of dialogue, although the songs are complete. **I** and **K** come from a fairly clean copy of *Outtakes 1,* but haven't been speed-corrected. **L** uses a tape that fades out after 47 seconds. The longer version is on the CD-R compilation *Vinyl to the Core.*

2003: The entire show, including the debuts of **H** and **J,** was bootlegged on the CD boxed set *The Beatles at the Beeb.*

21. Radio performance

Date: 1 June 1963
Time: 9:30 a.m.–1:30 p.m.
Location: BBC Paris Studio, London
Producer: Terry Henebery
Host: Lee Peters
Broadcast: 18 June 1963, 5:00–5:29 p.m.
BBC Light Programme
Pop Go the Beatles #3

[A.] **intro** (0:21)
[B.] **A Shot of Rhythm and Blues** (2:04)
[C.] **outro/intro** (0:46)
[D.] **Memphis, Tennessee** (2:16)
[E.] **intro (Happy Birthday to You)** (0:43)
[F.] **A Taste of Honey** (1:54)
[G.] **intro** (0:10)
[H.] **Sure to Fall (in Love with You)** (2:08)
[I.] **outro** (0:01)
Greenback Dollar (Carter-Lewis and the Southerners)
[J.] **intro** (0:16)
[K.] **Money (That's What I Want)** (2:38)
[L.] **outro** (0:05)
[M.] **intro** (0:10)
[N.] **From Me to You** (1:47)

Although this episode was the second to be taped, it was the third *Pop Go the Beatles* to be broadcast. After Ringo reads a fan request for "A Taste of Honey," Paul's twenty-first birthday is noted with a brief rendition of "Happy Birthday to You"—presumably this explains why the episode was held over for broadcast until June 18, Paul's actual date of birth. Speaking of birthdays, Lee Peters apologizes for prematurely announcing

Ringo's birthday in the previous episode (see following entry)—indicating that both his pieces of speech were taped independent of these June 1 recording sessions.

RELEASE HISTORY

1978: The vinyl bootleg *Youngblood* contained poor-quality recordings of **B** (incomplete), **D,** and **H** (a later pressing of this LP replaces **D** and **H** with performances from the January 1, 1962, Decca audition).

1982: The bootleg LP *Wonderful Picture of You* included fragments of **B–D** (a different section of **B** than *Youngblood*) in fair quality and way too fast.

1987: Thankfully, an excellent-quality tape surfaced on the LP *The Beatles at the Beeb, Volume 3,* comprising **A, B,** the end of **D,** and **E–K.** The Pyramid CD of this title omitted **I** (no big loss, as it's merely Lee Peters back-announcing the song's title).

1993: *The Complete BBC Sessions* box did a good job of reconstructing this session, including the debuts of **M** and **N** (from a slow, fair-quality tape), and a version of **D** edited from three sources. **I** was still missing, however.

1994: Apple included a nice copy of **H** on *Live at the BBC.*

1999: The *Mythology, Volume 1* boxed CD set contained a longer version of **C** (still a bit incomplete), as well as a complete copy of **D** (in inferior sound).

2000: Good-quality tapes of **C, D, M,** and **N,** all complete and speed-corrected, appeared on the bootleg CD *The Beatles Broadcast Collection, Trailer 1.*

2003: The entire show, including the debut of **L** and the Carter-Lewis and the Southerners number, was bootlegged on the CD boxed set *The Beatles at the Beeb.*

22. Radio performance

Date: 1 June 1963
Time: 1:30–5:30 p.m.
Location: BBC Paris Studio, London
Producer: Terry Henebery
Host: Lee Peters
Broadcast: 11 June 1963, 5:00–5:29 p.m.
BBC Light Programme
Pop Go the Beatles #2

[A.] **Too Much Monkey Business** (1:47)
[B.] **outro/intro** (0:29)
[C.] **I Got to Find My Baby** (1:57)
[D.] **outro** (0:02)
[E.] **intro** (0:22)
[F.] **Youngblood** (1:57)
[G.] **outro/intro** (0:12)
[H.] **Till There Was You** (2:11)
[I.] **intro** (0:28)
[J.] **Baby It's You** (2:44)
[K.] **outro** (0:28)
[L.] **intro** (0:09)
[M.] **Love Me Do** (2:26)

Although this episode was taped directly after episode #3, it was broadcast first on June 11. The boxed set *The Complete BBC Sessions* presents these songs in a different order, apparently based on printed references. I'm sticking to the order listed above, based on the source tape as found on *The Beatles at the Beeb, Volume 2.*

"I Got to Find My Baby" is followed by some unusual chat from Lee Peters, who reads a card sent in by some fans wishing Ringo a happy birthday. It's unusual because Peters says, "It was his birthday last Friday"; counting back from the broadcast date, that would be June 7. Unfortunately, Ringo was born on July 7.

RELEASE HISTORY

1978: A poor-quality, incomplete tape of **F** served as the title cut of the vinyl bootleg *Youngblood.*

1982: Good-quality copies of **A** (incomplete), **C,** and **F** (the intro obscured by the first few notes from an unrelated performance of "Twist and Shout") were booted on the LP *Beautiful Dreamer.* The same year, the radio special *The Beatles at the Beeb* included a mediocre-sounding tape with most of **B** and all of **C.**

1987: Most of this program (**A–C, E–J,** and **L–M**) was released in excellent sound on the bootleg LP *The Beatles at the Beeb, Volume 2.* The Pyramid CD of this title is missing part of **E;** it was copied in rearranged order on *The Complete BBC Sessions.*

1994: Apple's *Live at the BBC* CD gave us excellent copies of **B** (incomplete), **C, F, I** (cross-faded from the previous track), and **J.**

1995: **J** was released as the lead track of a CD single, with the bass frequency boosted compared to the album version.

2003: The entire show, including the debuts of **D** and **K,** was bootlegged on the CD boxed set *The Beatles at the Beeb.*

23. Radio performance

Date: 17 June 1963
Time: 10:30 a.m.–1:00 p.m.
Location: Studio 5, Maida Vale Studios, London
Producer: Terry Henebery
Host: Lee Peters
Broadcast: 25 June 1963, 5:00–5:29 p.m.
BBC Light Programme
Pop Go the Beatles #4

[A.] **intro** (0:01)
[B.] **I Saw Her Standing There** (2:49)
[C.] **outro/intro** (0:29)
[D.] **Anna (Go to Him)** (3:01)
[E.] **outro** (0:30)
[F.] **intro** (0:36)
[G.] **Boys** (2:27)
[H.] **outro/intro** (0:27)
[I.] **Chains** (2:14)
[J.] **outro** (0:08)
Faraway Places (the Bachelors)
Jailer Bring Some Water (the Bachelors)
[K.] **intro** (0:17)
[L.] **P.S. I Love You** (1:59)
[M.] **intro** (0:41)
[N.] **Twist and Shout** (2:24)
[O.] **outro** (0:10)

This episode of *Pop Go the Beatles,* the last of the initial four, is a bit disappointing, considering the material. Although the performances are fine, the song selection amounts to one long advertisement for the *Please Please Me* LP. Generally the songs follow their LP arrangements, including a fade-out for "Chains" and both middle eights in "I Saw Her Standing There." Two notable exceptions are "Boys," which comes to a full ending, and "P.S. I Love You," which has an extra chord tacked on at the end (Dmaj7 with an A in the bass).

There is also quite a bit of chat with host Lee Peters, who asks Paul how his twenty-first birthday party went. Although the party wouldn't be held until the day following the taping, Paul plays along and pretends it was a success; in fact it would turn into a disaster after John pummeled Bob Wooler. There's also a cute moment when Ringo reads out a request from some schoolgirls in the lower fourth class at Blackburn House, Liverpool. Paul interrupts by pointing out, "That was our sister school," and John affects an upper-class accent to add, "I was at college just near there, you know." Ringo, by far the most working-class Beatle, mocks him: "College puddin'! Well, you're posh."

RELEASE HISTORY

1987: An excellent copy of most of the broadcast (**A–I** and **K–M**) was included on *The Beatles at the Beeb, Volume 3.* For a change, neither the Pyramid CD nor *The Complete BBC Sessions* is missing anything compared to the original LP, although the latter has the song order altered slightly.

1995: Although nothing from this show was used on Apple's *Live at the BBC,* the "Baby It's You" CD single included an excellent copy of **G.**

1998: A bootleg CD, *Radio Sessions 62–65,* appeared purporting to contain the original, rejected lineup of Apple's CD. Minor sonic upgrades of **L** and **N** are included, which seems to indicate that Apple owns a really nice tape of this broadcast.

2000: Slight upgrades of **F–I,** plus the first appearance of **J,** were included on the bootleg CD *The Beatles Broadcast Collection, Trailer 1.*

2003: The entire show, including the debut of **O** and the Bachelors' numbers, was bootlegged on the CD boxed set *The Beatles at the Beeb.*

24. Radio performance

Date: 19 June 1963
Time: 8:45–9:45 p.m.
Location: Playhouse Theatre, London
Producer: Ron Belchier
Host: Brian Matthew
Broadcast: 23 June 1963, 10:31–11:30 a.m.
BBC Light Programme
Easy Beat

[A.] **Some Other Guy** (2:01)
[B.] **intro** (0:30)
[C.] **A Taste of Honey** (1:57)
[D.] **outro** (0:02)
[E.] **intro** (0:03)
[F.] **Thank You Girl** (2:01)
[G.] **intro** (0:31)
[H.] **From Me to You** (1:49)
[I.] **outro** (0:06)

All *Easy Beat* shows were taped in front of a studio audience, and this one turned out to be one of the Beatles' best early live performances. They were still a few months from their ensemble concert-playing peak, which extended from late 1963 through early 1964, but their stage act was becoming noticeably tighter and more polished while remaining energetic.

After the first song, Paul chats briefly with Brian and whitewashes the unfortunate events of the previous night's birthday party, claiming "we had a great time." Neither of the last two songs includes a harmonica part, unlike their released counterparts.

RELEASE HISTORY

1986: An excellent tape of this entire performance (**A–I**) was one of the highlights of *The Beatles at the Beeb, Volume 1.* The only flaw is the speed, which starts out too slow but gradually speeds up until the end, by which time it runs correctly.

1993: The Great Dane box *The Complete BBC Sessions* has a hard edit from **C** to **F,** but is otherwise complete.

1994: Apple's *Live at the BBC* included speed-corrected versions of **A** and **F,** joined by a cross-fade.

25. TV interview **J**

Date: 22 June 1963
Time: 8:30–9:15 p.m.
Location: Television Theatre, London
Producer: Neville Wortman
Host: David Jacobs
Broadcast: 29 June 1963, 6:35–7:00 p.m.
BBC TV
Juke Box Jury
Length: 6:26

John had the honor of making a solo appearance on BBC TV's record-judging panel show *Juke Box Jury,* hosted by disc jockey David Jacobs. Alongside fellow panelists Bruce Prochnik (Oliver Twist in the musical *Oliver!* on Broadway), Caroline Maudling (filling in for originally announced guest Zsa Zsa Gabor), and Katie Boyle (*Eurovision Song Contest* hostess), John gave a hit or miss designation to eleven songs, eight of which made it to air.

In fact, John's appearance became instantly notorious as he voted miss to each and every record on the broadcast, although he did give specific musical reasons for most of them. No videotape or kinescope of the original show has survived, but home-recorded tapes captured John's reactions to all but the first song.

"SO MUCH IN LOVE," THE TYMES

"I thought it was a Rolf Harris at first. And then I thought, 'Oh, it's the Drifters' . . . the style was all right, but it wasn't good enough in that idiom."

"THE CLICK SONG," MIRIAM MAKEBA AND THE BELAFONTE SINGERS

"If it was in English, it'd mean even less. It's intriguing because it's foreign, y'know . . . but you can pick 'em out a mile away, all the gimmicks and all the different styles."

"ON TOP OF SPAGHETTI," TOM GLASER

"Well, I can't stand these 'all together now' records . . . I prefer the recent Little Eva. 'Smokey Locomotion,' folks. But not that, y'know. It's like . . . an outing. A coach trip."

"FLAMENCO," RUSS CONWAY

"I like pianos and things, y'know, but not sort of pub pianos playing flamenco music . . . it still sounds honky, y'know. Didn't sound anything like flamenco . . . he hasn't pinched the best bits out of real Spanish music, I don't think. Sorry."

"FIRST QUARREL," PAUL AND PAULA

"Well, I liked their first record ["Hey Paula"]. And the—because I liked the octave singing, her singing, y'know, one above him. And it wasn't bad. I didn't buy it. And the second one, y'know, wasn't worth bothering. This—and this had 'Jim' in. Y'know, and I—all these American records are always about 'Jim' and 'Bobby' and 'Alfred' and all this."

"DON'T EVER LET ME DOWN," JULIE GRANT

"At the beginning I thought, y'know, 'Oh, it's one of those with an intro,' but the intro wasn't strong enough, y'know. I like . . . girl singers. I like Shirelles and Chiffons, y'know. They're different."

John's harshest criticism is reserved for Elvis Presley's "Devil in Disguise," as he complains about the lyrics, rhythm, and singing, agreeing with someone's comparison of the latter to Bing Crosby. Katie Boyle asks, "If he did sound like Bing Crosby, would it be bad?," and an incredulous John responds, "Well, for Elvis, yes."

As soon as the taping ended, John was rushed to Battersea Heliport where a waiting helicopter carried him to Abergavenny, Wales, for that evening's Beatles performance. After the show was broadcast a week later, the music papers printed letters from people complaining of John's negativity and from fans defending him for speaking his mind.

RELEASE HISTORY

1999: A good-quality off-line tape of this appearance lasting 5:04 was included on the bootleg CD boxed set *Mythology, Volume 1.* A fair-quality tape lasting 3:20 circulating among collectors contains material not found on the CD. The length listed above combines the unique elements from both sources.

26. Radio performance

Date: 24 June 1963
Time: 5:30–6:30 p.m.
Location: Playhouse Theatre, London
Producers: Jimmy Grant, Bernie Andrews
Host: Brian Matthew
Broadcast: 29 June 1963, 10:00 a.m.–noon
BBC Light Programme
Saturday Club #247

[A.] I Got to Find My Baby (1:57)
[B.] intro (0:37)
[C.] Memphis, Tennessee (2:18)
[D.] Money (That's What I Want) (2:30)
[E.] Till There Was You (2:13)
[F.] intro (0:28)
[G.] From Me to You (1:51)
[H.] Roll Over Beethoven (2:25)

As demand for Beatles appearances ballooned, the BBC began to book the group left and right for TV and radio programs. To fill the void between the two series of *Pop Go the Beatles,* another session for *Saturday Club* was quickly booked (their second in just over a month). The Beatles were also developing an on-air rapport with presenter Brian Matthew, which made their appearances on this series extremely enjoyable.

Their choice of material was interesting this time around; not only did they have Berry on the brain (three of the songs were written by Chuck), but three of these songs would be recorded at EMI the following month for their second album. Only their recent number 1 single, "From Me to You" (performed here with overdubbed harmonica), would be familiar to casual listeners.

John dedicates "Memphis" to "Good old Harry . . . and his box." The Beatles had been making mysterious references to this chap and his container in earlier episodes of *Pop Go the Beatles,* and Brian Matthew tries to get to the bottom of it all. John's explanation: "The truth about Harry and his box is that very pardon, often the parky walk through. Don't we? Y'know what I mean?"

RELEASE HISTORY

1972: The vinyl bootleg *Outtakes 1* (aka *Studio Sessions, Volume 1*) contained fair-quality, incomplete versions of **D, E, G,** and **H.**

1984: A very good copy of **H,** including Brian Matthew's spoken intro (suffering from tape glitches), was on the picture disc LP *Directly from Santa Claus.*

1987: The vinyl bootleg *The Beatles at the Beeb, Volume 2* included an excellent tape of **A–C** and **F–H.** The Pyramid CD of this title omits a portion of **F.**

1993: Great Dane's *The Complete BBC Sessions* box copies **D** and **E** from *Outtakes 1,* and the remainder from the Pyramid CD.

27. Studio session

Date: 1 July 1963
Time: 5:00–10:45 p.m.
Location: EMI Studio 2
Producer: George Martin

[A.] She Loves You—RM from unknown takes (2:18)
[B.] I'll Get You—RM from unknown take (2:02)
Mixed: 4 July 1963

[C.] She Loves You—RS1 (fake stereo) (2:21)
[D.] She Loves You—RS2 (fake stereo) (2:24)
Mixed: 8 November 1966

For their first studio session in nearly four months, the Beatles had an ace up their sleeves. Their original plan was to follow up two chart-topping singles with a charming but slight composition with the working title "Get You in the End." Luckily, John and Paul pushed themselves to write something better, and with five days to spare, "She Loves You" was born. Lyrically, the song was nothing special (engineer Norman Smith recalls seeing the lyric sheet before hearing the song and predicting disaster), but it all came together in the studio.

From Ringo's opening tom-tom salvo to the final glistening tripartite harmony, "She Loves You" is like nothing that came before in the Beatles' repertoire, and it would provide the engine to drive their career from transitory fame to superstardom. They certainly spent a long time getting it right, evidenced by the amount of tape used (more than one 30-minute reel, number of takes unknown), and the many edits (some hear as many as seven) needed to produce the final master take (**A**). It also sounds as though they added an extra layer of vocal overdubs to strengthen the crucial "yeah yeah yeah" refrains.

Less care was taken with the flip side, "I'll Get You" (**B**), down to leaving in one of the more obvious lyrical clashes in their catalog ("I'm gonna change/make your mind" in the bridge). They did overdub some trademark Fab handclaps and harmonica, but the song is severely out-classed by its companion. "She Loves You" would go on to sell more copies in Britain than any other single to that date, a record wholly deserved. It would also remain in the Top 40 from the week of its release in late August until the following March.

For such an important single, EMI was unusually careless with the original session tapes, all three reels of which were apparently gone by 1966. To include the song on stereo copies of the Christmas 1966 *Collection of Beatles Oldies* LP, Geoff Emerick prepared a fake stereo mix (**C**) with some tasteful reequalization (bass frequencies left, treble right). Thankfully, he rejected "RS two, version two" (**D**), which tries to achieve the same thing by panning portions of the song (mostly guitar licks and vocal riffs) from right to left. Both mixes have been bootlegged from John Barrett's cassette collection, complete with Emerick's mix announcements. According to Barrett's notes, these mixes were made from an EP master reel, presumably that for the 1965 EP *The Beatles' Million Sellers.*

RELEASE HISTORY

1963: **A** and **B** were released on the Beatles' fourth Parlophone single. No true stereo mixes of either song were ever made, nor will they be, since the session tapes are long gone. Various releases have contained fake stereo mixes of both songs, and the original mono mixes were contained on *Past Masters, Volume 1.*

1966: Stereo copies of *A Collection of Beatles Oldies* included **C.** A rechanneled mix of "I'll Get You" was prepared by EMI on December 24, 1970, but it's unclear whether it was ever released anywhere.

1992: The version of **A** included on *Past Masters, Volume 1* exposed all the edits in the song a bit too blatantly, so engineer Peter Mew was called upon to create a "sonic restoration" that disguises the splices somewhat. It was first released on the CD-EP of *The Beatles' Million Sellers,* but is more readily available on the CD *The Beatles 1962–1966.*

1999: Copies of **C** and **D** including Geoff Emerick's announcements surfaced among John Barrett's cassettes. They are both included on the bootleg CD *Turn Me On Dead Man: The John Barrett Tapes.* The versions booted on *Abbey Road Tape, Volume 1* sound worse than elsewhere (and have reversed channels), but retain all the silence in **C** between the slate and song, which other releases trim.

28. Radio performance

Date: 2 July 1963
Time: 6:30–9:30 p.m.
Location: Studio 5, Maida Vale Studios, London
Producer: Terry Henebery
Host: Rodney Burke
Broadcast: 16 July 1963, 5:00–5:29 p.m.
BBC Light Programme
Pop Go the Beatles #5

[A.] **That's All Right (Mama)** (2:53)
[B.] **outro** (0:02)
[C.] **There's a Place** (1:49)
[D.] **outro** (0:03)
[E.] **intro** (0:11)
[F.] **Carol** (2:35)
[G.] **intro** (0:31)
[H.] **Soldier of Love (Lay Down Your Arms)** (1:59)
[I.] **outro** (0:02)
[J.] **intro** (0:09)
[K.] **Lend Me Your Comb** (1:46)
[L.] **intro** (0:33)
[M.] **Clarabella** (2:38)
[N.] **outro** (0:02)

Before the fourth episode in the initial *Pop Go the Beatles* run had aired, the series was picked up for a further eleven installments. After a two-week break, it came roaring back with this excellent edition, complete with a new host who used the unlikely stage name Rodney Burke.

The Beatles always professed their love for Elvis Presley's earliest records, particularly his Sun material, and Paul does a sensational job handling "That's All Right (Mama)." It's nearly matched by the guitar fireworks in "Carol," although John has his usual difficulties translating Chuck Berry's lyrics into English. As Burke points out, "Lend Me Your Comb" is a suitable title for the mop-tops to perform, and they rock it up a bit more than Carl Perkins' original, perhaps thrilling at the chance to sing "bugger" on the air!

The Jodimars, a spin-off group of Bill Haley and his Comets, recorded "Clarabella" in 1956, and while it's hardly the most sophisticated song, Paul "whistles" it here with aplomb, while John plays blues harp for one of the few times on a nonoriginal composition. The moment when the harmonica comes wailing in alongside Paul's screaming vocal is perhaps the most exciting in *Pop Go the Beatles* history.

Most people's favorite Beatles at the Beeb performance, however, is "Soldier of Love (Lay Down Your Arms)," and it's hard to argue with that choice. The Beatles were not alone in their love for R & B singer-songwriter Arthur Alexander (the Rolling Stones would cover his sole Top 40 pop hit, "You Better Move On"), but John makes "Soldier of Love" his own with a soulful vocal, supported by Paul and George's polished harmonies. Lucky listeners of KRLA Radio in Los Angeles got to enjoy this recording when DJ Dave Hull aired an illicit tape on July 8, 1965.

RELEASE HISTORY

1973: The bootleg LP *Peace of Mind* included horrible-quality copies of **F** and **K,** misidentified for years as a Radio Luxembourg broadcast from January 18, 1963. (The Beatles did in fact appear on Radio Luxembourg January 21, 1963, but didn't perform.)

1974: An incomplete and poor-quality recording of **H** was released on *Rare Beatles* (aka *Happy Birthday*) and *Soldier of Love.*

1980: A bootleg EP titled *Four by the Beatles* contained an excellent tape of **F, H, K,** and **M,** with much of the surrounding chat intact. This tape was also used on the LP *Broadcasts.*

1982: A good-quality copy of **A** surfaced on the LP *Beautiful Dreamer.* The radio special *The Beatles at the Beeb* played a portion of this, as well as **E–H** and **J–M.**

1987: The LP *The Beatles at the Beeb, Volume 3* used two source tapes for this show. **A–C** are in very good quality, with very heavy and muddy bass. The first two notes of **C** are missing, but this same recording is available complete from a later broadcast (see the entry for *Pop Go the Beatles,* # 12, August 1, 1963). The rest of the show **(D–N)** is in excellent quality. The Pyramid CD of this title (used on *The Complete BBC Sessions* box) trims or omits a lot of the dialogue (**B, D, E, I, J,** and **N**) compared to the vinyl.

1994: Apple was shrewd enough to release every unreleased song from this excellent program. *Live at the BBC* has **A** (with much of the bass filtered out), **F, H** (unfortunately cross-faded near the end), **L** (edited), and **M.** On the plus side, all the songs are speed-corrected and generally sound great.

1995: The remaining song, **K,** was included on *Anthology 1,* in excellent sound.

2003: The entire show, including a more complete version of **D,** was bootlegged on the CD boxed set *The Beatles at the Beeb.*

29. Radio performance

Date: 3 July 1963
Time: 8:00–9:00 p.m.
Location: Playhouse Theatre, Manchester
Producer: Geoff Lawrence
Host: Gay Byrne
Broadcast: 4 July 1963, 1:00–1:30 p.m.
BBC Light Programme
The Beat Show

[A.] **A Taste of Honey** (1:53)
[B.] **Twist and Shout** (2:26)

Sandwiched among engagements in London was this return to the north to perform three songs in front of an audience at BBC Radio's Manchester venue. The first song, "From Me to You," has yet to surface, but the rest of the Beatles' sole appearance on the aptly titled *Beat Show* does exist from a shabby-sounding off-air tape.

RELEASE HISTORY

1993: These songs circulated on a fair-quality tape for a number of years before Great Dane included them on *The Complete BBC Sessions*. One strain of this tape, although marred by nasty glitches, does include the final drumbeat of **B,** which is missing from Great Dane's set. It's been restored on the CD-R *The Complete BBC Sessions—Upgraded.*

30. TV interview

Date: 19 June–6 July 1963
Interviewer: Gianni Bisiach
Broadcast: 23 December 1963
RAI 1
tv 7
Length: 1:47

Sometime during the summer of 1963, Italian TV reporter Gianni Bisiach interviewed the Beatles backstage at an unknown venue. My best guess at the date would be June 30 at the ABC Cinema in Great Yarmouth, the opening night of their seaside resort season. The group interview was probably filmed backstage prior to the concert; only John has changed into his stage suit.

Each Beatle gives his name and age (Paul is twenty-one and Ringo still twenty-two, narrowing down the date considerably), and they discuss fan mail (sufficient to require fan club secretaries to sort through by this point) and their Pierre Cardin–designed jackets. Asked what else occupies his life beyond music, Ringo replies, "Cars and girls and things like that, y'know."

This interview may not have been aired until Beatlemania was more of a worldwide phenomenon, as the circulating video comes from a December 23 broadcast. It includes footage of the Beatles' *Mersey Sound* performance of "Twist and Shout" and the Royal Variety Performance (the latter filmed directly off a TV screen). Also included are interviews with fans and some silent footage from the Cheltenham Odeon concert (see the November 1 entry).

RELEASE HISTORY

This footage circulates on video.

31. Radio performance

Date: 10 July 1963
Time: 10:30–1:30 p.m.
Location: Studio 5, Maida Vale Studios, London
Producer: Terry Henebery
Host: Rodney Burke
Broadcast: 23 July 1963, 5:00–5:29 p.m.
BBC Light Programme
Pop Go the Beatles #6

[A.] **intro** (0:08)
[B.] **Sweet Little Sixteen** (2:20)
[C.] **A Taste of Honey** (1:57)
[D.] **intro** (0:04)
[E.] **Nothin' Shakin' (but the Leaves on the Trees)** (2:57)
[F.] **outro/intro** (0:21)
[G.] **Love Me Do** (2:27)

[H.] intro (0:10)
[I.] Lonesome Tears in My Eyes (2:35)
Mad Mad World (Carter-Lewis and the Southerners)
[J.] intro (0:08)
[K.] So How Come (No One Loves Me) (1:53)
[L.] outro (0:10)

Halfway through a week-long stint in Margate, the Beatles spent one morning and afternoon in London taping the next two installments in their *Pop Go the Beatles* series. They continued to reach into their bag of oldies, all staples of their Cavern and Hamburg set lists, rather than simply play songs from their own singles and LPs.

This time they came up with a pair of obscure but impressive numbers: Eddie Fontaine's "Nothin' Shakin'" and "Lonesome Tears in My Eyes," which John explains is "a Dorsey Burnette number, brother of Johnny Burnette . . . recorded on my first LP in 1822!" It was actually performed originally by the Johnny Burnette Trio, which included Dorsey, and was cowritten by the brothers. Ringo eschews cymbals on this number, while John plays guitar lines he would later "borrow" for the "Ballad of John and Yoko."

Ironically, their only recorded Everly Brothers cover, "So How Come (No One Loves Me)," features John and George duetting rather than John and Paul, whose early harmonizing so often resembles that of Don and Phil.

RELEASE HISTORY

1971: The LP *Yellow Matter Custard* was the first bootleg to contain BBC performances, among them mediocre-quality copies of **E, I,** and **K.**

1972: A good-quality tape of **G** (with the intro chopped off) appeared on the vinyl bootleg *Outtakes 1* (aka *Studio Sessions, Volume 1*).

1978: Original pressings of the bootleg LP *Youngblood* included an incomplete copy of **B** in fair sound. The reissue copied the version from *Beautiful Dreamer* (see below).

1981: Upgrades of **E, I,** and **K** surfaced on the vinyl bootleg *Airtime,* although **K** was slightly less complete than on *Yellow Matter Custard.*

1982: *Beautiful Dreamer* included a good-quality (but slow and glitchy) tape of **B.** This and the three songs from *Airtime* were all part of the radio special *The Beatles at the Beeb.*

1987: Vinyl copies of the bootleg *The Beatles at the Beeb, Volume 4* included **A, B** (including the glitch), **D, E, H** (incomplete), **I, J,** and **K** (the last two incomplete). The boxed CD set *The Complete BBC Sessions* copies this, but reconstructs **E** and **K** using *Yellow Matter Custard,* supplemented by **G** from *Outtakes 1.*

1994: Apple unearthed a truly excellent copy of this program and included all six songs, including the debut of **C** and more complete recordings of **G** and **H,** on *Live at the BBC.*

2000: The bootleg CD *The Beatles Broadcast Collection, Trailer 1* included a reconstruction of this entire show, using all previous best sources and adding **L** and a complete **J,** both from a good-quality off-line tape.

2003: The entire show, including the debut of **F** and the Carter-Lewis and the Southerners number, was bootlegged on the CD boxed set *The Beatles at the Beeb.*

32. Radio performance

Date: 10 July 1963
Time: 1:30–3:30 p.m.
Location: Studio 5, Maida Vale Studios, London
Producer: Terry Henebery
Host: Rodney Burke
Broadcast: 30 July 1963, 5:00–5:29 p.m.
BBC Light Programme
Pop Go the Beatles #7

[A.] intro (0:01)
[B.] Memphis, Tennessee (2:15)
[C.] outro/intro (0:38)
[D.] Do You Want to Know a Secret (1:45)
Sweets for My Sweet (the Searchers)
[E.] intro (0:42)
[F.] Till There Was You (2:14)
[G.] intro (0:28)
[H.] Matchbox (1:57)
[I.] outro (0:01)
[J.] intro (0:27)
[K.] Please Mr. Postman (2:13)
Da Doo Ron Ron (the Searchers)
[L.] intro (0:06)
[M.] The Hippy Hippy Shake (1:50)
[N.] outro (0:16)

The songs in this edition of *Pop Go the Beatles* are a bit more familiar than those in the two previous episodes, with two of the titles officially recorded for their second LP later in the month and a third issued on an EP in 1964. Luckily, there is plenty of chat with Rodney Burke to entertain, including George reading a bizarre request, Burke reminding fans to send in postcards and not letters, and Ringo's cheerfully manic intro: "Hello there, kiddies! I'd like to sing a song for you today called 'Matchbox'!"

This week's guest artist, fellow Liverpudlian group the Searchers, perform their first single, "Sweets for My Sweet." Helped by the exposure and praise from John (who called it "the best disc ever from a Liverpool group" on its release), it climbed all the way to number 1 by August.

RELEASE HISTORY

1980: Excellent-quality copies of **B, D, F, H,** and **M** were included on the LP *Broadcasts*.

1981: The remaining song, **K,** appeared in very good sound on the vinyl bootleg *Airtime*.

1982: The radio special *The Beatles at the Beeb* featured **B, D, H, K,** and **M** (some of which were incomplete), probably copied from previous bootlegs.

1987: Vinyl copies of *The Beatles at the Beeb, Volume 4* contained a very good-quality (but slow) tape of nearly the entire program (**A–M,** but including only the first two words of **E**). The Pyramid CD of this title (copied on *The Complete BBC Sessions* box) was speed-corrected but omitted **E** and **I.**

1994: Excellent-sounding versions of **B, G, H,** and **M** were released on Apple's *Live at the BBC* CD, although the end of **B** is cross-faded with the following track.

2000: The bootleg CD *The Beatles Broadcast Collection, Trailer 1* included an excellent tape of **C–D,** plus the first Searchers number (**C** is slightly incomplete).

2003: The entire show, including the debut of **N** and both Searchers numbers, was bootlegged on the CD boxed set *The Beatles at the Beeb*.

33. Home demo

Date: ca. July 1963
Location: 20 Forthlin Road, Liverpool (?)

[A.] Tammy (0:41)
[B.] Over the Rainbow (1:22)
unknown song fragment (0:02)
[C.] Instrumental #1 (0:22)
unknown song fragment (0:04)
[D.] Instrumental #2 (2:29)
[E.] Michelle (1:00)
cymbal crash (0:02)
[F.] Instrumental #3 (0:08)
cymbal crash (0:03)
[G.] Instrumental #4 (1:20)
[H.] Instrumental #5 (1:06)
[I.] Three Coins in a Fountain (1:34)
unknown song fragments (0:10)
nursery rhymes (1:42)
[J.] Rockin' and Rollin' (backing track) (0:58)
[K.] Rockin' and Rollin' (playback—2 false starts) (0:15)
[L.] Rockin' and Rollin' (playback w/overdubs) (1:49)
unknown song fragments (0:34)
[M.] Rockin' and Rollin' (playback w/overdubs) (1:12)

This reel of homemade recordings is part of a collection once owned by Alf Bicknell, the Beatles' chauffeur from 1964–1966. He apparently obtained them from John, left them in his garage (thus the unofficial moniker "the garage tapes") for twenty-two years, and eventually sold them at a Sotheby's auction to an anonymous bidder (reportedly Paul McCartney). Luckily for us, somewhere between Alf and Paul, copies were made and have found their way to bootlegs, with each successive release getting a generation closer to the original source.

The dating of this tape is uncertain; I've placed it here because the bulk of the tapes date from July, but it was likely taped over a period of months or years, perhaps beginning much earlier than 1963. The location seems more certain, since the recordings all focus around Paul and family. The tape opens with Paul listening to the radio and singing along in exaggeratedly comical operatic fashion to versions of "Tammy" and "Over the Rainbow" (the latter also features Paul's Elvis impression).

This is followed by several minutes of Paul's solo guitar practice, entirely instrumental. Between songs we can hear unrelated material being taped over. The first piece (**C**) is haphazard and atonal, but the second (**D**) is a rockabilly number resembling Eddie Cochran's "Somethin' Else" (it's also similar to many of the instrumentals on the April 1960 Beatals rehearsal tape). The most interesting portion of the tape (**E**) is about a minute of the "French thing" Paul would eventually fashion into "Michelle." The structure of the verse is in place, but Paul soon wanders into random chords.

A brief Japanese-sounding riff (**F**) is followed by a jazzy improvisation in B major (**G**) and an exercise (**H**) that alternates chords with individual plucked and hammered-on notes. Finally, Paul runs through a tentative but chordally sophisticated version of "Three Coins in a Fountain" (**I**). The next portion of the tape has what sounds like Paul's brother Michael and a young girl (their stepsister Ruth?) singing about a ballet dancer and reciting "Mary, Mary quite contrary."

The tape ends with an early attempt at multitracking a generic blues boogie, "Rockin' and Rollin'," by means of making tape copies off a speaker while adding live overdubs. First we hear an instrumental "backing track" (**J**) consisting of piano, bass, and electric guitar. As John asks if the recorder is on (**K**), there are a couple of false start playbacks of a completed backing tape. Ringo replies, "Okay, we're going" (apparently he's manning the second machine), and trumpet, drums, and more guitar are played live (**L**), ending with a flourish well past the conclusion of the original backing track.

This tape was copied to the second machine again for Paul to add a lead vocal, and then back yet again to the original tape (**M**) for John and Paul to add some "doo wah" response vocals. By this time, the tape is at the fourth or fifth generation, and the original backing is a distant murk.

All these instruments would have been available at the McCartney home, since Paul started on trumpet, Mike owned a drum kit, and they had a family piano. Just before the final overdub take, there are fragments of two songs taped off the radio or records, the first of which seems to be the inspiration for "Rockin' and Rollin'." The original tape reportedly continues with several more minutes of radio broadcasts, including Helen Shapiro's 1961 hit, "Walkin' Back to Happiness."

RELEASE HISTORY

1992: The bootleg CD *The Garage Tapes* included fair-quality copies of **A–M.** This reel was part of the Alf Bicknell collection and sold for £11,500 at the August 22, 1989, Sotheby's auction.

1995: **A–M** appeared on the bootleg CD *Maybe You Can Drive My Car* in slightly better quality.

2001: Another minor upgrade of **A–M** was bootlegged on the CD *Alf Together Now.*

34. Speech — J, G

Date: ca. 15 July 1963
Location: Mendips, 251 Menlove Avenue, Liverpool (?)
Length: 6:00

During a rare day off, it seems John and George went home to Liverpool and visited Cynthia and three-month-old Julian at Mendips, John's childhood home where his aunt Mimi still lived. They brought a portable tape recorder, and, for whatever reason, taped themselves chatting and listening to an album (Julian can be heard cooing in the background as well). This recording comes from the Alf Bicknell collection, though it's not clear which of the reels it was originally on.

Most of the conversation is buried by the music (instrumental versions of an unknown song and "Never on Sunday"), but George can be heard discussing the group's upcoming schedule. He tells Cynthia that they'll be recording a show on Thursday for broadcast Sunday and complains that they'll have to wear stage suits because it's in front of an audience. This suggests a live radio performance, and *Easy Beat* would seem to fit the bill (actually recorded Wednesday the seventeenth for broadcast on Sunday the twenty-first).

George then says they're going to London "tomorrow" and will be there until Thursday (on Friday the nineteenth they moved on to Wales for two concerts). "Never on Sunday" ends, and George asks if that's the end of the LP side. The tape is shut off and resumes with a silly dialogue between John and George. A few weeks later, George would tell an interviewer: "Just lately we've all been having a bit of fun with a tape-recorder. John writes down the words—you can't really call it poetry or verse—and then I read it out on the tape. It's weird stuff. I'm not sure that anybody else would know what it's all about!"

That seems to be the case here. Although the signal is heavily overloaded and distorted, the exchange seems to go along these lines: "You're just fantastic, Nina. Quite a uniquey model." "Will I take that for the compliment?" "Believe me, I could pay you a higher one, you're so ugly. Darling, I think you've had your hair dyed long enough now, how about going bald."

RELEASE HISTORY

1995: This tape first appeared on the bootleg CD *Maybe You Can Drive My Car* in fair quality.

2001: A minor upgrade was bootlegged on the CD *Alf Together Now.*

35. Radio performance

Date: 16 July 1963
Time: 3:00–5:30 p.m.
Location: BBC Paris Studio, London
Producer: Terry Henebery
Host: Rodney Burke
Broadcast: 6 August, 1963, 5:00–5:29 p.m.
BBC Light Programme
Pop Go the Beatles #8

[A.] **intro** (0:13)
[B.] **I'm Gonna Sit Right Down and Cry (over You)** (2:02)
[C.] **outro/intro** (0:28)
[D.] **Crying, Waiting, Hoping** (2:10)
[E.] **Kansas City/Hey Hey Hey Hey!** (2:39)
[F.] **intro** (0:04)
[G.] **To Know Her Is to Love Her** (2:50)
[H.] **outro** (0:04)
It's Too Late Now (the Swinging Blue Jeans)
[I.] **intro** (0:29)
[J.] **The Honeymoon Song** (1:40)
[K.] **intro** (0:02)
[L.] **Twist and Shout** (2:25)
[M.] **outro** (0:10)

The Beatles' brutal July schedule continued with a triple-booking for the BBC, which saw them whip through uniformly excellent performances of seventeen numbers for *Pop Go the Beatles.*

In this edition, they revisit two songs from their Decca audition that highlight how far they've come in eighteen months. Buddy Holly's "Crying, Waiting, Hoping" and the Teddy Bears' "To Know Her Is to Love Her" both sound smooth and assured where they once sounded antsy and rushed. Even more amazing is a cover of Elvis' "I'm Gonna Sit Right Down and Cry (Over You)," which really should have been recorded at Abbey Road for an official release. It's a touch less frenzied than the 1962 Star-Club performance, but Ringo turns in one of his best performances ever, flailing away from start to finish tirelessly.

George reads a request from "the sheriff of Blackpool" for "the Honeyboot Sog." Although his pronunciation is explained away as the result of a stuffy nose, it's unwittingly accurate, for a soggier, sappier song would be hard to find in the Beatles' entire repertoire. The song was written for the film *Honeymoon,* but apparently Paul chose the number merely because he was impressed by the guitar volume pedal used by the guitarist of the Marino Marini Quartet, whose version they re-create.

RELEASE HISTORY

1971: Mediocre-quality versions of **B, D, G,** and **J** were included on one of the earliest bootlegs, *Yellow Matter Custard.*

1972: **E** surfaced on *Outtakes I* (aka *Studio Sessions, Volume 1*), incomplete and in good quality.

1981: An upgrade of **D** was included on the bootleg LP *Airtime.*

1982: The radio series *The Beatles at the Beeb* featured **D, G,** and **J,** the latter two in improved sound quality.

1987: *The Beatles at the Beeb, Volume 4* contained a very good tape of most of this program (**A–G** and **I–M**), although **E** was still missing the first couple of notes. This was copied on Great Dane's *The Complete BBC Sessions* box.

1994: Several songs from an excellent-sounding source were released on Apple's *Live at the BBC* CD: **B, D, E** (now with a complete intro, but with the ending cross-faded!), **G,** and **L** (the intro covered by screams from the previous track). Somehow a stray fragment of dialogue (**H**) made a unique appearance on the CD *The Ultimate Collection, Volume 3: The Radio Years at the Beeb.*

2003: The entire show, including the Swinging Blue Jeans number, was bootlegged on the CD boxed set *The Beatles at the Beeb.*

36. Radio performance

Date: 16 July 1963
Time: 6:00–8:30 p.m.
Location: BBC Paris Studio, London
Producers: Terry Henebery, Ian Grant
Host: Rodney Burke
Broadcast: 13 August 1963, 5:00–5:29 p.m.
BBC Light Programme
Pop Go the Beatles #9

[A.] **intro** (0:14)
[B.] **Long Tall Sally** (1:54)
[C.] **outro/intro** (0:24)
[D.] **Please Please Me** (1:54)
[E.] **intro** (0:40)
[F.] **She Loves You** (2:18)
[G.] **outro/intro** (0:23)
[H.] **You Really Got a Hold on Me** (2:56)

[I.] **outro** (0:02)
Searchin' (The Hollies)
[J.] **intro** (0:11)
[K.] **I'll Get You** (2:00)
[L.] **I Got a Woman** (2:48)
[M.] **outro** (0:16)

The circulating copy of this episode contains no chat from the Beatles, with five out of the six songs introduced by Rodney Burke reading out requests, babbling about "Long Tall Sally" ("Well, it can't be the one I know. She's a pally, Sally, but she doesn't dally"), and making a deliberately painful attempt to sing "What Kind of Fool Am I?"

This would have been eased somewhat by the listeners' first chance at hearing both sides of the group's new single, released ten days after the broadcast. They haven't quite got the words to "She Loves You" down ("[mumble] it's up to you"), and while they sing the wrong opening line to "You Really Got a Hold on Me," at least they all sing the same erroneous lyric! Elsewhere, John's guitar solo nearly collapses during "Long Tall Sally," but he does a great job re-creating Elvis' cover of the Ray Charles tune "I Got a Woman," right down to the baritone mutterings that precede the Preslian 12/8 time coda.

RELEASE HISTORY

1971: An incomplete recording of **L** appeared on *Yellow Matter Custard* in good sound.

1972: **B** and **D** were included on *Outtakes 1,* and an incomplete version of **F** was on *Outtakes 2* (aka *Studio Sessions, Volumes 1 and 2*).

1982: A mediocre copy of **K** surfaced on *Beautiful Dreamer.* None of the songs from this edition made it onto *The Beatles at the Beeb* radio special.

1987: The entire show (**A–M**) was released in excellent sound on *The Beatles at the Beeb, Volume 5,* and subsequently copied on *The Complete BBC Sessions* box.

1994: Apple released **B** (cross-faded at the end with screaming) and **L,** both in excellent quality, on the CD *Live at the BBC.*

2003: The entire show, including the Hollies number, was bootlegged on the CD boxed set *The Beatles at the Beeb.*

37. Radio performance

Date: 16 July 1963
Time: 8:45–10:30 p.m.
Location: BBC Paris Studio, London
Producer: Terry Henebery
Host: Rodney Burke
Broadcast: 20 August 1963, 5:00–5:29 p.m.
BBC Light Programme
Pop Go the Beatles #10

She Loves You (rebroadcast of version F from episode #9)
[A.] **outro/intro** (0:26)
[B.] **Words of Love** (1:56)
[C.] **outro** (0:03)
My Whole World Is Falling Down (Russ Sainty and the Nu-Notes)
Wipeout (The Nu-Notes)
[D.] **intro** (0:05)
[E.] **Glad All Over** (1:51)
[F.] **intro** (0:18)
[G.] **I Just Don't Understand** (2:47)
[H.] **outro** (0:07)
Unforgettable Love (Russ Sainty and the Nu-Notes)
Walkin' Tall (Russ Sainty and the Nu-Notes)
[I.] **intro** (0:26)
[J.] **Devil in Her Heart** (2:22)
[K.] **outro** (0:01)
Da Doo Ron Ron (Russ Sainty and the Nu-Notes)
[L.] **intro** (0:32)
[M.] **Slow Down** (2:36)
[N.] **outro** (0:02)

Despite the repetition of "She Loves You" from the previous week's broadcast and zero chat from the boys, this *Pop Go the Beatles* succeeds in highlighting the breadth of the Beatles' live repertoire.

John and Paul duet beautifully on a Buddy Holly ballad, "Words of Love," which they would record with a slower pace and more acoustic feel for the LP *Beatles For Sale.* George has a ball with the goofy Carl Perkins rockabilly tune "Glad All Over," and he takes the lead on the obscure girl-group number "Devil in Her Heart." Originally recorded by the Donays as "Devil in His Heart," the song would be taped at Abbey Road two days later for *With the Beatles* once they'd worked out the lyrics (there is plenty of confusion on this version).

"Slow Down" is a Larry Williams rocker familiar from the *Long Tall Sally* EP, although here John enunciates the lyric "now you don't care a dime for me" clearly. Perhaps the most unexpected cover in the entire Beatles BBC canon is "I Just Don't Understand," a torch song in waltz-time originally sung by film star Ann-Margret. John's singing drones on and the band is unable to rise above the repetitive melody, but if Rodney Burke is to be believed, at least two requests came in specifically for this song.

RELEASE HISTORY

1971: *Yellow Matter Custard* included good-quality recordings of **E, G,** and **M.**

1972: The two remaining songs, **B** and **J,** appeared (both incomplete) from a good-quality source on *Outtakes 2* (aka *Studio Sessions, Volume 2*).

1982: About half of **G** was included on the radio special *The Beatles at the Beeb,* probably taken from a bootleg.

1987: A decent-quality tape of this entire program (**A–N**) was released on the LP boot *The Beatles at the Beeb, Volume 5.* The Pyramid CD of this title (copied on *The Complete BBC Sessions* box) is missing **N.**

1994: Excellent versions of **E, G,** and **M** (with the ending cross-faded into the following track slightly) appeared on Apple's *Live at the BBC* CD.

1995: An excellent copy of **J** appeared on the "Baby It's You" CD single.

2003: The entire show, including the Nu-Notes numbers, was bootlegged on the CD boxed set *The Beatles at the Beeb.*

38. Radio performance

Date: 17 July 1963
Time: 8:45–9:45 p.m.
Location: Playhouse Theatre, London
Producer: Ron Belchier
Host: Brian Matthew
Broadcast: 21 July 1963, 10:31–11:30 a.m.
BBC Light Programme
Easy Beat

[A.] **intro** (0:03)
[B.] **I Saw Her Standing There** (2:35)
[C.] **intro** (0:02)
[D.] **A Shot of Rhythm and Blues** (2:09)
[E.] **intro** (0:09)
[F.] **There's a Place** (1:46)
[G.] **intro** (0:01)
[H.] **Twist and Shout** (2:24)
[I.] **outro** (0:06)

Less than a month after their previous appearance on *Easy Beat,* the Beatles returned for another four-song set, performed as usual in front of an exuberant audience. This time, there is no chat with host Brian Matthew, at least not on the circulating tape. We do get to hear the only recorded live versions of Arthur Alexander's "A Shot of Rhythm and Blues" and the group's own "There's a Place."

RELEASE HISTORY

1974: The obscure bootleg *Stockholm* included a poor-quality recording of **C–H,** running too slow.

1982: The vinyl bootleg *Wonderful Picture of You* contained an incomplete but upgraded tape of **C** and **D.**

1988: After circulating on tape for a while, the complete program finally surfaced on bootleg LPs. *Meet the Beeb* had **A–F,** and *The Beatles at the Beeb w/Pete Best* included **A–I.** Both releases were only mediocre quality.

1993: Great Dane's *The Complete BBC Sessions* box uses two sources for this; the first half (**A–E**) is probably from *Meet the Beeb,* while **F–I** were apparently taken from *Stockholm,* but not speed-corrected. In the editing, most of **E** and a bit of **I** were lost (both consist of nothing but audience screams).

39. Studio session

Date: 18 July 1963
Time: 7:00–10:45 p.m.
Location: EMI Studio 2
Producer: George Martin

[A.] You Really Got a Hold on Me—edit of RM7, 10, and 11 (2:58)
[B.] Money (That's What I Want)—edit of RM6–7 (2:46)
[C.] Devil in Her Heart—RM6 (2:23)
Mixed: 21 August 1963

[D.] You Really Got a Hold on Me—edit of RS7, 10, and 11 (2:58)
[E.] Devil in Her Heart—RS6 (2:23)
Mixed: 29 October 1963

[F.] Money (That's What I Want)—RS7 (2:46)
Mixed: 30 October 1963

The first session for the LP *With the Beatles* was originally scheduled for the fifteenth, but bumped forward three days so the Beatles could enjoy a day off in their hometown. No new songs had been written (or at least completed; "All My Loving" was begun during the Roy Orbison tour that ended June 9) in time for the session, so four cover versions were selected from their recent BBC Radio repertoire (all four had been performed within the last month).

"You Really Got a Hold on Me" was taped first, in five takes with John singing lead. Takes 6 and 7 were overdubs of George Martin's piano onto take 5. Takes 8, 9, and 10 were edit piece overdubs, apparently of John's "baby" exhortation after the final verse. Take 11 was a separate edit piece overdub, labeled on the session sheet as "ending," but it seems to be of the opening riff. The master would be assembled from takes 7, 10, and 11.

The mono mix (**A**) has audible edits at 0:13 and 0:25, plus the splice to take 10 at 2:21 between the words "hold" and "on me." The latter is easier to hear on the stereo mix (**D**), which doesn't seem to have the first two edits. What it does have is an edit piece of the opening seven-note riff, played by piano in the left channel and guitar on the otherwise vocals-only right channel.

Even more convoluted is the recording history of the next song taped, "Money (That's What I Want)." The backing track was recorded in five takes, presumably all featuring live vocals. Takes 6 and 7 were overdubs on take 5. Take 6 is listed as EDIT (PIANO) on the session sheet, and seemingly consisted of George Martin playing the opening piano riff while Ringo tapped time with his drumsticks.

Take 7 is an overdub of the whole song; judging from the stereo mix, the original instrumental track was fed to one channel of the new tape, George Martin's piano overdub to the second, and the original vocals plus handclap overdubs to both. That would explain why the stereo mix (**F**) has vocals and handclaps centered and lacks the tapping intro, as it was mixed from take 7. The mono mix (**B**) uses the take 6 edit piece (ending at 0:14), and thus includes the tapping. The band's entrance also comes at slightly different times on each mix.

What it doesn't explain is all the extra work done to the song after this initial session. On July 30, George Martin taped a "piano test" take, and then another complete overdub (take 8) and five edit piece overdubs for the start of the song, some of which are labeled (NATURAL PIANO). These were all apparently third-generation overdubs on take 7, as they have the designation (TRACK THREE) on the session sheet; none of them seem to have been used.

Mono mixing was done August 21, but on September 30, at the end of a mono mix tape, there is something noted in the tape log as (SI PIANO RM7) (VERSIONS 1–3). Stereo mixing took place over two days, October 29 and 30. Also unexplained is the fact that the mono mix seems to be missing the downward piano glissando before the solo, as well as George Martin's playing error at 2:13 (he goes to the pounding B chord a couple of bars early). This would seem to suggest that the mono mix contains a completely different piano overdub for the body of the song (perhaps from September 30), but with the session tapes long gone, it remains a mystery.

"Devil in Her Heart" is a lot more straightforward, thankfully. It required three takes of the basic track and three overdub takes of George's second lead vocal and Ringo's maracas onto take 3. The session ended with three takes of "Till There Was You," but time ran out; they would return to the song during their next session.

RELEASE HISTORY

1963: **A–C** were released on mono copies of *With the Beatles* and are currently available on EMI's CD of that title. **D–F** were included on stereo copies of the LP.

40. Speech — J, G

Date: 22–27 July 1963
Location: Royal Pier Hotel, Weston-Super-Mare

[A.] 1 Kings, 17 (4:43)
[B.] 1 Kings, 18 (2:45)
[C.] Psalm 23 (1:14)
[D.] Psalm 24 (1:14)
[E.] Out in the Street (8:31)

One good way to kill time during long stays on the road was making home recordings with a portable tape recorder. Not necessarily musical recordings, as this tape from one of the Beatles' seaside residencies attests.

Stuck in their hotel room, John, George, and Gerry Marsden each grabbed a copy of the hotel's Bible and began to read from it in exaggerated goonish voices, John's outlandishly twisted inflections causing particular hilarity. 1 Kings 17 is read through in turn by George, Gerry, and John, each taking a verse at a time. For 1 Kings 18, the order switches to John, Gerry, and George. Psalm 23 is read out in sing-song fashion, while Psalm 24 dissolves into chaos as words are skipped over haphazardly. Both end with a group "amen!"

Interviewed for *New Musical Express* around the first week of August, George recalled, "We had a gear time with the recorder a few weeks ago, when we were with Gerry and the Pacemakers at Weston-Super-Mare. We were in a car and Gerry was wearing a big hat and dark glasses, asking people the way to the local golf course. We got some dead-funny replies. Just like *Candid Camera* it was, only in sound!"

Amazingly, this recording has survived (**E**), and while John and George are occasionally heard, it's Gerry who runs the show. The first victim is a very accommodating lady who patiently points them toward a sanatorium. "Ooh! I don't wanna go there!" squeals Gerry.

Next is a woman who tells them to take the main road: "Down the lane road?" asks Gerry. He tells George to be quiet: "I can't hear the lady!" She continues: "Well, if you turn left, like that, you get on to a parallel road to this." Gerry continues to play dumb. "It's called Parallel Road?" Finally she gives up in frustration: "I'm sorry, I've got a hair appointment, I must go." Gerry replies politely: "Oh, at present? Thank you very mooch for all your helpful kind!"

Pedestrian #3 is a gentleman with a broad Wiltshire accent. Gerry relates their tale of woe: "We've been trying for about an hour to find this golf course." George adds, "We went to the wrong one, y'see." Gerry wants to know if you can turn right at the KEEP LEFT sign. Another female passerby is accosted, and John relays the instruction to "start it [the tape] again." As he explains that they "should have been playing at four o'clock, and it's twenty to five," Gerry slips into an Irish brogue, causing the others to crack up. The lady does not seem to notice, and tells them to catch a bus. "We can't get a bus with the car!" exclaims Gerry. Gracious to the last, he tells her: "If we win the match, I'll remember you."

Also presumably from this tape is an off-air recording of "Love Me Do" from the July 23 broadcast of *Pop Go the Beatles,* which proves that the Beatles themselves created the first-ever Beatles at the Beeb bootleg!

RELEASE HISTORY

1992: The bootleg CD *The Garage Tapes* included poor-quality copies of **C** and **D.** This reel was part of the Alf Bicknell collection and sold for £5,500 at the August 22, 1989, Sotheby's auction.

1995: **A–E** appeared on the bootleg CD *Maybe You Can Drive My Car* in slightly better quality.

2001: Another minor upgrade of **A–E** was bootlegged on the CD *Alf Together Now.*

41. Amateur footage

Date: 22–27 July 1963
Location: Royal Pier Hotel, Weston-Super-Mare, and Brean Down beach
Length: 9:11

Dezo Hoffmann visited the Beatles during their residence in Weston-Super-Mare for a series of photo sessions. Among his equipment was the 8 mm movie camera the Fabs had toyed with in Liverpool (see the March 25 entry), and it was put to good use again.

The footage opens with members of Gerry and the Pacemakers signing autographs for fans, riding donkeys on the beach (the Beatles would be photographed doing the same), and playing ball by the seaside. In the hotel's courtyard, the entourage are seen sunning themselves (mostly shirtless apart from John), to the obvious delight of teenage girls who take snapshots of the scene from behind a wall.

On the twenty-seventh, the Beatles and Dezo drove to the beach at Brean Down for a highly successful photo session, with the group dressed in striped bathing costumes and straw hats. The Beatles' driver (presumably Mal Evans) commandeered the camera to capture the proceedings, and the film shows how difficult it must have been to keep the foursome in line. It's not that far removed from the "field sequence" in *A Hard Day's Night,* as the mop-tops tackle one another, strike muscleman poses, and dance the Charleston.

On the way back to the hotel, a go-kart track was spotted, and naturally the Beatles wanted to take a spin, taking turns filming one another as they raced in circles. Back at the hotel, the final task was to shoot a series of photos to advertise Ty-Phoo Tea. Now dressed in suits, each Beatle is seen attempting to spell out the letters of the product's name and jumping from a staircase railing. The footage concludes with a shot of the colorful marquee outside the Odeon Cinema.

RELEASE HISTORY

This silent color footage circulates on video. Excerpts were first aired in the UK December 3, 1982, during a profile of Dezo Hoffmann on Channel 4's *The Tube.* A bit of this footage was used in the *Anthology* documentary during a sequence set to "It Won't Be Long."

42. Studio session

Date: 30 July 1963
Time: 10:00 a.m.–1:30 p.m.
Location: EMI Studio 2
Producer: George Martin

[A.] Piano/drum instrumental (1:15)
[B.] Please Mr. Postman—monitor mix of take 3 (2:40)
[C.] Please Mr. Postman—monitor mix of take 9 (2:33)
[D.] It Won't Be Long—monitor mix of take 7 (2:18)
[E.] It Won't Be Long—monitor mix of take 10 (?) (1:58)
unknown song fragments
[F.] Hello Little Girl—monitor mix of unknown take (1:49)
unknown song fragment
Twist and Shout (The Isley Brothers)
[G.] Hello Little Girl—monitor mixes of take 15 (1:48)
It's Up to You (Billy J Kramer)

[H.] Please Mr. Postman—RM9 (2:32)
Mixed: 21 August 1963

[I.] Please Mr. Postman—RS9 (2:31)
Mixed: 29 October 1963

The portable tape recorder that had traveled to Liverpool and Weston-Super-Mare now made its way into Abbey Road Studios and documented a portion of the Beatles' morning session of July 30. This reel was part of the Alf Bicknell collection and sold for £5,200 at the August 22, 1989, Sotheby's auction.

This long day began with the recording of "Please Mr. Postman." Two takes were recorded, with the instruments on one track and John's lead and Paul and George's backing vocals on a second. With take 3, John added a second lead vocal onto take 2; this arrangement was similar to their earlier BBC performances of the song, opening with a brief guitar lick and concluding with a fabricated A to Dm to A ending.

While waiting to hear a playback of this "best" take, Paul played a jazzy piano improvisation (**A**), joined by someone (probably John) on drums. This was captured on the portable tape recorder, most likely by George, along with the playback of take 3 (**B**). Unsatisfied with the result, they decided to reconfigure "Please Mr. Postman" to conform more closely with the Marvelettes' original.

They recorded four more takes of this new arrangement, with a stop-time intro, drum breaks throughout, and an extended coda that would be faded out. Takes 8 and 9 were overdubs on take 7 of John's second vocal plus handclaps. A playback of this new "best" take (**C**) continues a couple of seconds beyond where the released versions fade out. The mono mix of this song (**H**) lasts a touch longer than the stereo (**I**).

With this complete, they tackled John and Paul's new composition, "It Won't Be Long," an exciting number that would have made a great single but served equally well as the lead-off track for *With the Beatles.* The song featured call-and-response vocals between John's lead and Paul and George's backing.

Ten takes were needed to perfect the backing, two

of which were apparently overdubs or edit pieces for the ending. Take 7 was good enough to provide the basis of the finished recording, and a playback (**D**) includes the take announcement and count-in. A second unknown take, presumably the last of the session (**E**) was also played back. This is sung much more loosely than take 7 and cuts off just before the ending. Both takes reveal how little of the lead guitar George played at first: Only the descending riff between the two lines of each verse isn't an overdub.

The song needed more work, but the BBC beckoned. However, as long as they were in the control booth, the Beatles requested to hear playbacks of some of their associates' recent work. The Fourmost had been at EMI on July 24 to record John's "Hello Little Girl," and George Martin runs back the basic track of their performance (**F**) followed by what may be a couple of attempts at mixing the final take (**G**), complete with overdubs of a guitar solo doubled by what George Harrison correctly identifies as a celeste. This is followed by a playback of Billy J Kramer and the Dakotas' "It's Up to You," and the tape reportedly continued with a bit of their cover of "Da Doo Ron Ron." Both songs were probably taped during an EMI session July 16 or 22.

RELEASE HISTORY

1963: **H** and **I** were released on mono and stereo pressings of *With the Beatles*. **H** is available on EMI's CD of that title.

1992: The bootleg CD *The Garage Tapes* included **A–E,** in fair quality and at the correct speed.

1995: A slightly improved (but very slow) tape of **A–G** was booted on the CD *Maybe You Can Drive My Car.*

2001: Another minor upgrade of **A–G** (omitting the Billy J Kramer and Isley Brothers numbers) was bootlegged on the CD *Alf Together Now* at the correct speed.

43. Radio interview

Date: 30 July 1963
Time: 2:30 p.m.
Location: Playhouse Theatre, London
Interviewer: Phil Tate
Broadcast: 30 August 1963, 5:00–5:29 p.m.
BBC Light Programme
Non Stop Pop
Length: 2:18

Upon arriving at the Playhouse Theatre to record a session for *Saturday Club,* the Beatles were interviewed by bandleader Phil Tate for the "Pop Chat" segment of the series *Non Stop Pop.* The circulating tape includes an intro from the show's host and has jaunty theme music running underneath.

Ringo says that although they have a base in London (the Hotel President on Russell Square), they have no plans to relocate from Liverpool. In fact, within a few weeks they would move into a flat on Green Street in Mayfair, and eventually buy their own homes in and around London. Asked about the Lennon/McCartney partnership, John admits that most of their best songs, "the ones that anybody wants to hear," were written jointly.

George answers a listener's query about the origin of their hairdos: "Paul and John went to Paris and came back with it something like this. And I went to the baths and came out with it like this." Finally, Ringo is asked to request a record, and he chooses Billy J Kramer's "Bad to Me."

RELEASE HISTORY

1988: This interview first surfaced on the vinyl bootleg *Meet the Beeb* but was rebroadcast later that year in the November 5 episode of BBC Radio's *The Beeb's Lost Beatles Tapes*. It's available from that source in very good quality on the bootleg CD *The Beatles Broadcast Collection, Trailer 1.*

1993: A lesser-quality and incomplete version of this recording was released on the CD *The Beatles Tapes, Volume 2: Early Beatlemania 1963–1964.*

44. Radio performance

Date: 30 July 1963
Time: afternoon
Location: Playhouse Theatre, London
Producers: Jimmy Grant, Bernie Andrews
Host: Brian Matthew
Broadcast: 24 August 1963, 10:00 a.m.–noon
BBC Light Programme
Saturday Club #255

[A.] **Long Tall Sally** (1:49)
[B.] **She Loves You** (2:12)
[C.] **Glad All Over** (1:51)
[D.] **intro** (0:52)
[E.] **Twist and Shout** (2:26)
[F.] **intro** (0:43)
[G.] **You Really Got a Hold on Me** (2:37)
[H.] **I'll Get You** (1:56)

The Beatles' long day continued with the taping of their fifth appearance on *Saturday Club*. An excellent-quality tape of this show seems to be in the BBC's possession, but they have doled it out in bits and pieces (see release history). Until the whole thing turns up, we'll have to settle for a rendition of "She Loves You" that sounds as though it's being sung underwater.

The intro for "Twist and Shout" has Paul reading a request that is sent in an elaborate box, though when Brian Matthew asks if it's Harry's box, Paul feigns innocence: "What box?" John reads another request (**F**) while piano and guitar (Paul and George, or a prerecorded backing?) ramble in the background. "You Really Got a Hold on Me" begins with a half-length musical introduction, but it's not clear whether that's the result of editing.

RELEASE HISTORY

1984: A fair-quality version of **A** appeared on the vinyl bootleg *Directly from Santa Claus.*

1993: The boxed CD set *The Complete BBC Sessions* included fair-quality tapes of **A, B, C,** and **H.** All but **B** are slightly incomplete and run too slow.

1994: Apple released **F** and **G** in excellent quality on the CD *Live at the BBC.*

1996: Excellent-quality versions of **C, D,** and **H** were broadcast on part one of the BBC Radio special *The Beatles at the BBC* on New Year's Eve. Host Alan Freeman speaks over the beginning and very end of **C,** while **D** has had the title "Twist and Shout" replaced with "I'll Get You" from the September 7 *Saturday Club* to make it seem as though Brian Matthew is introducing that song. This broadcast appears on the CD-R *The Beatles at the BBC—Parts 1 & 2,* suffering from interference and light static.

1998: BBC Radio 2's *Saturday Club 40th Anniversary Special,* broadcast October 3, included **D** and **E** complete and in excellent quality.

1999: The boxed CD set *Mythology, Volume 1* included **C** and **H** from the 1996 special and **D** and **E** from the 1998 special, all in excellent quality and free of static. Unfortunately, **C** has had the first few seconds removed to omit Alan Freeman's narration.

45. Studio session

Date: 30 July 1963
Time: 5:00–11:00 p.m.
Location: EMI Studio 2
Producer: George Martin

[A.] **Till There Was You—RM8** (2:12)
[B.] **Roll Over Beethoven—edit of RM7/8** (2:42)
[C.] **It Won't Be Long—edit of RM17/21** (2:09)
[D.] **All My Loving—RM14** (2:05)
Mixed: 21 August 1963

[E.] **Till There Was You—RS8** (2:11)
[F.] **Roll Over Beethoven—edit of RS7/8** (2:42)
[G.] **It Won't Be Long—RS17** (2:09)
[H.] **All My Loving—RS14** (2:05)
Mixed: 29 October 1963

[I.] **All My Loving—unedited RS14** (2:06)

The evening session began with George Martin's piano experiments for "Money (That's What I Want)" (see the July 18 entry), presumably while the Beatles returned from the BBC and perhaps even got in a quick meal.

Picking up where they'd left off twelve days earlier, they completed "Till There Was You" in five further takes, with Paul singing and playing bass, Ringo on bongos, John on acoustic rhythm, and George playing a gorgeous lead on his nylon-stringed classical guitar. It was the only song on the album without any overdubs.

George's second featured number for the LP was taped next. "Roll Over Beethoven" required five takes, plus two attempts at overdubbing the guitar solo, handclaps, and George's second lead vocal. Take 8 was an edit piece of the entire group playing the song's final chord.

Then it was back to "It Won't Be Long"; after listening to their portable tape, the Beatles had selected take 7 as superior, so all further overdubs were done on this take. Takes 11–17 added John's second lead vocal throughout the song, while 18–23 were edit piece overdubs of the song's ending, with take 21 being the "best." The mono mix (**C**) splices in the phrase "till I belong" from take 21 at 1:59. The stereo mix (**G**) seems to be from take 17 without any edits.

The album's most celebrated song is Paul's "All My Loving," written "as a poem" during the Roy Orbison tour, with music added later. Ten takes were required (1–11, with no take 5) for the backing, with John playing fast and furious triplets and George a short but sweet guitar solo. Three overdub takes on take 11 added Paul's second vocal, harmonizing with himself on the final verse (a role George would fill during live performances).

Onstage, Paul would give a five-beat count-in to "All My Loving." In the studio, however, Ringo cued the opening vocal with five taps of his hi-hat cymbal. This was trimmed from the master reels before release, but for some reason an uncut stereo mix (perhaps a straight dub of take 14 before the session tape was destroyed) was sent to Odeon, EMI's West German affiliate, in 1965. This anomaly (**I**) includes the five hi-hat taps and Paul's intake of breath before he starts singing.

RELEASE HISTORY

1963: **A–D** were released on mono copies of *With the Beatles* and are currently available on EMI's CD of that title. **E–H** were included on stereo copies of the LP.

1965: **I** appeared on the German LP *Beatles Greatest*. It wasn't available in the UK until 1980 on *The Beatles Box*.

46. Radio performance

Date: 1 August 1963
Time: 1:30–4:00 p.m.
Location: Playhouse Theatre, Manchester
Producer: Ian Grant
Host: Rodney Burke
Broadcast: 27 August 1963, 5:00–5:29 p.m.
BBC Light Programme
Pop Go the Beatles #11

[A.] **Ooh! My Soul** (1:37)
[B.] **outro/intro** (0:35)
[C.] **Don't Ever Change** (2:04)
[D.] **outro** (0:05)
Country Line Special (Cyril Davies Rhythm & Blues All Stars)
My Babe (Cyril Davies Rhythm & Blues All Stars)
[E.] **Twist and Shout** (2:31)
[F.] **intro** (0:19)
[G.] **She Loves You** (0:06)
[H.] **intro** (0:29)
[I.] **Anna (Go to Him)** (2:50)
[J.] **A Shot of Rhythm and Blues** (2:15)

Regular *Pop Go the Beatles* producer Terry Henebery handed over the task to his assistant, Ian Grant, for the last five installments, probably to the Beatles' great delight. (George later recalled that Henebery "was a jazz fan and he hated the Beatles!") While most editions were taped in London, their increasingly demanding schedule allowed for this session in Manchester, on a free day between concerts in Nelson and Liverpool. Two nights later, they would play their final show as a group at the Cavern Club.

Rodney Burke refers to the new location with a corny joke (**B**) following Little Richard's "Ooh! My Soul": "Oh, my arms. We've just flown into Manchester here from London to record this show." George then says how great it is to be playing in Liverpool again and introduces "one of the oldies," "Don't Ever Change." This was actually a hit the previous year for the Crickets, and it was written by one of John and Paul's revered songwriting teams, Gerry Goffin and Carole King. It's sung here as a rare duet between George and Paul.

Most of the chat between songs is missing from the circulating tapes of this episode, as are all but a few seconds of "She Loves You." They also taped performances of "Lucille" and "Baby It's You" this day that were never aired.

RELEASE HISTORY

1971: Good-quality tapes of **C** and **J** were included on the earliest BBC bootleg LP, *Yellow Matter Custard*.

1972: A mediocre copy of **I** was released on the bootleg LP *Outtakes 2* (aka *Studio Sessions, Volume 2*). Although the beginning of the song is chopped off, no longer tape has surfaced yet.

1982: The vinyl bootleg *Beautiful Dreamer* contained a version of **A** that was basically complete (with a bit of "Slow Down" from *Pop Go the Beatles* #11 stuck on the beginning), but with a shrill noise throughout. The same year, the radio special *The Beatles at the Beeb* included very good tapes of **C** (slightly incomplete) and **J.**

1987: A very good tape of **A–E** surfaced on the bootleg *The Beatles at the Beeb, Volume 5,* although **A** was missing a few seconds at the beginning.

1993: Great Dane's *The Complete BBC Sessions* used the *Beeb, Volume 5* tape for most of this, with the following exceptions: **A** was repaired using the first few seconds (including the "Slow Down" fragment!) from *Beautiful Dreamer;* **C** used the superior tape from the 1982 radio special, with the missing intro and outro added from *Volume 5;* **I** came from *Studio Sessions,* and **J** was probably copied from the 1982 special.

1994: Apple's official release, *Live at the BBC,* contained excellent (but slightly fast) tapes of **A–C** and **J.**

2003: The entire show, including the debut of **F–H** and both Cyril Davies Rhythm & Blues All Stars numbers, was bootlegged on the CD boxed set *The Beatles at the Beeb.*

47. Radio performance

Date: 1 August 1963
Time: 4:00–6:00 p.m.
Location: Playhouse Theatre, Manchester
Producer: Ian Grant
Host: Rodney Burke
Broadcast: 3 September 1963, 5:00–5:29 p.m.
BBC Light Programme
Pop Go the Beatles #12

[A.] **intro** (0:14)
[B.] **From Me to You** (1:50)
[C.] **I'll Get You** (2:00)
[D.] **Money (That's What I Want)** (2:46)
[E.] **intro** (0:18)
There's a Place (rebroadcast of July 2, 1963, recording)
[F.] **outro** (0:01)
Do You Love Me? (Brian Poole and the Tremeloes)
[G.] **Honey Don't** (2:14)
[H.] **outro** (0:03)
I Can Tell (Brian Poole and the Tremeloes)
[I.] **intro** (0:44)
[J.] **Roll Over Beethoven** (2:19)

Like the previous edition, nearly all Beatles chat is missing from the circulating tapes of this *Pop Go the Beatles.* All that remains is George thanking some fans (**I**) for the gift of a scarf embroidered with a request for "Roll Over Beethoven." The first three songs from this broadcast exist only in inferior quality (and **B** is edited to remove one "to you" from the coda), while the fourth song is merely a rebroadcast of "There's a Place" from episode 5.

But the most valuable number is John's rendition of "Honey Don't," a song later given to Ringo. This performance includes the "bop bop's" of Carl Perkins' original, but the EMI version is otherwise more faithful, being more laid-back, with acoustic guitar and a second guitar solo. John would sing this tune again for the BBC (see the May 1, 1964, entry).

RELEASE HISTORY

1972: The LP *Outtakes 2* (aka *Studio Sessions, Volume 2*) included fair-quality versions of **D** and **G** (the latter incomplete).

1987: An excellent tape of **E–J** (including the rebroadcast of "There's a Place") was booted on vinyl copies of *The Beatles at the Beeb, Volume 5,* although **G** was still incomplete. The Pyramid CD of this title omits part of **E** and all of **F** and **H.**

1993: The boxed set *The Complete BBC Sessions* contained a poor-quality tape of **A–B** (making their debuts), as well as **D** (from *Outtakes 2*), and **E–J** copied from a Pyramid CD.

1994: Apple's *Live at the BBC* contained an excellent version of **G,** complete at last.

2001: A fair-quality tape of **C** surfaced on the CD-R *The Complete BBC Sessions—Upgraded.*

2003: The entire show, including both Brian Poole and the Tremeloes numbers, was bootlegged on the CD boxed set *The Beatles at the Beeb.*

47a. Amateur footage

Date: 6–10 August 1963
Location: Hotel St. Saviour and the airport, Jersey
Length: 2:46

The Beatles spent the week of August 6–10 performing in the Channel Islands: four nights at the Springfield Ballroom in Jersey, bookended around a performance at Candie Gardens in Guernsey.

Apparently, Ringo's milkman was considering a trip to Jersey and loaned the drummer his 8 mm movie camera to capture scenes of island life. The result was this silent color footage, which mostly focuses on activities around the hotel pool. Ringo cavorts with an inner tube, Paul flexes his muscles, and John soaks up some sun in a lounge chair, playing dead for the camera and grabbing a pack of ciggies. A few onlookers stop by and take photos, and Ringo clambers over some rocks at the seaside, joined by Valerie Callam, an old acquaintance from his days at Butlins.

There is also a sequence of the group at the airport August 8, boarding their chartered flight for Guernsey along with Neil Aspinall and Liverpool poet Royston Ellis. It was Ellis' girlfriend, Stephanie, whose behavior that night inspired John to write "Polythene Pam" five years later.

RELEASE HISTORY

This silent color footage was used in the documentary *The Unseen Beatles,* available on DVD.

48. TV performance

Date: 14 August 1963
Location: Studio 4, Granada TV Centre, Manchester
Broadcast: 14 August 1963, 6:30–7:00 p.m.
Granada TV
Scene at 6:30

[A.] Twist and Shout (2:30)

The earliest surviving Beatles-related TV broadcast is this lip-synced performance of "Twist and Shout" (discounting the performance filmed at the Cavern in August 1962, which wasn't aired until November 1963). A similar rendition of "She Loves You" was taped the same day and broadcast the following week, but doesn't seem to have survived. The atmosphere is particularly dark, with shadows looming over the group, wearing black polo-neck sweaters. The effect is not unlike Robert Freeman's cover photo for *With the Beatles,* which would be shot a week later at the Palace Court Hotel in Bournemouth.

RELEASE HISTORY

This clip was rebroadcast in Granada TV's 1984 special *The Early Beatles,* with a splice at the end that brings the audio out of sync. An unbroken version also circulates, presumably from an earlier rebroadcast before the footage was damaged. Bits of this performance were used in the *Anthology* documentary.

49. Radio interview

Date: 23 August 1963
Location: Gaumont Cinema, Bournemouth
Interviewer: Klas Burling
Length: 6:10

In the midst of a six-night residency in Bournemouth, the Beatles were interviewed by Swedish radio producer and host Klas Burling. The interview was probably conducted between the Beatles' two performances as they ate dinner (full mouths are in evidence). It opens with each Beatle introducing himself by way of imitating the sound of the instrument he plays.

Burling tries to convince them to tour Sweden, but Ringo says they're so busy they won't get there until next year. Paul adds that the "gorgeous blondes" in Sweden are an incentive, and Burling pretends to be shocked: "That's Paul, and he's supposed to be the sweet boy in this family, no?" John quips, "His dad was a Mars bar." Asked whether screaming "Twist and Shout" is hard on his throat, John says that having to perform it twice a night has inured him to the vocal strain. Burling points out the "sick humor" in John's stage mannerisms, and Ringo says, "It's not sick, he's just a cripple." John hastens to point out that he's "quite normal, my Swedish friends!"

John and Paul talk about songwriting, the use of personal pronouns, and donating songs to Billy J Kramer. Paul recalls composing "She Loves You" in

Newcastle, and John reveals that with both of their last two singles, what began as the A-side was bumped to the B-side when they came up with a better song. Burling asks if writing songs is easy, and feeling left out of all the composer talk, Ringo butts in: "We find it difficult sometimes."

Although he's interrupted before giving the title, Paul says that a song has already been composed specifically for Ringo to sing on the new LP. If the legend about "I Wanna Be Your Man" is correct, only one verse had been written at this stage, as John and Paul supposedly finished off the lyrics in front of a flabbergasted Mick Jagger and Keith Richards on September 10.

Another intriguing possibility is that Paul is referring to "Little Child," which was evidently written with Ringo in mind. In his 1980 *Playboy* interview, John recalled fuzzily: "That was another effort by Paul and me to write a song for somebody. It probably was Ringo, because I think that's who we gave it to." Paul confirmed the story in his authorized biography *Many Years from Now.* They also considered donating "Little Child" to Mike Hurst, ex-member of the Springfields, Dusty Springfield's original group.

Paul says the album will be out in November, but doesn't know when it'll reach Sweden. Burling must have been persuasive, because by the middle of September he had convinced Brian Epstein to book the Beatles for a Swedish tour at the end of October.

RELEASE HISTORY

1972: Several excerpts from these interviews were broadcast in the BBC Radio special *The Beatles Story.* They were copied from this source on the bootleg CD *Attack of the Filler Beebs!, Episode 2.*

1995: Further excerpts appeared on the bootleg CD *The Ultimate Collection, Volume 2: Live, Live, Live.*

2003: The complete interview was included on the bonus CD included with the book *Yeah Yeah Yeah! The Beatles Erövrar Sverige.*

50. Composing tape G

Date: 19–24 August 1963
Location: Palace Court Hotel, Bournemouth

[A.] Don't Bother Me/instrumental (5:29)

During their residency in Bournemouth, the Beatles attended Billy J Kramer's twentieth birthday party (on the nineteenth), shot the cover photo for their second LP, and continued to play with their portable tape recorder. Feeling under the weather one day, George was visited by a doctor who prescribed a tonic and bed rest. To keep himself occupied, George decided to try writing a song; if John and Paul could do it seemingly at will, how hard could it be?

Once he had a rudimentary idea, George grabbed the tape recorder and his guitar and began strumming away. The sound is a bit muffled as the tape begins, but as he pulls the microphone closer, we can hear the bridge of "Don't Bother Me" taking shape. George whistles and hums the melody a few times as he tests out various chord changes, pausing occasionally to cough.

After a couple of minutes of this, he hits some harmonics and tunes up, then slips into some guitar exercises, fiddling around in the key of A. With the addition of lyrics, the song would be ready to record at the next Abbey Road session on September 11.

NOTE

A concert recording from the Beatles' Bournemouth residency was auctioned in 1998 but has yet to surface. It contains eleven songs ("Roll Over Beethoven," "Thank You Girl," "Chains," "From Me to You," "A Taste of Honey," "I Saw Her Standing There," "Baby It's You," "Boys," "She Loves You," "Twist and Shout," and "From Me to You [reprise]") and is reportedly of good quality.

RELEASE HISTORY

1992: The bootleg CD *The Garage Tapes* included 2:19 of this tape, in fair quality and at the correct speed. This reel was part of the Alf Bicknell collection and sold for £7,500 at the August 22, 1989, Sotheby's auction.

1995: The full tape appeared on the bootleg CD *Maybe You Can Drive My Car,* in slightly better quality but way too slow.

2001: A speed-corrected upgrade was bootlegged on the CD *Alf Together Now.*

51. Amateur footage

Date: 25 August 1963
Location: ABC Theatre, Blackpool

During a performance in Blackpool, another act on the bill, Chas McDevitt, filmed four and a half minutes of color 8 mm footage of the Beatles onstage and in their dressing room. The documentary *The Unseen Beatles* uses less than a minute of this silent film, auctioned by Sotheby's on September 14, 1999.

It begins with some concert action, shot from the wings: John does his "spastic clapping" and a brief dance, and the group bows after completing a number. Backstage, John (wearing his horn-rimmed glasses) and George seem to be performing dramatic interpretations of fan letters, and Shadows guitarist Hank Marvin drops by for a chat.

RELEASE HISTORY

This silent color footage was used in the documentary *The Unseen Beatles,* available on DVD.

52. TV performance

Date: 27 August 1963
Time: 9:30 a.m.
Location: Little Theatre, Southport
Producer: Don Haworth
Broadcast: 9 October 1963, 10:10–10:40 p.m.
BBC TV
The Mersey Sound

[A.] **Twist and Shout** (0:46)
[B.] **Twist and Shout** (1:11)
[C.] **Love Me Do** (0:41)
[D.] **I Saw Her Standing There** (0:34)
[E.] **She Loves You** (2:23)
[F.] **Twist and Shout** (0:20)
[G.] **Twist and Shout** (0:35)

Less than four months after their debut appearance on BBC TV, the Beatles were approached by a British Broadcasting Corporation producer from Manchester, Don Haworth, who was eager to make a TV documentary about their flourishing success. Naturally, they agreed to cooperate, and the project was announced in mid-August as "an hour-long documentary about the Beatles . . . A BBC camera team will 'live' with the Beatles for seven days during the next month, filming their life."

Whether or not that was the original plan, it was easier written than done, so instead special filming sessions were set up to simulate a concert, home life, travels, and backstage scenes. The show's working title was *The Beatles,* but it was retitled *The Mersey Sound* and pared down to a half hour, with the focus expanded to include other Liverpudlians such as the Undertakers and Bill Harry.

The concert scenes were shot first: the frenzied audience reaction from the group's August 26 Southport concert was intercut with the Beatles performing at the Little Theatre the next morning, with only the BBC crew present. It seems likely that they prerecorded the songs and then lip-synced them to get the sound balance just right; for one thing, their amps don't seem to be miked.

"Twist and Shout" is chopped up into four segments throughout the documentary: **A** fades in at the second verse and cuts off at the "ah" raveup; **B** carries on from this portion through the conclusion of the song. **F** is superseded by **A,** although it includes a bit of the guitar break that is buried under narration in its earlier appearance. **G** plays over the closing credits and offers nothing new.

"She Loves You" (**E**) is a performance of the entire song, complete with synchronized bow and closing curtain; it also features BBC stagehands throwing jelly babies and other objects from off-camera for authenticity!

The Beatles sport their collarless Pierre Cardin suits for the previous two songs, but "Love Me Do" (**C**) is performed in different outfits in front of the closed curtain; here, they're lip-syncing to the original single version with Ringo on drums, and not a newly recorded rendition.

The instrumental version of "I Saw Her Standing There" (**D**) appears as incidental music over various scenes of the group offstage; it definitely sounds like a Beatles performance, complete with George playing a climbing riff from his standard "Long Tall Sally" solo. Filming continued over the next three days (see following entry).

RELEASE HISTORY

The original *Mersey Sound* documentary circulates on video. The version released on the home video *The Beatles Firsts* is missing the footage of "Love Me Do," presumably because its soundtrack is from the EMI recording. The soundtracks of **A, B, E, F,** and part of **D** appear on the bootleg CD *Beatles at the Beeb—TV.*

53. TV feature

Date: 28–30 August 1963
Locations: Manchester and Liverpool
Producer: Don Haworth
Broadcast: 9 October 1963, 10:10–10:40 p.m.
BBC TV
The Mersey Sound
Length: 7:42

The bulk of the Beatles' nonperformance footage for *The Mersey Sound* was filmed August 28 in a dressing room at BBC TV's Manchester studios. As each Beatle is introduced, he is seen applying makeup and primping his hair for the ostensible "concert."

Individual interviews with John, Paul, George, and Ringo follow. All four seem grateful for the chance to discuss their career in a serious fashion, recounting the development of their stage look from Hamburg to the present day and relating the perils of fame. The group dynamics are also revealed as Paul earnestly explains that they dropped their leather outfits "because more often than not . . . too many people'd laugh. It was just stupid, and we didn't wanna appear as a gang of idiots." George points out that someone stole Paul's leather pants anyway, and John mutters that "they didn't laugh at 'em in Liverpool."

A series of vignettes illustrate "a day in the life of the Beatles" (well before the plot of *A Hard Day's Night* had been conceived). From August 30, we see Ringo being mobbed while leaving his Liverpool home and driving off with George. They must have gone to the airport, because we see all four descending from the steps of a plane. This "arrival" was actually filmed in Liverpool as well, at Speke Airport on the twenty-ninth.

Scenes of the group signing autographs for fans in Liverpool on the twenty-ninth are intercut with "backstage" footage from the twenty-eighth. They read fan mail, some of which is read in voice-overs, including letters from a girl who had seen their May 24 Walthamstow concert, and another who had entered a contest in the July issue of *Boyfriend* magazine to win a date with a Beatle.

The show concludes with the group's thoughts on their future, and these clips have been oft-repeated, not just for their prescient nature, but for how neatly they encapsulate each Beatle's public persona. John is short-tempered. ("People demand that you think how long are you gonna last. Well, you can't say, y'know.") Paul is artistically ambitious ("probably the thing that John and I will do will be write songs, as we have been doing as a sort of sideline now"), and George is fiscally minded ("I hope to have enough money to go in—into a business of my own by the time, um, we do flop"). As for Ringo, it's hard to watch his quote without being reminded of Barry Wom's ambition to "become two hairdressers." Fittingly, we're treated to the absurd sight of Ringo as a salon host, filmed in Liverpool's Home Bros clothing store on the thirtieth.

RELEASE HISTORY

The original *Mersey Sound* documentary circulates on video and was released in the home video *The Beatles Firsts*. It also features heavily in the *Compleat Beatles* and *Anthology* documentaries. The soundtrack of the interview portions was booted on the CD *Beatles at the Beeb—TV.*

54. TV performance

Date: 1 September 1963
Time: evening
Location: Studio 1, Didsbury Studio Centre, Manchester
Producer: Philip Jones
Hosts: Mike Winters, Bernie Winters
Broadcast: 7 September 1963, 7:40–8:30 p.m.
ITV
Big Night Out

[A.] intro (0:14)
[B.] From Me to You (1:24)
[C.] She Loves You (2:23)
[D.] Twist and Shout (2:32)
[E.] outro (0:33)
[F.] I Saw Her Standing There (0:42)

The Beatles' first appearance on the TV variety show *Big Night Out* was to have been videotaped on August 18 but was postponed in favor of a concert at the Princess Theatre in Torquay. A planned concert at the ABC Cinema in Great Yarmouth on September 1 was then canceled to make room for the TV taping.

The complete show has survived and gives a good sense of the kind of corny comedy and pleasant but dull song and dance routines teenagers would have sat through impatiently before the Beatles appeared to close the show. In one sketch, the caber-tossing Bernie

"MacWinters" launches into a quick rendition of "From Me to You," but the real thing was far superior.

After a brief intro, the Beatles, dressed in their collarless Pierre Cardin suits, appear on an archway-dominated set. They lip-sync three songs, beginning with an abbreviated version of "From Me to You." Hosts Mike and Bernie Winters then reappear to say good night ("We hope you enjoyed the show, wackers!") and introduce the traditional show-closing dance: This week it's the Monkey Twist! The set fills with gyrating dancers as the credits roll and the Beatles mime to "I Saw Her Standing There."

RELEASE HISTORY

The complete show circulates on video from a good-quality kinescope. Portions of **B** and **D** were included in the *Anthology* documentary.

55. Radio performance

Date: 3 September 1963
Time: 2:00–4:30 p.m. (except *5:00–7:30 p.m.)
Location: Studio 2, Aeolian Hall, London
Producer: Ian Grant
Host: Rodney Burke
Broadcast: 10 September 1963, 5:00–5:29 p.m.
BBC Light Programme
Pop Go the Beatles #13

[A.] **intro** (0:02)
[B.] **Too Much Monkey Business** (2:07)
[C.] **outro** (0:25)
[D.] **Love Me Do** (2:25)
[E.] **outro/intro** (0:32)
[F.] **She Loves You** (2:13)
[G.] **outro** (0:02)
A Shot of Rhythm and Blues (Johnny Kidd and the Pirates)
Dr. Feelgood (Johnny Kidd and the Pirates)
[H.] **I'll Get You** (2:02)
[I.] **outro/intro** (0:22)
[J.] ***A Taste of Honey** (1:56)
I Can Tell (Johnny Kidd and the Pirates)
[K.] **intro** (0:27)
[L.] **The Hippy Hippy Shake** (1:44)
[M.] **outro** (0:05)

One final marathon session was required to fulfill the requirements for *Pop Go the Beatles,* and the group recorded their contributions for the last three episodes in a single day. Although they taped the standard six songs per episode, the BBC decided to get more bang from their Beatle buck by repeating the same performance of "She Loves You" in the thirteenth and fifteenth editions. This led to a little shuffling around, with "A Taste of Honey" included as a bonus seventh song in this program.

The circulating tape still contains only six songs, however. We hear Paul reading out a request for "Till There Was You" (**C**), but the song is absent. Instead, the source cuts directly to the following number, "Love Me Do," performed as usual with John playing harmonica and faded out at the ending. John then reads a request from "Glynis and Sue" for George to cut his hair (**E**), but John confides that "he's had it cut, and it looks a right laugh!"

Performances of both sides of the latest single are followed by a Scottish request for "A Taste of Honey." A card from Ronnie Yates, student in form 5E of Paul and George's alma mater, Liverpool Institute, leads them to recall the nicknames of various masters (the Baz, Slimy, Stinky, Nobby, Pinhead, Weepy, and so on). To close the show, they dedicate a Cavern favorite, "Hippy Hippy Shake," to Ronnie; note Paul's dynamic swoops on bass guitar during the coda.

RELEASE HISTORY

1978: The original pressing of *Youngblood* contained fair-quality, incomplete versions of **B** and **L.** A reissue of this bootleg replaced both tracks with earlier performances of the same songs.

1982: A very good, complete tape of **B** was included in the radio special *The Beatles at the Beeb.*

1987: Vinyl copies of *The Beatles at the Beeb, Volume 6* contained an excellent-quality tape of the entire broadcast (**A–M**). The Pyramid CD of this title (copied on *The Complete BBC Sessions* box) has **C** and **K** slightly abridged.

1994: An excellent tape of **B** appeared on Apple's *Live at the BBC,* although it fades slightly early.

2003: The entire show, including the Johnny Kidd and the Pirates numbers, was bootlegged on the CD boxed set *The Beatles at the Beeb.*

56. Radio performance

Date: 3 September 1963
Time: 5:00–7:30 p.m.
Location: Studio 2, Aeolian Hall, London
Producer: Ian Grant
Host: Rodney Burke
Broadcast: 17 September 1963, 5:00–5:29 p.m.
BBC Light Programme
Pop Go the Beatles #14

[A.] **intro** (0:12)
[B.] **Chains** (2:19)
[C.] **outro/intro** (0:31)
[D.] **You Really Got a Hold on Me** (2:53)
That's What I Want (The Marauders)
[E.] **Misery** (1:51)
[F.] **outro/intro** (1:02)
[G.] **Lucille** (2:28)
[H.] **intro** (0:28)
[I.] **From Me to You** (1:49)
[J.] **outro/intro** (1:09)
[K.] **Boys** (2:09)
[L.] **outro** (0:01)

This show opens with "Chains," which gives Rodney Burke the opportunity to insert an awful pun about "chainspotting." John then reads a request from "Geoff the greengrocer" for "You Really Got a Hold on Me." "Lucille" is dedicated to Derry Wilkie, lead singer of the Liverpool group Derry and the Seniors, who had preceded the Beatles at the Kaiserkeller in Hamburg.

During episode #6 of the series, George had introduced "So How Come (No One Loves Me)," speaking the punctuation in the song's title. Due to supposed overwhelming demand, George returns here (**J**) to utter the word "brackets" several more times (he'd also said the word in episode #4). In introducing "Boys," Paul, John, and George try to top one another by reading requests in silly, goonish voices.

RELEASE HISTORY

1972: Good-quality versions of **B** and **K** (both incomplete) and **G** were included on the bootleg LP *Outtakes 2* (aka *Studio Sessions, Volume 2*).

1974: **D** surfaced in fair quality on the vinyl bootleg *Rare Beatles* (aka *Happy Birthday*).

1987: An excellent-quality tape of the complete program (**A–L**) was used on the LP *The Beatles at the Beeb, Volume 6.* The Pyramid CD of this title (copied on *The Complete BBC Sessions* box) has **E** and **J** slightly incomplete and is missing **L.**

1996: An upgraded tape of **G** was broadcast on part one of the BBC Radio special *The Beatles at the BBC* on New Year's Eve. It appears from this source on the bootleg CD *The Beatles Broadcast Collection, Trailer 1.*

2003: The entire show, including the Marauders number, was bootlegged on the CD boxed set *The Beatles at the Beeb.*

57. Radio performance

Date: 3 September 1963
Time: 8:00–10:30 p.m.
Location: Studio 2, Aeolian Hall, London
Producer: Ian Grant
Host: Rodney Burke
Broadcast: 24 September 1963, 5:00–5:29 p.m.
BBC Light Programme
Pop Go the Beatles #15

[A.] **intro** (0:15)
She Loves You (rebroadcast of version F from episode #13)
[B.] **outro/intro** (0:11)
[C.] **Ask Me Why** (1:53)
[D.] **intro** (0:30)
[E.] **Devil in Her Heart** (2:22)
[F.] **outro/intro** (0:40)
[G.] **I Saw Her Standing There** (2:38)
[H.] **intro** (0:16)
[I.] **Sure to Fall (in Love with You)** (2:18)
[J.] **intro** (0:33)
[K.] **Twist and Shout** (2:31)
[L.] **outro (Goodbye Jingle)** (0:20)

After a reprise of "She Loves You," the final *Pop go the Beatles* continues with a truncated version of "Ask Me Why," the second bridge and preceding refrain being omitted. Paul counts off "I Saw Her Standing There" in German for no good reason, and "Sure to Fall (in Love with You)" is dedicated to the BBC's secretary Audrey, and to host Rodney Burke "for being a great help throughout the forty-nine weeks."

The series' final number is suitably "Twist and Shout," which each Beatle in turn dedicates to his bandmates. This is followed by a farewell a cappella jingle from the lads (**L**), based on the theme from *The Flowerpot Men:* "Goodbye, George/Goodbye, John/Ringo, Paul, Ringo, Paul/Rodney Burke!"

The guest artist in this final installment was Tony Rivers and the Castaways, whose rendition of "Abilene" from this broadcast was bootlegged in fair quality on the 1988 LP *Meet the Beeb,* under the title "My Evelyne."

RELEASE HISTORY

1971: A good-quality tape of **I** was released on *Yellow Matter Custard.*

1972: Good-quality but incomplete copies of **G** and **I** appeared on *Outtakes 2* (aka *Studio Sessions, Volume 2*).

1987: An excellent recording of this show (**A–L**) was included on vinyl copies of *The Beatles at the Beeb, Volume 6* (although **L** was slightly incomplete; see below). The Pyramid CD of this title (copied on *The Complete BBC Sessions*) is missing a bit of **D.**

1999: A slightly longer (but inferior quality) tape of **L** was included on the CD-R compilation *Vinyl to the Core.*

2003: The entire show, including the most complete copy of **L,** was bootlegged on the CD boxed set *The Beatles at the Beeb.*

58. Radio performance

Date: 7 September 1963
Time: 1:00–4:00 p.m.
Location: Playhouse Theatre, London
Producers: Jimmy Grant, Bernie Andrews
Host: Brian Matthew
Broadcast: 5 October 1963, 10:00 a.m.–noon
BBC Light Programme
Saturday Club #261

[A.] **intro** (0:51)
[B.] **I Saw Her Standing There** (2:31)
[C.] **Memphis, Tennessee** (2:13)
[D.] **intro** (0:01)
[E.] **Happy Birthday, *Saturday Club*** (0:30)
[F.] **outro** (0:02)
Fools Rush In (Rick Nelson)
Sally Ann (Joe Brown and His Bruvvers)
Autumn Leaves (Joe Brown and His Bruvvers)
Take Good Care of My Baby (Bobby Vee)
Walk Right Back (The Everly Brothers)
All I Have to Do Is Dream (The Everly Brothers)
A Picture of You (Joe Brown and His Bruvvers)
Bye Bye Love (The Everly Brothers)
[G.] **intro** (0:29)
[H.] **I'll Get You** (2:03)
[I.] **intro** (0:07)
[J.] **She Loves You** (2:14)
[K.] **Lucille** (1:51)
[L.] **outro** (0:48)

Saturday Club celebrated its fifth anniversary show in style, with the Everly Brothers' first performance specifically for British radio, and birthday greetings from Roy Orbison, Cliff Richard, Del Shannon, Brenda Lee, and Rick Nelson. Of course, the Beatles taped an appearance, and since they don't interact directly with host Brian Matthew, we can presume he was occupied elsewhere during the session.

John was given an arranging credit for the rocked-up rendition of "Happy Birthday to You" (**E**), though it's actually modeled on a current UK hit, Heinz's "Just Like Eddie," which is in turn based on Eddie Cochran's rumbling guitar classics such as "Summertime Blues." After playing both sides of their current number 1 single, the Beatles close the show with a cover of Little Richard's "Lucille." Matthew's introduction suggests that Paul sings it in tribute to fellow guests the Everly Brothers, whose rendition had charted in 1960.

RELEASE HISTORY

1972: The BBC Radio documentary *The Beatles Story* broadcast an incomplete fair-quality tape of **K,** misidentified as a Lennon lead vocal. This was copied on the bootleg *Have You Heard the Word* the following year and appeared on several other boots, usually attributed to a late 1962 studio session.

1974: Good-quality versions of **C–E** appeared on *Rare Beatles* (aka *Happy Birthday*).

1982: A mediocre tape of **E** was broadcast in the radio special *The Beatles at the Beeb.*

1984: The picture disc LP *Directly from Santa Claus* contained a good-quality copy of **C.**

1987: **A** (slightly incomplete), **B–F,** and **K** surfaced in excellent quality on the bootleg LP *The Beatles at the Beeb, Volume 7,* along with several songs from other artists from the same broadcast.

1988: By this time, it seems the BBC had recovered a tape of the original broadcast, and **G–J** made their debuts in excellent sound on the October 8, 1988, episode of *The Beeb's Lost Beatles Tapes*. This entire edition of *Saturday Club* was retransmitted October 5, 1991.

1993: Great Dane included everything but **G** on their *The Complete BBC Sessions* box.

1994: Apple released **K** (with a slightly cross-faded ending) on *Live at the BBC*.

2003: The complete program (**A–L**) was booted in excellent quality on the boxed CD set *The Beatles at the Beeb*.

59. Newsreel footage

Date: 10 September 1963
Time: afternoon
Location: Savoy Hotel, London
Length: 1:00

On one of their increasingly rare days off, the Beatles attended a Variety Club awards banquet at the Savoy Hotel, marking their first appearance in a British Pathé newsreel. They are seen briefly mingling with the other guests before picking up awards for top vocal group and best vocal record ("From Me to You"). Also glimpsed are top female TV artist Millicent Martin (star of BBC TV's *That Was the Week That Was*), top disc jockey David Jacobs (host of BBC TV's *Juke Box Jury*), and top female singer Susan Maughan. Top male singer Cliff Richard is absent, but boxer Sonny Liston seems to be the guest of honor and gets the most screen time.

After the luncheon, the Beatles, Susan Maughan, and Billy J Kramer posed for photos at the adjacent Victoria Embankment Gardens. As John and Paul caught a taxi across town to their new London digs, they bumped into former Beatle press officer Andrew Loog Oldham. He'd left that post to take on the task of managing a promising new outfit, the Rolling Stones, and invited the songwriting Beatles to a Stones rehearsal later that day at the Ken Colyer Jazz Club.

The Stones' first single, a cover of Chuck Berry's "Come On," had been a minor hit, but a follow-up was needed. As Mick Jagger later put it, in a slightly different context, Lennon and McCartney were already "known for their hit-making potential ability" and were glad to donate a composition in progress, "I Wanna Be Your Man." Their supposedly remarkable proficiency at finishing off the lyrics on the spot pales when one considers that the song (in the Stones' rendition) consists of only two different lines, "I wanna be your lover baby, I wanna be your man" and "Tell me that you love me baby, tell me you understand," alternating with the title refrain.

RELEASE HISTORY

This newsreel, titled *Liston's Here!*, circulates on video.

60. Studio session

Date: 11 September 1963
Time: 2:30–6:00 p.m.
Location: EMI Studio 2
Producer: George Martin

[A.] All I've Got to Do—RM15 (2:00)
Mixed: 30 September 1963

[B.] All I've Got to Do—RS15 (2:00)
Mixed: 29 October 1963

Before setting out on a fortnight's holiday, the Beatles spent two days at Abbey Road Studios working on their second LP. Since their last session, five new songs had been written for the album, including George's first composition and a pair of Lennon/McCartney contenders for Ringo's spotlight number.

The latter were taped first: one take of "I Wanna Be Your Man" and two of "Little Child." As the session tapes from this date are long gone, it's impossible to say who sang lead on these takes. As noted earlier (see the August 19 entry), "Little Child" was written for Ringo to sing, and perhaps the final vocal assignments weren't settled until after these initial attempts. Remakes of both songs would begin the following day.

John once described his composition "All I've Got to Do" as "me again, trying to do Smokey Robinson"; however, Arthur Alexander seems to have been the chief inspiration. Rhythmically and harmonically, it sounds like a cross between "Anna (Go to Him)" and

"Soldier of Love." The backing was taped in fourteen takes, with John and George playing two different rhythm guitar patterns. The fifteenth take was an overdub onto the previous one, perhaps of backing vocals (John's lead vocal is single-tracked) or the slowly strummed opening chord.

RELEASE HISTORY

1963: **A** and **B** were released on mono and stereo pressings of *With the Beatles*. **A** is available on EMI's CD of that title.

61. Studio session

Date: 11 September 1963
Time: 7:00–10:15 p.m.
Location: EMI Studio 2
Producer: George Martin

[A.] Not a Second Time—RM9 (2:04)
Mixed: 30 September 1963

[B.] Not a Second Time—RS9 (2:03)
Mixed: 29 October 1963

After a dinner break, the session continued with another John Lennon composition, "Not a Second Time." The basic track of John's vocal, bass, drums, and rhythm guitar was taped in five attempts. Four overdub takes on the last of these added John's second vocal and George Martin's piano contribution, performed simultaneously. The tape log indicates that take 9 was to be edited, which explains why the song opens abruptly mid-note; presumably a musical introduction was trimmed. The mono mix of this song (**A**) fades a couple of notes later than its stereo counterpart (**B**).

The session concluded with the first seven takes of George's "Don't Bother Me," three of which were overdubs, but time ran out and they would begin anew the following day.

RELEASE HISTORY

1963: **A** and **B** were released on mono and stereo pressings of *With the Beatles*. **A** is available on EMI's CD of that title.

62. Studio session

Date: 12 September 1963
Time: 2:30–6:30 p.m.
Location: EMI Studio 2
Producer: George Martin

[A.] Christmas Messages to Australia—take 1 (mono) (0:34)
[B.] Christmas Messages to Australia—takes 2–3 (mono) (0:56)
[C.] Open Message to Australia—take 1 (mono) (0:38)
[D.] Hold Me Tight—rehearsal take (stereo) (0:35)
[E.] Hold Me Tight—takes 20–21 (stereo) (2:57)
[F.] Hold Me Tight—take 22 (stereo) (0:51)
[G.] Hold Me Tight—takes 23–24 (stereo) (3:03)
[H.] Hold Me Tight—rehearsal fragment (stereo) (0:04)
[I.] Hold Me Tight—take 25 (stereo) (0:20)
[J.] Hold Me Tight—take 26 (stereo) (2:37)
[K.] Hold Me Tight—rehearsal fragment (stereo) (0:01)
[L.] Hold Me Tight—take 27 (stereo) (0:14)
[M.] Hold Me Tight—take 28 (stereo) (1:37)
[N.] Hold Me Tight—take 29 (stereo) (2:43)
[O.] Hold Me Tight—RM26 (2:28)
Mixed: 23 October 1963
[P.] Hold Me Tight—RS29 (2:29)
Mixed: 29 October 1963

Sadly, the reel from this afternoon session (E50527) is the only multitrack session tape from the *With the Beatles* LP sessions not to have been scrapped. Fortunately for historians, the majority of it, including all its musical content, has been bootlegged.

A possible reason for the tape to have been retained (or perhaps misfiled) is that it opens with a few special messages taped for broadcast on Australian radio. The first three of these were spoken directly to Bob Rogers, a DJ at Sydney's 2SM Radio who would travel with the group on their 1964 tour. The Beatles sound supremely disinterested during these messages

(**A–B**), their mouths full of food as they read from prepared scripts. The fourth take (**C**) is a brief, generic "open message," greeting Australian listeners in general.

With that taken care of, the group began a remake of Paul's "Hold Me Tight," originally attempted in thirteen takes during the *Please Please Me* LP sessions. As the tape rolls, they run through an experimental arrangement of the intro (**D**), building up à la "Back in the USSR." Paul dismisses the drum pattern as too similar to Johnny Preston's "Running Bear," and John suggests reverting to a simple guitar boogie.

The first proper take (**E**) is a false start as Paul sings the wrong lyric. Norman Smith accidentally announces the next take as 23, but it should be 21. This is marred by a backing vocal blunder ("too tight") during the second verse, and Ringo neglects to thump the toms on the second middle eight. Apparently there had originally been a guitar solo at that spot, and we learn at the end of the take that nobody had informed Ringo of the change.

Take 22 (**F**) has George confirming that fact: "Yeah, there's just two middle eights, right?" John and George are late with their first vocal entry, so George Martin whistles them to a halt. John complains that he's having trouble playing the repeating riff and concentrating on his singing. The tape is switched off, perhaps for more rehearsal. Take 23 is another false start with Paul bungling the opening line, but take 24 (**G**) provides the basis for the released version.

The single layer of overdubs consists of handclaps (on both tracks of the tape) and further backing vocals. As the tape rolls again (**I**), John discusses the clapping blueprint: "one-two-cha-cha-cha" during the middle eights and four-in-the-bar elsewhere. The playback of take 24 is started, but catches them unprepared: "We missed the clap . . ." Take 26 (**J**) is a complete overdub take with no major flaws, although the backing vocals occasionally clash with the original lyrics ("now" and "so" sung simultaneously).

They carry on with take 27 (**L**), a false start, and take 28 (**M**), which breaks down when they botch the singing going into the third verse. Take 29 (**N**) is complete, and differs from take 24 in that they sing vocal harmonies over the final "you, you, you." Its only blemish is that during the second middle eight, they are a bar late in switching to the alternate handclap pattern.

The tape box labels take 29 as "best" but notes "2nd middle 8 Possible edit." While George Martin did prepare an edit of takes 26 and 29 on September 30, the released mono mix (**O**) appears to be entirely from take 26, while the stereo (**P**) is from take 29 (I can't detect any edit points on either mix). Also included on the raw studio reel are a couple of fragments (**H** and **K**) of earlier rehearsals that were erased by the "proper" takes.

RELEASE HISTORY

1963: **O** and **P** were released on mono and stereo pressings of *With the Beatles.* **O** is available on EMI's CD of that title.

1983: The multimedia presentation *The Beatles at Abbey Road* concludes with Ringo's portion of **C.** It can be heard on the bootleg CD *Abbey Road Video Show.*

1984: Most of **C** was included in the radio documentary *Sgt. Pepper's Lonely Hearts Club Band: A History of the Beatle Years 1962–1970.* John, Paul, and George's portion appears in episode 3 and was copied from this source on the CD-R compilation *Vinyl to the Core.* Ringo's portion appears at the end of episode 9.

1988: An incomplete version of **N** surfaced on the vinyl bootleg *Ultra Rare Trax, Volume 3 & 4;* it appeared the following year from a tape source on the CD *Hold Me Tight;* both sources run too slow.

1989: The bootleg CD *Unsurpassed Masters, Volume 1* included excellent but slow copies of **F** and **G.**

1991: **I** and **J** were included, both too slow, on the bootleg CD *Unsurpassed Masters, Volume 7.*

1992: A portion of **E** (take 20) appeared on the vinyl bootleg *Arrive Without Travelling,* and from tape source on its CD counterpart *Arrive Without Aging* the following year.

1994: An excellent but slow tape of most of this session was bootlegged on the CD *The Ultimate Collection, Volume 2: Studio Sessions, March 5 and September 12, 1963.* This included **E** (incomplete), **F, G, I** (slightly incomplete), **J,** and **L–N.**

2000: A slightly upgraded (but still slow!) tape of **D–N** came out on the bootleg CD-R *Studio Sessions.* A speed-corrected version of the entire disc is circulating.

2005: Excellent copies of **A–C** first appeared on the bootleg CD *Message to Australia.*

63. Studio session

Date: 12 September 1963
Time: 7:00–11:30 p.m.
Location: EMI Studio 2
Producer: George Martin

[A.] Don't Bother Me—take 10 (stereo) (2:46)
[B.] Don't Bother Me—takes 11–12 (stereo) (1:13)
[C.] Don't Bother Me—take 13 (stereo) (2:34)

[D.] Don't Bother Me—RM15 (2:25)
Mixed: 30 September 1963

[E.] Don't Bother Me—RS15 (2:25)
Mixed: 29 October 1963

After grabbing a quick dinner, the Beatles returned to Studio 2 to continue working on George's "Don't Bother Me." The remake began with "take ten" (actually the eighth attempt), and all four takes needed to perfect the backing track have survived.

George sings a live vocal and plays a guitar solo on each complete take, while John plays rhythm guitar with a tremolo effect on his amp. As take 10 (**A**) begins, George is humming the song in an attempt to demonstrate the correct tempo. Although it's a complete performance, the playing is sloppy toward the end of the song, and George seems to realize this as he sings a tongue-in-cheek ad-lib over the coda: "Oh yeah, rock-and-roll now . . ." With no ending worked out, the song is actually faded out in volume from the control room as they perform it.

Take 11 (**B**) has a new feature as the band inserts a pause after the intro to spotlight George's vocal entry. He calls a halt to the song after singing one line, complaining about the rapid tempo. The next take breaks down when Ringo accidentally inserts the pause at the top of the second verse. George seems to be having trouble coordinating his singing and playing: "It's mad—it's hard enough for me trying to sing it, never mind . . . tryin' to do the . . ."

As take 13 begins (**C**) the band is still rushing a bit, and George cautions them off-mic "not too fast" just before beginning his vocal (this aside is audible on both released mixes). With no major flaws, the performance was chosen as suitable for overdubbing. George added his second lead vocal while John played tambourine, Paul woodblock, and Ringo what is colorfully described in the LP's liner notes as a "loose-skinned Arabian bongo." This overdub continued through take 19, with 15 being the "best."

The stereo mix (**E**) contains the end of the "four" from George's count-in, which is absent (or inaudible) in mono (**D**). A curious variation of **E** was released on a 1970s Canadian pressing of *Meet the Beatles!,* which has the word "don't" repeated during the final verse. This oddity is caused by a tape glitch and isn't a true alternate mix.

The session concluded with a remake of "Little Child," with the backing track perfected by take 13. This apparently consisted only of bass and drums (there may be a rhythm guitar buried in the background), plus John and Paul's vocal duet. With takes 14 and 15, John's harmonica and Paul's piano were overdubbed on take 13. John then had three attempts at playing his harmonica solo as an edit piece, with plenty of leakage from the playback speaker he was using as a monitor.

On September 30, takes 15 and 18 would be edited to produce a master take (the splices are obvious at 0:53 and 1:12), but overdubbing would continue October 3.

RELEASE HISTORY

1963: **D** and **E** were released on mono and stereo pressings of *With the Beatles.* **D** is available on EMI's CD of that title.

1983: A portion of **B** was included in the *Beatles at Abbey Road* presentation, and is contained on the many boots of that show (the best being *Abbey Road Video Show*).

1989: An excellent but slow tape of **B** and **C** (slightly incomplete) appeared on *Unsurpassed Masters, Volume 1.*

1991: An excellent but slow tape of **A** debuted on the bootleg CD *Unsurpassed Masters, Volume 6.*

1994: An excellent and complete (still slow) tape of **A–C** was released on *The Ultimate Collection, Volume 2: Studio Sessions, March 5 and September 12, 1963.*

2000: A slightly upgraded (but still slow!) tape of **A–C** came out on the bootleg CD-R *Studio Sessions.* A speed-corrected version of the entire disc is circulating.

63a. Amateur footage

Date: 16 September–3 October 1963
Location: Benton, Illinois
Length: 0:22

George became the first Beatle to set foot in the United States when he visited his sister, Louise, and her husband, Gordon, in Illinois. Although he was disappointed that nobody he encountered seemed to know who the Beatles were, George had a great time camping in the woods, sitting in with local band the Four Vests, and purchasing a new Rickenbacker guitar. Naturally, he brought along a home movie camera to document the trip. A few short clips have recently surfaced, including an extreme close-up of George's goofy grin, and Louise doing a cancan with her brother.

RELEASE HISTORY

This silent color footage circulates on video from an April 21, 2006, broadcast on Wild Chicago's *Illinois Road Trip*.

64. Studio session

Date: 3 October 1963
Time: 10:00 a.m.–1:00 p.m.
Location: EMI Studio 3
Producer: George Martin

[A.] Little Child—RM21 (1:44)
Mixed: 23 October 1963

[B.] Little Child—RS21 (1:44)
Mixed: 29 October 1963

This short overdub session was conducted in the absence of George, who was still en route from his visit to America. It began with takes 14 and 15 of "I Wanna Be Your Man," both of which were overdubs of vocals onto take 13 (Ringo's second lead, John and Paul's backing, and plenty of extraneous "woo's," clapping, and shouting).

"Little Child" was also completed with overdub takes 19–21 onto the edit prepared September 30. This overdub was apparently the doubled "come on come on" vocal sections that pop up on the left channel in stereo (**B**) during the middle eights. The vocal track fades out a couple of words earlier in mono (**A**), but the final "oh yeah" is still barely audible.

RELEASE HISTORY

1963: **A** and **B** were released on mono and stereo pressings of *With the Beatles*. **A** is available on EMI's CD of that title.

65. Radio interview

Date: 3 October 1963
Time: afternoon
Location: NEMS Enterprises, London
Producer: John Fawcett Wilson
Host: Tony Hall
Interviewer: Michael Colley
Broadcast: 3 November 1963, 3:00–4:00 p.m.
BBC Light Programme
The Public Ear
Length: 2:23

George rejoined his bandmates in time for this BBC Radio interview conducted at NEMS's first London headquarters. *The Public Ear* was assembling a feature story on the Liverpool music scene and naturally focused on the city's star pupils.

Each Beatle helpfully introduces himself by announcing his name and instrument played; John adds, "Sometimes I play the fool." George denies reports that they earn £7,000 a week (Paul: "I wish we did") and explains that record royalties can take months to arrive. He points out that they were content to perform for a pittance for several years, although he admits "the money does help, let's face it."

John says he's too impatient to sit and practice guitar, and is more interested in songwriting and the group's overall sound than achieving technical perfection. Paul pegs George as the keenest musical student, but George says he doesn't practice either, and thinks they are "all crummy musicians, really."

RELEASE HISTORY

1988: This interview was broadcast in the November 12 episode of BBC Radio's *The Beeb's Lost Beatles Tapes*. It's available on the bootleg CD *The Beatles Broadcast Collection, Trailer 1.*

1994: The Beatles' self-introductions were released on Apple's *Live at the BBC* CD as "Beatle Greetings," misdated as an October 9 recording.

66. TV performance

Date: 4 October 1963
Time: 6:15–7:00 p.m.
Location: Studio 9, Television House, London
Producer: Vicki Wickham
Host: Keith Fordyce
Interviewer: Dusty Springfield
Broadcast: live
Associated-Rediffusion TV
Ready, Steady, Go!

[A.] **intro** (0:32)
[B.] **Twist and Shout** (1:54)
[C.] **chat w/George** (0:46)
[D.] **Look Who It Is** (2:15)
[E.] **"Mime Time"** (2:48)
[F.] **chat w/Ringo** (1:20)
[G.] **chat w/Paul** (1:29)
[H.] **I'll Get You** (1:59)
[I.] **chat w/John** (1:08)
[J.] **She Loves You** (2:15)
[K.] **viewers' questions** (1:55)

Ten weeks into its run, the legendary British pop showcase *Ready, Steady, Go!* featured the country's top recording act. Dressed in their collarless suits, the Beatles lip-synced three numbers while crowded onto a small platform and surrounded by well-behaved dancing teens.

The show opens with regular host Keith Fordyce introducing that week's "commere (the mother of a compere)," singer Dusty Springfield. She in turn introduces the first number (**B**), after which she steps up on the platform to chat with George, who shows off his new Rickenbacker and claims they wear fiberglass wigs.

In a charming performance, Helen Shapiro sings "Look Who It Is" (**D**) while walking down a line of three Beatles, singing a verse to each in turn. John wiggles his eyebrows, Ringo puts his head on her shoulder, and George pleads on bended knees. Elsewhere in the studio, Paul judges a Mime Time competition (**E**) in which four girls lip-sync to Brenda Lee's "Let's Jump the Broomstick," with the champion receiving an Elvis Presley LP. Paul votes fourteen-year-old Melanie Coe, a regular dancer on the show, the winner. In a strange twist of fate, Melanie would run away from home early in 1967, and Paul would read her story in the *Daily Mail* and be inspired to write "She's Leaving Home."

Later in the show, Dusty poses more questions sent in by viewers. Ringo talks about his rings, bracelet, shoe size, and why he doesn't like Donald Duck, tossing in some quacking to demonstrate. Paul confirms that he sleeps with his eyes open, although "I haven't seen myself do it," and denies that he plucks "his well-shaped eyebrows."

After "I'll Get You," Dusty asks John if the group had any other names (Quarry Men), if he wears false teeth (no), and if he was once shot at for stealing apples (yes). She jokes that he still has a scar from the incident, and John replies, "No, they're scabs," and then asks to see Dusty's scabs! She wisely ends the interview and they perform "She Loves You." Fordyce then returns to read out some prize-winning questions sent in by readers. Asked to choose between a night out with Brigitte Bardot or £1,000, John (the married man) opts for the money, while Paul and Ringo choose Brigitte, and George wants "both, please."

RELEASE HISTORY

A, B, E, G, I, and **J** were released on the home video *Ready, Steady, Go! Volume 2.* The Japanese laser disc *Ready, Steady, Go! Special Edition* included **B,** a bit of **C,** and **F–K.** The other segments circulate on video.

67. Radio performance

Date: 9 October 1963
Time: 10:00–11:00 p.m.
Location: BBC Paris Studio, London
Producer: Bill Worsley
Host: Ken Dodd
Broadcast: 3 November 1963, 2:30–3:00 p.m.
BBC Light Programme
The Ken Dodd Show

[A.] intro (0:04)
[B.] She Loves You (2:17)
[C.] outro (0:12)

Liverpool comedian Ken Dodd worked with the Beatles on several occasions, and they appeared on his BBC Radio variety show on John's twenty-third birthday to plug their recent single. Photographer Dezo Hoffmann was present during the rehearsals, which began at 6:30 p.m., and took some publicity pictures of Dodd and the Beatles goofing around onstage (Dodd plays a violin while Ringo thumps on a pail).

He also got some nice candid shots of John (wearing glasses), Paul, and George sharing a microphone to rehearse their number watched by the BBC Variety Orchestra. For the actual show, an enthusiastic studio audience screamed its way through "She Loves You."

RELEASE HISTORY

1993: This show was booted in fair quality on *The Complete BBC Sessions* box, running too slow and missing the last few seconds of **C.**

2001: The CD-R *The Complete BBC Sessions—Upgraded* included a speed-corrected and complete copy of this broadcast, from a fair-quality tape that had been circulating for years.

68. TV interview

Date: 13 October 1963
Location: London Palladium
Broadcast: 13 October 1963
ITV
Length: 0:49

An ITV news crew interviewed the Beatles in their dressing room at the Palladium prior to their critical performance that evening. In this brief clip, Paul explains that they have gotten used to the screaming crowds, and Ringo reveals that the police always beseech them not to incite the fans by waving from windows.

RELEASE HISTORY

This interview circulates on video among collectors.

69. TV performance

Date: 13 October 1963
Time: 8:25–9:25 p.m.
Location: London Palladium
Host: Bruce Forsyth
Broadcast: live
ATV
Val Parnell's Sunday Night at the London Palladium

[A.] intro (0:28)
[B.] From Me to You (1:48)
[C.] intro (0:37)
[D.] I'll Get You (2:01)
[E.] intro (0:17)
[F.] She Loves You (2:15)
[G.] intro (1:13)
[H.] Twist and Shout (2:36)
[I.] outro (Twist and Shout/Startime) (1:28)

In late June, it was announced that the Beatles would be appearing on ATV's live variety show *Sunday Night at the London Palladium* when it returned in the fall. By the time the date rolled around, they had released the biggest-selling single in the history of British pop music and their album was enjoying its twenty-fourth of thirty consecutive weeks topping the chart. Their *Twist and Shout* EP had received the first-ever silver EP award in the UK for selling 250,000 copies.

Yet such was the prestige of appearing on the Palladium that the normally unflappable group was nervous and wary. They carefully rehearsed a four-song routine on the evening of the twelfth, and just before going onstage, the tension of the moment got to poor Ringo, causing a quick evacuation of his stomach contents.

Sadly, no video or kinescope of this key performance has been found, leaving a series of photographs as our only visual record. The Beatles performed in their collarless Pierre Cardin suits, Ringo on a large cubical drum riser, beneath giant glittering silver letters spelling out BEATLES. The circulating audio recordings all come from home viewers who taped the show for posterity.

Host Bruce Forsyth teased the crowd by having the Beatles appear fleetingly at the top of the show (not heard on the circulating tape) and then apparently doing his introduction in a Beatle wig. ("I thought I'd be a dead ringer for Ringo!") If anything, the group's corny patter before "She Loves You" comes off as over-rehearsed, and John's "spastic clapping" impression prior to "Twist and Shout" must have raised a few eyebrows among first-time Beatle viewers.

But the music is fresh and spirited, particularly a charming "I'll Get You," with the audience clapping along. After the Beatles' final song, the Jack Parnell Orchestra vamps a few bars of "Twist and Shout," allowing the Fabs to climb aboard the Palladium's famed revolving rostrum to wave good-bye over the closing theme. For better or worse, the Beatles had definitely "made it to the top" in British show business terms.

RELEASE HISTORY

1987: Slightly incomplete versions of **G** and **H** appeared on the bootleg LP *The Beatles at the Beeb, Volume 7* in good quality (misidentified as coming from an episode of *Easy Beat*). This source was copied on the CD-R *Vinyl to the Core*.

1995: A very good (but still off-line) copy of **D,** plus a fragment of its intro, was released on the CD *Anthology 1,* running too slow.

1997: A fair-quality recording of the entire program (**A–I**) surfaced on the bootleg CD *Road Runner.* This off-line tape includes a child giggling in places and suffers from backwards leakage of material from the other side of the tape; about half of **G** is missing as well. Only 52 seconds of **I** are included, but a complete recording circulates on tape.

1999: A distorted but upgraded copy of **B–H** was included on the bootleg boxed CD set *Mythology, Volume 1.* It sounds better than *Road Runner,* but still far below *Anthology.*

70. Newsreel footage

Date: 13 October 1963
Location: London Palladium
Broadcast: 14 October 1963
ITV
Length: 0:36

ITV's crew also captured the aftermath of the Palladium show, filming the Beatles' escape from the venue through a crowd of screaming teenagers who chased their car down the road as it sped away. Although such scenes were now commonplace at Beatles concerts, the London media were just beginning to catch on. The following morning, newspaper reports dubbed the phenomenon "Beatlemania."

RELEASE HISTORY

This silent footage circulates on video; a bit of it can be seen in the *Anthology* documentary.

71. Home demo — J

Date: ca. July–early October 1963
Location: London (?)

[A.] I'm in Love (1:27)

This recording features John's solo vocal and piano performance of a composition with the working title "I'm So Glad." It's more of a composing tape than a polished demo, as the lyrics seem to be half-finished. The demo was found on the same reel containing recordings of Cynthia and baby Julian (a bit of which was aired on *The Lost Lennon Tapes* in 1988).

It begins with the eventual second verse, followed by a partial rendition of the first verse, a completed bridge, and a mumbled third verse leading to the ending. The circulating tape plays back in F-sharp major, but John was clearly playing in the key of G. When the tape is speed-corrected to the proper pitch, John's voice sounds much closer to 1963-era Lennon. The chords used, G, Em, B, C, and D, are also the exact same chords in the verses and chorus of "I Want to Hold Your Hand," another song written by John and Paul on the piano around this time.

With completed lyrics and the addition of an introductory section, John would offer the song to Billy J Kramer (see following entry).

RELEASE HISTORY

1992: **A** was broadcast in episode 92-13 of the radio series *The Lost Lennon Tapes*. It was bootlegged on the LP *Arrive without Travelling* and copied on the CD *Arrive without Aging* in 1993.

72. Studio session — J

Date: 14 October 1963
Location: EMI Studios
Producer: George Martin

[A.] I'm in Love—take 32 w/false starts and chat (stereo) (3:39)

John and Paul ended up contributing two numbers for Billy J Kramer's next single, but only "I'll Keep You Satisfied" would make the cut. John was present when this and "I'm in Love" were recorded at Abbey Road, and his voice pops up from the control booth during Kramer's attempt to sing the latter.

This was most likely taped in Studio 2, apparently using the studio's new four-track tape machine, which the Beatles would try out for the first time in a few days. The song has been lowered from the key of G to Eb to make it easier for Kramer to sing, but he still struggles a bit with the opening phrases. After a false start caused by an errant bass note, John coaches Billy over the studio intercom. A second false start is caused by Dakotas guitarist Robin MacDonald playing a B minor instead of a C minor chord.

John teases Billy about his singing—"Adam Faith, ya fool!"—and Kramer apologizes. George Martin chimes in: "I give you full permission to come to the Beatles session on Thursday and shout at John whenever you like." Norman Smith announces take 32, a complete attempt that includes a second overdubbed vocal in places.

Within a few days, the group, the Fourmost, would have a crack at recording the song in a slightly new arrangement. The intro has new lyrics, the guitar solo is omitted, and "feeling on top of the world" has been changed to "sitting on top of the world"; the key is also raised to E major. Their version was released as a follow-up single to "Hello Little Girl," and reached number 15 on the *Melody Maker* chart.

RELEASE HISTORY

1991: **A** was released on the CD *The Best of Billy J Kramer and the Dakotas*.

72a. Amateur footage

Date: 15 October 1963
Location: Floral Hall, Southport
Length: 0:09

The *Anthology* documentary includes various undated clips from 1963 intercut with other home movies (including Dezo Hoffmann's; see the March 25 and July 22–27 entries) in a montage set to "It Won't Be Long." Timing the exact amount of footage is difficult due to speed manipulation, but the scenes include a 9-second shot of the group performing in their collarless suits, filmed from the wings at Floral Hall, Southport, October 15.

Backstage footage from an unknown venue shows John wearing an ice bucket on his head, walking into a wardrobe and emerging with George, draped in coat hangers. George lights John's cigarette, and George and Paul are seen playing their guitars while the others throw rubbish at them. Other unidentified home movies used in the same sequence show John rafting and frolicking on the rocks at some seaside resort, George snorkeling with a bird perched on his arm, and various "on the road" scenes (in the car with Neil, eating meals) from the same period.

RELEASE HISTORY

This silent color footage was used in the *Anthology* documentary.

73. Radio interview

Date: 16 October 1963
Location: Playhouse Theatre, London
Interviewer: Peter Woods
Broadcast: 16 October 1963, 7:00–7:31 p.m.
BBC Light Programme
Radio Newsreel
Length: 2:30

Events began to happen in a fast and furious fashion. Two days after Beatlemania was hatched at the Palladium, it was announced that the Beatles had been invited to perform for the Queen Mother and Princess Margaret at the annual Royal Variety Performance. The following day, the group rehearsed for a BBC Radio performance in London and, naturally, a BBC reporter was on hand to glean their reactions.

Paul agrees that they seem to have reached the top swiftly, but neither he nor John want to speculate how much is due to their musical talent and how much to their personality and "funny haircuts." Ringo admits their style of music is hardly revolutionary, merely their own unique take on rock-and-roll. George feels that their career has a couple of years left, but thinks "it'd just be ridiculous" if it continued at the same pace. Little did he know he was only beginning a solid six months of uninterrupted and escalating pandemonium!

Future opposition leader Edward Heath had recently been quoted as calling the Beatles' Liverpool speech patterns "unrecognizable as the queen's English." Paul responds that "we don't all speak like them BBC posh fellers, y'know . . . right up North." George is characteristically more direct: "We just won't vote for him."

RELEASE HISTORY

1984: A portion of this interview was included in the radio documentary *Sgt. Pepper's Lonely Hearts Club Band: A History of the Beatle Years 1962–1970.* It appears from this source on the CD-R *Vinyl to the Core.*

1988: A longer version was broadcast in the November 12 episode of BBC Radio's *The Beeb's Lost Beatles Tapes.* It's available on the bootleg CD *The Beatles Broadcast Collection, Trailer 1.* The 1984 and 1988 broadcasts each contain exclusive material.

74. TV interview

Date: 16 October 1963
Location: Playhouse Theatre, London
Broadcast: 16 October 1963
ITV
Length: 0:56

Also present at the Playhouse was an ITV reporter to film a Beatles interview for broadcast in that evening's news bulletin. As one of his bandmates swipes at the back of his head, Paul explains that they may go for a new look at the Royal Variety show, but haven't worked out their act yet. John is adamant about one thing: No matter what Mr. Heath says, they won't be speaking any differently. He lapses into an exaggerated idiot-Scouse: "Oh, no, like, we'll keep, like, the same kind of thing, like, won't we?"

RELEASE HISTORY

1995: The audio portion of this interview was released on the CD *Rare Photos & Interview CD, Volume 1.* The clip was included on the video compilation *Beatlemania,* and most of it was used in the *Anthology* documentary.

75. Radio performance

Date: 16 October 1963
Time: 9:00–10:00 p.m.
Location: Playhouse Theatre, London
Producer: Ron Belchier
Host: Brian Matthew
Broadcast: 20 October 1963, 10:31–11:30 a.m.
BBC Light Programme
Easy Beat

[A.] **intro** (0:13)
[B.] **I Saw Her Standing There** (2:30)
[C.] **outro/intro** (0:19)
[D.] **Love Me Do** (2:24)
[E.] **intro** (0:07)
[F.] **Please Please Me** (1:54)
[G.] **intro** (0:40)
[H.] **From Me to You** (1:50)

[I.] intro (0:02)
[J.] She Loves You (2:15)
[K.] outro (0:12)

It seems appropriate that at the juncture when everything was changing exponentially, the Beatles devoted a BBC Radio performance to taking stock of their career so far. To this end, they performed all four of their singles in succession for the wildly enthusiastic *Easy Beat* audience one day before recording their fifth single, which would provide an important American breakthrough.

While harmonica was a key ingredient of the first three of these singles, it's retained only in the live arrangement of "Love Me Do." Following "Please Please Me," Brian Matthew informs the audience that the Beatles have been selected for the Royal Variety show, and they are modestly delighted. (Paul: "All the fellows and I are knocked out." George: "Aye, very nice!")

RELEASE HISTORY

1987: A very good-quality tape of this entire show (**A–K**) was included on the bootleg LP *The Beatles at the Beeb, Volume 7.* It was copied on *The Complete BBC Sessions* box, although a far inferior tape was used for the last 3 seconds of **H.** This problem was rectified on the bootleg CD *The Beatles Broadcast Collection, Trailer 2.*

1994: **B** was released on Apple's *Live at the BBC* CD in excellent quality.

76. Studio session

Date: 17 October 1963
Time: 2:30–5:00 and 7:00–10:00 p.m.
Location: EMI Studio 2
Producer: George Martin

[A.] The Beatles' Christmas Record (mono) (5:02)
[B.] I Want to Hold Your Hand—take 1 (mono) (0:12)
[C.] I Want to Hold Your Hand—take 2 (mono) (0:06)
[D.] I Want to Hold Your Hand—take 9 (mono) (0:32)
[E.] I Want to Hold Your Hand—unknown take (mono) (0:06)
[F.] This Boy—unknown take w/take 12 announcement (mono) (0:14)
[G.] This Boy—take 12 (stereo) (1:02)
[H.] This Boy—take 13 announcement (mono) (0:02)
[I.] This Boy—take 13 (stereo) (2:12)

[J.] I Want to Hold Your Hand—RM1 (2:23)
[K.] This Boy—edit of RM1/RM2 (2:11)
[L.] I Want to Hold Your Hand—RS17 (2:23)
[M.] This Boy—RS15 (2:33)
Mixed: 21 October 1963

[N.] I Want to Hold Your Hand—RS1 (2:23)
Mixed: 7 November 1966

[O.] I Want to Hold Your Hand—RS from take 17 (#1) (2:23)
[P.] This Boy—RS from takes 15 and 17 (2:07)
[Q.] I Want to Hold Your Hand—RS from take 17 (#2) (1:22)

The Beatles' penultimate recording session of 1963 produced both sides of a new single plus a Christmas message to be mailed out to members of the Official Beatles Fan Club. The latter was apparently taped first (even though Paul says, "We've been [recording] all day before we started on this special message").

It opens with a bit of "From Me to You" played on the celeste, and then all four launch into a slightly demented version of "Good King Wenceslas," accompanied by sleigh bells. John reviews what a "gear year" 1963 has been and thanks the fans for sending him birthday presents before crooning his own "Chrimble" ditty (to the tune of "Happy Birthday to You"). Paul implores people to stop sending them jelly babies and rambles on until John cuts him off with a line from his poem "On Safairy with Whide Hunter." ("Stop shouting those animoles!") Paul sings a mock-German "Wenceslas," and Ringo is allowed to say only a few words prior to his own jazzy "Wenceslas" rendition. George is unimpressed: "Thank you, Ringo. We'll phone you." He thanks the fan club secretaries and sings a final verse of "Wenceslas," and all four launch into "Rudolph, the Red-Nosed Ringo" to close the disc.

John and Paul had written a pair of outstanding new tunes for the single, and the obvious A-side, "I Want to Hold Your Hand," was taped first. This was the group's first four-track recording, and the backing consisted of bass, drums, and John's rhythm guitar on one track, George's lead guitar on a second, and John and Paul's live vocals on a third. A lot of time was spent perfecting the opening chords, with Paul being particularly fastidious about getting them right.

Prior to the first take (**B**) John says to "do it slower," but Paul vetoes him and asks for a "clean beginning," wanting each chord to ring out distinctly. Before the second take (**C**), he instructs the others to "build up the beginning," but John still thinks it should start louder. Paul works on the dynamics further before take 9 (**D**), instructing Ringo to "keep his bit dead," and after a false start, clarifies that he wants them to attack the first chord and then hold back a touch.

Another fragment (**E**) has Paul vocalizing the opening and again requesting a "clean" start. Takes 14, 15, and 16 were all false starts as they labored to get what Paul was hearing in his head. It all paid off with take 17, and they added a fourth track of handclaps and an occasional bass guitar riff, completing the song.

They moved on to "This Boy," a song John and Paul had written in a hotel room during a recent concert appearance. The song was recorded in similar fashion to its flip side, with John substituting acoustic for electric rhythm guitar and John, Paul, and George sharing a microphone to sing the three-part harmonies. Take 2 lasted 2:25, the extra length accounted for by a brief guitar solo that was quickly dropped from the arrangement.

Their biggest problem wasn't singing the sophisticated harmony, which they'd been practicing for days, but distinguishing between "this" and "that" boy. One take (**F**—perhaps take 4) breaks down after John's voice cracks in the bridge and he correctly sings "this boy" but inserts "that boy" just in case. The last two seconds of this are only available (buried) in Paul's experimental *Liverpool Sound Collage,* at 6:08 on track 1, "Plastic Beetle."

Prior to take 12 (**G**), Paul encourages John not to be nervous, but it's Paul who blows the take by singing too loud on the second verse. Take 13 (**I**) goes smoothly until John sings "thas boy" about halfway through; they carry on, but Paul mocks John during the coda, singing an exaggerated *"Thas* boy." Note that Norman Smith's "take twelve" and "take thirteen" (**H**) announcements have been excised from the release of these takes on Apple's "Free as a Bird" single, but can be found on the *Anthology* video. The final take had overdubs of John's second lead vocal (on the bridge) and a slide guitar part from George (on the coda).

It's not clear which take produced the master; Mark Lewisohn indicates that take 15 was the final "best" and 16 and 17 were overdub takes. John Barrett's notes have 15 and 17 listed as best, presumably indicating they were to be edited together. Edits are audible at 1:27 and (less obvious) at 2:06.

On October 21, both songs were mixed into mono and stereo, although the stereo mixes remained unreleased until 1976. The stereo mix of "I Want to Hold Your Hand" (**L**) has the lead guitar centered, with vocals, handclaps, and the bass overdub in the right channel. "This Boy" has a similar setup, with the fourth track appearing at right for the second vocal, but centered for the slide guitar part. The raw tape of this mix that circulates (**M**) includes a false start of the playback, Norman Smith's "RS fifteen" announcement (not the fifteenth remix, but a stereo remix from take 15), and a bit of studio chat from the original tape, including the "take fifteen" announcement.

In November 1966, both songs were again mixed into stereo for the *Collection of Beatles Oldies* project. "I Want to Hold Your Hand" (**N**) now had vocals, handclaps, and second bass centered, with lead guitar in the right channel. "This Boy" was mixed in error (the title mistaken for "Bad Boy"), but had a similar stereo image. This mix was nearly released on the 1981 EP *The Beatles* but yet another administrative error led to a copy of the fake stereo mix from the *Love Songs* LP used in its place. When stereo outtakes of the song were released in 1995, they were mixed with centered vocals. The *Love* remix of "I Want to Hold Your Hand" (**Q**) has centered vocals and audience noise from the 1964 Hollywood Bowl concert added.

RELEASE HISTORY

1963: **J** and **K** were released on a single in the UK and are available on the "I Want to Hold Your Hand" CD single. **A** was released on a flexi-disc, titled *The Beatles' Christmas Record,* and mailed out to fan club members on December 6. It's included on Vigotone's CD *The Ultimate Beatles Christmas Collection.*

1966: ***N*** was released on the LP *A Collection of Beatles Oldies* in the UK. It's available on the CD collections *Past Masters, Volume 1,* The Beatles 1962–1966, and 1.

1976: **L** and **M** were released on an Australian single. When reissued on the 1983 Australian LP *23 Greatest Hits,* **L** was copied directly from the single, complete with the sound of the disc ramping up to speed at the start, but a clean transfer of the single can be found in the CD boxed set *Another Phase.* **M** was released on the CD *Past Masters, Volume 1.*

1995: **G** and **I** were released on Apple's "Free as a Bird" CD single.

1996: The *Anthology* home video included **B, D, F,** and **H,** plus a portion of **I.** They appear from this source on the bootleg CD *Abbey Road Video Show.*

1999: A tape of **M** with the mix announcement surfaced among John Barrett's cassette material and was included on the bootleg *Turn Me On Dead Man: The John Barrett Tapes.* The same year, a slightly longer but inferior-quality copy of **M** appeared on the bootleg CD *More Masters.* This includes the mix and take announcements and a bit of presong chat excised from earlier releases.

2000: **C, E,** and a portion of **B** were made available on the website thebeatles.com; they appear from that source on the CD *Studio Collection.* A portion of **F,** including 2 extra seconds at the end, was released on the CD *Liverpool Sound Collage.*

2003: **O** and **P** were released on the soundtrack of the *Anthology* DVD.

2006: **Q** was released on the *Love* CD.

77. TV performance

Date: 20 October 1963
Time: afternoon
Location: Alpha Television Studios, Birmingham
Producer: Philip Jones
Broadcast: 26 October 1963, 5:50–6:35 p.m.
ABC
Thank Your Lucky Stars

[A.] All My Loving (0:09)
[B.] Money (That's What I Want) (2:50)

The Beatles lip-synced three songs for their seventh appearance on ABC's *Thank Your Lucky Stars:* "All My Loving," "Money (That's What I Want)," and "She Loves You." Only the second of these (**B**) is circulating in full, and it shows the group performing on a slanted checkerboard stage in front of lights and a large sign reading BEATLES. The very end of "All My Loving" (**A**) has surfaced recently, suggesting the rest of the appearance may exist.

RELEASE HISTORY

This footage circulates on video in decent quality among collectors.

78. Studio session

Date: 23 October 1963
Time: 10:00 a.m.–1:00 p.m.
Location: EMI Studio 2
Producer: George Martin

[A.] I Wanna Be Your Man—RM16 (1:54)
Mixed: 23 October 1963

[B.] I Wanna Be Your Man—RS16 (1:56)
Mixed: 29 October 1963

Before departing for their Swedish tour, the Beatles put a finishing touch on "I Wanna Be Your Man," overdubbing a tambourine as take 16 onto take 15. The song's stereo mix (**B**) lasts a word or two longer during the fade than its mono counterpart.

The entire *With the Beatles* album was mixed into stereo in three hours flat on October 29, or more accurately, the best twin-track version of each song was copied to a master reel in the LP's running order, with EQ and echo added where necessary. In a few cases, different edits were used compared to the mono mixes ("It Won't Be Long," "Hold Me Tight," "You Really Got a Hold on Me," "Money (That's What I Want)").

With advance orders of nearly 300,000, the LP was awarded a silver disc four days before it went on sale. It entered the LP charts at number 1, remaining at the top for twenty-two weeks and even appearing on the singles chart in *New Musical Express,* the first album to do so since 1960.

RELEASE HISTORY

1963: **A** and **B** were released on mono and stereo pressings of *With the Beatles.* **A** is available on EMI's CD of that title.

78a. Newsreel footage

Date: 23 October 1963
Location: London Airport
Broadcast: 23 October 1963
ITV
Length: 0:14

With the Beatles now making headlines across Great Britain, ITV News decided to send a camera crew to cover their departure to Sweden. This first "Beatle/airport" footage of their career is relatively modest: just two quick shots of the group posing and waving goodbye from the airplane steps with not a single fan in view. Their return eight days later would be an entirely different story.

RELEASE HISTORY

This footage circulates on video.

79. Radio performance

Date: 24 October 1963
Time: 5:00 p.m.
Location: Karlaplansstudion, Stockholm
Producer/Host: Klas Burling
Broadcast: 11 November 1963, 10:05–10:30 p.m.
Sveriges Radio, channel 1
The Beatles pupgrupp från Liverpool på besök i Stockholm

[A.] **intro** (0:47)
[B.] **I Saw Her Standing There** (2:35)
[C.] **intro** (0:14)
[D.] **From Me to You** (1:52)
[E.] **intro** (0:15)
[F.] **Money (That's What I Want)** (2:42)
[G.] **intro** (0:09)
[H.] **Roll Over Beethoven** (2:10)
[I.] **intro** (0:16)
[J.] **You Really Got a Hold on Me** (2:55)
[K.] **intro** (0:10)
[L.] **She Loves You** (2:16)
[M.] **intro** (0:15)
[N.] **Twist and Shout** (2:36)
[O.] **outro** (0:06)

The Beatles arrived in Stockholm late in the afternoon of October 23 to a minimal welcome and were driven to the Hotel Continental for a press conference. The following day, they recorded a performance for Sveriges Radio in front of an enthusiastic but polite audience. The show, full title above, but better known as *Pop '63,* has survived in pristine quality. With no screaming during the songs, and the group peaking in performance ability, energy, and passion, this is perhaps the best document of the Beatles as a live rock-and-roll combo. The only flaw is that John's guitar starts out of tune and gets worse throughout the show.

Following Klas Burling's introduction, Paul counts in for a raucous "I Saw Her Standing There" (the now-standard truncated arrangement). After "Money," there is a break in the tape (omitting local group Hasse Rosen and the Norsemen's set). Paul does most of the talking between songs, but it's John who introduces the show's highlight: "You Really Got a Hold on Me." This is the only surviving live Beatles recording of this number, and despite some lyrical clashes, it's a gem, with impeccable drumming from Ringo, and airtight synchronized vocals on the stop-time "hold me" sections.

Engineer Hans Westman later recalled the recording setup: two vocal microphones, one for each Beatle's instrument, and four others for the audience and ambient sound. As soon as they launch into "I Saw Her Standing There," you can hear the VU meters shoot up into the red. The group's Vox amplifiers hadn't arrived in Sweden yet, forcing them to borrow the Norsemen's Fender amps for the occasion. Listening to playbacks, the Beatles claimed not to mind the distortion, and in fact, it merely lends an air of immediacy to the proceedings. These recordings are much hotter than anything achieved in the BBC's studio.

RELEASE HISTORY

1972: The BBC Radio documentary *The Beatles Story* broadcast **H, N,** and an incomplete version of **J.** All three were booted the following year on various LPs, usually misidentified as being recorded in Hamburg.

1973: A good-quality tape of the entire concert surfaced on the vinyl bootleg *Sweden 1963.*

1981: A very good-quality upgrade of the concert, running too slow, was booted on the LP *Airtime,* probably from a rebroadcast on January 6 of that year.

1988: The complete tape appeared in excellent quality on the bootleg CD *Stars of '63.*

1995: Apple's *Anthology 1* CD included slightly re-edited highlights of the concert (**B** without the count-in, **C–F,** an incomplete **I, J,** and **H**).

2000: The CD-R *Swedish Radio Show* contained a copy of the concert with slightly better equalization than *Stars of '63.* This improved source was copied on the slightly less obscure CD *Ultimate Live Masters.*

79a. Amateur footage

Date: 27 October 1963
Time: 3:00 p.m.
Location: Cirkus, Lorensbergsparken, Göteborg
Length: 0:09

Just over two minutes of silent color home movie footage exists of the Beatles' Gothenburg concert, although only a few seconds has been screened in public. Shot from the front row, it shows John and Paul singing a few words into a microphone and John playing some chords high on the neck of his Rickenbacker.

RELEASE HISTORY

This footage circulates on video from a 1989 Swedish TV broadcast.

80. TV performance

Date: 30 October 1963
Time: 7:00 p.m.
Location: Narren-teatern, Gröna Lund, Stockholm
Producer: Lasse Sarri
Host: Klas Burling
Broadcast: 3 November 1963, 7:00–7:30 p.m.
Sveriges Television
Drop In

[A.] **intro** (1:12)
[B.] **She Loves You** (2:16)
[C.] **intro** (0:36)
[D.] **Twist and Shout** (2:35)
[E.] **intro** (0:13)
[F.] **I Saw Her Standing There** (2:34)
[G.] **intro** (0:18)
[H.] **Long Tall Sally** (1:20)
[I.] **outro (Drop In)** (0:47)

The Beatles' appearance on Swedish TV's *Drop In* was equally as impressive as their earlier radio concert. It was videotaped at a theater in the Grona Lund amusement park, and like the radio broadcast, it was hosted by Klas Burling. Rehearsals occupied the morning, and a lunch break was followed by more dress rehearsals before evening taping in front of an audience.

As was often the case with TV appearances, the microphone balance is way out of whack, with the level on John's vocal and guitar mics overwhelming things a bit. After opening with their current hit single, Paul invites the audience to "join in" on "Twist and Shout," which had peaked at number 2 on the Swedish charts. They had been scheduled to perform only those two numbers, but Klas can see how well they are going down and asks for "one more number, please." They gladly comply with "I Saw Her Standing There," during which the house band, the Telstars, set up behind them in anticipation of playing the show's closing theme.

But confusion reigns: As the other presenters join hands at the front of the stage to say farewell, Klas turns to John and pleads for one more song, clapping in anticipation. Paul agrees and with the merest warning to his bandmates, screams, "I'm gonna tell Aunt Mary . . ." They are off and running in a breakneck "Long Tall Sally"—Paul seems possessed by the spirit of Little Richard and John has a death grip on his guitar as he plays the solo. Klas watches joyously from the sidelines, his cohosts looking stunned.

Realizing they're running overtime, Paul jumps straight from the first solo to the final choruses. Ringo becomes a human dynamo, his arms a blur as he propels the song into a crashing finale. Finally, the show can end, and the Beatles sing and clap along to the *Drop In* theme, with Ringo joining in on drums, as the credits roll. Not the Beatles' most celebrated television performance, but one of their most exciting.

RELEASE HISTORY

1974: The soundtrack to this show was first bootlegged on the LP *Stockholm*.

1994: Amazingly, it took twenty years for an upgraded tape to be bootlegged, on the CD *In Case You Don't Know*. This despite excellent video copies of the show circulating for years.

1996: The *Anthology* documentary included **F–I.** A composite using these upgraded versions appears on the CD-R *Telecasts One*.

81. Radio interview — P, R

Date: 31 October 1963
Time: morning
Location: Stockholm
Interviewer: Klas Burling
Length: 2:56

Before they departed for London, Paul and Ringo were interviewed by Klas Burling for Swedish radio. Paul describes the group's itinerary: a day off, then a five-week UK tour, with the Royal Variety Performance slotted in, followed by a Christmas residency at the Finsbury Park Astoria. Paul admits that traveling can be tiring, but says that the beautiful Swedish girls make it worthwhile. He and Ringo then share the few Swedish phrases they've learned: *aktiebolaget* (package tour) and *tack så mycket* (thanks very much), tossing in a bit of German for good measure. Asked to request a record, Ringo chooses "I Saw Her Standing There."

RELEASE HISTORY

2001: Forty-seven seconds of this interview was included on the bootleg CD *Swedish Fan Club Tape*.

2003: The complete interview was included on the bonus CD included with the book *Yeah Yeah Yeah! The Beatles Erövrar Sverige*.

82. Newsreel footage

Date: 31 October 1963
Time: evening
Location: London Airport
Length: 1:51

Having been whipped into a frenzy by the previous two weeks of national coverage, Beatlemania reached a new peak this evening as the Beatles' flight from Stockholm touched down at London Airport. It was the group's first overseas trip since attaining British superstardom, and a few hundred fans braved the pouring rain to welcome them back home.

A three-year tradition was also born as newspaper, radio, and TV newsmen covered the airport arrival. An Associated Press newsreel shows the plane taxiing up to the arrival building, and four amazed Beatles emerging to wave at the fans gathered on the roof. John does a little dance as they pose for photographers; fans hold up copies of the *Beatles Book Monthly* and the *Twist and Shout* EP; police escort the Beatles across the tarmac into a waiting car. The same scene would be played out hundreds of times in the months ahead.

Reporter Reg Abbis filed a breathless report for BBC Radio, struggling to be heard over the wail of the crowd: "What confusion here at London Airport! Hundreds and hundreds of young Beatle fans, shouting, yelling, waving umbrellas and hats. Shouting for their heroes, the four young men in dark clothes who've just disembarked from the huge white and blue twin-jet airliner which has flown them from Stockholm . . . Scores of people down there with the flashbulbs going as the Beatles try to force their way through. Massive security cautions here to bring them to the main building. The fans are virtually going wild here on the balcony! . . . And now comes the rush! Hundreds of fans rushing over the roof of the Queen's Building here to the exit to get downstairs and see their idols off the airport."

Also at London Airport that day on a talent-spotting visit were Ed Sullivan and his wife. It didn't take him long to spot that right in front of him was an explosive talent completely unexploited in the United States. He got in touch with Brian Epstein and arranged a meeting in New York for the following week.

RELEASE HISTORY

This footage circulates on video: 67 seconds from a silent AP newsreel and 44 seconds from an ITV News report (mostly silent apart from a few seconds of screaming). The BBC Radio report was rebroadcast in the 1972 series *The Beatles Story*.

83. Newsreel footage

Date: 1 November 1963
Location: Odeon Cinema, Cheltenham
Broadcast: 23 December 1963
RAI 1
tv 7
Length: 1:08

The Beatles' autumn tour opened with a bang this evening in Cheltenham; three segments of silent newsreel footage from this evening's performance circulate from an Italian TV report. These include bits of "Roll Over Beethoven" and "Till There Was You," shot from near the stage, and "Twist and Shout," shot from overhead in the balcony.

RELEASE HISTORY

This silent footage circulates on video.

84. Concert

Date: 4 November 1963
Time: evening
Location: Prince of Wales Theatre, London
Broadcast: 10 November 1963, 7:28–10:30 p.m.
ATV
The Royal Variety Performance

[A.] **From Me to You** (1:53)
[B.] **intro** (0:20)
[C.] **She Loves You** (2:17)
[D.] **intro** (0:32)
[E.] **Till There Was You** (2:21)
[F.] **intro** (0:32)
[G.] **Twist and Shout** (2:39)
[H.] **outro** (0:40)

"Beatles Rock Royals." Or so the legend would have it. Actually, their cheeky antics in front of the Queen Mother and Princess Margaret seem tame in retrospect, especially when viewing the footage of the occasion and not merely reading embellished written accounts.

Appearing seventh on a bill of nineteen, they launch right into "From Me to You," and a clearly nervous Paul greets the audience before a loud rendition of "She Loves You." As the polite, tempered applause dies down, Paul returns to the microphone, swallowing hard as he tests the waters with a joke: "This is from the show *The Music Man,* and it's also been recorded by our favorite American group, Sophie Tucker." The audience laughs approvingly at the showbiz reference (Tucker being a rather large American singer).

His confidence boosted, Paul sings a sweet and note-perfect "Till There Was You," and then John waits for the applause to subside. Looking the picture of innocence, he speaks: "Thank you. For our last number, I'd like to ask your help." He pauses to gather his breath. "Would the people in the cheaper seats clap your hands?" Mild chuckles. "And the rest of you, if you'd just rattle your jewelry." Startled cascade of laughter and applause. John gives an almost-embarrassed grin and crouches slightly.

The audience does clap along with "Twist and Shout," screamed as usual by John, with Paul giving encouraging whoops and Ringo riding the tempo slightly slower than usual. After their final bows to the audience and the royal box, they scamper offstage and emcee Dickie Henderson gives his assessment: "Aren't they fabulous? So successful, so young. Frightening."

Despite the mythology, it seems unlikely that Brian Epstein was standing in the wings worrying about John blurting out an obscenity. Not only was John too smart to decimate their career with such a stunt, it was Epstein himself, via Michael Braun's 1964 book *Love Me Do: The Beatles' Progress,* who first informed the world of the preshow anecdote: "Epstein recalled that at the Command performance he had asked John how he would get that kind of audience to join in. 'I'll just ask them to rattle their fucking jewelry,' John had said."

RELEASE HISTORY

1978: A very good-quality but slightly incomplete copy of this concert surfaced on the bootleg EP *By Royal Command.*

1987: A slightly lesser-quality but more complete copy appeared on the vinyl bootleg *The Beatles at the Beeb, Volume 7;* the first line of **A** was still truncated, however.

1995: **C–G** and part of **H** were released on the CD *Anthology 1* in excellent quality.

1996: The *Anthology* documentary included **A, E–G,**

and portions of **B, D,** and **H,** all in excellent quality. **A** is available from this source on the CD-R *Anthropology.*

2000: The entire show (**A–H**) was bootlegged in very good quality on the boxed CD set *Mythology, Vol. 1,* taken from a circulating videotape (which also includes Harry Secombe's intro for the ATV broadcast). In addition, various brief news clips circulate (all silent) of the Beatles rehearsing their set and lining up to receive royalty.

85. TV interview

Date: 5 November 1963
Time: morning
Location: back seat of a car, London
Broadcast: 7 November 1963, 9:10–9:40 p.m.
Associated-Rediffusion
This Week
Length: 2:09

The morning after their Royal performance, the Beatles filmed an interview for a TV news magazine, *This Week.* Unusually, the segments were filmed in the back seat of a rented car, driving around the streets of London. The group was interviewed two at a time, first George and Ringo and then John and Paul. Although nine minutes of interview footage was used, only ninety seconds or so is in the circulating clip.

George explains that the mop-top haircuts are not a gimmick, and John says he's had his "off and on for five years." "You should have seen it off!" adds Paul. Ringo laments that being constantly on the road means they don't have time for steady girlfriends, apart from John: "He's married." In addition to the interview footage, the report includes a brief scene of them clowning around in a dressing room and a night-time escape from a venue into a car with Neil Aspinall (probably filmed October 13 after the Palladium show).

RELEASE HISTORY

This interview was released on the home video *Casey Kasem's Rock 'n' Roll Goldmine: The Sixties.*

86. TV interview

Date: 7 November 1963
Location: Dublin Airport
Interviewer: Frank Hall
Broadcast: 7 November 1963, 7:55–8:00 p.m.
Radio Telefis Eireann
In Town
Length: 4:02

During their autumn tour, the Beatles made their only visit for performances in Ireland. They were met at the airport in Dublin by an RTE camera crew and interviewed on the tarmac by reporter Frank Hall.

John explains that their hairstyle was a fluke, apart from Ringo's, which was by design ("I designed it," says Ringo) to match the others'. Paul dismisses the "Liverpool sound" as a generalization that overlooks the diversity in styles among the artists. Hall asks about their Irish heritage, but Paul's reply is drowned out by a passing plane. John sticks his fingers in his ears, Paul yells, "Cut!", and they pause before continuing.

George's mother, maiden name Louise French, was of Irish blood, and had met the boys there along with one of George's cousins to see the concert and visit local relatives. Paul claims they all get along swimmingly, and as if on cue, they all pretend to pummel one another. After a question about their popularity, Ringo tries to give a thoughtful response but is upstaged by Paul and George hamming it up for the camera. Realizing he's being ignored, Ringo segues directly into a nonsequitur: "I forgot my mac, and so I said to John, 'If you don't fetch yours, it's gonna rain, y'see.' And he said . . ."

RELEASE HISTORY

1993: The audio portion of this interview, minus the first couple of seconds, was released on the CD *The Beatles Tapes, Volume 2: Early Beatlemania 1963–1964.* The full clip circulates on video, from a rebroadcast December 26, 1985, on RTE.

87. TV interview

Date: 8 November 1963
Time: afternoon
Location: Killeen
Interviewer: Jimmy Robinson
Broadcast: 8 November 1963, 6:25–6:35 p.m.
Ulster Television
Ulster News
Length: 0:44

As they drove from Dublin to Belfast, the Beatles were pursued by a TV crew from Ulster News, who finally managed to flag them down for a quick roadside interview.

The Beatles praise the reaction of Dublin fans, and George says that "six cars were arrested" at the show the previous night. John also tells the interviewer he resembles singer Matt Monro.

RELEASE HISTORY

This interview circulates among collectors on video from a December 9, 1980, rebroadcast on Ulster TV.

87a. Concert

Date: 9 November 1963
Location: Granada Cinema, East Ham, London

[A.] intro (0:06)
[B.] I Saw Her Standing There (0:40)

Granada TV filmed about twenty minutes of material at this evening's Beatles concert for the series *World in Action.* Strangely, none of it featured the Beatles on camera (perhaps they were denied permission by Brian Epstein, or perhaps the focus was meant to be on fans). A bit of this footage was used in their 1984 documentary *The Early Beatles.* Underneath shots of a frenzied audience, the compere can be heard introducing the Beatles, who perform the opening number, "I Saw Her Standing There."

RELEASE HISTORY

1984: This footage was included in Granada TV's documentary *The Early Beatles,* which circulates on video. The soundtrack was included on the CD-R *We'd Like to Carry On.*

88. TV interview

Date: 12 November 1963
Time: afternoon
Location: Guildhall, Portsmouth
Interviewer: Jeremy James
Broadcast: 12 November 1963, 6:05–6:45 p.m.
Southern Television
Day by Day
Length: 2:23

Soon after arriving at the Guildhall for a pair of performances, the Beatles filmed a backstage interview for a regional TV news magazine. They were actually scheduled to tape a musical appearance for the show at a Southampton studio that afternoon, but it was replaced with the interview, perhaps because of Paul's impending attack of gastric influenza.

Throughout the chat, he looks considerably queasy, but they're clearly still intending to perform that night. Asked how they made it to the theater intact, Paul says they boarded a van outside town that smuggled them in; George adds that the best escape route will be determined just before they go offstage. In the end, Paul's illness got the best of him, and both shows would be postponed until December 3.

Ringo is wearing a heavy scarf to protect himself from catching a chill. John tugs at it and asks, "Been to college, have you?" "Yeah, it's me school scarf. Borstal High." The interviewer seems ignorant of their musical career, as John has to point out that most of their numbers contain harmony singing and that ballads have always been a part of their repertoire. George says the audience at the Royal Variety show was better than they'd expected, and John confirms that some of them did indeed rattle their jewelry.

RELEASE HISTORY

1995: A portion of this interview was released on the CD *Rare Photos & Interview CD, Volume 1,* and a second fragment appeared on *Volume 2* the following year. The complete interview was included on the video compilation *Beatles 1962 to 1970.*

89. TV feature

Date: 13 November 1963
Location: Westward Television Studios and ABC Cinema, Plymouth
Interviewer: Stuart Hutchison
Broadcast: 16 November 1963
Westward Television
Move Over, Dad
Length: 6:41

By the following day, Paul was well enough to rejoin the Beatles' tour for a concert in Plymouth. With a local TV crew covering the group's activities that day, Paul clowned around for the benefit of the cameras, holding up a newspaper with the story of his illness and pretending to faint into the arms of his bandmates.

In a short group interview with Stuart Hutchison, Paul downplays reports of his illness and explains their recent appearance in police helmets outside a Birmingham theater. Silent footage from inside the venue shows the Fabs goofing around backstage and then performing "Till There Was You" onstage.

RELEASE HISTORY

Forty-one seconds of silent footage was aired November 3, 2001, on the McCartney TV special. The complete footage circulates on video among collectors.

90. TV feature

Date: 16 November 1963
Location: Winter Gardens Theatre, Bournemouth
Interviewer: Josh Darsa
Broadcast: 21 November 1963
CBS
The CBS Evening News
Length: 5:08

Having already made a loose arrangement with promoter Sid Bernstein to present the Beatles at Carnegie Hall the next February, Brian Epstein flew to New York on November 5 to meet with Ed Sullivan in hopes of securing some appearances on his TV show for the same time period. He also met with Capitol Records promo man Brown Meggs to ensure the label would give its first Beatles single, "I Want to Hold Your Hand," a proper amount of promotion.

By the time Brian returned to London on the fourteenth, the Beatles' future was looking rosier. Beatlemania had not gone unnoticed in the States, and that week both *Time* and *Newsweek* magazines ran articles about the "temporary craze." All three U.S. TV networks dispatched their London-based camera teams to cover the Beatles' concert at the Winter Gardens Theatre in Bournemouth.

CBS filed a report anchored by Alexander Kendrick from the Beatles' London fan club headquarters, where employees are seen opening sacks of fan mail. A clip of Princess Margaret receiving the Beatles at the Royal Variety show is also included. The bulk of the footage comes from the Bournemouth concert, although not with natural sound (dubbed with the released version of "She Loves You").

The Beatles are seen exiting a van, running down a corridor of police into the theater, and performing parts of "I Saw Her Standing There," "All My Loving," and "You Really Got a Hold on Me." A couple of minutes of concert footage is included, along with a backstage interview (predictably focusing on their haircuts) with CBS correspondent Josh Darsa. Kendrick's narration understandably treats the whole thing as a novelty, but this report was the first chance most Americans had to see and hear the Beatles.

RELEASE HISTORY

This footage circulates on video from a February 8, 2004, rebroadcast on *CBS Sunday Morning*.

91. TV feature

Date: 16 November 1963
Location: Winter Gardens Theatre, Bournemouth
Host: Jack Paar
Broadcast: 3 January 1964, 10:00–11:00 p.m.
NBC
The Jack Paar Program

[A.] From Me to You (1:02)

Unlike the CBS reporter, Jack Paar didn't make fun of the Beatles' looks or music when he screened NBC's footage of the Bournemouth concert, even calling them "four nice kids" and praising their sense of humor. He reserved his one-liners for the screaming fans: "I understand science is working on a cure for this." "Does it bother you to realize that in a few years, these girls will vote, raise children, and drive cars?" "I just show you this in case you're going to England and want to have a fun evening."

And so on.

The good thing about this report is that it contains what is apparently the natural sound of their performance of "From Me to You" (**A**), along with a glimpse of John (not synced) singing a line or two. Unfortunately, the song is largely obscured by screaming and Paar's narration. Also included in this report (not listed in the timing above) was a clip of "She Loves You" from *The Mersey Sound* documentary (see the August 27 entry).

The ABC coverage, reported by William Sheehan, doesn't seem to have survived. Reports were aired on various U.S. network newscasts on the eighteenth, nineteenth, and twenty-first. A day later, the country would have something far weightier on its mind.

RELEASE HISTORY

2001: A fair-quality copy of **A** was included on the CD-R compilation *Live: Make as Much Noise as You Like!*, and the video circulates among traders in similarly shaky quality. A 1986 rebroadcast in the NBC special *Jack Paar Comes Home* omitted the Bournemouth footage; it is included on the DVD *The Jack Paar Collection*, but with the music mostly obscured by overdubbed screaming.

92. TV interview

Date: 20 November 1963
Location: ABC Cinema, Manchester
Broadcast: 6 January 1964, 6:30–7:00 p.m.
Granada TV
Scene at 6:30
Length: 1:30

A reporter from Granada TV interviewed the Beatles backstage at a concert in Manchester, standing against a flower-patterned wallpaper backdrop.

Asked to predict the fate of their American trip, John issues the wise declaration: "I can't really say, can I? I mean, is it up to me? No! I mean, I just hope we go all right." He figures the same formula that brought them success will work in the States: "Stand there and sing and twitch." George denies that stress is getting to them, Ringo doesn't mind having his solitude shattered by fans, while Paul's motto is "live for the day."

RELEASE HISTORY

1996: A slightly incomplete copy of this interview was released on the CD *Rare Photos & Interview CD, Volume 2.* The full clip circulates on video from a rebroadcast in Granada's 1984 special *The Early Beatles.* A bit of it was used in the *Anthology* documentary.

93. Newsreel footage

Date: 20 November 1963
Location: ABC Cinema, Manchester
Length: 6:21

[A.] **intro** (0:09)
[B.] **She Loves You** (2:11)
[C.] **intro** (0:12)
[D.] **Twist and Shout** (1:10)
[E.] **From Me to You (reprise)** (0:15)

"By generous permission of their famous manager, Brian Epstein," as the narration explained, the Beatles were filmed in concert during the Manchester stop on their autumn tour. Pathé used a special wide-screen process called Techniscope to produce a full-color newsreel, *The Beatles Come to Town,* complete with one and a half songs from that evening's concert.

The result was quite impressive and is easily the best document of what that first major tour was like, from the ecstatic fans to the group's nonchalant demeanor backstage and their now highly polished but energetic onstage performance. Outside the theater, eager fans queue to get in, clutching tickets and paraphernalia; inside, the cinema's manager inspects his troops.

Paul is seen arriving, and all four pose for photos backstage, holding aloft a huge stuffed panda bear; John would take this gift home to his infant son, Julian. As the tension mounts in the auditorium, the unruffled Beatles walk to their dressing room to prepare for the show. Paul mugs for the camera, combing his hair furiously.

Once onstage, pandemonium drowns out their rendition of "She Loves You"; girls weep and wail and one young bobby nods his head in time to the music. The last half of the show-closing "Twist and Shout" is followed by a well-practiced synchronized bow and the curtain closes to an instrumental reprise of "From Me to You," a standard feature of their set throughout late 1963 and early 1964.

The finished newsreel was distributed to British cinemas beginning December 22, having been delayed due to coverage of President Kennedy's assassination. The footage was also inserted into a 1965 feature film, *Pop Gear* (aka *Go Go Mania*), using a slightly different edit.

Nine minutes of silent offcuts from this newsreel still exist in Pathé's archive, including further concert scenes and some backstage activity, as the Beatles rummage through a sack of fan mail. Ringo opens a parcel containing a pink cushion with white polka dots, embroidered with the words FOR RINGO.

RELEASE HISTORY

1976: The complete soundtrack to this newsreel first surfaced on the vinyl bootleg *ABC Manchester.* It's appeared on many bootlegs, such as the LP *Recovered Tracks* and the CDs *Live in the United Kingdom 1962–1965,* and Silent Sea's *The Beatles in Concert, Addendum 1: 1957–1964.*

The newsreel circulates on video in excellent quality and was briefly available on the home video *Beatles Firsts.* Much of it was also included in the *Anthology* documentary.

94. Interview

Date: 21 November 1963
Location: ABC Cinema, Carlisle
Length: 0:34

From entertainment to fashion to royalty, the Beatles' influence moved on to the political arena when they were mentioned in the House of Commons this afternoon. The question was raised whether government funds should be wasted on police protection for the group, and naturally they were interviewed backstage for their reaction to this nonevent. John's reprisal is to cheerfully pass on a rumor that the MP making the proposal had suffered a nervous breakdown: "I heard that he was a bit funny."

RELEASE HISTORY

This interview clip circulates on video.

95. TV performance

Date: 25 November 1963
Time: afternoon
Location: Studio 4, Granada TV Centre, Manchester
Interviewer: Gay Byrne
Broadcast: (A–C only) 26 December 1963, 6:30–7:00 p.m.
Granada TV
Scene at 6:30

[A.] **I Want to Hold Your Hand** (2:21)
[B.] **This Boy** (2:06)
[C.] **chat w/Ken Dodd** (3:14)
[D.] **chat w/Ken Dodd—uncut** (15:19)

To promote their new single, the Beatles taped a mimed performance of both sides for broadcast on various Granada TV shows. John and George chose to play their Jumbo Gibson acoustic guitars rather than electrics on both songs. To symbolize the tremendous amount of coverage Beatlemania was receiving, the set was dressed as a huge newspaper, with Ringo's drum riser disguised as a "Beatax" camera.

Taped on the same set, with Paul and Ringo seated on stools and the others standing, was an interview by host Gay Byrne with the Beatles and a fellow Liverpudlian, comedian Ken Dodd. They had become good mates with Dodd since appearing on his show, but that didn't stop the mutual ribbing. Asked if Dodd's "zany" unkempt hair contributed to his success, John quips, "No, I don't think it helped at all!"

Claiming that he's writing a film script for the group, Dodd elaborates on the ludicrous parts each member will supposedly portray. When he comes to George, not only does he get his name wrong (calling him "John" and then "Thingy"), Dodd casts him as an "evil-smelling peasant." "Why is he an evil-smelling peasant?" Byrne wonders. "Come and stand where I am!"

George's sweet revenge came with an ad-lib at the end of the chat. Asked if he will form a rock group of his own, Dodd tries to think up suitable names such as Kenny and the Cockroaches (John proposes the Dodderers). He also needs a stage name "like Cliff or Rock, something earthy." George's brilliant suggestion: "Sod."

The uncut rushes of this interview (**D**) still exist in Granada's archives, including a further twelve minutes of material. While Granada chose to air most of the best moments, they missed at least one gem: Asked to describe the differences in regional comedy styles, Dodd replies, "You can tell a joke in Manchester, and they don't get it in London. They can't hear it." The remainder is dominated by Dodd's silly tales of Scouseberry bushes, jam butty mines, and black pudding plantations.

A and **C** were first broadcast on *Late Scene Extra* November 27 and **B** followed on the same program December 20. All three items appeared in the Boxing Day edition of *Scene At 6:30,* as noted above.

RELEASE HISTORY

1996: The soundtrack to **C** was released on the CD *Rare Photos & Interview CD, Volume 2.* Most of **A** and **B** were included in the *Anthology* documentary. **A–C** circulate on video from a rebroadcast on Granada's 1984 TV special *The Early Beatles;* a bootleg DVD of the same title adds **D.**

96. Radio interview

Date: 29 November 1963
Location: ABC Cinema, Huddersfield
Interviewer: Gordon Kaye
Length: 2:12

Toward the end of their wildly successful autumn tour, the Beatles were interviewed backstage by Gordon Kaye for a closed-circuit hospital radio program, *Music Box.*

As long as the fans are paying, George professes not to mind their screaming. He pretends to like trad jazz, even as Paul accuses him of hating it, while Paul claims to enjoy Stravinsky and Beethoven. John suggests *The Man with the Green Bath-Chair* as a favorite film, but Paul opts for *"The Trial,* by Walt Disney." George has a hard time thinking of what he reads in his spare time, so Paul tries to cue him: "Tolstoy . . ." (George: "I read Telstar!"). Ringo recommends Beethoven's poems, the first appearance of a long-running gag.

These segments are intercut with fan interviews from outside the venue, which are the real highlight of this recording, particularly one young lass' description of each band member: "And Ringo Starr used to have a different 'aircoot all together. Just seen a picture of him in t'paper. That, uh, *Weekly News* or summat, and it looked . . . all curly 'air, wavy. Oo, it were different."

RELEASE HISTORY

1999: This interview, misidentified as a November 1 recording from Cheltenham, was included on the bootleg CD boxed set *Mythology, Volume 1.*

97. TV performance

Date: 2 December 1963
Time: morning/afternoon
Location: Studio C, Elstree Studio Centre, Borehamwood
Producer: Colin Clews
Hosts: Eric Morecambe, Ernie Wise
Broadcast: 18 April 1964, 8:25–9:00 p.m.
ATV
The Morecambe and Wise Show

[A.] **intro** (0:04)
[B.] **This Boy** (2:12)
[C.] **intro** (0:09)
[D.] **All My Loving** (2:02)
[E.] **outro** (0:04)
[F.] **intro** (0:07)
[G.] **I Want to Hold Your Hand** (2:17)
[H.] **chat** (2:25)
[I.] **Moonlight Bay** (0:44)
[J.] **chat/closing theme** (1:34)

Fondly remembered by British fans but somewhat of an enigma to Americans, the comedy duo of Eric Morecambe and Ernie Wise had a long-running and wildly successful TV career on ATV and the BBC. The Beatles taped an appearance in December for what would be the third edition in the fourth season of their self-titled series, to be broadcast the following April.

All three songs they played were making their live debuts; despite John's voice cracking, "This Boy" is a pleasant rendition, with Ringo using brushes in place of drumsticks. "All My Loving" features a novel vocal arrangement that would be retained in subsequent live versions: On the final verse, George takes the lead with Paul singing the harmony he had originally double-tracked on the record.

Later in the program, the Beatles perform their new single A-side and are joined onstage by Ernie, who introduces them to his partner. Eric pretends to mistake them for the Kaye Sisters and persists in calling the drummer "Bongo"! Not exactly the height of comedy, but Eric scores with a great ad-lib (based on everyone's reaction, it's clearly not a scripted gag). John says his dad used to tell him about Eric and makes a "when I was so high" gesture about two feet off the ground. "You've only got a little dad, have you?" retorts Eric.

The Beatles and Ernie don barbershop quartet outfits while Eric rushes offstage to change for their joint number. Accompanied by Ringo's drumming and pianist Kenny Powell, they launch into "Moonlight Bay," soon interrupted by a Beatle-wigged and madly twisting Eric. The show concluded every week with the opening line of a dirty joke: "There were these two old men sitting in deck chairs . . ." John is given the chance to deliver the joke and twists it to: "There was two old men sitting in a dirty deck chair."

RELEASE HISTORY

1989: I first surfaced on the 7-inch EP 1989 *Beatleg News Christmas Record.*

1993: **D** (with the opening bars replaced by a section from later in the song) and **G** appeared on the bootleg CD *Hollywood Bowl Complete.*

1995: **A–B** and **G–I** were released on the CD *Anthology 1,* although the first two notes of **G** were chopped off. **H** and **I** were also included in the *Anthology* video documentary the following year.

1999: **A–J** were included on the bootleg CD boxed set, *Mythology, Volume 1,* taken from a video of the complete appearance that circulates.

98. TV interview

Date: 7 December 1963
Time: 2:30–3:15 p.m.
Location: Empire Theatre, Liverpool
Producer: Neville Wortman
Host: David Jacobs
Broadcast: 7 December 1963, 6:05–6:35 p.m.
BBC TV
Juke Box Jury
Length: 20:44

The Beatles' group appearance on *Juke Box Jury* proved less controversial than John's solo outing (see the June 22 entry), as they voted the majority of songs as hits and found something positive to say about most of them. In 2001, the BBC put out a call for anyone who might have a video or film copy of the original show, having long since wiped it from their archives. All that turned up was an audio recording taped at home by a fan, which may or may not correspond with the versions that had already been circulating among collectors.

The first song ("I Could Write a Book" by the Chants, voted a hit) is missing from the circulating tapes. Despite John's dismissal of Elvis Presley's "Devil in Disguise," it had reached number 1 on the UK charts. The Beatles are no less severe when it comes to Elvis' latest single, "Kiss Me Quick." Paul praises his voice, but finds the material lacking. Ringo is more blunt: "Last two years, he's been going down the nick." George suggests releasing a real oldie like "My Baby Left Me," and John feels it'll be a minor hit on the strength of the Presley name (it would peak at number 11 in the UK and number 34 in the United States).

The next song is familiar to listeners of Beatles BBC broadcasts: "The Hippy Hippy Shake," covered here by another Liverpool group, the Swinging Blue Jeans. All four agree that while it's not up to the standard of Chan Romero's original, it will hit the charts (John says he also likes Bill Harry's version, which gets a knowing laugh from the hometown crowd). It would climb all the way to number 2 in the UK, stuck behind "I Want to Hold Your Hand," and even make the American top 30.

Paul Anka's "Did You Have a Happy Birthday" is wittily dissed by George, who says hearing that record might have spoiled his own birthday. John and Paul don't like Anka's voice, and Ringo finds the record "a drag." It flopped on both sides of the Atlantic. John says he'll buy Shirley Ellis' "The Nitty Gritty," even though he mistakes it for a Mary Wells disc at first. The others concur that the R & B style is right up their alley, but a bit too hip for the British listening public (right again, it reached number 8 in the United States and failed to chart in the UK).

Up next is "I Can't Stop Talking about You" by Steve Lawrence and Eydie Gorme, who had recently taken "I Just Want to Stay Here" to number 3 in the UK. They are lukewarm about the song, with Paul and George finding it just as catchy as the earlier hit, but John disappointed by the subpar effort of his favorite songwriting team, Goffin and King. Only Ringo votes it a miss, and only he was correct (although it reached number 35 in the United States).

Billy Fury's "Do You Really Love Me Too" is unfavorably compared to a Cliff Richard record that it resembles; only John and Paul like the song, but all four agree it will be a hit, which it was (number 15). The next song, in a bit of foreshadowing, is Bobby Vinton's "There! I've Said It Again." This is the song "I Want to Hold Your Hand" would knock from the top spot on *Billboard*'s chart the following month, launching a year of unprecedented U.S. chart domination by British acts. To the Beatles, it's just another bland Bobby Vinton effort, and all four correctly vote it a miss for the English record buyer.

A trio of schoolgirls from Coventry, the Orchids, are next with "Love Hit Me," a song that John finds too direct a clone of previous Crystals and Ronettes numbers. George and Paul are more enthusiastic, feeling it's about time records with that sound were produced in England rather than New York and LA, but all four ultimately vote it a miss. When it's revealed that the Orchids are present in the studio, they frantically apologize and switch their votes ("Didn't mean it! I'll buy two!"), but their initial instinct proved accurate.

With time running out, they give no opinions on the Merseybeats' "I Think of You," merely voting it a hit (they could scarcely do otherwise in Liverpool) before host David Jacobs reminds viewers to tune in that night at 8:10 for more Beatle fun. The fabulous theme tune, "Hit and Miss," closes out the show.

RELEASE HISTORY

1999: The final 9:13 of this show appeared from a poor-quality off-air tape on the bootleg CD boxed set *Mythology, Volume 1.* A fair-quality tape of the first 11:35 also circulates among collectors (the two sources overlap by only a few seconds).

99. TV performance

Date: 7 December 1963
Time: 3:45–4:30 p.m.
Location: Empire Theatre, Liverpool
Producer: Neville Wortman
Broadcast: 7 December 1963, 8:10–8:40 p.m.
BBC TV
It's the Beatles!

[A.] From Me to You (1:14)
[B.] I Saw Her Standing There (2:35)
[C.] intro (0:31)
[D.] All My Loving (2:06)
[E.] intro (0:28)
[F.] Roll Over Beethoven (2:10)
[G.] intro (0:29)
[H.] Boys (2:03)
[I.] intro (0:25)
[J.] Till There Was You (2:11)
[K.] intro (0:04)
[L.] She Loves You (2:15)
[M.] intro (0:24)
[N.] This Boy (2:13)
[O.] intro (0:04)
[P.] I Want to Hold Your Hand (2:16)
[Q.] intro (1:20)
[R.] Money (That's What I Want) (2:42)
[S.] intro (0:01)
[T.] Twist and Shout (2:15)
[U.] intro (0:02)
[V.] From Me to You (reprise)/Harry Lime (*Third Man* Theme) (1:16)

The *Juke Box Jury* audience, consisting of members of the Beatles' Northern Area Fan Club, got to stick around for a special concert, which would also be broadcast by the BBC as *It's The Beatles!* Technicians had a mere thirty minutes to set up between shows, and their lack of preparation is evident. The sound balance is lousy, with John's vocal microphone dominant and poor Ringo virtually inaudible during his rendition of "Boys." The visuals were apparently no better, with the cameras concentrating on Paul and the audience and ignoring John.

I say "apparently" because only about ten minutes of this program has survived on video, and the first section of this consists merely of audience reaction shots, spliced out of the show for an unknown reason. This includes fragments of **A–D, J, L, P, R,** and **T.** It's followed by the majority of **P–V,** although each of the songs except for the show-closing instrumental are slightly incomplete. Reuters also filmed portions of **P** and **T,** with sound, for a newsreel that lasts 3:24.

Most of the concert is available only from a home recording taped off a TV speaker during the original broadcast, complete with extraneous coughing. The Beatles certainly put their all into the performances, with the only noticeable blunder being John's omission of half a verse in "Twist and Shout." The audience is overwhelmingly enthusiastic, and the group feeds off this energy, particularly during "Roll Over Beethoven" and "I Want to Hold Your Hand."

John plays to the hometown crowd more than the TV audience, telling them repeatedly to "shut up!," introducing "Boys" as "a sort of special number, which we only do every night," and calling "Till There Was You" "a song from the musical *The Muscle Man,* sung by Peggy Leg." For "Twist and Shout," a large reproduction of the *With the Beatles* LP cover photo descends from the ceiling, and the closing credits roll over the group's standard show-closer of the era, an instrumental reprise of "From Me to You," with a few licks from the theme to the movie *The Third Man* thrown in for good measure.

The Beatles' long day concluded with a pair of concerts at the Liverpool Odeon. Backstage, they watched both BBC shows in disappointed amazement, on a TV set brought over from the NEMS department store.

RELEASE HISTORY

1978: A fair-quality off-line recording of **A–V** was included on the vinyl bootlegs *Youngblood* and *December 1963.* Although **V** is incomplete on both sources, it's a bit longer on *December 1963.*

1999: The off-line source tape appeared on the bootleg CD boxed set *Mythology, Volume 1* in good quality; unfortunately, not only was **V** still incomplete, the beginning of **A** was now missing!

The fragmentary video circulates among collectors; its soundtrack (the portion from **P–V**) is best found in very good quality on the bootleg CD *Ultimate Live Masters.* A good-quality copy of "Twist and Shout" (preceded by the intro to "Money") also circulates from a July 9, 1981, broadcast on the 900th edition of BBC TV's *Top of the Pops.* The Reuters newsreel clip of **P** circulates on video from a rebroadcast on MSNBC's *Time and Again,* October 9, 1999.

100. Newsreel footage

Date: 9 December 1963
Location: Southend-on-Sea
Broadcast: 9 December 1963
ITV
Length: 0:31

TV news crews from the BBC and ITV were present at the Beatles' Southend concert this evening. The BBC obtained an interview with the group in their Odeon Cinema dressing room. ITV had to settle for some footage of the Beatles being smuggled into the venue in the back of a police van. This is the earliest footage of John wearing the leather cap that he had recently bought at a boutique in Chelsea.

RELEASE HISTORY

This silent footage circulates on video, and a bit of it was included in the *Anthology* documentary.

101. Radio interview

Date: 10 December 1963
Time: evening
Location: Gaumont Cinema, Doncaster
Interviewer: Dibbs Mather
Broadcast: ca. January 1964
Dateline London #61
Calling Australia #453

[A.] intro (0:22)
[B.] chat (8:40)
[C.] outro (0:14)

Australian reporter Dibbs Mather would conduct several interviews with the Beatles for various BBC Transcription Service overseas radio shows. The first was taped backstage during a stop in Doncaster on the Beatles' 1963 autumn tour, and the screams of Beatlemania can be heard penetrating the dressing room walls throughout.

Ringo reminisces about his days "hanging around corners" in Liverpool gangs, which came to an end when he discovered music. George claims not to be bothered by their loss of privacy, and says that they're able to return to Liverpool only about once a fortnight (that frequency would rapidly dwindle from here on out). Apart from the monetary luxuries it affords, George feels that the group's fame hasn't really altered him or his parents. He predicts that their unprecedented success should taper off soon, but expects them to be in the running for at least two more years.

Recalling that they used to have "about ten [names] a week," Paul explains how John conceived the name Beatles and denies that they've consciously tried to set any trends. He says they have enough financial security now not to worry about future plans, but as they'll be "having a bash at a film next year," surmises that one or more of them might branch into a movie career.

To Mather's chagrin, John is in an obstinate mood and thwarts all attempts at a serious discussion, giving one-word responses and denying details of his life and personality included in their press material: "We don't normally write those things." He does, however, consent to read one of his poems, "The Neville Club." American author Michael Braun was currently following the Beatles around England to compile material for a book, *Love Me Do.* During an interview at John's London flat around this date, John read him other poems such as "No Flies on Frank," and Braun encouraged him to compile the material and publish it in book form.

RELEASE HISTORY

1985: This interview was released on the LP *'Round the World,* later reissued on CD. Kevin Howlett's book *The Beatles at the BBC* transcribes large sections of the disc's contents that have yet to be released.

102. Newsreel footage

Date: 14 December 1963
Time: 4:00 p.m.
Location: Wimbledon Palais, London
Length: 1:14

Beatlemania was on display in full force this afternoon as the group played host to their Southern Area Fan Club. Newsreel cameras documented the mayhem, which began with the Beatles sitting behind the Palais bar, shaking hands with all three thousand fans who showed up. Also glimpsed are a couple of songs ("You Really Got a Hold on Me" and "Boys") from the special concert for the fans, who were kept safely away from the stage by a tall metal fence.

RELEASE HISTORY

This silent footage circulates on video among collectors.

103. TV performance

Date: 15 December 1963
Time: afternoon
Location: Alpha Television Studios, Birmingham
Producer: Philip Jones
Host: Brian Matthew
Broadcast: 21 December 1963, 5:50–6:35 p.m.
ABC
Thank Your Lucky Stars

[A.] **intro** (0:19)
[B.] **I Want to Hold Your Hand** (2:31)
[C.] **All My Loving** (2:13)
[D.] **Twist and Shout** (2:39)
[E.] **award presentation** (0:27)
[F.] **She Loves You** (1:40)

This edition of *Thank Your Lucky Stars,* titled "Lucky Stars on Merseyside," featured Liverpool acts such as Cilla Black, Billy J Kramer and the Dakotas, Gerry and the Pacemakers, the Searchers, and of course the Beatles, who lip-synced four songs.

The show opens with corny narration from host Brian Matthew about the grimy Liverpool docks and includes a 16-second videotaped glimpse of the Beatles' arrival at the studio. Although he doesn't sing on the record, John mimes along cheerfully with "All My Loving." On the opening line of "Twist and Shout," he clearly substitutes his own (perhaps rude) phrase in place of the song's title, which causes Paul to grin madly. After George Martin brings out gold discs for their two most recent singles, the Beatles perform an edited rendition of "She Loves You" over the closing credits, ending up huddled around Ringo's drum kit.

RELEASE HISTORY

The complete show circulates in very good quality on video.

104. Radio performance

Date: 17 December 1963
Time: 3:00–6:30 p.m.
Location: Playhouse Theatre, London
Producers: Jimmy Grant, Bernie Andrews
Host: Brian Matthew
Broadcast: 21 December 1963, 10:00 a.m.–noon
BBC Light Programme
Saturday Club #272

All My Loving (commercially released version)
[A.] **intro** (1:04)
[B.] **This Boy** (2:16)
[C.] **outro** (0:02)
[D.] **All I Want for Christmas Is a Bottle/intro** (0:40)
[E.] **I Want to Hold Your Hand** (2:19)
[F.] **Till There Was You** (2:14)
[G.] **outro** (0:01)
[H.] **Roll Over Beethoven** (2:14)
[I.] **intro** (1:20)
She Loves You (rebroadcast of September 7, 1963, recording)
[J.] **Chrimble Medley (Shazam!)** (0:30)
[K.] **outro** (0:08)

Although the Beatles' seventh appearance on *Saturday Club* included only four newly taped numbers (plus a song recycled from their previous session and a track from their new LP), it contained plenty of silly interplay with host Brian Matthew and a few extra musical treats.

After berating "Brian Bathtubes" for not playing a request they had sent in, John and George read requests for "This Boy," including one "for myself and my friend Pearl Dandy." ("I didn't know you knew Pearl Dandy!" marvels John.) Telling people to listen for the differences, George points out that it'll be a new performance, not just a spin of the single version.

Dora Bryan had a novelty seasonal hit with "All I Want for Christmas Is a Beatle," which was covered on this show by Susan Maughan. It was followed by the Fabs' own a cappella version (**D**), and a request for their current number 1 single. Later on (**I**), they sing a Christmas ditty to the tune of Freddie and the Dreamers' current hit "You Belong to Me." George follows this up with a line of "From Me to You," but Paul admonishes him: "That's not a carol." Ringo saves the day: "No, it's a standard!"

The show closes with a "muddley" of Beatles song titles (plus "Rudolph, the Red-Nosed Reindeer") accompanied by a riff from Duane Eddy's "Shazam!," followed by a plug for their upcoming Boxing Day special (see following entry).

RELEASE HISTORY

1982: **A** and **B** were broadcast in the radio special *The Beatles at the Beeb* in very good quality.

1984: The vinyl bootleg *Directly from Santa Claus* included very good copies of **B, E, J,** and part of **I.**

1988: A very good tape of this entire program (**A–K**) was released on the bootleg LP *The Beatles at the Beeb, Volume 8.* The Pyramid CD of this title omitted **C** and **G;** this source was used on *The Complete BBC Sessions* box, with the order slightly shuffled.

1993: **D** and a slightly incomplete copy of **I** were released on the CD *The Beatles Tapes, Volume 2: Early Beatlemania 1963–1964.*

105. Radio performance

Date: 18 December 1963
Time: 7:00–10:30 p.m.
Location: BBC Paris Studio, London
Producer: Bryant Marriott
Host: Rolf Harris
Broadcast: 26 December 1963, 10:00 a.m.–noon
BBC Light Programme
From Us to You #1

[A.] **From Us to You** (0:54)
[B.] **intro** (0:29)
[C.] **She Loves You** (2:19)
[D.] **outro** (0:02)
[E.] **intro** (0:03)
[F.] **All My Loving** (2:04)
[G.] **Roll Over Beethoven** (2:18)
[H.] **George intro of Jeanie Lambe/Alan Elsdon** (0:08)
[I.] **intro** (0:09)
[J.] **Till There Was You** (2:12)
[K.] **outro** (0:04)
[L.] **intro** (0:07)
[M.] **Boys** (1:46)
[N.] **Money (That's What I Want)** (2:42)
[O.] **outro** (0:04)
[P.] **intro** (0:03)
[Q.] **I Saw Her Standing There** (2:35)
[R.] **outro** (0:02)
[S.] **intro** (0:08)
[T.] **Tie Me Kangaroo Down Sport** (2:46)
[U.] **outro/intro** (0:26)
[V.] **I Want to Hold Your Hand** (2:21)
[W.] **outro** (0:18)
[X.] **From Us to You** (0:44)

After the success of the *Pop Go the Beatles* series, it was natural that the BBC would design a new showcase for the Beatles. While their schedule no longer allowed for recording a weekly series, an occasional Bank Holiday special proved feasible. Guest artists would provide the balance of each two-hour show's music, and the Beatles would still chat between songs with the various hosts. The specials were given the working title *Beatletime,* but eventually fell under the banner *From Us to You.* The Beatles recorded a theme song (**A**) based on their hit single, with the appropriate pronoun replacement.

For this first edition, Australian singer and comic Rolf Harris was a suitable host, as he was already set to emcee the Beatles Christmas show in London. His interaction with the stars is limited to a bit of banter before each of the songs; George also introduces guest star Jeanie Lambe's performance of "Blue Skies" (**H**). Most of the songs are faithful to the records, although Ringo keeps playing through the last verse of "Roll Over Beethoven" where he usually lays off a bit. "Boys" fades out early, while the handclap overdub on "I Want to Hold Your Hand" ends with the group giving themselves a round of applause.

The show's highlight is a Beatle collaboration on Harris' hit song "Tie Me Kangaroo Down Sport" (**T**). Backed by Paul's bass and George's guitar, Rolf plays wobble board and sings Beatle-related lyrics that are only a few steps advanced from Tony Sheridan's "Sweet

Georgia Brown" rewrite. ("Don't ill treat me pet dingo, Ringo" is about the best.) John, Paul, and George contribute a few "ooh's," but have more fun mocking Rolf when he blanks on the lyrics to one verse.

RELEASE HISTORY

1988: A very good tape of **A–G, I–O,** and **Q–X** (with the first note of **V** missing) was released on the bootleg LP *The Beatles at the Beeb, Volume 8.* The source tape appears on *The Complete BBC Sessions* box, running slightly fast.

1996: An upgraded tape of **S–U** (with **U** slightly incomplete) was broadcast on part one of the BBC Radio special *The Beatles at the BBC* on New Year's Eve. It appears from this source on the bootleg CD *The Beatles Broadcast Collection, Trailer 1.*

1997: A complete version of **V** was broadcast on part two of the BBC Radio special *The Beatles at the BBC* on New Year's Day. It appears from this source on the bootleg CD *The Beatles Broadcast Collection, Trailer 1.*

2001: A good-quality tape of **H** surfaced on the CD-R *The Complete BBC Sessions—Upgraded.*

2003: The entire show, including the debut of **P,** was bootlegged on the CD boxed set *The Beatles at the Beeb.*

106. TV interview

Date: 20 December 1963
Location: Astoria Cinema, London
Broadcast: 25 December 1963
ITV
Length: 0:45

The Beatles Christmas Show was a sixteen-night extravaganza hosted by Rolf Harris, who reprised his Beatle-themed version of "Tie Me Kangaroo Down Sport" at each show. The Beatles performed a nine-song set and appeared in a pair of comedy sketches. As it was likely any dialogue would be drowned out by screams, the show's writer, Peter Yolland, went backstage during their November 26 performance in Cambridge to tape the group reading their lines for playback over the PA system during the show.

During rehearsals in London on December 20, photo calls and press interviews were held, including this short interview for ITV News. John is sporting the top hat he would wear as "Sir Jasper," the villain of the melodrama sketch. Each Beatle sends out holiday greetings to the fans (a shirt-sleeved George says, "Send me jacket back, it's cold!"), and they all sing a medley of "Garry Chrimble to You" and "Doo-dah, the Red-Nosed Reindeer," very similar to the rendition on their Beatles fan club flexi. John then holds out his hat to appeal for donations.

RELEASE HISTORY

1979: A fair-quality excerpt of this interview was included on the vinyl bootleg *The Beatles vs. Don Ho.*

1998: An upgraded copy of the soundtrack appeared on the bootleg CD *The Ultimate Beatles Christmas Collection.* A version released on the 1995 CD *Rare Photos & Interview CD, Volume 1* is slightly less complete than the bootleg. The footage was released on the commercial video *Beatlemania* with the singing excised (due to extreme copyright paranoia), but the complete clip circulates.

107. TV interview

Date: ca. 20 December 1963
Location: Astoria Cinema, London
Interviewer: Terry Carroll
Broadcast: 24 December 1963
Southern Television
Day by Day
Length: 0:29

Also present at the Astoria was a crew from Southern TV's *Day by Day.* Asked about their upcoming trip to America, John says they're going in January, although he doesn't know why. Ringo corrects John about the date of the trip, and George tips his cigarette ash onto John's head.

RELEASE HISTORY

1993: The audio portion of this interview, slightly incomplete, was released on the CD *The Beatles Tapes, Volume 2: Early Beatlemania 1963–1964.* The clip circulates on video in fair quality; a further six minutes reportedly exists.

1964: AND SO IS MY HAIR

TIMELINE

January 3	The Beatles make their U.S. prime-time television debut (via film) on NBC's *The Jack Paar Program.*
	U.S. release of "Please Please Me"/"From Me to You" single.
January 6	The Beatles go clubbing with Alma Cogan at the Talk of the Town.
January 10	U.S. release of *Introducing the Beatles* LP.
January 13	Ringo spends his day off visiting family.
January 14	John, Paul, and George fly from London to Le Bourget Airport in Paris. Ringo misses the connecting flight from Liverpool but jets over the following morning.
January 16	Opening night at the Olympia Theatre, Paris.
	After their concert, the Beatles celebrate the news that "I Want to Hold Your Hand" will be number 1 on the American *Cashbox* singles chart the following week.
January 20	U.S. release of *Meet the Beatles!* LP.
January 28	John and George fly from Paris to London for a brief visit before returning to Paris; George dines with the visiting Ronettes and Phil Spector.
January 29	Recording session at EMI's Paris studio.
February 3	The Beatles visit the American Embassy in Paris to obtain work permits and visas for their imminent visit to the United States.
	U.S. release of *The Beatles with Tony Sheridan and Their Guests* LP.
February 5	The Beatles fly from Paris to London Airport.
February 7	UK release of *All My Loving* EP.
	Pan Am Flight 101 performs one of the most famous feats in aviation history, carrying the Beatles, Cynthia, Neil, Mal, Brian, Phil Spector, and various journalists from London to JFK Airport, arriving on schedule at 1 p.m. and making the 1960s what they are today.
	Saturation coverage by paper, magazine, radio, TV, and newsreels of the Beatles' first American press conference, held at JFK Airport. Traveling by limo from the airport, the Beatles check in to the Plaza Hotel. (Their entourage occupies the entire twelfth floor.)
February 8	While John, Paul, and Ringo pose for photos in Central Park, George stays in bed with the flu.
	Afternoon rehearsals for the Beatles' debut on *The Ed Sullivan Show,* held at CBS Studio 50; Neil fills in for a flu-stricken George.
February 9	An audience of 73,000,728 people witnesses cultural history as the Beatles nonchalantly swing through a five-song set on *The Ed Sullivan Show,* broadcast live from CBS Studio 50. After the telecast, the Beatles celebrate with Murray the K at the Peppermint Lounge.
February 10	Award presentations from Capitol, photo shoots, and interviews at the Plaza Hotel occupy the bulk of the Beatles' day.
February 11	A snowstorm convinces the Beatles to travel by train from New York to Washington, D.C.
	The Beatles' first American concert, at Washington Coliseum, is taped by a camera crew from CBS. That night, the Beatles attend a somewhat disastrous and embarrassing reception at the British Embassy.
February 12	The Beatles ride the rails back to New York for two concerts at Carnegie Hall.
February 13	The Beatles fly from New York to Miami.
February 14	During the morning, the Beatles splash around at a private swimming pool for a famous series of *Life* magazine photos.

February 16 The Beatles perform six songs in front of an audience of 3,500 at the Deauville Hotel for CBS's *The Ed Sullivan Show.* Afternoon dress rehearsal and live broadcast in the evening are both videotaped. The Beatles attend a postshow party thrown at the Deauville by hotel owner Maurice Landsberg.

February 17 Paul and George try waterskiing and Ringo proves a somewhat shaky yachtsman.

February 18 Posing for photos with Cassius Clay and viewing Elvis's *Fun in Acapulco,* the Beatles' first drive-in movie experience.

February 20 U.S. release of "Twist and Shout"/"There's a Place" single.

February 21 After several days of fun in the sun at Miami Beach, the Beatles fly back to New York, continuing on to London that night.

February 22 Upon their morning arrival at London Airport, the Beatles receive a hero's welcome, heavily covered by film, TV, and radio.

Paul attends a performance of *The Jew of Malta,* a play featuring his actress-girlfriend, Jane Asher, in Canterbury.

February 23 The Beatles attend a party thrown by singer Alma Cogan at her Kensington flat.

February 24 Ringo spends the night visiting relatives in Liverpool, flying back to London the next morning.

February 25 At EMI Studio 2, the Beatles begin taping songs for their first film and its soundtrack LP.

March 2 The first day of filming for *A Hard Day's Night,* on location aboard a train departing from Paddington Station.

March 5 The Beatles attend an Oxfam dinner thrown by Jeffrey Archer at Brasenose College, Oxford.

March 10 The Beatles reunite briefly with Tony Sheridan at Brian Epstein's apartment.

March 16 George attends a Cilla Black recording session for BBC Radio's *Saturday Club.*

U.S. release of "Can't Buy Me Love"/"You Can't Do That" single.

March 19 The Beatles attend a Variety Club luncheon at the Dorchester Hotel and accept the award for Show Business Personalities of 1963.

George and Hayley Mills attend the midnight premiere of the film *Charade* at the Regal Theatre, Henley-on-Thames.

March 20 UK release of "Can't Buy Me Love"/"You Can't Do That" single.

March 22 John attends the launch party for his first book, *In His Own Write,* held at the offices of Jonathan Cape Publishing in London.

March 23 John's first book, *In His Own Write,* is published in the UK by Jonathan Cape.

U.S. release of "Do You Want to Know a Secret"/"Thank You Girl" single.

U.S. release of *The Beatles—Souvenir of Their Visit to America* EP.

The Beatles attend the Carl-Alan Awards at the Empire Ballroom and accept two awards.

March 27 The Beatles are treated to a four-day weekend break for Easter. John and George stay at a castle in Ireland, Ringo travels to Bedfordshire, and Paul remains in London.

U.S. release of "Why"/"Cry for a Shadow" single.

March 29 John and George return to London from Ireland.

April 1 Paul visits a sick relative at Walton Hospital. Meanwhile, John meets his father, Freddie, for the first time since 1947.

April 4 This week's *Billboard* singles chart shows a Beatle domination that is unprecedented and unmatched to this day. As "Can't Buy Me Love" hits number 1, the Beatles also occupy numbers 2, 3, 4, 5, 31, 41, 46, 58, 65, 68, and 79.

April 8 George and Ringo attend a party at London's Pickwick Club in honor of Anthony Newley.

April 10 U.S. release of *The Beatles' Second Album* LP.

April 11 More *Billboard* chart domination by the Beatles, with 14 songs in the top 100 singles chart, one more at number 131, the number 1 and 2 albums, and two more LPs at number 70 and 112.

April 16 Recording the single "A Hard Day's Night" at EMI Studio 2.

April 22 The Beatles attend a party thrown in their honor at Australia House, good publicity for their impending Australasian tour.

April 23 John leaves filming early to attend a luncheon at the Dorchester Hotel to celebrate his authorship of *In His Own Write.*

John and Ringo attend Roy Orbison's twenty-eighth birthday party.

April 24 Filming for *A Hard Day's Night* is completed, followed by a cast wrap party.

April 27 U.S. release of "Love Me Do"/"P.S. I Love You" single.

John's first book, *In His Own Write,* is published in the United States by Simon & Schuster.

April 28 The Beatles lip-sync seven songs and perform a humorous skit for Rediffusion-TV's special *Around the Beatles,* filmed in front of an audience at Wembley Studio 5A/B.

April 29 The Beatles pose for photos with their wax facsimiles at Madame Tussaud's.

May 2 The Beatles depart for a well-deserved month-long vacation. John, Cynthia, George, and Pattie travel to Honolulu (via Amsterdam and Edmonton); Paul, Jane, Ringo, and Maureen fly to the isle of St. Thomas (from Luton via Paris, Lisbon, and Puerto Rico).

May 5 Their cover blown, John and George leave Hawaii and fly to Tahiti to evade Beatles fans.

May 11 U.S. release of *4 by the Beatles* EP.

May 21 U.S. release of "Sie Liebt Dich"/"I'll Get You" single.

May 26 John and George return to London after flying from New Zealand to Los Angeles for a brief visit.

May 27 Paul and Ringo return to Luton Airport from the Virgin Islands.

John and George attend Cilla Black's birthday party (at Brian Epstein's apartment) and her performance that night at the London Palladium.

May 28 Paul and Ringo view a rough cut of the Beatles' first movie, *A Hard Day's Night.*

May 29 UK release of "Ain't She Sweet"/"Take Out Some Insurance On Me Baby" single.

Paul attends Billy J Kramer and the Dakotas' recording session for the Lennon/McCartney song "From a Window" and contributes a backing vocal.

May 30 The Beatles hold a press conference at NEMS's offices in London.

June 1 U.S. release of "Sweet Georgia Brown"/"Take Out Some Insurance On Me Baby" single.

June 2 Paul and Jane attend Cilla Black's performance at the London Palladium.

June 3 Ringo collapses with inflamed tonsils during a photo shoot at Prospect Studios in Barnes for the *Saturday Evening Post* photographer John Launois. After he is rushed to University College Hospital, a brief panic sets in to find a replacement drummer for the tour beginning the next day. The Beatles finally settle on Jimmy Nicol, due more to convenience (he lived in Barnes and had played on an album of instrumental Beatles covers) than parity with Ringo's talent.

June 7 The Beatles fly from Amsterdam to London and catch a flight to Hong Kong.

June 10 The Beatles fly from Hong Kong to Australia, landing early the next morning in Darwin for refueling and ultimately arriving at Sydney Airport.

June 11 Ringo checks out of University College Hospital.

June 12 Ringo flies from London to Australia, stopping over in San Francisco the following day.

June 15 Ringo rejoins the Beatles onstage for two concerts at Melbourne's Festival Hall.

June 19 UK release of *Long Tall Sally* EP.

June 21 The Beatles fly from Sydney, Australia, to Wellington, New Zealand.

June 26 U.S. release of *A Hard Day's Night* LP.

June 28 The Beatles fly from New Zealand to Brisbane, Australia (via Sydney).

July 1 The Beatles fly from Brisbane to Sydney for a brief layover following their Australasian tour.

July 2 The Beatles return to London Airport from Sydney, via Singapore and Frankfurt.

John and Paul attend Cilla Black's recording session for the Lennon/McCartney song "It's for You"; Paul stays late to play piano on the recording.

July 3 The Beatles completed their aborted photo session of June 3 by posing in front of a doorway in Lyall Mews, London.

July 4 The Beatles view a completed print of *A Hard Day's Night.*

July 6 U.S. release of "Ain't She Sweet"/"Nobody's Child" single.

The Beatles and Princess Margaret attend the world premiere of *A Hard Day's Night* at the London Pavilion Cinema, followed by a party at the Dorchester Hotel.

July 10 Two hundred thousand people line the streets of Liverpool for the Beatles' hometown return/local premiere of *A Hard Day's Night.*

UK release of *A Hard Day's Night* LP.

UK release of "A Hard Day's Night"/"Things We Said Today" single.

July 11 George is photographed in front of Brian Epstein's apartment building for *Beatles Book Monthly.*

July 12 George is involved in a minor car crash in London en route to the Beatles' Brighton concert.

July 13 U.S. release of "A Hard Day's Night"/"I Should Have Known Better" single.

July 15 John purchases Kenwood, a twenty-seven-room house in Weybridge, for £27,000.

July 17 George purchases Kinfauns, a bungalow in Esher, for £20,000.

July 20 U.S. release of "I'll Cry Instead"/"I'm Happy Just to Dance with You" single.

U.S. release of "And I Love Her"/"If I Fell" single.

U.S. release of *Something New* LP.

July 28 The Beatles fly from London to Arlanda Airport, Stockholm, for a brief Swedish tour.

July 30 The Beatles fly back to London Airport from Stockholm.

August 3 Paul and Jane Asher dine at the Talk of the Town nightclub in London.

August 11 The Beatles begin sessions for their fourth LP, *Beatles For Sale,* at EMI Studio 2.

August 12 The Beatles, members of the Rolling Stones, and other NEMS-managed acts attend a party at Brian Epstein's house.

August 18 The Beatles fly from London to San Francisco (with stopovers in Winnipeg and Los Angeles) for their first full-fledged North American tour.

August 24 U.S. release of "Matchbox"/"Slow Down" 45.

The Beatles attend a Hollywood charity party, shaking hands with dozens of celebrities and their children.

August 25 During their brief rest from touring, John entertains visiting film stars while the other three Beatles drop by Burt Lancaster's home for a private screening of the Pink Panther film *A Shot in the Dark.*

August 28 Following their show in New York, Bob Dylan visits the Beatles in their hotel suite and gives them their first real taste of marijuana.

September 9 The Beatles spend two unscheduled days in Key West, Florida, rather than Jacksonville, because of Hurricane Dora.

September 14 U.S. promo-only release of *The Beatles Introduce New Songs* 45 to DJs.

September 19 During a rare day off, the Beatles visit a private ranch in Missouri and try horse riding.

September 21 The Beatles fly from New York to London.

September 24 Ringo and partner Barry Patience form a construction, design, and decorating company, Brickey Building Ltd.

September 27 Ringo is a panelist judging the finals of the National Beat Group Competition.

Paul and Jane attend a first-anniversary party in London for the mod group Pretty Things.

September 30 Ringo sits in on a session with his former group, Rory Storm and the Hurricanes.

October 1 Paul attends a screening of the latest James Bond film, *Goldfinger,* in London.

October 2 Paul visits Alma Cogan's session for the song "I Knew Right Away" in London.

October 4 Brian Epstein's autobiography (ghostwritten by Derek Taylor), *A Cellarful of Noise,* is published.

October 5 U.S. release of *Ain't She Sweet* LP.

October 6 John, Paul, and Ringo go clubbing at the Ad Lib.

October 7 Walter Shenson visits the Beatles to discuss plans for their second movie.

October 8 Ringo passes his driving test at the Enfield town driving test center.

October 9 Opening night of the Beatles' UK fall tour.

October 26 Paul, Jane, Ringo, and Maureen socialize at the Ad Lib.

October 28 Jean Shepherd interviews the Beatles for *Playboy* magazine in their Exeter hotel suite.

November 6 UK release of *Extracts from the Film* A Hard Day's Night EP.

UK release of *Extracts from the Album* A Hard Day's Night EP.

November 14 John and Ringo attend Georgie Fame's show at London's Flamingo Club.

November 23 U.S. release of "I Feel Fine"/"She's a Woman" single.

U.S. release of *The Beatles' Story* LP.

November 27 UK release of "I Feel Fine"/"She's a Woman" single.

November 28 John tapes an interview at his new house with Chris Hutchins for both the *New Musical Express* and BBC Radio's *The Teen Scene.*

November 29 John and George dine with members of the Miracles at the Crazy Elephant restaurant in London.

November 30 Ringo visits the offices of the music paper *Melody Maker* and is photographed for the front page of the next edition.

December 1 Ringo checks into University College Hospital to have a tonsillectomy.

December 4 UK release of *Beatles For Sale* LP.

December 9 George and Pattie take a brief vacation in the Bahamas.

December 10 Ringo leaves the hospital following a successful tonsillectomy.

December 15 U.S. release of *Beatles '65* LP.

December 18 UK release of *Another Beatles Christmas Record,* the Beatles' second annual Christmas flexi-disc for fan club members.

December 19 George and Pattie fly back to London from their Bahamian holiday.

December 24 Opening night of "Another Beatles Christmas Show" at the Hammersmith Odeon.

December 25 The Beatles spend Christmas at their respective homes rather than returning to Liverpool.

December 31 The Beatles attend a New Year's Eve party thrown by EMI recording manager Norman Newell at his home in Marylebone.

1. Open-end interview

Date: early January 1964
Location: EMI Studios, London
Producer: Jack Wagner

[A.] Edit 1 (2:55)
[B.] Edit 2 (2:07)

To promote their upcoming U.S. visit, the Beatles dropped by Abbey Road one afternoon during the first week of 1964 to tape an interview for Capitol Records to distribute to American DJs. It was open-ended, meaning only their responses would be captured on the tape (presumably the questioning was done via headphones). A transcript of questions and answers would then be printed on the sleeve of the promotional record for disc jockeys to read from and imply that they were exclusively interviewing the group.

The raw tape was edited into two separate releases: **A** was issued simultaneous to their visit, on a disc containing three songs from Capitol's *Meet the Beatles!* LP. It includes John telling the "flaming pie" story, Paul describing the Palladium and Royal Variety show concerts, and George announcing that their new single, "I Want to Hold Your Hand," has topped the charts in Australia.

Paul jokes that it was his father who instigated the mop-tops by telling his son to ditch his square hairstyle. Playing along with the interview's conceit, George says they are "over here" [in America] to appear on *The Ed Sullivan Show* and rest in Miami. He also says they will be starting a film soon, which should be out in the States by year's end.

The second edit (**B**) followed in April to promote *The Beatles' Second Album,* on a disc including three cuts from that LP. The content overlaps slightly, as George's chat about the success of their "new single" is repeated, with the title chopped out to make it appear as though he's referring to "Can't Buy Me Love." They go on to say the single is also selling in Finland, Sweden, Ireland, and Israel. This edit also features Ringo on the origins of their stage suits, and Paul's explanation of the use of pronouns in their song titles.

The scripts provided by Capitol are full of misidentifications as to which Beatle is speaking, but the interviews served their purpose well enough. An incomplete hybrid of the two discs, with questions overdubbed, has appeared on various releases such as *Timeless II ½* and *The Beatles Are Coming.* Also of note is a broadcast in 1983's syndicated radio series *Ringo's Yellow Submarine* where Ringo acted as the DJ and interviewed himself. It's been booted on the LP *Mellow Yellow.*

RELEASE HISTORY

1964: **A** was released on a 7-inch 33⅓ rpm promo disc, *Open-End Interview with the Beatles.* The same year, **B** was released on a similar disc, *The Beatles' Second Open-End Interview.*

1977: **B** was bootlegged on the EP *Television Out-takes.*

1986: **A** was bootlegged on the LP *Great to Have You with Us,* available on CD as *John, Paul, George & Ringo—Through the Years.*

2. Studio session

Date: 3 January 1964
Location: Studio Hamburg (formerly Studio Rahlstedt)
Producer: Paul Murphy

[A.] Sweet Georgia Brown—new lead vocal (stereo) (2:02)

Polydor Records hadn't exactly been exploiting their catalog of Beatles/Tony Sheridan recordings, apart from an EP released in the UK in July 1963. However, the band's fame was becoming too big to ignore, and with the imminent possibility of successful trips to France and the United States in store, Polydor decided it was time to cash in. They discovered a few more recordings in their vaults that featured Beatles playing but had never been issued, namely "Nobody's Child," "Ain't She Sweet," and "Take Out Some Insurance On Me Baby," plus "Sweet Georgia Brown," which had found its way onto an obscure German EP.

All four were joined for a February release on a French EP, but first Polydor producer Paul Murphy had a brainstorm: Since "Sweet Georgia Brown" existed as a two-stage recording, with the lead vocal independent of the backing, why not hire Tony Sheridan to recut his lead vocal, singing novelty lyrics relating to the Beatles' new celebrity?

This Tony was happy to do, returning to the same studio where the original had been taped (now renamed Studio Hamburg) to croon such inanities as "In

Liverpool, she even dared/to criticize the Beatles' hair/with their whole fan club standing there," and exclaim, "Not too commercial, boys, not too commercial!" over the piano solo. Interestingly, at the same session, Tony recorded a new six-minute solo guitar and vocal rendition of "Nobody's Child," which would be coupled with **A** on a German single.

When Atlantic Records in the United States snapped up the rights to these four newly discovered songs, they did further tinkering in the studio before release, editing "Nobody's Child" and "Take Out Some Insurance," and hiring studio musicians to add overdubs to "Ain't She Sweet" (drums), "Sweet Georgia Brown" (drums and guitar), and "Take Out Some Insurance" (drums, guitar, and harmonica). The drummer may have been Bernard Purdie, which would explain his later outlandish claims to have secretly replaced Ringo's drumming on a number of Beatles recordings.

RELEASE HISTORY

1964: **A** was first released in mono on a French EP, *Ain't She Sweet,* and stereo on a French 10-inch LP, *Les Beatles.*

2001: The CD *Beatles Bop—Hamburg Days* contained both mixes, as well as other edits and overdubbed variations.

3. Radio interview — G, R

Date: 5 January 1964
Location: Green Street, London
Producer: John Fawcett Wilson

[A.] **Take 1** (0:44)
[B.] **outro** (0:04)
Broadcast: 12 January 1964, 3:00–4:00 p.m.
BBC Light Programme
The Public Ear

[C.] **Take 2** (0:36)
Broadcast: 11 June 1972, 5:00–5:55 p.m.
BBC Radio 1
The Beatles Story
episode 4, "The Start of Beatlemania"

Decca promo man and DJ Tony Hall was a good pal of the Beatles and lived in a flat across from the group in late 1963 when they moved to London. By January, only George and Ringo still lived in the apartment, and the duo got together with Hall to record a response to his comment on the December 29 edition of BBC Radio's *The Public Ear.*

Hall was a fellow fan of American R & B and soul music and had written in to request the BBC play more of the Beatles' current favorite artists. George reads out his and Ringo's supporting wish to hear singers "like Mary Wells, Miracles, and not to mention Marvin Gaye." After the first take (**A**), Ringo chides George for "wrecking the gag," which is met by much laughter.

In take two (**C**), we learn the gag was for Ringo to interrupt with "Marvin Gaye?" and George to reply, "I told you not to mention Marvin Gaye!" The blown take was funnier, however, and was included in the original broadcast. The "correct" take went unaired until the 1972 BBC Radio documentary series *The Beatles Story.*

RELEASE HISTORY

1988: **A–B** were rebroadcast in the December 3 episode of BBC Radio's *The Beeb's Lost Beatles Tapes.*

1998: **A–C** were bootlegged on the CD-R *Attack of the Filler Beebs!, Episode 1.*

2000: The bootleg CD *The Beatles Broadcast Collection, Trailer 1* included an upgrade of **C,** but slightly incomplete and with "Please Mr. Postman" added in the background.

4. Radio performance

Date: 7 January 1964
Time: 2:30–4:00 p.m.
Location: Playhouse Theatre, London
Producers: Jimmy Grant, Bernie Andrews
Host: Brian Matthew
Broadcast: 15 February 1964, 10:00 a.m.–noon
BBC Light Programme
Saturday Club #280

[A.] **intro** (0:03)
[B.] **All My Loving** (1:56)
[C.] **Money (That's What I Want)** (2:40)
[D.] **outro** (0:02)
[E.] **intro** (0:18)
[F.] **The Hippy Hippy Shake** (1:47)
[G.] **intro** (1:44)
I Want to Hold Your Hand (rebroadcast of December 17, 1963, recording)
[H.] **Roll Over Beethoven** (2:17)
[I.] **outro/intro** (0:29)
[J.] **Johnny B. Goode** (2:50)
[K.] **outro** (0:03)
[L.] **intro** (1:00)
[M.] **I Wanna Be Your Man** (2:09)
[N.] **outro** (0:01)

Seventeen days after their previous appearance was broadcast, the Beatles were back at the Playhouse Theatre to record another set for *Saturday Club.* As they'd be spending most of January and February out of the country, it seemed prudent to bank this performance well ahead of time to air during the dry spell.

As it was rehearsed and taped in ninety minutes flat prior to the usual two-per-night houses at the Beatles Christmas show, there was only time to record six new numbers (a recycled song from December made up the difference) and almost no chat with Brian Matthew. Besides reading requests for "The Hippy Hippy Shake," the Beatles interact with Matthew only once (and even then, his responses seem to have been added later in the studio).

Speaking over the intro to "Money," Matthew points out how much cash they must currently be reaping in America. John pokes fun at the delayed broadcast: "It's amazing that you can hear us, seeing as we're in America now." Asked about their upcoming film, Paul admits that none of them are actors, although Ringo teases that "John can act the goat." John replies, "If I wasn't in America, I'd punch you!"

The unique Beatle performance of "Johnny B. Goode" (**J**) is extremely disappointing, and it's clearly been a long time since they'd performed it. John sings the whole thing about a quarter-tone flat and fumbles the lyrics ("there stood a country cabin made of sod and wood"?), while George's guitar solo ends in utter disarray. By contrast, "I Wanna Be Your Man" sounds fresh and energetic. Ringo stuck with "Boys" until mid-December, but finally learned his new song in time for the Christmas stage show and has great fun with it here.

RELEASE HISTORY

1974: A poor-quality version of **J** appeared on the bootleg LP *Rare Beatles* (aka *Happy Birthday*), running too slow.

1982: Upgraded but incomplete copies of **J** surfaced on the bootleg LP *Beautiful Dreamer* and the radio special *The Beatles at the Beeb.*

1988: A very good recording of nearly the entire show (**B–N**) was included on the vinyl bootleg *The Beatles at the Beeb, Volume 9.* The Pyramid CD of this title (copied on *The Complete BBC Sessions* boxed set) omits **D** and **N.** All sources are missing the first note of **H.**

1994: **J** was released on Apple's *Live at the BBC* CD.

2003: The entire show, including the debut of **A,** was bootlegged on the CD boxed set *The Beatles at the Beeb.*

5. TV performance

Date: 12 January 1964
Time: 8:25–9:25 p.m.
Location: London Palladium
Host: Bruce Forsyth
Broadcast: live
ATV
Val Parnell's Sunday Night at the London Palladium

[A.] **intro** (0:09)
[B.] **I Want to Hold Your Hand** (2:25)
[C.] **intro** (0:04)
[D.] **This Boy** (2:23)
[E.] **intro** (0:57)
[F.] **All My Loving** (2:05)
[G.] **intro** (1:33)
[H.] **Money (That's What I Want)** (2:02)

[I.] intro (0:01)
[J.] Twist and Shout (1:25)
[K.] finale (Twist and Shout/Startime) (1:46)

Sadly, the Beatles' second appearance on *Sunday Night at the London Palladium,* like their first, is only represented by a home viewer's audio recording. After spending most of the day rehearsing at the Palladium, the group closed the live broadcast with a slightly expanded five-song set. To accommodate the extra song, they performed truncated versions of "Money" (omitting the third verse) and "Twist and Shout" (beginning with the instrumental break; an arrangement that would carry over to future tours).

After both sides of the latest single are played, Paul steps to the microphone and apologizes for not having a new joke to insert in the act, while John tells the screaming crowd to "shut up." Following "All My Loving," we hear Bruce Forsyth tell the audience to "hold on," followed by intermittent silences and screams. It's a bit hard to follow without the visuals, but this was presumably the "card-carrying skit" pictured in the book *The Complete Beatles Chronicle.* After the final two numbers, the Jack Parnell Orchestra plays a brass-heavy rendition of "Twist and Shout" as Forsyth welcomes the Beatles onto the show's revolving platform in time for the closing theme, "Startime."

RELEASE HISTORY

1973: **A–K** were first bootlegged in fair quality on the LP *Sunday Night at the London Palladium;* this source was copied on the bootleg CD *Live in the United Kingdom 1962–1965,* omitting **K.**

1999: The tape source for **A–K** was included on the bootleg CD boxed set *Mythology, Volume 1,* still only in fair quality and running a bit too fast.

6. Composing tape — J

Date: 1–14 January 1964
Location: Flat 3, 13 Emperors Gate, London (?)

[A.] If I Fell—take 1 (0:13)
[B.] If I Fell—take 2 (2:35)
[C.] If I Fell—take 3 (0:29)
[D.] If I Fell—take 4 (0:39)
[E.] If I Fell—take 5 (0:11)

While most of the new songs for *A Hard Day's Night* would be written during upcoming tours of France and the United States, John got a head start early in January. This series of rough demos for "If I Fell" was recorded over an audio letter, sent by a fan who had apparently seen the Beatles in Coventry on November 17; her message was taped New Year's Eve 1963.

As the tape begins, John has already started a take (**A**), but this is cut off for a complete attempt (**B**). The verse melody line sung by John would eventually be given to Paul, with John taking a lower harmony. Even in falsetto, it's clearly too high for John as he strains to reach the notes. The song's structure and lyrics are almost finalized, and the ending consists of a repeated riff that would be spun off into a song of its own, "I Should Have Known Better."

The third take (**C**) is sung an octave lower, a more comfortable range for John's voice, and consists of the final verse. The fourth (**D**) and fifth (**E**) takes are incomplete falsetto run-throughs beginning with the first verse; these may be remnants of an earlier session prior to the composition of the opening stanzas.

RELEASE HISTORY

1992: **A–E** first appeared on the bootleg CD *The Garage Tapes,* running too fast and in poor quality. This reel was part of the Alf Bicknell collection and sold for £6,500 at the August 22, 1989, Sotheby's auction.

1995: A slight upgrade of **A–E** was included on the bootleg CD *Maybe You Can Drive My Car.*

2001: The bootleg CD *Alf Together Now* contained yet another minor upgrade of **A–E.**

7. Newsreel footage

Date: 14–15 January 1964
Location: London Airport and Le Bourget Airport, Paris
Broadcast: 14–15 January 1964
ITV
Length: 0:44

Three of the Beatles flew out of London and arrived to a scaled-back reception in Paris; a blanket of fog over Liverpool had prevented Ringo from joining the others for their flight in London. ITV News was on the scene at both ends, filming John, Paul, and George's London departure on January 14 (broadcast that evening), as well as their arrival in Paris that night and Ringo leaving London the next morning (both clips aired on January 15).

RELEASE HISTORY

This silent footage circulates on video among collectors; a bit of it was used in the *Anthology* documentary.

8. Radio interview J, P, G

Date: 14 January 1964
Time: 6:00 p.m.
Location: Le Bourget Airport, Paris
Length: 0:46

Upon their arrival at Le Bourget, John, Paul, and George were interviewed for French radio. Asked to name some of their fave-raves, John chooses Carl Perkins, Chuck Berry, Ben E. King, the Shirelles, Little Richard, and Marlon Brando, hastening to add that he "n'aime pas" trad jazz. Paul adds Ray Charles and Brigitte Bardot, while George favors "Le Hitchcock" and "La TV." Paul explains that Ringo is held up in Liverpool because of heavy fog but will arrive the next day.

RELEASE HISTORY

1986: This interview was included on the vinyl bootleg *A Paris*. It also appears on the CD-R *City of Light*.

9. Newsreel footage J, P, G

Date: 15 January 1964
Time: afternoon
Location: Champs-Élysées, Paris
Length: 0:31

After sleeping in until 3 p.m., John, Paul, and George were finally roused from bed and convinced to take a photo-opportunistic stroll down the Champs-Élysées. Reuters newsreel footage shows them surrounded by PR man Brian Somerville and a host of press, but hardly being besieged by fans, although one girl stops to get autographs. Paul takes snapshots and John, wearing his button-down cap, makes goofy faces as they walk past a cinema showing *West Side Story* (in its ninety-eighth week!). Stopping at the Café George V, they peruse a rack of postcards.

RELEASE HISTORY

This silent footage circulates on video. A 24-second excerpt was aired on BBC News January 16, 1964.

10. Concert

Date: 16 January 1964
Time: 3:00 p.m.
Location: Olympia Theatre, Paris

[A.] **From Me to You** (1:50)
[B.] **outro** (0:06)
[C.] **I Saw Her Standing There** (2:36)
[D.] **intro** (0:14)
[E.] **This Boy** (0:03)
[F.] **Twist and Shout** (2:35)
[G.] **From Me to You (reprise)** (0:08)
[H.] **intro** (0:16)
[I.] **Long Tall Sally** (1:53)
[J.] **intro** (0:02)
[K.] **From Me to You (reprise 2)** (0:06)

When this tape surfaced, it was unclear which of the Paris shows it represented (possibly more than one, as "From Me to You" appears after the encore of "Long Tall Sally"). A logical guess is that it was taped by Europe 1 on the same day as the previously circulating *Musicorama* broadcast (see entry below).

This would make it the matinee show of the first day at the Olympia, January 16, which was performed for an audience of students; that would explain the audience's enthusiastic reaction compared to the other tape. The crowd claps along with "I Saw Her Standing There," spurred on by Paul's constant interjections. ("Yeah! Hey!") Although George's introduction remains intact, the recording of "This Boy" cuts off after the opening chords. Following the normal show-closing instrumental reprise of "From Me to You," a chant of "Une autre!" continues (**H**), leading to an exciting encore performance of "Long Tall Sally," featuring a savage guitar solo from George.

To confuse matters, this exact situation ("Twist and Shout" followed by cries of "Une autre" and an encore of "Long Tall Sally") is described in the book *Love Me Do* as occurring on the warm-up show in Versailles on the fifteenth; an article in *New Musical Express* has something similar happening during the first house on the seventeenth.

According to *Love Me Do,* French television was filming the students' reactions during the matinee show of the sixteenth. Fifty-two seconds of silent footage shot by a Reuters news crew is circulating from this performance, including glimpses of "This Boy" and "Boys." This circulates in tandem with 49 seconds of silent footage that seems to be from a different venue, perhaps the Versailles concert. It opens with a shot from the wings as the curtain rises (the curtains at the Olympia close from the sides) and contains portions of "Roll Over Beethoven" and "She Loves You."

RELEASE HISTORY

1999: This show (**A–K**) appeared in excellent quality on the CD-R *The Lost Paris Tapes;* portions had been broadcast in December 1993 on a French radio special. The silent Reuters newsreel footage circulates on video.

11. Radio interview

Date: 16 January 1964
Time: evening
Location: Olympia Theatre, Paris
Interviewer: Michel Lemaire
Broadcast: RTBF Radio, Belgium
Les Moins de 20 Ans
Length: 0:55

Backstage on opening night at the Olympia, the Beatles were briefly interviewed for Belgian radio, along with coheadliner Sylvie Vartan. Each Beatle gives his name and instrument (George plays "solo guitar," John plays "better guitar"), and then George requests "I Want to Hold Your Hand." During the interview with Vartan, conducted in French, "I Want to Hold Your Hand" can be heard playing distantly in the background; it sounds to me like the record, but it's possible that it's the Beatles onstage, in which case it may be the same performance as **E** in the following entry.

RELEASE HISTORY

2001: Both interviews were included on the CD-R *City of Light.*

12. Concert

Date: 16 January 1964
Time: 9:00 p.m.
Location: Olympia Theatre, Paris
Broadcast: 19 January 1964, 1:00–2:00 p.m.
Europe 1
Musicorama

[A.] **From Me to You** (1:45)
[B.] **outro** (0:09)
[C.] **This Boy** (2:16)
[D.] **outro** (0:09)
[E.] **I Want to Hold Your Hand** (2:17)
[F.] **outro** (0:09)
[G.] **intro** (0:02)
[H.] **She Loves You** (2:18)
[I.] **intro** (0:32)
[J.] **Twist and Shout** (2:35)
[K.] **intro** (0:02)
[L.] **From Me to You (reprise)** (0:07)
[M.] **outro** (0:29)
[N.] **Long Tall Sally** (0:14)
[O.] **intro** (0:02)
[P.] **From Me to You (reprise 2)** (0:05)
[Q.] **outro** (0:11)

All signs point to this radio broadcast (**A–M**) being from the evening performance of the sixteenth at the Olympia. Some sources report it as a live broadcast on the nineteenth, but edits in the tape (including a sentence (**F–G**) split between Paul and John) indicate it was pretaped. The radio station's recording equipment overloaded the power supply, causing the Beatles' amps to blow three times during the show, which would explain the need to edit the tapes prior to broadcast.

In addition, 1:11 of ITV News footage (aired January 17) circulates of what is unquestionably the evening performance. It includes segments of **J–L** with sound that matches this tape. It also shows the mayhem backstage as photographers fight to get in the Beatles' dressing room between shows.

An alternate version of this footage, from a German newsreel, includes an extra 38 seconds of backstage Beatle antics. The boys straighten their ties in the camera lens, and John shines his shoes and his leather cap (which is pulled down over Paul's eyes). Buried under the narration are further musical performances, including a bit of **C** and the end of "Long Tall Sally" and a second reprise of "From Me to You" (**N–Q**), also presumably from this concert.

Both film and radio broadcast illustrate the restrained reaction of the well-dressed socialites attending the opening night house; rather than rhythmic clapping, "Twist and Shout" is punctuated by derisive whistling. The chilly reception paled into insignificance later that night at the hotel when they received the good news they had been awaiting: "I Want to Hold Your Hand" was about to climb to the top of the U.S. singles chart in *Cashbox.*

RELEASE HISTORY

1986: The *Musicorama* broadcast (**A–M**) first surfaced on the vinyl bootleg *A Paris* in very good quality.

1989: The *Musicorama* broadcast (**A–M**) appeared from tape source on the bootleg CD *Live in Paris 1964 and in San Francisco 1966.* The ITV News clip circulates on video, and a portion of it was used in the *Anthology* documentary. Its soundtrack appears on the CD-R *Blackpool Night Out '64—Upgraded.* **N–Q** appear on the soundtrack of the German newsreel *Tumult Und Die Beatles,* which circulates on video.

13. Radio interview

Date: 24 January 1964
Time: 3:00 p.m.
Location: Hôtel George V, Paris
Interviewer: Harold B. Kelley
Broadcast: 25 January 1964
American Forces Network
Weekend World
Length: 13:58

Waking the Beatles in Paris was no easy task; the late hour of the Olympia shows combined with postconcert celebrations meant that they rarely awoke before noon, although Dezo Hoffmann was able to get them up at 9:30 one morning for a *Paris Match* photo shoot. On this day, two American reporters had a 1 p.m. appointment to interview the group at their hotel suite, but it was well over an hour before they emerged from their bedrooms wearing robes.

One of the reporters, Harold Kelley, was there to tape an interview for U.S. troops stationed in West Germany, broadcast the following day on AFN's *Weekend World.* Kelley's introduction tries to create the illusion that the Beatles have dropped by the studio, but John later gives the game away; asked what causes Beatlemania, he replies, "George's dressing gown is definitely a big attraction."

The interview opens with Paul's recounting of the group's history, from school through the Royal Variety show, with John tossing in a mention of Michael Braun, the journalist who had been covering their activities for the book *Love Me Do.* George explains that the so-called Liverpool sound is merely rock-and-roll with louder rhythm sections and more shouting. Chat about the evolution of the mop-top is followed by Paul's analysis of Beatlemania: a combination of originality, timing, gimmicks, and luck.

Asked about the Parisian audiences, George explains that many teenage girls aren't allowed out at night without chaperones, resulting in a far larger proportion of males than in British audiences. After Kelley inserts a pause to spin "I Want to Hold Your Hand," Paul relates how the song was written, though he's rather cagey about it. While it had actually been written on the piano in the Asher family's music room, Paul weaves the tale of walking along with John one day and coming upon a "disused house" with keyboards in the basement. John also reveals that the "yeah yeah yeah" catchphrase in "She Loves You" was merely an afterthought, but proved so popular, "we'll have to write another song with it."

Kelley asks about their upcoming U.S. visit, and Paul says they'll be making three appearances on *The Ed Sullivan Show,* one from Miami, and playing at Carnegie Hall. George explains how Sullivan happened to glimpse Beatlemania at London Airport when they returned from Stockholm the previous October. Finally, they discuss the logistics of their first movie, with Paul admitting that "we've gotta compose six songs specifically for the film. We gotta get down to that, too. There's a job."

RELEASE HISTORY

1988: An edited version of this interview was included on the vinyl bootleg *Re-introducing the Beatles.*

1998: The complete interview was included on the CD-R *Attack of the Filler Beebs!, Episode 1.*

14. Recording session

Date: 29 January 1964
Time: morning/afternoon
Location: EMI Pathé Marconi Studios, Paris
Producer: George Martin

[A.] **Komm Gib Mir Deine Hand—take 1 (mono)** (0:08)
[B.] **Komm Gib Mir Deine Hand—take 2 (mono)** (0:09)
[C.] **Komm Gib Mir Deine Hand—take 7 (mono)** (0:04)
[D.] **Komm Gib Mir Deine Hand—take 9 (mono)** (0:04)
[E.] **Komm Gib Mir Deine Hand—take 10 (mono)** (0:04)
[F.] **Komm Gib Mir Deine Hand—unknown take (mono)** (0:06)
[G.] **Sie Liebt Dich—unknown take (stereo)** (0:09)
[H.] **Can't Buy Me Love—monitor mix of takes 1–4 (mono)** (6:03)
[I.] **Can't Buy Me Love—edit of takes 1–2 (mono)** (2:08)
[J.] **Can't Buy Me Love—take 2 (stereo)** (2:13)
[K.] **Can't Buy Me Love—take 3 (stereo)** (0:41)
[L.] **Komm Gib Mir Deine Hand—RM1** (2:23)
[M.] **Sie Liebt Dich—RM1** (2:16)
Mixed: 10 March 1964

[N.] **Komm Gib Mir Deine Hand—RS1** (2:23)
[O.] **Sie Liebt Dich—RS1** (2:15)
Mixed: 12 March 1964

Despite their success on the charts with Tony Sheridan, Beatlemania had yet to catch on in West Germany, and Odeon Records, EMI's German subsidiary, thought it knew why: The songs were sung in English! While this hadn't prevented them from having hits in Sweden and Finland, and would prove to be irrelevant within a few months, George Martin reluctantly set up a Paris recording session for the Beatles to record a single sung in German.

The initial plan had been to merely translate both sides of the "She Loves You" single, and in fact a translation of "I'll Get You" had been done (titled "Glücklich Wie Noch Nie," roughly "Happy like never before"). But the Beatles put it off so long that it was decided their more recent hit would make a better A-side, thus "Komm Gib Mir Deine Hand" ("Come give me your hand") was chosen as the A-side, with "Sie Liebt Dich" on the flip. The translations were reportedly done by German DJ Camillo Felgen, but for publishing purposes he used the pseudonyms "Jean Nicolas" and "Heinz Hellmer" (for "Hand") and "Lee Montague" (for "Dich").

Two sessions were booked for EMI's Paris studio, on January 29 and 31, and engineer Norman Smith made a four-track copy of the backing track to "I Want to Hold Your Hand" on the twenty-fourth at Abbey Road Studio 1 before flying overseas to meet with George Martin. Getting the Beatles to participate was another matter: John and George had flown to London on a rare day off, the twenty-eighth, and returned early the next morning. Martin and Smith arrived for the late morning session and waited for the artists. And waited. Martin was finally forced to storm over to the hotel and drag them across town.

Once the session started, they made the most of it and actually had fun, judging from the existing tapes. The first task was for John and Paul to sing the new lyrics for "Komm Gib Mir Deine Hand." Onto a new twin-track tape (reel E51593) went the original musical backing along with the live vocal overdubs. This took eleven attempts, not all of them complete. Getting the pronunciation just right meant doing it in bits and pieces.

Several fragments from the session appeared on the website thebeatles.com in 2000. **A** consists of Smith's "take one" announcement while John and Paul get in some last-minute rehearsal of the line "Du nimmst mir den Verstand." **B** has the announcement for "take two" and a few words from John ("Oh yeah . . . come out like that anyway") followed by the backing track starting up. **C** has the take announcement plus a Bugs Bunny imitation from Paul. **D** was the second attempt at an edit piece, and John urges, "Let's get it," while Paul practices the line "Schoen wie ein Diamant." **E** is the announcement of another edit piece take, while **F** comes from the end of an unknown attempt; as the backing track dies away and shuts off, John shouts a bit of nonsense.

In the end, takes 5 and 7 of "Komm Gib Mir Deine Hand" were edited together and the result was copied onto a second twin-track tape (E51592) with a simultaneous handclap overdub, producing the final master. As the multitrack tape for "She Loves You" was already destroyed, the Beatles had to record the song from scratch, doing so in thirteen takes onto reel E51593. It's easily distinguished from the original by differing guitar fills (John had played his Gibson J-160 on "She Loves You," but uses his Rickenbacker here).

Take details are unknown, but it also took a number of attempts to record the vocals for "Sie Liebt Dich," one of which (**G**) breaks down in laughter. These were also done by making twin-track copies of the backing with live vocals, and the master is edited from the best attempts. Both songs were mixed into mono and stereo back at Abbey Road and sent to West Germany for rush-release on a single that shot straight to number 1.

Neither song was released in the UK at the time, but in America, a ravenous market for new Beatles material, both songs were issued. Swan Records, which had released "She Loves You," found they had the rights to its German counterpart and released **M** on a single May 21, 1964, backed with "I'll Get You." Surprisingly, it popped into the top 100 at number 97 for one week. Capitol was sent mono and stereo copies of "Komm Gib Mir Deine Hand" and decided to add the song to its next ragbag LP, *Something New.* Note that mono copies have a slightly longer fade on **L** than the *Past Masters* version, while stereo copies have a stray word ("coming") in the vocal channel of **N** that would be faded down for its eventual UK release on the *Rarities* LP. The latter LP also contained the first true stereo mix of "Sie Liebt Dich" (**O**).

With plenty of studio time remaining, they decided to record a song Paul had written on the hotel piano. "Can't Buy Me Love" originally began with the first verse, but George Martin suggested the chorus would provide a better introduction. A "monitor mix" tape of much of this session recently surfaced (**H**) from the preparations for the 1983 *Beatles at Abbey Road* presentation. It includes the complete first take, as well as the announcements and count-ins for takes 2 and 4, all of which was unavailable on the previously circulating in-line sources.

Take 1 opens with Norman Smith's announcement of the working title: "Money Can't Buy Me Love." The arrangement consists of John on acoustic guitar, Paul on bass, Ringo on drums, and George playing lead guitar, plus magnificent bluesy call-and-response vocals. John botches his backing vocal entry on the second verse, singing an even bluesier harmony than intended, and comments on it following the take: "I had the wrong note." At this point, Paul sings "my love" rather than "my friend."

The second take (**J**) is marred by Paul's lyrical flub on the third verse, but this pales in comparison to George's calamitous guitar solo. It's little wonder that for *Anthology 1* (**I**), the guitar solo from take 1 was spliced in its place. The third take (**K**) drops John and George's backing vocals and lowers the key from D major to C major. It breaks down when Paul sings a line from the first verse during the second verse. The next take was satisfactory, and with overdubs back in London the following month, "Can't Buy Me Love" would be ready for release as the Beatles' sixth single.

RELEASE HISTORY

1964: **L** and **M** were released on a single in West Germany. Both are available on the CD *Past Masters, Volume 1.* **L** and **N** were included on mono and stereo copies respectively of the LP *Something New* in the United States.

1978: **N** and **O** were released on the LP *Rarities* in the UK, with **N** being a slightly different mix to that on *Something New.*

1988: An excellent-quality tape of **J** surfaced on the bootleg CD *Ultra Rare Trax, Volume 2,* missing a couple of seconds at the end (John's coughing fit).

1991: The bootleg CD *Unsurpassed Masters, Volume 7* included excellent copies of **J** and **K,** both running too slow. **J** had the complete ending but chopped off a bit of Paul's count-in. A speed-corrected copy of **K** can be found on the CD-R *City of Light.*

1995: **I** was released on Apple's *Anthology 1* CD.

1996: The *Anthology* home video included **G** preceded by portions of **A** (the words "German version") and **E** (the phrase "edit piece take ten"). They appear from this source on the bootleg CD *Abbey Road Video Show.*

2000: **A–F** popped up as snippets on the website thebeatles.com and were bootlegged the following year on the CD-R *Studio Collection,* which also includes **G** and **L–O.**

2002: **H** first appeared in good quality on the bootleg CD *Complete Controlroom Monitor Mixes, Volume 1.* A similar tape on volume 2 of this set offers no extra material, although the quality is better in places.

15. Radio interview

Date: Late January 1964
Location: Hôtel George V, Paris
Interviewer: Bernard Redmont
Broadcast: WIND-AM, Chicago
Fake or Phenomenon
Length: 5:52

As a bit of promotion for their upcoming American tour (hardly necessary at this point), the Beatles spoke with radio correspondent Bernard Redmont in their Paris hotel suite. The interview was an exclusive for Group W stations and was used in documentaries on Chicago's WIND and New York's WINS.

John says that "Beatles" is a play on words, but adds that "a rose by any other name would smell as sweet." Asked to explain their success, George points to the overall British pop music scene, which by late 1962 was stagnant and placid, leaving rock-and-roll fans hungry for a new sound. Paul professes not to mind the fans' screaming during shows, as it energizes their performance. He also feels they play loud enough to be heard over the audience (this would change when they moved from theaters to stadiums).

John briefly recounts their history and admits that while they dreamed of stardom, it always seemed unattainable. Paul says he still has trouble connecting what he reads about the group in the papers with reality. Even if the mania were to abate, Ringo thinks they would continue playing clubs in Liverpool for the sheer joy of performing. Redmont wonders if they're looking forward to appearing in America, and the response is a unanimous "Yeah!" John adds, "We think about it all the time, don't we?"

Redmont then quotes from William Mann's *London Times* article of the previous December 27, including the infamous description of the "pandiatonic clusters" of "This Boy." Paul is baffled, denying the use of "periodontic" or "hypodermic clusters." (George: "Maybe that's why the needle got stuck on my copy.") John talks about Cynthia and Julian, and Ringo says none of them have time to go steady, being constantly on the road.

RELEASE HISTORY

2001: This interview appeared on the CD-R *City of Light,* reassembled from the poor-quality WIND broadcast and a shorter but good-quality broadcast from WINS-AM's *Meet the Beatles* special of February 9, 1964.

15a. Amateur footage

Date: 16 January–4 February 1964
Location: Olympia Theatre, Paris
Length: 0:55

The DVD *World Tour 1966: Home Movies,* mostly comprised of drummer Mickey Jones' personal footage of Bob Dylan tours, also includes his color home movies of Trini Lopez and the Beatles performing at the Paris Olympia. This silent footage includes glimpses of "Roll Over Beethoven" and John doing his "spastic clapping" routine.

RELEASE HISTORY

2002: This footage was released on the DVD *World Tour 1966: Home Movies.*

16. Composing tape J, P

Date: 18 January–4 February 1964
Location: Hôtel George V, Paris

[A.] One and One Is Two (1:54)

In addition to writing songs for their next single and film soundtrack, John and Paul spent time in Paris attempting to come up with another composition for Billy J Kramer. Chris Hutchins of the *New Musical Express* was in their hotel suite in the predawn hours of January 18 when song publisher Dick James was visiting. Paul played him what he had of the song "One and One Is Two" on the piano installed in their suite.

James requested a taped demo of the number be flown to London as soon as the song was finished. Journalist Michael Braun picked up the tale from there as Paul struggled to complete the lyrics some days later. With the others throwing out ideas (George: "Can't you do something with 'do' or 'Jew'?" John: " 'I'm a lonely Jew.' How's that?"), Paul scribbled out three suitable verses to go with the simplistic chorus. He and John taped three run-throughs, with Paul playing acoustic guitar and singing and John plonking along on piano.

Last-minute lyrical changes preceded the fourth and final take (**A**), which was performed with the same instrumentation (John's piano contribution is barely audible). The tape was duly sent off to London the next morning and the best take was cut onto an acetate for Kramer to learn. "Billy J is finished when he gets this song" was John's comment in Paris, and Kramer wisely rejected the tune.

The Fourmost already had minor success with another Lennon/McCartney song first attempted by Kramer, "I'm In Love," and decided to have a go at "One and One Is Two." Even with Paul sitting in on bass, they weren't able to make it work. Eventually a South African group, the Strangers with Mike Shannon, cut the song. They performed the song in the key of Eb (the demo plays back slightly on the flat side of E major), adding an extra chorus and guitar solo and altering the chords and lyrics slightly. Their single was released in the UK only, where it flopped, rightfully forgotten as one of the weakest Lennon/McCartney throwaways.

RELEASE HISTORY

1988: **A** first appeared on the bootleg LP *Ultra Rare Trax, Volume 3 & 4,* taken from a scratchy acetate.

1991: **A** was included on the bootleg CD *Acetates,* running slightly slower and missing the very ending (merely the sound of the tape being switched off). This version also has heavy noise reduction.

17. Newsreel footage

Date: 5 February 1964
Time: 1:00 p.m.
Location: London Airport
Broadcast: 5 February 1964
ITV
Length: 3:31

A couple hundred fans welcomed the Beatles back from Paris this afternoon. News footage of the arrival circulates from two sources. A 50-second silent Associated Press newsreel shows the group emerging from the plane (George unfurls a Union Jack, assisted by Ringo), walking across the tarmac, and eventually emerging from the terminal to dash into a limo.

ITV News filed a longer report (lasting 2:41) that includes further scenes of their stroll to the arrivals building, signing autographs as they go (fans scramble onto a luggage conveyor belt to get a closer look). Once inside, they sit down for an interview with an ITV reporter, discussing their French concerts and imminent U.S. visit.

George says the main difference in French audiences was the lack of female screams; Paul adds that they seemed to enjoy more boisterous rockers, which is why they added "a wilder number" than usual as an encore ("Long Tall Sally," not "Gone With the Wind," as John gibes). Paul demonstrates the only French phrase he knows: *"Je me lève à sept heures."* ("I get up at seven o'clock.")

Ringo says he'll be reciting some of Beethoven's poems at the City of London Festival. This is an inside joke poking fun at an unknown pop singer who had claimed in an interview to be reading a book of Beethoven's poetry. Ringo goes on to quote from Capitol's first bit of Beatle promotion: "You can even be a Beatle Booster, folks! Fifty cents!" (50-cent buttons with that slogan were sold in the United States beginning in early January). The reporter informs them of Detroit University's "Stamp Out the Beatles" movement, started by some students who find the group's haircuts "un-American." John is unfazed: "Well, it was very observant of them, 'cause we aren't American, actually."

RELEASE HISTORY

1993: The ITV interview was released on the CD *The Beatles Tapes, Volume 2: Early Beatlemania 1963–1964.* It circulates on video, as does the silent AP newsreel footage.

18. Interview

Date: 5 or 7 February 1964
Location: London Airport
Length: 1:51

This interview was conducted between the Paris and New York trips, either incoming or outgoing at London Airport. The female interviewer may be *Evening Standard* reporter Maureen Cleave, who was present on the morning of the seventh to join the trip to America, or June Harris, who reportedly interviewed George on February 6.

She asks whether they saw any Christian Dior–designed Beatle wigs, and Paul replies that they were creeped out by the sight of several rows of bewigged but stone-faced French lads at the Olympia. He teases Ringo about his inability to digest French food (too much garlic for the drummer's delicate digestive system), and George selects women's boots as the only cutting-edge French fashion they observed. Asked what sights he wants to see in America, John jokes, "The Eiffel Tower."

RELEASE HISTORY

2001: This fair-quality interview was included on the CD-R compilation *City of Light.*

19. Newsreel footage

Date: 7 February 1964
Time: 2:30 p.m.
Location: London Airport
Length: 2:09

When four thousand cheering fans saw the Beatles off to America, the band had no idea that a nearly identical scene was awaiting them at the other end of their journey. They knew that a U.S. Beatles fan club had started, and that they were currently topping the *Billboard* charts. On the other hand, they knew that some college students in Detroit had proposed "stamping out the Beatles," and that no previous British rock star had successfully made a lasting impact across the Atlantic.

A Pathé newsreel, *Beatles off to America,* documents the departure, which looks like most other airport scenes apart from the presence of Cynthia Lennon, there to accompany her husband for the entire trip. John wears his leather cap and Ringo a scarf as the boys wave farewell to weeping fans at the parapet atop the terminal.

In addition to the Beatles, Cynthia, and Brian Epstein, photographer Harry Benson and journalists George Harrison *(Liverpool Echo)* and Maureen Cleave sat in first class, along with American record producer

Phil Spector, who would feature heavily toward the end of the Beatles' story. Relegated to coach were roadies Mal Evans and Neil Aspinall, photographers Dezo Hoffmann and Robert Freeman, and journalist Michael Braun, still working on his firsthand account of *The Beatles' Progress* for a trade paperback.

RELEASE HISTORY

The Pathé newsreel *Beatles off to America* circulates on video, as does 50 seconds of silent ITV News footage.

20. Newsreel footage

Date: 7 February 1964
Time: 1:30 p.m.
Location: Kennedy International Airport, New York City

It's one of the most familiar images of the Beatles' career: three thousand fans waiting on the roof of JFK Airport in New York as a Pan Am jet discharges four pleasantly surprised passengers. George is first to emerge, then John (who removes his leather cap after the wind nearly whips it away), followed by Paul and Ringo. They spend several moments taking it all in and waving before turning themselves over to the NYPD for an escort to customs.

All three U.S. TV networks filmed the arrival, along with Associated Press and Pathé newsreel cameras. More importantly, young documentary filmmakers Albert and David Maysles were here to film the first scenes for what would become an outstanding inside look at America's first taste of Beatlemania. Granada, an independent British TV company, had hired the Maysles, but financial participation from Brian Epstein's NEMS Enterprises meant that the camera crew would be granted unprecedented access to film the Beatles' travels and offstage activities.

Some of the Maysles footage was first aired February 12 on ITV in the UK in a forty-minute special called *Yeah! Yeah! Yeah! The Beatles in New York.* The commonly circulating video comes from an hour-long U.S. version, broadcast on CBS November 13 as *What's Happening! The Beatles in the U.S.A.* A full "director's cut," which has been screened at some film festivals, runs eighty minutes. Extra footage has also been included in the DVDs *The First U.S. Visit* and *Anthology.*

The finished documentary has several uncanny parallels with *A Hard Day's Night,* which isn't too surprising as Alun Owen wrote the screenplay for the latter after observing the Beatles on tour. Both films show the group creating havoc on a train journey, cooped up inside hotel rooms, dancing in nightclubs, bantering with the press, and performing in a TV studio. While most of the similarities can be put down to the Beatles' "train and a room and a car and a room and a room and a room" lifestyle, the Maysles' handheld fly-on-the-wall shooting technique may have influenced Richard Lester's direction.

RELEASE HISTORY

The Pathé newsreel *Beatles Conquer America,* containing 27 seconds of arrival footage, circulates on video; basically the same footage is used in the American newsreel *Beatlemania Grips Gotham.* The Maysleses' footage was included in the TV special *What's Happening! The Beatles in the U.S.A.,* which circulates on video.

21. Press conference

Date: 7 February 1964
Time: 2:00 p.m.
Location: Kennedy International Airport, New York City
Length: 6:26

Once they had cleared customs, the Beatles were lined up in front of a Pan Am logo, behind a bank of microphones, facing a swarm of TV cameras, still photographers, newspaper and magazine writers, and radio reporters. Their press officer, Brian Somerville, lost his cool trying to maintain order amid the chaos. Meanwhile, in the front row, brash WINS-AM disc jockey Murray "The K" Kaufman angered many of his colleagues by attempting to hold his own private rap session with the Liverpudlians, who in turn were ignoring shouted questions from the back.

Although the enormity of the situation was still sinking in, the Beatles were quick on their feet, and by the end of the questioning, only the most skeptical journalists would remain unpacified. The event went roughly like this:

George: How d'you do?
Paul: All over here, quick. This way—John . . .
Q: Over here!
Paul: (parroting in a New York accent) Ova heah!
Q: Over here! Fellas! Fellas!
Q: Hey, Ringo!
Ringo: Yeah?
George: John—Ringo, can you get 'round there?
Q: Come over—
Q: Move back a little bit so the mic . . .
Q: All right, now, come on, sit down! Let the other newsmen get in here. All right . . .
Q: Are you a little—are you a little embarrassed by the lunacy you cause?
John: No, it's great!
Ringo: No, it's marvelous!
Paul: We love it!
John: We like lunatics.
B. Somerville: Look, ladies and gentlemen—
Q: You're in favor of lunacy?
John and Ringo: Yeah!
John: It's healthy.
Q: You're enriched by it, is that it?
B. Somerville: Can we PLEASE have quiet?!
Q: Quiet, please!
Q: Hey, hat!
Q: John, don't . . .
George: Let the feasting begin!
B. Somerville: Unless you keep quiet we can't even have a press conference! Would you please shut up? Y'know, 'cause . . .
Q: That's an American expression!
Ringo: Please be quiet.
Q: Shut up!
B. Somerville: Well, we'll just stand here until you're quiet.
Q: Please!
B. Somerville: Please be quiet!
Q: Get [?] outta there. Get Ike Pappas outta there!
Q: Get him out.
B. Somerville: If you're going to ask a question, would you be quiet please?
Q: Could you please sing something?
All: No!
Ringo: Sorry!
B. Somerville: Next question!
Q: There's some doubt that you can sing.
John: No, we need money first.
Q: How much money do you expect to take out of this country?
John: About half a crown. Two dollars or something.
B. Somerville: Sorry, I can't hear the question.
John: Depends on the tax.
Ringo: Five-eleven . . . five-six.
[Murray the K starts to interview them individually.]
Murray: How was your trip over?
Ringo: Fine. Very nice.
George: A bit bumpy over, uh . . . Alaska.
Murray: Have you ever seen a reception like this in any of the—
George: No, it's the best ever, we've ever had.
[Someone asks the same question of John.]
John: Um . . . I don't think so, not quite like this one.
George: Nice to be here! Nice to be here, great. And . . .
Ringo: We're havin' a good time.
[Someone asks why they are so popular.]
Paul: We can't tell you.
Ringo: Wish we knew.
Paul: No idea.
John: Good pub—good press agent.
B. Somerville: There's a question here . . .
Q: Hey, will you tell Murray the K to CUT that CRAP out?
Ringo: Cut that crap out!
John: Hey, cut that crap out!
Paul: Hey, Murray! Hey, Murray!
Q: Is that a question?
Q: Does all that hair help you sing?
John: What?
Q: Does all that hair help you sing?
John: Definitely, yeah.
Paul: Keeps you—
Q: Do you feel—do you feel like Samson, if you lost your hair, you'd lose what you have—"it"?
John: Dunno, I dunno. Dunno.
Ringo: No, I don't think so.
Q: How many are bald that you have to wear those wigs?
Ringo: All of us.
Paul: I am. I'm bald.
Q: You're bald?
John: Oh, we're all bald, yeah.
Paul: Don't tell anyone, please, y'know.
John: And deaf and dumb, too.
B. Somerville: There's a gentleman there with his—
Q: One psych—
B. Somerville: Quiet, please!
Q: All right, quiet!
Q: One psychiatrist recently said you're nothing but four Elvis Presleys.
John: He must be blind.
Ringo: (swinging his hips madly) It's not true! It's not true!
Q: Do you know American slang? Are you guys "for real"?
Paul: Huh?
Q: Do you know American slang? Are you "for real"?
Paul: For real.
John: Come and have a feel. Oh, sorry about that.
[Someone asks what their ambitions are.]

Paul: Uh . . .
Ringo: To be rich.
George: To go to America! That got a laugh!
Ringo: Any more?
Q: Listen, I got a question here: Aren't you afraid of what the American Barbers Association's gonna think of you?
Ringo: Well, we've run quicker than the English ones, we'll have a go here, y'know.
John: Did you understand that?
Q: Do you hope to get a haircut at all while you're in the States?
All: No!
Paul: No, thanks.
George: I had one yesterday.
Ringo: And that's no lie. It's the truth!
George: Honest.
Q: You know, I think he missed.
Ringo: No.
George: No he didn't, no.
Ringo: You should've seen him the day before.
B. Somerville: Okay, one here . . .
Q: What do you think your music does for these people?
John: Uh . . . well . . .
Ringo: I don't know.
Q: Makes them spend their money.
Ringo: It pleases them, I think. Well, I—they must do, 'cause they're buying it.
Q: Why does it excite them so much?
Paul: We don't know, really.
John: If we knew, we'd form another group and be managers.
Q: What about all this talk that you represent some kind of a social rebellion?
John: It's a dirty lie! It's a dirty lie.
[Someone asks why they speak with English accents but sing with American accents.]
John: That is English, actually.
Paul: That's the trick.
George: It's not English, it's Liverpudlian, y'see.
Q: . . . very American . . .
Paul: Well the Liverpool—the Liverpool accent, the way you say some of the words . . . y'know, you say "grass" instead of "grahss."
John: Grahss?
Paul: Well, that sounds a bit American. So there you go.
Ringo: Liverpool's the nearest part of England to America.
John: Anyway, it sells better.
Ringo: It's the capital of Ireland.
Paul: Anyway, we wrote half your folk songs in Liverpool.
Ringo: Yeah, don't forget.
Q: In Detroit, Michigan, college students are handing out car stickers saying "Stamp Out . . ."
Paul: Yeah, well, we've got two answers to that, which—we . . .
Ringo: Pardon?
Paul: I'll tell you in a minute! No, we're—first of all, we're bringing out a "Stamp Out Detroit" campaign, which—
Q: What about this "Stamp Out the Beatles" campaign?
John: What about it?
Q: D'you think it'll have any success?
Ringo: How big are they?
John: Well, it's . . .
George: But we're on your side!
Q: What do you think of Beethoven?
Ringo: Great. Specially his poems! I keep crackin' that gag every day. I'm sick of that one.
B. Somerville: Can we have the last questions now, gentlemen?
John: My favorites.
Paul: I hate them. Terrible group.
Q: Have you decided when you're going to retire?
John: Next week.
Ringo: I don't know.
Paul: No, probably . . .
Ringo: We're gonna keep goin' as long as we can.
George: When we get fed up with it. Y'know, we're still enjoyin' it now.
Ringo: Any minute now.
Q: —Make so much money and then—
George: No.
Ringo: No.
George: No, as long as we enjoy it, we'll do it. 'Cause we enjoyed it before we made any money.
Paul: (identifying each member for the benefit of the press) Paul . . . Ringo . . . George . . . and John!

So far, so good. Outside the terminal, four Cadillac limousines waited to speed the Beatles into Manhattan (13 seconds of footage of this transfer is included on the video *The First U.S. Visit,* taken from the Pathé newsreel *Beatles Conquer America*). In the confusion, Brian Epstein was left behind and forced to hail a taxi. Fans popped up all along the route from the airport and swarmed the Plaza Hotel, where the Beatle entourage would be occupying the ten-room Presidential Suite on the twelfth floor.

RELEASE HISTORY

The preceding reconstruction (which still has some holes) is based on examination of the following sources: The LPs *The Beatles American Tour with Ed Rudy* and *1965 Talk Album—Ed Rudy with New U.S. Tour;* the

CDs *Inside Interviews: Beatlemania* and *Rare Photos & Interview CD, Volume 3;* the videos *Imagine: John Lennon, The Compleat Beatles, The Road, The First U.S. Visit, Anthology,* and *Fun with the Fab Four;* the newsreel *Beatles Conquer America;* episodes of the TV series *Grandstand, Time and Again,* and *American Bandstand;* the radio series *The Beatle Years;* the BBC radio documentary *The Beatles Story;* the WINS radio documentary *Meet the Beatles;* and various video clips. Undoubtedly other potential sources also circulate.

22. Radio interview

Date: 7 February 1964
Time: evening
Location: Plaza Hotel, New York City
Interviewer: Murray Kaufman
Broadcast: 9 February 1964, 7:00 p.m.
WINS-AM, New York City
Meet the Beatles
Length: 4:09

After the Beatles enjoyed a room service dinner, the Ronettes dropped by for a visit; George at least had met them a few weeks earlier, along with Phil Spector. Accompanying them this time was Murray the K, armed with a tape recorder, for his first one-on-one interviews with the Beatles.

He would become an almost inescapable presence throughout the tour, but this initial encounter is comparatively subdued as they get to know one another. John says they are in America to appear on three TV shows, perform two concerts, and buy some records. Murray wonders why they turned down an offer (made by promoter Sid Bernstein) to play Madison Square Garden, which seats ten times as many people as Carnegie Hall. John figures it's because Brian didn't want to overexpose them.

George chats about the film they'll be making, and John jokes that during their two scheduled days of rest in Miami they'll build sand castles. (Murray's New York ears hear this as "sun castles.") They deny rumors putting their personal wealth at a million pounds each, but Paul expresses a desire to be "a rich hobo." Murray, obviously digging their sense of humor, replies, "That's the best kind, baby! Rich or poor, it's always good to have money!"

At one point, George explains that he's tired, having "been up for days. Hacking." In fact, his throat does sound ragged throughout the interview, and when a doctor was summoned to examine him, George was found to have a high temperature and likely case of influenza. The others could only hope that bed rest and heavy medication would get George well enough to perform on *The Ed Sullivan Show* two days hence.

RELEASE HISTORY

This interview circulates in good quality among collectors.

23. Radio interview

Date: 7 February 1964
Time: evening
Location: Plaza Hotel, New York City (via telephone)
Interviewer: Brian Matthew
Broadcast: 8 February 1964, 10:00 a.m.–noon
BBC Light Programme
Saturday Club #279
Length: 5:51

Once Murray departed, the Beatles still had to wait for a phone call from London, where midnight was fast approaching. Brian Matthew would be calling to interview them for the following morning's edition of *Saturday Club.* It turned out to be one of the most well-documented phone calls in history. Not only were engineers taping from the other end of the line, BBC Radio reporter Malcolm Davis was in the suite taping the responses, and the Maysles crew were rolling film for their documentary.

The interview as eventually heard consisted of answers taped by Davis, sent via a higher-quality phone line to London. These were edited together and Matthew dubbed his questions on top of this in the studio the following morning. Also included in the broadcast was a nine-minute report by Davis that includes just over a minute from his raw tape of the answers. (This includes three tiny bits not in the Matthew edit: Paul's "Paul here," John's "Ringo?," and George adding "joint" to the description of their three number 1 records in New York.)

After a false alarm (see following entry), Matthew gets through and chats first with Paul, who is amazed at the rapturous welcome they received: "They were all just sort of hanging all over the airport . . . thousands of press men, and thousands of New York cops and things . . . it was just ridiculous, y'know!" The novelty of American radio's saturation live coverage also impresses Paul, who marvels, "As we were going along, he was reporting it! . . . just as we were gettin' out of the car, he said, 'And we hear they've arrived now.' Fantastic!"

He tells Matthew that they just met the Ronettes and that a DJ ("Murray the K!" John shouts in the background) thinks he can hook them up with the Miracles. They're also hoping to catch the Isley Brothers while in town. John takes the phone to relate his impression of Americans: "They just seemed all out of their minds!" He says they've been watching themselves arrive on TV for the last hour or two, and that only George took a trip to Liverpool during their day off in England, but is paying for it now. Matthew jokingly lobbies for a role in their film, and John offers him a part "pushing a barrow or something."

Ringo describes the chaotic press conference at the airport, and finally a raw-throated George comes on the line. He lists the Beatles songs currently in the U.S. charts (" 'My Bonnie,' which is a laugh . . .") and is reminded by Matthew of their upcoming (pre-taped) appearance on *Saturday Club* the following week. In signing off, George relays a message to the show's producer, Bernie Andrews: "Tell him to get his hair cut!"

RELEASE HISTORY

1988: Malcolm Davis' report was included on the bootleg LP *The Beatles at the Beeb, Volume 8.* It was released on the CD *The Beatles Tapes, Volume 2: Early Beatlemania 1963–1964,* probably copied from the bootleg. The same year, the complete phone interview (as originally broadcast) was aired in the November 12 episode of BBC Radio's *The Beeb's Lost Beatles Tapes.* It's available from this source on the bootleg CD *The Beatles Broadcast Collection, Trailer 1.*

24. Documentary footage

Date: 7 February 1964
Time: afternoon and evening
Location: Plaza Hotel, New York City
Length: 6:37

We are fortunate that the Maysles film crew was allowed access to the Beatles' suite within the first few hours of their stay in America. The Fabs are seen watching *CBS Evening News* coverage of their airport press conference just a few hours earlier. They laugh uproariously at their own quips, and after anchor Walter Cronkite signs off ("That's the way it is, Friday, February 7, 1964"), Ringo switches to NBC.

The phone rings, and Ringo answers: "We're waiting for a very important call from London which you're blocking the line on." It turns out to be reporter Maureen Cleave, who had flown across the Atlantic with them. *The Huntley-Brinkley Report* begins, but their "important call" finally comes through, and Paul greets the caller: "Hello, Brian Bathtubes!" (They didn't miss anything, as Chet Huntley patronizingly refused to air any of the airport footage.)

Paul reads a transcript of their airport press conference in the evening paper, and they are all amused by a radio commercial for "the kind of wine that quenches a man's thirst . . . the Atomic wine . . . they took their time when they made this wine!" "It's a funny place, this America, though, isn't it?" reflects Paul. He tries to get the cameraman to "defy convention" and include a shot of the sound engineer's hand holding the microphone, which he reluctantly does, to their great delight.

They seem a bit overwhelmed, unsure what to do with themselves. George reiterates that he's tired, and John is still laughing at Murray the K's antics: "What was he saying about 'happening'?" Ringo says it's really eleven o'clock, and Paul informs the others that his watch is still set to London time. One thing they all agree on is that if they try going to bed early, they'll all be up before sunrise. In the end, only George would turn in early, due to his encroaching flu, but none of the others would attempt to leave the hotel on their first night in America.

RELEASE HISTORY

Three minutes and forty-nine seconds of this footage was included in the TV special *What's Happening! The Beatles in the U.S.A.,* which circulates on video. Most of it, plus an extra 52 seconds of footage, was released on *The First U.S. Visit.* Forty-one seconds of unique footage ("defy convention!") appears in BBC TV's *Grandstand* report, which circulates on video (see the February 22 entry).

25. Radio interview J, R

Date: 8 February 1964
Time: morning
Location: Plaza Hotel, New York City (via telephone)
Interviewer: Bud Ballou
Broadcast: WOLF-AM, Syracuse
Length: 0:46

Syracuse DJ Bud Ballou was one of many who got through to the Plaza Hotel for a phone interview before Brian Epstein was able to put a stop to the practice. Here Ringo and John say a few words before departing for lunch, leaving George to recuperate: "Yeah, we're keeping him in bed now. We're all going out to eat, but he's gotta stay in." Not surprisingly, Ballou tries to give WOLF credit for discovering the Beatles ahead of the game, claiming that his station was "one of the very first in the nation" to play "I Want to Hold Your Hand." Ringo is polite but unimpressed, while John merely urges the handful of listeners who haven't bought Beatle records yet to get on the ball.

RELEASE HISTORY

1986: This good-quality interview was released on the LP *The History of Syracuse Music, Volume 12/13.*

26. Newsreel/documentary footage J, P, R

Date: 8 February 1964
Time: early afternoon
Location: Central Park and limo, New York City
Length: 6:18

As George's sister Louise, visiting from Illinois, took care of her little brother, a secret operation managed to smuggle his bandmates out to Central Park. Secret to fans, that is, but not the press, since the object was to give still and newsreel cameras a chance to shoot the group in a location other than their hotel suite.

With the Maysles brothers rolling, John, Paul, and Ringo posed over and over with their arms spread wide ("Do it once more!" Ringo: "I haven't stopped!"), pointing at the sky ("Hey, Beatles! Where do the birds fly?") and shouting while standing on rocks at the edge of a lake. They enjoyed a lunch of cheeseburgers and malted milks at a boathouse café. More film is shot outside the boathouse, as Paul decides to "reintroduce" his Pepsi transistor radio for the sake of continuity.

In the back of the limo, filming continues with squad car 654 escorting John, Paul, and Ringo to CBS Studio 50 for a 1:30 rehearsal of *The Ed Sullivan Show* (they also took a quick trip through Harlem, but were disappointed at being unable to get out and explore the Apollo Theater). Paul tunes in to WINS and hears plugs for a "Battle of the Beatles" and the documentary *Meet the Beatles,* airing the following evening at 7 p.m. The ad promises a recording of the Beatles "reading their own poetry," which baffles Paul: "We ain't writ no poetry." Of course, John had, and the WINS documentary would include a tape of his recitation of "The Neville Club" from the *Dateline London* interview (see the December 10, 1963, entry).

Paul also talks back to a Kent cigarette ad touting the "Micronite Filter." "Marvelous radio over here," muses Ringo. As they approach the studio, John notices that fans are lining the streets, though he assumed their arrival was a secret. As the car stops momentarily, a group of girls runs up and pounds at the window, shrieking and waving. Paul is flirtatious ("Hi, girls!"), but John worries how they'll get in the building and suggests making a dash for it.

RELEASE HISTORY

This footage was included in the TV special *What's Happening! The Beatles in the U.S.A.,* which circulates on video; most of it, plus an extra 1:06 of Central Park footage, was released on *The First U.S. Visit* (some of it during the closing credits). The latter release has the limo scene spliced in the wrong spot chronologically, making it appear as though it was filmed on the way from Kennedy Airport to the Plaza the previous day. Twenty-two seconds of silent footage of the Central Park jaunt appears in BBC TV's *Grandstand* report, which circulates on video (see entry #59). Thirteen seconds, including unique footage of Ringo, John, and Paul leaving the Plaza and entering a car, is included in the newsreel *Beatlemania Grips Gotham.*

27. Radio interview **G**

Date: 8 February 1964
Location: Plaza Hotel, New York City (via telephone)
Interviewer: Ed Rudy
Length: 13:35

George's illness didn't keep him down for long. By afternoon's end, he was well enough to travel to the CBS studio to pose for publicity photos with the Beatles and Ed Sullivan. Around 4 p.m., he went to a suite at the Savoy-Hilton where a representative of the Rickenbacker guitar company sold him one of their first twelve-string electric guitars.

While remaining in bed, George also participated in Beatlemania by proxy, chatting with Murray the K and other disc jockeys and reporters via telephone. One such aspirant was Ed Rudy, a newsman who was putting together a documentary LP of their visit and actually managed to record John calling him "the fifth Beatle." But compared to Murray Kaufman, his access was severely limited. His biggest coup was taping this lengthy phone conversation with George, which would take up one side of the album.

At one point, Rudy tells George, "If it seems strange that I don't answer you, I'm trying to get you as clear as possible without interrupting you." The reason for this would become clear when Rudy released a promotional version of his album turning this conversation into an open-end interview, complete with script. One Miami DJ who took advantage of this recording was WQAM's Charlie Murdock, who released parts of it as an "exclusive" interview on the souvenir EP *Yeah Yeah Yeah—The Beatles in the U.S.A.*, dubbing in the questions himself.

The interview is sort of a Beatles primer, with George relating the origins of the group's name, haircut, and musical style. He describes the differences between mods and rockers, saying most American teens would be looked on as the latter in England, as mod fashion hadn't caught on yet in the States. Rudy misunderstands: "Rocker kind of means square, doesn't it?" He's also uncertain of how to refer to "Johnny Lennon. Or Jack—what do you call him? Jack or John?" For his part, George is puzzled by Rudy's use of the term "double date" ("How d'you mean?").

Rudy jokingly calls George a "has-been" merely because most of the Beatles' ambitions (London Palladium, play for the queen, top the U.S. charts) have already been achieved. Asked if he'd consider emigrating permanently to America, George diplomatically says they still have to visit places like Australia, New Zealand, and South Africa, where their popularity is ascending, and that it wouldn't be fair to the British fans to pack up and leave.

RELEASE HISTORY

1964: This interview was released on the LP *The Beatles American Tour with Ed Rudy,* the open-end version appeared on the promo LP *Beatlemania Tour Coverage.*

27a. Radio interview **G**

Date: 8 February 1964
Location: Plaza Hotel, New York City (via telephone)
Interviewer: Jack Diamond
Broadcast: WSPR-AM, Springfield
Length: 4:59

While convalescing at the Plaza, George also spoke with Jack Diamond of the Springfield, Massachusetts, station WSPR, even taping a brief promo for Diamond, "your leader in the Springfield area."

George reveals that this is his second trip to the United States, and that he loves American TV and radio. He says the Beatles will return to England on the eighteenth (this was before their Miami vacation got extended) and release a new single in March, and goes on to describe the premise of their upcoming movie. After explaining what Beatle Boots are, George adds that it was in fact Paul's cousin who gave him a haircut ("I had one yesterday") just before they left London.

RELEASE HISTORY

This interview circulates in good quality among collectors.

27b. TV promo

Date: 8 February 1964
Time: afternoon
Location: Studio 50, New York City
Broadcast: CBS
Length: 0:05

When George arrived at the TV studio for a photo call, Ed Sullivan took the opportunity to tape a brief promo for the February 14 Miami Beach telecast. It features all four Beatles and Ed, flanked by photographers, gazing up at a camera positioned onstage. While Sullivan plugs his upcoming guests, the Beatles remain silent.

RELEASE HISTORY

This footage circulates on video.

28. Radio interview

Date: 8 February 1964
Time: evening
Location: Plaza Hotel, New York City (via telephone)
Interviewer: Murray Kaufman
Broadcast: live
WINS-AM, New York City
Length: 7:23

The Beatles fell head over heels for American radio, and Brian Epstein had to continually lecture them about giving away free publicity to any station that got through to the Plaza suite. Special dispensation was apparently given to WINS disc jockey Murray the K. For whatever reason, he got preferential treatment from the start, and the Beatles spent a couple of hours this evening participating in his live *Swingin' Soiree* show, requesting and announcing records and generally acting loony.

Some of this was filmed from Murray's end by the Maysles brothers at the WINS studio. Murray would become such a major presence in the film, they would name the finished documentary after one of his sayings, "What's Happening!" Ringo is heard discussing "Love Me Do," and Paul (with a touch of echo added for style) introduces Marvin Gaye's "Pride and Joy."

George seemed to be the most willing (and John the least) to gab with Murray, as a 2:10 excerpt from the show released on Murray's souvenir EP demonstrates. WINS had been giving away Beatles sweatshirts, and George asks Murray if he's wearing one right now, telling him to get rid of the "cuckoo" Submarine Race Watchers sweatshirt he'd worn the previous evening (photos from Miami Beach a few days later show George and Ringo sporting their S.R.W. shirts).

Murray asks how he'd fare in England, and George says that while there are no British DJs who wear "ski pants and funny hats," there is "a mad fellow" called Jimmy Saville who carries a bag of tricks and rides around on a chariot. Murray is intrigued: "On a chariot? Well, that's snappy. That's boily, baby." He plays George the lengthy "Harambe" chant of the Submarine Race Watcher, telling him that's how a girl knows you're happenin'. George isn't so sure. "I think the girl would have gone by the time you'd finish saying that."

There's also an off-air recording of each Beatle doing a WINS promo for Murray, which comes from a later rebroadcast (early in 1965). Murray reprimands John for not including the word "baby" in his promo: "Will you try that again, old boy?" John retorts, "Okay, old man!" Paul plugs "the Murray K Show" [sic] and jokingly tells Murray he's fired. Ringo exclaims, "It's the gear, baby!" Murray is puzzled by the expression, but seems happy to learn a new bit of slang.

RELEASE HISTORY

1965: The interview with George was released on the EP *The Beatles & Murray the K: As It Happened,* copied on the LP and CD *Timeless II.* The WINS studio footage was included in the TV special *What's Happening! The Beatles in the U.S.A.* and released on *The First U.S. Visit.* The remainder circulates in fair quality from an off-air tape.

29. TV performance

Date: 9 February 1964
Time: 2:30 p.m.
Location: Studio 50, New York City
Producer: Bob Precht
Host: Ed Sullivan
Broadcast: 23 February 1964, 8:00–9:00 p.m.
CBS
The Ed Sullivan Show

[A.] intro (0:27)
[B.] Twist and Shout (2:34)
[C.] intro (0:04)
[D.] Please Please Me (1:55)
[E.] outro (0:17)
[F.] intro (0:03)
[G.] I Want to Hold Your Hand (2:24)
[H.] outro (0:46)

The Beatles got an early start this morning, with a 9:30 call for camera rehearsals. By now, George was well enough to attend (Neil Aspinall had stood in for him the previous day). The closing credit sequence of *The First U.S. Visit* includes an 8-second clip of the Beatles arriving at the studio (the Roseland Ballroom can be seen on West Fifty-second Street in the background), presumably from unused footage filmed by the Maysles brothers. After lunch, they went into makeup at 2 p.m. for the dress rehearsal, which would be videotaped in front of 728 lucky fans.

Journalist Michael Braun, who was present, described the occasion as "rehearsal for that evening's show as well as the taping of two additional songs for the program in three weeks' time." That does seem to be the case, as the two unique songs (**B** and **D**) are performed with a different stage design compared to "I Want to Hold Your Hand." More significantly, the latter song features the exact same camera cues and angles used in the live broadcast that night, so it's presumably from the end of the dress rehearsal itself.

When it was eventually broadcast, the Beatles opened the show (after the first commercial break). Ed's intro (**A**) refers to how "darn sorry" everyone on the show is to be saying good-bye to "these youngsters from Liverpool, England." It's not clear whether this was taped during the dress rehearsal or at a later date. "Twist and Shout" and "Please Please Me" receive enthusiastic cheers. Although neither had been released on a single in the United States yet, both appeared on the *Introducing the Beatles* LP, which was getting tons of airplay.

Ed packed the episode full of British acts, and it wasn't until Pinky and Perky, Morecambe and Wise, Acker Bilk, Gordon and Sheila Macrae, Dave Barry, Cab Calloway, and Morty Gunty had graced the stage that the Beatles returned to close the show. After "I Want to Hold Your Hand" (**G**), Ed strolls over to shake hands with each Beatle (climbing on Ringo's drum riser) and eggs on the audience: "Now, all right . . . come on, let's hear it!"

Everything had gone smoothly, and the Beatles insisted on visiting the audio control booth to confer with the sound engineers. The proper microphone levels and balances were marked on the mixing board with chalk, and the Beatles returned to their hotel to unwind before the "really big shoo."

NOTE

For this and their two subsequent performances (that evening and the eleventh in Washington, D.C.), the Beatles' guitars are tuned a half step below concert pitch. Most likely this was accidental, because after John took delivery of a new Rickenbacker guitar in Miami on the fourteenth and fifteenth, they were suddenly back in tune for both *Ed Sullivan* broadcasts of the sixteenth. Presumably the error was discovered when putting strings on John's new guitar, which would take the place of his earlier model from that point onward.

RELEASE HISTORY

In 2003, this entire show was released on an excellent-quality DVD, *Ed Sullivan Presents the Beatles.* A kinescope of the August 23 rebroadcast of the Beatles' set also circulates on video (it has a slightly different audience shot bridging **B** and **D** in addition to a different intro from Ed). All three songs were released on the video *The First U.S. Visit,* although shots of the evening audience are inserted between **D** and **G,** and **H** is intercut with unrelated footage. The *Anthology* documentary includes **D.** The entire soundtrack (**A–H**) was bootlegged on LPs such as *Ed's Really Big Beatle Blasts* and *The Beatles Conquer America.* It's best found in excellent quality on the bootleg CD *The Ultimate Collection, Volume 1: TV Appearances.*

30. Documentary footage

Date: 9 February 1964
Time: 6:15 p.m.
Location: Plaza Hotel, New York City
Length: 8:02

Before the all-important live *Ed Sullivan* broadcast, the Beatles went back to their Plaza suite for a break. Unfortunately, they didn't have much chance to rest in peace, as not only were the Maysles crew filming, but the ubiquitous Murray the K was hanging around, phoning in to WINS with an on-the-spot report and doing his best to rope the Beatles into saying a few words on the air.

Paul wisely stays out of it, shouting a station ID across the room (mutating "WINS 1010" into "Winston Churchill"), and John slumps on the couch, clearly wanting to be left alone. Ringo is full of enthusiasm as always, telling Murray to play "swingin' records . . . None of that drag stuff." John wants to hear "Corrina, Corrina," perhaps thinking of Bob Dylan's version on the LP *The Freewheelin' Bob Dylan.* George asks to hear a James Ray song, "Got My Mind Set on You," which of course would top the charts in George's 1987 cover version. They're also seen listening to the Impressions' new single, "Talking About My Baby," no doubt another George request.

Murray enthuses about the *Ed Sullivan* dress rehearsal, plugs WINS' *Meet the Beatles* documentary (coming up in forty-four minutes), and shouts at John to "Wake up! You gotta go on soon!" The weary Lennon gets his revenge when there is some confusion over one of their song titles:

Murray: What's the name of that song, mate?
John: "Love Me Do," wacker!
Murray: Ah, you see . . . ah, this is the wacker speaking here. The wacker over here, and . . .
John: Wacker the K.
Murray: Yeah, Wacker the K!

At this point, a member of the Beatles' party marvels, "We have ten million people listening to this?" George takes the phone to chat about the condition of his throat with the DJ (possibly Paul Parker), who segues directly into reading ad copy for a furniture sale, causing much hilarity. Murray finally hangs up, and Ringo tells the others to get ready, or they'll be late.

John is seen playing a chord sequence similar to the verse of "Strawberry Fields Forever" on a melodica, and George informs Cynthia, who has decided to stay in the room, what time and channel to watch them on. (This clip is seen only in *The First U.S. Visit.*) Paul and George enact a skit using their transistor radio earpieces as hearing aids, and they finally march out the door, moments away from a career-defining performance.

RELEASE HISTORY

This footage was included in the TV special *What's Happening! The Beatles in the U.S.A.,* which circulates on video. Most of it, plus an extra 41 seconds of footage, was released on *The First U.S. Visit.*

31. Newsreel footage

Date: 9 February 1964
Time: ca. 7:00 p.m.
Location: Studio 50, New York City
Length: 0:50

This brief newsreel interview was filmed outside the *Ed Sullivan Show* studios, most likely as the Beatles were on their way in for the live telecast (judging from their clothing and the lighting). Paul defines "Beatles" thusly: "Well, you've seen those little crawly things, haven't ya? Well, we're big crawly things." Asked to name a favorite song, George plucks "White Christmas" out of thin air. John tries to top this with "God Rule the Wenceslas Kingdom," but the reporter is intrigued by George's response: "That's not rock-and-roll!" George demurs, and the boys croon a bit of it to demonstrate, with John holding out his cap to solicit donations.

RELEASE HISTORY

1998: 22 seconds of this interview were included on the bootleg CD *The Ultimate Beatles Christmas Collection;* the full clip circulates on video among collectors.

32. TV performance

Date: 9 February 1964
Time: 8:00–9:00 p.m.
Location: Studio 50, New York City
Producer: Bob Precht
Host: Ed Sullivan
Broadcast: live
CBS
The Ed Sullivan Show

[A.] **intro** (0:23)
[B.] **All My Loving** (2:06)
[C.] **intro** (0:04)
[D.] **Till There Was You** (2:08)
[E.] **intro** (0:03)
[F.] **She Loves You** (2:18)
[G.] **outro** (0:41)
[H.] **intro** (0:13)
[I.] **I Saw Her Standing There** (2:35)
[J.] **intro** (0:04)
[K.] **I Want to Hold Your Hand** (2:25)
[L.] **outro** (1:04)

When 73 million people switched to their CBS affiliate at 8 p.m. on the evening of February 9, 1964, many were already Beatle fans. Some were tuning in out of curiosity, others tolerating it for the sake of their children. Here's what they saw.

The curtain opens and an announcer introduces the show and its sponsors. Ed takes center stage and cuts right to the chase: "You know, something very nice happened, and the Beatles got a great kick out of it. Just received a wire, they did, from Elvis Presley and Colonel Tom Parker wishing them a tremendous success in our country." The suspense is prolonged with words from Aero Shave and Griffin Shoe Polish, then it's back to Ed, master of understatement. "Now, yesterday and today, our theater's been jammed with newspapermen and hundreds of photographers from all over the nation, and these veterans agree with me that the city never has witnessed the excitement stirred by these youngsters from Liverpool who call themselves the Beatles. Now, tonight, you're gonna twice be entertained by them: right now, and again in the second half of our show. Ladies and gentlemen . . ."

The rest is lost in a wash of screams, and at 8:03, the camera cuts to four musicians surrounded by enormous white arrows, as though anyone needed guidance in where to fix their gaze. Paul counts to five and sings, "Close your eyes . . ." as the country falls to its collective knees. There is no trace of the nervousness that permeated the Decca audition, their first EMI session, or the Royal Variety show. Just a group seizing the moment, playing with energy and charm, not rushing the tempo, singing with confidence.

Paul is a grinning bobblehead doll come to life, bouncing off his left foot. George twists his right foot to and fro, receiving a cheer when he steps to the microphone to sing the last verse of "All My Loving" to Paul's harmony. ("His throat is okay!") A close-up of Ringo, nodding his head in time and singing along, is the cue for more screaming. John bends at the knees, taking it all in but showing little overt emotion. As the song ends, all four bow in perfect synchronization.

Now it's time to win the parents over. Paul croons "Till There Was You" in pure and sweet tones, and George recreates his melodic guitar solo flawlessly. Cut to the audience, where a girl is watching intently through binoculars, licking her lips. Her friend's tongue is stuck out in an imagined French kiss. Captions appear on the screen identifying each Beatle: PAUL (the girls are too busy drooling at him to notice the monitors), RINGO (applause as they start to catch on), GEORGE (cheers and whistling), JOHN—SORRY, GIRLS, HE'S MARRIED! (screams of surprise and dismay).

As the last chord of "Till There Was You" dies out, they bow again smartly and deliver the knockout blow. Paul's "One, two!" and a quick tom-tom roll are the only warnings heralding "She Loves You." Although John's vocal microphone level is way too low (a helpful studio janitor had wiped those messy chalk marks from the mixing board between dress and air), it doesn't matter. The audience claps along in time, and each "ooh" and shake of the head cements their image for good.

By 8:10, it is over. The Beatles have sung three songs, spoken no words, and already thousands of kids across the country have decided to take up the guitar and form a band. Ed informs viewers that the Beatles will "be back in the second half of the show after you've enjoyed Georgia Brown, the star of *Oliver!,* Tessie O'Shea, one of the stars of *The Girl Who Came to Supper.* But right now, a word about Anacin."

Undoubtedly, most families choose to discuss what they have just seen rather than enjoy the aforementioned acts. Magician Fred Kapps performs a card trick, Frank Gorshin does impressions, McCall and Brill perform a comedy sketch. Ads for All detergent, Pillsbury, and Kent cigarettes fill more time, and at 8:46, Ed is back to remind everyone he's got the Beatles for three straight weeks.

The microphone levels are still not sorted out, but the Beatles sing both sides of their Capitol single, which millions of people have heard by now. They still don't say a word to the audience, but drop their instruments after the final bow to shake hands with a triumphant Sullivan before disappearing backstage. Ed thanks the New York Police Department for handling "thousands of youngsters," and the acrobatic team of Wells and the Four Fays are left to close the show, perhaps the least enviable slot in the history of show business.

RELEASE HISTORY

In 2003, this entire show was released on the excellent-quality DVD *Ed Sullivan Presents the Beatles*. Much of it (**A–F, H,** and **K**) was released on the video *The First U.S. Visit*. The *Anthology* documentary includes **A** and **B.** The entire soundtrack (**A–L**) was bootlegged on LPs such as *Ed's Really Big Beatle Blasts* and *The Beatles Conquer America*. It's best found in excellent quality on the bootleg CD *The Ultimate Collection, Vol. 1: TV Appearances*. **B** and part of **A** were officially released on the CD *Anthology 1*.

33. Radio interview — P, G

Date: 9 February 1964
Time: evening
Location: Studio 50, New York City
Interviewer: Carroll James
Broadcast: WWDC-AM, Washington, D.C.
Length: 0:53

As the Beatles changed in their dressing rooms (52 and 53) following the show, legendary jazz trumpeter Dizzy Gillespie was backstage trying to gain entrance. Brian Somerville had no idea who he was, but luckily journalist Al Aronowitz, writing for the *Saturday Evening Post,* vouched for him and he was allowed in for a visit.

Washington, D.C., disc jockey Carroll James, who had been one of the first to play "I Want to Hold Your Hand" in the United States, had watched the show with George's sister, Louise, and was also backstage. When he saw Dizzy arrive, Carroll quickly switched on his tape recorder to capture the meeting.

Dizzy tries on Carroll's Beatle wig and Paul cries, "Good ol' Dizzy!" For his part, Dizzy says he hasn't heard their music, but "just came by to *look* at them. To see what this was all about." George starts to chat about how he seems to be recovered from his flu, but a CBS security guard comes over and makes Carroll shut off his recorder.

RELEASE HISTORY

1984: This interview was released on a mail-order EP, *The Carroll James Interview with the Beatles*. A slightly longer version circulates on tape.

34. Documentary footage

Date: 9 February 1964
Time: evening
Location: Plaza Hotel and Peppermint Lounge, New York City
Length: 5:11

With police clearing the route ahead of time, a limo rushed the Beatles from the *Ed Sullivan* studio back to the Plaza. The Maysles crew was waiting and filmed a bit of Paul walking down the hallway listening to his Pepsi radio. Also waiting was Murray the K, who joined the party for a late dinner at the Playboy Club.

After dinner, John, Cynthia, Paul, Ringo, Murray, and the film crew went to the Peppermint Lounge to twist the night away. Well, John and Paul actually sat at a table and tried their best to enjoy "the Four Younger Brothers, alias the American Beatles," a sort of tribute/rip-off act.

As the house band launches into "Money (That's What I Want)," Ringo climbs onto the dance floor, followed closely by a disheveled and ragged-looking Murray. Ringo works it on out with dancer Geri Miller, unleashing a pugilistic dance style. Murray does his best to keep up, but by "Peppermint Twist," he is back at the table cooling off with a drink. At 4 a.m., they finally leave the club and are filmed returning through the Plaza lobby, up the elevator, and back to their suite, where Mal is waiting up for them. John jokingly shields Cynthia with his coat as they stumble into their room.

RELEASE HISTORY

This footage was included in the TV special *What's Happening! The Beatles in the USA,* which circulates on video; most of it, plus an extra 14 seconds of the Peppermint Lounge sequence, was released on *The First U.S. Visit.*

35. Newsreel footage

Date: 10 February 1964
Time: afternoon
Location: Terrace Room, Plaza Hotel, New York City
Length: 1:55

Most of this day was devoted to meeting the press at a reception hall in the Plaza Hotel. A series of news conferences, award ceremonies, and individual interviews for radio, TV, print, and newsreel outlets kept the group occupied and unable to venture out and enjoy New York City for the entire day.

The Associated Press shot silent footage that afternoon when Capitol's Alan Livingston presented the group with gold records for the "I Want to Hold Your Hand" single and *Meet the Beatles*! LP. An AP reporter also interviewed the quartet, reading to them from that morning's review of their *Ed Sullivan* debut from *New York Times* music critic Theodore Strongin: "He said you had 'unresolved leading tones, a false modal frame, ending up as a plain diatonic.'" John's reply: "Well, we're gonna see a doctor about that." Paul points out that it's merely a rehash of William Mann's *London Times* article about "Aeolian cadences" and such. Ringo gives a fatalistic account of the origin of their haircut: "It just happened, y'know. Just wake up one day, and there you are!"

RELEASE HISTORY

This AP newsreel circulates on video among collectors. A 22-second excerpt was broadcast on BBC TV News February 11, 1964.

36. TV interview

Date: 10 February 1964
Time: afternoon
Location: Terrace Room, Plaza Hotel, New York City
Broadcast: CBS
Length: 2:31

This interview was conducted in the same location as that in the previous entry, with a reporter for CBS News doing the questioning this time. The most commonly seen portion comes at the start, as they are asked what the name "Beatles" means. John replies, "That's just a name. Y'know, like 'shoe.'" "We could have been called 'the Shoes' for all you know," adds Paul.

John laments that they are just as eager to meet their admirers as the fans are to meet them, but whenever they try to wave, police tell them to stop "inciting" the crowds. Ringo says they are a bit nervous about their upcoming Carnegie Hall concert, and John says they'd hoped more of the American artists they admired would be in town to meet them (Marvin Gaye, the Miracles, Mary Wells), but that most seem to be out on the road.

Ringo praises the New York City police detail protecting them, and Paul offers a "No comment" when asked about the most interesting offer he's received. Floundering for relevant questions, the reporter asks what they think of Britain's Keeler-Profumo political sex scandal. "It's great, yeah," says George cheerfully. Paul theorizes that the lukewarm critical reaction to their *Ed Sullivan* appearance might be explained by the broadcast's poor microphone balance, but stresses that the studio audience's reaction was "fantastic."

RELEASE HISTORY

1993: The majority of this interview was released on the CD *The Beatles Tapes Volume 2: Early Beatlemania 1963–1964,* missing a few seconds from the clip released on the video *Beatles 1962 to 1970.*

1995: A different excerpt of the interview was released on the CD *Rare Photos & Interview CD, Volume 1.*

37. Radio interview — J, P, R

Date: 10 February 1964
Location: Plaza Hotel, New York City
Interviewer: Ed Rudy
Length: 6:36

The Beatles' busy day wound up with a cocktail reception that merely meant more opportunities to be questioned by the eager American press. Ed Rudy was there to tape further "exclusive" Beatle interviews for his commercial and open-end LPs.

Ringo outlines plans for the rest of the year, the majority of which would change (trips to Israel and South Africa ended up being canceled). Paul commends the previous night's ecstatic audience, explains the origins of Ringo's stage name, and says they've achieved most of their ambitions (Palladium, America, Ed Sullivan). He also talks about their upcoming film and their night out at the Peppermint Lounge.

Asked what he thinks of American teenagers, John borrows a phrase from Murray the K: "They're what's happening, baby!" He points out that all the advance publicity could have killed them if they hadn't been prepared to live up to their advance billing. Rudy is skeptical about that, but John freely admits that their popularity is a fad that could pass at any moment: "We don't think we're gonna last forever. We're just gonna have a good time while it lasts, y'know."

Rudy asks for a definition of "the Beatle sound" and John says there is no such thing; the main difference between them and other rock groups is that their hit material is self-penned. Although Ringo hasn't composed any songs ("It's hard to write something on the drums, isn't it?"), they all contribute to the arrangements, worked out in the studio: "Because you write a song, and you get a sound in your head that you think it's gonna sound like, and it usually turns out different, y'know. We've given up trying to plan it too much before we go in."

RELEASE HISTORY

1964: These interviews were released on the LPs *The Beatles American Tour with Ed Rudy* and *1965 Talk Album—Ed Rudy with New U.S. Tour.* A further two minutes, apparently from Ed's promotional open-end LP, also circulates from a fair-quality off-air tape from KXOK in 1965, with DJ Johnny Rabbit reading the questions.

38. Radio interview — J, P, G

Date: 10 February 1964
Time: evening
Location: Baroque Room, Plaza Hotel, New York City
Interviewer: Fred Robbins
Broadcast: Radio Luxembourg *Assignment: Hollywood*
Length: 20:10

Radio personality Fred Robbins had a Sunday night show on New York's WNEW titled *Robbins' Nest,* but it was through Radio Luxembourg that the Beatles had heard his syndicated series, *Assignment: Hollywood.* He interviewed John and George for that show at the Plaza press reception, and Paul at what sounds like a much quieter location afterward.

John explains that Cynthia isn't present at the reception because she'd "probably just get lost in the crowd, y'know." Name-dropping his "good friend" Cliff Richard, Robbins repeatedly probes John to explain the reasons behind their success and their secret for remaining level-headed despite all the adulation. John puts it down to a historical cycle: "They've been doing it for years. They did it for—what is it, Rudy Valentini . . . or whatever his name was."

Asked to list his musical influences, John names the usual suspects (Presley, Berry, Perkins, Little Richard), but Robbins barks up the wrong tree when he names crooners such as Tony Bennett and Andy Williams. John scoffs, "*nothing* like that!," but he does admit to a fondness for Peggy Lee ("I can listen to her all day") and having seen the light about Ella Fitzgerald. John also relates the origins of the fans' jelly bean–tossing ritual, and Robbins suggests the Beatles go into the candy business to capitalize.

At one point, Robbins asks "Johnny" what his parents have to say, and he starts to reply that he has only a father, but amends that: "I haven't got any! You'll have to goof that bit." Indeed, the final broadcast edit omits this embarrassing exchange as well as a near-reference to wife-swapping and a few other extraneous pauses.

George is clearly familiar with *Assignment: Hollywood,* as he expresses a wish for some of the sponsor's product: "I could do with a bit of Noxzema, 'cause I'm feelin' a bit scabby today." He reveals that most of the Beatles' income goes directly into NEMS, with each Beatle receiving a stipend of 30 or 40 pounds each week to spend on necessities. After some chat about how the Beatles chose their name and hairstyles, George tosses in a Murray the K quote ("You're what's happenin', baby!") and says he doesn't want to get married for a few years.

Robbins' final interview is conducted while Paul tries to enjoy a meal. Not only does he sound distracted, Paul is clearly exhausted by the day's events and has trouble collecting his thoughts. ("When you've got a hectic day . . . it can be hectic." "Y'know, there's so many people who've proven it's a good—proven? Proven, I don't know whether that's right.") He sums up his reaction to New York City with what he admits is a corny remark: "It's breathtaking." Rather than go out and have their breath taken away, the weary Beatles remained in their suite for the rest of the night, recuperating and mentally preparing for their first American concert the next day.

RELEASE HISTORY

1984: These interviews were released on the cassette *Historic Interviews: The Beatles' First Day in America,* sold primarily through the Beatlefest catalog. The follow-up cassette, *Historic Interviews, Volume 2,* contains the broadcast edit of John's interview.

38a. Documentary footage

Date: 11 February 1964
Time: afternoon
Location: train from New York City to Washington, D.C.
Length: 11:01

The Maysles crew did some filming in Brian Epstein's suite at the Plaza as he conducted business with the help of Brian Somerville and newly hired assistant Wendy Hanson. On the morning of February 10, he is seen dictating a telegram of thanks to Elvis Presley and Colonel Tom Parker. He also takes a call from London informing him that "She Loves You" is now at number 7 in America (why he needed to learn this from overseas is unclear). He correctly predicts it'll climb all the way to number 1. Brian then leaves the Plaza and chats in the back of a cab about American radio and the musical *Hello, Dolly.*

On the morning of the eleventh, Brian throws on a scarf to "see the boys off to Washington," as Hanson informs a caller. Due to a heavy snowstorm blanketing the Northeast, the Beatles insisted on taking a train down to Washington for their concert that evening rather than flying. A private sleeper car, the King George, was hastily booked for their use, and they boarded it at Penn Station in New York around 1 p.m. Brian would stay behind to deal with further business matters and fly down in time for the concert. Cynthia Lennon and, predictably, Murray the K would make the train journey along with the Beatles.

Several scenes were filmed by the Maysles brothers on the trip down, including the Beatles experimenting with David Maysles' tape recorder. John listens to his own voice through headphones, with a slight delay, and enthuses, "Do 'Be-Bop-A-Lula'!" (reminded of Gene Vincent's recording, slathered in heavy tape echo).

Ringo worries about the weather, hoping they will be able to return to New York and fly to Miami without any further snowstorms. He also flirts with a charming little girl from Virginia, who kisses him on the cheek, compliments his singing, and invites him to visit her in Richmond. He escorts her down the corridor to meet his mates (Paul asks teasingly, "Are you engaged to Ringo Starr?").

Paul pokes fun at American TV's propensity for slipping advertisements into regular programming. He imitates a kids' show host who, in the midst of battling the dreaded Battu, suddenly wished for some "Creamy Porridge Oats" to give him strength. Even more on-target is his pitch for Coca-Cola worked into a newscast about a tense situation in China.

RELEASE HISTORY

Most of this footage was released on the DVD *The First U.S. Visit;* some is available only in the TV special *What's Happening! The Beatles in the U.S.A.*

39. Newsreel/Documentary footage

Date: 11 February 1964
Time: 3:00 p.m.
Location: Union Station, Washington, D.C.
Length: 4:41

A British Pathé newsreel team awaited the group's arrival at Washington's Union Station, along with three thousand zealous fans. Apparently Pathé editors decided that two newsreels about the Beatles was enough for one week, as their 2:05 of footage exists only in the form of silent offcuts. It includes scenes of fans trudging through the heavy snow outside the station, a WWDC WELCOMES THE BEATLES banner, and the Beatles, Murray, and Brian Somerville emerging from the train.

Associated Press cameras also shot 2:17 of footage covering basically the same material: the train pulling in, fans waving and holding signs and albums, and the Beatles walking slowly down the platform, engulfed by a crowd of reporters and onlookers. The Maysles crew filmed a fur-hatted and bewildered Ringo declaring, "It's great being here in New York!" "Washington," the cameraman informs him. "Oh, is that where it is? I don't know, I just keep moving."

RELEASE HISTORY

The Pathé newsreel outtakes and AP newsreel circulate on video, as does the TV special *What's Happening! The Beatles in the USA,* which contains the Maysles footage (most of which was released on the home video *The First U.S. Visit*).

40. Press conference

Date: 11 February 1964
Time: afternoon
Location: Washington Coliseum, Washington, D.C.
Length: 5:58

After checking in to their seventh-floor suite at the Shoreham Hotel (where Cynthia Lennon opted to stay behind, missing the concert), the Beatles were chauffeured to the Washington Coliseum. When they arrived, a press conference was held onstage (actually a boxing ring). The Beatles stood behind a cluster of microphones, while their press agent Brian Somerville took questions and repeated them into the microphones for all to hear.

Several fragments circulate from a tape made by disc jockey Carroll James, who dubs in most of the questions himself. George recounts the group's history, which leads them all to sing: "We've been together now for forty years . . ." This line, from the music-hall standard "My Old Dutch," was one of many Beatle inside jokes that cropped up in countless interviews. Someone asks whether they squabble with one another, and John replies, "Only in the morning!" Another reporter wonders if their hairdos looked the same before they all met. John: "Only in the morning!" Asked what they think of President Johnson, Ringo queries, "Does he buy our records?"

Also circulating is Bill Seaby and Paul Palmer's report for radio station WCAO. This includes further exchanges covering topics such as who writes their songs (George: "Brian Sommerville does the lyrics"), the origins of the names Beatles and Ringo, and the possibility of the Beatles being knighted (John: "Can you imagine Sir Ringo?").

A bit of this press conference was also filmed by network news (see following entry), including a slight overlap with these excerpts.

RELEASE HISTORY

1984: Some press conference fragments were released on a mail-order EP, *The Carroll James Interview with the Beatles;* they also circulate from a tape source.

2004: The WCAO recordings first appeared on the CD-R *Baggy Sweegin' U.S.A.!*

41. TV interview

Date: 11 February 1964
Time: afternoon
Location: Washington Coliseum, Washington, D.C.
Length: 5:23

This footage apparently originates in a shared network news feed and captures a bit of the press conference followed by individual interviews with reporters from CBS and NBC. The CBS reporter asks whether they'll be meeting President Johnson's daughters (George: "Didn't know they were on the show!"). The White House actually issued a press statement explaining that as it was a school night and they had homework, the Johnson girls would not be able to attend (never mind that the following day was a holiday).

The CBS reporter concludes by asking if they've heard of Walter Cronkite; although they'd watched him the night they arrived in New York, only George recognizes the name (John guesses he's on NBC). John recalls a reporter from NBC who had compared them to woolly mammoths the previous day in New York. Meanwhile, another NBC reporter steps to the bank of microphones as the Fabs sort out who is from what network and Paul lights everyone's cigarette.

The reporter presses them for a reason behind their popularity ("must be the weather," says John) and asks about their upcoming schedule. At this point, they are still planning to return to London on the seventeenth, the day after their second live *Ed Sullivan Show* appearance. They reel off a list of places in which they've topped the charts (United States, Hong Kong, Sweden, Australia, Denmark, Finland, France) and John reflects how odd it is to see "funny records" from early in their career topping the chart in other countries.

The reporter pounces upon this comment, asking if they call their own records "funny," but George patiently clarifies that by "funny," John meant it was "peculiar" that old records such as *Please Please Me* should still be able to sell so well. The reporter then asks whether they find their own songs to be musical. John spells it out for him: "Obviously they're musical, because it's music, isn't it? Y'know, instruments make music, and that's—it's a record. Even if it's not classical."

RELEASE HISTORY

1993: The soundtrack to this interview was released on the CD *The Beatles Tapes, Volume 2: Early Beatlemania 1963–1964;* the footage circulates in mediocre quality on video (my copy has a blue tint).

41a. Radio interview — J, G, R

Date: 11 February 1964
Time: afternoon
Location: Washington Coliseum, Washington, D.C.
Interviewer: Bill Seaby, Paul Palmer
Broadcast: WCAO-AM, Baltimore
Length: 3:42

Bill Seaby and Paul Palmer conducted individual interviews with at least three Beatles following the press conference. George says the Beatles' music is aimed at teenagers but doesn't place any age limit on their potential audience. John talks about their imminent recording plans and explains why the American market is currently saturated with Beatles records on several labels. Ringo briefly discusses the group's evolution ("There was five altogether, then one died, and then I replaced the other drummer").

RELEASE HISTORY

2004: These interviews first appeared on the CD-R *Baggy Sweegin' U.S.A.!*

41b. Radio interview

Date: 11 February 1964
Time: afternoon
Location: Washington Coliseum, Washington, D.C.
Broadcast: WMUC-AM, College Park
Length: 0:21

Cornered just after the press conference, John agreed to tape a couple of promos (backed with "She Loves You" and "I'll Get You" in postproduction) for WMUC, a radio station in College Park, Maryland, he probably never heard once in his life.

RELEASE HISTORY

2004: These promos first appeared on the CDR *Baggy Sweegin' U.S.A.!*

42. Radio interview

Date: 11 February 1964
Time: 5:05 p.m.
Location: Washington Coliseum, Washington, D.C.
Interviewer: Carroll James
Broadcast: WWDC-AM, Washington, D.C.
Length: 9:02

After the press conference, the Beatles dropped by WWDC's remote studio at the Coliseum for a highly entertaining interview with Carroll James. WWDC had supposedly been the first U.S. station to air "I Want to Hold Your Hand" when a young listener, Marsha Albert, wrote in to request the song. James arranged for a BOAC stewardess to fly over a copy from London and had Albert introduce the first airing on December 17, 1963, even taping the moment for posterity. Dubs of the song spread to other U.S. stations, hastening Capitol's rush release of the single the day after Christmas.

After recounting his previous brief encounter with the group in New York (see the February 9 entry), James asks some questions from listeners. John chooses steak and chips as his favorite food, and Paul describes a wild scene at their Belfast concert the previous November when "police on mounted dogs" failed to hold back the crowd behind crash barriers. Ringo says he owns "about two thousand, seven hundred and sixty-one" rings, and invites fans to send more to the Fan Club offices in London: "Make sure they're gold, I only wear gold!"

George admits that none of them are sports fans, although he enjoys watching motor racing. Ringo can't think of any drummers he admires, but John suggests "Big Deaf Arthur," who apparently plays with "Small Blind Johnny." After a chat about jelly beans, tea bags, and foreign languages (Paul speaks "fluent Shoe," and gives a demonstration), Marsha Albert is introduced to the Beatles.

James points out that John is called Chief Beatle ("Look, I don't call you names!") and asks him who is responsible for their haircuts ("It's bigger than both of us, Carroll"), but George steals the show with his quick and earnest response to the final question. Asked what career he had in mind at school, George replies, "I was going to be a baggy-sweeger." The others collapse in mirth as George goes on to give a job description: "Y'see, in every city there—they have twenty-five baggy-sweegers, and their job is go out to the airport each morning and then baggy-sweeging all along the line, man!"

RELEASE HISTORY

1984: This interview was released on a mail-order EP, *The Carroll James Interview with the Beatles.* An edited version (6:19) appears on the bootleg LP *The Beatles Conquer America.*

43. Radio interview R

Date: 11 February 1964
Time: evening
Location: Washington Coliseum, Washington, D.C.
Interviewer: Murray Kaufman
Broadcast: live
WINS-AM, New York City
Length: 3:05

As Carroll James was onstage introducing opening acts such as the Caravelles, Tommy Roe, and the Chiffons, Murray the K was backstage conducting a live broadcast for WINS radio. Ringo took a few minutes while getting ready to exchange "what's happenin', baby!'s" with Murray.

Ringo says they hope to reconnect with Tommy Roe after the show, having toured with him the previous year across Britain. Murray marvels at the impending meeting with British ambassador Sir David Ormsby Gore at a reception that evening. Ringo seems amused that the diplomat would impress a hip American disc jockey: "Have you had him on the show? He's swingin'!"

They discuss the train journey that brought them to the nation's capital, and Murray hints that listeners will learn of "a great surprise" in the upcoming weeks. Most likely this scoop was the invitation extended for Murray to visit the group in London in April (when he would participate in the *Around the Beatles* TV special and introduce them at the *New Musical Express* Poll-Winners' Concert).

Struggling to fill airtime, Murray reports on the color of Ringo's eyes (baby blue, baby!) and reminisces with Ringo about their escapades on the Peppermint Lounge dance floor. After some chat about the Coliseum's revolving stage, Murray finally lets Ringo depart for the dressing room. He tries to get Ringo to do a station ID, but after the tongue-lashing Brian had given his boys, none of them would fall for that trick again: "Everything's happenin', baby! With Murray the K on—I'm not allowed to say that!"

RELEASE HISTORY

This interview circulates in poor quality from an off-air home recording.

44. Concert

Date: 11 February 1964
Time: 8:31 p.m.
Location: Washington Coliseum, Washington, D.C.

[A.] **intro** (2:21)
[B.] **Roll Over Beethoven** (2:11)
[C.] **intro** (0:16)
[D.] **From Me to You** (1:48)
[E.] **intro** (0:57)
[F.] **I Saw Her Standing There** (2:38)
[G.] **intro** (0:46)
[H.] **This Boy** (2:13)
[I.] **intro** (0:34)
[J.] **All My Loving** (2:04)
[K.] **intro** (0:54)
[L.] **I Wanna Be Your Man** (2:04)
[M.] **intro** (1:03)
[N.] **Please Please Me** (1:51)
[O.] **intro** (0:33)
[P.] **Till There Was You** (2:04)
[Q.] **intro** (0:05)
[R.] **She Loves You** (2:14)
[S.] **intro** (1:31)
[T.] **I Want to Hold Your Hand** (2:20)
[U.] **intro** (1:07)
[V.] **Twist and Shout** (1:15)
[W.] **intro** (0:03)
[X.] **Long Tall Sally** (1:51)
[Y.] **outro** (0:02)

If the Beatles' *Ed Sullivan Show* performance was a Rolls-Royce gliding smoothly along a country lane, their American concert debut was a Jaguar screaming out of control down the M1. Their excitement at playing in the birthplace of most of the music they loved was matched by the crowd's excitement at being the first to see a live Beatles show. The atmosphere led to an adrenaline-fueled effort, with every song played harder, faster, louder, edgier than on TV two days earlier.

The show was videotaped for posterity by a CBS camera team, but not for network airing. Instead, kinescope transfers were made, edited together with performances by the Beach Boys and Lesley Gore, for screening in U.S. cinemas on the weekend of March 14 and 15. What is apparently the only surviving copy of the kinescope cuts off abruptly during the penultimate number, "Twist and Shout."

The original 2-inch videotape was unearthed in New York in 1995, allowing a first glimpse of the final song, "Long Tall Sally." Bits and pieces appear in *Anthology,* but hopefully Apple will release the entire video source someday. The Maysles crew was also present, and their *What's Happening!* documentary includes footage of Brian Epstein watching the concert, as well as "She Loves You" from an alternate angle to the CBS cameras.

The Beatles' entrance onstage is marked by a shower of jelly beans, a hail of deafening cheers, and a volley of blinding flashbulbs. While plugging in and tuning up, they realize Ringo's drum kit, on a rotating platform, is facing the opposite direction of the amplifiers. John says, "Turn these drums around," and Mal Evans and Brian Somerville run up to set things right.

A few hours earlier, John had scribbled down a set list for the concert on Shoreham Hotel stationery. How better to introduce yourself to a U.S. audience than with a Chuck Berry rocker? George plays the opening lick to "Roll Over Beethoven" tentatively, but Ringo is having none of that. His drum entrance kicks the song into high gear, and they are off and running. Unfortunately, one of the vocal microphones seems to be faulty, but George switches to a new one and continues singing, joined by John and Paul for the final chorus.

After a brief pause, John and Paul share a microphone for "From Me to You," then introduce "I Saw Her Standing There" with their "spastic clapping" schtick. During the latter half of the guitar solo, Ringo goes nuts, slamming the cymbals forcefully to propel the band forward. Before the next song, Mal Evans reappears to spin the drum kit around 180 degrees, and the others set up accordingly.

A beautifully impassioned rendition of "This Boy" is followed by "All My Loving." Paul then carries a microphone over to "our drummer . . . RINGO!" His rendition of "I Wanna Be Your Man" is largely inaudible, but the gleeful look on Ringo's face as he belts his heart out says it all. Another about-face for the next three songs, and then they rotate 90 degrees to their left, facing the side audience for the first time.

Paul thanks the fans "for buying this particular record . . . and giving us a chance to come here and see you in Washington," and they respond gratefully, clapping and singing along with "I Want to Hold Your Hand." The only way to follow this all up is with a couple of ravers. When Paul introduces "a number by the Isley Brothers," the crowd cheers, not for the mention of the R & B group, but because they know "Twist and Shout" is coming.

The Beatles' version of "Long Tall Sally," however, had not been heard in the United States yet and got no screams of recognition. One hundred and eleven seconds of manic caterwauling, stinging guitar solos, and cataclysmic drumming later, 8,092 sets of lungs were crying for more. Three hundred and sixty-two policemen held them back as forty red-coated attendants escorted four sweat-drenched and spent Beatles offstage.

RELEASE HISTORY

For many years, only the kinescope of this show (containing **A–V**) circulated on video. Its soundtrack was first bootlegged in fair quality on the 1974 LP *The Beatles: Live in Washington D.C.* (minus **U–V**) and eventually on the 1994 CD *In Case You Don't Know* (complete) in very good quality. Portions of the kinescope were released on the videos *The Beatles Firsts* (**B–F, L, P,** and **T**) and *The First U.S. Visit* (**F, L,** and **R**).

The videotape source was discovered too late to be included in the 1995 TV broadcast of *Anthology,* but Apple included video versions of **D** and the previously unheard **W–Y** on separate electronic press kits that year. "Long Tall Sally" was booted from this source on the CD *Lost and Found.* The home video release of *Anthology* includes **F** and **N** from the videotape source, and **R** from a combination of kinescope and color home movie footage.

45. Newsreel footage

Date: 11 February 1964
Time: evening
Location: British Embassy, Washington, D.C.
Length: 3:21

The evening went steadily downhill once the concert had finished. The Beatles were obliged to put in an appearance at a masked charity ball in the British Embassy, hosted by Sir David Ormsby Gore and his wife. The event started off amicably enough as the hosts met the Fabs in their private residence. With news cameras rolling, the Beatles and Brian Epstein then descended a staircase and entered the lobby, choked with press and onlookers.

A reporter grabs the first available Beatle and positions him in front of the camera, asking, "Which one are you?" "Eric," replies John. The poor journalist proceeds to introduce Eric to the American public, but John gets him off the hook: "I'm John. It was only a joke." John relays his favorable impression of the

Washington audience and U.S. reception in general, but is unimpressed when told of a parody group, the Cockroaches: "I haven't heard them, but it's already been done about eighty times in England. Sorry, Cockroaches!"

A "Pop Movies" newsreel contains 48 seconds of silent footage from the Embassy ball, depicting the Beatles mingling with guests and autographing copies of *Meet the Beatles!* Further footage used in *Anthology* shows John surrounded by reporters, giving Ed Rudy a one-word response (see following entry), and walking off to the ballroom.

RELEASE HISTORY

1993: The soundtrack to this interview was released on the CD *The Beatles Tapes, Volume 2: Early Beatlemania 1963–1964.* The footage (1:23) circulates on video and a bit of it was used in the documentary *The Complete Beatles.* The "Pop Movies" newsreel circulates on video in mediocre quality. A further 1:10 of footage is included in the *Anthology* documentary.

46. Radio interview — J, R

Date: 11 February 1964
Time: evening
Location: British Embassy, Washington, D.C.
Interviewer: Ed Rudy, Bill Healey
Length: 2:12

Also present at the Embassy were Ed Rudy and his colleague, *Radio Pulsebeat News* correspondent Bill Healey. They were able to get only a single word out of John ("John, this is the first time a rock-and-roll group has been honored at the embassy. Uh, what do you have to say about that?" "Really?" This exchange can be seen in *Anthology,* buried under narration), as well as brief interviews with Ambassador Ormsby Gore and Embassy press secretary Frank Mitchell.

Mostly they hang around Ringo, who talks about their visits to the Playboy Club and Peppermint Lounge ("All the press were there!") and denies he is a sex symbol ("You're joking! . . . You can see my face!"). Ringo is also heard chatting with military attaché Roger St. John, who had posed in a Beatle wig earlier in the evening (Ringo tells him to buy it, because "We need the ten percent!"). In rather plummy and vague but cordial tones, he lavishes praise on the Beatles' *Ed Sullivan* performance: "I watched you on the box . . . I enjoyed it very much, because you were having a very good go at everybody. And what you were putting over was good."

Ringo accepts the compliments graciously, but as he goes on to chat about Parisian audiences, one can hear constant interruptions for him to sign autographs and shake hands. Paul later recalled the "Hooray Henrys" who began to taunt them after tossing back a few too many. John was even blunter: "Some bloody animal cut Ringo's hair. I walked out, swearing at all of them, I just left in the middle of it."

Actually, by most accounts, John threatened to leave when Embassy officials condescendingly pressured them into announcing the winners of the evening's charity raffle ("Come along now! Come and do your stuff!"), but Ringo talked him into staying. A young lady did indeed snip off a lock of Ringo's hair from behind as he was talking to someone else. The Beatles stuck out the ordeal until 1 a.m., and Lady Ormsby Gore apologized as they left, but the embassy would issue an official statement proclaiming that the evening had gone swimmingly.

RELEASE HISTORY

1964: These interviews were released on the LPs *The Beatles American Tour with Ed Rudy* (two of Ringo's segments, and Frank Mitchell talking with Bill Healey) and *1965 Talk Album—Ed Rudy with New U.S. Tour* (the others).

47. Documentary footage

Date: 12 February 1964
Time: morning
Location: train from Washington, D.C., to New York City
Length: 6:34

The train journey down to Washington had been so much fun, it was arranged for the Beatles to return to New York via the rails, so after a quick trip to pose in front of the U.S. Capitol, they were headed north. Once again, the Maysles brothers were invited along to film the shenanigans.

Only George and Ringo seem to have much energy, hamming it up incessantly for Dezo Hoffmann and the other photographers and reporters present. John stays rooted to his chair, but does joke around with George, swapping jackets and performing an impromptu cigarette ad (recalling Kent's promotion of a "micronite filter," John plugs Marlboro's "microknee finger"). John also launches into a comic routine about drug addiction, cut from the original film for obvious reasons. Meanwhile, Paul sulkily tells the cameraman, "I'm not in a laughing mood, even."

George is in a great mood, stretching out on the overhead luggage compartment and posing as a refreshment car porter, complete with borrowed hat, jacket, and tray of beverages. It's Ringo who steals the show, however, sneaking behind chairs, sweeping up the floor, and loading himself up with a dozen camera bags to mock the frenzied photojournalists.

RELEASE HISTORY

All of this footage was released on the DVD *The First U.S. Visit*.

48. Newsreel footage

Date: 12 February 1964
Time: afternoon and evening
Location: Penn Station, Plaza Hotel, and Carnegie Hall, New York City
Length: 5:17

When the Beatles returned to New York, the Associated Press went into overdrive covering every aspect, accumulating footage from camera crews all over the city. At least three of these newsreels are circulating, the first of which shows fans at Penn Station waiting for the train to arrive, singing a chorus of "We Love You, Beatles" to pass the time. Unfortunately for them, the Beatles' car was brought in on a separate track, and they escaped via taxi to a limo and arrived an hour later at the Plaza Hotel. The newsreel team beat them there easily, filming hordes of girls waiting outside and the limo discharging its famous passengers, who sprint through a wedge of policemen into the lobby.

A second newsreel shows some of the five thousand fans who congregated in the street outside Carnegie Hall, lined up behind police barriers clutching copies of *Fabulous* magazine and wearing Beatle buttons. A group of greasy-haired lads grin for the camera and hold up cardboard anti-Beatle signs. The third newsreel begins after nightfall; by now, well-dressed girls are lined up to enter Carnegie Hall, while a sizable delegation of male students from Fordham University (wearing Yankee Doodle hats) march up and down in protest.

Their signs bear such slogans as FLUSH THE PUDDING BASINS, PRO-FUMO-GATE THE BEATLES, and BEATLES UNDERMINE ARTISTIC INTEGRITY (the latter slogan was accurately borrowed by a character in the 1978 film *I Wanna Hold Your Hand*). Before the Beatles could arrive and witness such negativity, the protesters were reportedly rushed by a flock of girls who destroyed the signs. It's likely they wouldn't have had time to notice, as when they do arrive, they are whisked into a side entrance, with Brian Somerville and Brian Epstein close behind.

During a press conference before the show, Swan Records presented the Beatles with a gold record for the single "She Loves You." The Carnegie Hall concerts were a great success, with three thousand attending each performance. One hundred and fifty extra fans per show were crammed into the hall seated on folding chairs on the stage itself, beside and behind the Beatles as they played. Heavy police presence ensured there was no rioting or damage to the hallowed concert hall. Capitol Records had planned to tape the show for potential LP release, but the plan was thwarted shortly beforehand when the American Federation of Musicians refused permission for the recording to go ahead.

RELEASE HISTORY

This AP newsreel footage circulates on video among collectors.

48a. Radio interview — J, R

Date: 7–12 February 1964
Location: New York City
Broadcast: WMCA-AM, New York
Length: 4:37

Sometime during the New York visit, John recorded a batch of promos for radio station WMCA, home of the "Good Guys" disc jockey team. Fourteen of these clips (all 30 seconds or shorter) have survived; in addition to reading promos for each of the Good Guys' shows (Joe O'Brien, Jack Spector, B. Mitchel Reed, Dan Daniel, Harry Harrison, and Johnny Dark), John sings a couple of WMCA jingles. He and Ringo also recorded generic spots nominating listeners as new "Good Guys."

RELEASE HISTORY

These promos are collected on the CD-R *New York Radio 1964–1969.*

49. Radio interview — P

Date: 14 February 1964
Location: Miami Beach
Interviewer: Ed Rudy
Length: 0:10

After the second Carnegie Hall show, the Beatles spent a night on the town, leaving their hotel at 1:30 a.m. to visit the Headliner Club and Improvisation coffeehouse and meet starlets such as Tuesday Weld, Jill Haworth, and Stella Stevens. They slept in the next morning until their 2 p.m. flight to Miami on National Airlines Flight 11.

Their arrival shortly before 4 p.m. was covered live by Charlie Murdock and Jack Sorbi of Miami radio station WQAM, and 3:18 of their coverage is included on the *Yeah Yeah Yeah—The Beatles in the USA* souvenir EP. Nearly seven thousand fans greeted the group, reportedly smashing twenty-three glass windows and doors at the airport trying to reach their idols (one girl who gets to shake hands with them actually exclaims, "I'll never wash my hand again!"). A few seconds of silent footage also exists of the Miami Airport arrival. After a press conference, they were driven to the Deauville Hotel, where they would stay for the next nine days (the WQAM disc includes a 0:34 report from the lobby as fans rush the elevators).

The first couple of days in Miami were a mixture of work and play; as *The Ed Sullivan Show* would be broadcast from the hotel, they were able to jump in the hotel pool or swim in the ocean, and then rehearse in their bathing trunks and robes. Murray the K was along to provide entertainment, and accompanied them to the local Peppermint Lounge to see Hank Ballard and the Midnighters. At the Deauville, they also took in a performance by the Coasters and were insulted by comedian Don Rickles.

Murray's biggest coup was arranging for the group to sail on the yacht of local millionaire Bernard Castro. At 2 p.m. on the afternoon of the fourteenth, the *Southern Trail* set sail (once a couple of stowaway journalists had been ejected). John and Ringo snapped color photos (many of which were used in the *Anthology* book and documentary), Paul demonstrated "Can't Buy Me Love" for Murray on a piano in the yacht's main cabin, and they spent an enjoyable couple of hours splashing in the Atlantic.

While Murray the K was never more than a few steps behind the Beatles in Miami, Ed Rudy was able to obtain updates on the group's activities only from Mal Evans and Neil Aspinall. These two snippets of Paul describing the day's events ("We went out on a—on a yacht today, y'know, and we sort of bathed around a bit") seem to be the only bits of Beatle chat Rudy recorded during the entire Miami trip.

Also probably filmed on this day were two short bits of color home movie footage used in *Anthology.* The first, lasting 13 seconds, shows John hanging over the edge of a boat wearing a giant red straw hat; the second, a mere 7 seconds, has Ringo snatching a pair of sunglasses from his face (both are played in slow motion).

RELEASE HISTORY

1964: These interviews (two with Paul, plus one each with Mal and Neil not included in the timing above) were released on the LP *The Beatles American Tour with Ed Rudy.* The silent home movie footage was released on the *Anthology* video documentary.

50. TV performance

Date: 16 February 1964
Time: 2:30 p.m.
Location: Deauville Hotel, Miami Beach
Producer: Bob Precht
Host: Ed Sullivan

[A.] **intro** (0:02)
[B.] **She Loves You** (2:18)
[C.] **intro** (0:05)
[D.] **This Boy** (2:15)
[E.] **intro** (0:27)
[F.] **All My Loving** (2:05)
[G.] **outro** (0:14)
[H.] **intro** (0:13)
[I.] **I Saw Her Standing There** (2:35)
[J.] **intro** (0:03)
[K.] **From Me to You** (1:48)
[L.] **intro** (0:47)
[M.] **I Want to Hold Your Hand** (2:22)
[N.] **outro** (1:10)

A surviving videotape of the Miami dress rehearsal for *The Ed Sullivan Show* clearly demonstrates the need to have dress rehearsals. As the Beatles launch into "She Loves You," John realizes his microphone is pointing in the region of his collar. He tries to adjust it throughout the song, but ends up having to hunch over while singing. He's distracted enough to sing the second verse again in place of the third, but as he can't really be heard anyway, it's not a big deal.

The rest of the first set goes smoothly, highlighted by a nice rendition of "This Boy." Paul greets the audience with "good afternoon" before "All My Loving." As the curtains open for the second set, they have already begun "I Saw Her Standing There," but this time Paul's vocal microphone has been shut off and he's inaudible until after the guitar solo. Despite all the problems, they turn in an energetic "From Me to You," after which John and Paul do their "clap your hands" routine to introduce "I Want to Hold Your Hand" (and John tells the audience to "shut up while he's talking!").

After a final bow, the Beatles are praised by Ed Sullivan, when he can get a word in between the screams of fans: "Please be quiet, because I know you'll want to hear what I'm gonna say here. These are four of the nicest youngsters . . . we've ever had on our stage."

RELEASE HISTORY

This broadcast circulates on video in excellent quality from the original videotape. The *Anthology* documentary includes a portion of **L.** The entire soundtrack (**A–N**) was first bootlegged on the LP *The Beatles Conquer America,* but is best found in excellent quality on the bootleg CD *The Ultimate Collection, Volume 1: TV Appearances.* All copies seem to have a glitch at the beginning of **B.**

50a. Radio interview G

Date: 16 February 1964
Time: evening
Location: Deauville Hotel, Miami Beach (via telephone)
Interviewer: Jack Diamond
Broadcast: WSPR-AM, Springfield
Length: 5:16

Between the dress rehearsal and live broadcast of *Ed Sullivan,* George once again spoke with WSPR disc jockey Jack Diamond via telephone from the Deauville. Diamond informs George that six of WSPR's current top 70 records are Beatle numbers, including two "album cuts," "Love Me Do," and "Do You Want to Know a Secret." Both were featured on the Vee Jay album *Introducing the Beatles,* and both would soon be released as singles.

When Diamond laments that it's snowing in Massachusetts, George says it's 75 degrees in Miami, but adds that he just got off the phone with someone in England, where it's freezing. He assures Diamond that the Beatles will return to America soon, explaining that initially, their visit was just to promote records by appearing on *The Ed Sullivan Show.* By the time they arrived, of course, their single and LP were topping the charts, and demand was great enough to add concerts in Washington, D.C., and at Carnegie Hall. Diamond wraps up by wishing them luck on *Ed Sullivan,* and George says he hopes the microphones will be turned on this time!

RELEASE HISTORY

This interview circulates in very good quality among collectors.

51. TV performance

Date: 16 February 1964
Time: 8:00–9:00 p.m.
Location: Deauville Hotel, Miami Beach
Producer: Bob Precht
Host: Ed Sullivan
Broadcast: live
CBS
The Ed Sullivan Show

[A.] **intro** (0:13)
[B.] **She Loves You** (2:16)
[C.] **intro** (0:04)
[D.] **This Boy** (2:16)
[E.] **intro** (0:35)
[F.] **All My Loving** (2:05)
[G.] **outro** (0:07)
[H.] **intro** (0:27)
[I.] **I Saw Her Standing There** (2:34)
[J.] **intro** (0:06)
[K.] **From Me to You** (1:48)
[L.] **intro** (0:21)
[M.] **I Want to Hold Your Hand** (2:24)
[N.] **outro** (0:48)

Amazingly, the Beatles' second appearance on *The Ed Sullivan Show* nearly matched their debut in viewing figures, with 70 million people tuning in. Brian Epstein opted to stay in his suite at the Deauville to watch the live broadcast, donning a "Stamp Out the Beatles" sweatshirt for the occasion. Although the studio audience is relatively sedate compared to both the New York crowds and Miami dress rehearsal, at least the technical problems have been solved. Microphone levels are consistent, although they still aren't adjusted to the correct height for the second set, forcing John to sing "I Saw Her Standing There" from a squatting position.

Heavyweight boxing champion Sonny Liston is present (his wife worked in the Deauville's beauty salon), and is acknowledged by Ed along with former champ Joe Louis. After performances by Allen & Rossi, Mitzi Gaynor, the Nerveless Nocks, and Myron Cohen, Ed introduces the Beatles' show-closing set with an awkward joke: "You know, Sonny Liston, actually, some of these songs could fit you in your fight. One is 'From Me to You.' That's one song they're gonna sing. And another one could fit Cassius, 'cause that song is 'I Want to Hold Your Hand.' "

Before their final song, in the place of their "clap your hands" routine, Paul opts to tell his "favorite American group, Sophie Tucker" joke, which had gotten a big laugh at the Royal Variety show. Here it's met with a deafening silence, bombing even worse than Ed's earlier attempt at wit. At the end of the show, Ed passes along a compliment from Richard Rodgers, "one of America's greatest composers," who was apparently "one of your most rabid fans."

RELEASE HISTORY

In 2003, this entire show was released on an excellent-quality DVD, *Ed Sullivan Presents the Beatles.* Three of the songs (**D, F,** and **K**) were released on the video *The First U.S. Visit,* in slightly scrambled order. The *Anthology* documentary includes part of **D.** The entire soundtrack (**A–N**) was bootlegged on LPs such as *Ed's Really Big Beatle Blasts* and *The 1964 & 1965 Ed Sullivan Shows.* It's best found in excellent quality on the bootleg CD *The Ultimate Collection, Volume 1: TV Appearances.*

52. Radio interview

Date: 13–17 February 1964
Location: Miami Beach
Interviewer: Murray Kaufman
Broadcast: WINS-AM, New York City
Length: 8:13

In the Beatles' twelfth-floor suite at the Deauville Hotel, John and Cynthia shared a room, Paul and Ringo another, Neil and Mal a third. This left space in George's room for Murray the K, and with WINS footing his share of the bill, he would stay with the group a few days, most likely leaving on the seventeenth, the day the Beatles were originally scheduled to return to New York.

Over the course of the stay, he would record numerous interviews for his *Swingin' Soiree* show; an unedited tape exists of Murray reading an ad for Fisher Nuts and introducing records by the Willows, Dale and Grace, and Nat King Cole (mocked by Paul in the background when he trips over his words). Leading into a Dion disc, Murray discusses the former doo-wop singer's switch to harder R & B material. Paul approves, and George plays a bit of less-than-soulful harmonica ("Just leave your number, George"). Murray acquires a bit of Liverpudlian slang when Ringo declares they are all "nesh" for the cold weather.

Also on this tape is a slightly longer recording of Murray's farewell to Paul, which was released on an

EP the following year (missing only the first word). Paul seems baffled that Murray is leaving the sunshine state so soon, but Murray laments that WINS won't pay to keep him in Miami any longer. After ten days of hearing those call letters, Paul teases, "I've forgotten what station yours was, Murray . . . what station was yours?" Out of breath from a swim in the Atlantic, Paul sincerely thanks Murray and his station for their Beatle-boosting efforts.

The EP also contains an interview with Ringo conducted on the beach earlier in the week. The drummer is puzzled as to why he seems to be the most popular Beatle in America (basically a reversal of the situation in England). He also recounts his history with the group, from meeting them in Hamburg in 1960 through his temporary stints filling in for Pete Best to the day when he got a call from Brian Epstein to join for good.

Further extracts that seem to be from this interview circulate from an off-air recording. Ringo praises the enthusiastic audiences in Washington and at Carnegie Hall, which inspired the group to go "potty" trying to match the energy of the crowd. Murray is thrilled to pick up more British lingo: "Potty, baby? That's what's happenin', huh?" Ringo misplaces one of his rings momentarily but luckily finds it in his bag. (". . . When Ringo loses a ring, baby, forget it! Everything else stops right about here.")

RELEASE HISTORY

1965: Interviews with Ringo and Paul were released on the EP *The Beatles & Murray the K: As It Happened,* copied on the LP and CD *Timeless II.* The unedited tapes described above were available for download on a website, and the fair-quality broadcast recording circulates among collectors.

53. Newsreel footage

Date: 18 February 1964
Time: 1:00 p.m.
Location: Fifth Street Gym, Miami Beach
Length: 0:22

While the Beatles were busy conquering America, a young boxer named Cassius Clay was preparing to conquer his opponent Sonny Liston in an upcoming heavyweight title bout. The fight's promoter, Harold Conrad, accompanied Liston to the February 16 *Ed Sullivan* broadcast, and approached the Beatles afterward about a possible photo opportunity with the fighters.

In the end, Liston refused to participate, but the media-savvy Clay (soon to be known as Muhammad Ali) eagerly agreed. The meeting took place this afternoon at Clay's training camp, with Dezo Hoffmann and other photographers present, as well as newsreel cameras. In these fragmented clips, Cassius is seen exchanging playful jabs with the Fabs and hoisting Ringo (wearing a WINS "Submarine Race Watchers" sweatshirt) aloft.

RELEASE HISTORY

This silent footage circulates on video among collectors.

54. Radio interview

Date: 19 February 1964
Location: Deauville Hotel, Miami Beach
Interviewer: Lee Alan
Broadcast: KNUZ-AM, Detroit
Length: 6:08

With this one final interview, the Beatles were able to enjoy two full days of relaxation on the beach in Miami away from microphones and cameras. In fact, KNUZ Radio's Lee Alan was allowed up to the Deauville for an interview only because the Beatles were so fond of Detroit's contribution to pop music.

Alan thanks them for taking a break from their vacation to chat with him (they sing a couple of illustrative bars from Connie Francis's 1962 hit "Vacation" at each mention of the word). Alan recognizes Ringo but then guesses wrong twice trying to identify Paul, much to his chagrin. ("Listen, kids, don't ever listen to him again. He's off his head. He doesn't know one from the other, kids!")

He asks when they first heard of Detroit University's Stamp Out the Beatles campaign. Paul says at the airport press conference, George says in *Cashbox* before they arrived, John says at school when he was seven years old! Paul points out that not all college students have it in for them, as they've been presented with a plaque by a University of Miami fraternity (the Gamma Phi chapter of the Sigma Chi fraternity, to be exact). A question about the group's history means another opportunity to sing, "We've been together now for forty years . . ."

Noting that they'd just been listening to a Martha and the Vandellas B-side, Alan names some Motown artists, which the Beatles cheer. When he mentions their "counterparts," the Four Seasons, however, they are less enthusiastic, preferring artists such as the Miracles, Marvin Gaye, Esther Phillips, and the Ronettes. The interview wraps up with the Beatles giving thanks to fans and to Ed Sullivan, and saying they'll probably be back to the States "about September."

RELEASE HISTORY

1964: This interview was issued in two parts on a giveaway single, *A Trip to Miami.*

55. Radio interview

Date: 21 February 1964
Location: Deauville Hotel, Miami Beach
Interviewer: Jack Milman
Broadcast: WQAM-AM, Miami
Length: 2:45

WQAM reporter Jack Milman taped this exclusive "farewell" message at the Deauville as the Beatles prepared to leave Miami. George speaks first, thanking the fans for buying the records, and the police for keeping the visit organized. Paul thanks Ed Sullivan for making them feel at home ("Good ol' Eddie!" shouts John), and specifically praises Sgt. Buddy Dresner for treating them to "one of the biggest meals I've ever eaten." He also acknowledges the Deauville Hotel, the fans on the sand outside, and Maurice Landsberg, owner of the hotel ("He wasn't on the sand," quips John).

John thanks school reporters and the University of Miami for presenting them with a plaque making them honorary members of a fraternity. He also mentions the owners of all the private homes they visited, insisting they shall "remain omnibus." Finally he thanks the press for being so kind, "and the ones who weren't kind, well, keep trying." Ringo closes the message with kudos to disc jockeys and Capitol Records for promotion and plugging, along with the mayor and citizens of Miami.

RELEASE HISTORY

1964: This interview was included on a souvenir EP, *Yeah Yeah Yeah—The Beatles in the U.S.A.,* distributed by WQAM Radio.

1984: The interview was released on the LP *The Beatles Talk Downunder (and All Over), Volume 2.* It has been reissued on the CD *Inside Interviews: Talk Downunder: Sydney to Seattle.*

56. Documentary footage

Date: 21 February 1964
Time: afternoon
Location: Deauville Hotel, Miami Beach, Miami Airport, and flight to New York City
Length: 9:34

After a long absence of filming, the Maysles crew finally caught up with the Beatles as they were packing to leave Miami. John and Cynthia are absent (probably packing in their own room) and Murray the K is long gone, but the camera rolls in Paul and Ringo's room, with George hanging around to watch, and Brian Somerville and Neil Aspinall doing their best to assist.

Paul has trouble closing his overstuffed suitcase, so he sits on it while George zips it shut. Ringo is in even worse shape, as Paul keeps finding items of clothing the drummer has forgotten to pack (George helpfully offers to carry one in his coat pocket). Joking around for the cameras, Paul "interviews" Ringo while George holds a heart-shaped chocolate box over his head. Paul plays the role of a portrait painter, holding up a fan's drawing and a vaguely Ringo-shaped design ("I've done an abstract!") on the cover of a brochure.

Ringo beats on a pair of bongos and combs his hair in a mirror while Paul feeds seagulls on the balcony. George whistles and sings "The Jet Song" and "Maria" from *West Side Story,* and he improvises a talking blues while strumming his out-of-tune acoustic guitar. All three also wave and shout from the balcony to fans on the beach below ("Which one are you?").

Once everything was packed up, the Beatles and company checked out of the Deauville and caught the

5:18 flight to New York City. Sixty-eight seconds of silent newsreel footage captures their departure, being driven from the terminal building to the Pan Am jet (N806PA), where they wave good-bye while boarding.

The Maysles crew apparently traveled all the way back to England with the group. Some outtake footage from inside the plane appears at the end of part 2 of the *Anthology* documentary, made to look as though it was shot on the way over from London February 7. But it must have been shot as the Beatles boarded the plane in Miami: Ringo is wearing sunglasses, not a scarf; Cynthia has an entirely different outfit on; John isn't wearing his leather cap.

RELEASE HISTORY

The TV special *What's Happening! The Beatles in the U.S.A.,* which circulates on video, includes 4:52 of this footage. The DVD *The First U.S. Visit* includes much of this, plus some unique footage; its soundtrack mutes the *West Side Story* tunes, probably for legal reasons. George's "Talking Guitar Blues" has been booted in many places and is best found on the CD-R compilation *Vinyl to the Core.* The 22 seconds of airplane footage appears on the *Anthology* home video documentary, and the Miami Airport clip circulates on video.

57. Radio interview R

Date: 21 February 1964
Time: evening
Location: Kennedy International Airport, New York City
Interviewer: Ed Rudy
Length: 0:07

Ed Rudy, who hadn't been able to get close to the group in Miami, was able to record an interview only with a weary and disinterested Neil Aspinall en route to Miami. During the half-hour layover in New York, the Beatles held one final American press conference, and Rudy captured Ringo's farewell message to the States: "Oh, it's fantastic again. Y'know, it's marvelous. Great! Y'know, it's [a] marvelous place! We hope to come back as soon as we can!"

The documentary *The First U.S. Visit* includes 16 seconds of footage of the Beatles climbing the steps to their Pan Am "Jet Clipper Beatles" for one last wave to American fans (the footage is intercut with their performance of "I Want to Hold Your Hand" from the February 23 *Ed Sullivan Show* broadcast).

RELEASE HISTORY

1964: This interview and the Neil Aspinall chat were released on the LP *The Beatles American Tour with Ed Rudy.* The airport footage was released on the video *The First U.S. Visit.*

58. Newsreel footage

Date: 22 February 1964
Time: 8:10 a.m.
Location: London Airport
Length: 8:56

While the Beatles' send-off to America had been a big deal, their return as conquering heroes was an order of magnitude greater, as nearly ten thousand girls welcomed them home, many of them arriving the previous evening to stake out a prime spot. Footage of the arrival was shot for ITV News (3:38), Associated Press (0:53), and Pathé (3:37) newsreels. The Maysles crew filmed from behind as the Fabs deplaned (0:48), and the BBC covered the whole thing for *Grandstand* (see following entry).

The Pathé newsreel, titled *Beatles Welcome Home,* is the most extensive. It's a real production including narration by Bob Danvers-Walker and excerpts of Beatles songs ("It Won't Be Long," "All My Loving," "I'll Get You," and "I Want to Hold Your Hand"), as well as alternate footage of an ITV News interview (see entry below). It opens with scenes of fans camping out overnight at the airport (leaving behind a ton of litter) and awakening at dawn, and includes remarkable images of unconscious fans being lifted like rag dolls over a fence. British Pathé's online archive also contains

10:36 of silent offcut footage from their newsreel, covering the day's events.

Otherwise, most sources show the same events: the Pan Am JET CLIPPER BEATLES drawing slowly near, the Beatles emerging carrying booty from their visit (mostly record albums), climbing aboard a transport that shuttles them to the customs building, and eventually reemerging only to disappear into a limo.

RELEASE HISTORY

These newsreels circulate on video, and the Maysles clip appears in the TV special *What's Happening! The Beatles in the U.S.A.,* and on the home video *The First U.S. Visit.*

59. TV interview

Date: 22 February 1964
Time: 8:10 a.m.
Location: London Airport
Interviewer: David Coleman
Broadcast: 22 February 1964, 1:00–5:15 p.m.
BBC TV
Grandstand
Length: 10:08

The BBC was so eager to capitalize on the Beatles' triumphant return, they devoted over thirteen minutes of their weekend sports roundup, *Grandstand,* to covering the airport arrival.

The report opens with illustrative clips of events from the Beatles' first two days in New York, including some unused footage licensed from the Maysles brothers (see the February 7 entry). Airport coverage includes interviews with eager fans, followed by 3:48 of "as it happened" footage of the Beatles exiting their plane (preceded by Brian Somerville), standing on the steps to wave for a long time, then boarding the shuttle bus.

Once inside, they are filmed having a lengthy (6:20) chat with sports announcer David Coleman. They all seem shocked that so many people are there to greet them so early in the morning. John adds that they've "only just got up," but Ringo corrects him: "We haven't been to bed yet." George contrasts the larger venues where they performed in the States with the cinemas they usually play, complaining about the dreadful acoustics in the Washington Coliseum. Ringo recounts the hair-snipping incident at the embassy ball: "I was just talking, having an interview—just like I am now!" John and Paul, hovering behind him, assist in the reenactment as Ringo waxes philosophical about the whole thing: "Tomorrow never knows!" John laughs and mentally files away the phrase.

They joke that Miami had nothing on New Brighton, but Paul claims to have caught a fish with "all things on his back and big teeth." Coleman reveals that Wilfrid Brambell has now been cast in the role of Paul's grandfather for their upcoming film. The announcement is news to them, although (apart from Ringo) they seem to have known it was in the works.

Coleman wonders what they thought of Cassius Clay, and they all found his antics entertaining but doubt he'll be able to defeat Sonny Liston. Paul confides that when someone at Clay's training camp asked him who he thought would win, he whispered, "Liston." John doesn't miss a beat, singing, "Liston . . . do you want to know a secret?" Coleman tries to continue the sports theme, asking their opinions of Liverpool's football cup chances, but they show little knowledge or interest. Ringo says he's been to only one football match in his life, and Paul admits, "We support whoever's winning at the time."

With "I Want to Hold Your Hand" falling to number 14 the previous week, the Beatles had no singles in the British top 10 for the first time in almost six months. They don't seem too shattered, and Coleman asks if they have anything in the works. Paul says they'll be recording next week, but the others try and hush him up. Coleman realizes the location is probably also a secret: "And we daren't ask you where." John replies, "Decca."

RELEASE HISTORY

This *Grandstand* report circulates in good quality on video among collectors.

60. TV interview

Date: 22 February 1964
Time: morning
Location: London Airport
Broadcast: 22 February 1964
ITV
Length: 3:31

ITV News also got a chance to interview the Beatles, in the same location as the BBC's interview (but facing the opposite direction). ITV included 3:31 of the interview in their report, while Pathé's *Beatles Welcome Home* newsreel contained 2:09 of footage (filmed from a slightly different angle).

They all praise Miami's warm and sunny climate (Ringo: "I didn't know what it meant till I went over there"), as well as the millionaires' houses they were allowed to "borrow" for recreational purposes. Assuming they've returned from America millionaires themselves, the interviewer asks if they have time to spend all that money. All four respond as one: "What money?"

John is asked if his wife enjoyed the trip, and he pretends to play dumb: "Who? Who?" Ringo says it's a secret, but of course John's marriage had been public knowledge for several months. Paul is asked about the taste of American fans, but John interrupts: "He never bit any." They also chat about meeting Cassius Clay and about having to add older material to their set list for the benefit of American audiences.

RELEASE HISTORY

Most of the ITV footage was included in Granada's 1984 special *The Early Beatles,* which circulates on video; its soundtrack was released on the CD *Rare Photos & Interview CD, Volume 2.* The Pathé interview footage circulates on video, and most of its soundtrack (1:37 worth) was released on the CD *The Beatles Tapes Volume 2: Early Beatlemania 1963–1964.*

61. Radio interview

Date: 22 February 1964
Time: morning
Location: London Airport (via telephone)
Interviewer: Brian Matthew
Broadcast: 22 February 1964, 10:00 a.m.–noon
BBC Light Programme
Saturday Club #281
Length: 4:04

For the third consecutive week, the Beatles appeared on *Saturday Club,* this time via a telephonic interview from London Airport. Brian Matthew taped the chat, and it was hurriedly edited to fit in the final twenty minutes of the show that very morning.

Paul takes the phone first and describes the return welcome as superior even to their New York arrival; Matthew notes the clearly audible fans still screaming in the background. George is weary but glad to be home, and Matthew wishes him a happy impending twenty-first birthday. Admitting that he thinks Sonny Liston will win, George nonetheless hopes Cassius Clay will be able to triumph, if only for claiming to be Chubby Checker's cousin!

Ringo also chats about his Clay encounter, revealing that he felt "like a feather in his arms" and joking that he declined the chance to spar because he "didn't want to hurt" Cassius. Matthew informs John that *Saturday Club* producer Bernie Andrews had a haircut as directed two weeks earlier, and John scoffs, "Oh, dear. Well, he's out the club, then." After airing the interview, Matthew spun a disc specially for George's birthday, the Miracles' "Shop Around," a number requested by George's mom.

RELEASE HISTORY

1988: A very good recording of this interview was included on the vinyl bootleg *The Beatles at the Beeb, Volume 9,* and is also on the Pyramid CD of this title. It's been released (copied from the bootleg) on the CD *The Beatles Tapes, Volume 2: Early Beatlemania 1963–1964.*

62. Newsreel footage

Date: 23 February 1964
Time: morning
Location: River Thames
Broadcast: 23 February 1964, 6:05–6:15 p.m.
ITV News
Length: 1:16

Twenty-four hours after returning home from America, the Beatles were back at work, filming location scenes for a skit in their *Big Night Out* appearance (see following entry). An ITV News crew covered the occasion as the group, bundled in heavy coats and scarves, boated down the Thames. With fans cheering and running alongside the banks, George adds some commentary along the lines of a rowing race: "And it's Cambridge in the lead. And you can hear the distant screaming from a thin bridge in the near future."

The clip continues with the Beatles being helped ashore, police trying to hold back fans behind a gate outside the TV studio, and a few seconds of studio rehearsal of the skit's conclusion, with Mike and Bernie Winters.

RELEASE HISTORY

This footage was released on the compilation video *Beatles 1962 to 1970.*

63. TV performance

Date: 23 February 1964
Time: evening–10:30 p.m.
Location: Studio 1, Teddington Studio Centre
Producer: Philip Jones
Hosts: Mike Winters, Bernie Winters
Broadcast: 29 February 1964, 6:35–7:25 p.m.
ABC
Big Night Out

[A.] **opening sketch** (3:28)
[B.] **arrival/customs sketch** (2:20)
[C.] **intro** (0:03)
[D.] **All My Loving** (2:04)
[E.] **intro** (0:06)
[F.] **I Wanna Be Your Man** (1:53)
[G.] **intro** (0:11)
[H.] **Till There Was You** (1:23)
[I.] **fan mail sketch** (1:06)
[J.] **intro** (0:05)
[K.] **Please Mr. Postman** (2:30)
[L.] **intro** (0:24)
[M.] **I Want to Hold Your Hand** (2:23)

Promoting nothing more than their return to the shores of the British Isles, the Beatles' second appearance on *Big Night Out* was a mixture of mimed musical performances and weak comedy sketches. Video copies of the show are circulating, both from its initial UK broadcast and an August 14, 1965, U.S. airing on New York's WOR-TV.

The show opens with a sketch (**A**) supposedly set in the Beatles' flat, with bewigged hosts Mike and Bernie Winters comprising the extra members of "The Mike Winters Six." They try to think up a new name (rejecting "Beatles" as terrible) while debating whether to watch *Big Night Out* ("that show with those two fellows that keep gettin' blown up every week"). Naturally, when the boys and Bernie go into the next room to make tea on a faulty gas cooker, an explosion sends them flying through the kitchen wall, where they introduce the show.

"Please Mr. Postman" plays over the opening credits (**B**) as the Beatles are seen "returning from the U.S." They are helped out of the boat (see previous entry), climb into a motor coach (whose driver takes off before they are seated, causing Paul to tumble backwards), and are driven to a customs office, where Bernie Winters doesn't bother to inspect their cases. "I know what's in them. Money!"

While a thin joke, this would have at least been a good lead-in to a performance of "Money (That's What I Want)." Mark Lewisohn indicates that the song was included in the original broadcast and omitted for overseas sales, but it isn't included in any circulating copy (he lists it between **K** and **M,** but this sequence plays without any edits). The remaining sketch (**I**) has the Beatles reading viewer mail asking for Bernie Winters to sing various Beatle songs (such as "All My Luggage"); of course, the requests turn out to have been written by Bernie himself.

For the musical spots, the Beatles perform in front of a giant Union Jack in the shape of a heart, surrounded by each Beatle's name. John mimes lead vocals even on songs where he has none (**D, F**). For "Till There Was You," he is relegated to the shadows along with George and Ringo while Paul lip-syncs to a heavily edited tape of the song up front. After "Please Mr. Postman," Mike and Bernie come out to say good night, and the stage fills with twisting dancers as the Beatles mime to "I Want to Hold Your Hand" over the closing credits.

RELEASE HISTORY

1973: The soundtrack to the U.S. rebroadcast was bootlegged from a good-quality off-line recording on the LP *Sunday Night at the London Palladium.* It's available on the CD-R *Telecasts Two,* probably taken from one of the circulating video copies. The *Anthology* documentary includes a bit of **A,** plus portions of **F** and **K.**

64. TV interview G

Date: 25 February 1964
Location: 13 Monmouth Street, London
Broadcast: 25 February 1964
ITV
Length: 3:45

Mail poured in from all corners of the globe to congratulate George on his twenty-first birthday, some fifteen thousand cards in all, plus countless gifts. Unsurprisingly, this was all given media coverage, with camera crews duly filming sacks of mail arriving at George's home in Liverpool and at the Beatles' Fan Club headquarters in London.

At the latter location, George is also seen sorting through mail with the help of Fan Club secretaries Anne Collingham and Bettina Rose. This is followed by a brief interview with George (who thanks the fans for his presents) and two minutes of silent offcuts of the interview.

RELEASE HISTORY

1996: The soundtrack of this interview was released on the CD *Fab Four CD & Book Set.* The footage was released on the video compilation *Then and Now.*

65. Studio session

Date: 25 February 1964
Time: 10:00 a.m.–1:30 p.m.
Location: EMI Studio 2
Producer: George Martin

[A.] You Can't Do That—take 6 (mono) (2:38)

[B.] Can't Buy Me Love—RM1 or RM3 (2:10)
[C.] You Can't Do That—RM3 (2:33)
Mixed: 26 February 1964

[D.] Can't Buy Me Love—RS1 (2:10)
[E.] You Can't Do That—RS1 (2:33)
Mixed: 10 March 1964

[F.] Can't Buy Me Love—RS from take 4 (1:42)
[G.] You Can't Do That—RS from take 9 (2:32)
[H.] Can't Buy Me Love—RS from take 4 (#2) (1:10)

Back at Abbey Road Studios for the first time in four months, the Beatles' first task was to complete two tracks for their next single. This was accomplished in the morning session, beginning with vocal and guitar overdubs on the "best" Paris recording of "Can't Buy Me Love."

George was enamored of his brand-new Rickenbacker twelve-string guitar and would use it on nearly every song in these sessions (even the early takes of "And I Love Her"). "Can't Buy Me Love" was no exception, as he erased his original Paris guitar track to include the twelve-string chiming chords on the intro, choruses, and coda. Playing the kind of solo he wanted proved difficult on the twelve-string, so George did the next best thing. On the guitar track, he played the solo once using his six-string Gretsch. Then he doubled the performance (differing only on a note or two), using the empty space in Paul's second vocal track. A close listen reveals microphone leakage of his original Paris solo (playing a totally different melody line) on the rhythm track as well!

With that song wrapped up, they turned to the B-side: John's superlative moaner, "You Can't Do That." Roles were switched a bit, allowing John to play lead guitar on the song; thus his six-string Rickenbacker got its own track. The rest of the backing (bass, drums, and George on the twelve-string Rickenbacker) went on a second track, while John's main lead vocal went on a third. Take 6 (**A**) was probably rejected for Ringo's sloppy drum fill heading into the guitar solo, although John's solo itself is also nothing to write home about.

By take 9, John had nailed down his dense and jagged solo, while Paul and Ringo had perfected the stop-start rhythm and George the jangling riff. The song's fourth track was filled with an overdub of John's second lead vocal (for the bridges only), Paul and George's girl-group backing vocals, Ringo's conga drum, and Paul's four-in-the-bar cowbell.

The following day, George Martin mixed both songs into mono for the single. According to Mark Lewisohn, RM2 and RM4 of "You Can't Do That" were destined for the United States, with RM3 made for the UK, while only one mono mix was necessary for "Can't Buy Me Love." However, tape box information indicates that EMItape E51867 (a reel not listed in John Barrett's log) included at least five mono mixes of "Can't Buy Me Love," with RM3 best for the UK, and RM4 and RM5 prepared for U.S. consumption. Whatever the case, there don't seem to be any differences among the mono mixes of either song released worldwide.

On March 10, both songs were mixed into stereo for the first time, along with "Long Tall Sally" and "I Call Your Name." Copies of all four mixes were probably sent to Capitol in the United States for use on *The Beatles' Second Album*. They opted not to include "Can't Buy Me Love" on the album, and had already made a fake stereo mix of "You Can't Do That" for the LP, using their mono single master. The other two songs did appear on the LP in unique stereo mixes.

Session sheets show that George Martin remixed both "Can't Buy Me Love" and "You Can't Do That" into stereo on June 22, along with the rest of the numbers for the LP *A Hard Day's Night*. However, John Barrett's log indicates that neither mix was "cut out" of the mix tape when assembling the LP master reel, so presumably it's the March 10 stereo mixes we hear on the album.

The mono mix of "Can't Buy Me Love" (**B**) has the cymbal accentuated (through compression and treble) and the twelve-string/lead guitar track mixed quieter than in stereo (**D**). Speculation that extra drumming was overdubbed on March 10 seems unfounded. George Martin did, however, add some piano to "You Can't Do That" during a May 22 session, as a four-track copy into take 10. This take was never used, although it still exists in the tape vault.

Ron Furmanek remixed both songs into stereo for the documentary *The Making of "A Hard Day's Night"* in 1995. "Can't Buy Me Love" (**F**) is heard in five different fragments throughout the tape (four with unique portions). This mix has the drums/bass/acoustic guitar track centered, the twelve-string/lead guitar track mixed left, the main vocal track left-of-center, and the second vocal/lead guitar track right-of-center. The new mix of "You Can't Do That" (**G**) is heard in its entirety at the end of the tape (albeit with screaming noises overdubbed). This centers the drums/bass/twelve-string track and isolates the second vocal/percussion track in the left channel.

RELEASE HISTORY

1964: **B** and **C** were released on a single worldwide; both are available on EMI's CD of *A Hard Day's Night*. **D** and **E** were released on stereo copies of the LP *A Hard Day's Night* in the UK. **D** is available on the compilation CDs *The Beatles 1962–1966* and *1* (with the stereo spread slightly narrowed).

1970: **D** was released for the first time in the United States on the LP *Hey Jude.*

1976: **E** made its U.S. stereo debut on the LP *Rock 'N' Roll Music.*

1995: **A** was released on the CD *Anthology 1.* The same year, **F** and **G** were included on the home video *The Making of "A Hard Day's Night."*

2003: **H** was released on the soundtrack of the *Anthology* DVD.

66. Studio session

Date: 25 February 1964
Time: 2:30–5:30 p.m.
Location: EMI Studio 2
Producer: George Martin

[A.] And I Love Her—take 2 (mono) (1:50)

The afternoon session began with a brand-new number written by Paul, "And I Love Her." After a false start or breakdown, the Beatles completed a take (**A**) with Paul singing and playing bass, John on acoustic guitar, George on his twelve-string Rickenbacker, and Ringo on drums.

The arrangement is quite different to the finished product, opening with stridently strummed acoustic guitar, accompanied by tom-tom and hi-hat on the first verse. The full drum kit kicks in for the second verse, along with bass guitar and pizzicato arpeggiations from the twelve-string. With no contrasting section composed yet, a third straight verse is followed by the familiar half-step modulation and a Rickenbacker solo. The last verse is a repeat of the third in the new key, and the ending trails off haphazardly.

It's clearly a song with potential, and they rightly decided a minor overhaul was in order, leaving it for the next day. The session concluded with the first three takes of John's "I Should Have Known Better," but this would also have to wait for the following day.

RELEASE HISTORY

1995: **A** was released on the CD *Anthology 1.*

67. Studio session

Date: 26 February 1964
Time: 2:30–5:30 p.m.
Location: EMI Studio 2
Producer: George Martin

[A.] I Should Have Known Better—take 8 (mono) (0:15)
[B.] I Should Have Known Better—take 11 (mono) (0:14)

[C.] I Should Have Known Better—RM1 (2:40)
Mixed: 3 March 1964

[D.] I Should Have Known Better—RS1 (2:42)
Mixed: 22 June 1964

[E.] I Should Have Known Better—RS from take 22 (0:31)
[F.] I Should Have Known Better—RS from take 22 (#2) (0:29)

In the morning, George Martin and Norman Smith mixed "Can't Buy Me Love" and "You Can't Do That" into mono for the upcoming single. After lunch, the Beatles got back down to work, continuing where they'd left off the previous night. "I Should Have Known Better" was remade (starting over at take 1 according to John Barrett's tape log, although Mark Lewisohn says they commenced with take 4).

A couple of excerpts from this session were included in the *Anthology* documentary's outtake medley. After a "take seven" announcement (which may belong to this session or that for "This Boy," which it follows), we hear take 8 breaking down (**A**). At this point, John is trying to play the harmonica bits live, leaving George to carry the rhythm on his twelve-string Rickenbacker. Running out of breath halfway through the song's first line, John complains, "I can't breathe after I've done that mouth organ bit. Can we skip the mouth organ?"

They would do just that starting with take 9, John switching to acoustic guitar and leaving the harmonica aside for the moment. Take 11 (**B**) breaks down when John can't hear the chord changes: "A bit less of George. I feel as though I'm singing in a sock!"

By take 22, they had perfected a backing of drums/bass/acoustic guitar on one track and John's main vocal on a second. The third track was filled with John's second lead vocal (presumably he made a goof on the last bridge, as the second vocal is mixed out at that spot on all mixes). The final track had John's harmonica overdubs, plus George's twelve-string solo and chiming chords on the middle eights.

While overdubbing the harmonica introduction, John ran out of breath, leaving a gap in the repeating phrase. This was fixed in the mono mix (**C**) by editing, but left alone in stereo (**D**). In 1982, Capitol engineers created a new stereo variation edited to match the mono mix; this was released on the *Reel Music* compilation LP. Ron Furmanek also remixed the song from multitrack for *The Making of "A Hard Day's Night."* This mix (**E**) appears in two segments: 18 seconds of verse two and 13 seconds of the final bridge. Compared to the original stereo mix, it has the twelve-string/harmonica track moved from right to left, the rhythm track moved from left to center, and the two vocal tracks split a bit wider.

RELEASE HISTORY:

1964: **C** and **D** were released on mono and stereo copies respectively of the LP *A Hard Day's Night* in the UK (all U.S. copies included **C**). **C** is available on EMI's CD of the same title.

1970: **D** was released for the first time in the United States on the LP *Hey Jude.*

1995: **E** was included on the home video *The Making of "A Hard Day's Night."*

1996: **A** and **B** were included in the *Anthology* home video; both were bootlegged on the CD *Abbey Road Video Show.*

2003: **F** was released on the soundtrack of the *Anthology* DVD.

68. Studio session

Date: 26 February 1964
Time: 7:00–10:15 p.m.
Location: EMI Studio 2
Producer: George Martin

[A.] And I Love Her—take 11 (stereo) (0:12)

After dinner, the Beatles tackled "And I Love Her" again, improving the song with each attempt. By take 11 (**A**), the instrumentation has been lightened considerably. Ringo now plays bongos rather than his full kit, and John and George are both playing acoustic guitars. Paul plays bass and sings, but botches the lyrics ("I'd love her" rather than "You'd love her, too"), and Norman Smith calls out for take 12. They would get as far as take 19 before calling it a night.

RELEASE HISTORY

1996: **A** was included in the *Anthology* home video and was bootlegged on the CD *Abbey Road Video Show.*

69. Studio session

Date: 27 February 1964
Time: 10:00 a.m.–1:00 p.m.
Location: EMI Studio 2
Producer: George Martin

[A.] And I Love Her—take 21 announcement (stereo) (0:02)
[B.] Tell Me Why—take 4 (mono) (0:15)

[C.] Tell Me Why—RM1 (2:05)
[D.] And I Love Her—RM1 (2:28)
Mixed: 3 March 1964

[E.] And I Love Her—RM2 (2:27)
[F.] And I Love Her—RS1 (2:28)
[G.] Tell Me Why—RS1 (2:07)
Mixed: 22 June 1964

[H.] Tell Me Why—RM from take 8 (1:42)
[I.] And I Love Her—RS from take 21 (2:27)
[J.] Tell Me Why—RS from take 8 (1:34)
[K.] And I Love Her—RS from take 21 (#2) (1:12)

A productive morning began with the culmination of three days' work on "And I Love Her." With John's help, Paul had written a middle eight section (with the singer addressing his love directly rather than a third party). George had worked out a gorgeous Spanish guitar solo, as well as a plucked riff to open and close the song.

Only two more takes were needed; what is apparently Norman Smith's announcement for the last of these (**A**) appears in the *Anthology* outtake medley preceding the snippet of take 11. The backing consisted of Paul's bass, John's acoustic rhythm, and Ringo's bongos on one track. George's guitar work had a track of its own, leaving two tracks for Paul's vocals, one of which was accompanied by claves (rhythm sticks).

The song's first mono mix (**D**) was sent to United Artists and Capitol; it appears on all mono U.S. releases and in the original film soundtrack of *A Hard Day's Night.* This has Paul's vocal single-tracked throughout except on the title line and the middle eight. Ron Furmanek re-created this in a new stereo mix (**I**) for *The Making of "A Hard Day's Night."* This mix has George's guitar left, second vocal right, and the other two tracks centered.

A second mono mix (**E**) was done for British record release the same day as the initial stereo mix (**F**). Both these mixes have Paul's vocal double-tracked throughout the song except on the first "bright are the stars that shine, dark is the sky." An odd variation of **F** was released on the German *Something New* album, with the ending edited to extend the closing riff (this curiosity was included on *The Beatles Box* in the UK and the *Rarities* LP in the United States).

"Tell Me Why" was John's attempt at "knocking off" an upbeat girl group–style song for the film. He had a nifty knack for knocking off such numbers, and with some swinging drumming from Ringo and luscious three-part harmonies, the song packs a mighty wallop. It was taped in eight takes, the fourth of which (**B**) broke down near the start when George had trouble hitting his vocal pitch.

The standard bass, drum, and guitars backing went on one track while John, Paul, and George sang live on a second. The third track was reserved for a bassy piano overdub, and further vocals went on the final track. But they wanted even more vocals on the bridge ("well, I'm beggin' on my bended knees . . ."), so this was "punched in" on the piano track (from 1:27–1:44 in the song).

The mono mix released on record (**C**) has John's vocal single-tracked for the "calls" of each verse and for the first half of the bridge. The mono mix used in the film (**H**) is similar, but uses the alternate "piano track punch-in" as the bridge vocal (John sings the line quite differently than on the two main vocal tracks). This mix also has the piano mixed louder than **C.**

The original stereo mix (**G**) leaves all four tracks open throughout, allowing us to hear both main vocals, the punched-in vocal, and some squeaky guitar strings at the conclusion. Ron Furmanek's remix (**J**) for *The Making of "A Hard Day's Night"* centers the rhythm, moves the piano/vocal track from right to left, and separates the two main vocal tracks slightly. Like the mono mixes, it leaves the verse "calls" single-tracked. It appears in two segments of 56 and 51 seconds (with 8 seconds of overlap).

RELEASE HISTORY:

1964: **C** and **E** were released on mono copies of the LP *A Hard Day's Night* in the UK and are available on EMI's CD of the same title. In the United States, **D** was released on a single and mono copies of *Something New,* as well as all pressings of United Artists' *A Hard Day's Night* LP. **F** and **G** appeared on stereo copies of *A Hard Day's Night* in the UK and of *Something New* in the United States. **H** was included on the film soundtrack of *A Hard Day's Night;* it's available on the CD-R compilation *Vinyl to the Core.*

1995: **I** and **J** were included on the home video *The Making of "A Hard Day's Night."*

1996: **A** and **B** were included in the *Anthology* home video; both were bootlegged on the CD *Abbey Road Video Show.*

2003: **K** was released on the soundtrack of the *Anthology* DVD.

70. Studio session

Date: 27 February 1964
Time: 2:30–7:15 p.m.
Location: EMI Studio 2
Producer: George Martin

[A.] If I Fell—RM1 (2:17)
Mixed: 3 March 1964

[B.] If I Fell—RS1 (2:17)
Mixed: 22 June 1964

[C.] If I Fell—RS from take 15 (0:36)
[D.] If I Fell—RS from take 15 (#2) (2:17)

Saving the best for last, "If I Fell" concluded this session in grand style. The lilting melody of John's demo was enhanced tenfold when sung as a duet with Paul. By take 15, the backing was perfected, with John's acoustic guitar, Paul's bass, and Ringo's drums on one track, John and Paul's blissfully wedded vocals on a second, and George's twelve-string Rickenbacker gently ringing on a third track. To strengthen the vocals even further, John and Paul sang the whole song through again on the fourth track, with George adding more twelve-string touches after the first verse and at the very end.

Paul had trouble reaching the high note on the word "vain" the second time around, so George Martin mixed out the faulty vocal track on the words "new love was in vain" for the mono mix (**A**). This mix also left John's introductory vocal single-tracked. The stereo mix (**B**), done more than three months later, was a bit of a rush job (pretty much the whole LP had to be mixed for stereo in a day). In addition to leaving both of John's vocals up for the intro, this mixes out the wrong vocal track on "was in vain," exposing Paul's cracking voice for all to hear. Ron Furmanek's remix (**C**) moves the twelve-string from right to left, splits the vocal tracks slightly, and centers the rhythm track.

The Beatles were unbowed under the pressure of creating a movie soundtrack from thin air. After just three days of work, six strong new original compositions had all been turned into unrivaled studio recordings of astonishing brilliance.

RELEASE HISTORY

1964: **A** was released on mono copies of the LP *A Hard Day's Night,* and is available on EMI's CD of the same title. **B** was released on stereo copies of *A Hard Day's Night* in the UK and of *Something New* in the United States.

1995: **C** was included on the home video *The Making of "A Hard Day's Night."*

2003: **D** was released on the soundtrack of the *Anthology* DVD.

71. Radio performance

Date: 28 February 1964
Time: 6:30–9:00 p.m.
Location: Studio 1, BBC Piccadilly Studios, London
Producer: Bryant Marriott
Host: Alan Freeman
Broadcast: 30 March 1964, 10:00 a.m.–noon
BBC Light Programme
From Us to You #2

[A.] From Us to You (0:58)
[B.] intro (0:05)
[C.] You Can't Do That (2:32)
[D.] intro (0:20)
[E.] Roll Over Beethoven (2:15)
[F.] outro (0:08)
[G.] intro (0:39)
[H.] Till There Was You (2:12)
[I.] outro (0:05)
[J.] intro (0:14)
[K.] I Wanna Be Your Man (2:08)
[L.] outro (0:06)
[M.] intro (0:56)
[N.] Please Mr. Postman (2:21)
[O.] outro (0:07)
[P.] All My Loving (2:05)
[Q.] outro (0:05)
[R.] intro (1:03)
[S.] This Boy (2:12)
[T.] intro (0:22)
[U.] Can't Buy Me Love (2:06)
[V.] outro (0:28)
[W.] From Us to You (0:57)

Wedged in the middle of TV, recording, and filming commitments was this recording session for another BBC Radio "Bank Holiday Beatles Special." It fell under the same title as the previous one, *From Us to You* (with a fresh recording of the theme tune). Taking the place of previous host Rolf Harris was another Australian: disc jockey Alan Freeman, late of BBC Radio's *Pick of the Pops.* Guests on this edition of *From Us to You* included the Hollies, Peter and Gordon, and the Rolling Stones.

The Beatles' BBC Radio sessions were ceasing to resemble live concerts and edging closer to duplicating their polished studio work. Not only were they abandoning the notion of performing unfamiliar material from their repertoire (a listener's request to hear "Youngblood" is denied), they were taking advantage of the studio setting.

For instance, "This Boy" and "Can't Buy Me Love" both have double-tracked lead vocals, and the latter also has a double-tracked guitar solo. "You Can't Do That" includes a cowbell overdub, while George plays his new twelve-string guitar on that song, "I Wanna Be Your Man," "Can't Buy Me Love," and even the theme tune, "From Us to You"! Not everything is a slavish imitation of the record, as both "I Wanna Be Your Man" and "This Boy" come to a full stop rather than fading out. But in general, this show has very little to offer musically over the familiar albums and singles.

The chat is not much more entertaining, with forced "adversarial banter" between Alan Freeman and the Fabs. John does take the opportunity to plug his book, *In His Own Write,* explaining that "It's about rubbish . . . with drawings, of course." They also play both sides of their freshly recorded single, mixed a mere two days earlier. Things being what they were in 1964, by the time the show aired, the single was already number 1 in the UK.

According to Kevin Howlett's book *The Beatles at the BBC,* this show "is the only Beatles session from which five songs were actually kept in the main BBC Sound Archive on a one-sided LP disc." The disc apparently contains the following, in this order: **A** (short edit with a different voice-over stating "It's the Beatles!"), **U,** one line of **V, G** (incomplete), **H, I, D–F, R** (incomplete), **P, Q, J–L,** a bit more of **V,** and a short edit of **W** with an alternate voice-over.

This archive disc was rebroadcast some years later, an airing that appears on the obscure vinyl bootleg *Shout.* It opens with the following introduction: "What you're going to hear is a BBC Radio program of thirteen and a half minutes' duration. And the program was called *From Us to You.* It features the Beatles, but it's hosted by a certain gentleman who works now not far from these studios in London. I'm not going to tell you who he actually is, but I'll give you a clue." This is followed by a snatch of the *Pick of the Pops* theme tune, "At the Sign of the Swinging Cymbal."

RELEASE HISTORY

1973: **D–F, J–L, P, Q,** and incomplete versions of **R** and **W** were bootlegged in very good quality on the LP *Mary Jane.* These are all from the last half of the archive disc.

1980: The bootleg LP *Rough Notes* included excellent copies of **N, S,** and **W.**

1981: Very good versions of **S** and **U** appeared on the vinyl bootleg *Airtime.*

1982: The radio special *The Beatles at the Beeb* included **D–F, H–L, P, Q, U,** and incomplete versions of **A, G, R, V,** and **W.** All were in excellent quality, and all were sourced from the archive disc.

1988: A very good-quality off-air tape of nearly the entire program (**A, D, G, J,** and **R** are all slightly incomplete) appeared on the bootleg LP *The Beatles at the Beeb, Volume 9.* This recording is missing **I, L,** and **Q,** all of which are outros from Alan Freeman that may have been recorded specially for the archive disc version.

1993: Great Dane's bootleg CD boxed set *The Complete BBC Sessions* reconstructed the entire show, but used incomplete versions of **A** and **G** and omitted **L.**

1994: Apple's *Live at the BBC* CD included excellent quality versions of **A** (edited), **D, E, G** (incomplete), **H, K, P,** and **U,** all sourced from the archive disc.

1998: The CD-R *Attack of the Filler Beebs!, Episode 2* included a complete version of **G,** edited from the off-air tape and archive disc sources.

72. Studio session

Date: 1 March 1964
Time: 7:00–10:00 p.m.
Location: EMI Studio 2
Producer: George Martin

[A.] I Call Your Name—studio chat (0:02)

[B.] I'm Happy Just to Dance with You—RM1 (1:54)
[C.] I Call Your Name—RM1 (2:10)
Mixed: 3 March 1964

[D.] Long Tall Sally—RS1 (2:01)
[E.] I Call Your Name—RS1 (2:06)
[F.] Long Tall Sally—RM1 (2:01)
Mixed: 10 March 1964

[G.] Long Tall Sally—RM1 (#2) (2:00)
[H.] I Call Your Name—edit of RM1 (#2)/RM2 (2:07)
Mixed: 4 June 1964

[I.] I'm Happy Just to Dance with You—RS1 (1:54)
[J.] I Call Your Name—edit of RS1 (#2)/RS3 (2:06)
[K.] Long Tall Sally—RS1 (#2) (2:00)
Mixed: 22 June 1964

[L.] I'm Happy Just to Dance with You—RS from take 4 (0:31)
[M.] Long Tall Sally—RS from take 1 (2:00)

With one day to go before filming started, only five songs had been completed for the film soundtrack, so a Sunday morning session was arranged to tape a few more candidates. Capitol Records also wanted to compile a follow-up LP to *Meet the Beatles!* but were a couple of songs short; they would pounce on any song not headed for the soundtrack.

The session began with George's vocal spotlight for the film, "I'm Happy Just to Dance with You." John and Paul wrote this specifically for George, and both later admitted there was no way they would have sung it. Presumably if George had rejected it, Tommy Quickly or Cilla Black might have ended up with another Lennon/McCartney reject.

The backing was recorded in four takes, with bass and drums on one track and John's rhythm guitar and George's twelve-string Rickenbacker on a second (chiming the opening chords). George then overdubbed two lead vocals on the remaining tracks, accompanied by John and Paul on one of them. Ringo also added some extra tom-tom work on one of the vocal tracks.

The original mono (**B**) and stereo (**I**) mixes sound similar. Ron Furmanek remixed the song for *The Making of "A Hard Day's Night,"* which includes two segments of 11 and 20 seconds (**L**). Compared to the original stereo mix, the bass/drum track has been moved from left to center, while the vocal track with tom-tom is moved to left of center. As neither excerpt of the remix includes backing vocals, it's unclear which of the two vocal tracks they appeared on.

With the supply of new original compositions depleted, they turned to an old standby, Little Richard's "Long Tall Sally," which Paul had been singing live since before he joined the Quarry Men. The studio version retained their standard concert arrangement, with John taking the first guitar solo and George the second, but had the luxury of adding piano. George Martin played this on the basic track to retain a live feel, and it paid off with everyone turning in an outstanding first-take performance that nearly manages to make Little Richard's original sound docile in comparison.

The song has Paul's solo vocal on one track and the piano on a second throughout. A close listen to the stereo mixes reveals that the track inputs for each guitar were actually swapped live during the take. The song begins with drums, bass, and John's guitar in the left channel and George's in the right, occupying its own track. After John's solo, his guitar moves to the right and George's joins the bass/drum track, so that both solos will occupy the same stereo position. This attention to detail shows that George Martin at least cared how the stereo mixes sounded, even if the Beatles may not have yet.

With some time remaining on the clock, they decided to reclaim an old song previously donated to Billy J Kramer. "I Call Your Name" was one of John's very first compositions, written in his bedroom at Menlove Avenue, with help from Paul. In 1963, he added a newly written bridge for Kramer's session. To this, the Beatles' version adds a guitar solo backed by a slightly "blue-beat" rhythm, although it sounds more Scouse than ska. This arrangement was evidently created on the spot, as prior to take 1, John can be heard speculating whether they should use Kramer's intro and solo, "'cause it's our song anyroad, innit?" (**A**).

The backing consisted of drums/bass/rhythm guitar on one track, John's main vocal on a second, and George's twelve-string guitar on a third. This was perfected in seven takes, so John's second vocal and Ringo's cowbell were added to the last of these, filling the tape's fourth track. Playbacks revealed that take five's guitar solo was in fact superior, so it would be spliced into the body of take 7 to produce a master. For some reason, the stereo mixes also tack on the guitar intro from take 5 (see below for details).

"I Call Your Name" and "Long Tall Sally" were each mixed in mono and stereo in March; these mixes were sent to the United States for inclusion on Capitol's *The Beatles' Second Album.* Label copy for the album was approved March 12, a mere two days after mixing was completed. While Capitol knew the titles, they didn't have the actual tapes yet, and labels on the initial pressings have no timings for either song. Mono acetates were cut in Hollywood March 17, and the album was rushed into shops by April 10.

When it was decided to release the two songs on an EP titled *Long Tall Sally* in the UK, George Martin remixed both numbers for mono and stereo in June, confusingly numbering each mix as "RM1" or "RS1." With EPs being issued in mono only, the new stereo mixes went unused for several years.

Compared to both UK mixes, the U.S. mono mix of "Long Tall Sally" (**F**) has less echo added, while the U.S. stereo mix (**D**) oddly has more, plus a heavier bass sound. The U.S. mono mix of "I Call Your Name" (**C**) has the longest fade of any mix; it begins with take 7 and cuts to take 5 at 1:07 (before "name"). The UK mono mix (**H**) has the edit to take 5 at 1:04 (before the words "I call"). Both mono mixes return to take 7 after the solo (just before the words "don't you know").

The U.S. stereo mix (**E**) opens with take 5 and edits to take 7 at 0:07 (before "call"), then to take 5 at 1:05 (before "call"), and back to take 7 at 1:25 (before "can't take it"). The UK stereo mix (**J**) also opens with take 5, and jumps to take 7 at 0:11 (before "but you're not there"), to take 5 at 1:06 (before "name"), and concludes with take 7 at 1:23 (before "don't you know").

RELEASE HISTORY

1964: **C** and **F** were released on mono copies of *The Beatles' Second Album* in the United States; stereo copies included **D** and **E. G** and **H** were released on the EP *Long Tall Sally* in the UK (available on a CD-EP of the same title). **B** and **I** were released on mono and stereo copies respectively of the LP *A Hard Day's Night* (in the UK) and *Something New* (in the United States). **B** is available on EMI's CD of *A Hard Day's Night.*

1968: The Australian LP *Greatest Hits, Volume 1* apparently included the first release of **K.**

1976: **J** and **K** were released on the LP *Rock 'N' Roll Music;* both are available on the CD *Past Masters, Volume 1.*

1995: **L** was included on the home video *The Making of "A Hard Day's Night."*

2000: **A** was released on the CD *Liverpool Sound Collage.*

73. Studio session

Date: 25 February–1 March 1964 (?)
Location: EMI Studio 2 (?)
Producer: George Martin

[A.] "Train Music" (0:06)

During one of the opening scenes of *A Hard Day's Night,* Ringo switches on his transistor radio and a generic rock tune blares out for a few seconds before it's forcibly shut off by Richard Vernon's irritated passenger. The film's producer, Walter Shenson, eventually verified what many suspected: The music was actually performed by the Beatles, presumably during sessions for the soundtrack the week prior to the start of filming.

It's an entirely instrumental fragment, performed in E major with John playing a Chuck Berry–like boogie pattern and George wailing away on lead guitar.

RELEASE HISTORY

1999: This recording was included on the CD-R compilation *Vinyl to the Core,* lifted from the original mono film soundtrack.

74. Radio interview **P, G**

Date: 2–6 March 1964
Location: train
Interviewer: Roger Henning
Broadcast: 3DB, Melbourne
Length: 0:23

In December 1963, Brian Epstein had signed a contract for the Beatles to tour Australia the following June. London-based Aussie native Roger Henning had interviewed the group a couple of times (see the April 18, 1963, entry), and was able to record a bit of advance promotion during the first week of filming for *A Hard Day's Night.*

From aboard the train that served as the location for the movie's opening scenes, Paul and George offer brief greetings to fans in Melbourne. The extent of Paul's knowledge of Australia seems to be that "it's warm and sunny and they keep all the convicts out there."

Also in circulation are 26 seconds of silent ITV News footage from March 2, mostly consisting of Paul waving out the train window at fans from Paddington Station and elsewhere.

RELEASE HISTORY

1981: This brief interview was released on the LP *The Beatles Talk Downunder* and has been reissued on numerous CDs such as *Inside Interviews: Talk Downunder: Australia Beatlemania; Beatles Tapes, Volume 2: Early Beatlemania 1963–1964;* and *Talk Downunder, Volume 1.*

75. Radio interview **P, G**

Date: 16 March 1964
Location: London (via telephone)
Interviewer: Murray Kaufman
Broadcast: WINS-AM, New York City
Length: 1:45

Scandal erupted across the US Beatlemaniac community when gossip columnist Walter Winchell reported that Paul McCartney was indisputably secretly married to actress Jane Asher. While hosting a closed-circuit broadcast of the Beatles' Washington, D.C., concert film over the weekend of March 14 and 15, Murray the K was beseeched by fans to find out the truth. He did so via his "beeper phone," most likely on Monday the sixteenth, a day when only Ringo was needed on the film set. Paul admits that Jane is his girlfriend but says the rumor of their wedding is "a lie."

Two other phone-interview fragments with Murray probably originate from this same date. In the first, Paul reminds him that their new single, "Can't Buy Me Love," was the same song he had played to Murray on the piano during their yacht voyage in Miami. In the second, George confirms that he sings "Do You Want to Know a Secret," but tells Murray "don't spread it 'round," as he's not too proud of his vocal performance. The song had been included on the LP *Introducing the Beatles* in January, but was released on a U.S. single March 23.

RELEASE HISTORY

1965: A 53-second excerpt of this recording (Paul talking about Jane) was released on the EP *The Beatles & Murray the K: As It Happened,* copied on the LP and CD *Timeless II.* The other two segments circulate in fair quality among collectors.

76. Radio interview — J, G, R

Date: 18 March 1964
Location: Twickenham Film Studios, London
Producer: John Fawcett Wilson
Interviewer: George Harrison
Broadcast: 22 March 1964, 3:00–4:00 p.m.
BBC Light Programme
The Public Ear
Length: 3:12

BBC Radio's *The Public Ear* gave George Harrison a tape recorder and free rein to file a report from Twickenham, and he took the opportunity to interview his bandmates and plug some of their projects.

The show opens with an announcer reading out a letter from a fan, Barbara Garnet, requesting advance notice of any Beatle appearances. Ringo's warning follows, and he tells everyone to phone their friends and listen in. The highlight of the show is a segment on John's imminently published book *In His Own Write.* Ringo comments that he's never read anything like it, and George says it must be because Ringo's never read before. John also treats the listeners to a lively recital of his poem "Alec Speaking."

The show closes with George and Ringo reading the credits and adding their own names as coproducers. This segment may have actually been taped the following day (see next entry for details).

RELEASE HISTORY

1988: These recordings were broadcast in the December 3 episode of BBC Radio's *The Beeb's Lost Beatles Tapes.* They are available in excellent sound on the bootleg CD *The Beatles Broadcast Collection, Trailer 1.*

77. Radio interview — P, G

Date: 19 March 1964
Time: noon
Location: limo from Twickenham to Park Lane, London
Producer: John Fawcett Wilson
Interviewer: George Harrison
Broadcast: 22 March 1964, 3:00–4:00 p.m.
BBC Light Programme
The Public Ear
Length: 1:45

As the Beatles were chauffeured from the film set to an awards ceremony at the Dorchester Hotel, George played BBC reporter again and taped a conversation with Paul in the backseat.

He teases Paul about memorizing dialogue for the film, and Paul readily admits he waits until the last minute to learn his lines: "I feel it gives an air of impromptuity." Paul pretends to forget George's name, and he identifies himself as from *Public Ear,* apparently sticking out his ear to demonstrate ("Oh, yes it is a bit," agrees Paul). George thanks Paul for the interview and promises him a 3-shilling fee.

RELEASE HISTORY

1996: This interview was rebroadcast in a BBC Radio 2 special on New Year's Eve. It appears from this source on the bootleg CD *The Beatles Broadcast Collection, Trailer 1.*

78. Newsreel footage

Date: 19 March 1964
Time: early afternoon
Location: Dorchester Hotel, London
Host: Peter Haigh
Broadcast: 20 March 1964, 10:30–11:00 p.m.
BBC TV
The Variety Club of Great Britain Awards for 1963
Length: 6:55

The Beatles dropped by the Variety Club luncheon to accept the joint award for Show Business Personalities of 1963. A list of the other winners reveals the astonishing depth of up-and-coming British talent in 1963: Julie Christie, Sean Connery, Maggie Smith, Patrick Macnee, and Honor Blackman. Also honored were Wilfrid Brambell (concurrently playing Paul's grandfather in *A Hard Day's Night*) and Margaret Rutherford (then in her seventies and famous for portraying detective Miss Jane Marple).

BBC TV filmed the ceremony for airing the following evening; their coverage was narrated by Peter Haigh, the event's Barker (master of ceremonies). The show opens with Beatles fans waiting in the rain for their idols to arrive; John walks past the camera and holds up a copy of *In His Own Write* (upside-down at first). Inside, the group poses for photos with their awards, Paul takes over George's role and "interviews" his colleagues, and they meet Labour Party leader Harold Wilson, who would be presenting the awards to them at the ceremony.

Wilson also gave an ingratiating speech referring to his fellow Liverpudlians as "our friends, the Beatles"; this is omitted from the BBC telecast (presumably due to political content) but is included in a Pathé newsreel of the event, *Beatles Get Show Biz Top Award*. The BBC's coverage picks back up with Haigh's introduction of the group, who rise to accept the awards from Wilson. They each step to the microphone to say a few words, with John pretending to confuse the silver heart-shaped awards with "Purple Hearts." George gets off the best joke though, thanking "Mr. Barker" and "Mr. Dobson" (Barker & Dobson's being a brand of candy). Interestingly, most printed sources, including Hunter Davies, Ray Coleman, and Mark Lewisohn, attribute this quip to John, but the filmed evidence proves otherwise.

John hastens their departure by declaring that "the fella on the film wants us, and he says it's costing him a fortune." As the Beatles exit the room, a solitary female scream pierces through the open doorway, causing much hilarity among those remaining.

RELEASE HISTORY

1993: A 1:21 excerpt of the Beatles' acceptance speeches (omitting the "Barker/Dobson" joke) was released on the CD *The Beatles Tapes, Volume 2: Early Beatlemania*. The BBC footage and Pathé newsreel circulate on video, as does 1:22 of ITV News footage.

79. Radio interview **R**

Date: 20 March 1964
Time: morning/afternoon
Location: Twickenham Film Studios, London
Interviewer: Lyn Fairhurst
Broadcast: 12 April 1964, 3:00–4:00 p.m.
BBC Light Programme
Movie-Go-Round
Length: 1:12

The Beatles had been interviewed by Peter Noble the previous day for BBC Radio's film magazine *Movie-Go-Round*. Also included in the report was this follow-up solo chat with Ringo, conducted by Lyn Fairhurst.

While he stresses that they're enjoying the filming process, Ringo complains about the wake-up calls requiring them on the set early each morning. Since their lives are "back-to-front of the ordinary person," they are more accustomed to turning in at dawn, rather than being forced to rise with the sun. He also gives a brief synopsis of the movie's plot.

RELEASE HISTORY

This interview circulates in good quality from an off-air tape. Six reels of ¼-inch tape consisting of Peter Noble's interviews from March 19 were auctioned by Bonham's March 22, 1996, but failed to sell.

80. Newsreel footage

Date: 20 March 1964
Location: Studio 9, Television House, London
Broadcast: 20 March 1964
ITV
Length: 1:11

At this stage in their career, the Beatles made news by merely existing and showing up somewhere. In this case, it was at a TV studio to appear live on *Ready, Steady, Go!*, and ITV News devoted a full minute of an evening's newscast to show film of their arrival at the studio, a bit of action inside the studio (with sound), and their departure past a horde of delighted fans.

RELEASE HISTORY:

This footage was included on the compilation video *Beatles 1962 to 1970.*

81. TV performance

Date: 20 March 1964
Time: 6:15–7:00 p.m.
Location: Studio 9, Television House, London
Producer: Vicki Wickham
Host: Keith Fordyce
Interviewer: Cathy McGowan
Broadcast: live
Associated-Rediffusion TV
Ready, Steady, Go!

[A.] **It Won't Be Long** (2:08)
[B.] **award presentation and chat w/Paul** (1:39)
[C.] **artwork contest and chat w/Ringo** (4:14)
[D.] **chat w/John** (2:49)
[E.] **You Can't Do That** (2:29)
[F.] **chat w/George** (1:57)
[G.] **Can't Buy Me Love** (2:11)
[H.] **Please Mr. Postman** (2:30)

The Beatles' second live appearance on *Ready, Steady, Go!* opens with a mimed performance of the leadoff track from *With the Beatles.* Keith Fordyce then presents the group with an award from *Billboard* magazine in honor of their unprecedented feat of occupying the top three spots ("I Want to Hold Your Hand," "She Loves You," and "Please Please Me") in the singles chart. He adds that they will have the top four spots in the following week's chart (the week ending March 28, with the addition of "Twist and Shout"), and 10 percent of the top 100. Cathy McGowan then chats with Paul about the songs in their film and their visit to the Playboy Club in New York.

The studio is decorated with viewers' submissions for a Beatle artwork competition, and "This Boy" is played as the group walks around surveying the entries. Armed with markers, they also deface many of the pieces, adding mustaches, glasses, and antennae to their own images. John scrawls, "I love Elvis" and "Buy my book" while Ringo adds the letters "ne" to the end of the words "Ready Steady Go." The contest winner is Jeremy Ratter, whose pop art entry (John: "Pop art the sailor man!") wins him a pair of LPs. John presents Jeremy with his chosen albums, one by Charlie Mingus and one of Shostakovich, with a conciliatory "Each to his own!"

Cathy chats with Ringo about his clothing, asking if he's a mod. "No, I'm not a mod. Or a rocker. I'm a mocker." Although he admits the joke is borrowed from John, Ringo would immortalize it during a scene shot April 2 for *A Hard Day's Night.* John then chats with Fordyce about *In His Own Write* and is asked to choose a record. He settles on Marvin Gaye, the Miracles, or the Shirelles, but is roped by a passing Alma Cogan into choosing her cover of "Tennessee Waltz."

After a lip-synced "You Can't Do That," it's George's turn to talk with Cathy, mostly about their recent U.S. tour. George enthuses about American drive-in theaters and claims that his favorite film star is Margaret Rutherford, which inspires great laughter from the other Beatles ("She's a mod," says John sarcastically). Asked to pick his favorite records, George unsurprisingly selects "Motown, Tamla records, Mary Wells, Miracles, Marvin Gaye, Impressions, all that crowd."

The Beatles lip-sync their latest single (**G**), and to close the show, their recording of "Please Mr. Postman" plays while Paul signs autographs and Ringo dances in the same pugilistic style glimpsed at the Peppermint Lounge and in the "Le Circle" scene of *A Hard Day's Night.*

RELEASE HISTORY

E–G and a portion of **B** were released on the home video *Ready, Steady Go!, Volume 1.* The Japanese laser disc *Ready, Steady, Go! Special Edition* included **A–G.** The soundtrack to **E–G** also appeared on the vinyl bootleg *Ready, Steady, Go!*

82. Newsreel footage

Date: 23 March 1964
Time: 10:25–11:15 p.m.
Location: Empire Ballroom, London
Broadcast: live
BBC TV
The Carl-Alan Awards
Length: 1:51

The trophies continued to pour in for the Beatles. In addition to the Variety Club honor, the *Billboard* accolade, and five Ivor Novello songwriting awards, March saw them receive a pair of Carl-Alan Awards. These apparently had something to do with ballroom dancing and were bestowed for "best beat group" and "best vocal record for dancing" ("She Loves You").

In reality, it was little more than an excuse for the group to dress in black ties and accept the honors from the duke of Edinburgh, Prince Philip. BBC TV broadcast the proceedings live, and a Pathé newsreel titled *Duke Meets Beatles* covered the event, including a scene of John and Ringo struggling to wrest control of one of the awards from each other, much to the prince's amusement.

RELEASE HISTORY

The Pathé newsreel circulates on video, as does 19 seconds of BBC TV footage included in a *Panorama* profile on Brian Epstein, originally aired March 30.

82a. Newsreel footage **J, G**

Date: 28 March 1964
Location: Dromoland Castle Hotel
Length: 0:07

During a well-deserved Easter weekend vacation, John and George traveled to Ireland along with Cynthia and Pattie. During their stay at the Dromoland Castle Hotel, the two Beatles agreed to pose for newspaper photographers, goofing around with croquet mallets and having a swordfight on the hotel's grounds. The latter was also filmed and can be seen in this brief clip (George has the upper hand in the duel).

RELEASE HISTORY

This silent footage circulates on video among collectors.

83. TV performance

Date: 31 March 1964
Location: Scala Theatre, London
Producer: Walter Shenson
Broadcast: 24 May 1964, 8:00–9:00 p.m.
CBS
The Ed Sullivan Show

[A.] You Can't Do That (2:44)

The climax and musical payoff of *A Hard Day's Night* was a Beatles concert, ostensibly being performed for TV cameras. More importantly, it was performed for an audience of 350 "extras" who needed no direction from Dick Lester to re-create a Beatlemanic atmosphere.

In addition to performing "If I Fell," "Tell Me Why," "I Should Have Known Better," and "She Loves You," all used in the final cut, the Beatles also lip-synced "You Can't Do That." This didn't make it into the film, but the full song was offered as a preview to *The Ed Sullivan Show,* where it was broadcast following Ed's exclusive interview with the group (see the April 17 entry).

Note that the version tacked on to the end of the home video *The Making of "A Hard Day's Night"* is not quite as originally broadcast, with scenes from the *Follow the Beatles* documentary (see the April 29 entry) spliced in at the start and finish, extending the clip's length to 3:01.

RELEASE HISTORY

The May 24 *Ed Sullivan Show* broadcast circulates on video. The documentary *The Making of "A Hard Day's Night,"* available on home video, includes most of this footage.

84. Radio performance

Date: 31 March 1964
Time: 7:00–10:30 p.m.
Location: Playhouse Theatre, London
Producers: Jimmy Grant, Bernie Andrews
Host: Brian Matthew
Broadcast: 4 April 1964, 10:00 a.m.–noon
BBC Light Programme
Saturday Club #287

- **[A.] intro** (0:07)
- **[B.] Everybody's Trying to Be My Baby** (2:24)
- **[C.] intro** (0:09)
- **[D.] I Call Your Name** (2:05)
- **[E.] outro** (0:02)
- **[F.] I Got a Woman** (2:33)
- **[G.] intro** (2:04)
- **[H.] You Can't Do That** (2:32)
- **[I.] intro** (0:14)
- **[J.] Can't Buy Me Love** (2:06)
- **[K.] intro** (2:03)
- **[L.] Sure to Fall (In Love with You)** (2:14)
- **[M.] Long Tall Sally** (1:58)
- **[N.] outro** (0:01)

After filming at the Scala and grabbing a quick dinner, it was over to the Playhouse to rehearse and record their ninth appearance on *Saturday Club,* breaking only for a half hour at 9 p.m. for Brian Matthew to interview John for a separate program, *A Slice of Life.*

Musically, the Beatles perform both sides of their new single, two tracks recently recorded for an EP, a pair of Carl Perkins oldies, and a cover of Elvis Presley's cover of Ray Charles' "I Got a Woman." Many of the songs (**D, F, J**) feature double-tracked lead vocals, while "I Call Your Name" includes a spectacular lyrical blunder from John at the end.

Chat-wise, they read requests prior to "You Can't Do That," and George confirms that his mother not only listens to *Saturday Club* while gardening, but had sent in a request for his birthday (see the February 22 entry). George shouts out a greeting: "Hello, Mrs. Harrison! I'm twenty-one now!" John adds, "Get well soon!" Later in the show (**K**), Paul gives a dull and drawn-out description of a scene from *A Hard Day's Night.* Matthew's sarcastic verdict: "Hilarious."

RELEASE HISTORY

1974: An incomplete version of **F** was included on the vinyl bootleg *Soldier of Love* in good quality.

1980: The bootleg LP *Broadcasts* contained very good-quality copies of **F, L,** and **M.**

1982: **F** and **L** were included in the radio special *The Beatles at the Beeb.*

1988: A decent-quality tape of nearly the entire show (**B–N**) appeared on the vinyl bootleg *The Beatles at the Beeb, Volume 10.* The same year, excellent copies of **F–H, K,** and **L** were broadcast in the radio series *The Beeb's Lost Beatles Tapes,* although **G** and **K** were heavily edited and the opening word ("well") was missing from **F.**

2003: The entire show (**A–N**) was bootlegged on the CD boxed set *The Beatles at the Beeb.*

85. Radio interview — J, G, R

Date: 1 April 1964
Location: NEMS Enterprises, London
Interviewer: Bernice Lumb
Length: 10:30

Following a day of filming at the Scala Theatre, Paul traveled to Liverpool to visit a sick relative while John, George, and Ringo remained in London. In Brian Epstein's office at NEMS headquarters, they were interviewed by Australian journalist Bernice Lumb. The interview itself is rather chaotic, with George trying to outdo John in a battle of witticisms, and all three Beatles spouting dialogue from *A Hard Day's Night.* At one point, John admits, "We might sound as though we've had some, but we don't." (True enough: They wouldn't try marijuana for another four months). They break into song a few times, including "Tie Me Kangaroo Down, Sport" and rather demented versions of "On the Street Where You Live" and "Sixteen Tons." Topics of discussion include John's book, the film screenplay, pirate radio, and the upcoming tour of Australia. The film's title has yet to be decided, although this would shortly change (see following entry).

RELEASE HISTORY

1984: This interview was released on the LP *The Beatles Talk Downunder (And All Over), Volume 2.* It has been reissued in the Inside Interviews boxed CD set, on the disc *Talk Downunder: Sydney to Seattle.* These two releases also include Bernice's interviews with Brian Epstein and BBC disc jockeys Keith Fordyce and Alan Freeman.

86. Newsreel footage

Date: 3 April 1964
Location: Twickenham Film Studios, London
Length: 0:35

Unique and rather whimsical footage for the theatrical trailer to promote *A Hard Day's Night* was filmed on this day at Twickenham, featuring the Beatles bantering while seated in baby carriages. This includes the first known mention of the film's title (Paul says it), thirteen days before the song "A Hard Day's Night" was recorded, although that phrase had already been published in John's book, in the poem "Sad Michael."

RELEASE HISTORY

1995: The complete trailer has circulated for decades on video. It was eventually released on the home video *The Making of "A Hard Day's Night"*; curiously, a foreign print with subtitles is used, and the backing music, "Can't Buy Me Love," switches between mono (when the Beatles are talking) and stereo.

87. TV interview

Date: 3 April 1964
Location: Twickenham Film Studios, London
Interviewer: Adrian Cairns
Broadcast: 9 April 1964, 10:10–10:40 p.m.
Tyne Tees TV
Star Parade
Length: 2:39

During a break on the movie set, the Beatles filmed a TV appearance for Tyne Tees' (an independent network) weekly series *Star Parade,* which covered the motion picture industry. In a unique but distracting format, questions were posed by teenage fans, filmed separately in Newcastle, and the Beatles' answers were edited in. Ringo says if he hadn't been a Beatle, he might have remained an engineer; Paul denies reports that he is married to Jane Asher; George says he and Ringo "play marbles" while John and Paul write songs; John claims he had to get married because "when you've gotta go, you've gotta go." The footage ends with a bit of clowning between the Fabs and host Adrian Cairns.

RELEASE HISTORY

This footage circulates on video thanks to a partial rebroadcast from 3 December 1982 on BBC TV's *The Tube* as part of a profile of photographer Dezo Hoffmann.

88. Radio interview

Date: 7 April 1964
Time: afternoon
Location: Twickenham Film Studios, London
Interviewer: Tom Clay
Broadcast: WJBK-AM, Detroit
Length: 11:47

Detroit disc jockey Tom Clay dropped by the set at Twickenham this day as the Beatles filmed scenes in which they rescued Ringo from the clutches of Wilfrid Brambell and the police. While various messages for South African radio were taped in the background, Clay grabbed whichever Beatle wasn't needed on the set and recorded interviews that were later pressed onto a pair of fan club discs.

Clay corners John first to enthuse about the Peppermint West club in Hollywood and seems amazed that Ringo could have actually played drums and sung "Boys" simultaneously. In turn, John makes fun of Clay's outdated short jacket and politely listens to Clay's ramblings about a "Beatle Booster Ball" attended by thirteen thousand fans in Detroit. Before he and John can escape to the safety of the soundstage, Paul is roped into giving a loud smooch into the microphone.

As George introduces records for the South African correspondent, Ringo talks at length with Clay, mocking not only his jacket but his necktie and haircut. Clay raves about the Swinging Blue Jeans' recent cover of "Good Golly Miss Molly," but Ringo prefers Little Richard's original. Informed that John plays the harmonica on "Love Me Do," Clay sighs with girlish delight. As he featured prominently in the police station sequence, Ringo grouses that he's been working since eight that morning, while "them other bums just rolled in at twelve!" He says the film is only a day behind schedule with three weeks to go.

Neil arrives with a pot of tea, and Ringo graciously offers some to Clay's wife, who demurs and faces gentle chiding. Ringo tells Clay that he shares a flat in London with George, who breaks in with the disclaimer, "It's just a rumor!" "There's nothing wrong with it!" adds Ringo. George talks about how embarrassed he is by his vocal performance on "Do You Want to Know a Secret?" and tells Detroit fans that if the "Stamp Out the Beatles" contingent is still around, they should stamp right back.

RELEASE HISTORY

1964: Just over six minutes from this interview were included on the single "Remember, We Don't Like Them, We Love Them."

1965: Further extracts from the interview were included on the 7-inch 33⅓ RPM single *Official IBBB Interview.*

89. TV interview **P**

Date: 15 April 1964
Time: 8:30 p.m.
Location: Studio 4, Television Centre, London
Producer: Joe McGrath
Host: David Frost
Broadcast: 18 May 1964, 10:15–11:00 p.m.
BBC1
A Degree of Frost
Length: 5:15

Paul's first solo interview for BBC TV was videotaped this evening in London. The five-minute discussion was an anomaly among Beatles interviews from this era, since the questions were actually intelligent, and as a result, Paul concentrated on giving thoughtful answers. Asked about ambitions, Paul says the Beatles take things in small stages. (Frost: "Do you want to be prime minister one day?" Paul: "God, no!") Paul also discusses the benefits of having power, writing songs in idioms other than pop, and what the future holds. ("Retirement," says Paul. "It'll probably be in the year about 2010," quips Frost.)

RELEASE HISTORY

1994: The audio portion of this interview was included on the bootleg *The Beatles at the Beeb—TV,* and the whole thing circulates on video.

90. Radio interview

Date: 16 April 1964
Time: evening
Location: EMI Studio 2 (via telephone)
Interviewer: Ron Riley, Art Roberts
Broadcast: 18 April 1964, evening
WLS-AM, Chicago
Length: 22:07

Sometime during this evening's recording session, the Beatles accepted a phone call from Chicago disc jockeys Art Roberts and Ron Riley. This has previously been identified as an April 18 recording, but it's mentioned several times that they are busy recording the title song for their movie. Presumably the recording date was confused with the original broadcast date; Riley mentions a five-hour Saturday Night Spectacular at one point and April 18 was a Saturday.

Paul reveals the film's title (which wasn't announced to the press until the following day, so this was a bit of a scoop) and seems unsure whether "A Hard Day's Night" will be their next single, saying he wants to wait and hear how it turns out. There is a bit of confusion when Riley asks about art school; Paul clarifies that although he "dabbles," John is the group's artist. George takes the line next and talks about such tired topics as lack of privacy, their haircuts, favorite singers, and the press-promulgated "feud" with the Dave Clark Five.

Ringo chats about his rings, fan mail, his love for the States, and his lack of marriage plans. John claims his favorite food is Jell-O, although he's puzzled by the mention of a Hershey bar ("Sounds like a crowbar!"). He says they stopped using harmonica on their records because he kept forgetting to bring it to sessions (see the March 5, 1963, entry for one documented example). After discussing his book, the film, and a recent *Saturday Evening Post* article, John signs off on behalf of his bandmates, who have all returned to the studio.

RELEASE HISTORY

1979: A 5:03 excerpt of this interview (along with a 30-second introduction) was released in good quality on the promotional LP *The Ultimate Radio Bootleg, Volume 3.* A 21-minute poor-quality off-line recording also circulates; the length listed above is cumulative, ignoring overlap (both sources contain unique material).

91. Studio session

Date: 16 April 1964
Time: 7:00–10:00 p.m.
Location: EMI Studio 2
Producer: George Martin

[A.] A Hard Day's Night—take 1 (mono) (2:40)
[B.] A Hard Day's Night—takes 2–4 (mono) (2:53)
[C.] A Hard Day's Night—take 5 (mono) (2:38)
[D.] A Hard Day's Night—takes 6–7 (mono) (4:30)
[E.] A Hard Day's Night—takes 8–9 (mono) (2:30)
[F.] A Hard Day's Night—monitor mix of takes 1–6 (mono) (12:40)

[G.] A Hard Day's Night—RM10 (2:28)
Mixed: 23 April 1964

[H.] A Hard Day's Night—RS1 (2:32)
Mixed: 22 June 1964

[I.] A Hard Day's Night—RS from take 9 (2:39)
[J.] A Hard Day's Night—RS from take 9 (#2) (2:29)

Having come up with the perfect name for their film, John and Paul now had to write a song based around the lyric "a hard day's night." John arrived at Abbey Road this evening ready to record, with the lyrics scribbled on the back of a birthday card to his son, Julian (who had turned a year old April 8). The backing of drums, bass, and guitars, including George playing his twelve-string Rickenbacker, went on track 1 while John and Paul sang live vocals on track 2. The memorable opening chord had John and George playing an F major with added G on the top string (later doubled by acoustic guitar and piano overdubs), while Paul plucked a D on the bass.

Nearly the entire session tape has been bootlegged in excellent sound, albeit mixed into mono. The first attempt (**A**) has slightly different lyrics ("holding me tight, all through the night"). While the take is complete, Paul's errant bass line during the second bridge renders it unusable, as he points out afterward ("My middle eight was crap anyway"). A "monitor mix" tape of much of this session recently surfaced (**F**) from the preparations for the 1983 *Beatles at Abbey Road* presentation. It includes some chat prior to take 1 that is unavailable elsewhere, as well as the occasional isolation of various tracks of the tape.

There follow several takes (**B**) that make it no further than the opening chord. Takes 2 and 3 are both false starts as John has trouble hitting the right notes. Before Norman Smith can announce take 4, John counts in again for a full performance, which is an improvement on take 1. Unfortunately, it's wrecked by George's poor guitar solo, and they decide it'd be best to let him overdub that part once they have a decent backing track.

Take 5 (**C**) is erroneously announced as "take four"; it's also complete, but still a bit sloppy. George complains that he doesn't quite know how the ending should go. Take 6 (**D**) breaks down in the third verse when Paul muffs some bass notes, although he doesn't exactly volunteer the information. (John: "I heard a funny chord." George Martin: "So did I!" John: "Not 'alf, you didn't!") They keep the tape rolling as Paul runs through the middle eight to get the chord pattern straight in his head. Meanwhile, Ringo is instructed to tap on the hi-hat to keep time between the opening chord and the first verse. Take 7 is complete, but John breaks a guitar string and Paul still has trouble playing the middle eight.

John counts in for take 8 (**E**), but Paul puts the brakes on it immediately to give himself one last quick primer on the middle eight. His rehearsal pays off, as take 9 is played to perfection. The raw studio tape as bootlegged includes the first two minutes of this take, with only tracks 1, 2, and 3 playing. Track 3 had overdubs of acoustic guitar, bongos (played by engineer Norman Smith), second vocals from John and Paul, and a cowbell during the bridges. Track 4 contained a dual solo played by George on guitar and George Martin on piano, plus an extra bass riff after the solo (over the lyric "so why on earth should I moan").

Mono and stereo mixes were prepared April 20 for United Artists, but neither seems to have been used (the mono mix heard in the film matches that heard on record). The released mono mix (**G**) fades out a bit earlier on the single than the album, while the stereo mix (**H**) is longer still. A stereo remix by Ron Furmanek (**I**) has an even longer ending, extended by editing the closing eight-note riff to repeat ten times. While the original stereo mix has tracks 1–4 mixed left to right in that order (rhythm far left, guitar/piano solo far right), this remix has track 1 centered, track 2 left-of-center, track 3 right-of-center, and track 4 far left.

RELEASE HISTORY

1964: **G** and **H** were released on mono and stereo pressings respectively of the LP *A Hard Day's Night*. The former is on EMI's CD of that title.

1983: The beginning of **B** (takes 2 and 3, plus the count-in for take 4) was included in the multimedia presentation *The Beatles at Abbey Road.* It appears from this source on the bootleg CD *Abbey Road Video Show.*

1984: The count-in from **C** was included in the radio documentary *Sgt. Pepper's Lonely Hearts Club Band: A History of the Beatle Years 1962–1970.*

1988: The remainder of **B** (take 4 minus the count-in) appeared in excellent sound on the bootleg CD *Ultra Rare Trax, Volume 2.*

1989: An excellent but slightly slow copy of **D** surfaced on *Unsurpassed Masters, Volume 2.*

1994: The nearly complete session tapes (**A–E,** minus the first few seconds of **A** and the false starts in **B**) were included in excellent mono, but running a half step too slow, on the bootleg CD *The Ultimate Collection, Volume 3: Studio Sessions, 1964.*

1995: The full recording of **A** was released on the CD *Anthology 1.* The same year, the home video *The Making of "A Hard Day's Night"* included **I;** unfortunately, the version booted on the CD *It's All in the Mind, Y'know* has been collapsed to mono.

1999: The bootleg CD boxed set *Mythology, Volume 2* contained an extended edit of **G,** with the song's final line, "You know I feel all right," repeated five rather than three times. It has long been reported that United Artists' cassette and eight-track releases of *A Hard Day's Night* in the United States contained a version of this song with the guitar riff repeated two extra times, so if this is legitimately taken from one of those releases, perhaps the story got muddled somewhere. It's possible that this is a mono remix created June 9, 1964, and labeled EXTRA ENDING ONLY FOR FILM CO.

2002: **F** first appeared in good quality on the bootleg CD *Complete Controlroom Monitor Mixes, Volume 2.*

2003: **H** was released on the soundtrack of the *Anthology* DVD.

92. TV interview

Date: 17 April 1964
Location: Les Ambassadeurs, London
Interviewer: Ed Sullivan
Broadcast: 24 May 1964, 8:00–9:00 p.m.
CBS
The Ed Sullivan Show
Length: 1:34

Ed Sullivan flew to London and filmed an interview with the Beatles this day in the garden of the Les Ambassadeurs club. The brief discussion centers around the Beatles' upcoming tours of Australia and America.

RELEASE HISTORY

1994: The audio portion of the interview was booted on the CD *The Ultimate Collection, Volume 1: TV Appearances.* The original broadcast also included an outtake from the film *A Hard Day's Night* (see the March 31 entry), and both items have circulated for years on video.

93. Studio session

Date: 19 April 1964
Time: evening–8:30 p.m.
Location: IBC Studios, London
Producer: Jack Good

[A.] Twist and Shout (mono) (2:30)
[B.] Roll Over Beethoven (mono) (1:48)
[C.] I Wanna Be Your Man (stereo) (1:47)
[D.] Long Tall Sally (stereo) (1:44)
[E.] Love Me Do/Please Please Me/From Me to You/She Loves You/I Want to Hold Your Hand (mono) (3:56)
[F.] Can't Buy Me Love (mono) (2:03)
[G.] Shout! (mono) (1:58)
[H.] Shout! (stereo edit) (1:28)
[I.] Boys (stereo) (1:49)
[J.] She Loves You/I Want to Hold Your Hand (mono) (2:19)

Despite Brian Epstein's assurance to the press that the performances in the TV spectacular *Around the Beatles* would not be mimed, the Beatles simply did not trust television audio engineers to reproduce their live sound faithfully. Too many instances of unbalanced microphone levels and inaudible drums had convinced them to prerecord new versions of the material in a proper recording studio, to be lip-synced during playback at the TV taping.

The set list was chosen to showcase each Beatle (one lead vocal apiece, although Ringo recorded an alternate, "Boys," which didn't make the cut), their history (a medley of their first five singles), and their new release. To cap it off, all four traded vocals on a raucous version of the Isley Brothers' "Shout!" While Mark Lewisohn has indicated that the number was part of their repertoire in 1960–61, John revealed a month later that they had to read from a lyric sheet (couldn't have been a big sheet with only six or seven lines in the whole song), so clearly it wasn't all that familiar.

The songs in the medley were clearly taped separately and edited together, which doesn't necessarily mean they performed complete versions of each. Most of the other songs were also arranged to omit verses, solos, and such, to keep them under two minutes each ("Twist and Shout" being the notable exception). The songs were recorded on three-track tape, and in addition to a mono dub that circulates, certain songs were remixed into stereo for *Anthology 1,* with vocals and handclaps left and instruments right.

While "Shout!" begins with a trio of B7 guitar chords on the broadcast version, the master tape must have been damaged in the intervening years, as all bootlegged versions contain only the last two of these. Even *Anthology 1,* which went back to the multitracks, had to use fakery by repeating the second chord (listen for Paul's two identical intakes of breath)! That's hardly the extent of the oafish butchering done to the *Anthology* version (**H**), which makes the Beatles sound incapable of performing a simple two-chord ostinato.

Another curiosity is that in the TV special, the edit point between "She Loves You" and "I Want to Hold Your Hand" comes at a different place than on the bootlegged source tape. This alternate edit can be heard in clearest form on a video (**J**) broadcast during the 2005 American Music Awards. The tape operator on this session was Glyn Johns, who would figure heavily in a more ill-fated Beatles TV special in January 1969.

RELEASE HISTORY

1984: The radio documentary *Sgt. Pepper's Lonely Hearts Club Band: A History of the Beatle Years 1962–1970* included **E** and **G.** The endings of both were obscured by Roger Scott's narration.

1985: **E** and **G** were included on the bootleg LP *Not For Sale;* while **E** was copied from the radio special, with the ending faded to omit narration, **G** was from a clean and complete source.

1986: **A–G** appeared in very good mono on the vinyl bootleg *Not Guilty* (with a brief gap during **A**). They've been copied on the CDs *Pollwinners go to Blackpool* (with brief silences between tracks that ruins the continuity) and *The Ultimate Collection, Volume 1: Miscellaneous Tracks* (with heavy noise reduction). Both sources repair the gap in **A** and fade **G** prematurely, but the original abrupt ending can be heard on the CD *Not for Sale.*

1995: **C, D, H,** and **I** were released on the CD *Anthology 1.* **C** and **D** were slightly longer than their previous mono counterparts.

2005: **J** was aired during the American Music Awards; the clip circulates on video.

94. Newsreel footage

Date: 22 April 1964
Time: evening
Location: Australia House, London
Length: 1:20

To promote their upcoming tour of Australia, the Beatles followed a busy day of filming with a visit to a cocktail party at Australia House. A newsreel depicts the group arriving in the pouring rain, having kangaroo badges pinned to their lapels, posing for photos with the Australian high commissioner, Sir Eric Harrison, and sampling Tasmanian apples. At one point, Ringo finds himself surrounded by Australian journalists and jokingly calls out to John for help.

RELEASE HISTORY

This footage, mostly silent, circulates on video; a 10-second clip with sound was broadcast, of all places, on Ringo's *Donahue* guest appearance.

95. Radio interview J, P, R

Date: 23 April 1964
Time: morning
Location: Thornbury Playing Fields, Isleworth
Interviewer: Murray Kaufman
Broadcast: WINS-AM, New York City
Length: 1:04

Sometime in mid-April, Murray the K flew to London to visit with the Beatles, introduce their upcoming set at the *NME* Poll Winners' Concert, and appear in their TV special *Around the Beatles.* Murray taped several interviews with the Beatles during the shooting of the "field scene" for *A Hard Day's Night* in Isleworth (Murray calls it "Twickingham" [sic]).

Murray exchanges a few "what's happening's" with Ringo and describes the scene: "They're doing various shots, the boys falling down on the ground and the whole bit. John's going to a luncheon with muddy shoes." (He's referring to Foyle's Literary Banquet; see following entry.)

RELEASE HISTORY

1965: These interviews were released on the EP *The Beatles & Murray the K: As It Happened,* copied on the LP and CD *Timeless II.*

96. Newsreel footage/interview J

Date: 23 April 1964
Location: Dorchester Hotel, London
Length: 0:46

By most measures, John's "literary luncheon" was a success—until someone introduced him as the guest of honor. Unprepared and reportedly hung over from partying at the Ad Lib the previous evening, John mumbles, "Oh, what—do I get up?" His impromptu "speech" is terse: "Uh, thank you very much, and God bless you. You've got a lucky face." The remarks are met with polite but disappointed laughter and applause.

When a reporter asks about his loss for words, John replies that he's "scared stiff" and "daren't" speak extemporaneously. He also professes not to care what he's remembered for when he's gone, and he notes that Ringo's phrase "a hard day's night" made its first printed appearance in his book (in the poem "Sad Michael").

RELEASE HISTORY

1999: John's "speech" and interview were included on the CD bootleg boxed set *Mythology, Volume 1.* A 1:15 ITV News report and 48 seconds of silent footage shot by BBC News also circulate on video.

97. Radio interview/Studio rehearsal

Date: 23 April 1964
Time: 10:00 p.m.
Location: Hall of Remembrance, London
Interviewer: Murray Kaufman
Broadcast: WINS-AM, New York City
Length: 29:33

Murray the K talked his way into a part in *Around the Beatles* introducing some of the acts, and he joined the first rehearsal session this evening at the Hall of Remembrance (a date not listed in Mark Lewisohn's *Complete Beatles Chronicle*). He brought along his tape recorder to give WINS listeners a running narrative of the proceedings.

As the tape opens, the Beatles are at their unamplified instruments, preparing to rehearse their lip-synced musical performances. While George plays riffs from "A Hard Day's Night" in the background on his twelve-string, John explains that they're working on "a TV show which you'll probably see in 1983. By the way it's going." The next few fragments capture playbacks of several numbers recorded at IBC (see the April 19 entry): "Twist and Shout," "Roll Over Beethoven," "I Wanna Be Your Man," and "Long Tall Sally." Interestingly, these studio recordings already have crowd noise overdubbed as "sweetening."

A break follows, with Ringo ordering a scotch for himself and a Coke for Murray. George plays an instrumental version of Buddy Holly's "Words of Love" while Ringo chats about their exhausting schedule, his recorded repertoire, and an upcoming performance at Wembley's Empire Pool. On April 20, thieves had broken into the flat shared by George and Ringo and stolen cash and jewelry; the drummer discusses this and their culinary habits (he cooked steak and chips the previous night; George prepared soup, eggs, and beans that evening). Producer Jack Good then calls the artists back to work: "John, George, Charlie, Paul, Fred, Albert! In positions, please!"

Murray describes the action as the Beatles struggle with the "medley of hits" spliced together at IBC. John is having trouble with the abrupt switch from harmonica to guitar after "Love Me Do": "I don't mind dropping it on the floor, it's just knowing." He suggests the cameras cut to Ringo at each segue to cover for the awkward miming transitions. Ringo points out that he has to change the drum pattern as well, but John feels nobody will notice. Jack Good has the last word, however: "No, we're going to do it the way we're going to shoot it."

After the medley and "Can't Buy Me Love" are perfected, they take five again. George strums "You Can't Do That," accompanied by someone (probably Paul) thumping on the drums. Murray calls it "the soul side" of their latest single and passes along a compliment from Ben E. King's guitar player, who George then imitates by strumming furiously. They continue with a rehearsal of "Shout!," which John jokingly introduces as "a number that we haven't recorded. And we're not likely to." Murray is knocked out and urges them to release it on a single, but John calls him "Muffy the Cow" and snaps that they release only original compositions as singles.

The evening concludes with a read-through of act V, scene 1 of *A Midsummer Night's Dream,* Beatle-style. It seems Murray was originally to play the role of Theseus, and one listen to his hammy performance here explains why his part was trimmed. As they depart for the evening, Murray reminds everyone that he'll see them tomorrow at the film wrap party for *A Hard Day's Night,* but nobody seems that interested. Jack Good approaches Murray to discuss the DJ's spot in the show, and Ringo revealingly jokes, "I'd like to cancel it." In the end, Murray's role in the show would be reduced to almost nil.

RELEASE HISTORY

1965: An excerpt of the "Shout!" playback from this recording was released on the EP *The Beatles & Murray the K: As It Happened,* copied on the LP and CD *Timeless II.*

2002: A 28-minute recording surfaced from a good-quality off-line tape on the CD-R *As It Happened, Baby!* An upgraded 3:40 tape, including 1:12 of new material, is on the CD-R *We'd Like to Carry On.*

98. Radio interview — G

Date: 25 April 1964
Time: evening
Location: unknown hotel, London
Interviewer: Gene Loving
Broadcast: WGH-AM, Tidewater
Length: 3:49

American disc jockey Gene Loving traveled to London with George's sister, Louise, and the two of them convened with George in a London hotel on this day for a taped interview. Topics discussed include George's lead vocals on Beatle records, the just-completed film (wrapped the previous day), George's Jaguar XKE, and the following day's concert.

RELEASE HISTORY

1986: This interview was released on the LP *All Our Loving,* later reissued on CD.

99. Radio interview — J, P, R

Date: 26 April 1964
Time: afternoon
Location: Empire Pool, Wembley
Interviewer: Gene Loving
Broadcast: WGH-AM, Tidewater
Length: 5:47

Gene Loving was able to tape further interviews backstage at the Empire Pool, Wembley, while the Beatles prepared for their performance at the *New Musical Express* Poll-Winners' Concert. John chats about the film, the Beatles' cars, and the Ivor Novello awards they had recently won; Paul yet again denies marriage rumors.

The longest segments are spent with Ringo, who discusses favorite drummers (he has none), touring the States, favorite groups (the Impressions and the Shirelles), and his eating habits. During Ringo's interview, the Rolling Stones can be heard in the background performing "I'm Alright" onstage.

RELEASE HISTORY

1986: These interviews were released on the LP *All Our Loving,* later reissued on CD.

NOTE

Following the concert, Gene Loving flew to Liverpool and taped interviews with George's parents and Cavern Club doorman Paddy Delaney (Loving calls him "Pat Dulaney," an error that is carried over to the record sleeve). These non-Beatle interviews are substantially longer on the CD release of *All Our Loving* when compared to the LP.

100. Concert

Date: 26 April 1964
Time: 2:30 p.m.
Location: Empire Pool, Wembley
Broadcast: 10 May 1964, 4:05–5:35
ABC
Big Beat '64

[A.] intro (2:06)
[B.] She Loves You (2:12)
[C.] intro (0:03)
[D.] You Can't Do That (2:19)
[E.] intro (0:34)
[F.] Twist and Shout (2:28)
[G.] intro (0:31)
[H.] Long Tall Sally (1:54)
[I.] intro (0:30)
[J.] Can't Buy Me Love (2:01)
[K.] outro (0:15)
[L.] award presentations (0:49)

The Beatles performed an energetic five-song set to close the *New Musical Express* Poll-Winners' Concert, though it wasn't without problems. John's microphone isn't tightened properly and he has to keep readjusting it during the first song; Paul and George have similar problems during the next song. It is also the first time they have played live in over two months, due to recording sessions and filming, and they are a bit rusty. John mixes up the verses to "She Loves You" and forgets entirely about the bridge to "You Can't Do That," rushing back to the mic to continue singing it. In the latter song, George begins to sing the backing vocals over John's guitar solo, but Paul isn't paying attention, so he gives up. Keen-eyed viewers will also spot John being whacked in the face by incoming debris halfway through "Twist and Shout." At the end of the event, the Beatles return to accept their four huge trophy cups from Roger Moore; John pretends to drink from his, while Ringo uses his as headgear.

RELEASE HISTORY

1988: The vinyl bootleg *The Beatles at the Beeb, Volume 13* included good-quality copies of **A–H,** running slightly slow in places.

1995: A very good copy of the musical material (**A–K,** with **A** slightly incomplete) was booted on the CD *Jellybeans Hailing in Dreamlike Noise.* A similar-sounding copy is included on the bootleg CD *Pollwinners Go to Blackpool.*

1999: The entire appearance (**L** followed by **A–K**) appeared on the CD bootleg boxed set *Mythology, Volume 1,* taken from a circulating video. Unfortunately, the quality isn't quite up to par with earlier releases. The *Anthology* documentary includes part of **J.**

101. Radio interview **P, G, R**

Date: 27 April 1964
Location: Studio 5A/B, Wembley Studios (via telephone)
Interviewer: Paul Drew
Broadcast: WQXI-AM, Atlanta
Length: 16:19

Despite having a prearranged phone interview, Atlanta DJ Paul Drew had a hard time getting through to the Beatles. After calling Wembley TV Studios, where a dress rehearsal for *Around the Beatles* was occurring, he was told to call Brian Somerville at NEMS. Somerville in turn passed him back to Wembley, telling him to ask for Neil Aspinall. With a bit of convincing, the overseas operator was finally able to get Ringo on the line.

Drew informs Ringo that "Boys" was the number 1 record in Atlanta (as a highlighted album track from *Introducing the Beatles,* not a single) and ascertains that he's able to sing and play drums simultaneously. Ringo explains how he came up with the phrase "a hard day's night" and says he had to sell his car after fans stripped it for souvenirs. He names some favorite vocalists (Chuck Jackson, Marvin Gaye, Betty Everett) and reveals that he's written a country-and-western song ("Don't Pass Me By") but has already "forgotten most of it anyway."

Ringo is able to round up George, who comes to the phone to talk about his Jaguar XKE, which is capable of doing 160 mph. Drew makes the uncannily accurate prediction that George will take up sports-car racing as a hobby someday. George praises the Searchers and selects "You Can't Do That" as his favorite Beatles song. He then goes off to look for John and Paul, but it's Neil who returns to inform Drew to call back in about fifteen minutes.

Paul takes the next call and denies a report that he is secretly married, instigated by one Norman Moss. "Tell him to come 'round, I'll thump him . . . He's an idiot." He chats about Murray the K's visit, the group's ability to speak German, the *New Musical Express,* the upcoming North American tour, and the film, and goes off to look for John. Unfortunately, Neil comes back with the news that John is now getting made up and won't be able to come to the phone. Neil obligingly answers a few questions on John's behalf, and Drew decides not to push his luck any further.

RELEASE HISTORY

These interviews are available in good quality on the CD-R *The Day the Beatles Came to Town.*

102. TV performance

Date: 28 April 1964
Time: 9:00–10:15 p.m.
Location: Studio 5A/B, Wembley Studios
Producer: Jack Good
Broadcast: 6 May 1964, 9:45–10:45 p.m.
Rediffusion-TV
Around the Beatles

Following days of rehearsal, *Around the Beatles* (at least, the portions requiring the Beatles' presence) was apparently filmed in just over an hour this evening. It opens with a rendition of "We Love You Beatles" by the Vernons Girls, played over the credits as the live audience files in to fill the studio floor and scaffolding surrounding the stage.

This is followed by the Beatles' Shakespearean debut, performing the "play within a play" from act V, scene 1 of *A Midsummer Night's Dream.* Paul and John take the roles of doomed lovers Pyramus and Thisbe, hamming up their parts enjoyably. Ringo plays the fierce Lion, while George is Moonshine, complete with "lanthorn," thorn-bush, and dog.

They stick to the general outline of the Bard's text, altering the dialogue when necessary. "Then know that I, one Snug the joiner, am/A lion-fell, nor else no lion's dam; For, if I should as lion come in strife/Into this place, 'twere pity on my life" becomes "Then know that I, one Ringo the drummer, am; For, if I was really a lion, I wouldn't be making all the money I am today, would I?" Members of Sounds Incorporated fill in for Theseus, Demetrius, and Hippolyta, interrupting the "play" with heckling comments, such as "Roll over, Shakespeare!" and "Don't call us, we'll call you."

Eventually, their constant interruptions and the screams of the audience become distracting, but seeing a golden-wigged and deep-voiced John tell Paul "My love thou art, I think" makes it all worthwhile. The "lovers" conclude with "Thus Thisbe ends: Adieu, adieu, adieu," segueing into "I Do Like to Be Beside the Seaside."

Throughout the show, the Beatles are seen enjoying the various guest performers from a box above the stage, with Paul introducing P. J. Proby and all four clapping and singing along with Long John Baldry's rendition of "Got My Mojo Workin'." Other acts include Cilla Black ("You're My World" and "Heatwave"), Millie Small ("My Boy Lollipop"), and Sounds Incorporated. It was originally announced that Jerry Lee Lewis would appear on the show, and he certainly would have livened up the parade of miming singers and dance routines by American troupe the Jets.

The Beatles save the day somewhat with their own musical set, although their attempts at lip-syncing are horrendous. Ringo doesn't open his mouth until the second line of "I Wanna Be Your Man," and John and George both miss their cues in "Shout!" John also pretends to sing all of "Can't Buy Me Love," but this might be to cover for Paul's double-tracked vocal. They speak only twice; Paul explains the concept of the medley, and John introduces the final number by repeating his Foyle's speech: "Thank you very much, and God bless you. You've got a lucky face. The end." "Shout!" works especially well in the live setting, climaxing in a frenzied call and response with the audience.

The show was a great success, screened on TV stations around the world (in Australia and New Zealand in early June, on ABC in the United States November 15).

RELEASE HISTORY

This program circulates on video (most commonly from the U.S. edit), complete with all acts. The "Pyramus and Thisbe" scene was released on the video *Fun with the Fab Four;* its soundtrack can be heard on the CD-R *Telecasts Three.* The Beatles' musical set (with John's "lucky face" comment moved to the very end, following "Shout!") was released on the video 45 *The Beatles Live!*

103. Radio interview

Date: 24–28 April 1964
Location: London
Interviewer: Murray Kaufman
Broadcast: WINS-AM, New York City
Length: 4:07

Murray the K taped further Beatle interviews throughout his week in London. John reads a couple of pieces from his book published in the United States that week, "I Sat Belonely" and "A Surprise for Little Bobby." Paul talks about seeing a film the previous night, and Murray assures him he'll find a place for the group to party during their August trip to New York. Finally, Murray wishes John and Cynthia a happy vacation and says he'll see the group again at their Forest Hills concert.

RELEASE HISTORY

1965: John's recital of "I Sat Belonely" and the chat with Paul were released on the EP *The Beatles & Murray the K: As It Happened,* copied on the LP and CD *Timeless II.* The remainder of these interviews circulate from a poor-quality off-air tape.

104. Radio interview

Date: 28 April 1964
Location: Studio 5A/B, Wembley Studios
Interviewer: Klas Burling
Length: 5:29

Also present at the taping of *Around the Beatles* was Swedish producer and host Klas Burling, who recorded interviews with all four for broadcast on Swedish radio.

Paul recounts their first trip to the United States, and Ringo expresses puzzlement at his own enormous popularity there. Paul also reveals the titles of all the new songs used in *A Hard Day's Night* (although John has to remind him of "I'm Happy Just to Dance With You"). George talks about his twelve-string Rickenbacker guitar and says he doesn't think they will be able to visit Sweden again until after Christmas, so busy is their schedule (they ended up squeezing in a two-day trip in July). He admits to being a lazy songwriter, but says he might have another composition on the next Beatles LP. His next composition, "You Know What to Do," never made it beyond a rough studio demo recorded in June.

John says he's considering buying a house when he

has time to settle down (he would purchase Kenwood three months later), and talks about donating compositions to other artists. Although "World Without Love" and "Love of the Loved" were written as early as 1960, John admits they are running out of old songs to give away. He also plugs his book, figuring that since it's not exactly written in standard English, Swedish readers should have little trouble understanding it. Asked to pick a couple of requests, John chooses "World Without Love," and "You Can't Do That," the B-side of 'Can't Buy Me Gloves.' "

RELEASE HISTORY

1972: A short segment of George's interview was included in the BBC Radio documentary *The Beatles Story*. It appears from this source on the CD-R *Attack of the Filler Beebs!, Episode Two.*

2001: Three excellent-quality excerpts from these interviews were included on the bootleg CD *Swedish Fan Club Tape*. The full interviews circulate in lesser quality among collectors.

104a. Open-end interview

Date: late April 1964
Location: London (via telephone)
Length: 4:48

Perhaps inspired by the success of Capitol's earlier "open-ended" radio promo discs, United Artists used the same technique to plug *A Hard Day's Night*. Their initial effort was a 10-inch disc containing a telephone interview with the Beatles, which seems to have been taped (from the other end) in front of an audience.

John explains that Ringo thought of the film's title and that the drummer's Harpo Marx–style clowning will steal the picture. Paul says the group will definitely meet U.S. fan club members on their summer tour, and George announces that they will be present for both the New York and Los Angeles movie premieres (neither proved to be true). He adds that they are signed with United Artists for two more films, one of which may costar Bob Hope. John jokes that he makes his mother-in-law take out the trash, and he says his poetry is written for anyone who can understand it.

A very limited number of discs were mailed out in early July (only two copies are known to have survived), by which time it was decided to record a new interview, in person this time rather than over the phone and focusing more exclusively on the making of *A Hard Day's Night* (see the July 11 entry).

RELEASE HISTORY

1964: This interview was issued on a promotional 10-inch one-sided LP, *Special Transatlantic Open-End Telephone Conversation* (United Artists SP 2298).

1990: The interview was copied on a 7-inch picture disc, *Open-End Interview:* A Hard Day's Night, created to promote the book *Picture Discs of the World Price Guide.*

105. Documentary footage

Date: 22 February–29 April 1964
Location: various locations, London
Broadcast: 3 August 1964, 7:50–8:20 p.m.
BBC1
Follow the Beatles
Length: 24:57

During the filming of *A Hard Day's Night,* United Artists cameraman Adrian Console was given the task of shooting silent footage documenting the making of the movie. The BBC purchased about twenty minutes of this footage, which together with two scenes from the finished product (not included in the circulating copy) and a bit of newsreel footage made up this TV special titled *Follow the Beatles.*

The soundtrack consists of narration from Robert Robinson and interviews with members of the production team (although not the Beatles, George Martin, or Brian Epstein). Producer Walter Shenson, director Dick Lester, screenwriter Alun Owen, hairdresser Betty Glasow, cameraman Gilbert Taylor, choreographer Lionel Blair, journalist Alexander Walker, and actors Norman Rossington and Wilfrid Brambell all weigh in on what it was like to make a film with the Beatles.

The earliest footage is of the group's February 22

arrival at London Airport, presumably shot by BBC or freelance cameras. But the most interesting scenes come from Abbey Road Studio 2 during recording of the soundtrack numbers.

On February 26, the Beatles are seen reading through the movie script for the first time. They present new material to George Martin while gathered around Paul at the piano. As George is playing his Ramirez classical guitar, they are probably running through the new arrangement of "And I Love Her" first attempted that day. From the morning session of the twenty-seventh, they are seen recording the final version of that song (John pulls faces at the camera as he strums his acoustic guitar), as well as "Tell Me Why" (shot through the glass partition of the control booth above).

Filming began with train scenes March 2 through March 6 and March 9, and this is when the bulk of the footage was shot. Brian Epstein sees the train off and John pores over his script inside while George is made up. Wilfrid Brambell is seen scrubbing dishes and George drinking and flirting with girlfriend-to-be Pattie Boyd. Paul is content to chat with fans through the compartment window. At one point, the Beatles' old friend Astrid Kirchherr can be glimpsed visiting the set with her camera.

On March 12 at Twickenham, the Beatles' measurements were taken for the preparation of wax effigies at Madame Tussaud's museum. Backstage scenes from this date show them playing with an assortment of glass eyes (John munches on one!) and preparing for a scene. John snips off a lock of his own hair and shaves his own reflection and a camera lens while George signs autographs. The following day, they arrived at Gatwick Airport for a 10 a.m. shoot of the movie's final scene. They are seen running into a helicopter from various angles; Gilbert Taylor then lies on his back underneath the chopper to film its ascent.

Filming switched to the Scala Theatre from March 23 through April 2, including the "TV concert" sequence (see the March 31 entry). The documentary includes scenes of the Lionel Blair dancers, the Beatles waiting in the wings (Ringo plays cards, John and Paul nervously strum their guitars), and the performance itself from several alternate angles.

On April 5, the movie's opening scenes were filmed at Marylebone Station. The Beatles are chased through the car park and across the platform by an eager crowd of extras (at one point, Paul sports his "disguise" of a false mustache and beard, shaking his fist at the camera).

Chronologically, the final scene included in *Follow the Beatles* was filmed the morning of April 29, before the Beatles departed for a tour of Scotland. It shows the group dropping by Madame Tussaud's wax museum in London to pose alongside their doppelgängers for the benefit of still and newsreel photographers. Three years later, they would do so again in more notable surroundings, on the front cover of their *Sgt. Pepper's Lonely Hearts Club Band* LP.

RELEASE HISTORY

This documentary circulates in decent quality on video, and much of the footage was released in the home video *The Making of "A Hard Day's Night."* Extracts of the Marylebone and Scala footage were recycled in an American "behind the scenes featurette" that also circulates on video.

106. Radio interview

Date: 29 April 1964
Location: ABC Cinema, Edinburgh
Broadcast: Forth Radio Network
Length: 2:08

Before their monthlong holiday, the Beatles performed a quartet of shows in Scotland, two each night in Edinburgh and Glasgow. Between shows in Edinburgh, a female reporter from the Forth Radio Network interviewed them backstage.

Paul says that they've played in Scotland before (as recently as October), and the audiences are always "knockout." He's not frightened of anything but being hit by flying debris, but Ringo confesses to being a bit nervous, at least until the curtains open.

Each Beatle gives a greeting to listeners who are in the hospital. Paul says to "keep your chin up . . . if it's in a plaster, keep it higher up, 'cause you never know!" George offers a helpful "never mind," and John says not to let the nurses bully you. Ringo shows promise as a greeting card writer: "Always remember, the sooner you're better, the sooner you're out." The recording closes with John ad-libbing a typically demented Scottish air.

RELEASE HISTORY

1999: This interview was bootlegged on the CD boxed set *Mythology, Volume 2.*

107. Radio performance

Date: 1 May 1964
Time: 6:30–9:30 p.m.
Location: BBC Paris Studio, London
Producer: Bryant Marriott
Host: Alan Freeman
Broadcast: 18 May 1964, 10:00 a.m.–noon
BBC Light Programme
From Us to You #3

[A.] **From Us to You** (0:55)
[B.] **intro** (0:49)
[C.] **I Saw Her Standing There** (2:37)
[D.] **outro** (0:01)
[E.] **Kansas City/Hey Hey Hey Hey!** (2:14)
[F.] **intro** (0:25)
[G.] **I Forgot to Remember to Forget** (2:06)
[H.] **outro** (0:03)
[I.] **intro** (1:16)
[J.] **You Can't Do That** (2:32)
[K.] **outro** (0:05)
[L.] **Sure to Fall (In Love with You)** (2:10)
[M.] **intro** (0:44)
[N.] **Can't Buy Me Love** (2:05)
[O.] **intro** (0:14)
[P.] **Matchbox** (1:53)
[Q.] **intro** (0:01)
[R.] **Honey Don't** (2:20)
[S.] **outro** (0:03)
[T.] **From Us to You** (0:10)

As they had in January, the Beatles recorded a BBC Radio appearance to be broadcast when they would be out of the country. They left it to the last possible minute, booking a session the night before their holiday trips began. As the Whit Monday Bank Holiday fell halfway through their vacation, the show became the third in their *From Us to You* series, with Alan Freeman reprising his role as host from the previous edition.

Following the newly recorded theme song, the Beatles sing a pair of echo-drenched a cappella renditions of "Whit Monday to You," a rewrite of "Happy Birthday to You" (**B**), the second ending in a vocal harmony flourish. There's a bit of forced "confusion" between George and Freeman over the title of "I Forgot to Remember to Forget," a number from Elvis Presley's first LP. More legitimate is George's confusion over pronouncing "Carmarthenshire" in a listener's address. Introducing a double-tracked vocal performance of "Can't Buy Me Love," Paul reads out the abbreviation for Gloucestershire: "Funny place, Glouc!"

Ringo has a silly bit of business getting on Freeman's nerves by repeating everything he says while trying to introduce "Matchbox." Ringo tosses in the line "I got news for ya, Johnny!" during the song, one of three Carl Perkins covers in the show. John had sung "Matchbox" before turning it over to Ringo around 1963, and would do the same with "Honey Don't" a few months after this performance. It's similar to John's earlier BBC rendition, complete with "bop bop's," but the tempo is a bit more relaxed.

RELEASE HISTORY

1972: The BBC Radio series *The Beatles Story* included about a minute of **G**, misidentified as being sung by Paul. It was copied from this source on the bootleg LP *Have You Heard the Word.*

1978: The bootleg LP *Youngblood* included a nearly complete copy of **G**, in fair quality.

1984: Most of **F** surfaced along with a complete good-quality version of **G** on the vinyl bootleg *Directly from Santa Claus.*

1988: A very good tape of nearly the entire broadcast (**A–C** and **E–T**) appeared on the bootleg LP *The Beatles at the Beeb, Volume 10.* The whole thing runs a half step too fast, but was speed-corrected for the boxed CD set *The Complete BBC Sessions.*

1994: Apple's *Live at the BBC* CD contained a version of **G** that manages to sound both hissy and muffled (whatever noise reduction was applied proved useless).

2003: The entire show (**A–T**) was bootlegged on the CD boxed set *The Beatles at the Beeb.*

108. Newsreel footage J, G

Date: 5 May 1964
Location: Honolulu Airport
Length: 1:28

On May 2, the Beatles split into two parties for a month of vacation. Paul and Ringo took Jane and Maureen to the Virgin Islands, where they played on a hired yacht. Paul got sunburned, tried spear fishing, and wrote a couple of songs ("Things We Said Today" and the mysterious "Always and Only"), and they all went to see the film *Boys' Night Out,* starring Kim Novak and James Garner.

John and George went with Cynthia and Pattie to Hawaii, but vacationing in the United States proved impossible as the press had scoped out their hotel location ahead of time. It was hastily arranged for them to fly to Tahiti instead, and journalists awaited them as they departed from Honolulu Airport.

This newsreel shows the party arriving by car and boarding their flight; John and George reluctantly emerge to wave to the dozen or so fans on the observation deck. A reporter asks George why they aren't staying longer, and he snaps, "Why didn't you leave us alone? How would you like to have a microphone stuck in your hand when you're on holiday? We're off duty now, and we want it that way."

RELEASE HISTORY

This footage circulates on video among collectors.

109. Radio interview J, G

Date: 25 May 1964
Location: Los Angeles
Broadcast: KFWB-AM, Los Angeles
Length: 0:39

John and George spent an enjoyable few weeks in Tahiti, snorkeling, fishing, sailing, and producing a homemade film, which sadly doesn't seem to have survived, with John playing a missionary. John also wrote several stories and poems for his next book, including a Sherlock Holmes parody, "The Singularge Experience of Miss Anne Duffield." John also reportedly composed five songs on the holiday, most likely "Any Time At All," "When I Get Home," "I'll Cry Instead," "No Reply," and "I'll Be Back." This is corroborated by Paul's authorized biography, which has Paul contributing to only the latter two songs. Presumably he helped John finish them off back in London in the days leading up to the next batch of recording sessions, at which all five were taped.

The return flight took John and George to Los Angeles, where they enjoyed a relatively anonymous afternoon of sightseeing on the Sunset Strip. At some point, probably at the airport before returning to England, local radio stations caught up with them. In addition to KRLA's Dave Hull, a DJ from rival station KFWB cornered the Fab Two. John and George taped this brief message relaying greetings to KFWB's Wink Martindale. John obviously recognizes the name from Wink's spoken-word hit single, "Deck of Cards" (or "Deck of Dubs," as he calls it).

The recording was chopped up and interspersed with some of George's comments from the Doncaster *Dateline London* interview (see the December 10, 1963, entry) and bookended by a pair of KFWB jingles, set to the tunes of "She Loves You" and "It Won't Be Long." The result was pressed on a Capitol Custom single given away to promote the opening of Wallichs Music City in Canoga Park during the week of June 5–13. The flip side was "You Can't Do That."

RELEASE HISTORY

1964: This interview was included on a promotional single, *Music City/KFWBeatles.* It was copied on the 1985 LP *The Golden Beatles,* also issued on CD.

110. Studio session — P

Date: 29 May 1964
Location: EMI Studios
Producer: George Martin

[A.] From a Window (1:52)

The final Lennon/McCartney composition donated to Billy J Kramer was primarily written by Paul. Having rejected "One and One Is Two," Kramer agreed to record "From a Window" after Peter and Gordon turned the song down. Paul attended the session at Abbey Road, which came in handy. When Kramer had trouble hitting the high G note that ends the song, Paul stepped in to sing the final syllable: ". . . niiiight."

RELEASE HISTORY

1964: **A** was released on a single that reached number 12 in the UK and number 23 in the United States. It's available on the CD *The Best of Billy J. Kramer & the Dakotas.*

111. Radio interview — J, P, R

Date: 30 May 1964
Location: NEMS Enterprises, London
Interviewer: Jim Stagg
Broadcast: KYW-AM, Cleveland
Length: 6:19

Once their vacations were over, the Beatles assembled at the Soho offices of NEMS Enterprises to hold a press conference chiefly for foreign reporters (they would meet the British press the following day). Various American radio stations sent over disc jockeys along with contest-winning fans, among them representatives from stations in Cleveland and Boston.

In these clips, KYW's Jim Stagg, who would travel with the Beatles on their summer tour of North America, introduces contest winner Lynette Carlo to Paul. Lynette wonders whether he enjoys interviews, and Paul says he does, although certain questions get tiring after the umpteenth asking. He also professes not to mind rumors too much, even the persistent one about his marriage to Jane Asher, which he again denies. Although he claims not to like the idea of marriage (it "seems like something for old people to me"), Paul insists that if he did, the risk of losing popularity wouldn't dissuade him from getting hitched.

Ringo gripes about the fact that every time he wants to go on a date like any healthy young man, people assume he's chosen a bride. John admits that rumors used to drive him up the wall, but says he's gotten over it. He reveals that the previous day, he'd walked around London with George Martin and a couple of friends and there were no mob scenes. Paul concurs that chance encounters with fans never end up with rending of garments, but rather with a friendly chat.

RELEASE HISTORY

These interviews circulate from a fair quality off-air recording; some of them overlap with those in the following entry.

112. Radio interview

Date: 30 May 1964
Location: NEMS Enterprises, London
Broadcast: WBZ-AM, Boston
Length: 27:14

Boston's WBZ Radio was represented by an unknown reporter and local fan Rosemary Hannigan. The Boston reporter captured many of the same responses on Jim Stagg's tapes (but edited out most of his questions), causing a few minutes of overlap with the previous entry.

George explains how the group met, how Ringo thought of the title *A Hard Day's Night,* and reveals that he's written a couple of new songs for the next LP. Ringo enthuses about visiting Boston on the upcoming tour—"We should do ten shows there!"—accepts gifts from American fans, and says he has no plans to marry Maureen. He chats about his vacation in the Virgin Islands and explains that the Dingle, where he grew up, is a district of Liverpool akin to the Bronx. He describes the format of their upcoming tours and says the studio recording process is open enough that anyone can contribute ideas to their songs. Even if a song is finished, they'll start over from scratch if a better concept is introduced. And what is Ringo's reaction when told that psychic Jeane Dixon has predicted that George will become interested in religion one day? "I don't think so!" he exclaims with confidence.

John is asked about the 1961 recording of "Ain't She Sweet," released by Polydor as a single that week in the UK. He is less than enamored of the performance, but as long as people realize it's ancient history, isn't ashamed to have it out. The DJ informs John that a bootleg recording of their *Around the Beatles* performance of "Shout!" is being aired in New York and Boston (most likely thanks to Murray the K bringing back a copy). Although John admits they had never played it before, the DJ thinks it should be recorded for a single. Being in Tahiti meant being far from any regular broadcasts of rock music, and John says he's looking forward to getting back to America, the land of twenty-four-hour pop radio. He scotches the notion that they will be attending any premieres of *A Hard Day's Night* in the States, however.

Paul confesses that nobody has ever proposed marriage to him, and when Rosemary Hannigan jumps at the opportunity, he jokingly accepts: "It's the new rumor!" He says they try to answer fan mail at every stop on their tours, and actually listen to some of the fans' suggestions. Like John, he thinks "Ain't She Sweet" is "a terrible record," but realizes they're powerless to prevent its release. Asked about "Sie Liebt Dich," recently issued as a U.S. single, Paul confirms that its backing had to be entirely retaped, and that they've recorded only two songs in German.

RELEASE HISTORY

These interviews circulate from a fair-quality off-air broadcast hosted by Bruce Bradley on a Thursday during WBZ's Beatle Week.

113. Newsreel footage

Date: 31 May 1964
Location: Prince of Wales Theatre, London
Length: 0:24

The Beatles' sole concert between their vacation and World Tour was part of a series of "Pops Alive!" shows presented by Brian Epstein at the Prince of Wales Theatre. Although the performance included no songs new to their set list, they had to rehearse beforehand to work out some of the kinks after a month off.

Prior to the concert, they held a press conference and clowned around behind the theater bar for the benefit of cameras. In this newsreel clip, Paul drapes a towel over his arm, John pretends to swig from a bottle of booze, and George stuffs a rag in Ringo's face.

RELEASE HISTORY

This silent footage circulates on video.

114. Studio session

Date: 1 June 1964
Time: 2:30–7:15 p.m.
Location: EMI Studio 2
Producer: George Martin

[A.] **Matchbox—RM1** (1:55)
[B.] **I'll Cry Instead—edit 1 of RM from take 6/RM from take 8** (2:04)
[C.] **I'll Cry Instead—edit 2 of RM from take 6/RM from take 8** (1:43)
Mixed: 4 June 1964

[D.] **Matchbox—RS1** (1:55)
[E.] **I'll Cry Instead—edit of RS from take 6/RS from take 8 (1:44)**
Mixed: 22 June 1964

In late April, it was reported that an LP would be released to accompany the Beatles' first film, containing the eight new songs featured in the movie plus "soundtrack music" (essentially what United Artists ended up issuing in the United States). A later report indicated that the extra material would be older numbers heard in the film, such as "She Loves You," "I Wanna Be Your Man," "Don't Bother Me," and "All My Loving."

That plan changed when John and Paul returned

from their vacations with several new compositions ready for recording. The first three days of June were set aside for recording sessions at Abbey Road to tape the new material before setting out on tour. At a party following their May 31 concerts, the Beatles had met Carl Perkins and invited him to drop by the studio the following day. Carl later reported that he jammed some of his rockabilly classics with the Beatles; if so, nobody seems to have thought to tape it. He did stick around to watch Ringo sing "Matchbox," a traditional blues number Carl had recorded for Sun Records in 1957.

"Matchbox" had long been a staple of the Beatles' live sets, with Pete Best or John singing lead, but Ringo had sung it as early as July 1963 for a BBC session. They recorded a backing track in five takes, with instruments on one track and Ringo singing a live vocal on a second. On take five, Ringo overdubbed two more lead vocals to fill the remaining tracks, accompanied both times by guitar solos from George and once by piano.

With three Ringos singing and two guitar solos, George Martin had plenty of options when remixing, which makes the mono mix (**A**) puzzling. It brings the sloppier guitar solo to the fore and leaves in a section where Ringo is out of sync with himself (on the line "watch how your puppy dog run"). The stereo mix (**D**) is much nicer, muting the second solo after the first few notes and burying the errant vocal track.

The next song taped was John's "I'll Cry Instead," recorded in a peculiar fashion. Six takes of "section A" were followed by two more takes of "section B"; the best take of each section would then be edited together. One theory is that Richard Lester's rough cut of *A Hard Day's Night* was complete, and he wanted one more song to lay over a chase sequence near the end, lasting just over two minutes. Perhaps performing the song in two parts made it easier to edit to whatever length would be required.

In any case, both parts had the same instrumentation: bass/drums/electric guitar on one track, John's main vocal on a second, his acoustic guitar on a third, and overdubbed tambourine and second lead vocal on a fourth. Each part (takes 6 and 8) was mixed separately into mono; the mixes were then edited together, beginning with verse 1, verse 2, the bridge, and verse 3 from take 6. At 1:09, after the words "I'll cry," there is an edit to take 8 for verse 4 (same lyric as verse 1), a repeat of the bridge, and verse 5 (same lyric as verse 3). This edit (**B**) was copied June 9 and sent to both United Artists and Capitol in the United States, both of whom released it.

For whatever reason, Lester decided against using the song in the scene, preferring to stick with "Can't Buy Me Love" (which lasts 2:09 and thus fits nicely). The song would be kept on the soundtrack album, however, and was mixed into stereo later that month. As before, stereo mixes of takes 6 and 8 would be edited together, but this time, George Martin (whether deliberately or mistakenly) made the edit in a different place, shortening the song considerably.

The stereo version (**E**) has an edit at 1:08 (after the words "until then") that cuts to the last bridge of take 8, thus omitting verse 4. At some point, Martin must have realized that the mono and stereo lengths no longer matched, and he trimmed the UK mono mix (**C**) to match the stereo version. As the United Artists' LP was already on its way to stores by this point, it was too late to fix the problem for the United States, although Capitol did receive the shorter stereo mix for its *Something New* LP. Any version of "I'll Cry Instead" claiming to be a "long stereo edit" is merely a forgery created by bootleggers.

Before breaking for dinner, the Beatles raced through another cover, Larry Williams' "Slow Down," in six takes. Drums, bass, and rhythm guitar occupied one track, John's main vocal another track, and his second vocal plus George's lead guitar a third. On one vocal track, John sings the line "now you don't care a dime for me" correctly; on the second, he seems to be singing "now you got a boyfriend down the street." The tape's fourth track would be filled by George Martin three days later in their absence.

RELEASE HISTORY

1964: **A** was released on the *Long Tall Sally* EP in the UK; it's available on EMI's CD-EP of that title. **B** was included on mono copies of *Something New* in the United States, while stereo copies contained **D.** In the UK, **C** was included on mono copies of the LP *A Hard Day's Night;* it's available on EMI's CD of that title. **E** was also issued on stereo copies of *A Hard Day's Night* in the UK.

1976: **D** made its UK debut on the album *Rock 'N' Roll Music.* It's available on the CD *Past Masters, Volume 1.*

115. Studio session

Date: 1 June 1964
Time: 8:00–11:15 p.m.
Location: EMI Studio 2
Producer: George Martin

[A.] I'll Be Back—take 2 (mono) (1:07)
[B.] I'll Be Back—take 3 (mono) (2:01)
[C.] I'll Be Back—takes 12–14 and take 15 announcement (mono) (0:35)

[D.] I'll Be Back—RM2 (2:19)
[E.] I'll Be Back—RM3 (2:21)
[F.] I'll Be Back—RS1 (2:21)
Mixed: 22 June 1964

[G.] I'll Be Back—RS from takes 2–3 (2:30)
[H.] I'll Be Back—RS from take 16 (2:11)

The evening session was dedicated to recording "I'll Be Back," a superb ballad written mainly by John with assistance from Paul. Although the lyrics and melody were complete, the first few takes were spent devising a suitable arrangement. Take 2 (**A**) is an attempt to perform the song in fast waltz-time, which causes Ringo some confusion and makes the phrasing of the bridge lyrics awkward. They try take 3 (**B**) in straight 4/4 time, which works out better. In lieu of an ending, John says they'll know the song is over "when I start going 'oh oh' about eight times."

The preceding takes are performed with two electric guitars, but by take 12 (**C**) they have switched to acoustics, which lends a more appropriately melancholy air. The take breaks down immediately because Paul is distracted and forgets to sing, and takes 13 and 14 are similarly stopped short, the latter when Paul apparently causes the lyric sheet to blow off the stand.

Take 16 would be "best," with a backing of drums, bass, and John's acoustic guitar on one track, John and Paul's vocal duet on a second, and George's acoustic, plucking the lead riff, on a third. The fourth track was overdubbed with further acoustic guitar and a second vocal for the bridge, completing the song. The stereo (**F**) and U.S. mono (**E**) mixes run at about the same speed, while the UK mono mix (**D**) seems to be sped up slightly.

RELEASE HISTORY

1964: **D** was released on mono copies of the LP *A Hard Day's Night* in the UK and is available on EMI's CD of that title. **E** was included on mono copies of the album *Beatles '65* in the United States. **F** appeared on stereo copies of *A Hard Day's Night* in the UK.

1995: **A** and **B** were released on the CD *Anthology 1.*

1996: **C** was included on the soundtrack of the *Anthology* video documentary. It's been booted on the CD *Abbey Road Video Show.*

2003: **G** and **H** were released on the soundtrack of the *Anthology* DVD.

116. Studio session

Date: 2 June 1964
Time: 2:30–5:45 p.m.
Location: EMI Studio 2
Producer: George Martin

[A.] When I Get Home—RM2 (2:14)
[B.] When I Get Home—RM3 (2:15)
[C.] When I Get Home—RS1 (2:15)
Mixed: 22 June 1964

The second day of recordings began with a morning session that saw the taping of the first seven takes of John's "Any Time At All" and three takes of Paul's "Things We Said Today." The former song would be seen through to take 11 at the end of this afternoon session, but both songs would have final overdubs the following day (see entry for details).

The afternoon session started with another of John's songs, "When I Get Home," perfected by take 11. Including overdubs, the song contains bass, drums (plus overdubbed cymbal crashes on the intro), two guitars, piano, John's lead vocal with backing from Paul and George, and a second vocal from John on the bridge. On one of the vocal tracks, John sings the phrase "till I walk out that door" a bit early. During mixing, the early vocal track was muted at that spot on both the stereo (**C**) and UK mono (**A**) mixes. For some reason, the U.S. mono mix (**B**) mutes the other vocal track instead at that point, highlighting the early vocal.

RELEASE HISTORY

1964: **A** was released on mono copies of the LP *A Hard Day's Night* in the UK and is available on EMI's CD of that title. **B** was included on mono copies of the album *Something New* in the United States. **C** was released on stereo copies of *A Hard Day's Night* in the UK.

117. Newsreel footage

Date: 3 June 1964
Time: 3:00–4:00 p.m.
Location: EMI Studio 2
Broadcast: 3 June 1964
ITV
Length: 0:33

This was a rather hectic day, due to Ringo's sudden illness during a morning photo session. Replacement drummer Jimmy Nicol was hastily summoned to EMI, and instead of their planned recording session, the group rehearsed with him, taped a few demos, and added some overdubs to existing songs. Before that could take place, the quartet had to pose for photographers and an ITV News camera.

Seated at Ringo's drum kit in front of some studio baffles, a bewildered Jimmy plays for a few seconds before the others enter, John welcoming him, George playfully punching him in the head, Paul holding up a suitcase. The second half of the clip (silent) has the group ostensibly "rehearsing" with their instruments (George plays a classical acoustic guitar, John his Rickenbacker 325).

RELEASE HISTORY

1995: The audio portion of this clip was booted on the CD *Jimmy Nicol and the Beatles.* The footage circulates on video, and bits of it were included in *Anthology* and *Beatles 1962 to 1970.*

118. Studio session

Date: 3 June 1964
Time: 5:30–9:30 p.m.
Location: EMI Studio 2
Producer: George Martin

[A.] You Know What to Do—demo take 1 (mono) (1:57)
[B.] No Reply—demo take 1 (mono) (1:44)

[C.] Things We Said Today—RM1 (2:34)
Mixed: 9 June 1964

[D.] Any Time At All—RM2 (2:09)
[E.] Any Time At All—RM3 (2:10)
[F.] Any Time At All—RS1 (2:10)
[G.] Things We Said Today—RS1 (2:35)
Mixed: 22 June 1964

[H.] Any Time At All—RS from take 11 (1:14)
[I.] Things We Said Today—RS from take 3 (2:33)

Although it was reported after the fact that this day's session had been "scheduled for vocal dual-tracking only," it's likely that had Ringo not fallen ill, they would have recorded a fourteenth number for inclusion on *A Hard Day's Night.* They had already decided to pair the two cover songs, "Matchbox" and "Slow Down," with two songs already released in North America, "Long Tall Sally" and "I Call Your Name," on an EP for the British market.

Two demos were recorded this evening, one each by John and George. The tape of this session was misfiled and only came to light in 1993; two of the songs were released on *Anthology 1.* First up was George's second completed composition, "You Know What to Do," not much of an improvement on "Don't Bother Me." For this rudimentary demo (**A**), George sings and plays guitar, accompanied by Paul on bass and John shaking a tambourine. Paul then sang lead on a 33-second busked version of Cilla Black's recent hit "You're My World" (not "It's for You," as has been reported elsewhere).

John had promised his composition "No Reply" (**B**) to NEMS-managed singer Tommy Quickly, although the Beatles would end up releasing it instead on their next album. John and Paul sing a less-than-serious duet, injecting the phrase "your face" whenever possible. Judging from the playing styles, it sounds as though Paul drums on this demo, with George taking over on bass and John stuck on rhythm guitar.

The session ended with the final overdubs on two previously taped songs. "Any Time At All" has a rhythm track of bass, acoustic guitar, twelve-string Rickenbacker, and drums. John sings most of the song, but Paul chimes in for the second "any time at all" in each refrain, perhaps because the notes are too high for John to reach comfortably. The vocals are double-tracked (extra guitar for the final chord was added to one of these tracks), while a piano part occupies the fourth track, including a solo doubling the twelve-string guitar, à la "A Hard Day's Night." The U.S. mono mix (**E**) has the piano mixed considerably lower than the other two mixes.

"Things We Said Today" was also polished off with further overdubs; the finished product includes two acoustic guitars, bass, drums, piano, electric guitar, tambourine, and two solo vocal tracks from Paul. One of them (centered in stereo) has an obvious punch-in at 1:27 (you can hear the phrase "on and on" end twice). With the album as complete as it could get, John, Paul, and George went home to get a few hours' rest and contemplate the prospect of touring without Ringo.

RELEASE HISTORY

1964: **C** and **D** were released on mono copies of the LP *A Hard Day's Night* in the UK; both are available on EMI's CD of that title. In the United States, mono copies of the album *Something New* included **E. F** and **G** appeared on stereo copies of *A Hard Day's Night* in the UK and *Something New* in the United States.

1995: **A** and **B** were released on the CD *Anthology 1.*

2003: **H** and **I** were released on the soundtrack of the *Anthology* DVD.

119. Newsreel footage

Date: 4 June 1964
Time: morning
Location: London and Copenhagen Airports
Broadcast: 4 June 1964
ITV
Length: 1:07

Although George privately resented it, the tour went on without Ringo, with newsreels filming at seemingly every possible juncture. ITV News footage of the rainy London departure and arrival in Denmark circulates; in the latter, John, Paul, George, and Jimmy are given bouquets of flowers as they deplane, and one fan holds aloft a troll doll.

RELEASE HISTORY

This silent footage was included on the compilation video *Beatles 1962 to 1970.*

120. Studio session

Date: 4 June 1964
Time: 2:30–7:00 p.m.
Location: EMI Studio 2
Producer: George Martin

[A.] Slow Down—RM1 (2:53)
Mixed: 4 June 1964

[B.] Slow Down—RS1 (2:53)
Mixed: 22 June 1964

[C.] Slow Down—RS from take 6 (0:27)

While the Fab Three were getting to know Jimmy, George Martin was spending a few hours in Abbey Road mixing songs into mono for the upcoming EP and LP. He also added a piano part to "Slow Down" prior to mixing it. The mono mix (**A**) fades the main vocal track early, omitting John's "ow" exclamation near the end, which is audible in stereo (**B**).

RELEASE HISTORY

1964: **A** was released on the *Long Tall Sally* EP in the UK; it's available on EMI's CD-EP of that title. **B** was released on stereo copies of the LP *Something New* in the United States; it didn't appear in the UK until 1976's *Rock 'N' Roll Music* LP. It's available on the CD *Past Masters, Volume 1.*

2003: **C** was released on the soundtrack of the *Anthology* DVD.

121. Interview

Date: 4 June 1964
Location: Copenhagen Airport
Length: 1:21

This report from an unknown Danish broadcast covers John, Paul, George, and Jimmy's arrival in Copenhagen and includes a brief interview. John seems to think that Ringo caught tonsillitis from someone, and Paul talks about the "-tles" that BEA airlines added to their logo for the flight that day. Jimmy says he's "been on similar scenes" but has never experienced anything akin to the six thousand fans who welcomed them to Denmark (wait till he sees the crowds in Adelaide!).

RELEASE HISTORY

1993: A 19-second excerpt from this interview was released on the CD *The Beatles Tapes, Volume 2: Early Beatlemania 1963–1964,* misidentified as a Swedish radio interview. The full interview circulates in very good quality among collectors.

121a. TV interview

Date: 4 June 1964
Location: Copenhagen
Length: 0:35

In this brief interview for Danish TV, the interviewer wonders if the Beatles' rise to the top has finally peaked. Asked where they are headed next, Paul extends the answer to the end of the year: Amsterdam, then Hong Kong, then Australia, then a tour of Britain, then a Christmas show at the Hammersmith Odeon!

RELEASE HISTORY

This footage was included in an early cut of the *Anthology* documentary, which circulates on DVD.

122. Concert

Date: 4 June 1964
Time: 9:30 p.m.
Location: KB Hallen, Copenhagen

[A.] I Saw Her Standing There (2:24)
[B.] I Want to Hold Your Hand (2:19)
[C.] intro (0:28)
[D.] All My Loving (2:09)
[E.] intro (0:24)
[F.] She Loves You (2:21)
[G.] intro (0:30)
[H.] Till There Was You (2:15)
[I.] intro (0:06)
[J.] Roll Over Beethoven (2:25)
[K.] intro (0:44)
[L.] Can't Buy Me Love (2:14)
[M.] intro (0:27)
[N.] This Boy (2:18)
[O.] intro (1:19)
[P.] Twist and Shout (2:34)
[Q.] outro (0:05)

Following an afternoon rehearsal at Tivoli Gardens, the Beatles played two concerts at KB Hallen in Copenhagen. An incomplete audience tape of the late show, apparently supplied by Danish fan Arno Guzek, includes eight of the nine songs performed (**B–Q**), with a break in the tape following "Can't Buy Me Love." Prior to the final song, Paul absentmindedly introduces the newest Beatle: "Big hand for our drummer Ring—uh, Jimmy!" The concert's opening song (**A**) surfaced several years later from a poor-quality source.

One minute of silent footage also circulates from one of the two Copenhagen concerts (from an ITV News report broadcast June 5), including shots of police dealing with fans outside the hall.

RELEASE HISTORY

1976: **B–Q** surfaced in fair quality on the vinyl bootleg *John Paul George and Jimmy.*

1989: A poor-quality copy of **A,** along with **B–Q,** appeared on the bootleg CD *Danmark & Nederland June 1964.* The silent footage was included on the compilation video *Beatles 1962 to 1970.*

123. Newsreel footage

Date: 5 June 1964
Time: 1:15 p.m.
Location: Schiphol Airport, Amsterdam
Length: 1:45

John, Paul, George, and Jimmy flew from Copenhagen to Amsterdam where four thousand fans greeted them at Schiphol Airport. AVRO Radio reporter Joop van Zijl covered the arrival live for Hilversum-1's *Radiojournaal,* and a few minutes of his report were released on a limited edition LP, *De Bietels Tussen De Bollen,* issued by the Dutch Beatles Fan Club.

Associated Press and Reuters camera crews were there to film the arrival, but the most commonly seen source comes from a Dutch Polygon newsreel, which includes 1:26 of footage. This footage was sold to the UK for Pathé's *Beatles Take Over Holland* newsreel, and the United States for Universal's *Beatles in Dutch* newsreel; both sources are less complete than the Polygon. An additional 19 seconds of footage circulates from Dutch TV.

The Beatles are met at the steps of the plane by four girls in traditional Dutch outfits and given bouquets (Paul slips coming down the stairs). They are presented with fur hats that they wear while strolling across the tarmac through a throng of police and journalists, en route to the press conference.

RELEASE HISTORY

1984: The radio coverage was included on the Dutch fan club LP *De Bietels Tussen De Bollen.* The silent newsreel footage circulates on video.

124. Press conference

Date: 5 June 1964
Time: 1:30 p.m.
Location: VIP Room, Schiphol Airport, Amsterdam
Length: 1:29

The airport press conference was covered by national media, and circulating TV news footage opens with the Beatles, Derek Taylor, and Neil Aspinall being ushered into the VIP lounge. Seated behind a table, the group is introduced in turn by Paul: "Jimmy, Paul, George, and John"; John then points to an empty spot to his left and adds, "Ringo." A reporter asks why they don't want to perform live on TV, and George points out the instances when they have (Palladium, Sullivan). John says it's because TV sound engineers are "stupid," but Paul puts it in more diplomatic terms: "They've been trained for, say, twenty years with big bands and orchestras. And they can get their sound perfectly. But when we come on, with amplifiers and things, it's very hard for them to get the sound."

Forty seconds from the press conference is also included in the *Radiojournaal* report (see previous entry). Someone asks how Ringo is doing, and George thinks he'll rejoin them in London on the seventh for the flight to Hong Kong, but John has heard it won't be until the tenth.

RELEASE HISTORY

1984: The radio coverage was included on the Dutch fan club LP *De Bietels Tussen De Bollen.* The TV footage circulates on video from a recent rebroadcast.

125. TV interview

Date: 5 June 1964
Time: afternoon
Location: Doelen Hotel, Amsterdam
Broadcast: VARA-tv (?)
Length: 1:42

From the airport, four limousines brought the Beatles to their luxury suite at the Doelen Hotel in downtown Amsterdam. Here they were interviewed by a somewhat hapless TV reporter.

Actually, the interview seems to be merely an excuse for the journalist to obtain autographs from the foursome. He stumbles over John's name a bit, and John replies, "Yes, that's me, John Leonard." He approaches Paul by calling him "George." As Paul signs his name, he's asked whether he also plays guitar left-handed, and he responds, "Actually, it's done by mirrors." Jimmy says it hasn't been decided yet whether he'll continue on to Hong Kong. By the time he hands the autograph book to George, the reporter has given up trying to determine which Beatle is which: "And the last one. Please."

RELEASE HISTORY

This footage circulates on video from a recent rebroadcast.

126. TV performance

Date: 5 June 1964
Time: 8:00 p.m.
Location: Café-Restaurant Treslong, Hillegom
Director: Ben de Jong
Host: Herman Stok
Interviewer: Berend Boudewijn
Broadcast: 8 June 1964, 8:30–9:10 p.m.
VARA-tv
The Beatles in Nederland

[A.] **intro** (1:27)
[B.] **interview** (11:27)
[C.] **intro** (0:37)
[D.] **She Loves You** (2:16)
[E.] **intro** (0:15)
[F.] **All My Loving** (2:03)
[G.] **intro** (0:28)
[H.] **Twist and Shout** (2:30)
[I.] **intro** (0:28)
[J.] **Roll Over Beethoven** (2:40)
[K.] **intro** (0:42)
[L.] **Long Tall Sally** (2:01)
[M.] **intro** (0:55)
[N.] **Can't Buy Me Love** (2:10)
[O.] **outro** (0:39)

By 4 p.m., the Beatles were at a TV studio south of Amsterdam (actually a restaurant with a semicircular theater) to rehearse for a VARA-tv special, taped in front of an audience of 150 that evening.

Their insistence on lip-syncing may have been due to covering for Jimmy Nicol's lack of familiarity with the material as much as their lack of faith in the ability of television sound engineers. In any case, their vocal microphones were left open to allow for spoken introductions between songs, and Paul and George chose to take advantage of this fact by singing along with the record playback, giving the performance an odd "live double-tracking" feel.

The show opens with a lengthy interview conducted in two languages and rooms. Host Herman Stok sits in the audience soliciting questions in Dutch, which Berend Boudewijn translates to English for John, Paul, George, and Jimmy, seated at the nearby bar drinking and smoking. Paul and George turn up their noses at the idea of marriage, claiming it's "too expensive." John says his wife cost "about fifty pounds in Nairobi." "But she was second-hand, wasn't she?" jokes George.

One fan wants to know what they think of British groups such as the Swinging Blue Jeans, the Dave Clark Five, and Freddie and the Dreamers. Their usual plug for the Searchers and the Rolling Stones is met with some groans; evidently both groups had yet to catch on in the Netherlands. Jimmy looks ill at ease; although he tries awkwardly to join in with the horseplay, he can't keep up with the others' wit and mostly remains silent until directly addressed.

John says that Ringo's health is improving, but when he realizes the camera has cut back to the audience, quickly adds, "Oh, we're off. He's ill!" They dismiss the Tony Sheridan recordings, scoff at the notion of playing big band arrangements, and disparage exercise and sport. Asked to itemize their instrumental prowess, Paul says, "I play a little piano. It's about that big."

Eventually, they set down their shot glasses and stroll into the theater to perform six songs to an enthusiastic crowd. Perhaps too enthusiastic. During "Roll Over Beethoven," a number of fans leave the bleachers to dance the twist in the background. People begin to throw debris onstage, some of which George places on his head. More dancers materialize during "Long Tall Sally," trying their best to be seen on camera front and center.

Paul begins to introduce the final number, and John hands him a licorice pipe someone has tossed onstage. As soon as they launch into "Can't Buy Me Love," a swarm of fans engulfs the Beatles, jostling them away from the microphones. The goal of most of the fans seems to be to appear on TV acting goofy next to a Beatle. With the help of Mal Evans, Herman Stok does his best to clear them away, but it's futile. John, Paul, and George vanish into the crowd, and Derek Taylor (the newly hired Beatle press officer) watches with amusement as technicians clear away the microphones before the song is even finished playing. A wide shot of the studio shows half-empty bleachers, with Jimmy Nicol left to carry on alone on the drum riser, now surrounded by the audience.

RELEASE HISTORY

1976: The musical performances (**D–O**) appeared in mediocre quality on the vinyl bootleg *John Paul George and Jimmy.* They were copied from this source on the bootleg CDs *Danmark & Nederland June 1964* and *The Beatles and Jimmy Nicol.*

1984: The interview (**B**) was included on the Dutch fan club LP *De Bietels Tussen De Bollen,* along with a report from the radio show *Balans* that includes interviews with fans at the TV taping and a bit of "Twist and Shout."

1999: The complete soundtrack appeared on the CD-R *Telecasts Three* in very good quality, taken from a video of the entire show that circulates. Footage of "Long Tall Sally" (with audio taken entirely from the record) and a bit of the interview were included in the *Anthology* documentary.

127. Newsreel footage

Date: 6 June 1964
Time: 11:30 a.m.–1:00 p.m.
Location: Ansall Canal, Amsterdam
Broadcast: 8 June 1964, 8:30–9:10 p.m.
Nederland-1, VARA-tv
The Beatles in Nederland
Length: 2:15

As with their airport arrival, the Beatles' trip down the canals of Amsterdam was filmed by AP, Reuters, and Polygon cinema newsreels, with the latter also being excerpted for Pathé and Universal newsreels in the UK and the United States. Footage was included in the original broadcast of *The Beatles in Nederland* special (although it's not in the circulating copy), and excerpts were intercut with footage of "Long Tall Sally" from that broadcast in the *Anthology* documentary.

The ninety-minute trip takes John, Paul, George, Jimmy, and Neil Aspinall ten miles in a glass-roofed boat past some fifty thousand fans lining the banks of the canal. Teenagers are seen hanging from lampposts, draping RINGO QUICK RECOVER signs from bridges, and in a few cases, jumping in the canal and swimming after the boat, only to be hauled out by police. Paul tries on wooden shoes, George snaps photos, and John hoists a Dutch flag aloft, while Jimmy just seems mesmerized by the spectacle.

In addition to the 1:39 of Polygon footage and the brief clips in *Anthology,* a further 36 seconds circulates from a Dutch TV report, which includes shots of the group waving from the Doelen Hotel balcony in the daytime and at night.

RELEASE HISTORY

This silent footage circulates on video among collectors.

128. Concert

Date: 6 June 1964
Time: 4:30 p.m.
Location: Veilinghal Op Hoop Van Zegen, Blokker
Reporter: Bert de Winter
Broadcast: 6 June 1964, 7:10 p.m.
Hilversum-2, KRO-Radio
Echo (I only)

[A.] **intro** (0:57)
[B.] **I Saw Her Standing There** (2:30)
[C.] **intro** (0:03)
[D.] **I Want to Hold Your Hand** (2:15)
[E.] **intro** (0:17)
[F.] **All My Loving** (1:58)
[G.] **intro** (0:49)
[H.] **She Loves You** (1:52)
[I.] **Twist and Shout** (2:29)
[J.] **intro** (0:04)
[K.] **Long Tall Sally** (0:24)

The Beatles played two shows at an auction hall in Blokker, just north of Amsterdam, on a bill with eight other artists. The afternoon show, added at the last minute, was played to a less than half-full arena of 2,500, despite the Beatles' late arrival onstage.

Radio reporter Bert de Winter filed a report from the concert, an excerpt of which (**I**) was broadcast that evening in the news magazine *Echo.* Although he talks over most of it, "Twist and Shout" is heard in its entirety in the background. Unfortunately, the Beatles' vocals are basically inaudible. Several other songs with a similar ambience have surfaced, presumably from the raw tape of his report.

Paul can be heard introducing "All My Loving" and "Long Tall Sally," but otherwise the only voices heard are those of the audience, who sing along happily with each number and blow noisemakers. They do a good job carrying the tunes, although they fall into the trap of leaping to the chorus of "All My Loving" after the first verse rather than carrying on with the second verse. An unfamiliar Dutch voice can be heard making an announcement prior to "She Loves You"; according to one written report of the concert, "after almost every number, the impresario came onstage and stopped it until the fans sat down."

RELEASE HISTORY

1984: **A–G** and the first 1:20 of **H** were released on the Dutch fan club LP *De Bietels Tussen De Bollen* in good quality; they appear from this source on the bootleg CD *Jimmy Nicol and the Beatles.* The Dutch LP also included **I** in good quality from the *Echo* report.

1999: A fair-quality but slightly longer source tape of **H,** running too slow, was included on the CD-R *Vinyl to the* Core, which also included **I,** copied from the Dutch fan club LP, and **J–K,** previously unbooted.

NOTE

A so-called upgrade of this concert that's circulating from a radio rebroadcast claims to have the vocals restored on **A–H,** but it sounds to me like they're merely dubbed onto the Blokker tape from alternate sources (such as *Ed Sullivan*). The missing ending to "She Loves You" is poorly reconstructed from bits of Blokker and the vocal source tape. This broadcast does include improved copies of **I–K,** from tape source, although the end of **K** is obscured by narration.

129. Concert

Date: 6 June 1964
Time: 10:05 p.m.
Location: Veilinghal Op Hoop Van Zegen, Blokker

[A.] I Saw Her Standing There (1:53)
[B.] I Want to Hold Your Hand (0:20)
[C.] intro (0:32)
[D.] All My Loving (0:48)

Portions of the evening concert in Blokker were filmed by newsreel cameras, and similar footage was shared by newsreel companies in three countries. This includes people climbing in the rafters, fans singing along (to "All My Loving," among others) and an elderly bearded fellow clapping.

The footage centers around the Beatles' performance of "I Saw Her Standing There," beginning with the second verse. Only the Dutch Polygon newsreel includes the actual sound of the performance. On the British Pathé version *(Beatles Take Over Holland)* and American Universal newsreel *(Beatles in Dutch),* the LP version is dubbed in, complete with excised second bridge to match the shortened concert arrangement.

Some brief audio-only fragments from the evening show also exist, consisting of pieces of two songs, plus Paul's introduction to "All My Loving."

RELEASE HISTORY

1984: The Dutch fan club LP *De Bietels Tussen De Bollen* included **A** in very good quality, from the Polygon newsreel soundtrack; it was copied from this source on the CD-R *Vinyl to the Core.* The newsreel circulates on video in all three variations, Dutch, British, and American. Some of this footage was reused in the 1976 promo clip for "Back in the USSR."

1998: New recordings (**B–D**) appeared in very good quality on the bootleg CD *The Beatles in Holland.*

130. Newsreel footage

Date: 7 June 1964
Time: 11:15 a.m.
Location: London Airport
Length: 1:18

The Beatles returned to London this morning to board a connecting flight to Hong Kong, via Zurich, Beirut, Karachi, Calcutta, and Bangkok, easily the most countries visited by the Beatles as a group in one twenty-four-hour period. Joining the party at London was John's aunt Mimi, who would be accompanying her nephew to Hong Kong and then flying to New Zealand to visit relatives.

Reuters newsreel cameras filmed 1:21 of footage covering the departure, some of which appears (in slo-mo) in the *Anthology* documentary. It shows the Beatles, Derek Taylor, and Aunt Mimi boarding the flight and waving to the two hundred or so fans present, and a stewardess "taming" George's hair with an enormous novelty comb. An ITV News report captured 49 seconds of footage of the same events, from a different angle.

RELEASE HISTORY

This silent footage circulates on video.

131. TV interview — J, P

Date: 7 June 1964
Location: flight from London to Hong Kong
Interviewer: Bob Rogers
Broadcast: Channel 7, Australia
Length: 3:05

As the Beatles boarded their flight to Hong Kong, Australian cameraman Mayo Hunter was there to film the occasion. Sydney disc jockey Bob Rogers had already joined up with the group during the recent Abbey Road sessions and traveled to Denmark and the Netherlands; he would continue to follow the tour and issue daily reports for the "National Beatle Network" through the rest of June.

Hunter filmed Rogers conducting several interviews during the lengthy flight. As John throws pillows at him, Paul talks about what he expects to see in Hong Kong and jokes that he'll be turning sixteen in Sydney. Although the trip is long, John feels "they're looking after us well," while Aunt Mimi says she always thought John would have success with his writings and drawings rather than his music.

RELEASE HISTORY

This footage circulates on video, and a bit of it was used in the *Anthology* documentary. About a minute was used in the documentary *The Unseen Beatles,* released on DVD.

132. Newsreel footage

Date: 8 June 1964
Time: 4:40 p.m.
Location: Kaitak Airport, Hong Kong
Length: 0:59

After a full day in the air, the Beatles finally arrived in Hong Kong. In addition to the usual emerge from plane/wave from steps/cross tarmac scenes, this Reuters newsreel footage demonstrates the heavy military presence at the airport.

RELEASE HISTORY

This silent footage circulates on video among collectors.

133. Press conference/Interview

Date: 8 June 1964
Time: evening
Location: President Hotel, Kowloon, Hong Kong
Length: 42:08

The Fab Three Plus One held a press conference at the President Hotel in Kowloon, and a tape of the entire proceeding has been unearthed. The first 12 minutes of the recording consist of the Beatles' introduction by press officer Derek Taylor, who says Ringo will be joining the group on Thursday (June 11). This is followed by photo opportunities; at one point, two film actresses from Thailand by the names of Unchuli Anantakul and Busara Narumit appear and pose for pictures with the group.

The press conference itself occupies the next 17 minutes of the tape, and there are some interesting highlights amid the usual "hair and money" questions. An ironic moment, in light of future events, occurs when one reporter inquires why they aren't also visiting Manila, and John replies that nobody asked them to, and that he doesn't even know where it is! This is soon followed by a somewhat chilling exchange: "You're taking your mothers to Australia, is this right?" John's immediate response: "Well, Paul and I aren't." Some lighter moments include Paul allowing a reporter to pull on his hair to prove it's not a wig, and Derek cracking everyone up by replacing his genteel suburban accent with comically broad Scouse. We also discover that George is a fan of Segovia and learned some guitar from playing his records.

The final 12 minutes are taken up with individual radio interviews. John claims not to be too frightened by fans except when they throw things; Paul discusses writing songs for other artists; Jimmy Nicol says he likes Dave Brubeck but prefers Cannonball Adderley; and George faces an antagonistic and condescending interviewer with great nonchalance.

RELEASE HISTORY

1997: These recordings were released on the CD *Beatles Tapes IV: Hong Kong '64.* 18 seconds of silent Reuters newsreel footage also circulates on video, depicting the arrival of the starlets from Thailand.

134. Concert

Date: 9 June 1964
Location: Princess Theatre, Kowloon, Hong Kong
Length: 0:10

A brief glimpse of one of the Beatles' two Hong Kong concerts can be seen (in slo-mo) in *Anthology.* Apparently the exorbitant ticket prices set by the local promoter ensured that most local fans were left out in the cold, and the half-full audiences consisted mainly of the British military families stationed there.

RELEASE HISTORY

This silent footage was included in the *Anthology* documentary.

135. Radio interview

Date: 10 June 1964
Time: afternoon
Location: Kaitak Airport, Hong Kong
Interviewer: Bob Rogers
Broadcast: 2SM, Sydney
Length: 2:18

Interviews with Bob Rogers were taped this afternoon at Kaitak Airport in Hong Kong. John and George sing a bit of "Waltzing Matilda" and "Tie Me Kangaroo Down, Sport," and Paul discusses buying suits and a watch in Hong Kong, but says he wouldn't have much use for a boomerang in London. The *Anthology* documentary also includes a few seconds of footage shot this day of the group's departure.

RELEASE HISTORY

1981: These interviews were released on the LP *The Beatles Talk Downunder* and have been reissued on the CD *Inside Interviews: Talk Downunder: Australia Beatlemania.*

136. Radio interview J, P

Date: 11 June 1964
Time: 2:35 a.m.
Location: Darwin Airport
Interviewer: John Edwards
Length: 1:14

At a refueling stop in Darwin, the Beatles got their first glimpse of Australia, with four hundred fans on hand to welcome them at 2:30 in the morning. Also present was reporter John Edwards, who taped an interview with John and Paul as they emerged from the plane. Paul bums a light from Edwards and expresses amazement that anyone is there to meet them at such an early hour. John sketches out their itinerary for the next few months.

RELEASE HISTORY

1981: This interview was released on the LP *The Beatles Talk Downunder* and has been reissued on the CD *Inside Interviews: Talk Downunder: Australia Beatlemania.*

137. Newsreel footage/Radio coverage

Date: 11 June 1964
Time: 7:43 a.m.
Location: Mascot International Airport, Sydney
Length: 1:37

Despite a cold and soaking rain, a few hundred fans waited overnight outside Sydney's Mascot Airport to welcome the Beatles. Only the TV floodlights kept them warm, as reporters from various networks interviewed the crowds (footage of this was included on the video *Beatlemania,* and an excerpt was released on the CD *Beatles Tapes, Volume 3: The 1964 World Tour*).

When they finally land, an hour late, the rain is still pouring, but they decide to reward the faithful by waving from the back of a flatbed truck. While they have an umbrella each, George's is whipped away by the wind, and he is forced to make the most of a borrowed hat. A radio report describes the scene as they are whisked off to a hotel in dry limos: "The Beatles are just pulling up in front of us now, we're about five feet from them . . . G'day, Paul! There's Paul, screaming out 'I'm soaking' as he went past."

RELEASE HISTORY

1981: The brief (0:16) radio coverage was released on the LP *The Beatles Talk Downunder,* reissued on the CD *Inside Interviews: Talk Downunder: Australia Beatlemania.* The newsreel footage of their arrival appears in documentaries such as *The Compleat Beatles* and *Anthology,* as well as the Cinesound newsreel *Beatles and Bedlam,* which circulates on video.

138. Press conference

Date: 11 June 1964
Time: 4:30 p.m.
Location: Sheraton Motel Hotel, Sydney
Length: 29:10

Upon their arrival at the Sydney Sheraton, the Beatles changed out of their wet clothes and made a brief appearance on the balcony outside their suite (George wearing a towel in lieu of dry trousers) before retiring for a few welcome hours of slumber. Jimmy Nicol stayed awake to visit local relatives, but by late afternoon he joined the others back at the hotel for their first Australian press conference.

It's a high-spirited affair, with reporters struggling to keep up with the quick-flying wisecracks of John, Paul, and George. George's dry wit is in particular evidence. Asked what put them above other groups, he deadpans, "We got a record contract." After denying that they and Brian are millionaires, John says a lot of their income "goes to Her Majesty." *"She's* a millionaire," adds George. Paul says he wants to see kangaroos and dingoes; George ripostes, "Dingo? He's coming on Sunday."

Jimmy again speaks only when directly questioned; his silence prompts the facetious query, "Have you got an agreement that Jimmy mustn't speak?" The topics come fast and furious: the damp weather, Hong Kong concerts, their favorite Beatle records (John chooses "Long Tall Sally," George "You Can't Do That"), their film ("It's as good as anybody that makes a film who can't act," John estimates), their birthday gift policy, John's poetry, their world travels, stage act, and plans for the rest of the evening.

John says they won't be writing any songs inspired by visiting Australia: "No, we never write themes about anything, y'know. Just write the same rubbish all the time." Paul explains that their candidness is an attempt to avoid the hypocrisy of celebrities who claim not to smoke, drink, or stay out late. Recounting their rejections by Decca, Pye, and EMI, John says, "I don't blame 'em after hearing the tapes." A few seconds later, he points out that his socks don't match. It's that kind of press conference.

RELEASE HISTORY

1964: Five brief clips from this press conference were released on the LP *The Beatles Story.*

1981: The first 3:43 of this press conference (minus a 6-second exchange) was released on the LP *The Beatles Talk Downunder,* from newsreel footage that circulates on video. The LP was reissued on the CD *Inside Interviews: Talk Downunder: Australia Beatlemania.*

1984: A further 12:29 of the press conference was released on the LP *The Beatles Talk Downunder (and All Over), Volume 2,* again missing a 6-second exchange. The LP has been reissued on the CD *Inside Interviews: Talk Downunder: Sydney to Seattle.*

1995: An incomplete version released on the CD *The Beatles Tapes, Volume 3: The 1964 World Tour* does include the fragments missing from earlier releases. Footage of the press conference was released on the home video *The Beatles Down Under.* The complete footage circulates among collectors.

139. Radio interview — J, P

Date: 11 June 1964
Location: Sheraton Motel Hotel, Sydney
Interviewer: Bob Rogers
Broadcast: 2SM, Sydney
Length: 1:58

Following the press conference, Bob Rogers taped interviews with John and Paul about the "shocking" weather that dampened their Sydney arrival. John compares it to a torrential downpour he'd seen the previous month in Tahiti, and Paul laments that the weather spoiled their chance to display the new capes they'd had made in Hong Kong. Rogers reports that their next American release will be the single "A Hard Day's Night," and John, who had thought it would be "Long Tall Sally," grumbles that "they all make their own singles out of the LPs everywhere else."

RELEASE HISTORY

1981: These interviews were released on the LP *The Beatles Talk Downunder* and have been reissued on the CD *Inside Interviews: Talk Downunder: Australia Beatlemania.*

140. Radio interview

Date: 12 June 1964
Time: morning
Location: flight from Sydney to Adelaide
Interviewer: Bob Rogers
Broadcast: 2SM, Sydney
Length: 4:45

During the morning, the Beatles flew from Sydney to Adelaide, accompanied as usual by Bob Rogers, who took the time to tape further interviews, released on *The Beatles Talk Downunder.* These and many of the subsequent interviews on that LP are also available in unedited form on the bootlegs *A Knight's Hard Day* and *Fuck!* (The first brief segment, on the official releases only, was actually taped prior to arriving at Sydney Airport, as John is asked whether he wants a kangaroo when he arrives.)

As John talks about the treatment they've been getting from Australia's press, George uses a fish-eye lens to snap extreme close-up photos of Rogers: "We hate having our pictures taken with 'em . . . it's just all distorted, you look like a dustbin or something. So I'm doing one of you. Getting me own back." George explains that he appeared on the Sheraton Motel balcony with a towel wrapped around his waist because his only pair of pants was drying.

After a brief chat with Jimmy Nicol (which is also absent from the bootleg), Rogers moves on to Paul, who admits he tried to escape from the motel near midnight to do some sightseeing. His only complaint about Australia so far has to do with the rain: "Sydney wasn't very good weather, was he? . . . I think it must have been the mongoose season."

Newsreel footage from various sources documents the group's departure from Mascot Airport and the flight itself, including shots of Rogers conducting his interviews. A stewardess serves Paul with a basket of fruit, and he and John snap photos out the windows of the plane.

RELEASE HISTORY

1981: Incomplete versions of these interviews were released on the LP *The Beatles Talk Downunder* and have been reissued on the CD *Inside Interviews: Talk Downunder: Australia Beatlemania.*

1988: Unedited copies of most of these interviews were booted on the LP *A Knight's Hard Day.*

The silent newsreel footage was released on the video *Beatlemania* and included in the newsreel *Beatles and Bedlam.*

141. Newsreel footage

Date: 12 June 1964
Time: 11:57 a.m.
Location: Adelaide Airport
Length: 4:24

As they arrived at Adelaide, the Beatles must have wondered where all the fans were, as none of them were allowed on the airport grounds. They got their answer on the drive to Adelaide Town Hall, as an estimated 200,000 people lined the route to cheer, wave, and snap photos of John, Paul, George, and Jimmy. It was easily the largest crowd they'd ever seen, and they were overwhelmed by the enormity of the reception.

Newsreel cameras followed them every step of the way: stepping off the plane, signing autographs for members of the police escort, and climbing into a Ford convertible along with Derek (with the names JOHN RINGO PAUL GEORGE painted on the outside; the designer must have assumed Jimmy wouldn't make it this far). The convoy inches its way through swarms of people and hails of confetti and streamers, taking an hour to travel the nine miles from the airport to the town hall.

RELEASE HISTORY

This silent footage circulates on video; some of it appears in the Pathé newsreel *Beatles Conquer Aussies.*

142. Newsreel footage/Radio coverage

Date: 12 June 1964
Time: 1:00 p.m.
Location: Town Hall balcony, Adelaide
Interviewer: Bob Francis
Length: 3:33

The main reason the Beatles appeared in Adelaide at all was an eighty-thousand-name petition sent to tour promoter Kenn Brodziak. Bob Francis, a DJ for Adelaide's 5AD Radio, was one of the driving forces behind organizing and publicizing the petition, even arranging a financial tie-in from local department store John Martin's to raise the needed funds for renting Centennial Hall.

It must have been a sweet and triumphant moment for Francis to stand on the balcony of Adelaide Town Hall, looking out over a crowd some thirty thousand strong, and introduce each of the Beatles. A remarkable recording of the occasion makes plain what an impact the scene had on the normally unflappable Beatles. George, not one to mince words, calls it "the best reception ever," a sentiment with which Jimmy concurs: "This is the best I've ever seen, anywhere in the world!"

Francis informs John that Adelaide has a population of 1 million, and he interrupts: "They're all here, though, aren't they?" With obvious sincerity, he adds that the welcome is "definitely the best we've ever been to." The crowd begins chanting, "We want Paul!" and responds at an ear-splitting level as Paul steps to the microphone: "This is fantastic. Thank you!" George snaps photos of the crowd, and they wave from all three sides of the balcony before reluctantly retreating inside to attend a reception with the lord mayor.

RELEASE HISTORY

1981: The town hall speeches were released on the LP *The Beatles Talk Downunder* and have been reissued on the CD *Inside Interviews: Talk Downunder: Australia Beatlemania.* Silent newsreel footage of the event also circulates on video.

143. Newsreel footage

Date: 12 June 1964
Time: 1:30 p.m.
Location: Queen Adelaide room, Town Hall, Adelaide
Length: 1:09

Cameras followed the Beatles inside as they rubbed elbows with the lord mayor of Adelaide and his family, for once not minding having to mingle with the local upper crust. In this footage of the crowded affair, Neil keeps a close watch as John and Paul drink and sign autographs; Jimmy still has confetti in his hair from the festivities along the parade route.

RELEASE HISTORY

This silent footage was released on the video *Beatlemania.*

144. Press conference

Date: 12 June 1964
Time: afternoon
Location: South Australian Hotel, Adelaide
Length: 13:24

The Adelaide press conference begins with Derek Taylor and Jimmy Nicol both absent, although Jimmy would show up after a minute or so. The Beatles all reiterate how unique and magnificent the Adelaide welcome was, although George admits to feeling vulnerable to sharpshooters while riding in the open-topped car.

John explains the origins of their bat-wing capes and stresses that they've only ever had a single public relations man working for them at any one time (first Brian Somerville, then Derek Taylor). Jimmy relates his impromptu performance the previous night backing singer Francis Faye at Sydney's Chequers nightclub, while the others tease him about "going backstage" and being "given something in return."

They deny taking part in any "zany publicity stunts," but Paul recalls that before they were famous, they considered having a group member swim across the Mersey (John has no memory of such a scheme). George explains that their Christmas show wasn't really a traditional pantomime tale, but a pop show with their occasional appearance in a sketch "for a laugh." "Nobody laughed, mind you," John adds.

Someone asks if there is a Beatle-owned factory producing the enormous amount of Beatle merchandise, but George points out that much of it is nonlicensed junk manufactured by people trying to cash in. They are joined for the last few questions by a female Ringo lookalike; John offers the young lady his chair and she sits smiling nervously, spurning Paul's offer of a cigarette.

RELEASE HISTORY

1987: The majority of this press conference was included on the bootleg LP *300,000 Beatle Fans Can't Be Wrong.* A newsreel clip with extra material (but some overlap) circulates on video, and a TV report with exclusive material was released on the video *Beatlemania.*

145. Concert

Date: 12 June 1964
Time: 7:05 p.m.
Location: Centennial Hall, Adelaide
Broadcast: 13 June 1964, 8:30–9:30 p.m.
5DN Radio, Adelaide
Beatles Show

[A.] **intro** (2:03)
[B.] **I Saw Her Standing There** (2:34)
[C.] **intro** (0:01)
[D.] **I Want to Hold Your Hand** (2:20)
[E.] **intro** (0:46)
[F.] **All My Loving** (2:00)
[G.] **intro** (0:12)
[H.] **She Loves You** (2:14)
[I.] **intro** (0:23)
[J.] **Till There Was You** (2:11)
[K.] **intro** (0:03)
[L.] **Roll Over Beethoven** (2:23)
[M.] **intro** (0:56)
[N.] **Can't Buy Me Love** (2:07)
[O.] **intro** (0:21)
[P.] **This Boy** (2:12)
[Q.] **intro** (0:16)
[R.] **Twist and Shout** (2:34)
[S.] **intro** (0:24)
[T.] **Long Tall Sally** (2:04)
[U.] **outro (God Save the Queen)** (2:40)

The Beatles' first concert in Australia was taped by Sydney radio station 2SM and initially broadcast on Adelaide's 5DN the following night, being syndicated across the "National Beatle Network" of Australian stations on the evening of June 15.

As a gesture of thanks, Bob Francis is allowed to introduce the group onstage, and he attempts to extract a promise from the audience not to scream during the songs. The existing recording is decent but rather thin-sounding, with bass and drums nearly inaudible. Still, Jimmy seems to be keeping up much better than he had at the start of the tour.

The set list is identical to the Copenhagen show, with the addition of "Long Tall Sally" as a finale, by which time Paul's voice is starting to go. Also listen closely during the musical introduction to "This Boy"; unless my ears are deceiving me, John shouts, "Fuck off" just off-mic! When the show is over, Francis praises the crowd's behavior despite their obvious inability to follow through on the "no screaming" promise; they become hushed as "God Save the Queen" is played over the PA but raise the roof again immediately thereafter.

Some silent newsreel footage from one of the Adelaide concerts (there were two this day and two the following day) circulates on video.

RELEASE HISTORY

1985: A very good-quality copy of most of the concert (**A–S** and part of **T**) surfaced on the bootleg LP *Doll's House;* this tape suffers from serious speed fluctuations.

1987: A slightly more complete version (with bits of Bob Francis' announcements in **U** missing) appeared on the vinyl bootleg *300,000 Beatle Fans Can't Be Wrong;* this still has variable speed problems.

1998: A speed-corrected tape of the whole show (only missing "God Save the Queen" at the very end) was included on the Quarter Apple bootleg CD *300,000 Beatle Fans Can't Be Wrong.*

146. TV interview **R**

Date: 12 June 1964
Location: London Airport
Broadcast: 12 June 1964
ITV
Length: 0:57

Fresh from his hospital stay and ready to set off for Australia, Ringo filmed this brief interview at London Airport, admitting what a drag it was to be stuck in bed watching his mates fly around the world on TV and saying he will have to lay off the singing for a week.

RELEASE HISTORY

1996: The soundtrack of this interview was released on the CD *Fab Four CD & Book Set.* The footage was released on the video compilation *Beatles 1962 to 1970.*

147. Newsreel footage

Date: 13 June 1964
Time: afternoon
Location: San Francisco International Airport
Length: 3:15

Ringo, Brian Epstein, and Vivien Leigh (she just happened to be on the same flight) flew from London to San Francisco while Ringo's passport took a separate flight and met up with him in America. Awaiting his arrival in San Francisco were three hundred fans and one very cynical TV newsman, who opens this report by admitting, "Police and airport officials have been urging people not to come out here all day long. I genuinely didn't want to."

While waiting for Ringo to disembark from the plane, the grumpy newsman makes this dubious comparison: "We have been here before greeting Madame Nhu, accused murderers coming back from extradition, and now . . . Ringo Starr." He manages to catch a few words from Ringo as he enters the terminal; Ringo says he hopes the airport officials will let him greet the fans.

Clutching a stuffed koala bear, Ringo does make an appearance alongside Brian, standing on a table and waving to the screaming crowd, shushing them to no avail. After a brief layover, Ringo boarded a Qantas flight that would take him via Honolulu and Fiji to Sydney.

RELEASE HISTORY

1996: The soundtrack to most of this footage (2:17) was released on the CD *Rare Photos & Interview CD, Volume 3.* The footage was released on the home video *Live in San Francisco.*

147a. Newsreel footage

Date: 13 June 1964
Time: 4:00 p.m.
Location: South Australian Hotel, Adelaide
Length: 1:20

To placate the four thousand fans who had amassed outside their hotel, John, Paul, George, and Jimmy made a brief appearance (eight and a half minutes) on a columned balcony. Silent newsreel footage shows them waving to the streamer-heaving throng below and speaking briefly over microphones.

RELEASE HISTORY

This silent footage circulates on video among collectors.

148. Radio interview

Date: 13 June 1964
Time: 4:00 p.m.
Location: South Australian Hotel, Adelaide
Interviewer: Bob Rogers
Broadcast: 2SM, Sydney
Length: 5:15

After their balcony appearance, the Beatles reconvened inside their suite to tape an interview with Bob Rogers, beginning with some testing of what appears to be a faulty microphone. Paul jokes that there were three or four people waving back to them from below, while John puts the estimate closer to 4 million. They compare reactions in Adelaide to those in New York, and Bob asks if they'll be listening to the broadcast of their concert from the previous night. John and Paul reply to a telegram from some schoolgirls, and Jimmy relates his future plans, before George gets in a final word.

RELEASE HISTORY

1981: An incomplete version of this interview was released on the LP *The Beatles Talk Downunder* and has been reissued on the CD *Inside Interviews: Talk Downunder: Australia Beatlemania.*

1988: An unedited copy of this interview was booted on the LP *A Knight's Hard Day.*

149. Radio interview R

Date: 14 June 1964
Time: 7:00 a.m.
Location: Mascot Airport, Sydney
Interviewer: Garvin Rutherford
Broadcast: 2SM, Sydney
Length: 4:41

Easily the busiest Beatle day of the month, Monday, June 14, 1964, began with Ringo's arrival in Sydney at Mascot Airport. He was first interviewed by Garvin Rutherford, who asks about the origins of his various rings before estimating the crowd that had just greeted Ringo at seven thousand. Ringo feels that may be an overestimate, but goes on to discuss the outback, fans screaming during shows, whether he'll be able to sing during the tour, and his career as an engineer.

RELEASE HISTORY

1981: An incomplete version of this interview was released on the LP *The Beatles Talk Downunder* and has been reissued on the CD *Inside Interviews: Talk Downunder: Australia Beatlemania.*

1988: An unedited copy of this interview was booted on the LP *A Knight's Hard Day.*

150. TV interview/Newsreel footage R

Date: 14 June 1964
Time: morning
Location: Mascot Airport, Sydney
Length: 4:23

Ringo and Brian Epstein were then interviewed for Australian TV. Ringo talks about his rings yet again, and Brian relates his first impressions of meeting the Beatles and claims there is nothing too difficult about managing them. Ringo also discusses getting into the hairdressing business and asks the reporter how many people were at the airport to greet him. Upon being told three or four thousand, he points to Rutherford and exclaims, "There y'are. Told ya! Seven, he said!"

The newsreel *Beatles and Bedlam* includes silent footage of fans' overnight airport vigil, the press conference, and Ringo holding up his stuffed koala and passport while boarding his connecting flight to Melbourne.

RELEASE HISTORY

1996: The soundtrack of this interview was released on the CD *Fab Four CD & Book Set.* The interview circulates on video; a slightly incomplete version was released on the video *Beatlemania.* The *Beatles and Bedlam* newsreel also circulates on video.

151. Newsreel footage

Date: 14 June 1964
Time: 12:50 p.m.
Location: Adelaide Airport
Length: 2:02

The Beatles' return trip to Adelaide Airport was a somewhat faster replay of their arrival, with fans lining the route but police motorcycles clearing the way for a twenty-minute journey. Newsreels captured their grateful farewell to Adelaide, as they boarded a chartered Ansett Royal Mail Plane with Derek Taylor close at hand.

RELEASE HISTORY

This silent footage circulates on video among collectors.

152. TV coverage

Date: 14 June 1964
Time: afternoon
Location: Essendon Airport, Melbourne
Broadcast: live
ATN Channel 7
Length: 11:58

Anticipation was high in Melbourne for the long-awaited Beatles reunion. Channel 7 covered the day's events live, with commentator Brian Naylor reporting from Essendon Airport as the separate flights touched down. He was accompanied by a couple of young female fans to help identify George from John and Jimmy from Paul.

Ringo's flight is the first to arrive, and he clutches his omnipresent koala as he emerges with Brian Epstein close behind. They climb in the back seat of a car that slowly drives past a long line of fans behind the airfield fence. Naylor assumes that Ringo's delicate condition is the reason for using an enclosed car.

A couple of hours later, the scene is replayed and magnified: As the second flight taxis into position, a mobile camera rolls onto the tarmac to capture close-ups of the great moment. And here they are, bat-wing capes and all! Unlike Ringo, the others board a flatbed truck for optimum viewing and make not one, but two complete laps past the appreciative fans. Even Neil Aspinall gets into the act, waving and grinning cheerfully. Fans swarm across the parking lot to catch one last glimpse of the truck as it speeds off for the hotel.

RELEASE HISTORY

1995: 3:38 of the soundtrack to the TV coverage was released on the CD *The Beatles Tapes, Volume 3: The 1964 World Tour.*

1999: The complete soundtrack to the TV coverage was included on the bootleg CD *Australian Tour 1964,* taken from video that circulates among collectors.

153. TV/Radio coverage

Date: 14 June 1964
Time: 4:00 p.m.
Location: Southern Cross Hotel, Melbourne
Broadcast: live
ATN Channel 7
Length: 25:37

Crowds at the airport were mild compared to the mob outside the Southern Cross Hotel, which had swelled from three thousand when Ringo arrived to some twenty thousand as John, Paul, George, and Jimmy were en route. Channel 7's live coverage of the human sea flooding Exhibition Street is an unparalleled document of the simultaneous nightmare and marvel that Beatlemania caused at its zenith.

Mounted police make futile attempts at crowd control, but security and military officers are hopelessly outnumbered and swallowed by the throng. Girls pass out and there is no way for medical attention to reach them; the slightest provocation causes the crowd to chant, "We want the Beatles" and surge forward. Only a weakening human barricade separates the twenty thousand from the hotel's glass facade.

A motorcycle cop inches through the crowd, followed by a car with sirens blaring. People push forward to have a look, and the policeman is knocked from his cycle while onlookers kick at the car. But it's a decoy: The Beatles have wisely been driven to a back entrance. This fails to deter the crowd, who merely renew their impatient chanting with increased vigor. Some climb onto the shoulders of others for a better look, some into the trees, some onto the awning of a shop across the street.

Just in the nick of time, the five Beatles stroll out onto the viewing platform, Paul shivering in the cold, and walk to a bank of microphones to address the crowd. The din intensifies and drowns out Paul's cheery "Hello, everybody, how are yer?" Ringo shakes his mop-top and gives a shout. Jimmy and Ringo pretend to choke each other. George points out a sign reading WE LOVE YOU, COBBERS and gets the others to wave at the Channel 7 camera. The fans devour every second of it and every movement or comment brings a fresh round of screaming.

Swept up in the moment, John gives a Nazi salute. Paul and Ringo find this hilarious and join in; George drives home the point with a shout of "Deutschland Uber Alles!" Eventually, Neil nudges them back inside and Paul thanks the crowd one last time. But nobody is going anywhere, and a chorus of "We Love You, Beatles" pays off when various heads begin to poke from the window of the Beatles' suite.

In addition to the Channel 7 video, 1:06 of radio coverage and 1:10 of color home movie footage of the balcony appearance are circulating. But the TV report is unrivaled, highly recommended viewing material.

RELEASE HISTORY

1981: The radio coverage of the balcony appearance (lasting 1:06) was released on the LP *The Beatles Talk Downunder* and has been reissued on the CD *Inside Interviews: Talk Downunder: Australia Beatlemania.*

1987: 5:42 of the soundtrack to the TV coverage was released on the LP *From Britain . . . With Beat!,* later reissued on CD.

1999: 10:30 of the soundtrack to the TV coverage was included on the bootleg CD *Australian Tour 1964.* The complete coverage circulates on video, as does the silent home movie footage.

154. Press conference

Date: 14 June 1964
Time: evening
Location: Southern Cross Hotel, Melbourne
Length: 30:47

Five Beatles faced the press for a unique conference that was videotaped for TV. It begins with Derek Taylor setting out the ground rules (photos, questions from newspapers, then individual TV and radio interviews). He jokingly mentions "the brief but very grave illness of Ringo Starr," prompting Ringo to stuff a half dozen cigarettes in his mouth. As they pose for photos, Ringo clowns around further with John; they are clearly thrilled to have him back and vice versa.

Poor Jimmy goes ignored throughout and isn't addressed once during the conference (although he talks briefly to a reporter while John is responding to a question). Even the TV camera ignores him, zooming in to fit the four "real" Beatles in the frame. He does get a souvenir, though, when they are all presented with didgeridoos. John is puzzled ("I thought it was an animal!"), but Ringo is hip: "Who's got a wobble board? We'll have a session!"

Ringo continues to spot familiar faces (Mal Evans, *Liverpool Echo* columnist George Harrison) and informs the others that his favorite drink is no longer scotch and Coke, but bourbon. "Did you get that at hospital?" John wonders. Asked "How do you find your police escorts?," John replies, "They usually find us." Derek eventually wraps things up by announcing a break for the TV cameras to set up. Ringo observes that "the telly's been on all the time, I hate to tell you."

RELEASE HISTORY

1999: 21 minutes of this press conference was included on the bootleg CD *Australian Tour 1964,* taken from the soundtrack of a videotape that circulates in very good quality. Further footage from a film source also circulates.

155. Radio interview — J, G

Date: 14 June 1964
Time: evening
Location: Southern Cross Hotel, Melbourne
Interviewer: Alan Lappin
Broadcast: 3UZ Radio, Melbourne
Length: 3:00

Allan Lappin, from 3UZ Radio, taped separate interviews with John and George following the press conference. John chats about the Soviet Union, his book, the army, and mods and rockers, while George expresses enthusiasm for pirate radio stations.

RELEASE HISTORY

1981: These interviews were released on the LP *The Beatles Talk Downunder* and have been reissued on the CD *Inside Interviews: Talk Downunder: Australia Beatlemania.*

156. Newsreel interview

Date: 15 June 1964
Location: Southern Cross Hotel, Melbourne
Interviewer: Malcolm Searle (?)
Length: 8:21

While the Fab Four slept in, Brian Epstein accompanied the temporary fifth Fab, Jimmy Nicol, to Essendon Airport. Newsreel footage exists of an interview with Brian and Jimmy as well as the latter boarding the flight that would carry him back to anonymity. When they awoke, the Beatles attended an EMI Records reception at their hotel and performed the first two of six concerts at Festival Hall that evening. Sometime in between, John filmed an interview with an Australian reporter named Malcolm, possibly 3AK Radio's Malcolm Searle.

John says that while *A Hard Day's Night* had a script, the experienced actors were often infuriated by the Beatles' penchant for not sticking to their lines as written. Malcolm wonders if John believes in God, and he classifies himself as "agnostic." The group's complete lack of interest in sports was alien to an athletic country like Australia, and while John played football as a child, he concedes to being "agnostic about sport, too."

He clears up Mimi's misconception that parts of *In His Own Write* were written during his childhood, and recounts meeting Paul (at an "agnostic church social"). As soon as John, Paul, and George met Ringo in Hamburg, they knew he was the drummer for them, but they had to bide their time until an excuse to sack Pete Best came along. While Jimmy Nicol did an admirable job, John admits they all felt awkward not having Ringo around.

John reveals that most of *In His Own Write* was written during the Beatles' residency at seaside resorts in July and August 1963 to occupy the time spent in hotel rooms. His reply to critics who call the book "sick": "So what? There's a lot of sickness about, isn't there?" Malcolm asks how much they feel they owe Brian Epstein, and John jokes, "We owe him one-and-six exactly." More seriously, he says that Brian has done better than expected and is a close friend, if not the genius some make him out to be.

RELEASE HISTORY

1996: The last 2:45 of this interview was released on the CD *Fab Four CD & Book Set.* The full interview circulates on video.

157. Newsreel/Amateur footage

Date: 16 June 1964
Time: 1:00 p.m.
Location: Melbourne Town Hall
Length: 7:05

The Beatles' third day in Melbourne began with yet another balcony appearance, witnessed by nearly as many people as the first. The group had been invited by the lord mayor, Leo Curtis, to a 12:30 reception at the town hall. Arriving a half hour late, they fought their way through the crowd of fifteen thousand to the hall and were soon waving from the balcony along with Mayor Curtis and his daughter Vikki.

The event was captured not only in the raw news footage and the newsreel *Beatles at the Stadium,* but in a color home movie by one of the throng below. Both show Paul clowning around with a boomerang. As was usually the case with "VIP only" gatherings, the subsequent reception was a disheartening affair along the lines of the British Embassy fiasco in Washington, D.C. Only when they were ushered into a private room with just the mayor's family did the Beatles relax, with Paul leading everyone in a piano singsong.

RELEASE HISTORY

The newsreel and silent color home movie footage both circulate on video.

158. Concert

Date: 17 June 1964
Time: 6:00 p.m.
Location: Festival Hall, Melbourne

[A.] intro (0:55)
[B.] I Saw Her Standing There (2:33)
[C.] intro (0:02)
[D.] You Can't Do That (2:25)
[E.] intro (0:33)
[F.] All My Loving (2:00)
[G.] intro (0:22)
[H.] She Loves You (2:12)
[I.] intro (0:38)
[J.] Till There Was You (2:09)
[K.] Roll Over Beethoven (2:13)
[L.] intro (0:20)
[M.] Can't Buy Me Love (2:02)
[N.] intro (0:25)
[O.] This Boy (2:13)
[P.] intro (0:05)
[Q.] Twist and Shout (2:36)
[R.] intro (1:42)

The Beatles played six shows at the Melbourne Festival Hall, two full houses of 7,500 for three straight nights. The set list was amended slightly from Adelaide, with "You Can't Do That" substituted for "I Want to Hold Your Hand." Although Ringo was now back behind the drums, he was advised against singing just yet, so the shows remained a truncated ten numbers long. None of it seemed to matter to the delirious audiences, who showed their appreciation with nonstop cheering, flashbulbs, and a constant hail of streamers.

Two soundboard recordings of Melbourne shows are circulating, both apparently from the final night (despite conflicting information over the years). During this show, prior to "Long Tall Sally" (which itself has yet to surface), Paul announces, "Seeing as this is the last night that we're playing in Melbourne, we'd, uh, like to thank everybody for being so great to us. And we'd like to dedicate the last number to two people who've been very good to us while we've been here. They've looked after us. This last number we'd like to do especially for our two fan club presidents who are sitting right down here."

Portions of this show first surfaced from an unknown radio broadcast that actually includes material from both nights (see details below). An upgrade that surfaced in 1996 may be the master tape used for this broadcast, as it exhibits many of the same edits. The tape that appeared in 1999 (supposedly from a photographer in Delaware who had covered the tour) is unedited, but ends prior to the introduction of "Long Tall Sally." This version also includes one song from opening act Johnny Chester, plus Sounds Incorporated's full set.

RELEASE HISTORY

1975: Much of this concert first appeared in fair quality on the bootleg LP *Live In Melbourne, Australia 7/16/64,* taken from a radio broadcast that is heavily edited. **A, G, I, L, M, N,** and **R** are all incomplete; **E** is rearranged to include dialogue from **R** (which is then heard again!). "This Boy" and "Long Tall Sally" on this release are spliced in from the second June 17 show. **P** and **Q** are entirely absent.

1981: The LP *The Beatles Talk Downunder* included portions of several introductions from this show, in good quality (the five fragments are taken from **E, R, I, R,** and **R** again, in that order). This LP was released on CD as *Inside Interviews: Talk Downunder: Australia Beatlemania.*

1996: A very good-quality tape appeared on the bootleg CD *All the Best from Australia.* This included most of the show, but was still missing bits of **E–I, L–N,** and all of **O. R** is complete for the first time, but "This Boy" and "Long Tall Sally" are still spliced in from the second show. This tape runs a half step too slow.

1999: The bootleg CD *Australian Tour 1964* included **A–Q,** complete and in very good quality, but omitted **R** entirely. This source also runs a half step too slow.

159. Concert

Date: 17 June 1964
Time: 8:45 p.m.
Location: Festival Hall, Melbourne
Broadcast: 1 July 1964, 7:30–8:30 p.m.
TCN Channel 9
The Beatles Sing for Shell

[A.] **intro** (1:31)
[B.] **I Saw Her Standing There** (2:37)
[C.] **intro** (0:03)
[D.] **You Can't Do That** (2:33)
[E.] **intro** (0:28)
[F.] **All My Loving** (2:03)
[G.] **intro** (0:17)
[H.] **She Loves You** (2:15)
[I.] **intro** (0:32)
[J.] **Till There Was You** (2:12)
[K.] **intro** (0:01)
[L.] **Roll Over Beethoven** (2:16)
[M.] **intro** (0:52)
[N.] **Can't Buy Me Love** (2:05)
[O.] **intro** (0:24)
[P.] **This Boy** (2:13)
[Q.] **intro** (0:06)
[R.] **Twist and Shout** (2:38)
[S.] **intro** (1:21)
[T.] **Long Tall Sally** (2:02)
[U.] **outro** (0:43)

The sixth and final Melbourne show was videotaped by Australian TV for an hour-long special sponsored by Shell Oil. The only song not used in the broadcast was "This Boy," although it is on the circulating soundboard. According to Mark Lewisohn, the videotape was "slightly defective" during "Till There Was You" and "Roll Over Beethoven," which explains why they're fragmentary on the circulating video copy.

Despite a poor sound balance (John's guitar is twice as loud as George's), it makes for entertaining viewing. John does a little dance accompanied by a drum flurry during his "clap your hands" routine. Paul stops to scratch his nose during "Twist and Shout" and George tries to help him out! Prior to the final number, Paul acknowledges Ringo's return to the fold (he'd made a similar announcement in the previous show), triggering rapturous cheering.

With mere bars to go in "Long Tall Sally," an eager chap sprints onstage and heads straight for John to shake his hand. Having achieved his goal, the fellow is willingly led away by police; John merely laughs and finishes the song. After the familiar last bow, the Beatles return for an uncustomary "encore bow," presumably as a final farewell to the phenomenally welcoming city of Melbourne.

RELEASE HISTORY

1982: Six of these songs (**D, F, H, N, R,** and **T**) were bootlegged in very good quality on the LP *Tour Years,* taken from the soundtrack of the *Sing for Shell* broadcast. The circulating video copy of that broadcast also includes the last 1:09 of **B,** the first 11 seconds of **J,** and the final 27 seconds of **L.** The *Anthology* documentary includes portions of **D, F,** and **M.**

1989: An excellent tape copy of the entire show was booted on the Pyramid CD *Live in Melbourne 1964 and Paris 1965;* this starts at the correct speed but slows down gradually toward the end. **A** is missing some of the emcee's chat, and the second chord of **P** is also absent.

1996: The bootleg CD *All the Best from Australia* included **A–U,** complete but running a half step too slow throughout. A similar version on the CD *Australian Tour 1964* is in worse quality than this or the Pyramid release.

159a. Newsreel footage

Date: 18 June 1964
Time: 11:40 a.m.
Location: Mascot International Airport, Sydney
Length: 4:37

A late-morning flight brought the Beatles from Melbourne back to Sydney, where news cameras captured a scene very similar to that on June 11, with the group and Derek Taylor deplaning and waving to hysterical fans from atop a flatbed milk truck. The only differences are that this time it isn't raining, and Ringo and Brian Epstein are both present.

RELEASE HISTORY

This silent footage circulates on video among collectors.

160. Radio interview **P, R**

Date: 18 June 1964
Time: afternoon
Location: Sheraton Motel Hotel, Sydney
Interviewer: Bob Rogers, Mike Walsh
Broadcast: 2SM, Sydney
Length: 1:49

Back at the Sheraton Motel Hotel, the Beatles faced the press and celebrated Paul's twenty-second birthday with a pair of parties. The second, held after their two concerts, was attended by winners of a *Daily Mirror* newspaper contest and lasted well into the next morning.

This earlier celebration was for the benefit of radio station 2SM, who had Bob Rogers and a team of local "Good Guy" jocks covering the occasion. Paul talks with Bob about the station's gifts: a five-foot-tall stuffed kangaroo and a seemingly endless scarf, knitted by teams of schoolgirls and presented by DJ Mad Mel. Mike Walsh introduces Ringo to a new instrument: the kazoo, on which Ringo hums a bit of "From Me to You."

RELEASE HISTORY

1981: These interviews were released on the LP *The Beatles Talk Downunder* and have been reissued on the CD *Inside Interviews: Talk Downunder: Australia Beatlemania.* They also appear on the bootleg LP *A Knight's Hard Day,* but with no extra material.

161. Concert

Date: 18 June 1964
Location: Sydney Stadium
Released: 25 June 1964
Beatles at the Stadium
Length: 12:51

Cinesound newsreel cameras were allowed "by kind permission of Brian Epstein" to film one of the Beatles' six Sydney concerts, most likely on the opening night. The result, *Beatles at the Stadium,* used three minutes of concert footage along with various photographs and other clips (the December 7, 1963, Liverpool Empire concert, the June 16 Melbourne Town Hall appearance, and the June 21 arrival in New Zealand).

The Beatles, led by Neil Aspinall, are seen clambering onstage, performing a number of songs (including "This Boy" and "All My Loving"), and fighting their way through crowds after the concert as Mal Evans retrieves their equipment. Some natural sound from the concert is used, primarily snippets of "I Saw Her Standing There" and "You Can't Do That," none of which matches up to the images. Studio recordings are also overdubbed, including "Misery," a song that wasn't even in the set list.

British Pathé's online archive contains 9:49 of silent offcuts from the Cinesound newsreel. Most of the songs from both shows on this date are covered, along with plentiful shots of screaming and clapping girls in the audience.

RELEASE HISTORY

2001: The poor-quality concert excerpts appeared on the CD-R compilation *Live: Make as Much Noise as You Like!* The full newsreel circulates on video among collectors, as do the offcuts.

162. Newsreel footage

Date: 18–20 June 1964
Location: Sheraton Motel Hotel balcony, Sydney
Length: 0:14

At some point during their second stay in Sydney, all four Beatles ventured out onto the balcony of their top-floor hotel suite to wave to fans, with newsreel cameras filming from the street below.

RELEASE HISTORY

This silent footage was released on the *Anthology* home video documentary.

163. Radio interview

Date: 21 June 1964
Time: morning
Location: flight from Sydney to Wellington
Interviewer: Bob Rogers
Broadcast: 2SM, Sydney
Length: 3:39

A morning flight brought the Beatles from Sydney to Wellington, New Zealand; along the way, Bob Rogers taped further interviews. At the final Sydney concert the previous evening, eggs had been thrown at the support act, Johnny Devlin, and yolk and shells littered the stage as the Beatles went on.

George seems more worried about the fact that fans are still throwing jelly babies, and Ringo just wishes they'd fried the eggs first. Prior to boarding, the group had been presented with a giant stuffed kiwi; Paul confuses it with an emu, but John says he "knew it was a kiwi 'cause it started polishin' me shoes." Although his aunt Mimi is currently in New Zealand visiting relatives, John doesn't think they'll have a chance to meet up until they return to "Sydney. Or Eric or Dave, somewhere like that."

RELEASE HISTORY

1981: Incomplete versions of these interviews were released on the LP *The Beatles Talk Downunder* and have been reissued on the CD *Inside Interviews: Talk Downunder: Australia Beatlemania.*

1988: Unedited recordings of these interviews were included on the bootleg LP *A Knight's Hard Day.*

164. Newsreel footage

Date: 21 June 1964
Location: Wellington Airport
Length: 2:48

Seven thousand fans welcomed the Beatles to New Zealand, as did the omnipresent film crews. Scenes of their arrival were included in the Cinesound newsreel *Beatles at the Stadium,* showing the group with their stuffed kiwi, rubbing noses with Maori girls, and riding past the fans in a convertible car with tikis draped around their necks.

RELEASE HISTORY

Thirty-six seconds of this footage were included in the newsreel *Beatles at the Stadium,* which circulates on video. The remainder is silent offcuts, which reside in British Pathé's online newsreel archive.

165. Interview

Date: 21 June 1964
Location: Hotel St. George, Wellington
Length: 0:49

Upon the Beatles' arrival at Wellington's Hotel St. George, another press reception was held. This brief clip has the group clowning around with a reporter. ("How are you liking this applause? Is it going to your head at all?" Ringo: "No. Well, it goes to me ears, but . . .")

RELEASE HISTORY

1995: This interview was released on the CD *The Beatles Tapes III: The 1964 World Tour,* dated June 22.

166. Interview **J, G, R**

Date: 21 June 1964
Location: Hotel St. George, Wellington
Interviewer: Doreen Kelso
Length: 8:12

After the press conference, reporter Doreen Kelso taped interviews with at least three Beatles. George talks about local senses of humor, how to avoid fans, and the value of being rich. John discusses the age range of their fans, his book, art school, the Quarry Men, the haircuts, and manufacturers of Beatles memorabilia. Ringo, predictably, talks about the state of his voice and his ring collection.

RELEASE HISTORY

1995: These interviews were released on the CD *The Beatles Tapes, Volume 3: The 1964 World Tour,* mislabeled as June 24 recordings from Auckland.

167. Radio interview **J, P, R**

Date: 23 June 1964
Location: Hotel St. George, Wellington
Interviewer: Bob Rogers
Broadcast: 2SM, Sydney
Length: 7:06

More Bob Rogers/Beatles chat was recorded this afternoon in their Wellington hotel room, although George is absent (busy writing a letter home). Paul claims that New Zealand audiences are more conservative than most, although some girls did try to rush the stage at one of their shows, which Paul says he would have welcomed. They complain about the microphones at the concert and mention that Ringo is now able to sing "Boys" every night, giving them an eleven-song repertoire at last. Some risque jokes about fertility symbols are followed by a bit of classical guitar playing from Paul. A discussion of the Vienna Boys Choir, who are also in town, winds things up. (Paul: "They blow up a bit of a storm, those fellas." John: "Vienna Boys Choir-mania, I'd call it.")

RELEASE HISTORY

1981: An incomplete edit of this interview was released in very good quality on the LP *The Beatles Talk Downunder* and has been reissued on the CD *Inside Interviews: Talk Downunder: Australia Beatlemania.*

1988: An unedited copy of most of the interview, in fair quality, was split between the bootleg LPs *A Knight's Hard Day* and *Fuck!* This is still missing some of the recording as compared to *The Beatles Talk Downunder,* so all three sources are needed for a complete composite.

168. Radio interview **J, P, R**

Date: 25 June 1964
Location: Royal International Hotel, Auckland
Interviewer: Bob Rogers
Broadcast: 2SM, Sydney
Length: 4:51

Individual interviews with Paul, John, and Ringo were taped by Bob Rogers following a press conference at the Royal International Hotel in Auckland. Paul says he's not tired of meeting the press, while John greets three female fans and relates the story of a fan who climbed up eight stories of drainpipes in Sydney to gain entrance to the Beatles' hotel suite. Ringo is asked about the furor caused by opposition to an official civic reception for the group in Auckland that will cost the taxpayers 60 pounds ("My god, they should be broke after that"). He also claims to have enjoyed meeting the lord mayor at a similar function in Melbourne.

RELEASE HISTORY

1981: Incomplete edits of these interviews were released on the LP *The Beatles Talk Downunder* and have been reissued on the CD *Inside Interviews: Talk Downunder: Australia Beatlemania.*

1988: Unedited copies of these interviews were booted on the LP *Fuck!*

168a. Amateur footage

Date: 25 June 1964
Location: Auckland Town Hall
Length: 0:30

Despite the controversy, the Beatles' public appearance with Mayor Dove-Myer Robinson was a success. This silent home movie footage documents the occasion, with the group waving to seven thousand fans and twirling poi (balls on ropes used by a Maori dance troupe that performed for them).

RELEASE HISTORY

1994: This silent color footage was included in the documentary *Inside New Zealand,* which circulates on video.

169. Radio interview

Date: 26 June 1964
Location: New City Hotel, Dunedin
Interviewer: Bob Rogers
Broadcast: 2SM, Sydney
Length: 15:56

Bob Rogers was able to tape a lengthy and very entertaining interview with all four Beatles this evening at the New City Hotel in Dunedin.

The conversation begins with a description of the civic reception in Auckland, and George is asked what he's been doing all this tour ("I've been touring, Bob"). Bob inquires about their new EP, which he believes will contain "Matchbox," although Ringo says he thought it wasn't included in Australia (he's right, as the equivalent of the *Long Tall Sally* EP, titled *Requests,* substituted "Boys"). Discussion of Carl Perkins follows, which leads to talk of "Slow Down" and Larry Williams. Ringo considers raffling off his tonsils, and John says he is against the idea of topless swimsuits. (Paul: "You've had us wearing 'em." John: "I know, Paulie! You're so well-built.")

The topic turns to their upcoming film, with "If I Fell," "And I Love Her," and the title song being singled out for praise. George says his songwriting attempts are "laughed off" by the others and whistles a bit of "You Know What to Do." Paul sings a bit of Ringo's first composition, "Don't Pass Me By," although when asked why he doesn't give it to the Rolling Stones, Ringo refuses to answer.

Anti-Beatles sentiments in New Zealand are debated, while Paul seems bemused by the fans holding up signs for pianist Arthur Rubenstein, concurrently touring Australia. A mouthful of salad causes John to bite on something unusual, which leads to talk of New Zealand foods before the group signs off with a nonsensical ad-libbed "catchphrase."

RELEASE HISTORY

1981: An incomplete edit of this interview was released on the LP *The Beatles Talk Downunder* and has been reissued on the CD *Inside Interviews: Talk Downunder: Australia Beatlemania.*

1988: An unedited copy of most of the interview was bootlegged on the LP *Fuck!* (It's missing some of the ending compared to *The Beatles Talk Downunder.*)

169a. Interview

Date: 28 June 1964
Time: evening
Location: flight from Auckland to Sydney
Length: 4:48

After a concert in Christchurch on June 27, the Beatles left New Zealand on the twenty-eighth, via Auckland and Sydney. A New Zealand journalist named Ted chatted with the group during the flight, two at a time. George and Ringo complain about air travel, working in a plug for "Don't Bother Me" along the way, and rail against the people who threw eggs at the group during a Christchurch balcony appearance (more eggs were in their immediate future). Paul translates "About the Awful" from *In His Own Write* into standard English, and then John gives it a straight reading in the original Lennon.

RELEASE HISTORY

These interviews circulate in excellent quality among collectors.

169b. Newsreel footage

Date: 28 June 1964
Time: evening
Location: Kingsford Smith Airport, Sydney
Length: 0:27

A bit of footage exists of the Beatles' brief layover in Sydney, showing the group waving at fans from the airplane steps (John wears sunglasses, even though it's quite dark out).

RELEASE HISTORY

This footage circulates on video among collectors.

170. Newsreel footage

Date: 29 June 1964
Time: 12:30 a.m.
Location: Brisbane Airport
Length: 8:12

Just after midnight, the Beatles landed in Brisbane, the final stop on the month-long tour. Footage of the waiting crowd hints at trouble ahead: Not only does someone set off a smoke bomb, but one fan proudly displays a sign reading WELLCUM JON GORGE POORL WRINGO. When the Beatles deplane, with Derek Taylor and Neil Aspinall in tow, they climb onto a milk float and are driven past the crowd. Suddenly, a shower of eggs, fruit, and chunks of wood rains down, thrown by a group of disgruntled University of Queensland students from behind the safety of the barrier.

RELEASE HISTORY

This silent footage circulates on video; 38 seconds of it was used in the Cinesound newsreel *Beatles Back in Australia!*

171. Press conference

Date: 29 June 1964
Time: morning
Location: Lennons Hotel, Brisbane
Length: 0:45

At a press conference this morning at Brisbane's fortuitously named Lennons Hotel, the Beatles were naturally asked about the food-throwing incident at the airport. Ringo and Paul both say that given the chance, they'd hurl the eggs and tomatoes back at the culprits, and John adds he'd "mash the hell out of them." George says he thought Brisbane would have more skyscrapers, and Ringo expected to see flying doctors (referring to the Royal Flying Doctor Service, a medical transport organization founded in Queensland).

RELEASE HISTORY

The audio portion of a TV broadcast including these clips circulates in very good quality.

172. Radio interview — P, G

Date: 29 June 1964
Time: morning
Location: Lennons Hotel, Brisbane
Interviewer: Tony Macarthur
Broadcast: 4BK, Brisbane
Length: 3:01

4BK Radio DJ Tony Macarthur taped brief interviews following the press conference. Paul chats about their upcoming second American tour and dismisses the recordings done with Tony Sheridan for Polydor. George talks about the film and his favorite musicians (the Miracles, Marvin Gaye, and Mary Wells). Macarthur would go on to record a number of interviews with the Beatles for Radio Luxembourg in 1968 and 1969.

RELEASE HISTORY

1981: These interviews were released on the LP *The Beatles Talk Downunder* and have been reissued on the CD *Inside Interviews: Talk Downunder: Australia Beatlemania*.

173. Radio interview

Date: 1 July 1964
Time: morning
Location: Mascot Airport, Sydney
Length: 12:33

Before leaving Australia, the Beatles submitted to one last round of interviews with the press at Sydney's Mascot Airport. Ringo discusses the students who threw eggs at them, and other signs of the Beatles' supposedly declining popularity. When asked for a joke, Ringo wearily replies, "Oh, after two hours' sleep, there's no jokes, believe me." Paul sounds worn-out as well, but gamely denies another round of false rumors and offers a brief farewell message to the Australian fans.

John is so exhausted he has trouble putting together a sentence of more than a few words: "John, could you tell us how you felt now after the tour's all over?" "Tired." "And do you think you'd ever come back again?" "Haven't a clue." "What are you going to do when you get home? Rest, I suppose?" "No, work. We don't rest." He does show some interest when informed that the Animals have just scored a number 1 song ("The House of the Rising Sun") on the UK charts. George (who seems to be the only Beatle to have gotten a decent night's sleep) also expresses great enthusiasm for the Animals and reveals that they are fans of Bob Dylan ("We've got all his LPs"). He goes on to describe the antics of Screaming Lord Sutch, a pirate-radio DJ in England who would soon be visiting Australia, and he candidly admits he wasn't too keen on New Zealand, but did enjoy Brisbane and Adelaide in particular.

RELEASE HISTORY

1987: These interviews were released on the LP *From Britain . . . With Beat!,* later issued on CD.

174. Radio interview

Date: 1 July 1964
Time: morning
Location: Mascot Airport, Sydney
Interviewer: Bob Rogers
Broadcast: 2SM, Sydney
Length: 10:07

These interviews took place concurrently with those in the previous entry; for instance, during George's chat with Bob Rogers, you can hear the interview with John (described earlier) taking place in the background. George jokes that since Ringo will be turning twenty-four the next week, they'll shake his hand, give him a gold watch, and send him to retirement. John again professes his tiredness, but chats briefly about what questions they are asked most often, before bidding farewell to Bob.

Paul's interview begins with a question from a college reporter about whether he would like to do a university course. Paul responds, "No thank you. But if you get the chance, don't refuse!" He also talks with Bob Rogers about the Animals' chart topper, but says he's not worried about being replaced as the top pop group: "Last week it was Dave Clark, the week before it was Brian Poole. I've given up answering that question." Finally, Ringo tells Bob about meeting some of the egg-throwers, records a brief generic promo to introduce a song from the *A Hard Day's Night* LP, and claims he'll be happy with whatever people will give him for his birthday.

RELEASE HISTORY

1981: These interviews were released on the LP *The Beatles Talk Downunder* and have been reissued on numerous CDs such as *Inside Interviews: Talk Downunder: Australia Beatlemania* and *Talk Downunder, Volume 2.*

174a. TV interview

Date: 1 July 1964
Time: morning
Location: Mascot Airport, Sydney
Length: 0:58

A TV reporter chatted with each Beatle individually before they departed for London; these brief clips feature the group praising and thanking their Australian fan base. John even concedes that the egg-throwers turned out to be decent blokes when they met in person. George sings a bit of "We'll Meet Again," and Paul jokingly orders the reporter, crouching down to conduct the interviews, to "get your hand off my knee."

RELEASE HISTORY

This footage circulates on video; a bit of it was released on the DVD *The Unseen Beatles.*

175. Studio session P

Date: 2 July 1964
Location: EMI Studio 1
Producer: George Martin

[A.] It's for You (2:19)

Despite suffering from jet lag, John and Paul both attended a Cilla Black session at Abbey Road Studio 1 this evening. Cilla was recording a second remake of "It's for You," a song written for her by Paul, who stayed late to add a piano contribution to the recording.

RELEASE HISTORY

1964: This song was released as a single in the UK (where it reached number 8) and the United States (where it peaked only at number 79). It was also the title track of an EP in the UK that fall. It's now available on the CD boxed set *Cilla 1963–1973, The Abbey Road Decade.*

176. Newsreel footage

Date: 6 July 1964
Time: evening
Location: London Pavilion
Length: 1:27

A Hard Day's Night was given a Royal Premiere this evening at the London Pavilion, attended by Princess Margaret and her husband, Anthony Armstrong-Jones. AP, Reuters, and ITV were among the newsreel companies filming outside in Piccadilly Circus as thousands of ticketless fans filled the streets, struggling with police to get a prime view of their idols.

As the Beatles exit their limo, with Brian and Cynthia in tow, a photographer spins George around to face his camera. George's lips are easily read: "Hey, don't push me." Princess Margaret arrives and receives the film's stars, lined up in front of Beatle-print drapery. Paul looks nervous, exhaling deeply and straightening his tie as costar Wilfrid Brambell chats with the princess. The fans stick around to watch the boys leave the theater later that night; a policeman revives one girl with smelling salts.

RELEASE HISTORY

This silent footage circulates on video.

177. Radio interview **R**

Date: ca. 7 July 1964
Location: London (via telephone)
Interviewer: Murray Kaufman
Broadcast: WINS-AM, New York City
Length: 0:26

This telephone interview with Ringo was taped at some point following the Beatles' return to England, perhaps on his birthday. Murray asks how the tour of Australia went, and Ringo thanks everyone who sent get-well cards while he was hospitalized with tonsillitis.

RELEASE HISTORY

1965: This interview was released on the EP *The Beatles & Murray the K: As It Happened,* which has been reissued in the United States on *Timeless II* and the UK on *The Beatles Conquer America.*

178. Newsreel footage **R**

Date: 7 July 1964
Time: 2:00 p.m.
Location: Lime Grove Studios, London
Broadcast: 7 July 1964
BBC TV
Length: 0:12

As Ringo turned twenty-four, the Beatles were busy with radio and TV appearances to promote *A Hard Day's Night.* While they were at a BBC TV studio to film a performance for *Top of the Pops,* the Beeb's crew shot a few seconds of footage of the birthday boy for inclusion in that evening's newscast.

RELEASE HISTORY

This silent footage was included in the video compilation *Beatles 1962 to 1970.*

179. TV interview

Date: 7 July 1964
Time: 5:30–6:00 p.m.
Location: Television House, London
Broadcast: 7 July 1964, 6:30–7:00 p.m.
Granada TV
Scene at 6:30
Length: 1:10

Although this interview is obviously from this date, it's only an educated guess that it comes from this particular broadcast. Ringo says the only unusual present he's gotten this year is a ring from a bull's nose; Paul is asked about the racehorse, Drake's Drum, he bought for his father (whose birthday it also was); George says the film premiere in London the previous night went great; John says the "next big event" will be the premiere in Liverpool later that week.

RELEASE HISTORY

1995: The audio portion of this interview was released on the CD *Rare Photos & Interview CD, Volume 1.* It also circulates on video and has been released on the videotape *Beatlemania.*

180. TV interview/Newsreel footage

Date: 10 July 1964
Time: evening
Location: Liverpool
Broadcast: 10 July 1964, 6:30–7:00 p.m.
Granada TV
Scene at 6:30
Length: 7:34

Some 200,000 people were on hand throughout the day to greet the Beatles upon their return to Liverpool. Their arrival at Speke Airport, their trip to the town hall, and the film premiere at the Odeon Cinema all received wide coverage from TV and newsreel cameras, and much footage exists, including an interview conducted at the airport. It has often been misidentified as an interview conducted by BBC TV's Gerald Harrison for *Look North,* but as it was subsequently included in a Granada TV documentary, it's most likely from *Scene at 6:30.*

Paul claims that their only remaining ambition is to make a "good film." George asks Paul if he thinks the one they made is any good, and John says it's not as good as a James Bond flick. When asked why it's been so long since the last Beatles appearance in Liverpool, John testily replies, "The people that are moaning about us not being here are people that never even came to see us when we were here." (This exchange would later be parodied brilliantly in *The Rutles.*)

RELEASE HISTORY

1995: A slightly incomplete audio copy of the interview was released on the CD *The Beatles Tapes, Volume 3: The 1964 World Tour.* It circulates on video from a 1984 broadcast in Granada TV's documentary *The Early Beatles,* as does a 1:14 ITV News report (aired July 11), focusing on the town hall appearance. Further footage from this date was included in the *Anthology* DVD.

181. Radio promos — P, G, R

Date: 11 July 1964
Time: morning
Location: London (?)
Broadcast: 12–16 July 1964
BBC Light Programme
Length: 2:37

In his excellent book, *John Lennon: In My Life,* Pete Shotton recounts how he and John stayed up all night on July 10 at his flat in Liverpool reminiscing, causing John to miss an appointment early the next morning. This probably accounts for his absence on several recordings known to be from this period. Pete recalls the engagement as "a radio show in Manchester" but it seems likely the appointment was to tape promotional interviews for a radio appearance, for their film, and for German radio.

The radio show was the BBC's brand-new pop program *Top Gear,* and Paul, George, and Ringo taped promos for their upcoming appearance—not in Manchester, but reportedly at a flat in London's Shepherd Street shared by BBC producer Bernie Andrews and NEMS associate Terry Doran. The promo spot as broadcast lasted about 0:25, and a further 2:12 of outtakes and goofing around (Paul using his "posh announcer" and "Scouse" voices) also circulates.

RELEASE HISTORY

1988: These recordings were broadcast in the November 26 episode of BBC Radio's *The Beeb's Lost Beatles Tapes.* They are available in excellent sound on the bootleg CD *The Beatles Broadcast Collection, Trailer 1.*

182. Open-end interview — P, G, R

Date: 11 July 1964
Time: morning
Location: London (?)

Also probably taped on this day was an open-end interview to be sent to radio stations in the United States to promote local showings of *A Hard Day's Night.* Only the Beatles' answers were included on the finished disc so that DJs could read the questions from the enclosed script and appear to be interviewing the group exclusively. The complete program, including four songs from the film and commercials, lasted a half hour.

Paul jokingly explains John's absence away by claiming that he's gone down to the shipyards to have an estimate for a haircut. The three Beatles then chat about making the film, the tribulations of getting up early to shoot scenes, writing the songs, and trying not to laugh while acting. They also introduce each of the songs ("A Hard Day's Night," "And I Love Her," "If I Fell," and "I'm Happy Just to Dance with You") and discuss Beatle imitators and the pressures of fame.

RELEASE HISTORY

1964: This interview was included on a promotional LP, *United Artists Presents "A Hard Day's Night."* It appears on the cassette *Historic Interviews, Volume 2,* with the questions read by Fred Robbins (and a specific greeting from Paul, "Nice to be here, Fred," edited in). A slightly edited version with questions read by WGH's Gene Loving is on the CD *Moviemania!,* and a severe edit of this is on the CD *All Our Loving.*

1982: A 6:17 edit was nearly released by Capitol as "Fab Four on Film." It appeared on promotional copies of the "Beatles Movie Medley" single, but was replaced on the commercial release with "I'm Happy Just to Dance with You." This edit has a cameo appearance from John spliced in from the soundtrack of the film's trailer.

183. Radio interview — P, G, R

Date: 11 July 1964
Time: morning
Location: London Hilton (?)
Interviewer: Dieter Bröer
Broadcast: NDR
Length: 10:11

This interview for German radio's Nord Deutsche Rundsfunk network is placed here chiefly because of John's absence. It's usually said to have been recorded at the London Hilton.

Paul and George do their best to respond in German to interviewer Dieter Bröer's questions, although Ringo remembers how to order only *"zwei ei and kartoffeln"* (two eggs and potatoes). Similarly, Paul recalls consuming *"cornflakes mit milsch"* at Harald's Bar in Hamburg, while George enjoyed tea and "whiskey mit Coca-Cola." Ringo appreciated Hamburg's nightlife, which meant that when they finished marathon music sets, there would still be plenty to keep them occupied.

After naming all the clubs they played on the Reeperbahn, Paul says that their professional career really started with the Johnny Gentle tour of Scotland, but that a few months later, they earned decent money on their first trip to Hamburg. Ringo relates the plot of *A Hard Day's Night,* and Paul gives a literal translation of the title into German. Paul admits he's frightened by the prospect of marriage and tells Bröer to air some songs from the film along with the interview.

Although they have no plans to tour Germany, they talk a bit about their upcoming North American tour. To sign off, Paul launches into a word-for-word recitation of the "Ausweiskontrolle" announcement given at the start of curfew hours in Hamburg nightclubs. The books *Many Years from Now* and *Anthology* prove that he and George retained the entire speech some thirty-five years later.

RELEASE HISTORY

1965: Some of this interview was released on a flexi-disc included with the November 1965 issue of *OK,* a German magazine.

1983: An edited version lasting 3:43 was released on the 7-inch picture disc *Timeless II ½,* with the interviewer listed as Deutcher Bovick. This edit was copied on the LP *The British Are Coming* and the CD *The Gospel According to the Beatles.*

1992: A longer edit, lasting 5:01, was included on an EP given away with the book *Mach Schau!*

1999: The full interview was included on the bootleg CD boxed set *Mythology, Volume 2.*

184. Newsreel footage

Date: 12 July 1964
Location: Hippodrome Theatre, Brighton
Broadcast: 12 July 1964
ITV
Length: 0:38

The Beatles' 1964 summer seaside resort tour paled in comparison to the previous year's. They played a mere four venues, beginning this evening in Brighton, where they shared the bill with erstwhile deputy drummer Jimmy Nicol and his band, the Shubdubs.

ITV News cameras filmed the crowds filling the streets outside the venue (one fan holds aloft a STONES FOREVER placard), as well as a brief Beatles appearance at the stage door, chatting with the white-helmeted policemen who attempt to maintain order. If George looks a bit unhappy, it's because he'd been involved in a fender-bender while driving his new Jaguar to the concert.

RELEASE HISTORY

This silent footage was included in the video compilation *Beatles 1962 to 1970.*

185. Radio performance

Date: 14 July 1964
Time: 7:00–11:00 p.m.
Location: Studio S2, Broadcasting House, London
Producer: Bernie Andrews
Host: Brian Matthew
Broadcast: 16 July 1964, 10:00–11:55 p.m.
BBC Light Programme
Top Gear #1

[A.] **Long Tall Sally** (1:57)
[B.] **outro/intro** (0:09)
[C.] **Things We Said Today** (2:20)
[D.] **outro** (0:04)
[E.] **intro** (1:17)
[F.] **A Hard Day's Night** (2:32)
[G.] **outro/intro** (2:02)
[H.] **And I Love Her** (2:19)
[I.] **intro** (0:21)
I Should Have Known Better (commercially released version)
[J.] **intro** (0:02)
[K.] **If I Fell** (2:07)
[L.] **You Can't Do That** (2:29)
[M.] **outro/Top Gear** (0:17)

The Beatles made good use of the studio for the *Top Gear* premiere, double-tracking the lead vocals on all four songs making their BBC debuts (both sides of their new single plus two ballads from their movie). For some reason, "A Hard Day's Night" has had the guitar/piano solo spliced in from the released version. The show's producer, Bernie Andrews, has claimed that this was due to a no-show on the part of George Martin, who was scheduled to re-create his keyboard part. However, George Harrison would need no such accompaniment playing the solo three days later for another BBC session, or five days later on live TV.

The chat with Brian Matthew is silly and rambling as ever, as the group mock their own acting ability and Matthew's sunburned nose. When Ringo has trouble hearing from across the studio, John suddenly murmurs, "We've brought you the flowers. And the grapes." This was a Beatle inside joke about hospital visitation; a similar version appears in Michael Braun's book *Love Me Do*.

Later, the Beatles "launch the good ship *Top Gear*" and talk about songwriting, with Paul reciting a bit of Ringo's first and only composition to date, "Don't Pass Me By." Paul agrees to record the backing for Ringo's demo, but the drummer wants Paul to sing lead, lamenting "no one seems to want to record it." Also included in the original broadcast is the LP version of what Matthew introduces as "You Should Have Known Better."

The BBC seems to have recovered at least some of the original broadcast tape in recent years, as Kevin Howlett's book *The Beatles at the BBC* describes elements not available elsewhere, such as Paul requesting the disc "Mockingbird," and Matthew's reference to a Beatles rehearsal of "The House of the Rising Sun."

However, the most commonly heard excerpts from this program originate from BBC Overseas transcription discs for the series *Top of the Pops,* which cannibalized about half of the Beatles' appearance from *Top Gear*. One oddity concerns the chat (G) directly following "A Hard Day's Night." George keeps playing the final guitar riff while the others repeatedly tell him to stop. John, thinking of the film, says, "The train comes in now." In the original broadcast, the dialogue continues as follows:

Brian: We did that to prove that we weren't playing the record then, y'see, because otherwise there's no point in your being here, is there?
John: Yeah, we did that. 'Cause it sounds just like it, doesn't it?
Brian: Exactly, yes, very good.

Two alternate versions of this chat exist on Transcription disc sources, apparently from two different editions of *Top of the Pops* that used this song. Both feature Brian Matthew speaking new dialogue over an odd bit of Beatle laughter in the background.

OUTRO 2 (USED IN PREVIEW EPISODE #00)

John: The train comes in now.
Brian: We did that to prove that we weren't playing the record then, y'see, because otherwise there's no point in your being here, is there?
John: Yeah, we did that. 'Cause it sounds just like it, doesn't it?
Brian: Critical lot of fellows, there, aren't you? Here, Ringo, have a banana! Catch!

OUTRO 3 (EPISODE UNKNOWN)

John: The train comes in now.
Brian: Does it? Yes, well, go and get on it!

The "banana" reference ties in with the earlier mention of grapes. The Transcription disc version of "Things We Said Today" also includes Matthew speaking over the opening ("And they close with another of their film songs, 'The Things We Said Today' ") and closing ("John Lennon and Paul McCartney's composition 'The Things We Said Today' ") of the song itself, both of which are clean on the original broadcast.

RELEASE HISTORY

1971: Very good copies of **A, C, E, F,** and a bit of **G** appeared on the bootleg LP *The Beatles Last Album,* reportedly from a 1968 rebroadcast of the Transcription disc source.

1982: The radio special *The Beatles at the Beeb* included **A, C, E, F, G** (outro 3), and **H,** all in excellent quality, and all from the Transcription disc. Outro 3 can be heard on the bootleg CD *From Us to You* or the CD-R *Attack of the Filler Beebs!, Episode 2.*

1988: A very good-quality off-air tape of the entire program (**A–M,** although **A** and **E** are slightly incomplete) appeared on the bootleg LP *The Beatles at the Beeb, Volume 11.* This is the only place to hear the original outro in **G.** The same year, the radio series *The Beeb's Lost Beatle Tapes* broadcast the version of **G** with outro 2.

1993: Great Dane's *The Complete BBC Sessions* boxed CD set reconstructed the show using the available disc sources where possible (including outro 2 of **G**).

1994: The Transcription disc versions of **C, E** (incomplete), **F,** and **G** (outro 2, incomplete) were released in excellent quality on Apple's *Live at the BBC* CD.

1997: An excellent-quality copy of **K,** apparently from a newly discovered tape of the original program, was broadcast on part two of the BBC Radio special *The Beatles at the BBC* on New Year's Day. It appears from this source on the bootleg CD *The Beatles Broadcast Collection, Trailer 1.*

186. Radio performance

Date: 17 July 1964
Time: 2:15–6:15 p.m.
Location: BBC Paris Studio, London
Producer: Bryant Marriott
Host: Don Wardell
Broadcast: 3 August 1964, 10:00 a.m.–noon
BBC Light Programme
From Us to You #4

STUDIO SESSION:

[A.] **Long Tall Sally** (2:05)
[B.] **If I Fell** (2:19)
[C.] **Boys** (2:11)
[D.] **I'm Happy Just to Dance with You—backing track** (2:14)
[E.] **I'm Happy Just to Dance with You** (1:56)
[F.] **I Should Have Known Better—false start** (0:23)
[G.] **I Should Have Known Better—single-tracked vocal** (2:47)
[H.] **I Should Have Known Better** (2:48)
[I.] **Things We Said Today** (2:39)
[J.] **A Hard Day's Night** (2:45)
[K.] **Kansas City/Hey Hey Hey Hey** (2:44)
[L.] **From Us to You—unused take** (1:05)
[M.] **From Us to You** (1:06)

BROADCAST:

From Us to You (M w/voice-over)
[N.] **intro** (0:29)
Long Tall Sally (A)
[O.] **outro** (0:04)
If I Fell (B)
[P.] **outro** (0:03)
I'm Happy Just to Dance with You (E)
[Q.] **outro** (0:04)
[R.] **intro** (0:23)
Things We Said Today (I)
[S.] **outro** (0:03)
[T.] **intro** (0:02)
I Should Have Known Better (H)
[U.] **outro** (0:03)
[V.] **intro** (0:16)
Boys (C)
[W.] **outro** (0:03)
[X.] **intro** (0:02)
Kansas City/Hey Hey Hey Hey (K)
[Y.] **outro** (0:03)
It's for You (Cilla Black)
[Z.] **intro** (0:53)
A Hard Day's Night (J)
[AA.] **outro** (0:04)
From Us to You (M w/voice-over by John)

The fourth and final *From Us to You* is the only Beatles BBC program for which a complete studio session tape has survived. Presumably retained by a studio employee, it's obviously a copy of a copy of a copy. But despite the less than stellar sound quality, it gives us a few insights into their working methods in the radio studio.

Most BBC studios didn't have the capability of multitracking, so any overdubs were performed live during tape-to-tape copies, which is evident here as we can hear the playbacks start and stop. The first three songs were recorded in a straightforward manner, but for whatever reason, George elected not to sing during the recording of "I'm Happy Just to Dance with You." The backing heard here (**D**) would have been copied to a second tape for his first vocal pass, and that tape was copied back onto the original tape (**E**) to add his second vocal.

Similarly, we have the basic take of "I Should Have Known Better" with John's main vocal (**G**). John added his second lead vocal during a tape copy, with the result copied back (**H**) for the final layer, John's harmonica. Two other songs have overdubs, but we hear only the finished versions here: "Things We Said Today" has two lead vocals from Paul, plus handclaps and tambourine, while "A Hard Day's Night" has double-tracked vocals, cowbell, and a double-tracked guitar solo.

In addition to bits of between-song chat and stray guitar notes, the studio tape contains a couple of bloopers, both caused by John's penchant for lyrical blunders. His transposition of verses in "I Should Have Known Better" is caught in time to abort the take right away (**F**), but it's not until the end of "From Us to You" (**L**) that John sings "from me to you," necessitating a second full attempt.

During the broadcast, chat with host Don Wardell is minimal, although John amusingly reads a listener's name and address as "Ron, age two hundred and eight, Almond Tree Avenue." John also reads the host and producer credits during the show's closing theme.

RELEASE HISTORY

1978: A good-quality tape of the complete studio session (**A–M**), running too fast, appeared on the bootleg LP *From Us to You—A Parlophone Rehearsal Session.* It appears from a speed-corrected tape source on the CD-R compilation *The Complete BBC Sessions—Upgraded,* although the broadcast version of **A** is substituted for the studio tape, which had gaps in the introduction and middle.

1988: A decent off-air recording of most of the original broadcast (**N–W** and **Y–AA** plus the songs as aired) was included on the vinyl bootleg *The Beatles at the Beeb, Volume 11.* Great Dane's boxed CD set *The Complete BBC Sessions* copies this source tape (from the corresponding Pyramid CD) and adds the unique tracks from the studio session (**D, F, G, L**).

2003: The entire show, including the debut of **X** and Cilla Black's number, was bootlegged on the CD boxed set *The Beatles at the Beeb.*

187. Newsreel footage

Date: 19 July 1964
Location: ABC Theatre, Blackpool
Broadcast: 19 July 1964
ITV
Length: 0:40

An ITV News crew was on hand to film the Beatles' arrival at the ABC Theatre to make their third appearance on the *Big Night Out* variety show (the summer editions were titled *Blackpool Night Out*). As the show was an ITV series, the camera was also allowed in during afternoon rehearsals. The Beatles and Mike and Bernie Winters are seen running through the show's opening sketch, set in an operating room, and performed here in street clothes rather than costumes.

RELEASE HISTORY

This silent footage was included in the video compilation *Beatles 1962 to 1970.*

188. TV performance

Date: 19 July 1964
Time: 8:25–9:25 p.m.
Location: ABC Theatre, Blackpool
Producer: Philip Jones
Hosts: Mike Winters, Bernie Winters
Broadcast: live
ABC
Blackpool Night Out

[A.] Operating Table sketch (2:25)
[B.] intro/theme (0:15)
[C.] A Hard Day's Night (2:27)
[D.] intro (0:03)
[E.] Things We Said Today (2:33)
[F.] intro (0:30)
[G.] You Can't Do That (2:29)
[H.] intro (0:24)

[I.] If I Fell (2:13)
[J.] intro (0:06)
[K.] Long Tall Sally (1:57)
[L.] outro/theme (0:03)

Unlike the Beatles' other three appearances on *Big/Blackpool Night Out,* no videotape or kinescope of this one seems to have survived. Luckily, we have a complete audio recording of their musical performance, as well as an awful-sounding tape of the show's opening sketch (**A**). It features Ringo as a patient on a gurney, while Paul, George, and John relay instructions between hosts Mike and Bernie Winters, playing surgeons. The dialogue is difficult to make out, but the joke seems to be that there is no Pentathol or sleeping pills for the patient (and "there's no ether, either!"), so Bernie ends up singing "Rock-a-Bye Baby" to Ringo.

The five-song set opens with both sides of the group's new single, with George taking the harmony on "Things We Said Today," an arrangement similar to "All My Loving," which would be kept for the upcoming concert tour. Paul introduces "You Can't Do That" and John says they're doing a song from the film "to prove we're not miming," but a fit of giggles causes "If I Fell" to have a false start. This is followed by a raucous rendition of "Long Tall Sally," the title track of their latest EP, to close the show.

Overall, it's a highly polished set of numbers, and with a decent sound balance for a change; perhaps that's why *Blackpool Night Out* would be the only live British TV performance they would attempt in 1965. Note that their guitars are tuned down a half step for reasons unknown. Mark Lewisohn's *Complete Beatles Chronicle* lists a slightly different lineup for this show, substituting "And I Love Her" for "You Can't Do That"; presumably he relied on faulty written documentation, as the recording had yet to circulate.

RELEASE HISTORY

1993: **I** first appeared in very good sound quality on the bootleg CD *Hollywood Bowl Complete.*

1999: The bootleg CD boxed set *Mythology, Volume 2* included a mediocre-sounding copy of **C–L,** "speed-miscorrected" to run a half step too fast (although it matches the keys of the original records).

2001: A very good-quality tape of nearly the entire show (**B–K,** with the last chord of **K** missing) surfaced and was bootlegged on the CD-R *Blackpool Night Out '64—Upgraded.* The opening skit (**A**) circulates in fair quality but has yet to be booted.

189. TV interview — G

Date: 25 July 1964
Time: 5:40–6:05 p.m.
Location: Studio 4, Television Centre, London
Producer: Barry Langford
Host: David Jacobs
Broadcast: live
BBC1
Juke Box Jury
Length: 2:44

George and Ringo both taped appearances on BBC TV's *Juke Box Jury* this evening at Television Centre. George's appearance was broadcast live, while Ringo's was held over for the following week. Mediocre-quality off-line recordings of both broadcasts exist with the comments from the other panelists edited out.

Asked to rate several records "hit" or "miss," George gives thumbs-down to a cover version of "I Should Have Known Better" by the Naturals, claiming "a few chords that I didn't know were in it." He praises the Fourmost and Sounds Incorporated, as well as the Zombies' "She's Not There" ("I thought Harry and Billy Zombie, the vocalists, were great"). But most interesting are his comments about the Crystals' "All Grown Up," produced by Phil Spector. George says that Phil has "just about had his day . . . with all this overdubbing." Ironically, George and Phil would take that very approach in producing the album *All Things Must Pass* six years later.

RELEASE HISTORY

1999: The audio portion of this recording was bootlegged on the CD boxed set *Mythology, Volume 2.*

190. TV interview

R

Date: 25 July 1964
Time: 8:15–9:00 p.m.
Location: Studio 4, Television Centre, London
Producer: Barry Langford
Host: David Jacobs
Broadcast: 1 August 1964, 5:40–6:05 p.m.
BBC1
Juke Box Jury
Length: 5:29

Like the other three Beatle-related *Juke Box Jury* appearances, Ringo's exists only as a home-taped audio recording. Unlike the other three, this one is practically indecipherable, at least on the dismal-sounding copy I own.

The first song reviewed is "Thinking of You Baby" by the Dave Clark Five; although their press-generated "rivalry" has died down, Ringo is careful to praise "Good ol' Dave," while admitting he won't buy a copy. The song, voted a hit by the panel, would peak at number 23 in the UK. Chad and Jeremy's "A Summer Song," voted a miss overall, reached number 7 in the United States but flopped in England. Ringo says the Overlanders' "Don't It Make You Feel Good" "moves along," but it would fail to live up to the panel's hit forecast.

He's naturally enthusiastic about Cilla Black's "It's For You," predicting a number 1 placement: "You did it again, Cilla!" While her last two singles reached the top of the British chart, this one would stall at number 8. Being a fan of dance records, Ringo says, "I was moving, baby" to Simon Scott's "Move It Baby," but the panel was wrong again about its hit status. They had better luck with the Bachelors' "I Wouldn't Trade You for the World," which would climb to number 4 in the UK, and were also correct in pronouncing Sammy Davis Jr.'s "Not for Me" a miss.

RELEASE HISTORY

This recording circulates among collectors from a poor-quality off-line tape.

191. Radio interview

Date: 28 July 1964
Time: 12:30 p.m.
Location: Arlanda Airport, Stockholm
Interviewer: Klas Burling
Length: 1:56

The Beatles took a 10:10 flight this morning from London via Copenhagen to Stockholm. They landed at Arlanda Airport around 12:30 in the afternoon, and a radio interview was taped inside the plane by the group's old friend Klas Burling. This brief segment has the Beatles adopting joke names, with Paul pretending to be Dave Clark, George posing as George Chakiris, and John adopting the last name Jagger. As passports are collected, Ringo says he remembers Sweden well and asks if the girls are still around.

RELEASE HISTORY

1972: A bit of this interview was included in the BBC Radio documentary *The Beatles Story*. It appears from this source on the CD-R *Attack of the Filler Beebs!, Episode 2*.

2003: The complete interview was included on the bonus CD included with the book *Yeah Yeah Yeah! The Beatles Erövrar Sverige*.

192. Newsreel footage

Date: 28 July 1964
Time: 12:30 p.m.
Location: Arlanda Airport, Stockholm
Length: 2:38

At least two newsreel companies filmed the Beatles' emergence from their flight in Stockholm. Some three thousand fans wave and cheer as the boys are presented with bouquets of flowers by beauty queen Kerstin Dahlöf. John sports sunglasses, and Paul snaps his fingers in time as a student band plays "I Want to Hold Your Hand" and "A Hard Day's Night."

RELEASE HISTORY

This silent footage circulates on video among collectors.

193. Press conference

Date: 28 July 1964
Time: 3:15 p.m.
Location: Hotel Foresta, Stockholm
Length: 1:04

From the airport, they traveled to the Hotel Foresta, where a press conference was held. A brief audio recording exists, with such questions as "How many girlfriends do you have?" (Ringo: "As many as I can find!") and the probing follow-up, "How big are they?" (George: "Twelve-foot-three!") Ringo is also asked about his resemblance to Charles DeGaulle.

RELEASE HISTORY

This clip, apparently the audio portion of a TV broadcast, circulates in very good quality among collectors. Twenty seconds of silent newsreel footage from this press conference also circulates on video.

194. TV interview

Date: 28 July 1964
Time: afternoon
Location: Hotel Foresta, Stockholm
Interviewer: Torsten Ljungstedt
Length: 2:37

Following the press conference, John filmed a brief interview discussing *In His Own Write.* He humorously introduces his bandmates as "George Parasol, Ringo Stone, and Paul MaCharmley" and goes on to state that his poetry is not influenced by James Thurber or James Joyce ("James Stewart," Paul interjects). John begins to read his poem "Good Dog Nigel" but is interrupted by George, who says there's a better poem elsewhere in the book, and the two proceed to rip the book to shreds.

RELEASE HISTORY

This footage was included on the home video *Fun with the Fab Four,* but a slightly longer version circulates on video.

195. Newsreel footage

Date: 28 or 29 July 1964
Location: Johanneshovs Isstadion, Stockholm
Length: 1:14

The Beatles' first show in Stockholm was a bit unpleasant; not only was there a *Spiñal Tap* moment as an elevator lowering the band onstage got stuck for five minutes, but the microphones weren't grounded properly and gave Paul a mighty shock. The next two shows went okay, but pandemonium midway through the fourth and final concert brought it to a premature conclusion as fans charged the stage during "I Wanna Be Your Man."

Newsreel footage of one of the shows (most likely from the opening night) includes bits of the Beatles performing "Twist and Shout" interspersed with screaming fans; the audio consists of the introduction of the band and doesn't include any music. One of the Stockholm shows was reportedly taped by an audience member who played a few minutes of the tape at a 1997 Swedish fan convention.

RELEASE HISTORY

This Swedish newsreel circulates on video among collectors.

196. Radio interview

Date: 29 July 1964
Location: Stockholm
Interviewer: Klas Burling
Length: 8:48

Before they left Stockholm, Klas Burling recorded several Beatle interviews for Swedish radio. As Ringo and others party in the background, Paul relates the experience of making *A Hard Day's Night* and chooses "If I Fell" as his favorite song from the movie. He explains that "It's for You" was written during the filming, but given to Cilla Black because it wasn't right for the Beatles. Paul goes on to describe the upcoming American tour, including the ticker-tape parade planned for their San Francisco arrival.

Ringo is interviewed about why he always looks so sad, and he professes his ambition to open beauty salons. John and George request records (Timmy Shaw's "I'm Gonna Send You Back to Georgia" and the Impressions' "It's All Right," respectively), and Paul gives a final farewell to Klas and the Swedish fans.

RELEASE HISTORY

1972: Two segments (with Ringo and Paul) were included in the BBC Radio documentary *The Beatles Story*. They appear from this source on the CD-R *Attack of the Filler Beebs!, Episode 2.*

2003: 7:20 of Paul's interview was included on the bonus CD included with the book *Yeah Yeah Yeah! The Beatles Erövrar Sverige.* John and George's record requests may not come from Burling's tapes, as Kevin Howlett reports that they are on "a mysterious undated reel" in BBC Radio's archives. Of course, it's possible that a copy of Burling's interviews ended up there, as many of them were used in the BBC's *The Beatles Story*.

197. Studio session

Date: 11 August 1964
Time: 7:00–11:00 p.m.
Location: EMI Studio 2
Producer: George Martin

[A.] Baby's in Black—RM2 (2:04)
Mixed: 26 October 1964

[B.] Baby's in Black—RS1 (2:04)
Mixed: 4 November 1964

Such was the demand for new Beatles music in the summer of 1964 that one month and a day after the release of *A Hard Day's Night,* the group began sessions for a follow-up album. The first song recorded was John and Paul's waltz ballad "Baby's in Black."

The backing was taped in fourteen takes: John on acoustic guitar, Paul on bass, George on lead guitar, and Ringo on drums. Overdubs included John and Paul's vocal duet, Ringo's tambourine, and occasional extra vocals from John and Paul. George also added what has been referred to in some places as a "tone-pedal" part, although "volume pedal" would be more accurate; however, since George didn't have a foot pedal, he actually played the chords and notes while John manually turned the volume knobs for him.

Thirteen edit pieces of the song's opening were also attempted but went unused, as did the song's first mono remix three days later. There is no appreciable difference between the mono and stereo mixes of this song.

RELEASE HISTORY

1964: **A** and **B** were released on mono and stereo pressings respectively of the *Beatles for Sale* LP. The former is on EMI's CD of that title.

198. Studio session

Date: 14 August 1964
Time: 7:00–9:00 p.m.
Location: EMI Studio 2
Producer: George Martin

[A.] I'm a Loser—takes 1-2 (stereo) (2:29)
[B.] I'm a Loser—take 3 (stereo) (2:52)
[C.] I'm a Loser—takes 4-6 (stereo) (4:36)
[D.] I'm a Loser—take 7 (stereo) (0:55)
[E.] I'm a Loser—take 8 intro (stereo) (0:18)
[F.] Mr. Moonlight—take 1 and take 2 intro (mono) (0:11)
[G.] Mr. Moonlight—take 4 (mono) (2:38)

[H.] I'm a Loser—RM2 (2:29)
Mixed: 26 October 1964

[I.] I'm a Loser—RS1 (2:28)
Mixed: 4 November 1964

[J.] Mr. Moonlight—RS from take 4 (stereo) (2:31)

One final recording session was squeezed in before the North American tour. It began with John's latest composition, "I'm a Loser," recorded in eight takes, all of which are available to collectors.

The first two takes (**A**) have the backing spread across three tracks: bass/drums/acoustic guitar, John and Paul's vocals, and George's lead guitar. As the tape starts, Paul is reminding John that he'll leave a space in his count-in for John to overdub his harmonica entry. The first take breaks down immediately as Paul forgets to play, but take 2 is complete, although as Paul comments, finishes with a "frayed edge."

A bit more rehearsal precedes take 3 (**B**), which is also complete. John has switched from six-string to twelve-string acoustic, and a new introduction has been arranged with John and Paul's familiar stop-time vocal duet. John expresses his dissatisfaction with this performance as the take winds down: "It didn't work out the same, 'cause . . ."

Before the next take, George has decided he wants a track free to overdub his lead guitar part, so the remaining attempts occupy only two tracks of the tape. Track 1 contains drums, bass, and both guitars, while track 4 has John and Paul's vocals plus harmonica, which John is now opting to play live.

As take 4 starts (**C**), Paul complains about how corny his vocal harmony is. The take breaks down when John screws up the lyric during the first chorus. Apparently he's having trouble seeing the lyric sheet, so he asks for it to be repositioned. Take 5 is called to a halt by George Martin, as the "p" in John's "appear" causes a loud popping on the sensitive vocal microphone. The sixth take is complete, but John still gets the words wrong ("I would lose in the end"). Apparently, playing harmonica, guitar, and singing at the same time is a bit much for John, who cries out, "I'm all wrapped up!"

The tape rolls again (**D**) as John and Paul run through their vocal entry and George fusses with his guitar. But another plosive "p" causes George Martin to stop the proceedings and install a spit-screen in front of John's vocal mic. John's impatience is clear in his remarks prior to take 8 (**E**): "Okay, let's go, let's get out of here."

The eighth take went smoothly and had overdubs of George's lead guitar plus tambourine on track 2, and further vocals on track 3. The take lasted 2:49 but was faded early for both released mixes. The mono mix (**H**) is slightly longer, while the stereo (**I**) has the guitar/tambourine track mixed a touch louder.

With no other new compositions ready for recording, they looked back to their Cavern repertoire and selected "Mr. Moonlight." This time, with no overdubs anticipated, all four tracks of the tape were used: Paul's bass and Ringo's tom-heavy drums on track 1, John's rhythm guitar on track 2, John's lead vocal, backed by Paul and George, on track 3, and George's lead guitar on track 4. On the *Anthology* video, during an outtakes medley, we can hear how the session started (**F**): First, Norman Smith's "take one" announcement and then John's first attempt at the vocal introduction. (John: "Stop!"; Paul: "Nearly."; John: "Yes, not bad, that one.") And then we have Norman Smith's "take two" announcement.

This cuts directly to the start of take 4, including a bit of laughter and a comment from Paul ("No, don't know now . . .") that preceded the take. The *Anthology 1* CD includes a mono mix of take 4 (**G**) including this chat. It's preceded by take 1 minus Norman Smith's take announcements; despite what the CD booklet says, this is all in mono. John Barrett's 1982 stereo remix of take 4 (**J**) is lacking the brief chat before the take.

The performance itself is loose and fun, with lyrics sung in a different order to the eventually released version and plenty of vocal exclamations during the guitar solo. Although they would remake the song in October, they liked John's shouted vocal entrance from take 4 enough to splice it to the front of the master take.

RELEASE HISTORY

1964: **H** and **I** were released on mono and stereo copies respectively of the LP *Beatles for Sale;* **H** is available on EMI's CD of that title.

1984: A small excerpt of **E** was broadcast in the radio documentary *Sgt. Pepper's Lonely Hearts Club Band: A History of the Beatle Years 1962–1970,* preceding the regular stereo mix (**I**). It appeared from this source on the vinyl bootleg *Not for Sale,* preceding a stereo mix of "Yes It Is."

1991: **A** appeared in excellent quality on the bootleg CD *Unsurpassed Masters, Volume 6,* while a slightly incomplete copy of **B** appeared on *Unsurpassed Masters, Volume 7.* Both sources run a half step too slow.

1994: An excellent-quality tape of **A–E** was booted on the CD *The Ultimate Collection, Volume 3: Studio Sessions, 1964.*

1995: **F** (minus the take announcements) and **G** were released on *Anthology 1.*

1996: The video release of *Anthology* included **F** and the first 11 seconds of **G.** Both appear from this source on the bootleg CD *Abbey Road Video Show.*

1999: **J** surfaced among John Barrett's cassette material; it's been booted on CDs such as *Turn Me On Dead Man: The John Barrett Tapes* and the boxed set *Mythology, Volume 2.*

199. Studio session

Date: 14 August 1964
Time: 10:00–11:15 p.m.
Location: EMI Studio 2
Producer: George Martin

[A.] Leave My Kitten Alone—take 5 (mono) (2:54)

[B.] Leave My Kitten Alone—RM from take 5 w/false start (2:52)
Mixed: 23 April 1976

[C.] Leave My Kitten Alone—RS from take 5 (2:22)

In the eyes of most Beatle fans, the worst decision they and George Martin ever made when assembling an album was including "Mr. Moonlight" on *Beatles for Sale* instead of John's blistering performance of Little Willie John's "Leave My Kitten Alone."

The song's backing was recorded in five takes, with drums, bass, and guitars on track 1 and John's main vocal on track 3. Overdubs consisted of piano and tambourine on track 4, and John's second vocal on track 2. George then "punched in" a guitar solo on track 2; the beginning of this overdub erased a bit of John's second vocal ("leave her alone") and there is a distracting "fwip" at the end point of the overdub.

Despite all this work, they must have rejected the song immediately, as it wasn't remixed until 1976 when EMI went through the vaults after the group's contract expired. This rough mix (**B**) includes a false start caused by John's sticky fingers on the opening guitar phrase. The tape box lists take 4 as a breakdown, but Mark Lewisohn describes it as a false start; this may be take 4 or merely an unnumbered appendage of take 5. This mix cuts off abruptly during the coda (after John's "hey hey").

Interestingly, engineer John Barrett also noted that the "track cuts off before end" when listening to the reel on February 19, 1982, but this doesn't seem to correspond to the abrupt ending of the 1976 mix. The full take 5 lasted 2:57, and Geoff Emerick's 1984 remix for *Sessions* includes 2:54 of this before fading out. "Leave My Kitten Alone" was tentatively scheduled by EMI for release as a single in 1980, again in 1982, and to accompany the aborted *Sessions* project in 1985. It was finally released in 1995 on *Anthology 1.* A clean mono mix (**A**) appeared from John Barrett's collection in 1999, and at long last, a true stereo mix (**C**) was created for the *Anthology* DVD in 2003.

RELEASE HISTORY:

1983: A 1:16 excerpt of **A,** overlaid with stereo echo, was included in the multimedia presentation *The Beatles at Abbey Road.* It appears (slightly incomplete) from this source on the bootleg CD *Abbey Road Video Show.*

1984: **B** surfaced on the vinyl bootleg *File Under: Beatles;* the false start unique to this rough mix was also bootlegged on the LP *Not for Sale* and the CD-R *From Me to You,* tacked onto the *Sessions* mix.

1985: Geoff Emerick's remix of **A,** also mono with stereo reverb, was prepared for the *Sessions* project. This mix, which has a longer fade than any other, appears on Spank's bootleg CD of *Sessions.*

1988: Another variation of **A,** sounding cleaner than *Sessions,* but shorter and still not true mono (perhaps the basis of the *Beatles at Abbey Road* mix), appeared from tape source on the bootleg CD *Ultra Rare Trax, Volume 2.*

1995: A new "fake stereo" remix of **A** was released on *Anthology 1.*

1999: A clean mono mix of **A** appeared among John Barrett's cassette material. It's best found on the bootleg CD *Another Sessions . . . Plus.*

2002: The CD-R *As It Happened, Baby!* included **B** from a tape source, unfortunately with the very start clipped slightly.

2003: **C** was released on the soundtrack of the *Anthology* DVD.

200. Concert

Date: 16 August 1964
Time: evening
Location: Opera House, Blackpool
Length: 0:39

The last in a summer series of Sunday seaside concerts before setting off for North America, this show at Blackpool's Opera House also featured up-and-coming Shepherd's Bush band the High Numbers. A few months later, when they were no longer trying to cater so exclusively to a mod audience, the group would change its name back to the Who. Also on the bill were the Kinks, whose first hit, "You Really Got Me," had just been released.

The lucky fans who attended both shows were the only audiences to experience a Beatles/Who/Kinks concert lineup. One fan's home movie captured not only portions of the Beatles' appearance, but other seaside activities at an amusement park and along the pier.

RELEASE HISTORY

This silent color home movie circulates on video among collectors.

201. TV interview

Date: 18 August 1964
Time: afternoon
Location: Winnipeg International Airport
Interviewer: Bob Burns
Broadcast: Channel 7
Length: 5:32

Thirty-two concerts in twenty-five cities in thirty-two days. That's what the Beatles had to look forward to as they boarded a Boeing 707 in London at noon local time. Their first stop was Winnipeg, Manitoba, for refueling and a brief wave to some two thousand fans. Channel 7 sent reporter Bob Burns to the airport to cover the arrival and hopefully obtain an interview with the foursome.

He describes the scene as they emerge from the plane, including "Ringo with his inimitable [sun]glasses" (huh?). Burns then fights through the crowd of reporters to get a few words with the group, and points out to Paul that this is the first time all four Beatles have been on Canadian soil (although none of them actually walk past the end of the airplane's steps).

Asked to demonstrate his Liverpool accent, John offers up "knickers," and he agrees with Burns' mistaken notion that their first concert will be that night in San Francisco. They are interrupted by an autograph-seeker, and Burns moves over to congratulate Ringo on *A Hard Day's Night.* The Beatles reboard the plane before he can get to George, but Burns does interview one of the flight attendants, Janet, about the penetrating insights a seven-hour flight has afforded her.

RELEASE HISTORY

This footage circulates in fair quality on video.

202. Newsreel footage

Date: 18 August 1964
Time: 4:15 p.m.
Location: Los Angeles International Airport
Length: 1:27

A few hours after leaving Canadian airspace, the Beatles arrived in Los Angeles for a quick stop to go through customs, meet the press, and stretch their legs before the final part of their flight to San Francisco. The arrival and press conference were covered in a so-called *Hollywood Star* newsreel that also has footage of their return to LA a few days later.

A few of the one thousand fans waiting in the terminal are seen watching the Pan Am flight arrive. The Beatles then emerge from the customs building along with Brian Epstein and Neil Aspinall. They pose for photos and wave to fans from the building's staircase, all but Paul wearing sunglasses.

RELEASE HISTORY

This silent footage appears in the *Hollywood Star* newsreel that circulates on video.

203. Press conference

Date: 18 August 1964
Time: ca. 4:30 p.m.
Location: Los Angeles International Airport
Length: 8:08

Seated at a pair of tables in front of a large Pan Am backdrop, the Beatles gave their first press conference of the tour, a makeshift disorganized affair with reporters competing for questions and Derek Taylor nowhere to be seen.

Amid the chaos, John describes their musical background as "twelve-bar," Ringo reveals that he keeps his rings in a box, and Paul says that he and Jane Asher are "just good friends." They seem to be unconcerned with the fact that no lodging has been arranged for their return visit in five days ("As long as we get a bed each" George will be fine), but John disparages the "dirty lie" printed in a magazine called *Truth* that his wife is expecting another child. Eventually, Brian whispers something to John, who informs the press that "the airport man says we've got to go!"

RELEASE HISTORY

1964: A couple of brief audio clips from this press conference (Paul talking about "sneaky haircuts" and being friends with his bandmates) were released on the LP *The Beatles' Story.* The complete footage circulates on video; most of it appears in the *Hollywood Star* newsreel.

204. Radio interview

Date: 18 August 1964
Time: ca. 5:00 p.m.
Location: Los Angeles International Airport
Interviewer: Dave Hull
Broadcast: KRLA-AM, Los Angeles
Length: 4:16

Following the press conference, the Beatles dispersed for individual interviews with local radio, TV, and press reporters. KRLA disc jockey Dave Hull had interviewed John and George during their brief stopover in Los Angeles May 25, but now he had the chance to speak with all four. He would continue to tape interviews upon their return to LA a few days later.

Ringo clarifies that nothing is wrong with his throat at the moment, and that the scheduled tonsilectomy is only to prevent future infection. He also denies a report of litigation with Pete Best ("What could he sue me for?"). As Jane Asher's involvement with Paul was a major source of rumors, Paul clarifies that they aren't married, engaged, or living together, and that Jane will not have a role in the Beatles' next movie.

Asked to choose a favorite piece from *In His Own Write,* John selects "Act One, Scene Three," and then condemns the "damn fool magazines" for reporting false tales of Cynthia's pregnancy. Dave Hull had revealed the Beatles' Liverpool home addresses to his listeners, which resulted in their parents receiving a sudden deluge of letters from California. He apologizes to George, who kindly says his mother doesn't mind responding to fan mail.

RELEASE HISTORY

1964: These interviews were released on the LP *Hear the Beatles Tell All,* which has been bootlegged on the CD *The VJ Story.*

205. TV report

Date: 18 August 1964
Time: 6:25 p.m.
Location: San Francisco International Airport
Broadcast: KCRA-TV, San Francisco
Length: 4:38

By 5:25 p.m. the Beatles were airborne again for the one-hour flight to San Francisco. Awaiting them were nearly ten thousand fans crowded into a small fenced-off area dubbed Beatlesville. This was a halfhearted compromise between local police, who would have preferred whisking the group directly from the plane to their hotel, and Derek Taylor, who fought for the fans' right to see their idols in the flesh.

Local TV station KCRA covered the Beatles' visit to San Francisco, producing a half-hour special about the arrival, press conference, concert, and aftermath. Most likely, the original program no longer exists, but an audio recording taped by a home viewer does circulate. It includes a reporter's description of the scene as "some one hundred and fifty cynical—supposedly—newsmen and -women" surround the Beatles as they exit the plane. He also gets a brief word from Paul, but no response to the question "Are you afraid of going to Beatlesville?"

If he wasn't, he soon would be. The Beatles walked onto a platform, separated from the crush of fans by only a flimsy wire mesh and 180 members of law enforcement. They were able to wave briefly, but wisely decided to get the hell out of Dodge before the crowd broke through.

RELEASE HISTORY

2004: This recording appeared in good quality on the CD-R *We'd Like to Carry On.* Four minutes of mostly silent footage also circulates, covering the airport arrival and brief visit to Beatlesville.

206. Press conference

Date: 18 August 1964
Time: evening
Location: San Francisco Hilton
Length: 9:25

A couple of hours after checking in, the Beatles held their first full press conference of the tour at the San Francisco Hilton. John reveals that he has written a new poem, "Snore Wife and the Seventy Warts," during the flight from England. Discussion turns to the "Ringo for President" campaign, and who Ringo would choose as his cabinet—George offers to be the door, and John says he could be the cupboard. The tape ends with John's cries of "Help!" to press officer Derek Taylor, as the reporters and photographers get out of control. And this was only the first day!

RELEASE HISTORY

1964: A few seconds of the group identifying themselves ("Ringo, John, Paul, George! All together now!") was released on the LP *The Beatles' Story.*

1985: The complete recording was released on the LP *West Coast Invasion,* later reissued on CD (severely sped up).

207. Radio interview J, P

Date: 18 August 1964
Time: evening
Location: San Francisco Hilton
Interviewer: Larry Kane
Broadcast: WFUN-AM, Miami
Length: 2:39

Larry Kane of Miami's WFUN radio was one of three lucky American reporters chosen to cover the Beatles entire American tour, and fortunately he preserved all of his interview tapes, which were released as a series of LPs in the 1980s. In San Francisco, Kane met up with the group and taped some introductory conversations. Paul thanks American radio for helping to promote their records, and John talks about a controversial *Saturday Evening Post* profile by Al Aronowitz that had been recently published.

RELEASE HISTORY

1985: These interviews were released on the LP *West Coast Invasion,* later reissued on CD.

208. Concert

Date: 19 August 1964
Time: 9:29–10:02 p.m.
Location: Cow Palace, San Francisco
Broadcast: KCRA-TV, San Francisco

[A.] **intro** (0:13)
[B.] **Twist and Shout** (1:20)
[C.] **She Loves You** (2:14)
[D.] **outro** (0:03)
[E.] **A Hard Day's Night** (2:19)
[F.] **outro** (0:03)

The North American tour kicked off in style with a sellout crowd of seventeen thousand yelling their lungs out at the Cow Palace. KCRA's crew filmed three complete songs for their TV special.

A Reuters newsreel of the concert shows fans arriving and holding up a RINGO FOR PRESIDENT banner. Inside, a hail of jelly beans and flashbulbs marks the Beatles' entrance, and their performances of "Twist and Shout" and "You Can't Do That" are glimpsed. After the show, rather than stay another night in San Francisco, they returned to the airport for a short flight to Las Vegas.

RELEASE HISTORY

2001: Fair-quality excerpts of each song were included on the CD-R *Live: Make as Much Noise as You Like!*

2004: The complete recording appeared in good quality on the CD-R *We'd Like to Carry On.* The Reuters footage circulates from a Swedish newsreel and a slightly different edit, often misidentified as the Forest Hills concert.

209. Newsreel footage

Date: 20 August 1964
Time: 1:45 a.m.
Location: McCarran Field and Sahara Hotel, Las Vegas
Length: 1:28

The Beatles arrived in Las Vegas to a minimal greeting at the airport. Although they hadn't been scheduled to arrive until that afternoon, thousands of fans were already waiting outside the Sahara Hotel when the Beatles checked in at 2:30 a.m. This Associated Press newsreel clip shows the group arriving at the airport and fighting their way through a crowd of fans at the hotel.

RELEASE HISTORY

This silent footage circulates on video among collectors.

210. Radio interview — P, R

Date: 20 August 1964
Time: 3:30 p.m.
Location: Las Vegas Convention Center
Interviewer: Larry Kane
Broadcast: WFUN-AM, Miami
Length: 8:33

Just before two concerts at the convention center, Larry Kane taped further interviews with the group. (Kane's microphone on this and subsequent recordings often picked up questions posed by Jim Stagg and other reporters, but I will refer to them as Larry Kane interviews.)

Paul and Ringo plead for fans to throw streamers and not jelly beans at the concerts, and when asked about segregation, Paul says, "You can't treat other human beings like animals." They also profess their love for the Rolling Stones and James Bond novels, and Paul keeps working in a plug for Cilla Black's "It's for You."

RELEASE HISTORY

1985: This interview was released on the LP *West Coast Invasion,* later reissued on CD.

210a. Concert

Date: 20 August 1964
Location: Las Vegas Convention Center
Length: 1:11

[A.] Twist and Shout (0:28)

A Reuters film crew captured just over a minute of action from one of the Las Vegas concerts, including fans arriving and about half of the opening number (with distorted but natural sound), "Twist and Shout."

RELEASE HISTORY

This Reuters newsreel footage circulates on video.

211. Newsreel footage

Date: 21 and 22 August 1964
Time: afternoon
Location: Seattle-Tacoma Airport and Edgewater Inn, Seattle
Length: 1:11

The Beatles slept as usual this morning, then took an afternoon flight from Las Vegas northwest to Seattle. A latter-day documentary about their visit includes brief scenes, some on film, some on videotape, of their airport arrival and journey to room 272 of the Edgewater Inn, plus their departures at the inn and airport the following afternoon.

The main point of interest is a short interview with Paul upon their arrival. From the steps of the plane, he chats briefly about their stay in Las Vegas (they played the slot machines, but didn't win).

RELEASE HISTORY

This footage circulates on video from a rebroadcast on the KOMO-TV special *The Beatles in Seattle.*

211a. Radio interview — P, G

Date: 21 August 1964
Time: afternoon
Location: Seattle-Tacoma Airport
Interviewer: "Mad" Mel Potts
Broadcast: CFUN-AM, Vancouver
Length: 1:42

During the Australian tour, the Beatles had become acquainted with "Mad" Mel, a young Californian disc jockey who was working for Sydney station 2SM at the time. Mel had urged his listeners to knit woolen scarves that were then joined together (over ten thousand separate pieces) and presented to the group in Sydney.

By August, Mel was back in North America, working for Vancouver station CFUN, and he interviewed Paul and George upon their arrival in Seattle. Paul wishes Mel a happy nineteenth birthday and clearly remembers the scarf, as he claims they have knitted him a two-mile scarf. George describes "Barmy Mel's" appearance: pink socks, a bright red shirt, and red eyes to match!

RELEASE HISTORY

This recording circulates from its appearance on a website.

212. Radio interview — R

Date: 21 August 1964
Time: afternoon
Location: Seattle-Tacoma Airport
Interviewer: Larry Kane
Broadcast: WFUN-AM, Miami
Length: 1:30

The Beatles' arrival was also captured on tape by Larry Kane—Ringo jokes, "Not you again!" as he steps off the plane. Ringo says he didn't sleep during the flight, despite only two hours' sleep the night before. Instead he listened to records that one of the opening acts, the Exciters, had brought.

RELEASE HISTORY

1986: This interview was released on the LP *Things We Said Today,* later reissued on CD, along with Kane's play-by-play as the flight prepared for landing and the reactions of fans outside the Edgewater Inn.

213. Press conference

Date: 21 August 1964
Time: 9:00 p.m.
Location: Seattle Coliseum
Length: 14:17

The Beatles held a press conference backstage at the Seattle Coliseum during the opening acts' performances. It opens with Derek Taylor still trying to feel his way around how to conduct such affairs in America: "If that's what you wish. Still press, then the writing and the radio, and then the TV. Well, suit yourself. Whatever you like. Until it wears thin—till they start dying a bit, or you do."

We learn that the group dined on omelettes and didn't catch anything while fishing out their suite window overlooking Elliott Bay. The usual topics are discussed: the film, screaming fans, their longevity, Ringo's throat troubles. Asked why he gets the most fan mail, Ringo deduces, "Perhaps 'cause more people write to me."

Someone inquires about future plans, and Paul gives his stock answer of "John and I'll carry on songwriting." "I'm not doing it with you," snorts John, causing Paul to envision a headline: "Are the Beatles Breaking Up?" Although they were apparently unaware of what they were looking at, they had flown over Boulder Dam on the way to Seattle. Paul marvels, "That's what it was, he was flying 'round for hours!" and says he'd learned about the dam at school.

Talk turns to John's poetry, and he shuns the notion of writing about his personal experiences on tour. He is persuaded to give a rather reluctant reading of

"Good Dog Nigel." They continue to evince disgust at the wild rumors printed in gossip magazines, such as "Ringo asks John to share wife" and "Paul definitely married." The conference is eventually called to a halt with only eight minutes to showtime.

RELEASE HISTORY

1986: Excerpts of this press conference were released on the LP *Things We Said Today,* later reissued on CD.

1989: A complete recording of this press conference was released on a picture disc single titled *Seattle Press Conference.* Fourteen seconds of footage (with sound) from this press conference were included in the KOMO-TV special *The Beatles in Seattle.*

214. Concert

Date: 21 August 1964
Time: 9:30 p.m.
Location: Seattle Coliseum

[A.] **intro** (2:32)
[B.] **Twist and Shout** (1:15)
[C.] **intro** (0:02)
[D.] **You Can't Do That** (2:27)
[E.] **intro** (0:35)
[F.] **All My Loving** (1:59)
[G.] **intro** (0:15)
[H.] **She Loves You** (2:12)
[I.] **intro** (0:19)
[J.] **Things We Said Today** (2:10)
[K.] **intro** (0:03)
[L.] **Roll Over Beethoven** (2:11)
[M.] **intro** (0:48)
[N.] **Can't Buy Me Love** (2:03)
[O.] **intro** (0:38)
[P.] **If I Fell** (2:02)
[Q.] **intro** (0:07)
[R.] **I Want to Hold Your Hand** (2:15)
[S.] **intro** (0:34)
[T.] **Boys** (2:05)
[U.] **intro** (0:23)
[V.] **A Hard Day's Night** (2:19)
[W.] **intro** (0:28)
[X.] **Long Tall Sally** (2:01)
[Y.] **outro** (0:38)

The Beatles' Seattle concert is the first of three shows in a row to have been bootlegged in their entirety. Unfortunately, this particular performance exists only as an audience recording almost entirely drowned out by screams.

The tape opens with the MC's introduction; there is a second or two missing from "Twist and Shout" but the concert is otherwise intact from top to bottom. About the only thing this recording has going for it is the audience's rhythmic clapping, which accompanies "She Loves You" and "I Want to Hold Your Hand." Twenty-six seconds of silent newsreel footage from this concert (mostly of "Long Tall Sally") is included in the KOMO-TV special *The Beatles in Seattle.*

RELEASE HISTORY

1995: Most of this concert (**A–R** and the beginning of S) surfaced from a poor-quality audience tape on the bootleg CD *Atlanta * Munich * Seattle,* running a half step too slow.

2000: The CD-R *Northwest Nights* included the previously bootlegged portion of the concert, plus **T–Y** from a similarly slow source tape.

2004: A complete copy of S appeared on the CD-R *We'd Like to Carry On. The Beatles in Seattle* TV special circulates on video.

215. Press conference

Date: 22 August 1964
Time: 7:00–8:00 p.m.
Location: Press Room 19, Empire Stadium, Vancouver
Broadcast: CKNW, Vancouver
Length: 31:20

After departing from Seattle for Vancouver, the Beatles' flight was forced to return due to a snafu about passports. When they finally did arrive in Canada at 6 p.m., it was decided to skip the hotel in favor of a brief tour of the city and then a trip to Empire Stadium for their press conference and concert.

A lengthy recording from CKNW's radio coverage includes several minutes of interviews by Jack Cullen prior to the conference itself. Cullen talks with freelance Tampa journalist Fred Paul, WFUN's Larry Kane, and Vancouver reporter Orem Turner. He's joined by CKNW newsman Jack Webster for an exclusive interview with Fulton Mackey, an errand boy who salted Ringo's 19-cent hamburger!

Finally, the Beatles arrive and the press conference is joined in progress. One of the reporters asks if he can have the Beatles' suite at the Hotel Georgia for a party, since they have decided to fly on to Los Angeles directly after the show, and Paul replies, "You can have it as far as I'm concerned." The Vancouver press seems particularly interested in financial concerns, asking about the Beatles' revenue, their tax situation, their accountant, and their contract with EMI. Asked to name their favorite artists, they come up with Little Richard, Mary Wells, Marvin Gaye, the Miracles, and Chuck Jackson ("Derek Taylor," quips George). John also says Buddy Holly was a big influence and that the Crickets' name probably inspired the Beatles'.

Paul complains about Capitol's glut of Beatle releases in the North American market: "I think we've only ever made seven singles, and it seems to me like thousands." They also indulge in some cruel jokes at Pete Best's expense. Asked "Who was the boy that was ahead of Ringo," Ringo replies, "The one that died?" John matter-of-factly says, "We threw him out," while Paul shifts the blame to George Martin. One reporter wonders if they think they'll ever get a knighthood, and the future Sir Paul replies, "No." "Not if we can help it," adds John. The proceeding ends with the presentation of an oil-on-velvet portrait by a local artist.

RELEASE HISTORY

1972: The radio coverage and press conference were included in their entirety on the vinyl bootleg *Vancouver 1964.*

1978: This recording was legitimately released in part on the LP *Beatle Talk,* reissued on CD as *Beatles Tapes: The Beatles in the Northwest.*

2000: The radio coverage and press conference appeared from tape source on the CD-R *Northwest Nights.* Twelve minutes of footage from the press conference supposedly exists, but only 1:23 circulate on video.

216. Radio interview — P, G

Date: 22 August 1964
Time: evening
Location: Empire Stadium, Vancouver
Interviewer: Larry Kane
Broadcast: WFUN-AM, Miami
Length: 19:44

Backstage before the show in Vancouver, Larry Kane taped separate conversations with Paul and George (taking turns with Jim Stagg and others in asking questions).

Paul talks about the narrow escape from Seattle the previous night, when the decoy car was crushed by fans while the Beatles hid in the dressing room, eventually escaping in an ambulance full of sailors. He recounts an incident the previous November 10 in Birmingham when they posed for photos in police helmets, leading to a legend that they had once disguised themselves as officers to evade fans.

After discussing the origins of the jelly bean–throwing ritual, Paul again makes a plea for fans to throw streamers instead, noting what a festive atmosphere they created in Australia. With the Democratic National Convention about to open in Atlantic City, Paul's view of the American political scene is solicited. Although he tries to be diplomatic about it, he has a decidedly negative opinion of Republican presidential candidate Barry Goldwater.

Kane praises the Beatles' comic abilities in *A Hard Day's Night* and wonders whether they'll exploit said talent in their stage act. Paul admits they used to do more between-songs patter and jokes onstage, but it became futile when their every word was drowned out by screaming. Other topics discussed include boxing (he finds all but the biggest fights boring), automobiles (British make the best in the world, but he acknowledges Volkswagen's current massive success in the United States), exercise (he's too lazy), and yachting (makes him seasick).

George covers some of the same topics, including the Seattle concert and Barry Goldwater ("I thought he was Goldfinger!"), about both of which he shares Paul's opinions. Asked to choose his favorite Beatle records apart from "A Hard Day's Night," George chooses "I'll Cry Instead," "If I Fell," and (unsurprisingly) "You Can't Do That." In a separate segment apparently taped during the same sitting, Paul records brief radio introductions for the latest Peter and Gordon and Cilla Black singles, both Lennon/McCartney compositions. He and John would repeat the promotional exercise more formally in Los Angeles the following week.

RELEASE HISTORY

1985: These interviews, misidentified as recordings from Milwaukee, were released on the LP *'Round the World,* later reissued on CD. Another 12-second clip of Paul introducing "It's for You" (recording date unknown) appears on the LP *West Coast Invasion,* but not the CD.

217. Concert

Date: 22 August 1964
Time: 9:23 p.m.
Location: Empire Stadium, Vancouver

[A.] **intro** (1:15)
[B.] **Twist and Shout** (1:17)
[C.] **intro** (0:01)
[D.] **You Can't Do That** (2:24)
[E.] **intro** (0:33)
[F.] **All My Loving** (1:56)
[G.] **intro** (0:14)
[H.] **She Loves You** (2:11)
[I.] **intro** (0:16)
[J.] **Things We Said Today** (2:10)
[K.] **intro** (0:04)
[L.] **Roll Over Beethoven** (2:11)
[M.] **intro** (1:05)
[N.] **Can't Buy Me Love** (2:01)
[O.] **intro** (0:32)
[P.] **If I Fell** (2:06)
[Q.] **intro** (0:30)
[R.] **Boys** (1:59)
[S.] **intro** (0:38)
[T.] **A Hard Day's Night** (2:15)
[U.] **intro** (0:20)
[V.] **Long Tall Sally** (1:58)
[W.] **outro** (0:03)

The Vancouver concert was a bit of a debacle, with the police force woefully unprepared to handle the crush of twenty thousand fans continually straining to reach the stage. More than a hundred people required medical attention, with several injured seriously enough to be taken to the hospital. The potential disaster of the situation is well illustrated in CKNW's live radio coverage of the concert, from the show *On the Town.* From up in the press booth and down on the field, we get reports with such alarming commentary as "it's an absolute damn disgrace" and "I don't think you got five seconds from the time they leave that stage till the time that all those hurdles are down, and that there are sixteen people dead!"

An in-line recording of the whole show doesn't seem to reflect any concern on the part of the Beatles. John chuckles during "Twist and Shout" and Paul does likewise in "Things We Said Today," in which the line "these days such a kind, girl/seems so hard to find" somehow becomes "be my one and only/yes, you say you're mine." During "If I Fell," Paul seems to be blatantly singing poorly on purpose to crack up John. Paul also goofs around with the backing vocals in "Boys," throwing in some "be-bop-a-lula's."

The concert is interrupted twice during introductions to tell the crowd to move back or else: first by MC Red Robinson before "Can't Buy Me Love," then by Derek Taylor before "A Hard Day's Night." John's response to the latter is an impatient "Oh, come on, let's go on. Come on, count it in!" The Beatles' only concession to calming the situation is a seemingly impromptu decision to drop "I Want to Hold Your Hand" from the set list.

RELEASE HISTORY

1972: The entire concert (**A–W**), was bootlegged from a very good soundboard recording, along with 31 minutes of radio coverage, on the LP *Vancouver 1964.*

2000: The concert and radio coverage appeared from the original tape source on the CD-R *Northwest Nights.* While the soundboard runs a half step too slow, the radio coverage is at the correct speed. A few seconds of silent footage from this concert can be glimpsed in the *Anthology* documentary.

218. Press conference

Date: 23 August 1964
Time: ca. 7:00 p.m.
Location: Cinnamon Cinder, Los Angeles
Length: 12:58

Yet another press conference, this one conducted at a nightclub partly owned by Bob Eubanks, called the Cinnamon Cinder. Eubanks, a KRLA disc jockey, had arranged their Hollywood Bowl performance that night, and in addition to being the concert's MC, usurped Derek Taylor's role in presiding over the somewhat chaotic press conference.

There were a large number of teenage girls present, some representing fan clubs and some under the guise of *Datebook* magazine reporters. One of the girls can be heard keeping a reporter up to date as the conference begins. ("What's the girl's name?" "Jane Asher. Oh, don't embarrass Paul. He only likes her for a friend! Don't—don't—don't . . .")

The first question, about a psychiatrist in Seattle who claimed the Beatles were menaces, is met with George's "Psychiatrists are menaces, too." This is followed by the female fan amusingly trying to get their attention—"That's the way, George! Do you agree, Paul? Paul?"—before being rebuked by a newsman: "Siddown! . . . Now, look—don't start goin' up there, girlie!" More mundane questions and answers follow: The Beatles don't plan to play behind the Iron Curtain; they want to meet Paul Newman and Jayne Mansfield while in Hollywood; they don't like sports, except swimming; they have all of Elvis' early records.

RELEASE HISTORY

1996: This event has been preserved on film, 6 minutes' worth with sound, the rest silent footage, which circulates on video. Most of the portion with sound was released on *Rare Photos & Interview CD, Volume 2.* The *Hollywood Star* newsreel includes 3:14 of further silent footage shot from a different angle, and 1:21 of silent color home movie footage also circulates.

219. Radio interview R

Date: 23 August 1964
Time: ca. 7:30 p.m.
Location: Cinnamon Cinder, Los Angeles
Interviewer: Dave Hull
Broadcast: KRLA-AM, Los Angeles
Length: 2:26

After the press conference, KRLA's Dave Hull grabbed Ringo to record a quick interview before the Beatles were whisked away to the Hollywood Bowl.

Hull asks if Maureen Cox is Ringo's private secretary, and he clarifies that the rumor was born from a joking comment he made when Maureen retired from the hairstyling biz. He downplays her role as a steady girlfriend, stressing that their trip together in May was chaperoned. Ringo also doubts they'll be visiting Disneyland while in California, admitting he didn't even know where it was, and says the Canadian audience the previous evening was similar to most the world over.

RELEASE HISTORY

1964: This interview was released on the LP *Hear the Beatles Tell All,* which has been bootlegged on the CD *The VJ Story.*

220. Concert

Date: 23 August 1964
Time: 9:30–10:05 p.m.
Location: Hollywood Bowl, Los Angeles
Producers: Voyle Gilmore, George Martin

- **[A.] intro** (5:42)
- **[B.] Twist and Shout** (1:15)
- **[C.] intro** (0:02)
- **[D.] You Can't Do That** (2:25)
- **[E.] intro** (0:30)
- **[F.] All My Loving** (1:59)
- **[G.] intro** (0:17)
- **[H.] She Loves You** (2:11)
- **[I.] intro** (0:20)
- **[J.] Things We Said Today** (2:08)
- **[K.] intro** (0:03)
- **[L.] Roll Over Beethoven** (2:11)
- **[M.] intro** (0:48)
- **[N.] Can't Buy Me Love** (2:03)
- **[O.] intro** (0:28)
- **[P.] If I Fell** (2:04)
- **[Q.] intro** (0:05)
- **[R.] I Want to Hold Your Hand** (2:15)
- **[S.] intro** (0:51)
- **[T.] Boys** (1:58)
- **[U.] intro** (0:20)
- **[V.] A Hard Day's Night** (2:14)
- **[W.] intro** (1:02)
- **[X.] Long Tall Sally** (1:54)
- **[Y.] outro** (1:58)

After a slightly shambolic concert in Vancouver, the Beatles shaped up in time to deliver a sterling performance at the Hollywood Bowl. At the beginning of May, it was announced that Capitol had received permission from the American Federation of Musicians (denied for the Carnegie Hall show) to record the bowl concert for LP release.

Three-track tape was used, with bass and drums on one track, guitars on a second, vocals on a third, and the screams of 18,700 people on all three. Due to the placement of vocal microphones vis-à-vis amplifiers, there is plenty of guitar leakage on the vocal track, which explains George Martin's later comment: "[T]hey did some very bizarre mixing . . . I found guitars and voices mixed on the same track."

The master tapes were mixed into stereo at Capitol's Hollywood studios on the twenty-seventh, by which time the press was already reporting that "any releases from the session are considered unlikely. Overwhelming audience reaction ruined the technical quality of the tapes." Undeterred, Capitol assigned the release project #4877 and cut a mono acetate (the stereo mix with combined channels, not a unique mono mix) on September 3.

Within days, the Beatles were referring to the recording in interviews as "a souvenir . . . not for general release," and the album was shelved indefinitely. Capitol snuck out a bit of the first song on its November 1964 documentary album, *The Beatles' Story.* They also prepared a stereo acetate of the concert on September 30, 1966, but despite rumors every year or two, the release failed to materialize.

The multitrack master and stereo mixdown tapes were eventually sent to Abbey Road; judging by the tape reel number (E94024), this occurred sometime in mid-1969. Within a year, a copy had leaked to bootleggers, who took matters into their own hands, making this perhaps the most reissued Beatles concert of all time.

In 1976, the Beatles' contract with EMI expired, allowing them to exploit the group's unreleased catalog unhindered. George Martin was asked to reappraise the tapes of this and the 1965 Hollywood Bowl show, which he did January 18, 1977, at his AIR London studios. Once he found a working three-track machine, he transferred the recordings to 24-track tape, from which he was able to assemble an entertaining if slightly phony "composite concert," half from 1964 and half from 1965.

The result was released on the LP *The Beatles at the Hollywood Bowl,* which shot to number 1 on the British chart, dispelling all notions of the "technical quality" being ruined. If anything, the audience reaction only enhances the overall ambience of the recording, particularly the wild reaction to Ringo's number. Even more entertaining is the unedited show, which opens with the MC addressing the audience as "Hullabalooers."

Other documents of this concert include an audience tape (often misidentified as the Chicago performance of September 5), a bit of footage in the *Hollywood Star* newsreel, and a longer film, complete with decent sound but shaky camerawork, of the first six songs and the last three. A bit of the latter source ("All My Loving") was used in the *Anthology* documentary, and a "restored" version is circulating that synchronizes the stereo soundtrack from a bootleg to the film, repeating footage where necessary to cover for gaps.

RELEASE HISTORY

1964: The first 46 seconds of **B** were released in excellent stereo (with added echo) on the LP *The Beatles' Story.*

1970: This concert (**B–X**) was first bootlegged in very good quality mono on the LP *Shea, the Good Old Days.* A slightly upgraded copy on the bootleg *Back in 1964 at* *the Hollywood Bowl* was missing portions of **B** and **P.** Despite dozens of other permutations, no better copy of the full show appeared for twenty-three years.

1977: The LP *The Beatles at the Hollywood Bowl* included the following portions of this show in excellent stereo: the last half of **E, F–L** inclusive, the end of **S,** all of **T,** a bit of **U,** most of **W,** and all of **X.**

1993: The bootleg CD *Hollywood Bowl Complete* included an excellent-quality mono copy of this show, apparently from the tape used to prepare the original 1964 acetates. This has a bit of **S** edited out, and a cross-fade between sides omits a few seconds of **M.**

1997: The entire concert, with **A** and **Y** much longer than any previous release, appeared from an excellent-quality stereo tape source on the bootleg CD *The Complete Hollywood Bowl Concerts 1964–65.* The various newsreel film clips circulate on video.

221. Newsreel footage

Date: 24 August 1964
Time: 5:15 p.m.
Location: Mrs. Olson's residence, Brentwood
Interviewer: Saul Halpert
Length: 15:25

Most of this day was spent relaxing by the pool in their mansion hideaway, but the Beatles did have one function to attend. They put in an appearance at a garden party benefiting the Hemophilia Foundation of Southern California, held in Brentwood at the home of Capitol president Alan Livingston's mother-in-law. The Beatles sat on stools for about an hour and shook the hands of dozens of celebrities and their children, but were reportedly disappointed at the lack of major Hollywood stars.

KCBS-TV reporter Saul Halpert covered the event, filming an interview with a very relaxed-looking Derek Taylor (shirt half-unbuttoned) at the gate of the Bel Air mansion, and then moving to Avondale Avenue in Brentwood to capture the scene outside the party. Among the arrivals are gossip columnist Hedda Hopper, actors Edward G. Robinson and John Forsythe, and Los Angeles mayor Sam Yorty.

When the Beatles' car arrives, they are instantly surrounded by a swarm of journalists and onlookers (a police line holds back most of the fans across the street). John, George, Derek, and Brian all wear sunglasses; Neil and Mal are in tow as well. They pose for photos with some of the privileged offspring and then make their way into the party.

This footage was used by the Barbre Productions team, a camera crew who had also filmed the Cinnamon Cinder press conference the previous day. They would follow the Beatles around the United States for the next few weeks, filming concerts, press conferences, and interviews with fans, judges, policemen, janitors, taxi drivers, barbers, psychologists, and anyone remotely connected to the tour. It seems the footage from this day wasn't shot by them, however, but licensed from KCBS for inclusion in their production (which was apparently never completed).

RELEASE HISTORY

This footage circulates on video from reel 14 of the Barbre Productions collection.

222. Interview — J, P

Date: ca. 24 August 1964
Location: Reginald Owens' residence, Bel Air
Interviewer: Jack Wagner
Length: 6:19

Capitol Records producer Jack Wagner dropped by during the Beatles' stay in Bel Air to record some promotional items. As George and Ringo enjoyed the pool, John and Paul were interviewed at the piano for Capitol's *Teen Set* magazine. In addition to the full 6:11 recording, a 4:10 edit of the interview was prepared for Silver Platter Service, a series of preprogrammed radio LPs. It was included on the March 1965 edition (143–144), accompanied by a pair of songs from the Hollyridge Strings' new LP, *The Beatles Song Book, Volume 2.* This edit includes 8 seconds of unique material, including John and Paul greeting Jack by name.

It's quite an entertaining chat, with John and Paul in top wisecracking form. Asked to describe their approach to songwriting, John says, "We normally approach it on the M1." Paul elaborates by illustrating some of the piano riffs they supposedly present to each other, banging haphazardly on the keys to simulate a bitter disagreement. John and Paul then offer humorous demonstrations of various accents (Cockney, Liverpudlian, Irish, Scottish, and Welsh).

Recounting how they were introduced by Ivan Vaughan, John and Paul send out a greeting to their old mate, who is honeymooning in the United States (this appears only on the Silver Platter Service edit). Paul describes the Quarry Men as a "little group," which John takes literally: "Rather a large group, Paul. There was about fourteen of us, I think!"

John cheerfully offers up this prognostication of their destiny: "Well, probably we'll sell less records, less people'll go to see the film, we'll write less songs, and we'll all die of failure!" Paul tries to give a more serious answer, but John mocks his standard "John and I will carry on songwriting" response. Paul gives in and John launches into a dapper piano improvisation: "I hope Noel Coward's listening!" "And a hit is born!" adds Paul.

RELEASE HISTORY

1965: A 4:10 edit of the interview was included on the promotional LP *Silver Platter Service.* An edited version has been released on *Timeless II ½* and *The Beatles Are Coming.* The full interview circulates among collectors.

223. Speech J, P

Date: ca. 24 August 1964
Location: Reginald Owens' residence, Bel Air
Producer: Jack Wagner
Length: 0:40

Also recorded during Wagner's visit were promotional messages for a pair of Lennon/McCartney compositions donated to other artists. John introduces Cilla Black's "It's for You," and Paul does likewise for Peter and Gordon's "I Don't Want to See You Again." They also recorded a sign-off each to be played as outros for the songs. The messages were coupled on a 7-inch EP, *The Beatles Introduce New Songs,* distributed to radio stations by Capitol around September 14.

RELEASE HISTORY

1964: These messages appeared on the promotional EP *The Beatles Introduce New Songs.* They were bootlegged on the LP *Great to Have You with Us,* available on CD as *John, Paul, George & Ringo—Through the Years.*

2001: Paul's intro and outro were released on the compilation CD *The Ultimate Peter & Gordon,* taken from tape sources.

224. Radio interview P

Date: ca. 24 August 1964
Location: Reginald Owens' residence, Bel Air
Broadcast: *Here's to Veterans* #953
Length: 0:38

While in Los Angeles, Paul also agreed to record some brief song introductions for a veterans' administration radio series, *Here's to Veterans,* syndicated to radio stations via transcription discs.

The original program was aired November 30. It lasts 14:30 and opens with Paul's unenthusiastic greeting spoken over an excerpt of "I Want to Hold Your Hand." ("The Beatles sing for *Here's to Veterans.* Yahoo!") Paul goes on to introduce three songs from Capitol's *Something New* LP ("I'll Cry Instead," "Tell Me Why," and "If I Fell"), along with "Roll Over Beethoven." The show concludes with the Hollyridge Strings' rendition of "I Want to Hold Your Hand," over which Paul says farewell, "speaking for all the Beatles, from Hollywood, U.S.A." This original disc is extremely rare.

More common, thanks to its being widely counterfeited, is a 1968 *Here's to Veterans* program that clumsily reedits Paul's speech to make it seem as though he is introducing new songs. It helps that their latest LP is called *The Beatles.* Paul's original intro was: "And here's another song from our new album, *Something New.* The Beatles, my pals, and 'Tell Me Why.' "

This becomes "This is Paul McCartney of the Beatles speaking, and the next record you're gonna hear is another song from our new album *The Beatles*/ and . . ." This leads into "Ob-La-Di, Ob-La-Da." Also included in this broadcast are "I'll Cry Instead," "Eleanor Rigby," and "Hey Jude."

RELEASE HISTORY

1964: The original program was distributed on an LP, *Here's to Veterans,* as program no. 953.

1979: Melvin Records used a bit of this speech (from the 1968 program) on their bootleg LP *The Beatles vs.*

Don Ho, although here Paul introduces Don Ho's "Tiny Bubbles."

1999: The bootleg CD *I'm a Loser* included Paul's intros from the 1968 disc.

225. Radio interview **J**

Date: 25 August 1964
Time: evening
Location: Reginald Owens' residence, Bel Air
Interviewer: Larry Kane
Broadcast: WFUN-AM, Miami
Length: 17:31

Another well-deserved and well-enjoyed rest day was nearly spoiled by a trip to the Whiskey a Go Go nightclub, where one photographer who refused to stop taking flash photos had a drink thrown at him by George. The resulting photo made the front page of the following day's *Herald Examiner.*

Earlier that evening, most of the Fabs' entourage (except John) went to Burt Lancaster's home for dinner and a private screening of the Peter Sellers film *A Shot in the Dark.* John stayed behind to meet visitors and tape interviews, including this one with Larry Kane (Derek Taylor and *Liverpool Echo* reporter George Harrison are also present).

Topics of discussion include clothing, country music, Bob Dylan, Barry Goldwater, Shakespeare ("a drag"), the Stones ("good friends"), the garden party ("a job of work . . . harder than playing"), money, writing books ("I used to call it 'rubbish,' but it's 'books' now, isn't it?"), New Orleans, and their homecoming reception in Liverpool the previous month.

RELEASE HISTORY

1985: This interview was released in two segments on the albums *'Round the World* and *Not a Second Time* (issued the following year). Both titles have been reissued on CD.

226. Radio interview **J**

Date: 26 August 1964
Time: ca. midnight
Location: Reginald Owens' residence, Bel Air
Interviewer: Jim Steck
Broadcast: KRLA-AM, Los Angeles
Length: 13:14

The second interview of the evening was conducted by KRLA's Jim Steck and is one of the more thoughtful interviews of the period. John has a chance to explain how the group started (as a skiffle band) and talks at length about his educational background. Asked for a final word to the Los Angeles listeners, John says, "Good night and thanks for the bread," which probably sums up his feelings about the tour as well as anything.

RELEASE HISTORY

1964: This interview occupied the entire first side of the LP *Hear the Beatles Tell All,* which has been bootlegged on the CD *The VJ Story.*

227. Radio interview **P, R**

Date: 23–26 August 1964
Location: Los Angeles or Denver
Interviewer: Dave Hull
Broadcast: KRLA-AM, Los Angeles
Length: 0:39

The exact date of this interview is unknown, but it must postdate Seattle, as Dave Hull asks Paul whether George and Ringo caught anything while fishing out the window of the Edgewater Inn. Paul never answers, as he's busy telling Ringo about Dave's habit of giving out the Beatles' home addresses: "Not a nice trick, Dave."

RELEASE HISTORY

1964: This interview was released on the LP *Hear the Beatles Tell All,* which has been bootlegged on the CD *The VJ Story.*

228. Newsreel footage

Date: 26 August 1964
Time: 11:00 a.m.
Location: Los Angeles International Airport
Length: 1:06

As the Beatles departed Los Angeles, they were filmed at the airport signing autographs for a blond girl, who even gets to kiss George on the cheek. "Don't let the TV cameras see you," he cautions. "Or they'll have you engaged," John adds. She waves farewell to their plane as the cameraman shouts directions: "Throw him a kiss!"

Also covering the departure were KRLA disc jockeys Dave Hull and Jim Steck, who made a spur-of-the-moment decision to simply stroll aboard the Beatles' flight as if they were on the passenger list. Nobody seemed to notice until they had arrived in Denver that afternoon.

RELEASE HISTORY

This footage circulates on video from reel 14 of the Barbre Productions collection.

228a. TV interview

Date: 26 August 1964
Time: 11:00 a.m.
Location: Los Angeles International Airport
Length: 1:00

Local TV station KABC filmed an interview with Ringo at the airport (with Paul butting in at one point), talking about the incident at the Whiskey a Go Go and his love of country music. This clip was aired on ABC's *New American Bandstand,* October 10, 1964.

RELEASE HISTORY

2003: The audio portion of this footage was included on the CD-R American Bandstand *Salutes the Beatles,* but the footage itself has yet to appear on video.

229. Newsreel/Amateur footage

Date: 26 August 1964
Time: 1:35 p.m.
Location: Stapleton Field, Denver
Length: 2:28

More airport footage, this time of the Denver arrival. John and George wear shades and Paul and Ringo squint in the midday sun as the foursome pose for photos on the steps of the plane. Microphones are shoved in their faces as they make their way slowly to a waiting limo that carries them off in a massive motorcade. Fans (or local radio station shills) are then seen holding up a banner reading KDAB DIGS THE BEATLES.

RELEASE HISTORY

One minute and fifty-three seconds of this silent footage circulates on video from reel 10 of the Barbre Productions collection; the remainder circulates from a fuzzy color home movie.

230. Radio interview

Date: 26 August 1964
Time: afternoon
Location: Brown Palace Hotel, Denver
Interviewer: Dave Hull
Broadcast: KRLA-AM, Los Angeles
Length: 4:40

Upon their arrival at the Brown Palace Hotel, the Beatles' entourage piled into an elevator along with several hangers-on and policemen. A photographer also forced his way in and was met with a cry of "Get that bastard photographer out of here!" by a British voice. Sure enough, the elevator got stuck between floors, and the Beatles were forced to jump out and walk up a flight of stairs to their eighth-floor suite.

Meanwhile, Dave Hull and Jim Steck of KRLA had been confronted by Brian Epstein about stowing away on the flight. Derek Taylor decided to take mercy on the pair, not only giving them tickets to the concert at Red Rocks, but allowing them into the hotel to interview each of the Fabs. Hull made the interviews short but sweet, not wanting to press his luck further.

John discusses *A Hard Day's Night,* choosing the field scene as his favorite and explaining that even the ad-libbed moments failed to be spontaneous due to retakes. He denies that their next movie will be filmed in Hollywood or written by him, and says he hasn't moved into his new Weybridge home yet, as it's still being redecorated.

Ringo teases Hull for getting caught sneaking on the flight, relates how he thought of the phrase "a hard day's night," and talks about his upcoming tonsillectomy. Paul chats about Drake's Drum, the racehorse he purchased for his father, and George says even if they were planning to visit Disneyland, it'd be pointless to announce it. Both he and Paul concur with John's choice of best scene in *A Hard Day's Night.*

RELEASE HISTORY

1964: These interviews were released on the LP *Hear the Beatles Tell All,* which has been bootlegged on the CD *The VJ Story.*

231. Press conference/TV interview

Date: 26 August 1964
Time: evening
Location: Red Rocks Amphitheatre, Denver
Interviewer: Pat Murphy
Broadcast: KOA-TV, Denver
Length: 11:16

That evening, the Beatles held a press conference before going onstage at Red Rocks (an opening act can be heard performing faintly in the background). John denies that he's leaving the group and says they'll be back to the United States "next year at the earliest." Asked about their upcoming Jacksonville concert, George says they don't play to segregated audiences, and that "half of our show is colored, anyway" (support group the Exciters). Ringo admits that he's read only about five pages of John's book ("You're so popular over here, you should plug it, you fool!" scolds John).

After Derek Taylor takes a quick poll to discern how many legitimate journalists are present (most of the questions are posed by teenage female voices), Ringo hopes he's having a good influence on teenagers ("Who do you think you are, Bob Dylan?" teases John). A couple of disc jockeys ask the Beatles' opinions of Seattle's Paul Revere and the Raiders and Denver's Astronauts; they've only vaguely heard of either group. Someone asks Ringo why Pete Best "quit" the group, and John corrects him bluntly: "We just threw him out."

Following the conference, KOA-TV reporter Pat Murphy grills the Beatles about their apparent hostility toward the press back at the hotel. "We're only as rude as the people we meet," snaps John, while Ringo points out that the elevator was crowded enough before reporters had to jump in.

RELEASE HISTORY

1996: Some of the press conference and the Pat Murphy interview were released in the *Fab Four CD & Book Set,* taken from a slightly longer newsreel that circulates on video. An average-sounding tape circulates that includes a further 7:02 of the press conference.

232. Newsreel footage

Date: 26 August 1964
Time: 9:30 p.m.
Location: Red Rocks Amphitheatre, Denver
Length: 4:51

The Beatles were most impressed with the outdoor facility at Red Rocks, and apart from the thin mountain air, their performance went off without a hitch. Several minutes of silent concert footage exists, shot from the side of the stage. In addition to opening acts the Righteous Brothers and Jackie DeShannon, it includes segments of the Beatles' first six songs.

RELEASE HISTORY

This silent footage circulates on video from reel 4 of the Barbre Productions collection.

233. Radio interview

Date: 27 August 1964
Time: noon
Location: Stapleton Field, Denver
Interviewer: Jim Steck
Broadcast: KRLA-AM, Los Angeles
Length: 0:16

As the Beatles departed Denver, they also parted company with Dave Hull and Jim Steck, who had to fly back to LA at KRLA's expense. They take the opportunity to tape one final farewell message from Ringo, who asks, "Aren't you coming with us?" Steck responds dejectedly, "No. Not this time." The drummer bids adieu to Los Angeles listeners: "It's been fab bein' here. Great place you got here. Hope to come back."

RELEASE HISTORY

1964: This interview was released on the LP *Hear the Beatles Tell All,* which has been bootlegged on the CD *The VJ Story.*

234. Radio interview

Date: 27 August 1964
Time: afternoon
Location: flight from Denver to Cincinnati
Interviewer: Larry Kane
Broadcast: WFUN-AM, Miami
Length: 1:54

During the flight from Denver to Cincinnati, the Beatles were presented with a *Melody Maker* award as best international group. The occasion was documented by Larry Kane's tape recorder and then shipped off to an awards luncheon, presumably in London, to be played for the assembled guests. Each Beatle gives a short speech of gratitude, with George's "Hi there, Beatle People!" getting a big laugh from his bandmates.

RELEASE HISTORY

1985: This recording was released on the LP *East Coast Invasion,* later reissued on CD.

235. Newsreel footage

Date: 27 August 1964
Time: 5:05 p.m.
Location: Lunken Airport, Cincinnati
Length: 2:52

Eleven hundred fans were on hand to greet the Beatles at Cincinnati's Lunken Airport. Newsreels captured the plane's first appearance in the sky, touchdown on a distant runway, and pulling to a halt. Derek and Neil are first to emerge, followed by the Fabs, who pause at the top of the steps for the obligatory photocall.

RELEASE HISTORY

This silent footage circulates on video from reel 6B of the Barbre Productions collection.

236. Press conference

Date: 27 August 1964
Time: evening
Location: Cincinnati Gardens
Length: 2:56

The Beatles were driven straight from the airport to Cincinnati Gardens, arriving around 6 p.m. The standard backstage press conference preceded the concert and revealed nothing new. Asked what question he hates answering, Ringo chooses, "How's your book, John?" One reporter asks if the Dave Clark Five are copying them, but John points out that they use saxophones and organs, and Ringo insists, "They're nothing like us, y'know, if you listen."

RELEASE HISTORY

In addition to a 2:32 audio recording, a 24-second film clip circulates on video, most of which was used in *Anthology*. Two minutes and twenty-one seconds of silent footage also circulates from reel 6B of the Barbre Productions collection.

237. Amateur/Newsreel footage

Date: 27 August 1964
Time: 9:35 p.m.
Location: Cincinnati Gardens
Length: 2:17

Footage of the Beatles' Cincinnati concert exists from two separate sources, neither with sound. Footage from WKRC-TV's archives includes portions of "All My Loving," shot from the side of the stage, plus scenes of fans standing on their seats. In addition, reel 6B of the Barbre Productions collection includes 58 seconds of the concert, mostly from "She Loves You" (one version is synced to sound from an unrelated bootleg). The Beatles play in front of a large banner reading WSAI GOOD GUYS PRESENT THE BEATLES.

RELEASE HISTORY

This silent footage circulates on video among collectors.

238. Radio interview — P, R

Date: 28 August 1964
Time: 4:00 p.m.
Location: Delmonico Hotel, New York City
Interviewer: Bruce Morrow, Scott Muni
Broadcast: live
WABC-AM, New York
Length: 13:14

Some three thousand fans welcomed The Beatles back to New York when their flight from Cincinnati touched down just before 3 a.m. Any exhilaration they felt at returning to the site of their first American triumph was dampened by their struggle to fight through the crowd outside the Delmonico Hotel. In the fracas, a pair of hands grabbed the St. Christopher medal around Ringo's neck and tore it away. He escaped into the lobby with shirt and skin intact, but was upset by the loss of the medal, which was a twenty-first birthday gift from his aunt.

Radio station WABC saw an opportunity to crush their competition and jumped on it. From the Beatles' suite, they broadcast a plea for the medal to be returned, no questions asked. The reward: a kiss from Ringo! It didn't take long for the culprit to get in touch: a sixteen-year-old girl, Angie McGowan. WABC continued to hype the story throughout the morning as the Beatles slept in, and by 4:00 the next afternoon, they were back in the suite to arrange the reunion, aired live on the station.

As thousands of girls scream and weep enviously in the streets outside, Angie and three of her friends are introduced to Ringo and receive smooches. Ringo verifies that the medal is indeed his and signs autographs for the girls. He chats with DJ "Cousin Brucie" Morrow about their plan to fly to Forest Hills in a helicopter for that night's concert, and he halfheartedly endorses Lyndon Johnson for president: "Good fella. Leave them dogs alone!"

Scott Muni shows Ringo some entries in a WABC Beatle art contest, and he is underwhelmed, commenting that a portrait of Paul "looks as if he's got a few odd teeth in." Paul himself shows up soon after, causing a fresh wave of screaming from fans outside listening on transistor radios. The noise intensifies when Paul gives Angie a kiss as well. After a bit more schmoozing and self-promotion—"As a guest of our city, as WABC New York number one, so we had to find it—we just had to find it for him"—Morrow and Muni finally step aside to allow other journalists a shot at interviewing and photographing Paul and Ringo.

RELEASE HISTORY

This recording circulates in good quality among collectors from an off-air tape, and several minutes circulate on video, from WABC-TV news coverage.

239. Press conference

Date: 28 August 1964
Time: 5:30 p.m.
Location: Crystal Ballroom, Delmonico Hotel, New York City
Length: 14:06

During the New York press conference, the sheer repetition of questions is starting to take a toll on the usually high-spirited Beatles, as they are asked about their future plans three times during the proceedings ("They keep saying that every two minutes!" cries an exasperated John). Asked if the drink-throwing incident in LA was due to a worn-thin temper, George deadpans, "No. I was in very high spirits that evening, and I just thought I'd baptize him." One reporter wants to know if the cynical press conference scene in *A Hard Day's Night* correctly mirrors their attitude toward the press, and John hedges: "They're quite good, y'know, but they're gettin' a bit large these days." Probably the low point occurs when a teenager with a thick Brooklyn accent wonders whether George is the least popular Beatle. "He goes a bomb in Sweden" is John's assessment.

RELEASE HISTORY

1965: Excerpts from this press conference were released on the LP *1965 Talk Album—Ed Rudy with New U.S. Tour.*

1982: Six minutes of further extracts appeared on the LP *Like Dreamers Do.* Newsreel footage also circulates on video with even more portions. Although all three sources have some degree of overlap, all have unique material.

240. Radio interview P, R

Date: 28 August 1964
Time: evening
Location: Delmonico Hotel, New York City
Interviewer: Larry Kane
Broadcast: WFUN-AM, Miami
Length: 5:32

Soon after the press conference disbanded, Larry Kane taped a five-minute interview with Paul and a very short one with Ringo before they left the hotel. Paul compares this New York visit to the one in February and confesses that he and John have a lot of songs to write for their next album, while Ringo talks about the St. Christopher medal incident.

RELEASE HISTORY

1985: These interviews were released on the LP *East Coast Invasion,* later reissued on CD.

241. Radio interview

Date: 28 August 1964
Location: Delmonico Hotel and Forest Hills Tennis Stadium, New York City
Interviewer: Murray Kaufman
Broadcast: WINS-AM, New York City
Length: 7:14

Naturally, the "fifth Beatle" had to hook up with his four comrades once they hit town, and a group of recordings circulate from this visit featuring Murray the K interviewing and clowning around with the Beatles.

The first seems to be a telephone interview with Paul, conducted between the WINS studio and the Delmonico. After welcoming him back to the United States, Murray asks Paul about *A Hard Day's Night*'s critical success. While he had doubts about how it would be received, Paul is thrilled that even the most highbrow newspapers gave the film good reviews. He lauds Billy J Kramer's rendition of "From a Window," and he gives an echo-laden introduction to the disc for Murray to air.

The next fragment has Murray complaining that Beatle fans got on his case for treating the Rolling Stones well on their recent New York visit, but John confirms that he'd asked Murray to show them around town: "Shut up, all those people moaning. They're our mates!"

Murray probably attended that evening's show at Forest Hills, and he reportedly accompanied the group back to their suite that evening, so the remaining interviews may have been taped at either location. Ringo talks about a collection of his personal photographs (a sixty-four-page magazine titled *Ringo's Photo Album*), which was published late that year in America.

Paul asks if Murray is playing "It's for You," and Ringo says, "You must keep playing it, or we won't turn in." "To what?" Murray inquires innocently. Ringo begins to reply, "To ten—" but stops short before giving 1010 WINS yet another free plug. "We got tricked so many times last year," moans Paul. Later he and Murray have a conversation in "Meusurry" dialect about how wonderful the girls in "Breusooklyn" and "Queuseens" are. Paul also denies that Jane will have a role in their next film, and Murray emphasizes how impressed he and his wife were by Jane's poise and composure when they met in London.

RELEASE HISTORY

These interviews circulate in poor to good quality among collectors, from off-air recordings.

242. Radio interview J, G, R

Date: 28 August 1964
Time: evening
Location: Forest Hills Tennis Stadium, New York City
Interviewer: Larry Kane
Broadcast: WFUN-AM, Miami
Length: 6:42

Around 7:30 p.m. the Beatles were driven to a helicopter and airlifted to Forest Hills for their concert. Backstage, Larry Kane taped further interviews with the group. George chats about being "the quiet Beatle" and says he wouldn't mind having a winter home in America, "somewhere hot" like Florida or California. Brian Epstein also speaks with Larry about discovering the Beatles; at the end of Brian's interview, John walks over to add some words of greeting to the fans in Miami. Ringo says that New York City "moves more than London," and says he's gone on a few dates while in America, but "I'm not giving you any names."

RELEASE HISTORY

1985: These interviews were released on the LP *East Coast Invasion,* later reissued on CD.

243. Radio interview R

Date: 28 or 29 August 1964
Location: New York City
Interviewer: B. Mitchell Reed
Broadcast: WMCA-AM, New York
Length: 0:47

This aircheck contains two short snippets from Ringo's chat with one of WMCA's "Good Guys." The first has Ringo asking, "Hey, scooters. Can you really understand what the leaders say?," which presumably made some sense to listeners at the time. In the second, he describes the differences between mods and rockers.

RELEASE HISTORY

This recording circulates in good quality among collectors.

244. Radio interview P

Date: 28 or 29 August 1964
Location: Delmonico Hotel, New York City
Interviewer: Long John Wade
Broadcast: WDRC-AM, Hartford
Length: 0:32

At some point during their stay in the Delmonico, an ever-accommodating Paul recorded this message for WDRC Radio's Long John Wade: "This is Paul McCartney, your—your resident DJ and newscaster, reporting from the hotel bedroom of the Beatles in New York. And I've got with me now that famous man, who you've probably never heard of, John Wade. I know you don't really wanna listen to him, 'cause he's a load of rubbish, really. But here he is, sitting around, giggling. I told you he was an idiot, didn't I, folks?"

RELEASE HISTORY

This interview circulates among collectors from its appearance on a WDRC website.

245. Radio interview J, P, G

Date: 29 August 1964
Location: Delmonico Hotel, New York City
Interviewer: Larry Kane
Broadcast: WFUN-AM, Miami
Length: 8:19

After staying up late to get high with Bob Dylan, the Beatles slept in until the afternoon. Larry Kane was able to corner John and Paul for separate interviews before they left the hotel for their second New York show that night. John discusses an incident at the previous night's concert where a girl got onstage and hugged George, who struggled to carry on playing: "I could hear all wrong notes coming out!" He also professes his love for big cities like New York and London and says the acoustics at the Hollywood Bowl were outstanding. Paul weighs in on such issues as movie acting, inconsiderate journalists, folk music, and Jane Asher.

Kane also interviewed George about psychic Jeane Dixon's supposed prediction that the Beatles would die in a plane crash when they left Philadelphia the following week. It turned out to be a rumor, but George, already known to be the Beatle with the greatest fear of flying, says he'll travel on a bicycle that particular day.

RELEASE HISTORY

1985: These interviews were released on the LP *East Coast Invasion,* later reissued on CD.

246. TV interview

Date: 30 August 1964
Time: afternoon
Location: Lafayette Motor Inn, Atlantic City
Interviewer: Peter Woods
Length: 3:28

Flying on to Atlantic City directly from the final Forest Hills gig, via helicopter, the Beatles checked in to the Lafayette Motor Inn for a single concert and a couple more days off. At some point during the afternoon before their show, they were interviewed by Peter Woods, a British TV correspondent who happened to be staying in the same motel while in town to cover the Democratic National Convention.

The clip begins with a long intro during which the reporter runs down a list of complaints about having his peace and quiet ruined by Beatle fans. Then he is ushered into the Beatles' suite to chat with all four at once about the noisy fans; Paul says they are used to it, just like someone who worked in a bell factory all day would be immune to ringing.

RELEASE HISTORY

This footage was released on the home video *Beatles 1962 to 1970.*

246a. Concert

Date: 30 August 1964 (?)
Time: evening
Location: Convention Hall, Atlantic City (?)

[A.] **intro** (0:19)
[B.] **Twist and Shout** (1:15)
[C.] **intro** (0:01)
[D.] **You Can't Do That** (2:28)
[E.] **intro** (0:33)
[F.] **All My Loving** (1:54)
[G.] **intro** (0:04)
[H.] **She Loves You** (2:10)
[I.] **intro** (0:22)
[J.] **Things We Said Today** (2:06)
[K.] **intro** (0:01)
[L.] **Roll Over Beethoven** (2:11)
[M.] **intro** (0:18)
[N.] **Can't Buy Me Love** (2:00)
[O.] **intro** (0:32)
[P.] **If I Fell** (2:06)
[Q.] **intro** (0:04)
[R.] **I Want to Hold Your Hand** (2:20)
[S.] **intro** (0:09)
[T.] **Boys** (1:59)
[U.] **intro** (0:04)
[V.] **A Hard Day's Night** (2:17)
[W.] **intro** (0:44)
[X.] **Long Tall Sally** (1:54)
[Y.] **outro** (0:17)

Keep your pants on! This is not a newly unearthed Beatles concert recording. Rather, it was Ed Rudy's last desperate attempt to make money from his dubious "fifth Beatle" claim.

Yes, it is an authentic tape of a Beatles concert, presumably Atlantic City, based on Rudy's between-song fan interviews. But the only time a Beatle voice can be heard is in a few of the song introductions. Once the music starts, the original Beatle performances are overdubbed with "re-creations" by a hapless group of musicians dubbed the Liverpool Lads (who are hyped on the LP sleeve).

The best thing I can say about their renditions is that they know nearly 60 percent of the lyrics and manage to finish the songs within 15 seconds either way of the Beatles' underlying performances. The Lads' version of "Can't Buy Me Love" may be the most objectionable item committed to vinyl in the 1960s. The sound quality of the concert is on par with the worst audience tape you've ever heard, and the song order is scrambled (but all twelve songs are represented). As a special bonus, you get Rudy's studio interview with a Brian Epstein imitator.

The timings for **D** and **J** are approximate, as the only copy of this LP I could find had a deep gouge on one side, no doubt from the original owner's attempt to exact revenge on this vinyl nightmare.

RELEASE HISTORY

1965: This lamentable recording was unleashed upon an unsuspecting public on the LP *The Great American Tour 1965 Live Beatlemania Concert.* Nobody has had the guts to bootleg it yet.

246b. TV interview

Date: 30 August–1 September 1964
Location: Atlantic City
Broadcast: 18 September 1964, 7:00–7:30 p.m.
WABC-TV
Beatlemania
Length: 2:32

Before the tour had concluded, New York City's ABC-TV affiliate had assembled and aired a thirty-minute Beatles special, *Beatlemania,* cohosted by WABC radio disc jockeys Bruce Morrow and Scott Muni. An audio dub of the program has survived, and most of the material can be found elsewhere: The show opens with a screening of the *Making of* A Hard Day's Night featurette, followed by Morrow and Muni's August 28 interview of Ringo and Paul at the Delmonico.

Next up are some TV interviews from other cities, presumably shared by other local ABC stations. After some brief interviews from Pittsburgh (see the September 14 entry), there is a unique section filmed in Atlantic City. John explains how tour mate Jackie DeShannon got the Beatles hooked on Monopoly and compares the American and British versions of that board game. Paul says that he and John have written two songs on the tour so far, and Ringo uncharacteristically talks about his rings. Asked about their future dreams, George breaks into a refrain of "I dream of Jeannie with the light brown beard."

The special continues with footage of the San Francisco press conference and Cow Palace concert (no music from the show is heard), and after an ad from Pepsi-Cola, the show concludes with a spin of "She Loves You."

RELEASE HISTORY

These interviews circulate in very good quality among collectors.

247. Radio interview G

Date: 31 August–1 September 1964
Location: Lafayette Motor Inn, Atlantic City
Interviewer: Larry Kane
Broadcast: WFUN-AM, Miami
Length: 2:30

Rather than risk a journey outside the confines of their lodgings, the Beatles spent the last day of August watching TV and listening to music, playing cards and Monopoly, and shopping vicariously (salesmen brought items up for their perusal). Larry Kane taped interviews with Derek Taylor and Neil Aspinall about the previous night's show, when the crowd had again gotten out of control and several teenagers were hurt.

The first day of September was another day off spent in the motel, playing games and records, watching TV and a private screening of *A Hard Day's Night,* and participating in a late-night rockabilly jam session with tour mates the Bill Black Combo. The latter was taped using Larry Kane's recorder and sent by Ringo to a friend in Liverpool, but unfortunately hasn't been unearthed in the succeeding years.

Sometime over these two days, Kane also taped this short interview with George, who compares the United States to England and explains why he prefers wearing jeans on his days off.

RELEASE HISTORY

1985: Kane's interviews were released on the LP *East Coast Invasion,* later reissued on CD.

248. Press conference

Date: 2 September 1964
Time: 6:00 p.m.
Location: Convention Hall, Philadelphia
Length: 8:10

The escape route from Atlantic City this afternoon went as follows: motel service elevator, delivery van, limousine, and chartered bus for the short trip to Philadelphia. As their hotel reservation in the city had been canceled, the Beatles arrived at the venue and flew out directly after the show.

Over 8 minutes of footage from the backstage press conference in a meeting room at Convention Hall circulates, unfortunately without sound. It shows the group seated at a long table (John wears his striped jacket), and posing for photos with a police officer displaying a poster; George points to the BE SAFE! motto at the top.

RELEASE HISTORY

This silent footage circulates on video among collectors.

249. Radio interview

Date: 2 September 1964
Time: 6:30–9:15 p.m.
Location: Convention Hall, Philadelphia
Interviewer: Charlie Murdock
Broadcast: WQAM-AM, Miami
Length: 24:20

Miami disc jockey Charlie Murdock taped interviews with each of the Beatles as they killed time backstage at Convention Hall. Murdock had covered the group's February trip to Miami for radio station WQAM, and he arrived in Philly bearing copies of a promotional EP put together by the station, which included recordings of their airport arrival and an interview at the Deauville Hotel.

Each Beatle brightens considerably at the mention of Buddy Dresner's name when Murdock passes along greetings from their old pal on the Miami police force. Ringo thinks he should be promoted from sergeant, and he says if the "Ringo for President" campaign works out, he'll name Dresner chief of national security. Over the course of Ringo's interview, we get a good idea of how he spent the previous days off.

On August 31, they had stayed inside all day watching TV and playing Monopoly, which Ringo was no good at. He had better luck with a four-hour game of poker, winning $40 playing against Paul, disc jockeys, and photographers. Ringo stayed up until 8 a.m. and didn't rise until 5 p.m. on the 1st. After dinner and more Monopoly, the Beatles watched two films (their own and one other) from midnight till 4 a.m. Then came the country jam session with Paul, Ringo, Mal, and three members of the Bill Black Combo taking part. The Beatles capped off the night visiting a couple of local bars until 6 a.m. It's no wonder John and Ringo were suffering from insomnia for the next few days!

After the first Forest Hills show, opening act the Righteous Brothers had asked to be removed from the tour, disheartened at having their performance eclipsed by the arrival of the Beatles in a helicopter. Their replacement, singer Clarence "Frogman" Henry, joined the tour this night and Ringo was eager to watch him rehearse.

George chats about his continued correspondence with Buddy Dresner, to whom he had sent some Beatle-style shirts. After talking about life on the road and their movie career, he's asked to rate the British music scene and names the Searchers and the Rolling Stones as favorite groups, realizing how outrageous the Stones look to Americans. George also praises the Animals, particularly a recent TV performance that the Beatles all agreed sounded better than the record, despite their general distrust of TV sound engineers.

Murdock asks Paul what their act consists of, and he runs down the set list, accidentally omitting "Can't Buy Me Love"; he prefaces the list with "tonight, we'll be doing . . ." as though they made amendments from city to city! He chooses "Long Tall Sally," "This Boy," "If I Fell," and "A Hard Day's Night" as current favorites in the Beatle catalog, and he reveals that they arranged "A Hard Day's Night" in the studio after writing it to order "a couple of days" before the session. Finally, John says a few words about his books and says that he calls Cynthia every chance he gets, but won't tonight as they have no hotel to stay at.

RELEASE HISTORY

These interviews circulate in very good quality among collectors.

250. Radio interview — J, P, R

Date: 2 September 1964
Time: 6:30–9:15 p.m.
Location: Convention Hall, Philadelphia
Interviewer: Larry Kane
Broadcast: WFUN-AM, Miami
Length: 40:27

Larry Kane was able to record several interviews backstage in between the press conference and evening concert. The first three of these were separate chats with Paul, John, and Ringo.

Paul discusses the influence country music has had on the group, particularly Carl Perkins, and he and John both claim to read as much of the fan mail as possible. John explains why he thought today's press conference was superior to the one in "Atlanta" (he probably means Atlantic City) due to the higher ratio of reporters to fans: "Kids are to play songs to and wave at." Kane reflects on how natural the Beatles appeared in their film, but John admits they were ill at ease, particularly in the opening scenes. He also says that nobody scripts their witty press conference responses, but if someone came up with a good line, they wouldn't hesitate to use it. Ringo touches on a variety of subjects: country music, wanting to be a DJ, fan reaction, sports, Monopoly (he prefers playing cards), why he used to be quiet during press conferences, and fan clubs.

Since the group wasn't staying at a hotel, there was a lot of time to kill backstage, so Kane also took the opportunity to record a long and intelligent conversation with John and Ringo, which has been released in two distinct segments.

Ringo begins by explaining the meaning of "cheeky" (a term used in their film) and admits they learned most of their lines on the way to the studio, to try and keep things fresh. He also denies rumors that he's dating actress Hayley Mills, which began merely because they were photographed together at a party. "If I have a photo with President Johnson, they'll say we're going steady," he laments. Kane inquires about family members being taken advantage of, and John says insincere fan letters to his wife are easily spotted: "Hello, Mrs. Lennon, may I call you Cyn? Could you get me ninety-five autographed photographs of the boys?" Ringo complains that they are in a no-win situation when it comes to dating—if they do, marriage rumors circulate; if they don't, homosexual rumors circulate. John is shocked: "You can't have that on tape!" Ringo responds, "I'll have it on tape that I've been called a queer." After some further kind words to Sgt. Buddy Dresner, mixed-religion marriages are discussed, with John admitting he didn't even know Cynthia's religion when he proposed.

Part two of the conversation moves on to "worst questions asked" and adolescent girls growing old too fast, before John throws in a seeming nonsequitur: "I met a man who went to Glasgow with a bad egg. And nobody'd sit with him on the train." Asked about an impending nuclear war, Ringo is pessimistic, while John feels "only a nutter like Hitler" would press the button. They concede the Beatles have their fair share of arguments, but nothing bad enough to cause a split; Ringo says he couldn't stand it on his own. Things wind up with a discussion of Hollywood phonies, and their side of the Whiskey a Go Go drink-throwing incident.

RELEASE HISTORY

1985: The first three interviews were released on the LP *East Coast Invasion.* The first half of John and Ringo's conversation was released on the LP *'Round the World,* and the latter half was included on the LP *West Coast Invasion,* misidentified as a recording from August 23 at the Hollywood Bowl. All three LPs were subsequently issued on CD.

251. Concert

Date: 2 September 1964
Time: 9:30 p.m.
Location: Convention Hall, Philadelphia
Broadcast: live
WIBG-AM, Philadelphia (?)

[A.] intro (0:46)
[B.] Twist and Shout (1:18)
[C.] intro (0:02)
[D.] You Can't Do That (2:28)
[E.] intro (0:45)
[F.] All My Loving (2:00)
[G.] intro (0:22)
[H.] She Loves You (2:13)
[I.] intro (0:21)
[J.] Things We Said Today (2:09)
[K.] intro (0:03)
[L.] Roll Over Beethoven (2:10)
[M.] intro (1:00)
[N.] Can't Buy Me Love (2:01)

[O.] **intro** (0:37)
[P.] **If I Fell** (2:08)
[Q.] **intro** (0:02)
[R.] **I Want to Hold Your Hand** (2:20)
[S.] **intro** (0:40)
[T.] **Boys** (1:59)
[U.] **intro** (0:30)
[V.] **A Hard Day's Night** (2:16)
[W.] **intro** (0:38)
[X.] **Long Tall Sally** (1:54)
[Y.] **outro** (0:12)

The Philadelphia concert was apparently simulcast by radio station WIBG, giving us one of the few decent soundboard recordings from the Beatles' touring days. John's guitar is mixed way too loud, but the vocals are up front and the music isn't totally drowned out by screaming.

The group's performance is nothing special, with the usual giggling fit during "If I Fell" and inaccurate stage introductions. (John calls "She Loves You" "our second record in England. Third, fourth, I don't know!"; Paul announces "Boys" as "from our first Capitol album.")

In addition to the audio recording, the Barbre team were at it again, filming portions of "You Can't Do That," "All My Loving," "She Loves You," and "A Hard Day's Night," along with the Beatles' escape from the stage into a service elevator with Neil and Derek. Although this footage (8:06 worth) is silent, a version circulates that has been synchronized to the radio soundtrack.

RELEASE HISTORY

1971: This was one of the first Beatles concerts to be bootlegged, appearing on the LP *Live Concert at Whiskey Flats* in very good quality. Several variant titles gave the impression that the fictional Whiskey Flats venue was in Atlanta, which led to misinterpretation that this was the Atlantic City concert of a few days previous.

1993: The entire concert appeared from a very good-quality tape source on the bootleg CD *The Ultimate Live Collection, Volume 1.* The silent concert footage circulates on video from reel 19 of the Barbre Productions collection.

252. TV footage

Date: 3 September 1964
Time: 1:00 a.m.
Location: Weir Cook Airport, Indianapolis
Broadcast: 9 September 1964
WISH-TV, Indianapolis
Our Fair Beatles
Length: 2:11

Despite psychic Jeane Dixon's supposed prediction, the Beatles' flight from Philadelphia to Indianapolis failed to crash. Although they were arriving well past midnight, a few fans and plenty of press welcomed them at the airport.

Local CBS affiliate WISH would be covering the Beatles' every move over the next thirty-six hours to produce a TV special, *Our Fair Beatles,* beginning with their arrival. Bright TV lights flood the steps of the aircraft as Neil, Derek, and the Fabs emerge. They are interviewed, presumably by local radio reporters (the TV footage is silent) walking across the tarmac to a car. Paul listens to a portable transistor radio as a police motorcade escorts them to rooms 242 and 244 of the Speedway Motel.

RELEASE HISTORY

This silent footage is included in the *Our Fair Beatles* special, which circulates on video.

253. Radio interview **J, R**

Date: 3 September 1964
Location: Speedway Motel, Indianapolis
Interviewer: Art Schreiber
Broadcast: KYW-AM, Cleveland
Length: 5:12

After a sleepless night/morning at the motel, John phoned up KYW's news director, Art Schreiber, who had joined the entourage in New York, and invited him over for a chat. After discussing events in the news, such as civil rights and the Kennedy assassination, off the record, the tape was switched on for more mundane matters.

John recounts the items thrown onstage the previous evening in Philadelphia, including a half-empty milk carton and some cake, which he stepped in. More dangerous were the jelly beans, one of which hit George on his hand and caused him to stop playing, and two of which hit John in the head and chest. Although he stresses they are sick of jelly beans, John pleads for the fans to mail them if they must, rather than flinging them at the group.

Also probably from the same date are a couple of interview segments with Ringo, who says that he manages to avoid the flying debris thanks to his height advantage, except at shows performed in the round. Schreiber wonders if Ringo shakes his head during the show to incite the crowd, but he replies that it's an old habit (George thinks he's trying to shake his brain back into position). Ringo also talks about his desire to be a disc jockey, feeling he could never keep up with the steady stream of chatter American DJs exude.

RELEASE HISTORY

These interviews circulate in excellent quality among collectors.

254. Concert

Date: 3 September 1964
Time: 6:21 p.m.
Location: Indiana State Fair Coliseum, Indianapolis
Broadcast: WIFE-AM, Indianapolis (?)

[A.] intro (1:21)
[B.] **Twist and Shout** (1:20)
[C.] intro (0:03)
[D.] **You Can't Do That** (2:34)
[E.] intro (0:36)
[F.] **All My Loving** (2:03)
[G.] intro (0:16)
[H.] **She Loves You** (2:16)
[I.] intro (0:24)
[J.] **Things We Said Today** (2:13)
[K.] intro (0:05)
[L.] **Roll Over Beethoven** (2:15)
[M.] intro (1:00)
[N.] **Can't Buy Me Love** (2:05)
[O.] intro (0:36)
[P.] **If I Fell** (2:11)
[Q.] intro (0:04)
[R.] **I Want to Hold Your Hand** (2:25)
[S.] intro (0:47)
[T.] **Boys** (2:01)
[U.] intro (0:28)
[V.] **A Hard Day's Night** (2:19)
[W.] intro (0:45)
[X.] **Long Tall Sally** (0:53)

For the second show in a row, the Beatles were taped by a local radio station. This in-line recording sounds similar to the Philadelphia concert, with a slightly better mix but a recurrent tape defect through the last few minutes.

It opens with the introduction from MC Jack Sunday (real name Jerry Baker) and ends halfway through "Long Tall Sally," apparently when the thirty-minute reel ran out. This is the first of two shows, performed in the early evening twilight, which confuses Paul as he greets the crowd: "Good evening—afternoon!"

Our Fair Beatles includes 3:47 of footage from the show, including bits of the first three songs (overdubbed with this show's performance of "She Loves You") and most of "If I Fell" (with natural sound). The Barbre crew captured 6:19 of silent footage, shot partially from behind the stage, and concentrating on fans, police, and a young Coca-Cola vendor. This footage, which includes clips of "Twist and Shout," "All My Loving," "She Loves You," "Things We Said Today," and "If I Fell," also circulates in a version synced to the radio soundtrack.

RELEASE HISTORY

1993: The entire concert surfaced from a very good-quality tape on the bootleg CD *State Fair to Hollywood.* A minor-quality upgrade appeared later that year on the CD *The Ultimate Live Collection, Volume 1,* but this fades out **X** a few words earlier. The *Our Fair Beatles* special circulates on video, as does the silent concert footage from reel 19 of the Barbre Productions collection.

255. Press conference

Date: 3 September 1964
Time: ca. 7:00 p.m.
Location: Radio Building, Indiana State Fair, Indianapolis
Broadcast: 9 September 1964
WISH-TV, Indianapolis
Our Fair Beatles
Length: 13:12

The press conference in Indianapolis was held between shows and filmed for WISH-TV's *Our Fair Beatles* special. It's the usual affair, with some humorous moments. Asked where they stand on the draft, John quips, "About five-eleven." He also declares "Land of Hope and Glory" to be his favorite Lennon/McCartney composition—Paul elects "It's for You." George says he has recently written about three "bits" of songs, but nothing complete, although they sing a bit of his "You Know What to Do."

Asked about favorite groups, they praise the Animals ("nice fellas . . . from Newcastle"), the Detroit sound, and the Beach Boys ("very good harmonies"). Ringo, pressed to choose a favorite color, selects black, and John interjects, "They'll have a riot! Oh, wrong place, Philadelphia that, isn't it?" (in reference to that city's race riots the previous week). Asked about religion, Paul says if anything, he's agnostic; Ringo shoots back with "Are you? You look all right to me."

RELEASE HISTORY

1995: Portions of this recording were released on the CD *The Beatles Tapes III: The 1964 World Tour.* The majority of this press conference (10:51 worth) is included in the *Our Fair Beatles* special, which is traded on video, but some extra material is circulating (audio only, from an unknown vinyl or acetate source).

256. TV interview

Date: 3 September 1964
Time: ca. 7:30 p.m.
Location: Radio Building, Indiana State Fair, Indianapolis
Interviewer: Bill Aylward
Broadcast: 9 September 1964
WISH-TV, Indianapolis
Our Fair Beatles
Length: 4:36

Following the press conference, WISH-TV reporter Bill Aylward interviewed Paul and Ringo about other countries they'd been to (Paul erroneously lists Norway) and their responsibilities toward teenagers, with Paul saying he hates people who preach. George and John also speak briefly, comparing Liverpool districts with Aylward, when John continues his running gag from the day before: "I have an uncle went to Scotland with a bad egg in his pocket and nobody'd sit by him." Aylward wonders who writes his material, and John says, "Ed Sullivan. Couldn't think of anybody else. Sorry, Ed."

RELEASE HISTORY

The entire *Our Fair Beatles* special circulates on video, and a tiny clip of the Paul/Ringo interview is seen in the *Anthology* home video.

257. TV footage

Date: 4 September 1964
Time: 1:00 p.m.
Location: Weir Cook Airport, Indianapolis
Broadcast: 9 September 1964
WISH-TV, Indianapolis
Our Fair Beatles
Length: 1:17

A restless Ringo stayed up after the show until 4 a.m. talking with journalist Chris Hutchins. By 5 a.m., still wide awake, Ringo was able to talk a couple of Indiana state troopers into giving him a tour of Indianapolis and its surroundings, including a stop for breakfast at a roadside diner. Back at the motel, Ringo grabbed a couple of hours sleep before the Beatles moved on to the airport around 1 p.m.

WISH-TV was there to film groups of fans waiting outside the motel and at the airport to see them off, including a party of seven girls in matching outfits that spelled out BEATLES. Paul seems to be the only one interested in shaking hands and signing autographs, hanging back while the others board the plane.

RELEASE HISTORY

This silent footage is included in the *Our Fair Beatles* special, which circulates on video.

258. Newsreel footage

Date: 4 September 1964
Time: 4:30 p.m.
Location: Mitchell Field, Milwaukee
Length: 0:38

As the Beatles flew from Indianapolis to Milwaukee, close to one thousand fans awaited their arrival at Mitchell Field. A local TV crew interviewed some of them, including one teenage boy who admits his admiration for the group, but says he's "not gonna have a spaz attack over it."

Neither he nor any of the fans would be allowed to spaz, when the police and airport officials made an eleventh-hour decision to have the flight land out of sight of the crowd. The news cameras catch sight of the group deplaning and being whisked away, followed by Captain Kondracki's bullhorn announcement to the crowd: "The Beatles are already on their way to the hotel." The astonished crowd wails in despair and rejection.

RELEASE HISTORY

This footage circulates on video from a rebroadcast on WTMJ, channel 4, in Milwaukee.

259. Press conference — P, G, R

Date: 4 September 1964
Time: 5:00 p.m.
Location: Coach House Motor Inn, Milwaukee
Length: 0:17

While John rested in his room with a sore throat, his comrades faced the Milwaukee press, responding to accusations about whose fault the airport vanishing act was. This brief clip consists of a question about their opinion of American fans and Paul's reply (they're the same as European fans, but with a different accent).

RELEASE HISTORY

This footage circulates on video from a rebroadcast on WTMJ, channel 4, in Milwaukee.

260. Radio interview **P**

Date: 4 September 1964
Time: evening
Location: Coach House Motor Inn, Milwaukee
Interviewer: Larry Kane
Broadcast: WFUN-AM, Miami
Length: 3:58

After the press conference, Larry Kane and Art Riley taped an interview with Paul. The police's refusal to let them see their fans at the airport arrival in Milwaukee, and a similar ban already announced for Chicago, are both frowned upon by Paul.

It should be noted that the interviews with Paul and George on *'Round the World* said to be from this date are actually from August 22, 1964, in Vancouver. This probably also applies to Paul's plugs for Cilla Black and Peter and Gordon on that LP (see entry for complete details).

RELEASE HISTORY

1986: This interview was released on the LP *Not a Second Time,* later reissued on CD.

261. Concert

Date: 4 September 1964
Time: 9:08 p.m.
Location: Milwaukee Arena
Length: 0:20

Another night, another concert, another $40,000. A few seconds of the mayhem appeared in a local TV station's coverage.

RELEASE HISTORY

This silent footage circulates on video from a rebroadcast on WTMJ, channel 4, in Milwaukee.

262. Newsreel footage

Date: 5 September 1964
Time: afternoon
Location: Mitchell Field, Milwaukee
Length: 0:12

The Beatles slept in till around noon, and by 2:15 a police escort waited to accompany them back to Mitchell Field. This time, fans would be allowed to wave from a distance, but more disappointment lay just ahead in Chicago.

RELEASE HISTORY

This footage circulates on video from a rebroadcast on WTMJ, channel 4, in Milwaukee.

263. TV/Newsreel footage

Date: 5 September 1964
Time: afternoon and evening
Location: Midway Airport and Stockyards Inn, Chicago
Length: 10:28

Five thousand fans were waiting along with the Barbre crew and local media at Midway Airport in Chicago when the Beatles touched down outside gate 34. Footage from an unknown Chicago TV station's report includes an interview with police captain Francis Dailey, two angles of the group deplaning with Derek

Taylor (John wears sunglasses), and a few words from Paul through the window of their limousine.

The silent Barbre footage follows the Beatles from the plane across the tarmac (mostly the back of Ringo's head) and into a car that trails their entourage to the hotel. Paul holds up a book or magazine with the Beatles on the cover as the cars pull up alongside each other en route. The Barbre crew also waited in the hotel parking lot to ambush the group as they were driven to the concert later that evening. The car almost drives off before Neil can hand Paul his Hofner bass, and he ends up practically shoving it in the back seat.

RELEASE HISTORY

This footage circulates on video from unedited TV rushes and from reel 19 of the Barbre Productions collection.

264. Radio interview J

Date: 5 September 1964
Time: evening
Location: Stockyards Inn, Chicago
Interviewer: Larry Kane
Broadcast: WFUN-AM, Miami
Length: 4:24

Tempers began to wear thin after the Beatles' entourage arrived at Midway Airport this afternoon. They had been scheduled to arrive at O'Hare, but city officials secretly switched locations in an attempt to control crowds of Beatlemaniacs. However, a local PR man leaked the info, infuriating one Colonel Jack Reilly, who worked for the mayor's office, and accused the Beatles' camp of leaking the location in "a cheap publicity stunt." In any case, the whole thing made the papers, radio, and TV, causing a minor disaster.

At their hotel, the Stockyards Inn, Larry Kane recorded this interview with John and Derek Taylor about the situation; they each insist that the Beatles try to go out of their way to see the fans but are often prevented by overzealous security.

RELEASE HISTORY

1986: This interview was released on the LP *Not a Second Time,* later reissued on CD.

265. Press conference

Date: 5 September 1964
Time: evening
Location: Stockyards Inn, Chicago
Length: 9:22

During this press conference, the tension is palpable, with John seeming particularly enraged. A reporter asks about the Chicago skyline, and John says it was good, but much the same as any other. This doesn't satisfy the reporter, who declares it's special, which John dismisses with "everybody likes their own hometown." He insists the airport switch wasn't their fault, but seems reluctant to put all the blame on the police (who, after all, they still needed for protection), claiming, "There's always somebody that does something." Paul complains about how biased a TV news report in Milwaukee the previous night seemed, making it appear that they wanted no part of their fans.

Another reporter innocently asks about some fans' feeling that the group prefers celebrity girlfriends, and John snaps, "It's the first time we've heard it. I mean, are you making it up or did somebody say that?" Someone else asks why they are so popular, and John begins to trot out his standard joke about "if we knew, we'd form another group and be managers," but he can't even bring himself to finish the sentence, sounding completely fed up. Things get even worse as they are asked where they'd like to visit next, and all four road-weary Beatles respond in unison, "Home!" "You mean you don't like the U.S.?" baits the newsman. John's disgusted reply: "No, don't be stupid."

Derek soon senses it's time to end things, but not before issuing his own statement of rebuttal to Jack Reilly. A journalist asks for the name of the person making the statement, and Paul tells him, "Derek Taylor," to which John adds sarcastically, "He's our twenty press officers."

RELEASE HISTORY

1995: Most of this press conference was released on the CD *Inside Interviews: Beatlemania.* The complete footage circulates on video, and a small clip was used in the *Anthology* documentary.

266. Concert

Date: 5 September 1964
Time: 9:20 p.m.
Location: International Amphitheater, Chicago

[A.] intro (0:30)
[B.] Twist and Shout (0:03)
[C.] intro (0:01)
[D.] You Can't Do That (0:05)

Despite all the brouhaha that preceded it, the Chicago concert was a rousing success, apart from Paul being whacked by a flying flashbulb. The show is documented by three separate film sources. The same TV crew who had covered the airport arrival was present to film 1:09 of concert footage with sound. This consists largely of the preshow excitement and the Beatles' arrival and tuning up onstage ("Listen to this crowd roar!"), but includes the dying chord of the first song and opening bars of the second (**A–D**).

The Barbre Productions team shot 3:15 of silent concert footage, including "You Can't Do That," "All My Loving," and "She Loves You." More exciting is the silent but gorgeous 16 mm color home movie shot from right in front of the stage. This lasts 2:43 and includes fragments of "Twist and Shout," "Boys," "A Hard Day's Night," and "Long Tall Sally," complete with Paul's watch-pointing "this next song will have to be our last" announcement.

RELEASE HISTORY

2001: The soundtrack of the TV footage, including **A–D,** was included on the CD-R compilation *Live: Make as Much Noise as You Like!* The TV footage circulates on video, as does the silent footage from reel 19 of the Barbre Productions collection. The home movies were released on the video *Minnesota Mania.*

267. Concert

Date: 6 September 1964
Time: afternoon
Location: Olympia Stadium, Detroit
Broadcast: WKNR-AM, Detroit

[A.] Can't Buy Me Love (0:35)

Just after midnight, a flight from Chicago brought the Beatles to the city that had once vowed to stamp them out. After sleeping in at the Whittier Hotel, they traveled to Olympia Stadium for a pair of concerts. WKNR Radio recorded some of the matinee show, from which a portion of "Can't Buy Me Love," buried under thousands of screams, was broadcast.

In addition, 22 seconds of silent color home movie footage circulates from one of the Detroit concerts, shot from Paul's side of the stage.

RELEASE HISTORY

2001: This fair-quality recording appeared on the CD-R compilation *Live: Make as Much Noise as You Like!* The silent concert footage circulates on video.

268. Press conference

Date: 6 September 1964
Time: evening
Location: Olympia Stadium, Detroit
Broadcast: WKNR-AM, Detroit
Length: 10:41

Between shows, a press conference was held in the Olympia dressing room, and WKNR's recording of the event was broadcast after the Beatles had left town.

Given a chance to praise Detroit music, something they had always done anyway, the group reels off a list of Motown artists: the Miracles, Shirelles, Exciters, Impressions, Tams, Marvin Gaye, Mary Wells, and Major Lance. As far as British groups, current faves include the Rolling Stones, the Animals, and the Searchers. A female reporter, not taking the hint, wonders if they like George Gershwin, Jerome Kern, or Cole Porter and is mocked by a male reporter, who adds the Yankees' first baseman Joe Pepitone to the list.

They continue to campaign against throwing jelly

beans, and Paul reveals that he was nearly skewered once by a flying silver kilt pin. George feels the police should confiscate candy at the gate, and Paul and John opt for streamers and balloons. John denies that he's writing the screenplay for their next film, and he says that he used to paint at art school, "but only 'cause I had to."

A question about Peter and Gordon gives Paul the chance to plug "I Don't Want to See You Again," and he trots out another Sophie Tucker reference when asked who the group's competitors are. Earlier, when asked who influenced their music, John had responded "Nicky Cuff," a rather obscure inside joke (Cuff was a musician whose groups always seemed to beat out the Quarry Men in skiffle competitions). American radio is lauded as superior to British, and they admit to being uninterested in sports. "Smoking's a good sport," offers Paul.

RELEASE HISTORY

This press conference circulates in excellent quality among collectors.

269. Radio interview — P, G, R

Date: 6 September 1964
Time: evening
Location: Olympia Stadium, Detroit
Interviewer: George Hunter
Broadcast: WKNR-AM, Detroit
Length: 3:52

Following the press conference, WKNR's reporter George Hunter briefly interviewed at least three of the Beatles. Paul has abandoned his "Stamp Out Detroit" revenge plot, and he is sure that he and John will continue writing songs together after the group disbands. George wants a career as an independent record producer, while Ringo interestingly feels he has no future as a film actor.

RELEASE HISTORY

These interviews circulate in very good quality among collectors.

269a. Radio interview

Date: 6 September 1964
Time: evening
Location: Olympia Stadium, Detroit
Interviewer: Bill Bonds
Broadcast: WKNR-AM, Detroit
Length: 4:43

WKNR newsman Bill Bonds recorded a follow-up interview with all four Beatles. They list the usual artists when asked who in Detroit has influenced them (the Miracles, Mary Wells, Marvin Gaye), but are more creative when naming their current competition. (George: "Elmer Bernstein!"; John: "Judy Garland!")

RELEASE HISTORY

This interview circulates in good quality among collectors.

270. Newsreel footage

Date: 7 September 1964
Time: 12:30 a.m.
Location: Malton Airport, Toronto
Length: 1:35

After the second show in Detroit, it was back to the airport for a late night flight to Toronto, where they landed at a quarter past midnight and emerged from the plane fifteen minutes later. Newsreel footage shows fans waiting behind a chain-link fence and the Beatles walking to a waiting limousine. Ringo sits up front while the others share the back seat (as usual, John is wearing sunglasses despite the late hour). Paul rolls down the window to talk with journalists before the car speeds off in a police motorcade, bound for the King Edward Hotel.

RELEASE HISTORY

This mostly silent footage circulates on video among collectors.

271. Press conference/Interview

Date: 7 September 1964
Time: 6:30 p.m.
Location: Maple Leaf Gardens, Toronto
Length: 6:43

Between shows at the Maple Leaf Gardens, a press conference was held on and in front of the stage, during which the Beatles met Miss Canada and were presented with a gold record by Capitol of Canada for their LP *Beatlemania! with the Beatles.*

This footage from an unknown source (perhaps a local TV station) includes a bit of the press conference, plus a shot of George playing a drumroll on Ringo's kit as they pose for photos. Most of it consists of an interview conducted on the crowded stage after the general questioning. John says his sore throat is getting better, Ringo talks about their chaotic early-morning entrance at the hotel, Paul praises the first-show audience, and George chats about the origins of the group. The reporter seems concerned that they are prisoners of their own fame, and John mocks him by pretending to interview George: "Pity you don't get out so much and see the bricks."

RELEASE HISTORY

1995: The soundtrack of the interview was released on the CD *The Beatles Tapes III: The 1964 World Tour.* The complete footage circulates on video among collectors.

272. Concert

Date: 7 September 1964
Location: Maple Leaf Gardens, Toronto

[A.] You Can't Do That (0:25)
[B.] intro (0:10)
[C.] All My Loving (1:56)
[D.] intro (0:16)
[E.] She Loves You (1:12)

The Beatles played 4 p.m. and 8 p.m. shows at the Maple Leaf Gardens, and some long-distance footage of one of the shows circulates (with natural but extremely muffled sound), along with scenes of their arrival at the gig in a police van. This may be raw footage shot for the report used on CBC-TV's *This Hour Has Seven Days* (see entry #274).

RELEASE HISTORY

2005: These recordings were included on the CD-R *Can You Hear Me?* The concert footage circulates among collectors on video.

273. Newsreel footage

Date: 8 September 1964
Time: morning
Location: Toronto International Airport
Length: 1:25

Aware of the recent bad press, the Beatles were sure to make themselves available to any fans waiting to see them off at the airport in Toronto. Newsreel footage shows them doing just that, standing on the tarmac with Neil and waving to fans behind a chain-link fence. Although George boards the plane right away (and gives a thumbs-up through the window), the others remain outside to shake the hands of police officers while Paul takes snapshots.

RELEASE HISTORY

This silent footage circulates on video.

274. TV feature

Date: 7–8 September 1964
Location: Toronto
Broadcast: 4 October 1964, 10:00–11:00 p.m.
CBC-TV
This Hour Has Seven Days
Length: 8:52

The Beatles' visit to Toronto was covered in the first edition of CBC-TV's groundbreaking public affairs series, *This Hour Has Seven Days.* In addition to interviews with fans (including some grannies and a Ringo semi-look-alike), the report has clips from the press conference, one of the concerts, and their airport departure.

The concert footage is shot close-up (including a few overhead shots!) and has what seems to be natural sound from the concert (only synced up for a few seconds). Amid the ear-piercing screams, 20 seconds of "All My Loving" and 1:12 of "She Loves You" can barely be made out. The soundtrack also includes a couple of brief interview clips, presumably taped during their stay.

During the press conference, we see the Beatles receiving glass ashtrays and answering a question about setting a bad example by smoking. There's also a shot of the group walking through a corridor (at the hotel or gardens) with police, which was used in the *Anthology* documentary.

RELEASE HISTORY

This show circulates on video in excellent quality from a July 8, 2001, rebroadcast on CBC-TV. The soundtrack is on the CD-R *We'd Like to Carry On.*

274a. Press conference

Date: 8 September 1964
Time: evening
Location: Montreal Forum
Length: 11:32

Following the first show in Montreal, CBC-TV filmed yet another Beatle press conference. The usual topics are covered, including Jane Asher (John: "I'm going out with her"), how much money they earn (George: "We ran out of fingers to count on"), and what they do while cooped up in hotels (George: "Ice skating"). Ringo denies knowing starlets Ann-Margret and Joey Heatherton, and John trots out the only bit of French he knows: *"Je me lève à sept heures."* After the general questioning, John is interviewed separately by a CBC reporter about *In His Own Write.*

RELEASE HISTORY

This footage, along with about a minute of their arrival in Montreal, circulates on video.

275. Radio interviews — P, G, R

Date: 8 September 1964
Time: evening
Location: Montreal Forum
Interviewer: Larry Kane
Broadcast: WFUN-AM, Miami
Length: 23:38

These interviews were taped between the matinee and evening concerts in Montreal. During these shows, security was extra-tight due to a death threat Ringo had received, and he sounds understandably shaken up (he's not sure what day of the week it is) as he chats about audiences, the latest single's sales figures (2.5 million), and his solo escapades in Indianapolis. He also praises the police in Toronto for letting them get near the fans, and he reveals that during their supposed two weeks of posttour vacation they have four days of recording penciled in.

George explains why he uses a twelve-string guitar on some songs, and also praises the Stones, as well as the Animals and the Searchers. He also discusses topics that have all been covered before—his favorite parts of their film, other groups asking for advice, and the Beatles' naturalness. If you listen very closely in the background during George's interview, you can hear John and Paul working on a new composition, "Every Little Thing" (backstage photos from the Montreal Forum show John strumming his new Gibson acoustic guitar).

Paul, sounding extremely tired and out of breath, says he never had any ambitions beyond music and relates the story of an extreme fan in Sydney. Larry asks what Paul looks for in a wife, and John interjects, "Two arms, two legs . . ."

RELEASE HISTORY

1985: The first half of George's interview, misidentified as a recording from Las Vegas, was released on the LP *West Coast Invasion,* later reissued on CD.

1986: The rest of the interviews were released on the LP *Not a Second Time,* later reissued on CD.

276. Concert

Date: 8 September 1964
Time: evening
Location: Montreal Forum

[A.] **intro** (0:16)
[B.] **Twist and Shout** (1:15)
[C.] **intro** (0:01)
[D.] **You Can't Do That** (2:24)
[E.] **intro** (0:33)
[F.] **All My Loving** (1:56)
[G.] **intro** (0:16)
[H.] **She Loves You** (2:07)
[I.] **intro** (0:20)
[J.] **Things We Said Today** (2:04)
[K.] **intro** (0:03)
[L.] **Roll Over Beethoven** (2:05)
[M.] **intro** (1:35)
[N.] **Can't Buy Me Love** (1:58)
[O.] **intro** (0:38)
[P.] **If I Fell** (2:10)
[Q.] **intro** (0:07)
[R.] **Boys** (1:44)
[S.] **intro** (0:39)
[T.] **A Hard Day's Night** (1:35)

This incomplete concert recording surfaced in 2003, proving that even after forty years, there is still Beatles material out there waiting to be discovered. Judging from the ambience and sound balance, it comes from a radio broadcast taped off a speaker. The music and vocals are up front, and crowd noise is at a minimum. Unfortunately, the currently circulating copy also seems to be several generations removed from the original, and it is only in fair quality at best. There is a break in the tape where "I Want to Hold Your Hand" would have been, and the introduction and song that follow are both fragmented. The end of "A Hard Day's Night" and the final song, "Long Tall Sally," are also absent.

Paul greets the audience with a "bonsoir," verifying the location (and making it likely this was the evening show rather than the matinee); John also tosses in a "merci beaucoup." The performance is a bit more energetic than usual, perhaps due to an extra shot of adrenaline in Ringo's system. Throughout the show, his only protection from the death threat was a lone security officer posted beside his drum kit.

Everyone seems to be in a good mood though, interrupting one another's stage announcements with silly banter, including longer than usual "clap your hands" instructions prior to "Can't Buy Me Love." Leading into the "Boys" guitar solo, Paul shouts, "Yeah, go, Ringo!," and after the song, Ringo and John thank each other profusely. John then introduces the title song from the film *"A Hard Day's Night,* starring Glenn Miller and his Brown Orchestra."

Following the concert, the Beatles flew on to Key West for a couple of days' rest originally scheduled for Jacksonville, but relocated due to Hurricane Dora.

RELEASE HISTORY

2003: This concert first appeared in fair quality on the bootleg CD *The Beatles in Montreal,* running about a half step too slow.

277. Press conference/Interview

Date: 11 September 1964
Time: 6:00 p.m.
Location: George Washington Hotel, Jacksonville
Interviewer: Jean Morris
Length: 3:40

The group's suite at the George Washington Hotel in Jacksonville wasn't quite ready when they arrived, so they dined on turkey sandwiches while holding the mandatory press conference, following which local reporter Jean Morris interviewed all four.

The respite seems to have buoyed their spirits, and they joke and quip freely. Someone asks if they have any nicknames for one another, and John says he calls George "Ray Coleman." Paul again refutes the rumor that he's married, to which Morris replies, "And you're available?" "You can get him on H.P.," claims John, who asks if Jean is related to Boris Morris (the title character in one of his poems for *A Spaniard in the Works*).

RELEASE HISTORY

1986: These interviews were released on the LP *Things We Said Today,* later reissued on CD. They also circulate on video, with a bit of extra press conference footage (culminating in a food fight).

278. Press conference

Date: 12 September 1964
Time: afternoon
Location: Madison Room, Hotel Madison, Boston
Length: 11:00

This press conference is another standard affair, with questions about Ringo's tonsils, police protection, their next movie project, and what sports they like. Told there is someone in the building who thinks he's Paul McCartney, Paul says, "As long as he isn't, I don't mind." Another person is said to look like Ringo, who replies, "God help him!" The only question with a local flavor is about Arthur Fiedler, conductor of the Boston Pops, who is said to find Beatles music relaxing; they claim to like his music, as well.

RELEASE HISTORY

This press conference circulates on video from reel 20 of the Barbre Productions collection.

279. Radio interview J

Date: 12 September 1964
Time: afternoon
Location: Madison Room, Hotel Madison, Boston
Interviewer: Larry Kane
Broadcast: WFUN-AM, Miami
Length: 1:32

Following the press conference, Larry Kane taped a brief interview with John, who professes not to mind the various cash-in albums of Beatles music by the Chipmunks and the Boston Pops, since "Paul and I get a lot of money" from the songwriting royalties. He also expresses a preference for indoor concerts, calling the previous night's show in Jacksonville "dreadful."

In addition to high winds, a remnant of the hurricane, Jacksonville had seen a final showdown with the Barbre Productions team. The Beatles and Brian Epstein demanded the camera crew be removed from the stadium. When police refused to intervene, Derek Taylor appealed to the crowd, saying the Beatles wouldn't perform unless something was done. The bluff worked, as the crowd began chanting, "Out! Out! Out!" until the police did their job (George later compared Derek's speech to "Hitler at the Nuremberg rally").

RELEASE HISTORY

1986: This interview was released on the LP *Not a Second Time,* later reissued on CD.

280. Radio interview — P, G, R

Date: 12 September 1964
Time: afternoon
Location: Madison Room, Hotel Madison, Boston
Interviewer: Gary LaPierre, Bob Kennedy
Broadcast: WBZ-AM, Boston
Length: 4:54

While Larry Kane was interviewing John, WBZ Radio's Gary LaPierre was speaking with Paul and Ringo (Kane's interview can be heard in the background of this one) about the overzealous police protection when the Beatles arrived at Hanscom Field early that morning. Paul admits that the police are usually right to whisk them away for safety's sake, but with a mere handful of fans greeting them in Boston, gripes that "it was stupid this morning." Ringo concurs, wishing they'd at least been able to drive past the fans and wave.

LaPierre expresses surprise at Paul's revelation that Bob Dylan is an influence on the Beatles' music (it wouldn't be evident until "I'm a Loser" was released a few months later). Paul adds that he and John have been writing songs together since they were fourteen (a slight exaggeration), admitting that most of their early efforts were below par. Elsewhere, WBZ's Bob Kennedy chats with George about the lack of decent tea in America.

RELEASE HISTORY

These interviews circulate in very good quality from a tape of WBZ's radio coverage.

281. Press conference

Date: 13 September 1964
Time: evening
Location: Baltimore Civic Center
Length: 3:06

Another day, another city, another between-shows press conference. Asked how it feels to be putting on the whole country, George famously responds, "How does it feel to be put on?" John says that groups that don Beatle wigs aren't imitating them, because "we don't wear Beatle wigs." George also reveals that the distinctive sound of his guitar solo on "Till There Was You" was due to nylon strings on a Spanish guitar.

RELEASE HISTORY

1965: These excerpts were released on the LP *1965 Talk Album—Ed Rudy with New U.S. Tour,* unfortunately with Rudy dubbing in the questions himself.

282. Radio interview — J, P, G

Date: 13 September 1964
Time: evening
Location: Baltimore Civic Center
Length: 7:28

Individual interviews were conducted following the press conference; these were done by an unknown reporter and included on the *Ed Rudy* LP. As usual, Rudy dubs in the questions in his own voice, leading to the ludicrous statement "George, your sister, Lucille, is an American citizen." George discusses his girlfriend, Pattie, fear of flying, homesickness, and phoning his parents; Paul talks about fan reaction, the next film, and his girlfriend, Jane; John says he doesn't know when they'll be back to the States because "that's all arranged over our heads."

RELEASE HISTORY

1965: These interviews were released on the LP *1965 Talk Album—Ed Rudy with New U.S. Tour.*

283. Radio interview P, R

Date: 13 September 1964
Time: evening
Location: Baltimore Civic Center
Interviewer: Carroll James
Broadcast: WWDC-AM, Washington, D.C.
Length: 4:20

Concurrent with the interviews in the previous entry (an identical announcement from Derek Taylor can be heard in the background on both sources), Washington DJ Carroll James interviewed both Paul and Ringo. Local fan club member Pam Johnson presents Paul with photos of the birthday party they held for him (complete with 5'11" cake). Paul also says that during their days off in Atlantic City they finished a half-written song and composed a brand-new one, though he won't divulge the titles. Based on other evidence, I'd guess these were "Every Little Thing" and "What You're Doing," respectively. Ringo talks about his rings, his throat, and his first composition ("Don't Pass Me By").

RELEASE HISTORY

1984: These two interviews were released on the mail-order EP *The Carroll James Interview,* although a slightly longer version of Paul's segment circulates.

284. Radio interview J, G

Date: 13 September 1964
Time: evening
Location: Baltimore Civic Center
Interviewer: Jim Stagg
Broadcast: KYW-AM, Cleveland
Length: 7:33

Cleveland disc jockey Jim Stagg shared tour coverage duties with KYW's news director Art Schreiber and was backstage in Baltimore to chat with John and George while the latter practiced on his Rickenbacker twelve-string guitar.

Asked whether radio exposure is easier to obtain in the United States or the UK, John feels the case could be made either way: Although England has only a handful of outlets, if your record gets played on one, it's liable to reach a much greater percentage of your potential audience. John praises the pirate stations for making the BBC scrap some of the soap operas they've had since "they invented radio" in favor of more pop programs. Stagg wonders why Radio Luxembourg DJs only play three-fourths of a song before moving on, and John feels it's a good way to foil home tapers who want to avoid having to buy their own copies.

John and George both offer views on the value of a college education; while John says he had fun at art school, he wouldn't have made it through a serious curriculum. George admits he was lucky, because he'd ignored his schoolwork in favor of practicing guitar, and it happened to pay off. Calling himself a "jack of all trades, master of none," George says he can play something on most string instruments, but wants to further his ability someday by taking guitar lessons.

Calling his own songwriting attitude "lackadaisical" and "defeatist," George reveals that he has a couple of compositions nearly finished (one of which was "You Know What to Do"), but expresses a stronger interest in becoming an independent record producer.

RELEASE HISTORY

These interviews circulate among collectors from a poor-quality off-air recording.

285. Radio interview J, R

Date: 13 September 1964
Time: evening
Location: Baltimore Civic Center
Interviewer: Larry Kane
Broadcast: WFUN-AM, Miami
Length: 16:59

Along with Ed Rudy's reporter, Carroll James, and Jim Stagg, Larry Kane was in Baltimore with his tape recorder as usual, and he talked for several minutes with John and Ringo. Besides guitar, John says he plays only a bit of piano and mouth organ, and that the most unusual gift from a fan was a bra, which "didn't fit." His opinion of Key West? "It was all right, for a swamp." His method to stop war? "I don't think there'll ever be a solution." Kane asks whether policemen bribe them by swapping autographs for protection (and offers to cut this portion from the tape if it's too controversial a topic). John dismissively says there are some lousy cops, but "you get bums everywhere."

Ringo laments that young men shouldn't be sent off to fight war when it's the politicians who have the problems with one another. He also discusses the group's naturalness (a topic that Kane seemed almost obsessed with at this point) and reveals that the train scene in *A Hard Day's Night* with Richard Vernon is based on a real incident that happened during a Beatles tour.

RELEASE HISTORY

1985: Ringo's interview, misidentified as a recording from Milwaukee, was released on the LP *'Round the World,* later reissued on CD.

1986: John's interview was released on the LP *Not a Second Time,* later reissued on CD.

286. Newsreel footage

Date: 14 September 1964
Time: 4:40 p.m.
Location: Greater Pittsburgh Airport
Length: 1:04

Some four thousand people greeted the Beatles' late-afternoon arrival in Pittsburgh, not all of them fans, as this news footage reveals. The reporter describes the scene as the Beatles emerge from the plane: "Here comes Ringo, right off the bat. And you can hear the group behind him . . . You can see things being thrown out over the booth. Tomatoes and all sorts of things. Apparently, there are some unfriendly Beatle fans in the area."

As John holds up a Beatle doll over his shoulder, Ringo makes a few comments while walking across the tarmac: "Looked like tomatoes to me. It's always the same, y'know, you got about two lunatics in a couple of thousand . . . But those—y'know, they always cull all the publicity, the two lunatics."

RELEASE HISTORY

This footage circulates on video among collectors.

287. Press conference/Radio interview

Date: 14 September 1964
Time: 6:00 p.m.
Location: Pittsburgh Civic Arena
Broadcast: 15 September 1964, midnight–6:00 a.m.
KQV-AM, Pittsburgh
The Dex Allen Show
Length: 37:35

The Pittsburgh press conference was held in conference room A of the arena. A lengthy aircheck of radio station KQV's live coverage circulates, from a rebroadcast in the wee hours of the following morning. Unfortunately, the fidelity leaves much to be desired, and the anchor's annoying need to narrate the proceedings ("now they're being asked about their film . . . now George is giving an answer") obscures much of the dialogue.

As still photos are taken, Paul whistles and sings the Zombies' current British hit, "She's Not There." In general, the questioning covers old ground, such as their taste in clothes, the "Ringo for President" campaign and his tonsils, pirate radio, and even that old chestnut, "Who writes the words and who writes the music?"

Commenting on the arena's retractable roof, John says, "I hope you don't lift [it] while we're playing!" Paul's favorite actors include Marlon Brando and Paul Newman, while John stays British and opts for Peter Sellers. Someone asks when "I'll Be Back" will be available in the United States, and John says he doesn't know why Capitol "cut it out" from the album (at that point, it was the only song from the British *A Hard Day's Night* LP not to be released in America).

John mentions Capitol's recording of the Hollywood Bowl concert: "It's lousy, but it's a souvenir." When asked if they plan to make a documentary film of the tour, John alludes to the Barbre Productions film crew that has been following them around the country: "Somebody has been doing it behind our backs, making a fortune, but we're not doing one."

After the general questioning, KQV's Steve Rizen interviews Paul for a couple of minutes, sharing a smoke and a glass of 7UP. With thousands of fans outside straining to get a glimpse of any Beatle activity, reporter Bill Clark implores them over the airwaves not to press against the plate glass windows. TV interviews follow, one of which (with a female reporter) is also picked up by KQV's microphones. Asked what he attributes their popularity to, George replies, "John's left leg."

RELEASE HISTORY

These recordings circulate in fair quality among collectors; 34 seconds of the TV interview appears in very good quality on WABC-TV's *Beatlemania* special.

288. Press conference

Date: 15 September 1964
Location: Sheraton Hotel, Cleveland
Broadcast: WKYC-TV, Cleveland
Length: 10:51

Two separate press conferences were held before the concert in Cleveland. The first, open to all members of the press, covers such fascinating topics as Ringo's rings, their last haircut, the Rolling Stones, and how much money they make. Paul spends most of his time doodling on a piece of paper. When someone asks what foods they miss from England, none of them can come up with a response, except Paul, who mumbles "sausages and mash" without even looking up from his drawing.

RELEASE HISTORY

This footage circulates on video, some of it from a rebroadcast on MSNBC's *Time and Again,* which also included NBC affiliate WKYC-TV's interviews with Brian Epstein and Derek Taylor from this date.

289. TV interview/Press conference

Date: 15 September 1964
Location: Sheraton Hotel, Cleveland
Interviewer: Don Webster
Broadcast: WEWS-TV, Cleveland
Upbeat
Length: 3:44

The second Cleveland press conference was held for the benefit of WHK Radio contest winners and was covered by a local TV station's pop music series, *Upbeat.* Several minutes of raw footage from the *Upbeat* camera circulates, beginning with the Beatles arriving and shaking hands with contest winners. They pose for photos as John tells the police to "put away their autograph books," and then newly hired *Upbeat* host Don Webster talks to John and George. They answer a few questions about jelly beans, their next film, and Hamburg, while John plays with a toy telephone.

RELEASE HISTORY

This footage circulates on video among collectors.

290. Radio interview

Date: 15 September 1964
Time: evening
Location: Public Auditorium, Cleveland
Interviewer: Art Schreiber
Broadcast: KYW-AM, Cleveland
Length: 0:50

Halfway through the Beatles' performance of "All My Loving" in Cleveland, a group of fans ran into the center aisle of Public Auditorium and began a rush toward the stage. Some girls were reportedly thrown to the floor and in immediate danger of being trampled. The police detail, who seemed to have been anticipating the moment, took over immediately. Deputy Carl Bare stepped to the microphone, interrupting the Beatles mid-song to announce, "This show is over!" Amid a hailstorm of boos and catcalls, the disbelieving group reluctantly allowed themselves to be ushered back to their dressing room.

John spotted KYW's Art Schreiber on the way and

invited him backstage to air the group's grievances. Schreiber phoned up the station and relayed this live report:

Art: We're in the—we're in the dressing room. Ringo, what—what happened? What did they say to you when they stopped the show?
Ringo: Well, I—y'know, just a few in the front started to sort of get pushing forward and that, and then the police went potty, and then the chief just ran on and said, "Get offstage." That's all I know.
Paul: And he threw George off.
Ringo: Yeah.
Art: He did what, Paul?
Paul: He threw George offstage. I think, y'know, they haven't got a sense of proportion. I mean, [I'm] sure they must get worse than that at a football crowd or something. Never stop those games.
Art: Well, was it because of something that you had done, some actions, or . . .
John: No, no! Five or six kids were breaking through the front lines, and that happens at every show. but these fellas got off their heads, 'cause they're amateurs, that's why.
Paul: Well, y'know, they think they know what's happening, but they've no idea.
John: We see it every night of the year, they don't. Y'know, and they think they know it all. They're just stupid.
Paul: It was the fella who came on, I don't know who he was—
George: We'd like to see 'em if they had a proper riot!

Obviously the Beatles knew better than anyone when they were in danger and when they weren't, but to be fair, the police had warned the crowd beforehand that if things got out of hand, the concert would be stopped immediately. It took another appeal from Derek Taylor to the fans, who promised not to stand up, to get the show rolling again, but the damage was done. As a result of the incident, Cleveland's mayor banned all rock groups from performing at the Public Auditorium.

RELEASE HISTORY

This interview circulates from a fair-quality rebroadcast on KYW circa February 14, 1965.

291. Radio interview — P

Date: 16 September 1964
Time: afternoon
Location: Congress Inn, New Orleans
Interviewer: Art Schreiber
Broadcast: KYW-AM, Cleveland
Length: 0:57

After a flight from Cleveland and a somewhat harrowing limousine trip from New Orleans's Moisant Field, the Beatles arrived at the Congress Inn after 3 a.m. and did their best to catch up on sleep throughout the morning as fans waited outside.

After an afternoon press conference at the hotel, Art Schreiber taped an interview with Paul, who had seen him struggling to get through the crowd outside earlier. Art relays the rumor among the crowd that the Beatles would be waving to them from the windows, but Paul says that, as usual, the police have advised them against it. Asked if he was frightened by the audience's charge in Cleveland, Paul replies that the large amount of police present made him feel well-protected.

RELEASE HISTORY

This interview circulates in excellent quality among collectors.

292. Concert

Date: 16 September 1964
Time: 9:25 p.m.
Location: City Park Stadium, New Orleans
Broadcast: 16 September 1977
WNOE-AM, New Orleans

Twist and Shout—studio recording w/overdubbed screams
You Can't Do That—studio recording w/overdubbed screams
[A.] intro (0:26)
All My Loving—Hollywood Bowl, August 23, 1964
[B.] intro (0:23)
She Loves You—studio recording w/overdubbed screams
[C.] intro (0:08)
Things We Said Today—Hollywood Bowl, August 23, 1964
Roll Over Beethoven—studio recording w/overdubbed screams
[D.] intro (0:42)
Can't Buy Me Love—studio recording w/overdubbed screams
[E.] intro (0:32)
If I Fell—studio recording w/overdubbed screams
[F.] intro (0:43)
Boys—studio recording w/overdubbed screams
[G.] intro (0:30)
A Hard Day's Night—Hollywood Bowl, August 30, 1965
[H.] intro (0:51)
Long Tall Sally—studio recording w/overdubbed screams

The New Orleans press conference was followed by a backstage meeting with one of the group's heroes, Fats Domino, whose bejeweled watch made quite an impression. Halfway through the Beatles' set that night at an outdoor arena, it was Cleveland revisited. Hundreds of kids broke through barriers and swarmed onto the field, only to be rounded up by mounted policemen like a herd of cattle.

Five minutes of silent footage from the concert exists, but for the most part it's too dark and the stage too distant to observe much of the performance, let alone the mayhem. After Jacksonville, the Barbre camera crew had been effectively banned from the venues and was forced to film the action from outside the grounds. The Beatles are seen arriving; police assist a fan who has collapsed and struggle to keep the crowd behind a rope barrier.

In addition, a recording recently surfaced claiming to be a radio broadcast of the entire concert. It turned out to be a "re-creation" aired on the concert's thirteenth anniversary, using mostly studio versions overdubbed with a screaming crowd loop, plus three songs from the then–newly released *The Beatles at the Hollywood Bowl* LP. Curiously, the spoken introductions (**A–H**) do seem to be from a legitimate tape of the concert itself.

Introducing the 1977 airing, the WNOE DJs play it straight, proclaiming the tape to be a legitimate Beatles concert "from 1965" in New Orleans. Apparently the city is correct, as John and Paul make several references to the chaos on the field, which erupted about halfway through the show. Prior to "Can't Buy Me Love," Paul interrupts himself: "Oh, well. I was gonna say something, but I won't bother." After the song, John comments further: "Thank you, folks! Those of you that are still alive."

In later interviews, they would refer to the "football match" between the rampant fans and mounted police in New Orleans, and this is evident in their final two stage announcements: John's "If you'd stop playing football in the middle of the pitch" (**G**) and Paul's "We'd like to say to everybody here tonight—including the football players—thank you very much for coming along!"

RELEASE HISTORY

The WNOE broadcast, including **A–H,** circulates in very good quality from an off-air recording. Five minutes and one second of silent footage also circulates on video from reel 7 of the Barbre Productions collection.

293. Press conference

Date: 17 September 1964
Time: evening
Location: Hotel Muehlebach, Kansas City
Length: 24:46

September 17 was supposed to be a day of sightseeing in New Orleans. All that changed when Charles O. Finley waved a $150,000 check in front of Brian Epstein, so the Beatles found themselves traveling to Kansas City instead.

The questions posed at the Kansas City press conference were standard, but they did give some inventive answers. When asked for the 414th time what they will do when the bubble bursts, Paul predicts that "John and I will carry on songwriting, and George will go into basketball." He also reveals that they did record an album while in Hollywood, but that it was meant as a souvenir of the concert and never for general release. Asked for their views on religion or politics, John says they're not interested in either.

Someone suggests a movie should be made about their days at the Cavern, but John feels they "couldn't put that kind of thing on the screen. Not yet, anyway." Who is the most exciting woman you've met in the world? John: "Ringo's mother's pretty hot." Photographer Curt Gunther, who had sweet-talked his way into a spot on the tour (and whose excellent photos appear in the book *Beatles '64: A Hard Day's Night in America*), wonders what they think of the press, and they joke, "Good, except for you. We're sick of you."

RELEASE HISTORY

1992: A portion of this press conference was released on a mail-order cassette titled *A Beatles Press Conference: Kansas City, Missouri, September 17, 1964.* The complete recording can be found on the CD *Beatles '64: Goin' to Kansas City.*

294. Radio interview

Date: 17 September 1964
Time: evening
Location: Hotel Muehlebach, Kansas City
Interviewer: Larry Kane
Broadcast: WFUN-AM, Miami
Length: 22:43

Larry Kane, another person they were probably sick of, recorded his final Beatle interviews of the tour at some point this evening. George talks about homesickness, rumors, U.S. radio, and what other instruments he can play (a bit of drums, piano, mandolin, and banjo). One would think that after a month, Kane (who was a reporter, not a DJ) could have come up with some fresh questions.

Paul and Ringo both discuss the New Orleans concert, when mounted policemen struggled to control the audience, while Paul is surprisingly fatalistic (as John had been in previous interviews) about any hope of diverting nuclear war. Kane opines that it's down to man's love for his fellow man, but Paul feels that "no matter how friendly you're gonna be, there's always gonna be someone who isn't." Ringo, while claiming he could do another two weeks in America, sounds worn out as he relates his prefame plans to emigrate to Houston, his feelings on the British monarchy, U.S. radio, and Capitol's promotion of "I Want to Hold Your Hand."

In a separate segment apparently from this same date, Kane informs Paul that on the day they perform in Dallas, presidential candidates Lyndon Johnson and Barry Goldwater will both be appearing at a convention. Making the obvious connection between Dallas and presidents, Paul says, "I've heard a lot about that place. You know what I mean? It should be hectic."

RELEASE HISTORY

1986: Paul's comment about Dallas was released on the LP *Things We Said Today,* later issued on CD.

1987: The other interviews were released on the LP *From Britain . . . with Beat!,* later issued on CD.

2003: Two unique segments (John talking about the New Orleans concert) surfaced on the CD included with Larry Kane's book *Ticket to Ride.*

295. Radio interview J, G

Date: 17 September 1964
Time: evening
Location: Hotel Muehlebach, Kansas City
Broadcast: WHB-AM, Kansas City
Length: 3:12

Following the press conference, a reporter from radio station WHB was able to tape brief interviews with two of the Beatles. George reveals that he drives a Jaguar XKE, but confesses that he doesn't drive it as fast as he'd like to because speeding tickets make for bad headlines. He praises the press conference ("sometimes it's boring, they just sit there and look at us") and says that expenses and British taxes will eat up most of the $150,000 they earn at that night's show.

John says that Cynthia isn't jealous of the group's popularity and has enjoyed watching their career blossom. He also jokes about the "football match" on the field in New Orleans the previous night: "We were announcing, y'know, 'It's a goal for the Beatles! That policeman just scored!' "

RELEASE HISTORY

These interviews circulate in fair quality among collectors.

296. Concert

Date: 17 September 1964
Time: evening
Location: Kansas City Municipal Stadium
Length: 1:10

Promoter Charles Finley ended up taking a bath on the Beatles' Kansas City performance, as only half the seats in Municipal Stadium were filled. Those who attended the show got their money's worth, as the Beatles added "Kansas City/Hey Hey Hey Hey!" to their set list as a special bonus. Otherwise, it was just another gig for the quartet, albeit a $5,000-a-minute gig. A bit of 8 mm color home movie footage of the concert's opening minutes circulates, shot from fairly close to the stage.

RELEASE HISTORY

This silent footage was released on the home video *The Royal Years,* issued by KCPT-TV in Kansas City.

297. Newsreel footage

Date: 18 September 1964
Time: 12:30 a.m.
Location: Love Field and Cabaña Motor Hotel, Dallas
Length: 2:03

The end was in sight as the Beatles arrived in Dallas for the final regular concert of the tour (only a charity show in New York on September 20 would follow). Newsreel footage exists of their predawn arrival and their struggle to get through a crowd to the lobby of their hotel. In addition, four minutes of silent footage is rumored to exist from their concert at the Memorial Auditorium this evening.

RELEASE HISTORY

This footage circulates on video among collectors.

298. TV interview

Date: 18 September 1964
Time: evening
Location: Dallas Memorial Auditorium
Interviewer: Bert Shipp
Broadcast: WFAA-TV, Dallas
Length: 1:50

This local TV interview is mainly of note because they are all wearing cowboy hats. Asked what kind of girls he prefers, John says, "My wife." Asked the same question, George answers, "John's wife."

RELEASE HISTORY

1986: This interview was released on the LP *Things We Said Today,* later issued on CD. It also circulates on video.

299. Press conference

Date: 18 September 1964
Time: 7:30 p.m.
Location: Dallas Memorial Auditorium
Length: 9:05

The Dallas press conference took place backstage before that evening's concert. Told that some girls ate the grass he walked on after their arrival, Ringo hopes they won't get indigestion. Commenting on the "Ringo for President" campaign, he quips, "Gotta watch yourself down here" [i.e., Dallas]. Along similar lines, a reporter wonders if they're ever scared and John says, "More so here, perhaps." A female voice asks George if he's trying to make the black turtleneck sweater his symbol, like Ringo's rings. George, wearing a shirt and tie, deadpans, "Yeah, that's why I'm wearing one now."

RELEASE HISTORY

1986: Six minutes of the press conference were released on the LP *Things We Said Today,* later issued on CD. It also circulates on video, with a further three minutes at the start of the press conference. The extra material mainly consists of posing for photographers and includes Ringo singing a snatch of the yet-unreleased "I'm a Loser."

300. Radio interview P, R

Date: 20 September 1964
Time: afternoon
Location: flight from Missouri to New York City
Interviewer: Art Schreiber
Broadcast: KYW-AM, Cleveland
Length: 2:36

From Dallas, the Beatles flew to Walnut Ridge, Arkansas, where they were met by American Flyers owner Reed Pigman, who had invited them to stay at his ranch in Alton, Missouri, during their final day off in America. Pigman flew them the rest of the way in his private plane, and the group, along with Brian, Neil, Mal, and Derek, spent the nineteenth relaxing, riding horses and go-karts, and posing for a wonderful series of Curt Gunther photographs.

Late the next morning, they returned to Arkansas and met up with their equipment and the rest of the touring party for a flight back to New York. En route, KYW's Art Schreiber taped a couple of messages with two of the travel-weary but accommodating Beatles. The recordings were apparently a special favor for a fan, Margaret Ann Snyder, who had attended their show in Baltimore.

Ringo and Paul both send out greetings to her, and Paul plays along with her belief that he had specifically waved at her during the concert: "I'd recognize her anywhere. She's the girl with the long fair hair, and her father's got a little black pen knife." Schreiber passes along a hello from his wife, Alice, and Paul pretends that he's having a secret affair with her.

RELEASE HISTORY

This interview circulates in excellent quality among collectors.

300a. Newsreel footage

Date: 21 September 1964
Time: morning
Location: Kennedy International Airport, New York City
Length: 2:43

The tour ended on a downer: After a charity show at the Paramount Theater (at which John later complained they were treated "like animals"), Brian and Derek had gotten into an enormous fight over the trivial matter of a limousine. Before retiring for bed, Derek slipped his note of resignation as Beatles press officer under Brian's door. John stayed up all night and ended up having breakfast with Bob Dylan.

Later that morning, the fatigued and battle-scarred party assembled at Kennedy International Airport for one last chance to face the U.S. press before flying back to London. While they waved at fans and signed autographs, the Beatles were filmed answering a few more inane questions shouted out by the assembled press. ("What was the high point?" George: "Sixteen thousand foot in the plane.")

RELEASE HISTORY

This ABC News footage circulates on video among collectors.

301. Radio interview

Date: 21 September 1964
Time: morning
Location: Kennedy International Airport, New York City
Interviewer: Art Schreiber
Broadcast: KYW-AM, Cleveland
Length: 2:59

Art Schreiber's tape captured a few farewell interviews at the airport. Ringo bids Art and his colleague Jim Stagg farewell, while George says they made "a bit" of money on the tour. More interesting is Art's brief chat with Derek, who confirms that he has resigned due to a "personal disagreement between me and Brian Epstein, which has nothing to do with the Beatles, who are still splendid." He chalks it up to show business, and Art wishes him good luck.

Brian would mend fences on the flight back, but was unable to persuade Derek to return to his position. Instead Taylor would move to Los Angeles, where he remained active in the music business and visited with the Beatles whenever one of them passed through. Not until late 1967 would he move back to London and join Apple, remaining there until the group split up in 1970.

RELEASE HISTORY

These interviews circulate in excellent quality among collectors.

302. Newsreel footage

Date: 21 September 1964
Time: 9:35 p.m.
Location: London Airport
Broadcast: 22 September 1964
ITV
Length: 1:08

Four weary-looking Beatles returned to London Airport and, as usual, cameras were waiting to film their deplaning. John wears sunglasses, despite the late hour, and Derek Taylor stands behind his now ex-employers on the stairway watching police deal with a fan on the tarmac.

RELEASE HISTORY

This footage circulates on video and was partially included in *Anthology.*

303. Studio session

Date: 29 September 1964
Time: 7:00–10:45 p.m.
Location: EMI Studio 2
Producer: George Martin

[A.] I Don't Want to Spoil the Party—RM1 (2:32)
Mixed: 26 October 1964

[B.] I Don't Want to Spoil the Party—RS1 (2:33)
Mixed: 4 November 1964

Scarcely a week after returning home, the Fab Four reconvened at EMI Studios to continue recording their fourth LP. Only four songs had been taped so far, and just a handful more were written in the meantime. Sandwiched between four takes of "Every Little Thing" and seven of "What You're Doing," they did manage to complete a single song—John's lovely country-style ballad "I Don't Want to Spoil the Party."

The backing was perfected in nineteen takes, with bass, drums, and acoustic guitar on one track, George's lead guitar on a second, and John and Paul's vocals on a third. For the verses, Paul sings the lower harmony (sounding deceptively like a second Lennon), and on the bridges Paul takes the high part. An overdub on the fourth track added smooth "ooh" backing vocals and tambourine. The mono and stereo mixes are nearly identical, with only slight differences in the level of George's guitar.

RELEASE HISTORY

1964: **A** and **B** were released on mono and stereo pressings of the *Beatles for Sale* LP, respectively. The former is on EMI's CD of that title.

304. Studio session R

Date: 30 September 1964
Location: EMI Studio 2
Producer: Brian Epstein

[A.] America (2:30)

Sometime this day at Abbey Road, probably before the Beatles' afternoon session, Ringo sat in on a session for his former group, Rory Storm and the Hurricanes. In a session produced by Brian Epstein, the group recorded "America," from the musical *West Side Story,* with Ringo playing percussion (clapping is audible toward the end) and perhaps adding to the chorus of backing vocals.

In the dubious tradition of Tony Sheridan's "Sweet Georgia Brown," Stephen Sondheim's original lyrics are scrapped in favor of more topical verses such as "The Beatles went out to America/Played 'Twist and Shout' in America."

RELEASE HISTORY

1964: This recording was released as a UK-only Parlophone single on November 13. It's available on the CD *Rory Storm & the Hurricanes: The Complete Works.*

305. Studio session

Date: 30 September 1964
Time: 2:30–5:30 p.m.
Location: EMI Studio 2
Producer: George Martin

[A.] Every Little Thing—RM1 (1:59)
[B.] Every Little Thing—RS1 (2:02)
Mixed: 27 October 1964

The second day of sessions began with the completion of "Every Little Thing," a song begun by Paul in London and completed with John's help on the recent North American tour. Takes 5 through 9 concentrated on laying down the rhythm tracks: drums, bass, and acoustic guitar on one, and George's twelve-string Rickenbacker on a second.

John and Paul sang a duet on the third track, in unison on the verses and harmonized for the choruses and coda. The remaining track had overdubs of further lead guitar from George, piano from Paul, and booming timpani from Ringo. The stereo mix (**B**) lasts a bit longer in the fade than the mono (**A**), allowing an extra word to be heard.

RELEASE HISTORY

1964: **A** and **B** were released on mono and stereo pressings of the *Beatles for Sale* LP, respectively. The former is on EMI's CD of that title.

306. Studio session

Date: 30 September 1964
Time: 6:30–10:30 p.m.
Location: EMI Studio 2
Producer: George Martin

[A.] What You're Doing—take 11 (stereo) (2:01)
[B.] No Reply—take 1 (mono) (0:40)
[C.] No Reply—take 2 (mono) (2:26)

[D.] No Reply—RM2 (2:13)
Mixed: 16 October 1964

[E.] No Reply—RS1 (2:14)
Mixed: 4 November 1964

[F.] No Reply—RS from take 8 (0:06)

The evening session commenced with five more takes of "What You're Doing," with drums, bass, and rhythm guitar on one track, George's twelve-string on a second, and Paul's main vocal on a third, augmented by slightly rough harmonies from John.

Take 11 (**A**) was chosen as "best" and had its fourth track filled with further vocals (on the bridge) and guitar. This take was ultimately rejected, but is not without its charms, particularly the Byrdsian chiming of George's twelve-string guitar, and an unexpected instrumental break that momentarily raises the key from D to G major.

"No Reply" concluded the session; despite the Beatles' June demo, the number had gone unreleased by NEMS artist Tommy Quickly, so they appropriated it for their own use (it was way too good a song to throw away). Initial takes had drums, bass, acoustic guitar, and piano (the latter played by George Martin) on one track, with John and Paul's vocals on a second.

Take 1 (**B**) is preceded by some chat, with John warning Paul not to slow down, or he'll cut off his drug supply! At this point, John and Paul are singing the verses as a duet, in unison, but John realizes he can't hit the high note on "I saw the light" and they stop. Before take 2 (**C**), John suggests they lower the key from C major to A, but is summarily vetoed. Instead, John takes a low harmony on "I saw the light" and "I nearly died," but it's not enough to salvage the take. Ringo seems lost on the middle eight, and John gets a fit of the giggles, singing "with another plank in my place" and accidentally adding another bridge where the coda should be.

The eighth and final take was chosen as "best" and had further adjustments to the arrangement: John now sings the verses solo, and George Martin's piano is left out for the time being. Overdubs of vocals, handclaps, and piano (the latter on the bridge only) went on the tape's third track, with dramatic cymbal and piano crashes on the fourth. About a minute into the song, one of John's vocals on "in my place" hits the wrong note (it almost sounds as though he's trying to harmonize with himself); this goof was mixed out in mono (**D**) but retained in stereo (**E**).

RELEASE HISTORY

1964: **D** and **E** were released on mono and stereo pressings of the *Beatles for Sale* LP respectively. The former is on EMI's CD of that title.

1995: **C** was released in excellent mono (the booklet claims it's stereo) on the CD *Anthology 1.*

1996: **B** was included in the *Anthology* home video set as part of the "studio outtakes" medley. It's available on the bootleg *Abbey Road Video Show.*

1999: A very good copy of **A** surfaced from engineer John Barrett's personal cassettes. It's booted on the CD *Turn Me On Dead Man: The John Barrett Tapes* and the boxed CD set *Mythology, Vol. 2.*

2003: **F** was released on the soundtrack of the *Anthology* DVD.

307. TV performance

Date: 3 October 1964
Time: afternoon
Location: The Granville Studio, London
Producer: Jack Good
Host: Jimmy O'Neill
Broadcast: (D–K) 7 October 1964, 8:30–9:00 p.m.
ABC (United States)
Shindig

[A.] **intro** (0:06)
[B.] **Kansas City/Hey Hey Hey Hey!—unsweetened** (2:23)
[C.] **outro** (0:12)

[D.] **intro** (0:07)
[E.] **Kansas City/Hey Hey Hey Hey!** (2:23)
[F.] **outro** (0:10)
[G.] **I'm a Loser** (2:19)
[H.] **intro** (0:03)
[I.] **Boys** (2:05)
[J.] **outro** (0:05)
[K.] **closing credits (Swanee River)** (0:36)

The Beatles spent the afternoon at London's Granville Studio videotaping a rare exclusive performance for American TV. Producer Jack Good had been thrilled by the reaction to the *Around the Beatles* special, and he was able to secure the Beatles for the fourth episode of his new ABC series *Shindig,* usually taped in Hollywood but relocated to London for the occasion.

The complete show survives from the original 2-inch videotape. It opens with the Beatles performing "Kansas City/Hey Hey Hey Hey!," followed by a commercial for the American Dairy Association. After performances by the Karl Denver Trio, Lyn Cornell, Tommy Quickly, Sandie Shaw, Sounds Incorporated, and P. J. Proby, host Jimmy O'Neill tells us about who's coming up next week (The Hondells and Manfred Mann), and introduces the Beatles' final set. They play a brand-new song, "I'm a Loser," followed by "Boys," and then join all the day's guests as Karl Denver sings "Swanee River" over the closing credit sequence.

Close examination of the performance shows that while the vocals (and some of John's harmonica) are live, the music is not. Certainly John's harmonica keeps playing after he removes his lips during "I'm a Loser," and George's guitar solo as heard in "Boys" doesn't seem to match what his fingers are playing. The extended intro to "Kansas City" and fade-out on "I'm a Loser" are also suspicious. Exactly when and where the backing tracks were recorded is unknown; it may have been the previous day, during rehearsals at Granville; it may have been at Abbey Road during the September 29 or 30 sessions; it may have been at IBC Studio, where the *Around the Beatles* backing tracks had been taped.

A few years ago, rumors began to circulate that video of the *Shindig* rehearsal might exist. This stirred up hopes that other songs busked between takes, such as "The House of the Rising Sun" (first reported in *Beatles Book Monthly* magazine, November 1964), would finally be heard. What eventually turned up was merely a copy of "Kansas City/Hey Hey Hey Hey!" (**B**) in improved fidelity and lacking an extra layer of applause, which was added in postproduction.

RELEASE HISTORY

1972: **E, G,** and **I** first appeared on the vinyl bootleg *Live in Europe & U.S. TV Casts.* Upgrades were booted on the LP *The Beatles Conquer America* in 1985.

1996: This entire performance was included on the bootleg *In Case You Don't Know . . . ,* taken from the soundtrack of a commonly circulating video. The *Anthology* documentary includes a copy of "Kansas City/Hey Hey Hey Hey!" from a kinescope source, rather than video.

308. Studio session

Date: 6 October 1964
Time: 7:00–10:00 p.m.
Location: EMI Studio 2
Producer: George Martin

[A.] **Eight Days a Week—take 2 (mono)** (0:49)
[B.] **Eight Days a Week—takes 4-5 (mono)** (3:24)

Sessions continued at Abbey Road for a potential single and eventual album track, "Eight Days a Week." In comparing Mark Lewisohn's liner notes for *Anthology 1* to the entry in his book *The Beatles Recording Sessions,* there seems to be some discrepancy about which takes were released. The CD booklet says takes 1, 2, 4, and 5 are included, but what can be heard is a portion of a full take (presumably take 2, although it may be an edit of elements from the first two takes) cross-faded with some dialogue, a false start (take 4) and finally the complete take 5.

Take 2 (**A**) has John and Paul's vocal on track 3 of the tape, beginning with a unique "ooh" introduction. It's accompanied by handclaps, acoustic guitar, and bass, all on track 1. The available recording fades after 49 seconds, but originally lasted a full 2:49, despite some lyrical flubs.

Take 4 (**B**) begins with "ooh" and claps again, but John misses his guitar entrance, and they try again. Take 5 has the "ooh" intro, no clapping, and acoustic guitar entering after one bar; this time, George joins in playing electric rhythm guitar. Apart from a different melody on the title line, the arrangement is otherwise similar to the finished version. Take 13 was the "best" take from this session and was mixed into mono on October 12, but the Beatles worked on the song further on the eighteenth.

RELEASE HISTORY

1995: **A** and **B** were released on the CD *Anthology 1.*

309. Studio session

Date: 8 October 1964
Time: 3:30–5:30 p.m.
Location: EMI Studio 2
Producer: George Martin

[A.] She's a Woman—take 1 (mono w/stereo reverb) (1:18)
[B.] She's a Woman—take 2 (stereo) (3:14)
[C.] She's a Woman—takes 3–4 (stereo) (3:38)
[D.] She's a Woman—take 5 (or 7?) (stereo) (6:19)

This day's session was entirely devoted to finishing off the lyrics to Paul's "She's a Woman," and then recording it for their next single. The basic backing consisted of guitars, drums, and bass on one track, and Paul's lead vocal on a second.

Take 1 (**A**) is played in a rockabilly style, without the syncopated chords of later takes. Take 2 (**B**) is complete, but Ringo has trouble deciding when to switch from hi-hat to ride cymbal, Paul's voice cracks at one point, and the guitars get awfully discordant toward the end. Take 3 (**C**) is a pair of false starts, as George's guitar is out of tune. Take 4 begins with another false start (Ringo doesn't come in cleanly), but before a new take number can be announced, they start the song again for a complete but very sloppy version. Paul gives a Roy Orbison growl as the tape fades out.

The infamous "long jam" outtake (**D**) is usually identified as take 7, because of what George Martin says before it begins: "Take five, is it? Take seven." I think Martin was actually correct the first time, but was confused by all the false starts in the previous two takes. If this was *after* take 6 (the released take, played perfectly), John wouldn't need to remind the others that the middle eight follows the solo, as he does here. In addition, Ringo neglects to go to the ride cymbal on the first bridge. Whichever take this is, it ends with three minutes of jamming and screaming from Paul after the final verse, prompting Ringo's comment, "Well, we've got a song and an instrumental there." Before the tape ends, John also reveals that he had dropped his guitar pick halfway through the take!

RELEASE HISTORY

1983: **A** was used in the *Beatles at Abbey Road* presentation; it appears from this source on the bootleg CDs *Abbey Road Video Show* and *Another Sessions . . . Plus.*

1988: **B** was booted, at the correct speed, on *Ultra Rare Trax, Volume 1.* **D** surfaced on the vinyl bootleg *Ultra Rare Trax, Volume 3 & 4;* it appeared the following year from tape source on the CD *Unsurpassed Masters, Volume 2.*

1991: **B** was included on *Unsurpassed Masters, Volume 6.* Note that this version ends with some dialogue from the beginning of **C** heard nowhere else. (Paul saying, "We can put some . . ." Only the last word of this is audible on *Studio Sessions, 1964*).

1994: **B–D** can all be heard in best quality on *The Ultimate Collection, Volume 3: Studio Sessions, 1964,* although the whole disc is mastered too slow.

310. Studio session

Date: 8 October 1964
Time: 7:00–10:00 p.m.
Location: EMI Studio 2
Producer: George Martin

[A.] She's a Woman—take 6 (3:02)

[B.] She's a Woman—RM1 (3:00)
[C.] She's a Woman—RS1 (3:00)
Mixed: 12 October 1964

[D.] She's a Woman—RM2 (2:59)
Mixed: 21 October 1964

[E.] She's a Woman—unedited RS 1 (3:01)

After a break for dinner, "She's a Woman" was completed by overdubbing on take 6. Paul probably retaped his main vocal on the tape's second track, and George played a guitar solo on the third. The final track was filled with piano, chocalho (shaker percussion), and doubling of both George's lead guitar and Paul's vocal. The raw studio tape of take 6 (**A**) has no echo added and fades a second or two later than any released mix.

Separate mono mixes were made for the U.S. and UK singles. The U.S. mix (**D**) fades out a bit earlier than the UK mix (**B**) and has heavy echo that drowns out much of the piano. The stereo mix has been released with (**E**) and without (**C**) Paul's original count-in.

RELEASE HISTORY

1964: **B** was released on the B-side of the UK "I Feel Fine" single; it's available on the CD single of that title. **D** was released on a U.S. single and all copies of *Beatles '65* (stereo pressings contained a "duophonic" mix).

1967: **C** was finally released on an Australian LP, *Greatest Hits, Volume 2.* It can be found on the CD *Past Masters,* Volume One.

1981: **E** (the same mix as **C,** but with Paul's count-in retained) was released on *The Beatles,* an EP included in EMI's boxed set of EPs. It's also on the CD release of that title.

1995: **A** was bootlegged in excellent quality (but running slow) on the Audifön CD *Anthology.*

311. Newsreel footage

Date: 9 October 1964
Location: Gaumont Cinema, Bradford
Length: 0:58

This was the opening night of the Beatles' twenty-seven-date UK Autumn Tour, and newsreel footage exists of their arrival at the Gaumont Cinema in Bradford.

RELEASE HISTORY

This clip can be seen in documentaries such as *Anthology* and *The Early Beatles.* Both sources also have dressing room footage from somewhere on the tour (possibly this night).

312. Newsreel footage

Date: 14 October 1964
Time: afternoon
Location: Studio Four, Granada TV Centre, Manchester
Length: 3:33

A lip-synced performance of "I Should Have Known Better" was videotaped this afternoon for Granada TV's *Scene at 6:30.* The videotape doesn't seem to have survived, but some silent film of the rehearsals and one complete run-through (shot from inside the control booth) still exists. John wears a harmonica in a brace around his neck (as he had on *Shindig*), and does a bit of silly dancing.

RELEASE HISTORY

This silent footage circulates on video, and a second or two was included in Granada TV's *The Early Beatles* documentary.

313. TV interview

Date: 15 October 1964
Location: unknown hotel, Stockton-on-Tees
Broadcast: 16 October 1964, 6:35–7:00 p.m.
Tyne Tees TV
North-East Newsview
Length: 2:56

A reporter from the local ITV program *North-East Newsview* filmed an interview with the Beatles in their Stockton-on-Tees hotel room; it was broadcast October 16, conflicting directly with the airing of their *Scene at 6:30* appearance noted above. Too bad there were no VCRs at the time! Since this was general election day, the main topic was politics, although none of the group showed any interest in the matter.

They seem most interested with preventing their income and cigarettes from being taxed, and they freely admit that none of them bothered to vote. Even though George gets in a good joke about Liberal Party leader Jo Grimond ("the situation looks pretty Grimond"), their only response about what they want from a new government is Ringo's "more wine!" The interviewer persists, asking whether they've read any of the candidates' speeches, and John says he'll wait for the film.

RELEASE HISTORY

1995: This recording was released on *Rare Photos & Interview CD, Volume 1,* although the circulating video is slightly more complete.

314. Studio session

Date: 18 October 1964
Time: 2:30–11:30 p.m.
Location: EMI Studio 2
Producer: George Martin

[A.] **Kansas City/Hey Hey Hey Hey!—take 2 (stereo)** (2:42)
[B.] **I Feel Fine—take 1 (stereo)** (1:40)
[C.] **I Feel Fine—take 2 (stereo)** (1:31)
[D.] **I Feel Fine—take 5 (stereo)** (2:22)
[E.] **I Feel Fine—take 6 (stereo)** (2:44)
[F.] **I Feel Fine—take 7 announcement and chat (stereo)** (0:14)
[G.] **I Feel Fine—take 8 (stereo)** (0:05)
[H.] **I Feel Fine—take 9 (stereo)** (2:26)

[I.] **I Feel Fine—RM3** (2:20)
[J.] **I Feel Fine—RM4** (2:19)
[K.] **I'll Follow the Sun—RM1** (1:46)
[L.] **Everybody's Trying to Be My Baby—RM1** (2:22)
Mixed: 21 October 1964

[M.] **Rock and Roll Music—RM1** (2:29)
[N.] **Words of Love—RM1** (2:09)
[O.] **Kansas City/Hey Hey Hey Hey!—RM1** (2:27)
[P.] **Kansas City/Hey Hey Hey Hey!—RS1** (2:37)
Mixed: 26 October 1964

[Q.] **Mr. Moonlight—edit of RM1 and RM2** (2:32)
[R.] **Eight Days a Week—edit of RM2 and RM3** (2:41)
[S.] **Eight Days a Week—edit of RS1 and RS2** (2:42)
Mixed: 27 October 1964

[T.] **I'll Follow the Sun—RS1** (1:47)
[U.] **Everybody's Trying to Be My Baby—RS1** (2:23)
[V.] **Rock and Roll Music—RS1** (2:30)
[W.] **Words of Love—RS1** (2:02)
[X.] **Mr. Moonlight—edit of RS1/RS2** (2:38)
[Y.] **I Feel Fine—edit of RS1** (2:17)
Mixed: 4 November 1964

[Z.] **I Feel Fine—unedited RS1** (2:18)
[AA.] **Eight Days a Week—RS from edit of takes 13 and 15** (1:53)
[BB.] **I Feel Fine—RS from take 9** (2:12)
[CC.] **I'll Follow the Sun—RS from take 8** (1:46)
[DD.] **Rock and Roll Music—RS from take 1** (2:28)

The four planned EMI sessions held between the U.S. and UK tours had produced only four of the needed fourteen remaining songs for their LP and single. So this Sunday afternoon session was squeezed into the middle of the tour, and after an industrious nine hours' work, eight more songs were completed.

The first task was taping edit pieces for the intro and outro of "Eight Days a Week." The intro piece went unused (they faded the song in during mixing instead), and the outro edit can be heard in **S** at 2:34 as the stereo picture changes (acoustic guitar moves from center to left, and drums from left to right). There are no major differences between the mono and stereo mixes.

"Kansas City/Hey Hey Hey Hey!" was the next song taped, with drums, bass, and John's guitar on track 1, George's lead guitar on track 2, and Paul's lead vocal on track 3. The first take was good enough to be released, but they tried for a second to be on the safe side. Judging from its release on *Anthology 1* (**A**), they went so far as to add backing vocals and handclaps on track 4 of the second take. These don't appear to be "flown in" and synced up from take 1, because that take also has piano playing on track 4, alongside the vocal overdub. The song's stereo mix (**P**) is 10 seconds longer during the fade-out than the mono (**O**).

"Mr. Moonlight" was then remade, with takes 5 through 8 having the rhythm on track 1 (bass, guitars, and conga) and John's main vocal on track 3. To the last and "best" take, backing vocals were added on track 4, with Paul's Hammond organ and emphasized "thumps" placed on track 2. John's opening vocal scream from the August 14 "best" (take 4) was edited onto the front of take 8 to produce the final master. The stereo mix (**X**) has an extra-long fade compared to its mono counterpart (**Q**).

A good portion of time was spent on what was now the leading single A-side contender, John's "I Feel Fine." Bass and drums went on track 1 of the tape, electric guitars on track 2, and John's guide vocal on track 3. Take 1 (**B**) is actually performed in the key of A, but breaks down following the guitar solo. John asks George Martin, "Did it sound too strange singing—" just as the tape cuts off, so perhaps vocals are the reason subsequent takes are played in the key of G.

Take 2 (**C**) runs smoothly until the guitar solo, when George's squeaky guitar strings are mistaken by John for a whistled signal from the control booth to stop playing. Take 5 (**D**) is preceded by Paul telling John not to let the opening guitar feedback last so long. The performance is complete, but ends with Paul's judgment: "Scrappy."

For take 6 (**E**), John has decided not to sing anymore and dub the vocals on later. The tape catches George practicing his "She's a Woman" guitar solo just before this complete instrumental take. The raw studio tape heard on bootleg includes some chat (**F**) preceding take 7, as George plays a riff from "Tequila." Take 7, a false start, has yet to be booted, and take 8 (**G**), another false start caused by a crackling guitar lead, appears only on the radio documentary *Sgt. Pepper's Lonely Hearts Club Band,* buried under dialogue.

That documentary also included the raw studio tape of take 9 (**H**), with overdubs and no fade. This also appears on the bootlegged session tape, directly following **F.** Overdubs consisted of vocals and a guitar solo on track 3, both of which were then doubled on track 4.

Four variations of "I Feel Fine" were released. The stereo mix (**Z**) on UK vinyl copies of *The Beatles 1962–1966* has a whispered "'s low enough" just before the song starts, which was trimmed from the common stereo mix (**Y**). The stereo mix has almost no echo, while the UK mono mix (**I**) has some, mostly on the vocal; it also lasts a couple of seconds longer than any other released mix. The U.S. mono mix (**J**) is absolutely drenched in echo.

Following a dinner break, four more songs were taped for *Beatles for Sale.* The backing for "I'll Follow the Sun" has acoustic guitar and percussion on track 1, with electric rhythm guitar on track 2 and vocals on track 3. John and Paul sing a duet, in unison on the verses (although it sounds like Paul double-tracked, it's not) and harmonizing on the bridges; Paul sings the refrains by himself. On the eighth and "best" take, George added a brief guitar solo to track 4 of the tape. There is little difference between the mono (**K**) and stereo (**T**) mixes.

Next up was a cover of Carl Perkins' "Everybody's Trying to Be My Baby," recorded in a single take with drums, bass, and rhythm guitar on track 1, George's lead guitar on track 2, and his main vocal on track 3, complete with live tape echo. The sole overdub was of tambourine and George's second vocal on track 4. Even more echo was added during mono mixing (**L**); as the U.S. mono mixes of "I Feel Fine" and "She's a Woman" (both mixed the same day, October 21) also have this extra layer of echo, maybe we should let Capitol and Dave Dexter Jr. off the hook a little and place the blame on Messrs. Martin and Smith!

Continuing with the string of classics by their rock heroes, Chuck Berry's "Rock and Roll Music" followed, another "one-take wonder," this time with drums and bass on one track, both guitars on a second, and John's tape-delayed solo vocal on a third. To fill the fourth track, John, Paul, and George Martin all simultaneously pounded the keys of the studio Steinway in an attempt to duplicate Johnnie Johnson's original piano part. In stereo (**V**), the piano track is mixed out from 1:47–1:53, perhaps to cover for a goof. It then moves from center to left during the "tango" verse.

The session concluded with John and Paul duetting on Buddy Holly's "Words of Love." The first three tracks were laid down in the same fashion as "Rock and Roll Music" (drums/bass; guitars; main vocal). For the fourth track, John and Paul doubled their vocals while adding some gentle Holly-styled clapping, and George doubled his lead guitar part. The mono mix of "Words of Love" (**N**) lasts several seconds longer during the fade than the stereo (**W**).

RELEASE HISTORY

1964: **K–O, Q,** and **R** were released on mono pressings of the *Beatles for Sale* LP and are available on EMI's CD of that title. **P** and **S–X** were released on stereo pressings of *Beatles for Sale.* **I** and **J** were released on singles in the UK and United States respectively; the former is on a CD single.

1966: **Y** was released on *A Collection of Beatles Oldies;* it's also on the CD *Past Masters, Volume 1.*

1973: **Z** was included on British copies of *The Beatles 1962–1966.*

1984: **G** and **H** were included in the radio documentary *Sgt. Pepper's Lonely Hearts Club Band: A History of the Beatle Years 1962–1970.* They appear from this source on the CD-R compilation *Vinyl to the Core.*

1988: **E, F,** and **H** surfaced on the vinyl bootleg *Ultra Rare Trax, Volume 3 & 4;* they appeared the following year from a tape source, but with reversed channels and running too slow, on the CD *Unsurpassed Masters, Volume 2.*

1991: **D** was included, slightly incomplete, on *Unsurpassed Masters, Volume 7.*

1994: **B–F** and **H** can all be heard in best quality on *The Ultimate Collection, Volume 3: Studio Sessions, 1964,* although the whole disc is mastered too slow.

1995: **A** was released on *Anthology 1.*

2003: **AA–DD** were released on the soundtrack of the *Anthology* DVD.

315. TV interview

Date: 20 October 1964
Location: Caird Hall, Dundee
Interviewer: June Shields
Broadcast: 23 October 1964, 6:10–6:45 p.m.
Grampian Television
Grampian Week
Length: 0:34

The Beatles filmed an interview with reporter June Shields backstage prior to their concert at Caird Hall in Dundee, Scotland. Wrapped in a heavy coat and thick scarf, John sings a "traditional Gaelic air," but then admits, "I just made it up on the spurt."

RELEASE HISTORY

This footage circulates on video among collectors from a recent rebroadcast.

315a. Concert

Date: 20 October 1964
Location: Caird Hall, Dundee
Length: 4:06

About four minutes of silent footage exists of the Dundee concert, perhaps shot by the Grampian TV crew (it's certainly not a home movie, as some shots are taken from the floor, others from the balcony). This is easily the best visual document of a UK Beatles package tour, as it includes short clips from all the opening acts (the Rustiks, Michael Haslam, Sounds Incorporated, Mary Wells, and Tommy Quickly). MC Bob Bain introduces the Beatles, who are seen performing "Twist and Shout," "Money (That's What I Want)," "Can't Buy Me Love," "Things We Said Today," "If I Fell," and "I Wanna Be Your Man."

RELEASE HISTORY

This silent footage circulates on video among collectors.

316. Studio session

Date: 26 October 1964
Time: 4:30–6:30 p.m.
Location: EMI Studio 2
Producer: George Martin

[A.] Honey Don't—RM1 (2:54)
[B.] Honey Don't—RS1 (2:57)
Mixed: 27 October 1964

The final two songs for *Beatles for Sale,* as well as the second annual Beatles Fan Club Christmas disc, were taped at Abbey Road during another hypothetical day off from the tour.

Ringo had yet to record a lead vocal for the new album, so Carl Perkins' "Honey Don't," traditionally sung by John (as recently as May 1 on the BBC), was handed over to the drummer, who had done so well with Carl's "Matchbox." The backing of bass and drums on one track, John's acoustic and George's electric guitars on a second, and Ringo's lead vocal on a third, was completed in five takes. Tambourine was then added to the last and "best" take, completing the song. Apart from the length, there are no notable differences between the mono and stereo mixes.

RELEASE HISTORY

1964: **A** and **B** were released on mono and stereo pressings, respectively, of the *Beatles for Sale* LP. The former is on EMI's CD of that title.

317. Studio session

Date: 26 October 1964
Time: 7:30–10:00 p.m.
Location: EMI Studio 2
Producer: George Martin

[A.] What You're Doing—unknown take (stereo) (0:19)
[B.] Christmas Message—take 1 (Hello Dolly) (mono) (1:10)
[C.] Speech—take 1 (mono) (3:16)
[D.] Speech—take 2 (mono) (3:26)
[E.] Speech—takes 3 + 4 (mono) (0:48)
[F.] Another Beatles Christmas Record (mono) (4:00)

[G.] What You're Doing—RM1 (2:29)
[H.] What You're Doing—RS1 (2:30)
Mixed: 27 October 1964

[I.] What You're Doing—RS from take 19 (0:36)

After an hour-long dinner break, the Beatles tackled "What You're Doing," using a somewhat less raucous arrangement than the previous month. The basic tracks were similar to "Honey Don't," with drums and bass on one track, acoustic and electric guitars on a second, and Paul's lead vocal on a third. A brief outtake (**A**) from the end of one performance (probably take 13, 16, or 19, the only complete ones) was included during the studio medley on the *Anthology* video. Paul asks George Martin, "What did it sound like with the bass doing a funny thing," presumably referring to his brief bass solo just before the coda. Martin replies regally, "It sounded rather magnificent."

Take 19 had various overdubs added to the fourth track: Paul's second lead, backed by John and George (with several lyrical clashes compared to the main vocal track), plus piano and lead guitar for the solo and coda. The mono (**G**) and stereo (**H**) mixes have slight differences in the level of the percussion tracks.

The Beatles' last Abbey Road recording of 1964 was a special message for their fan club members. Press officer Tony Barrow had again written a script, but they didn't exactly stick to it, with John in particular making a mockery of his lines (reading out page numbers and dialogue cues). Five takes, including one of marching feet, were needed to produce a usable recording.

The proceedings begin with a loose rendition (**B**) of "Hello Dolly" (John on harmonica, Paul on piano, and George on kazoo), which mutates into "Jingle Bells" near the end. Take 1 of the speech (**C**) follows, but doesn't get too far beyond Paul reading his portion stiltedly and complaining, "Go on, let's think of something." George Martin keeps the tape rolling as each Beatle dutifully reads his part, throwing in a joke here and there, but sounding rather listless.

The second take (**D**) is even more lackluster, although a rendition of "The Twelve Days of Christmas," Beatle-style, livens things up toward the end. ("One plastic bag, two Ringos, two tins of beans, and a Chrimble in a pear tree!") As they prepare for another take, George jokingly makes his true feelings known: "And I'd just like to say, we hate yer all, ya little scruffs!" Take 3 (**E**) is a false start, but Paul doesn't appreciate being interrupted. ("Sod off! I'm getting all sincere!")

The final edit (**F**) begins with marching feet and another rendition of "Jingle Bells." Paul thanks the fans for buying Beatles records and hopes they've enjoyed listening "as much as we've enjoyed melting them." John thanks everyone who bought his book and reveals that there will be "another one out pretty soon, it says here." George talks about their upcoming film, while Ringo, with mock-sincerity, thanks people "just for being fans." Paul leads a singalong of "Can You Wash Your Father's Shirt," and the Fabs march off into the new year shouting, "Happy Christmas!"

RELEASE HISTORY

1964: **G** and **H** were released on mono and stereo pressings, respectively, of the *Beatles for Sale* LP. The former is on EMI's CD of that title. **F** was released on a flexi-disc, titled *Another Beatles Christmas Record,* mailed out to fan club members on December 18.

1984: Portions of **C** and **D** were included in the radio documentary *Sgt. Pepper's Lonely Hearts Club Band: A History of the Beatle Years 1962–1970.*

1994: The bootleg CD *The Complete Christmas Collection* contained **B** and **C,** along with a very clean copy of **F.**

1995: **A** was included in the *Anthology* documentary in mono; it's available on the bootleg CD *Abbey Road Video Show.* A stereo mix appears on the *Anthology* DVD.

2002: The CD boot *The Seven Years of Christmas* included the first complete releases of **D** and **E,** along with **B, C,** and **F,** all in excellent quality. This CD also contains an alternate edit of **F,** which seems to be a work tape used in preparation of the 1983 multimedia presentation *The Beatles at Abbey Road* (the portion used in that show has been sliced out and reinserted in the wrong place).

317a. Interview

Date: 29 October, 1964
Location: ABC Cinema, Plymouth
Interviewer: Michael Rinehold
Length: 3:12

As they arrived at the ABC Plymouth in the midst of their UK tour, the Beatles held an informal press reception. A few minutes of footage was shot by a local BBC crew, with each Beatle being interviewed on camera individually. Paul says he isn't worried by the prospect of Beatlemania waning, Ringo explains that they got lost on the way to Exeter the previous night, and George claims he wants to be a fire-engine driver. Reporter Michael Rinehold asks John and Ringo if they voted in the recent election, and Ringo says they were too busy touring. "Tory?" replies a confused Rinehold.

RELEASE HISTORY

This footage circulates on video among collectors from recent rebroadcasts.

318. TV interview

Date: 31 October 1964
Location: Ipswitch
Interviewer: John McGregor
Broadcast: Anglia-TV
Length: 1:27

Anglia-TV reporter John McGregor was dispatched to film an interview with the Beatles prior to their concert at the Gaumont Cinema in Ipswitch (it may have actually been filmed in their hotel suite).

McGregor starts by asking where the Beatles got their name, and the most they will reveal is that "John thought of it." John denies yet again the rumor that he's leaving the group, and Paul demands to see the *News of the Beatles* paper where the reporter got this dubious info. McGregor happily obliges by producing the flimsy tabloid from his breast pocket, and while Paul munches an apple and peruses the article, the reporter asks Ringo if that's his real name. Nothing like doing your research!

Ringo explains how he got his nickname and shows off his rings for the camera. McGregor turns to John to ask another question, but John holds up his bare hands and interjects, "I'm not called Ringo." Paul follows quickly with "He's called Hando."

RELEASE HISTORY

The clip was broadcast back in 1964 and then went unseen for nearly thirty years, when the local station unearthed it. Thanks to a rebroadcast on July 21, 1993, it is now in circulation among video traders.

319. TV performance

Date: 14 November 1964
Time: 1:00–5:00 p.m.
Location: Teddington Studio Centre, Teddington
Producer: Philip Jones
Host: Brian Matthew
Broadcast: 21 November 1964, 5:50–6:35 p.m.
ABC
Lucky Stars Special

[A.] **I Feel Fine** (2:22)
[B.] **She's a Woman** (3:03)
[C.] **I'm a Loser** (2:26)
[D.] **Rock and Roll Music** (2:32)

This Saturday afternoon was spent in Teddington Studio Centre videotaping an appearance on *Thank Your Lucky Stars,* retitled *Lucky Stars Special* for the occasion. The show opened with a brief skit starring Ringo and host Brian Matthew and originally included at least one more brief skit featuring the group. The Beatles also lip-synced four songs from their new single and LP. John played his Gibson semiacoustic throughout, George an electric Gretsch, and Paul his Hofner bass.

The backdrop consists of the word BEATLES spelled out in lights, and after "I Feel Fine," the stage lighting is dimmed briefly as the group takes a bow. During the final verse of "She's a Woman," after Paul lip-syncs, "She's no peasant," John repeats the line (probably out loud), causing Paul to crack up.

The lights dim again as John quickly dons a mouth organ for "I'm a Loser," and they remain dimmed throughout the song. John takes the opportunity to act out the lyrics, following "clown" with a broad grin and "frown" with a grimace. After a break in the tape, a close-up of John's Gibson leads into the final song, "Rock and Roll Music." Various close-ups of the Beatles' instruments during this song make a mockery of their attempted miming: George changes chords at the wrong time, and Paul twiddles his fingers furiously as if playing a frantic bass solo rather than the simple riff that can be heard.

RELEASE HISTORY

B first surfaced in the mid-1980s on a bootleg video compilation, *Private Reel,* which consisted of various video transfers from Ringo's private collection. This fact, plus Mark Lewisohn's written description of the Beatles skits that have yet to surface, points to the existence of the complete program, so hopefully the whole thing will be released someday. A copy of the entire musical portion of this show now circulates among video collectors. The circulating tape appears to be the raw video of all four (lip-synced) songs, with no audience applause added yet (there was none present at the taping).

1996: The latter part of the opening skit was included on the *Anthology* video. (Matthew's comment: "Funny chaps—who are they? Well, maybe I'll find out as the show goes on.") That tape also includes **A,** although it's intercut with other footage.

320. Radio interview R

Date: 17 November 1964
Time: 7:30–11:30 p.m.
Location: Playhouse Theatre, London (via telephone)
Interviewer: Murray Kaufman
Broadcast: WINS-AM, New York
Length: 4:42

At some point during the taping of a new *Top Gear* appearance, perhaps while the others chatted with Brian Matthew or set up equipment, Ringo accepted a phone call from Murray the K in New York.

The recording opens in mid-conversation with talk of Ringo's tonsils. Murray praises the Maysles Films' *What's Happening!* documentary, which had been broadcast in the United States November 13. Ringo says he's seen only part of it (Granada TV had shown footage of only the trip's first few days). He also seems baffled that the "I Feel Fine" single is already being broadcast in the United States, as he hasn't even gotten a copy yet (the U.S. release date was November 23, but the song was on New York radio charts as early as November 10).

The *Around the Beatles* special had also been recently aired on U.S. TV (on November 15), and Murray complains that all his contributions were excised from the broadcast. "You don't go in America," jokes Ringo. Murray asks about their second film, but Ringo is reluctant to divulge the plot, saying that it could change. After wishing the American listeners well, Ringo departs to rejoin the others in the BBC studio.

RELEASE HISTORY

This interview circulates in fair quality among collectors.

321. Radio performance

Date: 17 November 1964
Time: 7:30–11:30 p.m.
Location: Playhouse Theatre, London
Producer: Bernie Andrews
Host: Brian Matthew
Broadcast: (**D–O** only) 26 November 1964, 10:00 p.m.–midnight
BBC Light Programme
Top Gear #20

[A.] **studio chat/I Feel Fine—false start** (0:48)
[B.] **I Feel Fine—single-tracked vocal** (1:05)
[C.] **studio chat** (0:40)

[D.] **intro** (0:02)
[E.] **I'm a Loser** (2:36)
[F.] **intro** (3:07)
[G.] **Honey Don't** (2:52)
[H.] **outro** (0:03)
[I.] **She's a Woman** (3:13)
[J.] **intro** (0:34)
[K.] **Everybody's Trying to Be My Baby** (2:22)
[L.] **outro** (0:02)
[M.] **I'll Follow the Sun** (1:49)
[N.] **intro** (2:41)
[O.] **I Feel Fine** (2:13)
[P.] **outro** (0:04)

In addition to posing for photos with host Brian Matthew and taking long-distance calls from Murray the K, the Beatles spent most of the evening taping several songs and chat for at least one BBC Radio show. The bulk of the material was used in *Top Gear,* and four of the songs would be recycled for *Saturday Club.* In addition, chat and songs from both shows were reedited and compiled on a 1965 Transcription disc for the overseas program *Top of the Pops.* Any material from these shows in excellent sound quality comes from this Transcription disc, although the original 1964 broadcasts do exist from decent-quality home tapes (with plenty of interference).

A 10-inch thirty-minute studio reel (marked "2 of 2") from the music session was discovered in 1988, and bits and pieces of it have been aired. **A** has producer Bernie Andrews and balance engineer Bev Phillips asking for another run-through of "I Feel Fine" to set levels; the Beatles comply but John botches the intro riff. **B** is the completed take prior to overdubbing of John's second lead vocal track; unfortunately, only a minute or so has been broadcast. In **C,** producer Bernie Andrews asks if they want to hear a playback of "I Feel Fine"; Paul thinks they should listen in the control booth, as it has a superior speaker, but John feels if it sounds okay on the crappy studio speaker, they'll know it's all right. This is followed by some chat that preceded a take of "She's a Woman" (complete with shaker percussion).

The show opens with a nice version of "I'm a Loser," with John playing acoustic guitar and harmonica. The chat that follows (**F**) has some unflattering references to America excised on the *Top of the Pops* disc. Conversely, two lines of dialogue that were excised from *Top Gear* are reinstated on *Top of the Pops.* (John: "So she has, she's got that all right." Brian: "Funny habits, you people.") The rambling discussion touches on the trials and hardships of being a Beatle, the number of cover versions on their new LP, and Paul's assertion that "it's a bit of a drag" when Capitol pulls singles from an album.

The version of "Honey Don't" on *Top of the Pops* is truncated to remove the final solo and chorus, but the full version can be found on the off-air tape. George talks about his sore throat (**J**) and says "even though it is conceited," he didn't write "Everybody's Trying to Be My Baby." Matthew praises "She's a Woman," calling it "better than the A-side," but John disagrees: "We had to finish it off rather quickly, and that's why they're such rubbishy lyrics." Ringo talks about a black opal ring he'd received in Australia, and George says he's not ready to get married. The show concludes with a plug for their upcoming Christmas stage show at the Hammersmith Odeon, followed by "I Feel Fine."

RELEASE HISTORY

1972: The BBC Radio documentary series *The Beatles Story* included incomplete versions of **F, J, K,** and **N,** all from *Top of the Pops.*

1978: The bootleg LP *December 1963* included **K** and **M** in fair quality and overdubbed with screaming to simulate an audience concert recording.

1980: **E, I, K, M,** and **O** were included in excellent quality on the bootleg LP *Broadcasts.*

1982: The radio special *Beatles at the Beeb* included **E, I, K, M,** and **O,** plus incomplete versions of **F, G,** and **N,** all from *Top of the Pops.*

1988: The bootleg LP *Beatles at the Beeb, Volume 12* included a good-quality off-air tape of nearly the entire original broadcast (**E–P**). Note that this omits the bit of **F** exclusive to the *Top of the Pops* edit. The same year, the series *The Beeb's Lost Beatle Tapes,* in addition to many of the *Top of the Pops* segments, broadcast **A, B,** and a portion of **C.**

1993: Great Dane's *The Complete BBC Sessions* boxed set contained **E–P,** assembled from various sources, but **F** and **G** were both incomplete; **A** and a portion of **C** were also included.

1994: Apple's *Live at the BBC* CD included **E, I, K, O,** and an incomplete version of **F,** all from *Top of the Pops.*

1995: **M** was released on the "Baby It's You" CD single.

1997: **A** and a complete version of **C** were broadcast on part two of the BBC Radio special *The Beatles at the BBC* on New Year's Day. They appear from this source on the bootleg CD *The Beatles Broadcast Collection, Trailer 1.*

1998: The CD-R *Attack of the Filler Beebs!, Episode 2* included **A, B,** and **F–H,** edited together from the off-air broadcast and *Top of the Pops* sources.

2003: The entire show, including the debut of **D,** was bootlegged on the CD boxed set *The Beatles at the Beeb.*

322. TV performance — J

Date: 20 November 1964
Time: morning
Location: Wimbledon Common, London
Producer: Joe McGrath
Host: Dudley Moore
Broadcast: 9 January 1965, 9:20–10:00 p.m.
BBC2
Not Only . . . But Also . . .
Length: 2:26

Dudley Moore and Peter Cook were able to acquire the biggest draw in British entertainment—a Beatle—for the premiere episode of their sketch/variety series, *Not Only . . . But Also . . .* Although he was no longer actively promoting his eight-month-old book, John agreed to participate by reading several poems from *In His Own Write.*

The first task was a location shoot on Wimbledon Common this morning; the fanciful footage would be aired while Moore read John's poem "Deaf Ted, Danoota (and me)." The finished clip is similar in tone to the "field" sequence of *A Hard Day's Night,* and fittingly, Norman Rossington, one of the movie's costars, joined John and Dudley in a romp across the grass, as they danced in circles, held balloons, and pushed one another in a swing. The vignette also owes a lot to *The Running Jumping and Standing Still Film,* a Peter Sellers–Spike Milligan short directed by Richard Lester.

The footage is mostly silent, with incidental music and the recited poem heard over the soundtrack, but the final line, "Sometimes we bring our friend Malcolm," was spoken on location by the trio; the film then cuts to a shot of their pal, with MALCOLM written across his forehead.

RELEASE HISTORY

See the November 29 entry for details.

323. TV performance

Date: 23 November 1964
Time: afternoon
Location: Wembley Studios, Wembley
Producer: Vicki Wickham
Host: Keith Fordyce
Interviewer: Cathy McGowan
Broadcast: 27 November 1964, 6:08–7:00 p.m.
Rediffusion-TV
Ready, Steady, Go!

[A.] **chat** (1:33)
[B.] **chat w/Paul** (0:48)
[C.] **I Feel Fine** (2:12)
[D.] **chat w/John and Ringo** (1:28)
[E.] **She's a Woman** (2:54)
[F.] **intro** (0:18)
[G.] **Baby's in Black** (2:02)
[H.] **chat** (1:40)
[H.] **Kansas City/Hey Hey Hey Hey!** (2:21)
[I.] **outro** (0:11)

This was the Beatles' final group performance for *Ready, Steady, Go!* All four songs are lip-synced, although the audience can be heard clapping and singing along throughout. Director Michael Lindsay-Hogg also makes brief use of a split-screen showing Paul and Ringo during "She's a Woman." That and the waltzing couples during "Baby's in Black" are about the only visual highlights of the show.

There are also several interviews between songs, largely obscured by the screaming audience swarming around the stage. Keith Fordyce chats with all four at some length, wondering if the Mersey sound is dead. John guesses that the American sound will be the next craze, but as long as people still like the Beatles, he doesn't care.

Cathy McGowan asks Paul what he does with his money, and he says he has bought a house in the middle of a swamp. He admits that he doesn't do all his own housework, but he "make[s] good gravy." Ringo says his songwriting technique is to hum a tune to himself and let the others work out the chords on a guitar. He also reveals that he will be having his tonsils removed the following week, but implores people not to phone him about it!

George discusses the problems of being recognized in public, but John feels their lives are "fabgearfaveravepic." Finally, Paul talks of upcoming plans: the Christmas show and then a holiday during which they need to write at least six songs for their next film. After their final song, the Beatles escape over a flight of stairs at the back of the stage.

RELEASE HISTORY

A basically complete copy of this appearance was released only in Japan on the laserdisc *Ready, Steady, Go!—The Beatles,* although it is interspersed in segments throughout the disc.

324. Radio performance

Date: 25 November 1964
Time: 7:00–10:30 p.m.
Location: Studio 2, Aeolian Hall, London
Producers: Jimmy Grant, Brian Willey
Host: Brian Matthew
Broadcast: 26 December 1964, 10:00 a.m.–noon
BBC Light Programme
Saturday Club #325

[A.] **intro** (0:05)
[B.] **Rock and Roll Music** (2:01)
[C.] **intro** (1:39)
I'm a Loser (rebroadcast of version D from *Top Gear* #20)
[D.] **outro** (0:01)
Everybody's Trying to Be My Baby (rebroadcast of version J from *Top Gear* #20)
[E.] **intro** (0:41)
I Feel Fine (rebroadcast of version N from *Top Gear* #20)
[F.] **intro** (0:28)
[G.] **Kansas City/Hey Hey Hey Hey!** (2:41)
[H.] **intro** (0:05)
She's a Woman (rebroadcast of version H from *Top Gear* #20)
[I.] **outro** (0:03)
[J.] **chat** (0:42)

The written records would seem to indicate that the Beatles recorded a second complete show for BBC Radio eight days after the *Top Gear* session, but that only two new songs were aired. It seems unlikely that a three-and-a-half hour session would yield only two usable songs and a few minutes of chat; could it be that the Beatles taped their contributions for both shows on November 17 and didn't attend this session? After all, each song has only one Beatle-chat-specific intro. (In a couple cases, there is no intro.) "I Feel Fine" seems to have two, but this is the result of clever editing (John and Paul's "okay" response to a request for the song in *Top Gear* could have been spliced in from anywhere).

In any case, this does include some chat specific to listeners of *Saturday Club,* so if it was all taped at once, they knew it would be included in both shows. After "Rock and Roll Music," the Beatles send greetings to the General Overseas listeners, who received the second half hour of *Saturday Club* each week. Matthew asks which country they enjoyed visiting most, and they all pick America, although George adds that Australia had plenty of fans. A few lines of dialogue excised from the original broadcast at this point were restored for *Top of the Pops:* Paul's "Hoppin' around" and Ringo's "Kangaroos in disguise," and a bit more discussion of John's green outfit. They discuss their upcoming film, wish everyone a happy Christmas, and introduce "I'm a Loser."

Further Christmas greetings (**E**) precede "I Feel Fine," after which Paul chats about the number of cover versions on their new LP (**F**) and introduces "Kansas City/Hey Hey Hey Hey!" Note that Matthew rerecorded some of his intros for *Top of the Pops* to reflect the spring 1965 broadcast date, changing "this year" to "last year" and inserting a reference to Ringo's marriage.

One extra piece of chat, most likely from this session, also appeared on episode 15 of *Top of the Pops,* aired the week of March 6, 1965. This bit (**J**), with Ringo's "long nose" coming between Brian Matthew and the microphone, was used as a trailer at the top of the show. It was reused in the 1988 series *The Beeb's Lost Beatles Tapes.*

RELEASE HISTORY

1978: The bootleg LP *December 1963* included **B** and **G** in fair quality and overdubbed with screaming to simulate an audience concert recording.

1981 **B** and **G** were included in very good quality on the bootleg LP *Airtime.*

1982: The radio special *Beatles at the Beeb* included **B, C, G,** and an incomplete version of **F,** all from *Top of the Pops.*

1988: The bootleg LP *Beatles at the Beeb, Volume 12* included a good-quality off-air tape of the entire original broadcast (**A–I**). Note that this omits the bit of **C** exclusive to the *Top of the Pops* edit. The same year, **J** was broadcast in *The Beeb's Lost Beatles Tapes.*

1993: Great Dane's *The Complete BBC Sessions* boxed set contained **B–J,** reassembled from various sources, although **F** is slightly incomplete.

1994: Apple's *Live at the BBC* CD included an excellent copy of **B** from *Top of the Pops.*

325. TV performance **J**

Date: 29 November 1964
Time: 8:30 p.m.
Location: Studio 1, Television Centre, London
Producer: Joe McGrath
Host: Dudley Moore
Broadcast: 9 January 1965, 9:20–10:00 p.m.
BBC2
Not Only . . . But Also . . .

[A.] intro (0:34)
"Deaf Ted, Danoota (and me)" film (shot November 20)
[B.] poetry recitals (5:11)
[C.] closing theme (Good-bye-ee) (2:13)

The studio sequences for *Not Only . . . But Also . . .* were videotaped this evening. After Dudley Moore introduces the filmed piece (see entry number 322), John reads his back cover blurb, "About the Awful," stumbling over a couple of the lines. Then Dudley, John, and Norman Rossington perform "All Abord Speeching," followed by Norman and John's recitation of "Good Dog Nigel," aided by an actual surrogate Nigel, who attempts to jump for joy out of John's arms.

Dudley praises Nigel's performance and then narrates the tale of "Unhappy Frank," portrayed here by Norman. Finally, John and Norman read "The Wrestling Dog," although rather than a live dog, this time a brief shot of John's drawing from *In His Own Write* is inserted to illustrate the tale. John appears again at the end of the episode (**C**), dancing across the stage as Dudley reintroduces the guest stars.

RELEASE HISTORY

The entire program was rebroadcast by BBC2 December 9, 1990, and all sequences involving John circulate on video.

1994: The soundtrack, minus the closing segment, appeared on the bootleg *The Beatles at the Beeb—TV.*

1996: The "Wrestling Dog" segment was included on the *Anthology* home video set.

326. Newsreel footage **R**

Date: 1 December 1964
Location: University College Hospital, London
Broadcast: 1 December 1964
ITV
Length: 1:18

Prior to checking into London's University College Hospital, Ringo held a press conference that was filmed by newsreel and TV cameras.

Ringo poses for photographers, hamming it up by opening his mouth to expose his tonsils and crooning a few notes. Then he chats with an ITV News reporter, who asks if the tonsils have been troubling him long. Ringo responds, "I feel fine! Plugging it, you know!" (i.e., the new Beatles single, "I Feel Fine"). He says he will pass the time in the hospital by watching TV, reading, and playing albums on a record player being brought in for him. He mentions Bob Dylan, the Supremes, James Brown, Yusef Lateef, and Chico Hamilton as probable platters to spin.

Finally, Ringo says the other Beatles won't be visiting him, even though they are all at home (George wouldn't leave for the Bahamas until the ninth), and he gets in one final plug for their upcoming Christmas show at the Hammersmith Odeon.

RELEASE HISTORY

1996: This clip is circulating on video, and the soundtrack has been released on *Fab Four CD & Book Set.*

327. Newsreel footage R

Date: 1 December 1964
Location: University College Hospital, London
Length: 0:41

This alternate interview clip, filmed by Reuters, comes from the same press conference. Ringo admits that some fans have asked to keep his tonsils as souvenirs, but he thinks the organs are too nasty looking. This prompts the press to request another look, and Ringo opens wide yet again. The reporter asks if Ringo will have a go at singing after the operation, and the drummer admonishes him: "I sang anyway. You haven't been buying the albums, have you?"

RELEASE HISTORY

This footage circulates on video.

328. Newsreel footage R

Date: 10 December 1964
Time: morning
Location: University College Hospital, London
Broadcast: 10 December 1964
ITV
Length: 0:47

As Ringo checked out of the hospital, an interview was conducted for ITV News while fans called out his name in the background. The interviewer asks how Ringo got along with the nurses, and how his voice is doing, although Ringo refuses to demonstrate by singing something. Ringo also denies that George has married, saying that he knows firsthand because George visited him during the previous week, and insisting that "none of us" are married. Ironically, just over a month later, Ringo would propose to Maureen Cox.

A bit of the ITV interview can be glimpsed in a Pathé newsreel titled *Tonsils Good-Bye,* which contains 1:26 of silent footage of Ringo fighting his way through a crowd of fans, reporters, and hospital personnel to a limousine. An alternate silent newsreel clip lasting 45 seconds captures the same action from a different angle.

RELEASE HISTORY

1996: The soundtrack of the ITV interview was included on *Fab Four CD & Book Set,* taken from a circulating video. The Pathé newsreel and alternate clip also circulate on video.

329. Radio interview

Date: 21–24 December 1964
Location: Hammersmith Odeon, London
Interviewer: Paul Drew
Length: 7:00

Atlanta DJ Paul Drew interviewed the Beatles backstage as they rehearsed for their second annual Christmas show. The circulating tape cuts in midway through a question about how they'll spend Christmas. George says they won't invite one another over for dinner, just drop in casually for visits. Since he still lives in an apartment and hates to cook, Ringo wants to go out for Christmas dinner. Paul has arranged for his father and new stepmother and stepsister to stay in a fancy London hotel. He's sure Jane will "pop in" as well.

Even assuming this interview was conducted on the first day of rehearsals, Paul left his shopping quite late, as he still hasn't decided what to give Jane. "A secret marriage license," jokes the reporter. Each Beatle selects highlights of the previous year, and Paul admits to driving 140 miles an hour, because "you're allowed to go any speed" on the motorway. Asked if there are any old Beatles recordings or photos that might pop up, John can only think of the Tony Sheridan sessions, but doesn't care if any skeletons are dragged from their closet, as "they're all clean skeletons."

Ringo confirms that the Beatles don't buy one another gifts and denies that he is married or engaged (that would change within a few weeks). George says he wasn't bothered by reporters on his Bahamian vacation, although he calls the press "a bit narrow-minded." John complains that people still congratulate him on having a new baby, no matter how often he disavows it. Paul also reiterates that he and Jane have no wedding plans. The interview concludes with a Beatle-sung verse of "We Wish You a Merry Christmas," complete with guitar accompaniment.

RELEASE HISTORY

1989: The final 17 seconds of this interview surfaced on the 7-inch EP *1989 Beatleg News Christmas Record,* taken from an alternate source with added narration.

1998: 18 seconds from this recording (including all of "We Wish You a Merry Christmas") were included on the bootleg CD *The Ultimate Beatles Christmas Collection.* The full seven-minute interview circulates in fair quality among collectors.

330. Radio interview

Date: 24–31 December 1964
Location: Hammersmith Odeon, London
Interviewer: Chris Denning
Broadcast: Radio Luxembourg
The Beatles
Length: 2:55

Radio Luxembourg debuted a weekly show titled *The Beatles* on January 5, 1965. The host, Chris Denning, cornered the Beatles for some exclusive chat in their Hammersmith dressing room during the final week of 1964. Since each episode was only fifteen minutes long including music, the interview material was presumably spread out over several installments, so it's unknown exactly when these recordings were aired.

Two interview segments circulate, with the Beatles wolfing down a meal and sounding tremendously bored with the interview and the Christmas show itself. George tries to put a good face on it, but John bluntly admits, "The sketches are lousy." Paul says they're playing the same songs in every set, and George points out that most of the numbers are new. This isn't quite true; while seven of the eleven songs were from the new LP and single, three of those were covers of rock-and-roll songs in the group's repertoire since Hamburg.

In the second segment, Denning asks about songwriting. John says he and Paul usually sit down with two guitars ("And Geoff, the singing piano," adds George), although sometimes they write separately and "make them more Beatley" by collaborating in the studio. Perhaps thinking of the Lennon-dominated *A Hard Day's Night* LP, John says, "Sometimes I do much more work than Paul, but we won't mention that, will we?"

Also recorded during this visit were record dedications to various Liverpool mates (including Nigel Whalley, Ivan Vaughan, Arthur Kelly, Tony Workman, Roy Trafford, and Rory Storm). The circulating tape includes John "sending a message" to Pete Shotton, who used to play washboard in the Quarry Men. George follows suit by cheekily dedicating "Love Me Do" to one of his classmates and fellow Quarry Men, Paul McCartney!

RELEASE HISTORY

1972: The two interview segments were broadcast in the BBC Radio series *The Beatles Story.* The first was bootlegged on the CD *The Beatles Broadcast Collection, Trailer 1.* The dedication segment was available on a website dedicated to the history of pirate radio and circulates among collectors.

1965: THEY ARE STANDING STILL

TIMELINE

January 8	John, Paul, and Ringo privately tour the annual boat show at Earl's Court after it has closed to the public for the day.
January 15	George and Ringo attend a party thrown by Melody Maker columnist Bob Dawbarn in London.
January 25	John and Cynthia join George Martin for a fortnight of skiing at St. Moritz in the Swiss Alps.
January 27	George attends his brother Peter's wedding in Liverpool.
January 28	George and Pattie fly to the continent for a brief vacation.
February 1	U.S. release of *4 by the Beatles* LP.
February 3	Ringo and Maureen Cox attend a luncheon for Paul Getty in London.
February 4	Paul and Jane Asher fly to Hammamet, Tunisia, for a ten-day vacation.
February 7	John and George Martin return from their Swiss Alps skiing trip.
February 11	Ringo marries Maureen Cox in London with John and George in attendance; Brian Epstein is best man.
February 14	Paul returns from Tunisia and Ringo returns to London from a brief honeymoon.
February 15	John Lennon passes his driving test and receives his license; it goes mostly unused the rest of his life. He poses for photos in George Martin's automobile at EMI to celebrate.
	The Beatles begin taping songs for their second film, *Help!,* and its soundtrack LP.
	U.S. release of "Eight Days a Week"/"I Don't Want to Spoil the Party" single.
February 16	The Beatles receive several gold records and awards during a ceremony at EMI House.
February 18	Northern Songs stock goes public.
February 19	Perhaps a follow-up to the ceremony of February 16, EMI chairman Sir Joseph Lockwood holds a party in the Beatles' honor at the Connaught Hotel. All four attend.
February 22	The Beatles fly to New Providence, the Bahamas, to begin shooting *Help!*
March 10	The Beatles fly from Nassau back to London, arriving early the following morning.
March 13	The Beatles fly from London to Salzburg, where they hold a press conference before traveling to their filming destination, Obertauern.
March 22	The Beatles fly from Salzburg to London.
	U.S. release of *The Early Beatles* LP.
April 6	During shooting at Twickenham, the Beatles receive an award from Radio Caroline.
	UK release of *Beatles for Sale* EP.
April 8	Paul and Jane attend the opening of the Pickwick's new basement nightclub, Downstairs at the Pickwick.
April 9	UK release of "Ticket to Ride"/"Yes It Is" single.
April 13	Taping the single "Help!" at EMI Studios.
April 19	U.S. release of "Ticket to Ride"/"Yes It Is" single.
April 28	At Twickenham, Peter Sellers presents the Beatles with their 1964 Grammy Award.
May 3	First of a three-day location shoot for *Help!* on Salisbury Plain.

May 9 The Beatles attend Bob Dylan's concert at Royal Festival Hall in London.

May 11 Shooting for *Help!* wraps as far as the Beatles' contributions are concerned.

May 16 John attends a party for singer Johnny Mathis held at the home of EMI producer Norman Newell.

May 18 Paul and Jane attend Gene Barry's show at the Talk of the Town nightclub in London

May 25 John and Cynthia fly back to London from a visit to the Cannes Film Festival.

May 27 The Beatles fly from London to various vacation destinations, returning early the following week.

June 2 George and Brian Epstein attend the world premiere of Richard Lester's film *The Knack (and How to Get It).*

June 3 John, Cynthia, George, and Pattie attend Allen Ginsberg's thirty-ninth birthday party.

June 4 UK release of *Beatles for Sale (No. 2)* EP.

June 7 BBC Radio broadcasts *The Beatles (Invite You to Take a Ticket to Ride),* the Beatles' final musical performance specifically for radio. Their contribution was taped May 26.

June 11 Paul returns to London from a fortnight in Portugal as the news of the Beatles' inclusion on the MBE awards list is revealed.

June 12 At Twickenham Film Studios, the Beatles participate in continuous interviews with world press discussing their upcoming MBE honors.

June 14 U.S. release of *Beatles VI* LP.

Paul and Jane Asher go clubbing at the Cromwellian Club.

June 20 The Beatles fly from London Airport to Paris for a brief European tour.

June 23 The Beatles journey by train from France to Milan.

June 25 The Beatles fly to Rome immediately following their second Genoa show.

June 29 The Beatles fly from Rome to Nice.

July 1 John's second book, *A Spaniard in the Works,* is published in the United States.

The Beatles fly from Nice to Madrid.

July 4 The Beatles fly from Barcelona to London.

July 7 Paul and George attend a party in London given by the Moody Blues.

July 13 Paul attends the annual Ivor Novello Awards banquet at London's Savoy Hotel.

July 14 Paul attends a play at the Palace Theatre in Watford; among the cast is his girlfriend, Jane Asher.

John, George, and Ringo visit the Bastille Day party at the Scotch of St. James nightclub.

July 19 U.S. release of "Help!"/"I'm Down" 45.

July 23 UK release of "Help!"/"I'm Down" 45.

July 24 Ringo purchases Sunny Heights, a mock-Tudor house within walking distance of John's home. He and Maureen don't move in until the end of the year.

July 29 The Beatles visit TVC Studios, where a new animated TV series about them is in production.

World premiere of *Help!,* the Beatles' second motion picture, at London Pavilion cinema. All four Beatles and Princess Margaret attend the premiere and the party afterward at the Dorchester Hotel.

August 2 Paul and Jane Asher go clubbing at the Scotch of St. James with members of the Byrds.

August 6 UK release of *Help!* LP.

August 8 John and George attend the Fifth National Jazz and Blues Festival at Richmond Athletic Association Grounds.

August 9 John produces a studio session for new NEMS group the Silkie, covering his composition "You've Got to Hide Your Love Away." Paul adds acoustic guitar and George contributes tambourine to the recording.

August 13 U.S. release of *Help!* LP.

The Beatles fly from London to New York City to begin their second tour of North America.

August 15	Concert at Shea Stadium in New York, filmed for a television documentary and attended by a record-setting crowd of 55,600.
August 23	The Beatles fly from Portland, Oregon, to Los Angeles to begin a five-day break from touring.
August 24	The Beatles halfheartedly rub shoulders with the Hollywood elite at a party thrown by Capitol Records.
August 27	Paul and George attend a morning recording session in Los Angeles by their pals the Byrds.
	Elvis Presley deigns to meet the Beatles at his home in Beverly Hills.
September 1	The Beatles fly from the United States back to London Airport, arriving early the following morning.
September 6	Paul and Jane attend the play *The Killing of Sister George* at the Duke of York's Theatre.
September 11	The Beatles return to their hometown of Liverpool for two days to visit family and friends.
September 13	Ringo and Maureen's first child, Zak Starkey, is born at Queen Charlotte's Hospital in London.
September 14	U.S. release of "Yesterday"/"Act Naturally" single.
September 22	Maureen and Zak arrive home from the hospital.
October 4	John and Paul attend an Alma Cogan recording session; she records a cover of their composition "Eight Days a Week." Later Paul visits relatives and friends in Liverpool.
October 5	The Beatles are photographed for a *Beatles Book Monthly* shoot at the flat shared by their road managers, Neil Aspinall and Mal Evans.
October 7	George is photographed by Leslie Bryce for *Beatles Book Monthly* at George's bungalow in Esher.
October 9	All four Beatles celebrate John's twenty-fifth birthday by attending a party thrown by Lionel Bart.
October 11	U.S. release of "Boys"/"Kansas City/Hey Hey Hey Hey!" single.
	Paul attends Marianne Faithfull's session at Decca Studios in London; she records a cover of Paul's composition "Yesterday."
October 12	Sessions begin for the *Rubber Soul* LP at EMI Studio 2.
October 15	Paul attends Ben E. King's performance at the Scotch of St. James nightclub. John and George arrive late and miss King's set.
October 24	Paul, George, and Ringo attend a party held by Brian Epstein at the Scotch of St. James nightclub.
October 26	The Beatles receive MBE awards from Queen Elizabeth in a ceremony at Buckingham Palace. Afterward, they hold a press conference at the Saville Theatre, covered by radio, TV, and newsreels, to describe their visit to the palace.
November 16	Paul attends Gene Pitney's concert at the Adelphi Cinema in Slough and ends up emceeing the show incognito.
November 23	The Beatles videotape a total of ten promotional clips for five songs on Twickenham Film Studio Stage Three.
November 25	The Beatles are allowed the run of the store at Harrods for two hours after closing time.
November 27	Paul attends a package show at the East Ham Granada Cinema featuring Manfred Mann, the Yardbirds, and the Scaffold (a music/comedy group including Paul's brother Michael).
December 1	The Beatles convene at Neil and Mal's flat in London to rehearse for their imminent British tour.
December 3	UK release of "We Can Work It Out"/"Day Tripper" single.
	UK release of *Rubber Soul* LP.
	Opening night of the Beatles' final UK tour.
December 6	UK release of *The Beatles' Million Sellers* EP.
	U.S. release of "We Can Work It Out"/"Day Tripper" single.
	U.S. release of *Rubber Soul* LP.
	The Beatles spend their day off visiting friends and relatives in Liverpool.

December 12 Ringo attends a Christmas party at the Scotch of St. James nightclub.

December 17 UK release of *The Beatles' Third Christmas Record,* the Beatles' third annual Christmas flexi-disc for fan club members.

December 19 Paul and Jane attend a preview performance of *Twang!,* a pop musical, at the Shaftesbury Theatre.

December 26 While visiting his father, Paul falls off his moped, suffering a minor laceration to his lip and chipping a front tooth.

A newly engaged George pays a surprise visit to his parents' new home in Liverpool.

December 31 For the second straight year, the Beatles attend a New Year's Eve party thrown by EMI recording manager Norman Newell at his home in Marylebone.

1. Radio interview P, R

Date: 6 January 1965
Location: London (via telephone)
Interviewer: Murray Kaufman
Broadcast: WINS-AM, New York City
Length: 5:29

On January 4, Reuters carried a story that must have caused severe anxiety among American Beatle fans. It began: "A spokesman for the Beatles confirmed today that the singing group could not consider any more visits to the United States because of a tax dispute with the American Government." This was part of a larger transatlantic game of "call my bluff" going on between the IRS and British booking agencies.

In 1964, with British acts suddenly cleaning up via American tours, the United States naturally felt it deserved a chunk of the pie. At the end of the year, the Labor Department suddenly decided to cancel work visas for several groups, such as the Zombies. After plenty of negotiations (Brian Epstein flew to New York on January 19 to chime in), the matter was resolved, but when this story was picked up by the *New York Times* on January 5, concerned Beatlemaniacs flooded WINS radio with phone calls.

The next day, Murray the K decided to clear up the matter by placing a call to London, probably to the Hammersmith Odeon, where the Beatles were halfway through their Christmas show. Paul and Ringo were at the other end to dismiss the story as "rubbish," with Ringo adding, "We're dyin' to come back!" With that cleared up, Murray chatted with the boys about the Christmas show, upcoming holiday plans, the rebuilt Ad Lib nightclub (recently damaged by a fire), and Ringo's missing tonsils.

RELEASE HISTORY

This interview circulates in mediocre quality among collectors from an off-line radio recording.

2. Newsreel footage J

Date: ca. 28 January 1965
Location: St. Moritz
Broadcast: 29 January 1965
ITV
Length: 0:33

Sometime during this ski vacation with George Martin, John and Cynthia were filmed on the slopes by newsreel cameras; one such clip was aired January 29 on ITV. It was during this trip that John began to compose "Norwegian Wood (This Bird Has Flown)."

RELEASE HISTORY

This silent footage circulates on video.

3. Press conference **R**

Date: 12 February 1965
Time: 1:00 p.m.
Location: David Jacobs' garden, Hove
Length: 4:24

The morning after their wedding, news of Ringo and Maureen's marriage was in all the papers, and their honeymoon location was leaked soon afterward. In hopes of getting some privacy, the newlyweds agreed to a brief session with the media, held in the back garden of Beatles lawyer David Jacobs. The proceedings opened with a general press conference, as they took questions from radio and newspaper reporters.

Ringo talks about the ring ceremony, plans for having a large family, and the possible effect his marriage will have on fans and the Beatles' career. He also reveals that he had decided to get married back in the fall, and that he proposed to Maureen in the Ad Lib nightclub. Ringo seems pleased that the wedding remained private, but dismayed that the honeymoon might become "a stage show," and he jokes that the only place he can get privacy is Vietnam!

RELEASE HISTORY

1965: Excerpts totaling 48 seconds were released on the EP *The Beatles & Murray the K: As It Happened,* but a poor-quality offline radio recording lasting four and a half minutes also circulates.

4. TV interview **R**

Date: 12 February 1965
Time: 1:00 p.m.
Location: David Jacobs' garden, Hove
Broadcast: 12 February 1965
ITV
Length: 2:42

Following the press conference, the couple filmed at least two separate interviews for TV and newsreel cameras. In the first, for ITV News, Ringo explains that Paul hasn't heard the news, being out of the country, but refuses to reveal Paul's whereabouts. Asked whether she'll keep away from the spotlight like Cynthia Lennon, Maureen cheerfully admits that she doesn't like reporters.

RELEASE HISTORY

1996: Most of this interview was released on *Fab Four CD & Book Set;* it also circulates on video.

5. TV interview **R**

Date: 12 February 1965
Time: 1:00 p.m.
Location: David Jacobs' garden, Hove
Broadcast: 12 February 1965
BBC TV
Length: 2:29

The questions here are similar to those asked in the previous interview and press conference, and rather stereotypically, Maureen is asked whether she will rearrange Ringo's home decor. The BBC reporter redeems himself slightly with a joke after Ringo mentions the Ad Lib club: "You mean, you made it up as you went along?" The clip ends with Ringo waving farewell to all the assembled press, shouting, "Goodbye! Hope not to see you out my window again!"

RELEASE HISTORY

1996: This interview was released on the CD *Rare Photos & Interview CD, Volume 3;* it also circulates on video.

6. Studio session

Date: 15 February 1965
Time: 2:30–5:45 p.m.
Location: EMI Studio 2
Producer: George Martin

[A.] Ticket to Ride—take 2 (stereo) (3:10)
[B.] Ticket to Ride—production acetate (mono) (3:04)

[C.] Ticket to Ride—RM1 (3:02)
Mixed: 18 February 1965

[D.] Ticket to Ride—RS1 (3:06)
Mixed: 23 February 1965

[E.] Ticket to Ride—RM2 (3:05)
Mixed: 15 March 1965

[F.] Ticket to Ride—RS from take 2 (#1) (3:07)
[G.] Ticket to Ride—RS from take 2 (#2) (3:06)
[H.] Ticket to Ride—RS from take 2 (#3) (0:46)
[I.] Ticket to Ride—RS from take 2 (#4) (3:05)

All four Beatles convened at Abbey Road Studios on this day to begin an industrious six days of recording, usually comprised of a session in the afternoon and a second one following a dinner break. At the end of those six days, they had eleven finished songs to choose from. Six of them were chosen for the film, one became a B-side, two became LP filler, and two were rejected entirely.

John's "Ticket to Ride" was the first song to be recorded during the afternoon session. The backing consisted of drums and bass on one track, and John's rhythm guitar and George's lead (playing the repeating riff on his twelve-string Rickenbacker) on a second. On a third track, John taped his lead vocal, with some very soulful backing from Paul. The fourth track was filled with some lead guitar notes and a solo (played by Paul), tambourine, handclaps (during the middle eight and coda), and John's second vocal for the choruses. The result was strong enough to be chosen as the A-side for their next single, released in April as a preview to the film and album.

Take 1 was a false start, but the second take was satisfactory. The raw studio tape of take 2 (**A**) has no echo added, and the bass is much clearer than any other mix; it also has no fade, so we can hear the instruments and vocals come to a gradual halt, as well as a stray "ride" at the very end, which may be a remnant of a rehearsal take erased by the final takes.

Mix **B,** from a "film production acetate" for use by United Artists, has a touch of echo and John's second vocal track practically mixed out. Mix **E,** used in the film, has even more echo, but less tambourine. Mix **C** is similar; note that the original LP mix is a couple of words longer than that available on the CD single. Mixes **D** and **F** are nearly identical, with echo and murky bass (both are a bit longer than any mono mix). Mix **G** centers the bass/drum track and moves the fourth track to the left.

The evening session began with the recording of Paul's "Another Girl," which he had written in Tunisia. The backing consisted of bass and drums on track 1, John's Fender and George's Jumbo Gibson acoustic on track 2, and Paul's lead vocal, backed by John and George, on track 3. Track 4 was overdubbed with more vocals from Paul and John, tom-tom from Ringo, and George playing his Gretsch at the end.

The day concluded with five takes of the backing track for George's "I Need You." On track 1 went Paul's bass, Ringo thumping the back of a Jumbo Gibson, George playing Spanish acoustic guitar, and John playing offbeats on Ringo's drum kit! This was accompanied by George's guide vocal on track 2. Overdubs began with his main vocal on track 3 (with harmony from Paul), and the two doubled their vocal efforts on track 4, alongside Ringo's cowbell. Both this and "Another Girl" would be completed the following day.

RELEASE HISTORY

1965: **C** was released on a single and **D** on stereo pressings of the album *Help!* The former is commercially available on a CD single, but as noted above, it is faded a bit early. **E** was included on the soundtrack of the film *Help!* as heard in theaters that summer.

1984: **A** was broadcast in the radio special *Sgt. Pepper's Lonely Hearts Club Band,* although the ending was buried under narration.

1987: **F,** a new digital remix created by George Martin, was released on the *Help!* CD.

1988: A clean version of **A** first surfaced in excellent sound on the LP *Ultra Rare Trax, Volume 3 & 4.* It appeared the following year from tape source on the CD *Ultra Rare Trax, Volume 3.*

1993: **G** was included on the soundtrack of an EPK promoting the CD release of *The Beatles 1967–1970.* It can be heard on the bootleg CD *Lost and Found.*

1998: Besides the first release of **B,** the bootleg CD *Help! Original Mix* also contained copies of **A** and **C–E,** making it a worthy purchase for fans of "Ticket to Ride" remixes.

2003: **H** was released on the soundtrack of the *Anthology* DVD.

2007: **I** was released on the soundtrack of the *Help!* DVD.

7. Studio session

Date: 16 February 1965
Time: 2:30–5:00 p.m.
Location: EMI Studio 2
Producer: George Martin

[A.] I Need You—production acetate (mono) (2:28)
[B.] Another Girl—production acetate (mono) (2:07)

[C.] Another Girl—RM1 (2:03)
[D.] I Need You—RM1 (2:25)
Mixed: 18 February 1965

[E.] I Need You—RS1 (2:26)
[F.] Another Girl—RS1 (2:03)
Mixed: 23 February 1965

[G.] I Need You—RS from take 5 (#1) (2:26)
[H.] Another Girl—RS from take 1 (#1) (2:03)
[I.] Another Girl—RS from take 1 (#2) (0:34)
[J.] I Need You—RS from take 5 (#2) (2:27)
[K.] Another Girl—RS from take 1 (#3) (2:04)

Once again, the day was split into afternoon and evening sessions. First order of business was the completion of "I Need You" with overdubs erasing the previous content of two tracks. George's second vocal, backed by John and Paul, went on track 4. More backing vocals from John and Paul, Ringo's cowbell, and George's twelve-string Rickenbacker guitar, using his newly acquired volume-control pedal, went onto track 2.

Mix **A** has a minimal amount of echo, and the vocal tracks mixed well forward. The mix heard in the film sounds similar (both mixes run too slow), but with the instruments a bit less buried; it's probably just a cleaner copy of this mix. Mixes **E** and **G** both have extra echo added, but the rhythm track sounds clearer on **G.**

"Another Girl" was then finished off with the addition of Paul's lead guitar track. Judging from the stereo mix, this is on the same track as George's acoustic and John's electric rhythm guitars, which means those would have had to be reperformed as well during the overdub. Mix **B** includes Paul's count-in and has a touch of echo, with the vocal track up front. Mix **C** has an extra guitar strum and some tapping at the very end not heard on any other mix. Mixes **F** and **H** are similar, with extra echo on the latter.

RELEASE HISTORY

1965: **C** and **D** were included on mono and **E** and **F** on stereo pressings, respectively, of the *Help!* LP. **A** was included on the soundtrack of the film *Help!* as heard in theaters that summer; it appears on the CD-R *Vinyl to the Core.*

1987: **G** and **H,** new digital remixes created by George Martin, were released on the *Help!* CD.

1996: **B** surfaced on the bootleg CD *Help! Sessions.*

1998: The acetate version of **A** was included on the bootleg CD *Help! Original Mix.*

2003: **I** was released on the soundtrack of the *Anthology* DVD.

2007: **J** and **K** were released on the soundtrack of the *Help!* DVD.

8. Studio session

Date: 16 February 1965
Time: 5:00–10:00 p.m.
Location: EMI Studio 2
Producer: George Martin

[A.] Yes It Is—take 1 (stereo) (2:57)
[B.] Yes It Is—take 2 (stereo) (1:24)
[C.] Yes It Is—takes 3–9 (stereo) (5:38)
[D.] Yes It Is—takes 10–11 (stereo) (0:18)
[E.] Yes It Is—take 14 (stereo) (2:51)
[F.] Yes It Is—production acetate (mono) (2:40)
[G.] Yes It Is—edit of takes 2 and 14 (mono/stereo) (1:49)

[H.] Yes It Is—RM1 (2:38)
Mixed: 18 February 1965

[I.] Yes It Is—RS1 (2:39)
Mixed: 23 February 1965

The entire evening session was spent completing John's "Yes It Is." All of the basic tracks feature Paul on bass, Ringo on drums, John on acoustic rhythm and guide vocal, and George on electric guitar, using his volume pedal again to crest the notes gently.

Take 1 (**A**) is complete but sloppy, as Paul makes some errors in the third verse and George doesn't really know what to play yet. They also finish by vamping on an E chord, but John insists, "We'll have to have an ending" just before the tape cuts off. As it rolls again (**B**), George searches for the right series of notes to play over the intro, and they begin take 2. Unfortunately, one of John's guitar strings snaps during the first bridge, so they have to stop again.

Take 3 (**C**) is a false start, and take 4 breaks down near the beginning as Paul wonders about the arrangement; John says to stick in an extra bar between the first two verses, a feature included in all subsequent takes. John plays a bad chord at the beginning of take 5, the band's entrance on take 6 is sloppy, and Paul errs again during takes 7 and 8. Take 9 is a complete run-through, with the ending worked out this time (right down to George's final four guitar notes).

Takes 10 and 11 (**D**) are both false starts, but take 14 is played to perfection, so a double-tracked Lennon lead vocal (with close harmony from Paul and George), further guitar notes, and a cymbal are overdubbed to complete the song. The raw studio tape of take 14 (**E**) begins with some chat and John goofing around on organ (singing a line from the bridge), probably during one of the overdubs.

Although "Yes It Is" wasn't used in the film, a production acetate was prepared, featuring a mix (**F**) with prominent vocals. The stereo mix (**I**) wasn't released until 1988, probably because of a tape dropout in the first line of the song. The first minute or so of take 2, mixed into mono (with stereo reverb), and the last 47 seconds of take 14 (supposedly remixed but sounding identical to **I**) were cross-faded (**G**) for release on *Anthology 2.*

RELEASE HISTORY

1965: **H** was released on a single; it's available on the "Ticket to Ride" CD single.

1984: **E** (the song only, with no chat) was broadcast in the radio special *Sgt. Pepper's Lonely Hearts Club Band.* It was copied from this source on the bootleg LP and CD *Not for Sale.*

1988: **I** was released on the CD *Past Masters, Volume 1.* The same year, **A, B,** and an incomplete version of **E** first appeared in excellent sound on the bootleg LP *Ultra Rare Trax, Volume 3 & 4.*

1989: **A, B,** and **E** (still incomplete) were booted from tape source on the CD *Hold Me Tight;* this release has a bit of chat prior to **A** not found elsewhere on CD (Norman Smith's take one announcement and Paul's "Say hey").

1991: A complete version of **E** appeared on the bootleg CD *Unsurpassed Masters, Volume 7,* running too slow.

1994: Excellent but slow tapes of **A–E** were included on the bootleg CD *The Ultimate Collection, Volume 3: Studio Sessions, 1965–66.*

1996: **G** was released on *Anthology 2.*

1998: **A** surfaced on the bootleg CD *Help! Original Mix.*

9. Studio session

Date: 17 February 1965
Time: 2:00–7:00 p.m.
Location: EMI Studio 2
Producer: George Martin

[A.] The Night Before—production acetate (mono) (2:31)

[B.] The Night Before—RM1 (2:31)
Mixed: 18 February 1965

[C.] The Night Before—RS1 (2:31)
Mixed: 23 February 1965

[D.] The Night Before—edit of RS2 (mono copy) (2:18)
Mixed: 18 April 1965

[E.] The Night Before—RS from take 2 (#1) (2:32)
[F.] The Night Before—RS from take 2 (#2) (0:40)
[G.] The Night Before—RS from take 2 (#3) (2:18)

Paul's "The Night Before" was completed during this afternoon session in just two takes. The basic rhythm had drums and bass on one track and John playing the group's new Hohner Pianet C electric piano on a second. This was supplemented by Paul's double-tracked lead vocal, backing vocals, maracas, and a dual guitar solo in octaves, played by Paul and George simultaneously.

Mix **A** has the drums mixed lower, with minimal echo (none on the guitar solo). The version chopped up for use in the film does seem to be a unique mix, with some echo and slight differences in the vocal track. This is probably a mono copy of an alternate stereo mix (**D**) that was prepared April 18 and taken away by United Artists. Mix **B** has no echo added, **C** has some, and **E** has even more.

RELEASE HISTORY

1965: **B** and **C** were included on mono and stereo pressings, respectively, of the *Help!* LP. **D** was included on the soundtrack of the film *Help!* as heard in theaters that summer; it appears on the CD-R *Vinyl to the Core.*

1987: **E,** a new digital remix created by George Martin, was released on the *Help!* CD.

1998: **A** surfaced on the bootleg CD *Help! Original Mix.*

2003: **F** was released on the soundtrack of the *Anthology* DVD.

2007: **G** was released on the soundtrack of the *Help!* DVD.

10. Studio session

Date: 17 February 1965
Time: 7:00–11:00 p.m.
Location: EMI Studio 2
Producer: George Martin

[A.] You Like Me Too Much—production acetate (mono) (2:35)

[B.] You Like Me Too Much—RM1 (2:33)
Mixed: 18 February 1965

[C.] You Like Me Too Much—RS1 (2:33)
Mixed: 23 February 1965

[D.] You Like Me Too Much—RS from take 8 (2:34)

The evening session was spent recording George's "You Like Me Too Much," which didn't make it into the film, even though a production acetate was prepared. The backing track probably consisted of Ringo on drums, Paul on bass, George on acoustic guitar, John on tambourine, and George Martin playing the Steinway piano during the intro. Two tracks were reserved for vocals from George (backed by Paul in spots), while the fourth track had overdubs of Pianet electric piano from John, a guitar solo from George, and further Steinway piano played by Paul during the solo and coda.

Mix **A** has no echo, with the vocals mixed more prominently, while the other mixes have varying degrees of echo, but otherwise sound nearly identical.

RELEASE HISTORY

1965: **B** and **C** were included on mono and stereo pressings, respectively, of the *Help!* LP.

1987: **D,** a new digital remix created by George Martin, was released on the *Help!* CD.

1998: **A** surfaced on the bootleg CD *Help! Original Mix.*

11. Studio session

Date: 18 February 1965
Time: 3:30–5:15 p.m.
Location: EMI Studio 2
Producer: George Martin

[A.] You've Got to Hide Your Love Away—edit of takes 1 and 5 (mono) (2:43)
[B.] You've Got to Hide Your Love Away—production acetate (mono) (2:09)
[C.] You've Got to Hide Your Love Away—RM1 (2:06)
Mixed: 20 February 1965

[D.] You've Got to Hide Your Love Away—RS1 (2:07)
Mixed: 23 February 1965

[E.] You've Got to Hide Your Love Away—RS from take 9 (#1) (2:06)
[F.] You've Got to Hide Your Love Away—RS from take 9 (#2) (2:06)
[G.] You've Got to Hide Your Love Away—RS from take 9 (#3) (2:07)

In the morning, George Martin and Norman Smith prepared mono mixes of the first four songs to be completed; mono mixes of the previous day's two songs would be created between the afternoon and evening sessions, probably while the group nipped off to the cafeteria for dinner.

This afternoon session was devoted to John's "You've Got to Hide Your Love Away." The backing consisted of John on his new Framus Hootenanny twelve-string acoustic guitar, Paul on bass, George's Spanish acoustic, and Ringo on drums (using brushes) on one track, and John's guide vocal on a second. A sampling of the session (**A**) was released on *Anthology 2.* It begins with take 1, a false start as John readjusts his mic, followed by the sound of Paul shattering a glass. We then cut to the full take 5, a pleasant alternate including a solo vocal from John.

Overdubs were added to take 9, the best performance. John retaped his lead vocal, and Paul's maracas, Ringo's tambourine, and George's twelve-string acoustic guitar occupied the third track. Johnnie Scott, the first session musician since Andy White to play on a Beatles record, completed the recording by adding a double-tracked flute solo (one alto, one tenor); one flute went on the remaining free track, and the other went at the end of John's vocal track.

Based on George Martin's production notes, the flute overdubs might have occurred on the twentieth. That would explain why the song wasn't mixed until the end of the day on the twentieth, while the other two songs recorded on the eighteenth were mixed at the start of the session. Mix **B** includes a count-in from John, but otherwise sounds similar to **D.** Mix **C** has a bit of extra echo on the vocal, and **E** has even more.

RELEASE HISTORY

1965: **C** and **D** were included on mono and stereo pressings, respectively, of the *Help!* LP.

1987: **E,** a new digital remix created by George Martin, was released on the *Help!* CD.

1996: **A** was released on *Anthology 2.* The same year, **B** surfaced on the bootleg CD *Help! Sessions.*

2003: **F** was released on the soundtrack of the *Anthology* DVD.

2007: **G** was released on the soundtrack of the *Help!* DVD.

12. Studio session

Date: 18 February 1965
Time: 6:30–10:30 p.m.
Location: EMI Studio 2
Producer: George Martin

[A.] If You've Got Trouble—take 1 (stereo) (2:45)
[B.] Tell Me What You See—RM1 (2:34)
Mixed: 20 February 1965

[C.] Tell Me What You See—RS1 (2:34)
Mixed: 23 February 1965

[D.] If You've Got Trouble—RM from take 1 (2:49)
Mixed: 21 April 1976

[E.] If You've Got Trouble—edit of take 1 (mostly fake stereo) (2:21)
[F.] Tell Me What You See—RS from take 4 (2:34)
[G.] If You've Got Trouble—RS from take 1 (#1) (2:46)
[H.] If You've Got Trouble—RS from take 1 (#2) (2:41)

After dinner, the group attempted to record a song for Ringo to sing in the film; unfortunately, it was a rather miserable Lennon/McCartney throwaway titled "If You've Got Trouble," and after a solitary take, they wisely abandoned it. The rhythm track consisted of drums, bass, and George's Gretsch. Ringo overdubbed his main lead vocal on track 3, while a guitar trio was added to track 2: Paul's Epiphone Casino, George's Gretsch again, and John's Fender. Track 4 was filled with Ringo's second vocal, John and Paul's backing vocals, and George's solo, played on his Fender Strat.

The song remained hidden in the vaults until April 1976, when a rough mono mix (**D**) was created for the first in-house compilation of outtakes prepared by EMI. This mix has a touch of extra studio chatter at the beginning compared to other versions.

In 1984, Geoff Emerick prepared an edited version (**E**) for the *Sessions* project, beginning with the second verse and first middle eight, then the first verse (with extra "oh oh" backing vocals flown in), and finally the guitar solo (with an extra exclamation of "rock on!" mixed out on all other variations) through the end of the song. Only the guitar solo is in true stereo on this mix, with the rest being rechanneled. Thankfully, this was rejected in favor of a true stereo mix with a touch of echo (**G**) for release on *Anthology 2.* More recently, a very clear tape with better stereo separation (**A**) surfaced on the various releases of the John Barrett tapes; another true stereo mix (**H**) is on the *Anthology* DVD.

The final song recorded this evening was Paul's "Tell Me What You See," completed in four takes but rejected for use in the film (not even making it as far as the production acetate stage). The backing consisted of Paul's bass, Ringo's drums, John's rhythm guitar, and George's guiro (a scraped percussion instrument) on a single track, with John and Paul singing a duet on a second. Paul played the Pianet on a third track and added a second vocal on the final track, accompanied by tambourine and claves. The mono and stereo mixes used on the *Help!* LP sound similar, while the CD remix (**F**) has some echo added.

RELEASE HISTORY

1965: **B** and **C** were included on mono and stereo pressings, respectively, of the *Help!* LP.

1984: **D** surfaced on the vinyl bootleg *File Under: Beatles.*

1985: **E** appeared on bootlegs of the *Sessions* LP; the tape source is on Spank's CD of that title.

1987: **F,** a new digital remix created by George Martin, was released on the *Help!* CD.

1989: **A** was included from a tape source, but with reversed channels and running too slow, on the CD *Unsurpassed Masters, Volume 2.* A speed-corrected upgrade appears on the bootleg CD *Another Sessions . . . Plus.*

1995: **G** was released on *Anthology 1.*

2002: The CD-R *As It Happened, Baby!* included **D** from a tape source.

2003: **H** was released on the soundtrack of the *Anthology* DVD.

13. Studio session

Date: 19 February 1965
Time: 3:30–6:20 p.m.
Location: EMI Studio 2
Producer: George Martin

[A.] You're Going to Lose That Girl—production acetate (mono) (2:18)

As the Beatles had been invited to a dinner party at the Connaught Hotel by EMI chairman Sir Joseph Lockwood, only a single afternoon session was held on this day, during which John's "You're Going to Lose That Girl" was recorded.

The backing consisted of John's Gretsch rhythm guitar, Paul's bass, and Ringo's drums on track 1 of the tape. Track 3 had John, Paul, and George's vocals, while track 2 was filled with electric piano and George playing a guitar solo. Finally, John doubled his lead vocal on track 4. All of this (including the alternate guitar solo and very faint electric piano) can be heard on the bootlegged film production acetate, containing a rough mono mix (**A**). They would return to the song on March 30.

RELEASE HISTORY

1985: **A** first appeared on the vinyl bootleg *Not Guilty,* slightly incomplete.

1996: **A** was included on the bootleg CD *Help! Sessions.*

14. Studio session

Date: 20 February 1965
Time: noon–5:15 p.m.
Location: EMI Studio 2
Producer: George Martin

[A.] That Means a Lot—take 1 (stereo) (2:58)
[B.] That Means a Lot—rehearsal fragments (stereo) (0:40)

[C.] That Means a Lot—RM from take 1 (2:42)
Mixed: 21 April 1976

[D.] That Means a Lot—RS from take 1 (fake stereo) (2:25)
[E.] That Means a Lot—RS from take 1 (0:43)

A wasted Saturday afternoon. The Beatles attempted to record Paul's new composition "That Means a Lot" on their final day at Abbey Road before setting off to make their film. Four rehearsal takes were recorded, and the tape was then rewound to be used for the finished product. The backing had drums, bass, John's Fender Strat, and George's Spanish acoustic guitar, all on track 1. Track 2 added more bass, Ringo's echoed tom-tom, and extra Fender guitar from John at the start.

Tracks 1 and 2 were then bounced across and combined on track 3. This freed up track 2 for John and George's vocals, backing up Paul's lead vocal on track 4 (why they did it this way rather than singing simultaneously on track 4 is a mystery). Finally, track 1 had an overdub of piano (George Martin), more backing vocals (John and George), a second bridge vocal (Paul), and maracas over the coda (Ringo).

This single take was then copied onto a separate tape, with the four tracks being reduced and the result called take 2. Further vocal and guitar work was apparently overdubbed, but the results weren't satisfactory, and the original take 1 was temporarily labeled as best and later mixed into mono and stereo.

The Beatles' version suffered a similar fate as "If You've Got Trouble," being locked in the vault until 1976, when a rough mix (**C**) was made (announced on the tape as "Can't You See"), and then newly remixed for the *Sessions* project in 1984. The latter (**D**) is an especially murky mix, being in mono with heavy stereo reverb; unfortunately, it's the mix Apple chose to release officially on *Anthology 2,* although it sounds a bit clearer there than previous bootleg releases.

More recently, a new tape has surfaced offering us the complete take 1 in true stereo, with no echo added, including the take announcement and no fade-out (**A**). Interestingly, the tape also has a bit of the rehearsal session that was partly erased by take 1. These fragments (**B**) consist of chat between Paul and George Martin followed by the end of a very loose run-through.

RELEASE HISTORY

1984: An incomplete copy of **C** surfaced on the vinyl bootleg *File Under: Beatles.*

1985: **D** appeared on bootlegs of the *Sessions* LP; the tape source is on Spank's CD of that title.

1989: **D** was included from a tape source, but running too slow, on the CD *Unsurpassed Masters, Volume 2.*

1995: **D** was released on *Anthology 1.*

1999: **A** and **B** surfaced among John Barrett's cassette material. They appeared in excellent quality on the bootleg CD *Turn Me On Dead Man: The John Barrett Tapes,* but the last 30 seconds of **A** were missing. Later that year, a more complete copy of **A** was included on the bootleg CD *More Masters,* unfortunately in lesser quality.

2002: The CD-R *As It Happened, Baby!* included **C** from a tape source.

2003: **E** was released on the soundtrack of the *Anthology* DVD.

15. Newsreel footage

Date: 22 February 1965
Time: morning
Location: London Airport
Broadcast: 22 February 1965
ITV
Length: 0:36

After taking Sunday off, the Beatles convened at London Airport this Monday morning to fly to the Bahamas, via New York City, to begin shooting their second movie. ITV News cameras filmed their departure, with the group and costar Eleanor Bron waving farewell to fans. On the way over the Atlantic, the Beatles enjoyed the effects of a fresh supply of marijuana, allegedly supplied by actor Brandon De Wilde. This set the tone for the stoned atmosphere that would pervade the entire *Help!* project.

RELEASE HISTORY

This silent footage circulates on video among collectors.

16. Radio interview

Date: 22 February 1965
Time: 7:00 p.m.
Location: Nassau Airport
Interviewer: Gene Loving
Broadcast: WGH-AM, Tidewater
Length: 7:00

Upon their arrival at Nassau Airport that evening, several interviews were conducted, including some with the Beatles' old acquaintances Gene Loving and Larry Kane, who had flown over from Virginia and Florida, respectively, for the occasion.

Gene speaks first with Paul, who is clearly in a very silly mood. After refusing to reveal their titles, Paul says the new film will have "about six or seven" songs on the soundtrack. John, standing nearby, picks this up and runs with it, interrupting Paul's discussion of his Tunisian holiday and Ringo's marriage by interjecting "about six or seven" every few seconds. Gene then tries to ask John when his next book will be coming out and is met with "about six or seven."

Amazingly, John then explains that they kept occupied on the flight over by getting stoned. Gene assumes he's kidding (and probably assumes he's referring to getting drunk), but John insists he's telling the truth. Gene tries one last time to get a coherent answer about how much of the Beatles' recent *Playboy* magazine interview was true, and John mumbles, "Most of it was true. Some of it wasn't. About six or seven."

Gene next turns to George, who appears to be in a sane state of mind, but his first answer is again interrupted by John's "about six or seven." George also explains that John sings lead on "I Don't Want to Spoil the Party," the latest American single, but can't remember what the flip side is. Incredibly, John comes up with the correct answer, "Eight Days a Week," and talks a bit about "She's a Woman" before Neil Aspinall calls him away. Finally, Gene asks Ringo a few questions about his new bride and his role in the film.

RELEASE HISTORY

1986: These interviews were released on the LP *All Our Loving,* later reissued on CD.

17. Radio interview

Date: 22 February 1965
Time: 7:00 p.m.
Location: Nassau Airport
Interviewer: Larry Kane
Broadcast: WFUN-AM, Miami
Length: 4:33

In the background of the Gene/Ringo interview (see previous entry), Larry Kane can be heard interviewing Paul and John (and the Ringo interview is audible during the tape of Larry's interview as well). The pair are only slightly more composed, as John ditches "about six or seven" in favor of a new catchphrase: "This thing's wide open, anything can happen, man." Meanwhile, Paul refers to Kane as "Larry Ellis," either jokingly or mistakenly; it's hard to tell. Larry also chats with George about Northern Songs going public and the upcoming North American tour, and with Ringo about a six-foot wedding cake prepared by fans in Miami.

RELEASE HISTORY

1985: These interviews were released on the LP *'Round The World,* later reissued on CD.

18. Radio interview — J, P, G

Date: 24 February 1965
Location: Interfield Road, New Providence
Interviewer: Gene Loving
Broadcast: WGH-AM, Tidewater
Length: 2:33

During the first full day of shooting (filming cycling scenes on Interfield Road), Gene Loving taped several more interviews with the cast and crew of *Help!* In addition to Brian Epstein, producer Walter Shenson, director Richard Lester, and hairdresser Betty Glasow, Gene taped a short conversation with John, Paul, and George.

John and George talk about the film so far, mentioning the hotel swimming pool scene shot the previous day, and George says that he "might" move out of London now that Ringo has left to get married. Actually, he had purchased a home in Esher back in July of 1964 and was already in the process of moving in. Paul, still in a strange mood, refuses to give serious answers to Gene's questions about the film, relaxing, and the difference in climate between the Bahamas and the Alps.

RELEASE HISTORY

1986: These interviews were released on the LP *All Our Loving,* later reissued on CD.

19. Radio interview — G

Date: 25 February 1965
Time: evening
Location: Balmoral Club, New Providence (via telephone)
Interviewer: Tom Clay
Broadcast: KBLA-AM, Burbank
Length: 4:55

After another day of filming, the Beatles and friends held a twenty-second birthday party for George in their temporary abode at the Balmoral Club. Meanwhile, in Los Angeles, former Detroit DJ Tom Clay was attempting to phone Nassau to deliver greetings from California fans. After the operator gets the club manager on the line, Tom gives his location and spells out his name carefully, and he agrees to talk with Brian Epstein: "He'll remember me."

Clay had interviewed the Beatles during the filming of *A Hard Day's Night* (see the April 7, 1964, entry), but Brian does not remember him until given further clues (although he's probably just being polite). Brian agrees to go fetch George from his party, but during the intervening silence, the operator assumes that the call is over and disconnects Clay. Brian is understandably a bit annoyed when reached a second time, but George finally arrives for a brief chat.

After conveying birthday wishes and asking about the next U.S. tour, Tom asks how Ringo is. George, perhaps dropping a hint, replies, "At this moment, he's having a good time at my party." Tom asks George to give the listeners a big kiss and then lets him return to the festivities.

RELEASE HISTORY

1965: The entire phone call was included on the 7-inch $33\frac{1}{3}$ RPM single *Official IBBB Interview.*

20. Amateur footage

Date: 27 February 1965
Location: Balmoral Island
Length: 2:48

The Beatles' financial advisor, Dr. Walter Strach, accompanied them on location in the Bahamas and Austria, and he brought along his color home movie camera to document his travels. Several minutes of footage from the Bahamas include candid scenes of the filming this day for the "Another Girl" sequence, with the Beatles standing on the beach playing their instruments (George mimes to Paul's lead guitar role).

RELEASE HISTORY

This silent color footage was released on a videotape called *The Making of* Help! Other non-Beatle footage on this tape includes home movies of the blimp scene and Foot and Algernon's car crashing into a tree. Also note that the trailer for *Help!,* released on the video *Help! Special Edition,* includes a couple of shots from the Bahamas that didn't make it into the final picture (George in a plastic bubble and the Beatles driving cars in a quarry).

21. Radio interview

Date: 2 March 1965
Location: Bahamas
Interviewer: Dave Hull
Broadcast: KRLA-AM, Los Angeles
Length: 27:53

This was the first of three consecutive days' filming on Cabbage and Victoria beaches, concentrating on the very last scenes in the film when Ringo is about to be sacrificed to Kali. Numerous interviews were taped over this period by Dave Hull (they greet him by name a couple of times, but the name is spliced out on the circulating tape).

John complains about the humidity, having to get up early, and the lack of nightlife in Nassau. He also discusses his upcoming book, *A Spaniard in the Works,* explaining the pun behind the title ("spanner" being the British equivalent of "monkey wrench") and revealing that the book is finished, but won't be out for another month (for some reason, the publication was delayed until June).

Paul relates a humorous story about his recent vacation in Tunisia, where communications with the outside world were less than satisfactory. Thus, a telegram from Brian Epstein read to him over the phone, which he heard as "Request early tea," actually read, "Rich [Ringo] wed early this morning," although the last word was printed as "morneg." He was unable to phone Ringo and relay his good wishes, but he did bring him a silver apple as a wedding gift. Paul also reveals that the sandals he is currently wearing were bought in a Tunisian market for $2, and that he shot home movies during his vacation. Additionally, he claims that only American tourists have been bothering the group while in the Bahamas, and they have been able to visit a few nightclubs.

George's interview was recorded while the crew was busy submerging the giant statue of Kali. Although he can't divulge the names of any of the eleven new songs recorded the previous month, George makes some attempt to describe them but can't come up with much beyond "some slow ones, some fast ones . . . mine are medium sort of rocker things." He also denies a rumor that *Bahama Ball* is a proposed movie title, preferring his own joke idea, *Who's Been Sleeping in My Porridge?*

Ringo also dispels a bunch of silly rumors: that he had been involved in an accident diving off a ship the previous day (which dates these interviews as March 2, assuming they were taped on the same day);

that during filming the previous week while the Queen Mother was passing by, he had jumped up and yelled, "Hi, Mum!" (her procession was actually over fifty yards from the film location); and that the scene with a car crashing into a tree was "a mishap" (it was part of the script). Hull closes by wishing luck to Mrs. Starkey, and newlywed Ringo admits he's still not used to hearing that name.

A second Dave Hull interview with John, on the LP *From Britain . . . with Beat!,* presumably comes from around this date. John clarifies who sings lead on "Rock and Roll Music" (he does), talks about raising Julian, and dispels a rumor that George had arrived at Ringo's wedding on a bicycle. He also chats about his recent skiing vacation and admits he was quite adept at falling over in the snow, except when it came time to do so for a publicity photo!

RELEASE HISTORY

1987: These interviews were released on the LPs *Moviemania!* and *From Britain . . . with Beat!,* both later reissued on CD.

22. Radio interview

Date: ca. 3 March 1965
Time: morning
Location: Bahamas
Interviewer: Derek Taylor
Broadcast: KRLA-AM, Los Angeles
Length: 32:40

In comparing these interviews to each other and to those in the previous entry, there are some consistent details when clothing is described (George's straw hat and jeans, Ringo's red-painted suit), but that could be for continuity purposes in the movie and doesn't mean these were all taped on the same day.

These interviews with Derek Taylor take the form of informal chats with an old friend and were recorded for syndication on American radio (in edited form, no doubt). Derek begins by testing his recorder and then talking with all four at an indoor location, probably their hotel room. After pleasantries are exchanged and family information is discussed, they talk about the basic format of the film, as well as rejected titles such as *High-heeled Knickers* and the aforementioned Goldilocks pun. John says his book will be out in "two minutes . . . two *months,"* and their upcoming North American tour is briefly discussed.

Later, Derek interviews each Beatle individually on the beach while filming continues in the background (Richard Lester can be heard shouting various orders through a megaphone). Paul says they won't be reusing old songs in the new film, as was done in *A Hard Day's Night* (although in the end, part of "She's a Woman" was included). He seems reluctant to discuss the incidental film score, but he reveals that all eleven of the new songs had been written since the beginning of the year, and fourteen songs were actually "ready to record"—perhaps the leftovers were the ones eventually recorded in June (Richard Lester recalls Paul playing the melody to "Yesterday" repeatedly during filming). Paul relates how John vetoed the line "never been a beauty queen" in "I Saw Her Standing There," and he says that actor John Junkin is thinking of recording a version of "She Loves You" in spoken conversational style (Peter Sellers eventually took up this idea). Derek compliments Paul's singing in "She's a Woman," but Paul admits he's glad it stayed on the B-side; we also learn that the UK album *Beatles for Sale* is available in the United States as an import, and Paul urges fans to "buy Britain!"

John mocks Derek's detailed description of John's outfit, and he points out how difficult it would be to write a song called "Who's Been Sleeping in My Porridge?" After more complaining about their early rise, John gets himself into a bit of trouble by referring to "fat American tourists" bothering him. This caused a minor stir when the tape was eventually aired on American radio, but I don't think John ever apologized for it. John praises the send-off they were given at London Airport and denies a rumor that he'd visited Hollywood with his wife recently (although in May, the couple would visit the Cannes Film Festival).

George (who sounds as though he has a mouthful of drool throughout this recording—maybe he has the munchies?) talks about the upcoming European and North American tours, reflecting that this year will be almost as hectic as 1964 had been, even though they will be playing less concerts. Leisure time and interior decorating are also discussed, as well as George's recent visit to Liverpool to attend his brother's wedding. Derek then proposes that the Bahamas would be a nice place to live, not least because it's a "good tax spot." George feigns innocence: "I leave all that to our financial advisors," but in fact that is the precise reason the location was chosen. Their advisor, Walter Strach, had set up a tax shelter in the Bahamas. In the end, George declares that despite the weather, he prefers living in London.

Ringo explains why his suit is painted red for the film, and he praises his fellow cast members Eleanor Bron, Roy Kinnear, Leo McKern, and the Beatles' favorite, Victor Spinetti. Derek congratulates Ringo on his marriage and cheekily asks for an official statement on the matter. Ringo obliges with "I married Maureen Cox," quickly adding, "and I'm very happy, and her name's now Maureen Starkey!" Derek is surprised to learn that the island they are on is British, and he quips that since moving to California, "I feel like an American. There's a contradiction in terms there."

RELEASE HISTORY

1986: These interviews were released on the LP *Here, There, and Everywhere,* later reissued on CD.

22a. Radio interview

Date: 2–9 March 1965
Location: Bahamas
Interviewer: Murray Kaufman
Broadcast: WINS-AM, New York City
Length: 24:13

Naturally, Murray the K didn't want to be left out of the fun, so he flew to Nassau and hung around the set of *Help!,* recording interviews during the lengthy down times during filming. After a short clip with George discussing Ringo's recent marriage, the scene shifts to the beach at Paradise Island, where the film's final scenes were shot March 3. Here Murray chats with Victor Spinetti and describes the action as Mal Evans's cameo is interrupted by a shark sighting.

The bulk of the interviews were taped March 7 or 8 on location at the "abandoned warehouse" (actually a hospital), where Murray talked with each Beatle individually. John plugs *A Spaniard in the Works,* although he can't recite any of it from memory, and he and Paul both reveal ambitions to write a musical with a rock-and-roll score. Paul also refutes columnist Dorothy Kilgallen's claim that he and Jane Asher have married.

Murray praises the *Help!* soundtrack songs they had all heard the previous evening, and George explains that they were nine of eleven recorded so far (the leftovers were "If You've Got Trouble" and "That Means a Lot"), two of which were his own compositions. George, Ringo, and Murray then play a word-association game they had tried the previous evening.

RELEASE HISTORY

These interviews circulate in fair quality among collectors.

23. Radio interview G, R

Date: 9 March 1965
Location: Paradise Island, Bahamas
Interviewer: Fred Robbins
Broadcast: Radio Luxembourg
Assignment: Hollywood
Length: 26:34

During the final day of filming in the Bahamas, Ringo and George both recorded long interviews with American reporter Fred Robbins, probably for his syndicated show *Assignment: Hollywood,* heard on Radio Luxembourg in England.

Ringo's interview lasts almost twenty minutes and mostly focuses on his recent marriage; it was probably taped while the group wasn't needed on set, since Paul is heard chatting to someone and singing "It's My Party" loudly in the background from time to time, and John is around, too. Naming the film is still a problem, as Ringo admits they have gone through a lot of titles but don't have one that fits yet. Robbins points out that Nassau is a beautiful place for a newly married man to be, and Ringo deadpans, "My being married doesn't alter the place." Robbins clarifies that maybe Maureen would have liked to come along, but Ringo points out that it wouldn't be much of a honeymoon with "people like you" (journalists) hanging around. Ringo reveals that his new bride is staying with her mother for the time being, and that they will be living with John and Cynthia until they get their own apartment. He says he will bring Maureen to Austria, since it's only for eight days.

Robbins asks whether Maureen is intimidated by Beatlemania, but Ringo says she is well-protected and that while she has to share Ringo Starr with the world, she has Richard Starkey all to herself. Interestingly, he hopes to have three children, and that's how many they ended up with (Zak, Jason, and Lee). Although he wasn't able to keep the honeymoon location a secret, at least the wedding was quiet, which was more important, since he feels "that's a woman's day." More marriage talk follows, before the topic finally changes to business ventures. Ringo hasn't given up his goal of running hairdressing salons, but for now he has only a building company.

The film is also discussed, and Ringo feels it should be better than *A Hard Day's Night* if all the gags work out; he also records a generic introduction to a song from the film (which indicates that this wasn't broadcast at least until the "Ticket to Ride" single was released in April). Beyond that, he doesn't want to give away any of the plot, lest it wreck the experience for viewers. He also reveals that the Beatles have been to see a movie, *How to Murder Your Wife,* while in the Bahamas (although he gets it mixed up with *How to Succeed in Business Without Really Trying,* and calls it "How to Murder Your Wife Without Really Trying"). The future vegetarian names his favorite foods as steak, chops, lamb, and egg and bacon, insisting that his tastes haven't changed just because he has more money, although he can afford better cars now. Ringo also reflects on the irony of companies giving him free drum kits now that he can afford to buy good equipment!

Turning back to matrimonial matters, Robbins asks what Ringo expects out of wedded life, and he responds that it's great to be able to share everything (although he incongruously claims, "Now I'm the boss"). This section of the interview was spliced into an open-ended disc sent to radio stations to promote *Help!,* although it's not clear whether Robbins was the interviewer for the rest of that disc (see the late May to early June entry for details).

George also chats with Robbins, although he doesn't seem to be in the mood for answering questions about whether he'll get married; nonetheless, Robbins keeps pressing the issue. At first George deflects it with a simple "it's good fun," then he suggests Fred should be talking to John, since he's been married a while. Finally, he exclaims that it doesn't matter if everyone else got married or divorced, he'll do what he wants when he wants.

RELEASE HISTORY

Both interviews were released on the cassette *Historic Interviews, Volume 2,* sold primarily through the Beatlefest catalog.

24. Location recording

Date: ca. 9 March 1965
Location: Bahamas
Length: 1:55

Fred Robbins also captured a couple of minutes of audio-verité during the rehearsal of a scene in which the Beatles splashed around in the water. The assistant director instructs John to dog-paddle, calling it a "dog dance," to which John replies, "Do the Dog, man!"

RELEASE HISTORY

This recording was released on the cassette *Historic Interviews, Volume 2,* sold primarily through the Beatlefest catalog.

25. Newsreel footage

Date: 11 March 1965
Time: 7:05 a.m.
Location: London Airport
Length: 1:34

On the evening of March 10, the Beatles boarded a return flight to London, arriving the following morning. Reuters newsreel footage shows fans on the observation deck holding up a banner reading WELCOME HOME BEATLES. Ringo reads it aloud and sings a few appropriate lines from "Hello Dolly" ("it's so nice to see you back where you belong") as the Beatles exit a car and walk into the passport office, waving to the crowd. They're also seen returning to the car, stopping briefly to speak with a reporter.

RELEASE HISTORY

This newsreel footage circulates on video among collectors, as does 1:03 of silent ITV News footage.

26. Amateur and Newsreel footage

Date: 13 March 1965
Time: 11:00 a.m.
Location: London Airport
Length: 0:55

After a day in London to get their bearings, the Beatles and crew were off to Austria for another week of location filming. This time, Cynthia and Maureen were permitted to accompany their husbands to get in a little skiing. Newsreel footage and Walter Strach's color home movies document the party's departure from London Airport, including glimpses of director Richard Lester and costar Victor Spinetti.

RELEASE HISTORY

The silent home movie footage was released on the video *The Making of "Help!,"* and the silent newsreel footage (filmed by ITV) was included in the video compilation *At the Movies*.

27. Newsreel footage

Date: 13 March 1965
Time: afternoon
Location: Flughafen Airport and unknown hotel, Salzburg
Length: 1:30

Besides the usual journalists and fans awaiting the Beatles' arrival in Austria, a group of students greeted them by holding up individual signs spelling out BEATLES GO HOME. A minute or two of silent footage documents this, as well as the Beatles stepping off the plane (John, wearing his familiar *Help!*-era hat and cape, does some mock band conducting) and being driven off in a station wagon to a local hotel to hold a press conference.

RELEASE HISTORY

This silent footage circulates on video among collectors.

28. Radio interview

Date: 13 March 1965
Time: afternoon
Location: Flughafen Airport and unknown hotel, Salzburg
Broadcast: 15 March 1965
WDR Radio
Length: 4:22

German radio also covered the Beatles' arrival and press conference in Salzburg. This tape begins with the flight arrival announcement and the reporter's description of the "Beatles Go Home" dissenters. As the group poses for photographs on the plane's steps, Ringo jokes that they can't come any farther without their passports. The interviewer welcomes Paul to Austria, and John seems surprised (almost disappointed) that the weather is so warm.

During the press conference, Ringo is asked whether he knows about the avalanche in Obertauern, where the filming will take place. He reveals that avalanche danger is the reason they didn't go straight to the location (they aren't "allowed to" until after 6 p.m.), but that he's not afraid of being trapped under snow because the chance is just as great that their plane will crash one day. Ringo also refuses to disclose the names of any new film songs, invites the interviewer to have a pull at his hair to prove it's not a wig, and shows off his ability to order potatoes in German. Asked how much income tax he paid the previous year, John replies, "A lot."

RELEASE HISTORY

This interview circulates on tape in very good quality, thanks to a rebroadcast on November 29, 1980.

29. Amateur footage

Date: 17 March 1965
Location: Obertauern
Length: 0:13

A temporary name for the movie was announced to the press this day: *Eight Arms to Hold You.* But nobody was really happy with it, and John and Paul couldn't stomach composing a song with that title. Luckily, they hit upon *Help!* less than a month later. The curling rink scene was filmed this morning at the Hotel Edelweiss in Obertauern. Some silent color home movie footage was also taken by Walter Strach documenting the explosion of the "fiendish thingy."

RELEASE HISTORY

This footage is available on a videotape called *The Making of "Help!"* Other non-Beatle footage on this tape includes some ski-lift scenes from the fifteenth or sixteenth and scenes from Salzburg Airport around the twenty-first.

30. Studio session

Date: 30 March 1965
Time: 7:00–10:00 p.m.
Location: EMI Studio 2
Producer: George Martin

[A.] That Means a Lot—take 20 (stereo) (1:12)
[B.] That Means a Lot—take 22 (stereo) (2:08)
[C.] That Means a Lot—takes 23–24 (stereo) (2:09)
[D.] That Means a Lot—test take (stereo) (0:53)

[E.] You're Going to Lose That Girl—RM from take 3 (2:16)
[F.] You're Going to Lose That Girl—RS3 (2:15)

Mixed: 2 April 1965

[G.] You're Going to Lose That Girl—RS from take 3 (#1) (2:16)
[H.] You're Going to Lose That Girl—RS from take 3 (#2) (2:17)
[I.] You're Going to Lose That Girl—RS from take 3 (#3) (2:17)

A one-off evening recording session to tidy up some of the songs from February (the film's title song, "Help!," wasn't written yet). The bulk of the time was spent in a futile effort to tape a good version of "That Means a Lot." All attempts used three of the tape's four tracks (bass/drums; Paul's vocal; John and George's guitars).

Since it was a remake, they started with take 20, even though there were only two previous takes, both in the key of E. Take 20 (**A**) is played in G and begins with Norman Smith's take announcement. Once Paul has found the right tempo, he counts in for an unspectacular performance punctuated by some bluesy "answering" guitar licks from George. This breaks down in the second verse, perhaps because Paul is having trouble singing in a higher key.

The following take (**B**) is back in E and has a nice "chiming" double guitar riff played by John and George (many bootlegs list this as take 21, but Mark Lewisohn writes that the lead guitar had "disappeared" for that take, so it must be 22). This take, performed at a slower tempo, also features some snare rolls from Ringo, and it staggers its way to the end, but Paul has to remind the others about just when the song should finish.

Takes 23 (a false start) and 24 (**C**) are attempts at using the chiming guitar lick in the key of G, but end up even sloppier than before, and take 24 makes it only to the third verse before the Beatles break down into a half-time parody of themselves. This cuts off abruptly and we hear Paul say, "It's just a test"—perhaps he wanted to give it one more go, or perhaps this is part of a rehearsal session otherwise erased by the proper takes. In any case, this unnumbered take (**D**) is a shambles right from the start when the band fails to follow Paul's count-in and he gives up immediately, singing loudly and off-key (John has abandoned his guitar in favor of banging away on a piano) for less than a minute, finally thanking engineer Norman Smith for rolling tape, which mercifully cuts off at that point.

Also recorded on this day were the final overdubs for "You're Going to Lose That Girl." The original track 2 was erased in favor of a fresh guitar solo, this time accompanied by bongos and acoustic piano. The result was mixed for release on the *Help!* LP.

RELEASE HISTORY

1965: **E** and **F** were released on mono and stereo copies of the *Help!* LP in the UK. U.S. mono copies of *Help!* contained **F** with combined channels, and U.S. stereo copies have **F** with a tiny burst of noise before the song starts. It's difficult to tell whether this is a print-through of the "y" in the song's first word, or the end of "three" from Paul's count-in, caused by a banding error.

1987: **G,** a new digital remix created by George Martin, was released on the *Help!* CD.

1992: **C** and **D** appeared from a good-quality tape on the vinyl bootleg *Arrive without Travelling.* The same tape appeared the following year on the CD *Arrive without Aging.* A worse-sounding (but slightly longer) copy of **C** and **D** showed up on *Hodge Podge* later this year.

1999: **A–D** were included on *Turn Me On Dead Man: The John Barrett Tapes* in excellent sound and most complete form yet (with reversed channels compared to earlier issues).

2003: **H** was released on the soundtrack of the *Anthology* DVD.

2007: **I** was released on the soundtrack of the *Help!* DVD.

31. Radio interview

Date: late March–early April 1965
Location: Twickenham Film Studios, London
Interviewer: Monika, Norbert, Dieter Weidenfeld
Broadcast: Radio Luxembourg
Length: 20:32

A long set of interviews from this time period were recorded for an unknown program on the German-language service of Radio Luxembourg. The hosts, Monika, Dieter, and Norbert, hold separate discussions with each Beatle, conducted mostly in German, to the degree that each Beatle feels comfortable. George is first, and he not only has the best command of the language, but sings a bit of a German song, "Am Sonntag Will Mein Süßer Mit Mir Segeln Gehn," accompanying himself on acoustic guitar. The song had been a hit for the Old Merry Tale Jazzband in June 1961, when the Beatles were in Hamburg. He also plays a bit of Leroy Anderson's "Belle of the Ball," a waltz used as theme music for Radio Luxembourg's German broadcasts beginning in 1957.

George goes on to relate their recent experiences in Salzburg, and how the film company wouldn't let them do much skiing in case of injury, so Austrian ski instructors were used as stand-ins. He also praises Dick Lester for making it easy on untrained actors such as the Beatles. George describes his hobbies as playing guitar, listening to records, and watching movies, with *The Ipcress Files* being a current favorite. Finally, he talks about trying to travel through London Airport with John in heavy disguise, only to be instantly recognized, much to their chagrin.

John's interview is next, and he seems to have forgotten most of what little German he'd picked up in Hamburg, although he is able to sing a line from the bridge of "Komm Gib Mir Deine Hand" flawlessly! He explains that although *Help!* is not based in reality like their first film, the Beatles still basically play themselves. Upcoming projects plugged by John include the June European tour and his second book; he also says that he and Paul don't have a backlog of unrecorded songs written, apart from some inferior compositions from their teenage years. As do his fellow band members, John complains about the filming schedule, which requires them to be up early, although upon reflection of his 8 to 6 workday, he realizes, "It's like going to the office."

Ringo, who seems to speak almost no German, also bitches about the 7 a.m. wake-up call, joking that since they don't go to bed until 6 a.m., it's their own fault if they're tired. He also chats about the significance of his ring to the plot of the film and accepts the hosts' congratulations on his marriage. Last to speak is Paul (he can be heard lurking in the background of Ringo's segment), who talks a bit about skiing in Obertauern and blames the nonappearance of the group in Germany for three years on Brian Epstein.

As for the dating of this recording, I've seen it listed anywhere from March to June, but there are a couple of clues. In discussing "Rock and Roll Music," Dieter says that it was released two weeks ago as a single in West Germany. I haven't found a definitive release date yet, although one source lists February 22, which is clearly too early (they didn't return to London until March 22). George also gives a specific introduction for "Ticket to Ride," which probably wasn't available in Germany until the middle of April.

RELEASE HISTORY

1977: This interview was rebroadcast on the Radio Luxembourg show *Da Capo,* which seems to be the source of all circulating copies.

1996: Short extracts were included on the bootleg *Die Beatles In Deutschland 1966!*

32. Newsreel footage

Date: 6 April 1965
Location: Twickenham Film Studios, London
Length: 0:47

This was the second consecutive day of filming the Indian restaurant scenes for *Help!,* on kitchen and dining room sets at Twickenham. On the dining room set, Pathé's newsreel cameras captured the Beatles receiving a bell-shaped award from pirate station Radio Caroline, ostensibly "for being the most consistent pop stars" over Caroline's first year of operations. It was mainly an excuse for Caroline disc jockey Simon Dee, who presented the award, to interview the group for his radio show.

Fifteen seconds of silent newsreel footage from the same day was filmed by ITV News for airing April 12. It depicts the foursome and director Dick Lester horsing around with cutlery on the kitchen set.

RELEASE HISTORY

Both the silent Pathé newsreel (titled *Beatles Win Caroline Award*) and the ITV News footage circulate on video among collectors.

33. Radio interview — P

Date: ca. 6 April 1965
Location: Twickenham Film Studios, London
Length: 1:25

In addition to Simon Dee, an unknown DJ from Radio London recorded Beatles interviews around this time. This interview recording may stem from either or neither, but was conducted somewhere in the midst of filming *Help!*

Paul expresses his hatred of the artifice used to introduce songs in musicals and feels they'll get around this problem by having scenes take place during recording sessions ("You're Going to Lose That Girl," "I Need You," "The Night Before") or eschewing straight performances in favor of having the music play over more surreal footage ("Ticket to Ride," "Another Girl"). Although he won't know for sure until he sees a final cut, Paul feels *Help!* is turning out to be a lot more madcap than their first movie. He praises supporting cast members, such as Eleanor Bron and Leo McKern, noting, "We're the only ones that can't act!"

RELEASE HISTORY

This interview circulates in very good quality among collectors.

34. TV performance

Date: 10 April 1965
Time: 1:30 p.m.
Location: Studio 2, Riverside Studios, London
Broadcast: 22 May 1965, 5:40–6:05 p.m.
BBC1
Dr. Who

[A.] Ticket to Ride (0:28)

The "Ticket to Ride"/"Yes It Is" single was released April 9 in Great Britain, and the Beatles wasted no time in promoting it, donating their subsequent weekend to that task. This afternoon, they videotaped lip-synced performances of both songs for BBC1's *Top of the Pops.* This was also the public debut of their new stage costumes, whose design was based on a military-style jacket Paul had tried on in the Bahamas.

Nothing seems to have survived of the original April 15 broadcast, but the first verse and chorus of "Ticket to Ride" were recycled in an episode of the sci-fi series *Dr. Who,* which does circulate. The episode, titled "The Executioners," featured a "time and space visualizer" device that allowed the doctor to view various people from the past, such as Abraham Lincoln, Shakespeare, and of course, the Beatles on *Top of the Pops.* After switching off the machine, assistant Vicki exclaims, "Of course I know about them, I've been to their memorial theater in Liverpool! I didn't know they played classical music!"

RELEASE HISTORY

This *Dr. Who* episode was released on home video in the *Daleks Limited Edition Boxed Set.*

35. Concert

Date: 11 April 1965
Time: afternoon
Location: Empire Pool, Wembley
Broadcast: 18 April 1965, 3:15–4:40 p.m.
ABC
Pollwinners' Concert

[A.] intro (1:57)
[B.] I Feel Fine (2:06)
[C.] intro (0:30)
[D.] She's a Woman (2:42)
[E.] intro (0:28)
[F.] Baby's in Black (2:11)
[G.] intro (0:27)
[H.] Ticket to Ride (3:00)
[I.] intro (0:43)
[J.] Long Tall Sally (2:00)
[K.] outro (0:18)
[L.] award presentations (1:18)

For the third year running, the Beatles performed at the *New Musical Express* Poll-Winners' All-Star Concert, held at the Empire Pool in Wembley. Wearing their new stage suits again, they turned in a highly energetic five-song set, with John and Paul seeming in particularly high spirits, and both John and Ringo chewing gum throughout.

After Mal adjusts the amps and John does a microphone check, they open with "I Feel Fine," John picking out the riff on his electrified Gibson J-160. Things get off to a bad start, with Paul and George's shared vocal mic being off for half the song, and nobody remembering exactly how to end it. While John changes to his Rickenbacker six-string, Paul introduces a nice performance of "She's a Woman," in a slightly shortened arrangement that jumps from the guitar solo directly to the coda.

Paul introduces the next song as " 'Baby's in Black'—pool!" and shouts words of encouragement to George before his solo. Unfortunately George seems a bit off his game during the show, and before the next song, John stops to ask if he's in tune. A very tight performance of "Ticket to Ride" follows, and then John gives Paul a quick shoulder rubdown before the last song, "Long Tall Sally." Ringo is in top form and Paul shouts his mop-top off in what is the last performance of this warhorse until it was brought out of retirement for their last few shows in August of 1966.

To close the proceedings (**L**), Tony Bennett hands out awards, and John comes out by himself to receive runner-up in British vocal personality. *NME* owner Maurice Kinn then announces, "Top British vocal group, indeed top vocal group in the world!," and the Fab Four are united onstage (John giving Paul a bear hug) to hold up their microphone-shaped awards and pose for the cameras, as John reads from his cup in a mock disgusted voice: "Runner-up!"

RELEASE HISTORY

1987: Very good copies of **D, H,** and most of **J** were booted on the LP *Dig It!*

1998: The full musical portion (**A–K**) was included on the bootleg CD *The* NME *Pollwinners' Concert 1965* in excellent quality, taken from the soundtrack of a video that circulates (and includes the award presentations).

36. TV performance

Date: 11 April 1965
Time: 11:05–11:50 p.m.
Location: Studio 1, Teddington Studio Centre
Host: Eamonn Andrews
Broadcast: live
ABC
The Eamonn Andrews Show
Length: 19:16

Once they were offstage and changed out of their stage suits, the Beatles traveled to Teddington TV Studio to appear live on *The Eamonn Andrews Show.* No film or video of this show seems to have survived, but a fairly good off-air recording of the first twenty minutes has survived (the original broadcast was forty-five minutes including commercials). Besides lip-syncing both sides of their new single, the group chatted with host Andrews and guests Katharine Whitehorn and Wolf Mankowitz, and because of the show's late-night time slot and adult appeal, the questions had a more serious slant than usual, with Andrews backing up his theories by reading quotes from Dr. Joyce Brothers and from Brian Epstein's *A Cellarful of Noise.*

However, that doesn't mean that the Beatles are prepared to answer them all seriously, and they mostly goof around with topics such as their movie career, the reasons behind their success, and their long-term plans. George jokes that Paul will play the role of

Cathy in a film adaptation of *Wuthering Heights,* and Ringo follows up a few minutes later with a pun ("Withered Heights") while discussing where they will be in ten years' time. Asked what type of comedy they prefer to watch, Ringo chooses Laurel and Hardy, George praises Peter Sellers, and Paul gives a shout-out to Peter Cook ("What good last week, Peter!"), whose series with Dudley Moore, *Not Only . . . But Also . . . ,* had just ended its first season on BBC TV eight days earlier.

Wolf Mankowitz joins the panel and attacks the Beatles for being immodest and treating their audiences with contempt. They agree up to a point, but insist that they are not as confident as they appear, revealing that before their concert appearance earlier that day they were quite nervous, not having performed live for three months. Mankowitz stubbornly reiterates that their records garner huge presales, while Paul makes several futile attempts to explain to him that no matter how many copies dealers order, it can still be a flop if the public doesn't like it.

RELEASE HISTORY

1999: After circulating on tape for a long time, this recording was bootlegged on the boxed CD set *Mythology, Volume 2,* although the first few seconds of the announcer's introduction are missing there.

37. Radio interview G

Date: ca. 12 April 1965
Time: 2:00 p.m.
Location: Twickenham Film Studios, London (via telephone)
Interviewer: Jerry G. Bishop
Broadcast: KYW-AM, Cleveland
Length: 6:00

Cleveland disc jockey Jerry G. Bishop would get to travel with the Beatles on their summer 1965 North American tour, but a few months earlier he was just another voice on the phone. He managed to get through to the Twickenham canteen and speak with George, the others having finished their lunch and returned to the set already.

Bishop informs George that the Beatles were voted the number 1 group by the station's listeners and that one of them, junior high student Debbie Krueger, has won the chance to pose a few questions. She asks George about his favorite food (roast lamb) and whether Ringo's voice has changed after having his tonsils removed (no). George also reveals that the film's working title, *Eight Arms to Hold You,* has been scrapped, but after conferring with someone away from the receiver, he isn't able to share the new title just yet.

He does say that the title song will be released as a single, and that "Ticket to Ride" will be the only "old" song in the film. While he's written a couple of songs for the movie, George isn't sure if either will be used (the sequence for "I Need You" had yet to be filmed), although they will be on the soundtrack LP in any case. Bishop congratulates the Beatles on having sold 141 million records worldwide and on "Ticket to Ride" entering the UK chart at number 1 that week.

On April 7, it was announced to the press that Ringo and Maureen were expecting a child, and George says the father-to-be was "knocked out" by the news, even though he's never changed a diaper. Noting that Cleveland is absent from the upcoming tour itinerary, Bishop wonders if it's because of the mayor's ban on rock concerts at that city's public hall. George recalls the incident the previous year that led to the ban but doesn't think it's related. Before returning to the film set, George confirms that neither he nor Paul are engaged or married, but that if anything happens, "you'll hear about it . . . I can assure you."

RELEASE HISTORY

This interview circulates in very good quality among collectors.

38. Radio interview

Date: ca. April 1965
Interviewer: Brian Matthew
Broadcast: week of 3 July 1965
Top of the Pops #32
Length: 2:07

This chat, in two segments, has survived as part of a *Top of the Pops* Transcription disc assembled by the BBC's overseas sales department. It may have been taped April 13 during Brian Matthew's interview for the show *Pop Inn,* conducted at Twickenham Film Studios.

In the first segment, John's second book, the upcoming American tour, and Bob Dylan are topics of discussion. Brian asks John and Paul whether they are writing a musical, and George, not wanting to be left out, insists that he and Ringo will be painting Buckingham Palace green, with black shutters. This segment ends with an introduction of "Ticket to Ride," with the Beatles mocking Brian's clumsy segue. ("That's pretty folk!")

The second segment is just a brief introduction from George, who says he's taking a break from painting to sing "Everybody's Trying to Be My Baby."

RELEASE HISTORY

1982: Both segments (minus the "Ticket to Ride" intro) were included in the radio special *The Beatles at the Beeb.*

1988: The first segment (complete) was broadcast in *The Beeb's Lost Beatles Tapes.*

1998: The first segment was booted (complete but in inferior sound) on *Attack of the Filler Beebs!, Episode 2.*

2004: Both segments were included on the CD-R set *The Complete BBC Sessions—Upgraded for 2004.*

39. Studio session

Date: 13 April 1965
Time: 7:00–11:15 p.m.
Location: EMI Studio 2
Producer: George Martin

[A.] Help!—take 1 (stereo) (0:36)
[B.] Help!—takes 2–3 (stereo) (2:08)
[C.] Help!—studio chat (stereo) (0:35)
[D.] Help!—take 4 (stereo) (2:15)
[E.] Help!—take 5 (stereo) (2:52)
[F.] Help!—take 6 (stereo) (0:40)
[G.] Help!—tuning and chat (stereo) (0:29)
[H.] Help!—take 7 (stereo) (1:48)
[I.] Help!—takes 8–9 (stereo) (2:55)
[J.] Help!—take 10 (stereo) (2:27)
[K.] Help!—take 11 (stereo) (0:14)
[L.] Help!—take 12 (stereo) (2:26)
[M.] Help!—monitor mix from takes 3–9, 11, and 12 (mono) (16:25)

[N.] Help!—RM4 (production acetate) (2:20)
Mixed: 18 April 1965

[O.] Help!—RS2 (2:16)
Mixed: 18 June 1965

[P.] Help!—RS from take 12 (#1) (2:16)
[Q.] Help!—RS from takes 9 and 12 (#1) (2:16)
[R.] Help!—RS from takes 9 and 12 (#2) (0:10)
[S.] Help!—RS from take 12 (#2) (2:16)
[T.] Help!—RS from take 12 (#3) (2:16)

After dinner, the Beatles convened at Abbey Road to record the title song for their film and album in progress, written during a day off on April 4. "Help!" was completed in just over four hours, so they must have rehearsed it or at least settled on an arrangement prior to the session. For the song's backing, Paul and Ringo played bass and drums on one track while John strummed the rhythm on his twelve-string Framus acoustic, accompanied by George's electric Gretsch, on a second track.

A tape of what seems to be this complete session is available on bootlegs, obviously recorded over some other performances of "Help!," although it's not clear whether this is on the master reel or the bootlegger's copy. In addition, a "monitor mix" tape of much of this session has recently surfaced (**M**) from the preparations for the 1983 *Beatles at Abbey Road* presentation. It includes a bit of chat and the count-in prior to take 4, which are unavailable elsewhere, as well as putting the take in context.

Take 1 (**A**) breaks down when one of John's strings snaps, although the control room doesn't stop rolling tape until Ringo points this out. Take 2 (**B**) is a false start aborted when George has trouble with the first descending guitar riff. Take 3 rolls along nicely until the transition to the second verse, where John switches chords a couple of bars too early. Until this point, George has been limited to playing some chords over the intro, syncopated offbeats on the chorus, and the descending lick that ushers in each verse. But George Martin points out that he's having trouble playing the latter part cleanly and suggests he should overdub it separately. George argues that if they want to double-track the vocals, with only two tracks remaining on the tape, he'd have to sing and play the lick simultaneously, which would be even harder. The tape is stopped while they hash it out.

When it starts up again (**C**), Paul is trying to devise a way to mark out the beats on the tape to make it easier for George; John points out that he has been thumping out the beat on the body of his guitar. Finally they begin take 4 (**D**), a complete and well-executed take with George leaving out the difficult lick for the time being. This take is only marred by a couple of minor errors from Ringo.

The next piece of tape (**E**) begins with George practicing the chords, followed by a complete take 5. John realizes his guitar is going out of tune, but before he can amend the problem, Paul counts in for take 6 (**F**). Halfway through the opening verse, George Martin halts things so that John can tune up. The following segment (**G**) captures John's increasingly futile attempts to do so (highly reminiscent of Neil Innes' live performance of "Protest Song"), and when John is nearly weeping with frustration, the tape stops again.

Take 7 (**H**) goes well until they botch the transition to the final verse, and John is still trying to get in tune as they prepare for take 8 (**I**). Before counting in, Paul optimistically enthuses, "This is it. It's the swinging take!" However, a few seconds into the take, George stops playing. Thankfully, take 9 proves satisfactory and is rewound so that two vocal tracks can be added, one of which also has Ringo playing tambourine.

Take 9 is then reduced to three tracks of a new tape, combining both vocal tracks to one to free up space for George's lead guitar overdub. Take 10 (**J**) is an unused reduction, and take 11 (**K**) is aborted when Norman Smith forgets to mix out one of the vocal tracks on the intro. Take 12 (**L**) proves best and has George's guitar overdub added, filling all four tracks.

Most likely a rough mono mix was done at the end of the session for the Beatles to scrutinize. Three more mono mixes, numbered RM 2–4, were created on April 18, along with the first stereo mix. These were sent to United Artists for use in producing the film soundtrack, and the best mono mix (**N**) appears on a "production acetate."

It was probably this mix that the Beatles mimed to during filming on April 22, but soon thereafter, it was decided that both vocal tracks needed to be replaced. This was done during a non-EMI session on May 24 (see entry for details), and the new vocals were used in the film and on the mono LP and single mix.

But when it came time to mix the song in stereo at EMI, George Martin faced a problem. The new overdubs had been done on a three-track tape, a format that couldn't be played back on any of Abbey Road's machines. So the mix used on the stereo LP (**O**), and indeed all subsequent stereo remixes, use the original vocal tracks from take 12.

Latter-day remixes include Martin's 1987 digital remix for the *Help!* CD (**P**), which adds a touch of echo, and a 1993 remix for a video soundtrack (**Q**), made by syncing all four tracks of take 9 with the lead guitar overdub from take 12. This centers the bass/drum track, isolates lead guitar left and the other guitars right, and splits the two vocal tracks slightly.

RELEASE HISTORY

1965: **O** was released on stereo pressings of the *Help!* LP.

1983: The multimedia presentation *The Beatles at Abbey Road* included **D.** This is available in excellent quality on the bootleg CDs *Turn Me On Dead Man: The John Barrett Tapes* and *Abbey Road Video Show.* It's also on the *Mythology, Volume 2* boxed CD set with a faked count-in.

1987: **P,** a new digital remix created by George Martin, was released on the *Help!* CD.

1988: **A–C** and **E** first surfaced in excellent sound on the LP *Ultra Rare Trax, Volume 3 & 4.* They appeared the following year from tape source on the CDs *Hold Me Tight* and (**A,** part of **B,** and **E** only, with reversed channels) *Unsurpassed Masters, Volume 2;* both sources run a half step too slow.

1991: The bootleg CD *Unsurpassed Masters, Volume 6* included an excellent but slow tape of **I.**

1993: **Q** was included on the soundtrack of an EPK promoting the CD release of *The Beatles 1967–1970.* It can be heard on the bootleg CD *Lost and Found* and the CD-R *Video 1.*

1994: Excellent but slow tapes of **A–C** and **E–L** were included on the boxed set *The Ultimate Collection, Volume 3: Studio Sessions, 1965–66.*

1998: In addition to the first release of **N,** the bootleg CD *Help! Original Mix* also contained speed-corrected tapes of **A–C** and **E–L,** plus a copy of **O.**

2002: **M** first appeared in good quality on the bootleg CD *Complete Controlroom Monitor Mixes, Volume 2.*

2003: **R** was released on the soundtrack of the *Anthology* DVD.

2006: **S** was released on the *Love* CD.

2007: **T** was released on the soundtrack of the *Help!* DVD.

40. TV appearance — J, G

Date: 16 April 1965
Time: 6:08–7:00 p.m.
Location: Studio 1, Wembley Studios, London
Producer: Vicki Wickham
Host: Cathy McGowan
Broadcast: live
Rediffusion-TV
Ready Steady Goes Live!
Length: 2:12

Although the Beatles were in the midst of enjoying a five-day Easter break from shooting, John and George appeared on live TV this day to promote "Ticket to Ride." The show was Rediffusion's *Ready Steady Goes Live!,* and the Fab Two traveled to Wembley Studios to be interviewed by Cathy McGowan. Although none of the interview seems to be circulating, a recording (audio only) exists from the end of the program, as Adam Faith performs "I Need Your Loving," and all the other guests sing along. John's and George's voices can be made out clearly among the crowd, which also includes Doris Troy, the Kinks, and Herman's Hermits.

RELEASE HISTORY

1996: After first surfacing on a vinyl bootleg single, this recording was booted on the CD *Free as a Bird.*

41. Promo clip

Date: 22 April 1965
Location: Twickenham Film Studios, London
Producer: Walter Shenson
Broadcast: 17 July 1965, 5:50–6:30 p.m.
ABC
Lucky Stars Anniversary Show

[A.] Help! (2:17)

Cleverly killing two birds with one stone, a lip-synced performance of "Help!" was filmed at Twickenham (in black and white) to serve as both a title sequence and a promotional film clip. In the movie, it is "projected" onto a screen that has darts thrown at it, and thus the promo clip has come to be known as "dartless," although "creditless" would be just as accurate.

The Beatles perform dressed in black on a minimalist set, designed to resemble a modern "pop" TV show. Ringo wears the oversized prop ring from the film, and John plays his six-string Gibson acoustic (he had played a twelve-string on the record).

RELEASE HISTORY

The full dartless clip was included in the Austrian TV documentary *John Lennon & Yoko Ono,* which served as the best source for many years. It now circulates among video collectors in excellent quality, thanks to its appearance in Apple's *Anthology 2* and *1* electronic press kits.

42. TV interview

Date: 28 April 1965
Time: afternoon
Location: Twickenham Film Studios, London
Interviewer: Peter Sellers
Broadcast: 18 May 1965, 8:30–9:30 p.m.
NBC
The Best on Record
Length: 1:25

At Twickenham this afternoon, the Beatles took a break from shooting the pub scene to film a special insert for American TV. Peter Sellers was enlisted to present them with a Grammy Award for "A Hard Day's Night" (best performance by a vocal group, 1964), and the brief clip was included as part of NBC's Grammy special.

With John, Paul, George, and Ringo lined up on bar stools, Sellers introduces things by speaking into one of the Victrola-shaped awards: "I don't know if you can hear me better now . . ." He then gives the "Grandma" award to Paul, and hands out three others from a box ("Thanks, Mr. Ustinov," quips John). Finally, in the manner of a magician's assistant, Sellers holds up the container for inspection: "As you can see, folks, the box is now empty." John then leads all five in what sounds like cod-Italian but metamorphoses into a singalong of "It's a Long Way to Tipperary."

RELEASE HISTORY

1999: This clip circulates on video due to its inclusion in more recent Grammy broadcasts, as well as a Peter Sellers documentary; the audio was booted on *Mythology, Volume 2.*

43. Radio interview **P**

Date: 29 April 1965
Location: Twickenham Film Studios, London
Interviewer: Chris Denning
Broadcast: Radio Luxembourg
The Beatles
Length: 0:51

Chris Denning turned up at Twickenham to tape further interviews for his Radio Luxembourg series, chatting with three of the Beatles while Ringo filmed a scene ostensibly in the basement of Abbey Road. In this brief clip, Paul talks about the newly chosen title track and explains that Dick Lester thought up the name *Help!* because nobody was happy with *Eight Arms to Hold You,* which he reveals was another Ringo-ism.

RELEASE HISTORY

1972: This interview excerpt was aired in the BBC Radio documentary *The Beatles Story.*

44. Newsreel/Amateur footage

Date: 3 May 1965
Location: Salisbury Plain, Knighton Down
Length: 3:20

The Beatles convened on Salisbury Plain this morning to begin three days of location filming for *Help!* The scenes portrayed a "recording session" (complete with a control booth window!) in the middle of an enormous field, surrounded by the famous protection of Her Majesty's Third Armoured Division. The group mimed to "I Need You" and "The Night Before" before fleeing the enemy attack, eventually commandeering a tank to make their narrow escape.

On this first day, the press were invited to take pictures and film of the proceedings; footage shot by ITV News (for broadcast that evening) and the Associated Press is circulating, as well as more of Walter Strach's color home movies. All three sources cover the same events, with the Beatles arriving on location (Paul gives a thumbs-up) and posing with their instruments for photographers (costar Leo McKern also takes a snapshot). The "troops" then gather around Ringo's drum kit, and George exchanges his guitar for a prop rifle; Paul opts to use his bass guitar to mow down the enemy.

RELEASE HISTORY

The 30-second ITV report is included in a circulating compilation titled *At the Movies.* One minute and twenty seconds of the AP newsreel footage was included as a bonus on the home video release of *Help! Special Edition.* One minute and thirty seconds of Walter Strach's color home movie was released on the video *The Making of* Help!; unfortunately, all the aforementioned footage is silent.

45. Radio interview

Date: 9 May 1965
Time: afternoon
Location: Dolphin Restaurant, London
Interviewer: Sandy Lesberg
Broadcast: New York (?)
Length: 13:02

Several street scenes for *Help!* were filmed on this day in various London locations, and in the evening the Beatles attended Bob Dylan's concert in the Royal Festival Hall. Somewhere in between, they also recorded an interview with an American journalist, Sandy Lesberg. Walter Shenson, producer of *Help!,* was present, and he had arranged the interview, being a New York associate of Sandy's. Most releases claim this was taped inside the Dolphin Restaurant, the exterior of which was one of the locations visited this day.

It's a very entertaining thirteen minutes, as each Beatle tries to outdo the other in wordplay and tomfoolery. There's also a running gag about the fact that their imminent film, LP, and single end with an exclamation point. Lesberg tries to nail down some facts about their summer tour of America, but the group remains blissfully ignorant of their itinerary. Perhaps Mr. Lesberg was writing a gossip column, as he alludes to Hedda Hopper and Walter Winchell, the latter of whom the Beatles profess to despise (he had repeatedly insisted that Paul was secretly married, despite Paul's protests).

Since they'll be playing some stadiums on their upcoming tour ("Tessie O'Shea Stadium," George quips), Paul suggests they play some "rounds" of baseball to limber up before each show. Ironically enough, they would do so the following two days on the film set—Paul can be seen playing catch against the wall during the scene in question. Walter Shenson helpfully mentions the Chicago venue as "Cominskey" [sic] Park, to which John makes a knocking sound and replies, "Come inski!"

Also in the sports vein, Paul describes an Irish game he and John had seen on American TV, similar to lacrosse but using shillelaghs to hit the ball. George, clearly on a roll, chimes in with "Bill Shillelagh" of "Rock around the Clock" fame. The actual sport they saw was probably hurling, in which a stick called a hurley (similar to a hockey stick) is used. George also makes repeated attempts to tell an off-color joke but is censored by the others before he can get to the punch line, which John eventually reveals as being, "Take the sack off, I wanna kiss her!"

RELEASE HISTORY

1996: This interview was released on *Rare Photos & Interview CD, Vol. 3.*

46. Studio session

Date: 10 May 1965
Time: 8:00–11:30 p.m.
Location: EMI Studio 2
Producer: George Martin

[A.] Bad Boy—RM1 (2:17)
[B.] Dizzy Miss Lizzy—RM1 (2:52)
[C.] Bad Boy—RS1 (2:17)
[D.] Dizzy Miss Lizzy—RS1 (2:52)
Mixed: 10 May 1965

[E.] Dizzy Miss Lizzy—RS from take 7 (2:52)

Capitol Records in the United States had a dilemma: No new Beatles albums had been released since December 1964, and they needed new product on the shelves. All they had were six songs left over from *Beatles for Sale* (two of which were already out as Capitol singles), and three songs from the February sessions that would not be used in the upcoming film (one of which had been used as the B-side to "Ticket to Ride"). This was not quite enough to fill an LP, even by Capitol's meager standards. So the call went out for a couple more usable songs, and the Beatles complied, shoe-horning in an evening session at Abbey Road after a full day of location filming.

With no new compositions ready, they dug into their old repertoire and came up with a pair of Larry Williams rockers—perhaps inspired by the top 30 success of their previous cover of "Slow Down" on the *Billboard* singles chart. First up was "Dizzy Miss Lizzy," with two takes of a backing track being recorded, followed by four takes of "Bad Boy." They then decided they could improve on "Dizzy Miss Lizzy" and laid down five more rhythm takes. Overdubs for both numbers included John's raucous lead vocal, further lead guitar from George, percussion from Ringo (tambourine for "Bad Boy" and cowbell for "Dizzy Miss Lizzy"), and electric piano from Paul.

This session ended with mono and stereo mixes of both numbers (one per song) being prepared past midnight, and the tapes were airmailed to California the following day. By May 12, the front cover proof for *Beatles VI* was approved, with the back cover finished two days later. The rush to have covers printed meant that the sleeve merely listed the song titles in roughly the order Capitol had received them, with "Bad Boy" and "Dizzy Miss Lizzy" tacked on at the end, along with a note reading "see label for correct playing order."

The 1987 remix of "Dizzy Miss Lizzy" (**E**) has a layer of digital reverb added to John's vocal. There is also a "backing track" version of that song on bootlegs such as *Hodge Podge 3,* which is merely an outfake created by OOPS-ing version E.

RELEASE HISTORY

1965: **A–D** were released in the United States on *Beatles VI.* Only **B** and **D** were released that year in the UK, on *Help!*

1966: **A** and **C** were finally released in the UK on *A Collection of Beatles Oldies.* **C** can be found on the CD *Past Masters, Volume 1.*

1987: **E,** a new digital remix created by George Martin, was released on the *Help!* CD.

47. Radio interview — J, P, R

Date: 11 May 1965
Time: ca. 3:00 p.m.
Location: Cliveden House, Maidenhead
Interviewer: Buddy McGregor
Broadcast: KNUZ-AM, Houston
Length: 3:52

This would be the Beatles' final day in front of the cameras for *Help!,* and the last of a two-day shoot at historic Cliveden House in Berkshire, which was doubling as the grounds of Buckingham Palace. Official Beatles photographer Bob Whitaker was among those allowed on the set, and he smuggled an American DJ, Buddy McGregor of Houston's KNUZ-AM, into what was supposed to be a set closed to outside press. The Beatles were in such a good mood that day celebrating the wrap that they probably wouldn't have cared. They spent some time playing softball on the grounds and challenged the film crew to a relay race. Team Beatle (supplemented by Neil Aspinall and Alf Bicknell) triumphed over three other teams, and McGregor captured some of the action on his tape recorder. Some footage of the race also appears on the 2007 DVD of *Help!*

After a lunch break, the group drove away from the set and wandered into the wooded ground for a joint or two, and then returned to giggle their way through the final scenes. McGregor cornered John, Paul, and Ringo for a brief interview while they sated their munchies by sucking Popsicles. Not surprisingly, the conversation is less than illuminating, as they recap the race, discuss Ringo's car and the Astrodome scoreboard, and debate the differences in British and American English. John explains the "Spaniard/spanner" pun in his new book title, and we learn that Popsicles are called "lolly ices" in Britain, although nobody can agree on the derivation of either term.

RELEASE HISTORY

1965: This interview was pressed onto a souvenir 45 rpm single complete with picture sleeve, titled *Buddy in Britain—A Chat with the Beatles,* which sold for 50 cents at Foley's department store in Houston.

1993: A home video called *The Lost Interview* was released, mostly comprised of stock newsreel footage and stills interspersed with McGregor telling his story to the camera. It includes a brief excerpt of the relay race (audio only), and ends with four minutes of the interview (again, audio only). As I don't have a copy of the single, I can't say whether that had extra material beyond what is on the video.

48. TV interview

Date: 24 May 1965
Location: Cannes
Interviewer: Merv Griffin
Broadcast: 1 June 1965
syndicated
The Merv Griffin Show
Length: 3:19

On May 22, John and Cynthia joined Dick Lester and his wife, Deirdre, for a long weekend at the Cannes Film Festival, where *The Knack,* Lester's follow-up film to *A Hard Day's Night,* was being screened (it would go on to win the Palme d'Or, much to Lester's astonishment). The day before they returned to London, John and Dick were interviewed by Merv Griffin, there to cover the festival for his TV talk show, syndicated across America by Westinghouse.

Although the footage isn't circulating, a home-taped audio recording shows what a playful mood the pair were in, dodging Merv's every effort to ask a serious question. Merv is a good sport and tries to joke along, noting that "Beatles at the Cow Palace . . . sounds like a condition of some kind." John plugs *Help!* and *A Spaniard in the Works,* claiming that Lester directed his book as well as their new movie. Merv asks whether the other Beatles know he's left the country, and John deadpans, "I think they'll have noticed."

RELEASE HISTORY

This recording circulates among collectors from a good-quality off-air tape.

48a. Studio session

Date: 24 May 1965
Time: 7:00–10:00 p.m.
Location: CTS Studios, London
Producer: George Martin

[A.] Help!—RM? (film mix) (2:16)
Mixed: 24 May 1965

[B.] Help!—RM4 (#2) (2:16)
Mixed: 18 June 1965

John flew back from Cannes just in time to attend this postsync session for the film *Help!* in London. Although dialogue may have been added to the soundtrack this evening, the main task was to tape new vocal tracks for the film's title song. The fact that this was done at a film dubbing studio may indicate that they didn't feel the miming was accurate enough in the filmed version. Or perhaps Abbey Road was booked, and using CTS (Cine Tele Sound) was a matter of expediency.

In any case, CTS had only three-track machines, so all three instrumental tracks from take 12 of "Help!" had to be bounced down to one track on a new tape. This left two free tracks on the reduction for the new vocals, this time without any tambourine. The new vocals can be distinguished from the old by the first verse: John sings "and now these days," where on the original vocals he had sung "but now these days."

A mono mix using these new vocals was created for use in the film (**A**); this leaves both vocal tracks up in the introduction. On June 18, George Martin decided to clean up the intro a bit for record release and prepared a new mono mix (**B**), which splices the first 10 seconds of the original take 12 vocals to the CTS vocal version.

Confused as to which mono mix you're listening to? If John sings "but now" in the first verse, and you hear tambourine, it's the production acetate mix. If John's vocal is double-tracked on the intro, it's the film soundtrack mix. Otherwise, it's the mix released on the single and LP. All three mono mixes also omit John's "thumping" on the body of his guitar, which is audible on all stereo mixes.

RELEASE HISTORY

1965: **A** was included on the soundtrack of the film *Help!* as heard in theaters that summer. **B** was released on a single worldwide and is available on EMI's "Help!" CD single.

1998: The bootleg CD *Help! Original Mix* included a copy of **A.**

49. Radio performance

Date: 26 May 1965
Time: 2:30–6:00 p.m.
Location: Studio 1, BBC Piccadilly Studios, London
Producer: Keith Bateson
Host: Denny Piercy
Broadcast: 7 June 1965, 10:00 a.m.–12:15 p.m.
BBC Light Programme
The Beatles (Invite You to Take a Ticket to Ride)

[A.] **Ticket to Ride (edited)** (0:38)
[B.] **intro** (0:19)
[C.] **Everybody's Trying to Be My Baby** (2:20)
Stay (The Hollies)
[D.] **I'm a Loser** (2:31)
You Know He Did (The Hollies)
Chug-A-Lug (The Hollies)
Dream Child (The Hellions)
[E.] **intro** (1:45)
[F.] **The Night Before** (2:27)
[G.] **outro** (0:02)
Nitty Gritty/Something's Got a Hold on Me (The Hollies)
[H.] **Honey Don't** (2:48)
[I.] **intro** (0:25)
[J.] **Dizzy Miss Lizzy** (2:42)
[K.] **outro** (0:04)
I'm Alive (The Hollies)
That's Why I'm Crying (The Ivy League)
[L.] **intro** (0:02)
[M.] **She's a Woman** (2:47)
[N.] **intro** (0:06)
[O.] **Ticket to Ride** (2:59)

After recording 268 songs for broadcast by BBC Radio in 51 programs, the Beatles' unique relationship with the Beeb came to an end this afternoon, as they recorded their final exclusive show, titled *The Beatles (Invite You to Take a Ticket to Ride).* Seven songs and chat with presenter Denny Piercy were taped for the Whit Monday broadcast, and it took some wrangling within the BBC to secure the Beatles for one last performance: At one point, they would agree only if the radio session could be taped at Abbey Road using more professional equipment and George Martin as producer.

In the end, it was recorded at the Piccadilly Theatre with Keith Bateson at the board, but none of the usual spirit of fun was missing from the words or music. John parodied his own lyric in "I'm a Loser" as "beneath this wig I am wearing a tie," and George threw in an "everydobby" during his vocal on "Everybody's Trying to Be My Baby." This was also their only BBC session to use electric piano, which they incorporated into "The Night Before" and "Dizzy Miss Lizzy."

Although Brian Matthew was sadly absent, Piercy filled in admirably as a foil to the Fab wit—they were familiar with him from their appearance on the Piercy-hosted *Parade of the Pops* way back in February 1963. He also held his own, catching everyone off-guard by sabotaging a heavy-handed intro for "Dizzy Miss Lizzy" with a glib "Let's hear it then, 'A Ticket to Ride'!"

RELEASE HISTORY

1972: The BBC Radio series *The Beatles Story* included an excellent copy of **J,** from a *Top of the Pops* transcription disc. It was copied from this source on the bootleg LP *Have You Heard the Word.*

1982: The BBC radio special *The Beatles at the Beeb* included excellent copies of **J** and **O,** both from Transcription disc sources.

1988: A very good tape of the entire broadcast (**A–O**) appeared on the bootleg LP *The Beatles at the Beeb, Volume 13.* The whole show was used on Great Dane's boxed CD set *The Complete BBC Sessions.*

1994: Predictably, only the two songs from the Transcription disc (**J** and **O**) were released on Apple's *Live at the BBC* CD. Both are slightly incomplete and crossfaded.

50. Open-end interview

Date: late May–early June 1965
Location: Twickenham Film Studios, London (?)
Length: 10:03

Although their on-camera work for *Help!* was complete, the Beatles had to return to Twickenham on several occasions during postproduction to overdub some dialogue to certain scenes. It was probably on one of these days at Twickenham that an open-end interview was conducted to promote the film in America, similar to the one recorded for *A Hard Day's Night.* (Although this time John showed up!) That one had actually been conducted a few days after the film's premiere, but it seems likely that this one was taped in late May or early June—for one thing, there is no mention of the Beatles' MBE awards. May 18 is the only verified date the Beatles were present for postproduction during this period.

The unheard interviewer is unknown, although it's probably not Wink Martindale, as the *Golden Beatles* sleeve claims; his name is mentioned in the KFWBeatles Promo that appears just before the open-end interview on that release (see the May 25, 1964, entry), so that's likely where the confusion occurred. There's a possibility that it was Fred Robbins, since a portion of his March 9 interview with Ringo (discussing his new marriage) is spliced into the middle of the open-end chat.

The origin of the film's title and some perfunctory description of the film open the disc, but the Beatles are clearly jaded and bored with the whole promotion machine and begin to subvert the process. Rather than describe the plot in their own words, they simply parrot the advertising taglines, such as "Will John live to sleep in his pit again?," which they are apparently reading from ad copy lying in front of them. After some discussion about the soundtrack and Beatle pressures, John responds to charges that the group was rude to some tourists in the Bahamas. He admits that they were only responding in kind to an obnoxious woman who interrupted their meal with a demand for autographs for her daughter. By the end of this interview, they have abandoned any pretense of taking it seriously, and Paul and John try to top each other by describing nonexistent scenes from *Help!* Unfortunately, the world will never get to see the Beatles in a vintage car derby or the touching love scene between George and Ringo on the beach at sunset!

RELEASE HISTORY

1965: The interview was first released on a promotional disc, *United Artists . . . Presents . . . "Help!"*

1985: It was reissued on *The Golden Beatles,* which also appeared on CD, but the interview was not taken from a tape source.

51. Newsreel footage **P**

Date: 11 June 1965
Time: evening
Location: London Airport
Length: 1:14

As summer approached, Paul enjoyed a fortnight's vacation at a villa in Albufiera, Portugal, soaking up the sun with Jane Asher and finishing up a new composition, "Yesterday." A phone call from Brian Epstein delivered a piece of news that necessitated Paul's return to London a day earlier than planned.

Cameras rolled as the couple deplaned, carrying a bag each, and entered the terminal. From there, Paul would place phone calls to Brian and to reporter Ronald Burns for BBC Radio's *Late Night Extra.* He is also seen signing autographs for policemen and being driven away with Jane. Having been tipped off a day or two in advance, Fleet Street already had their M.B.E.ATLES banner headlines prepared for the following morning.

RELEASE HISTORY

This silent footage circulates on video; 10 seconds was used in ITV's *Reporting '66: End of Beatlemania.*

52. TV interview

Date: 12 June 1965
Location: Twickenham Film Studios, London
Interviewer: George Yateman
Broadcast: 30 June 1965, 8:15–8:30 p.m.
WNDT-TV, New York
British Calendar: News
Length: 3:05

What was supposed to be a private screening of a rough cut of *Help!* at Twickenham Film Studios turned into a succession of print, TV, radio, and newsreel interviews for the Beatles to discuss being named Members of the Most Excellent Order of the British Empire (MMEOBEs?). The press conference was arranged to begin at 1:30 p.m., but John decided to stay in bed, perhaps ambivalent about accepting the award in the first place. Brian Epstein finally persuaded John to show up, and the event began seventy minutes late. Cameras captured at least four separate interviews, all available to collectors in various places.

The first and perhaps most widely seen clip was apparently filmed for U.S. public television. The interview is prefaced by some footage from *A Hard Day's Night* with an American voice-over, although the reporter, George Yateman, is British. He wonders whether the Beatles' $10 million in American record sales are responsible for their MBEs, and he asks whether they'll dress up to visit Buckingham Palace. John jokes that they'll wear drainpipe trousers, and Ringo says they won't bother to get haircuts. Yateman's overdramatic description of their rise to success "from obscurity in a cellar in Liverpool" is mocked by John, who says it's much easier to write songs now that they have nice soft cushions to sit on. Plugging their upcoming appearance on *The Ed Sullivan Show* to U.S. viewers, Paul wonders whether Ed or his wife, "Mrs. Ed," are watching; Ringo just hopes "Mr. Ed" is.

RELEASE HISTORY

This film clip was included in part in the documentary film *Imagine: John Lennon,* and is basically complete (some of the visuals near the end are replaced with other footage) on the video *Fun with the Fab Four.* It also circulates in original form among video collectors.

53. Newsreel interview

Date: 12 June 1965
Location: Twickenham Film Studios, London
Length: 0:40

An Associated Press newsreel is the source of this interview clip with an unknown reporter who inquires whether the Beatles' "teenage rebel image" will be hurt by this step toward nobility. They dispute having any such image, and Ringo even claims that he'd like to be a duke!

RELEASE HISTORY

This footage circulates on video, usually accompanying the George Yateman interview described earlier.

54. Radio interview

Date: 12 June 1965
Location: Twickenham Film Studios, London
Interviewer: Hugh Moran
Broadcast: BBC Radio
Length: 3:49

The third interview was conducted by BBC reporter Hugh Moran, who introduces each Beatle, with the phrase "Ringo Starr, MBE" causing uproarious mirth. Ringo reveals that he hasn't even told his mother yet about the award and hopes that it can be worn around the neck, rather than having to fill his suits with pinholes. Paul says if they have to wear top hats to the ceremony, maybe they can pull rabbits from them, and George tries to make a joke about confusing MBE with NDO (Northern Dance Orchestra). Moran makes one final attempt to get a serious answer about how they really feel about the award, but it's in vain—Ringo merely boasts of having a certificate for successfully swimming twenty-five yards.

RELEASE HISTORY

Although it was filmed by Reuters (a small clip can be seen in *Anthology*), this interview was primarily for BBC Radio, and as such was aired in part on *The Beeb's Lost Beatles Tapes* series as well as Westwood One's documentary *Sgt. Pepper's Lonely Hearts Club Band: A History of the Beatle Years 1962–1970.* The 2:15 Reuters soundtrack edit was released on *Fab Four CD & Book Set,* but all three sources are needed for a complete recording.

55. TV interview

Date: 12 June 1965
Location: Twickenham Film Studios, London
Interviewer: Richard Linley
Broadcast: 12 June 1965
ITV
Length: 2:02

The final clip was filmed for ITV News, and at this point, the Beatles have run out of material and basically repeat jokes from the previous interviews (about journalist Donald Zec, being drafted, and pronouncing MBE as an acronym). When George mentions Twickenham, John sneaks in a plug for *"Help!,* our new film . . ."

RELEASE HISTORY

1995: The audio of this interview was included on *Rare Photos & Interview CD, Volume 1.* This footage appears on video compilations such as *Beatlemania* and *Beatles 1962 to 1970,* and a very short segment is also seen in the *Anthology* home video.

56. Studio session

Date: 14 June 1965
Time: 2:30–5:30 p.m.
Location: EMI Studio 2
Producer: George Martin

[A.] I'm Down—take 1 (stereo) (2:51)

[B.] I've Just Seen a Face—RM1 (2:02)
[C.] I'm Down—RM1 (2:32)
[D.] I've Just Seen a Face—RS1 (2:02)
Mixed: 18 June 1965

[E.] I'm Down—RS1 (2:30)
Mixed: 28 April 1976

[F.] I've Just Seen a Face—RS from take 6 (2:02)
[G.] I'm Down—RS from take 7 (0:20)

British Beatles albums usually contained fourteen tracks; eleven had been recorded for *Help!* in February, but two of these were rejected and one never made it past a B-side. The recording of the title song in April brought the total back up to nine, and three days were booked at Abbey Road Studios to come up with the final five numbers. Three contenders were recorded on this first day, all Paul McCartney compositions and all excellent in different ways.

First to be recorded was "I've Just Seen a Face," with the backing track of drums, six- and twelve-string acoustic guitars, and Paul's lead vocal perfected by take 6. Overdubs consisted of electric guitar for the intro, maracas and a second vocal (Paul harmonizing with himself) for the choruses, and a nice acoustic solo from George. The original mono and stereo mixes (**B** and **D**) are basically identical, while a hint of echo is added for George Martin's 1987 remix (**F**).

Paul's "Long Tall Sally" rewrite, "I'm Down," came next, with Paul shouting his Little Richard vocal on track 3 of the tape backed by his own bass, John on a Vox Continental electric organ, George on electric guitar, and Ringo bashing away at his kit, all recorded on track 1.

Take 1 (**A**) can be heard in stereo (with the first two phrases of George's solo panned briefly to the left) on *Anthology 2,* and it's a very exciting performance—with no ending worked out, Paul tells the others to "keep going" as the final choruses roll around. When they finally grind to a halt, he utters the immortal phrase, "Plastic soul, man," which would inspire their next LP title.

Take 7 was the master, featuring overdubs of bongos, backing vocals, and an organ solo on track 2, with more backing vocals, a brief bit of organ (heard in the second chorus and near the end), and a new guitar solo on track 4. Interestingly, George's original solo can be heard leaking through other microphones in the center of the stereo mix (**E**), presumably from an earlier attempt played simultaneous to the track 2 overdubs. Although a stereo mix was prepared on June 18, 1965, the one eventually released in 1976 was a fresh remix from the four-track. The mono mix (**C**) has no "phantom" guitar solo, lasts a couple of seconds longer than the stereo, and was released on the B-side of their next single, "Help!"

RELEASE HISTORY

1965: **C** was released on a single around the world and can be found on the "Help!" CD single. **B** and **D** were included on mono and stereo pressings of the *Help!* LP in the UK (and *Rubber Soul* in the United States).

1976: **E** was released on the album *Rock 'N' Roll Music.* It's also available on the CD *Past Masters, Volume One.*

1987: **F,** a new digital remix created by George Martin, was released on the *Help!* CD.

1996: **A** was released on *Anthology 2.*

2003: **G** was released on the soundtrack of the *Anthology* DVD.

57. Studio session

Date: 14 June 1965
Time: 7:00–10:30 p.m.
Location: EMI Studio 2
Producer: George Martin

[A.] Yesterday—take 1 (mono w/stereo reverb) (2:31)

After a break for dinner, the versatile McCartney returned to the studio to tape "Yesterday," accompanied only by his Epiphone Texan acoustic guitar, tuned down a full step to make it easier to play and sing simultaneously. Indeed, as take 1 begins, Paul can be heard explaining to George that although he's playing a G-shape, the accompaniment will have to be in the key of F major.

That accompaniment would come not in the form of his fellow Beatles, but a string quartet scored by George Martin over the next two days; for now, Paul ran through the song on his own—just acoustic guitar on track 2 and vocal on track 3 of the tape. On this first take, Paul mixes up the order of lines in the second verse and chuckles at his mistake. Take 2 was flawless and would be completed later that week.

RELEASE HISTORY

1996: **A** was released on *Anthology 2.*

58. Studio session

Date: 15 June 1965
Time: 2:30–6:15 p.m.
Location: EMI Studio 2
Producer: George Martin

[A.] It's Only Love—takes 3 and 2 (mono w/stereo reverb) (1:55)

[B.] It's Only Love—RM1 (1:53)
[C.] It's Only Love—RS1 (1:53)
Mixed: 18 June 1965

[D.] It's Only Love—RS from take 6 (1:53)

While Paul had been inspired to create three new compositions, John, stuck in the midst of his self-proclaimed "fat Elvis" period, wasn't so fortunate. He did come up with one new song, "It's Only Love," and his later comment that it was one of his songs that he "hated the most" does a disservice to the lovely melody and great singing.

These strengths are even more evident in the simple early version (**A,** consisting of take 3, a false start, spliced in front of take two) released on *Anthology 2.* At this point, there is just the backing track of bass, drums, six- and twelve-string acoustic guitars, plus John's vocal. By take 6, electric guitars had been overdubbed, one of them annoyingly drenched in tremolo, along with a tambourine and second lead vocal for the choruses. The original mono and stereo mixes (**B** and **C**) contain a slight difference in John's second vocal track when compared to the 1987 remix (**D**).

RELEASE HISTORY

1965: **B** and **C** were included on mono and stereo pressings of the *Help!* LP in the UK (and *Rubber Soul* in the United States).

1987: **D,** a new digital remix created by George Martin, was released on the *Help!* CD.

1996: **A** was released on *Anthology 2.*

59. Radio interview **J**

Date: 16 June 1965
Time: 8:00–8:30 p.m.
Location: NEMS Enterprises, London
Interviewer: Wilfrid De'Ath
Broadcast: 3 July 1965, 10:10–10:40 p.m.
BBC Home Service
The World of Books
Length: 6:07

John's second book, *A Spaniard in the Works,* was due to go on sale across Great Britain on June 24. Since the Beatles would be touring abroad that week, John did most of his promoting during this pretour stretch of activity. After spending the day at Twickenham with his bandmates completing postsync work on *Help!,* John arrived at the NEMS offices in the evening to tape two interviews for BBC Radio.

The first and most important was for the July 3 broadcast of *The World of Books.* Host Wilfred De'Ath, clearly a fan of John's writing, steers the conversation away from pop music and toward strictly literary matters. This seems to catch John off-guard, and he has trouble formulating detailed answers at first; De'Ath's query about the use of onomatopoeia is met with, "I just haven't got a clue what you're talking about really. 'Automatic pier,' sounds like to me." After the usual questions about literary influences (Joyce, Chaucer, Lear, Carroll), John dismisses criticism about his sick sense of humor, insisting that he'd been writing and drawing the same way since school.

De'Ath points out that some of the stories have a social conscience, but the future war protester can only mumble, "I'm not a do-gooder about things, I won't go around marching . . ." before admitting that he does keep up with current events through the newspapers. John's reading from "The Fat Budgie" is followed by a discussion of his drawing technique.

This conversation was deemed interesting enough to be included in two other contemporary BBC Radio broadcasts, and even pressed onto a Transcription Services disc for overseas sale titled *John Lennon—Bookbeatle.* It's no doubt thanks to this disc that an excellent copy has survived the years and been included in numerous BBC and Lennon documentaries.

RELEASE HISTORY

2000: The longest available version of this interview was bootlegged on the CD *The Beatles Broadcast Collection, Trailer 2.*

60. Radio interview **J**

Date: 16 June 1965
Time: evening
Location: NEMS Enterprises, London
Interviewer: Tim Matthews
Broadcast: 21 June 1965, 7:15–7:45 a.m.
BBC Home Service
Today
Length: 0:31

John's second interview from this day was conducted by Tim Matthews for the June 21 edition of the newsmagazine *Today.* All that seems to exist from this is a 30-second excerpt of John reading "The National Health Cow."

RELEASE HISTORY

1984: This recording appeared in Westwood One's *Sgt. Pepper's Lonely Hearts Club Band: A History of the Beatle Years 1962–1970* radio special.

2000: The interview was included on the bootleg CD *The Beatles Broadcast Collection, Trailer 2.*

61. Studio session

Date: 17 June 1965
Time: 2:00–4:00 p.m.
Location: EMI Studio 2
Producer: George Martin

[A.] Yesterday—RM2 (2:02)
Mixed: 17 June 1965

[B.] Yesterday—RS1 (2:03)
Mixed: 18 June 1965

[C.] Yesterday—RS from take 2 (2:02)

This was the final day of recording sessions for the *Help!* album, and the first and most important task was the completion of "Yesterday." The string quartet overdubbed their part onto track 1, and then Paul made a second attempt at recording his lead vocal on track 4 of the tape. The only portion of this to be used was at the end of the first bridge, and since he was singing without headphones, Paul's original vocal can be heard over the playback speaker, giving the passage a double-tracked effect. The released mixes all have this second vocal at slightly varying volume levels, with the most prominent heard on the original stereo mix (**B**). The 1987 stereo remix (**C**) fades the song a split second early to cover up some extra bow squeaking at the end.

RELEASE HISTORY

1965: **A** and **B** were included on mono and stereo pressings of the *Help!* LP in the UK, and **A** was released as a single in the United States.

1987: **C,** a new digital remix created by George Martin, was released on the *Help!* CD.

62. Studio session

Date: 17 June 1965
Time: 4:00–5:30 p.m.
Location: EMI Studio 2
Producer: George Martin

[A.] Act Naturally—RM1 (2:27)
[B.] Act Naturally—RS1 (2:27)
Mixed: 18 June 1965

[C.] Act Naturally—RS from take 13 (2:27)

With the completion of "Yesterday," there were still two slots to fill on the album, and for the last time until 1970, the Beatles settled upon releasing a cover version. After briefly considering a song donated by their recording engineer Norman Smith, they decided instead to ensure Ringo had a lead vocal on the album. John and Paul's song "If You've Got Trouble" had been wisely rejected after its February recording. In its place, Ringo opted for a Buck Owens favorite of his, "Act Naturally." The rhythm track of George on acoustic guitar, Paul on bass, and Ringo on drums was completed in thirteen takes. To this, Ringo added his vocal, supported by harmony from Paul in places. George played some tasty country-style licks on his Gretsch electric, and Ringo added percussion, tapping on the rim of his snare. There are no real differences among any of the three available mixes.

After a break for dinner, a fourteenth number was attempted: Paul's "Wait," which he had written on location in the Bahamas. A backing track (bass, drums, rhythm guitar, and the "volume-swell" style of lead guitar that was the trademark of this album's sessions) and a shared lead vocal from John and Paul were completed, but for whatever reason, that was as far as they went, filling up only two tracks of the tape before calling it quits. To hear how the song sounded at this point, you can simply play the left channel from the standard stereo version on *Rubber Soul.* The next day, when final mixing was done, a mono mix of "Wait" was made, but this may have just been for reference and not release, as no stereo counterpart was created. In its place, the cover of Larry Williams' "Dizzy Miss Lizzy," originally recorded in May for the American market, was added as the fourteenth and final song on *Help!*

RELEASE HISTORY

1965: **A** and **B** were included on mono and stereo pressings of the *Help!* LP in the UK, and **A** was released as a single in the United States.

1987: **C,** a new digital remix created by George Martin, was released on the *Help!* CD.

63. TV interview J

Date: 18 June 1965
Time: 7:00–7:35 p.m.
Location: Lime Grove Studios, London
Interviewer: Kenneth Allsop
Broadcast: live
BBC1
Tonight
Length: 4:43

One last bit of promotion before the tour, as John appeared live on the British TV show *Tonight* to discuss *A Spaniard in the Works.* He had appeared on this series a year earlier when his first book was published, and at the time, presenter Kenneth Allsop had encouraged John to employ some of the imagination he used in writing poems when writing song lyrics. Thus John was more than happy to chat with Allsop once again, having composed weightier songs such as "I'm a Loser," "You've Got to Hide Your Love Away," and "Help!" in the interim.

The segment opens with John reading two poems, "We Must Not Forget the General Erection" and "The Wumberlog (Or the Magic Dog)." John then reveals that Michael Braun, author of *Love Me Do: The Beatles' Progress,* who had followed the group in the winter of 1963–1964, was the catalyst for having John's poetry published in book form. It was accepted by the publishers before the author's identity had been revealed; John admits that "they publish a lot of rubbish, anyway," his fame notwithstanding. Allsop wonders how it feels to be getting serious recognition for both his books (from literary critics) and his songs (covered by "respectable" artists such as Ella Fitzgerald). John insists those kinds of honors are only important to people who wouldn't be inclined to take him seriously otherwise. He says writing has always been just a hobby, compared to his musical profession, and when Allsop points out that other writers have encountered similar problems keeping track of multiple characters, John sounds surprised to be included in that category: "Oh. Other writers? Good."

RELEASE HISTORY

1994: The audio portion of this interview was bootlegged on the CD *The Beatles at the BEEB—TV.* The complete appearance also circulates on video and has been rebroadcast occasionally on BBC Television—it probably survived because their usual "wipe every tape" policy was overridden by their "keep the final episode of each series" policy. Strangely, none of it has been included in documentaries such as *Imagine: John Lennon* or *Anthology,* although the poems were aired during the Westwood One radio series *The Lost Lennon Tapes.*

64. Newsreel footage

Date: 20 June 1965
Time: morning
Location: London Airport and Hôtel George V, Paris
Length: 0:39

The Beatles' first tour of 1965 finally began early this morning as they boarded an Air France flight for Paris. Touring meant omnipresent newsreel cameras, beginning with their departure: a black limo arriving on the tarmac, Paul obliging as ever with autographs, then joining his bandmates (John and Ringo wearing sunglasses) to wave good-bye from the steps of the plane.

They arrived in Paris at 9:55 a.m. and stayed at their old haunt from 1964, the George V. Further footage shows them posing for the European press on the balcony of the hotel, occasionally turning to wave at fans on the boulevard below.

RELEASE HISTORY

This silent footage was released in the video compilation *Beatles 1962 to 1970.*

65. Concert

Date: 20 June 1965
Time: 3:00 p.m.
Location: Palais des Sports, Paris
Broadcast: 27 June 1965, 1:00–2:00 p.m.
Europe 1
Musicorama

[A.] intro (0:41)
[B.] Twist and Shout (1:18)
[C.] intro (0:03)
[D.] She's a Woman (2:47)
[E.] intro (0:30)
[F.] I'm a Loser (2:19)
[G.] intro (0:37)
[H.] Can't Buy Me Love (2:05)
[I.] intro (0:17)
[J.] Baby's in Black (2:10)
[K.] intro (0:41)
[L.] I Wanna Be Your Man (2:05)
[M.] intro (0:43)
[N.] A Hard Day's Night (2:21)
[O.] intro (0:26)
[P.] Everybody's Trying to Be My Baby (2:17)
[Q.] intro (0:19)
[R.] Rock and Roll Music (1:50)
[S.] intro (0:32)
[T.] I Feel Fine (2:05)
[U.] intro (0:25)
[V.] Ticket to Ride (2:57)
[W.] intro (0:46)
[X.] Long Tall Sally (1:52)
[Y.] outro (0:05)

Both of the Beatles' Paris concerts were broadcast on France's national radio station, Europe 1. While the evening show went out live as *Les Beatles (en direct du Palais des Sports),* this afternoon performance was taped for airing a week later on *Musicorama.*

Although it's their first full concert in six months, the songs are performed with high energy and few flaws. Perhaps that's because the set list is nearly identical to the Christmas shows, with the addition of "Ticket to Ride," and the substitution of "I Wanna Be Your Man" for "Honey Don't" as Ringo's spotlight number. The main problem seems to be getting everyone to end "I'm a Loser" and "I Feel Fine" at the same time.

Paul's attempts to communicate with the audience in their native tongue are slow and painful: "Et maintenant une chanson . . . chanson, chanson? Yeah, chanson, chanson . . . de . . . uh . . . un homme . . . uhh, in Les Beatles. It's too hard." George dedicates "Ticket to Ride" to Hubert Wayaffe, the show's MC, and Paul seems to slip an obscenity in at the end of "Long Tall Sally." ("Have some fuck tonight!")

RELEASE HISTORY

1974: This concert first appeared in fair quality on the vinyl bootleg *Paris Sports Palais.* This is still the only source for various bits and pieces of song introductions but is musically obsolete.

1986: The bootleg LP *A Paris* included much of this concert in excellent quality (**F–H, K–N,** and **Q–Y,** with **N, S,** and **W** being slightly incomplete). The source tape for this material was included on the bootleg CD *The Ultimate Collection, Volume 2: Live, Live, Live.*

1988: Swingin' Pig's bootleg CD *Live in Paris 1965* included an excellent-quality tape copy of the complete concert, mislabeled as the evening show. Unfortunately, the whole thing runs a half step too slow and nearly every introduction is incomplete, as is "Ticket to Ride."

1998: An assembly of the entire show, speed-corrected where necessary, appeared on the CD-R *Et Maintenant Une Chanson (New Version).* Its only flaw is that "Ticket to Ride," taken from a source other than Swingin' Pig, runs a half step too fast. Another assembly appears on the CD-R *City of Light* but doesn't speed-correct any of the Swingin' Pig material.

NOTE

A Paris also included portions of songs from the opening acts (Les Pollux, Evy, Moustique, Les Haricots Rouges, and the Yardbirds); this material can be found on the CD-R *City of Light.*

66. Concert

Date: 20 June 1965
Time: 9:00 p.m.
Location: Palais des Sports, Paris
Broadcast: 31 October 1965
Channel 2, France
Les Beatles

[A.] **intro** (0:26)
[B.] **Twist and Shout** (1:18)
[C.] **intro** (0:02)
[D.] **She's a Woman** (2:44)
[E.] **intro** (0:38)
[F.] **I'm a Loser** (2:22)
[G.] **intro** (0:26)
[H.] **Can't Buy Me Love** (2:05)
[I.] **intro** (0:29)
[J.] **Baby's in Black** (2:11)
[K.] **intro** (0:40)
[L.] **I Wanna Be Your Man** (2:05)
[M.] **intro** (0:31)
[N.] **A Hard Day's Night** (2:25)
[O.] **intro** (0:08)
[P.] **Everybody's Trying to Be My Baby** (2:13)
[Q.] **intro** (0:17)
[R.] **Rock and Roll Music** (1:58)
[S.] **intro** (0:21)
[T.] **I Feel Fine** (2:14)
[U.] **intro** (0:20)
[V.] **Ticket to Ride** (3:00)
[W.] **intro** (1:08)
[X.] **Long Tall Sally** (1:55)
[Y.] **outro** (1:04)

In addition to being simulcast on French radio, the evening show in Paris was videotaped for broadcast several months later on French television. For unknown reasons, the song order was scrambled during editing, as follows:

"Twist and Shout"
"She's a Woman"
"Ticket to Ride"
"Can't Buy Me Love"
"I'm a Loser"
"I Wanna Be Your Man"
"A Hard Day's Night"

"I Feel Fine" (all but the last few bars of this song are missing from most video copies)
"Baby's in Black"
"Rock and Roll Music"
"Everybody's Trying to Be My Baby"
"Long Tall Sally"

Not only does this stick most of the cover versions at the end, it places George's "The next song is gonna be our last one" announcement after only two songs! Probably for the benefit of the TV cameras, the Beatles run offstage following "Ticket to Ride," making the standard show-closer, "Long Tall Sally," a dubious "encore." (Paul: "Seein' as the demand was . . . nothing.") As often noted, the Paris audience is unusually boy-heavy, but they are no less enthusiastic than female fans. Instead of high-pitched wailing, we get plenty of audience participation, swaying in time to "Baby's in Black," and singing the "lo-ove" refrain throughout all of "Can't Buy Me Love," which throws the group off-track somewhat. Ringo's number engenders a chant of "Une autre!," and "Long Tall Sally" has everyone dancing in the aisles.

RELEASE HISTORY

1973: This concert first appeared in good quality on the vinyl bootleg *Live Paris Olympia,* taken from the rearranged videotape source missing **S** and all but the end of **T.**

1986: The bootleg LP *A Paris* included most of the concert in excellent quality, still missing **S** and most of **T.** The song order reflects the videotape, except that "Ticket to Ride" has been moved to its rightful penultimate spot. The source tape for this variation was included on the bootleg CD *Live in Melbourne 1964* and *Paris 1965,* which includes the longest version of **Y** available on CD.

1988: Swingin' Pig's bootleg CD *Live In Paris 1965* included the same source tape used on *A Paris,* mislabeled as the afternoon show. "I Feel Fine" has been spliced in from the afternoon show (running at the right speed, unlike its other appearance on the same disc)!

1998: An assembly of the entire show, restored to its original running order, appeared on the CD-R *Et Maintenant Une Chanson (New Version).* "I Feel Fine" and its intro are reinstated from a video source that suffers from a couple of glitches. A better reconstruction is on the CD-R *City of Light,* but "I Feel Fine" runs too slow.

NOTE

The rearranged show circulates on video in decent quality, as does the complete "I Feel Fine" from a separate source. A "remastered" version that circulates does restore the correct lineup, but the sound of the afternoon "I Feel Fine" is dubbed onto the soundtrack of the evening performance's video! Portions of **F** and **P** are included in *Anthology,* and a complete video clip of **P** was released by Apple in 1996 to promote *Anthology 2.*

67. Radio interview

Date: 20–22 June 1965
Location: Rolls-Royce and Hôtel George V, Paris
Interviewer: Jacques Ourevitch
Length: 3:31

Although they didn't perform on June 21, the Beatles remained in Paris through the morning of the twenty-second. During their stay, they gave at least two interviews that are available to collectors. The first, conducted by Jacques Ourevitch for French radio, captured John, Paul, and George in a Rolls-Royce and then all four back in their hotel suite. With translations into French (including overdubs apparently to correct some inaccuracies), the Beatles talk about the differences in French, British, and American audiences, their Napoleon-style haircuts, and police protection. John says that "even people who don't like the Beatles like Ringo," and Ringo thinks it's because he's ugly, but nice.

RELEASE HISTORY

1986: This interview was included on the bootleg LP *A Paris.* It was copied from this source on the CD-R *City of Light.*

68. Radio interview

Date: 20–22 June 1965
Location: Hôtel George V, Paris
Interviewer: Chris Denning
Broadcast: Radio Luxembourg
The Beatles
Length: 0:26 (first segment)

The Beatles also recorded their final exclusive interviews for Chris Denning's Radio Luxembourg series while staying at the George V. The first segment is a brief discussion of the reasons they were awarded MBEs. This is followed by several record requests, with Paul dedicating "Do You Want to Know a Secret" to journalists Bernard Levin, Wolf Mankowitz, and Donald Zec, followed by Ringo's play on the *Sun* newspaper by requesting "I'll Follow the Sun" for Don Short of the *Daily Mirror* and Judith Simons of the *Daily Express*. However, John tops them all by dedicating "Thank You Girl" to "Mister H. Wilson of Hampstead Garden Suburb"—i.e., prime minister Harold Wilson!

RELEASE HISTORY

1972: The MBE discussion was rebroadcast in the BBC Radio documentary *The Beatles Story*. It was copied from this source on the CD-R *City of Light*.

1987: The record dedications were included in a Christmas radio special, *Station of the Stars—Radio Luxembourg*.

69. Concert/Newsreel footage

Date: 22 June 1965
Location: Palais d'Hiver, Lyon
Length: 0:22

The Beatles traveled from Paris to Lyon, where they played two shows and stayed overnight. A bit of footage shows them posing for photos backstage and performing onstage.

RELEASE HISTORY

This silent footage circulates on video among collectors.

70. Newsreel footage

Date: 23–24 June 1965
Location: Milan
Length: 0:41

On the evening of June 23, the Beatles boarded a train for Italy. Newsreel footage documents their nighttime arrival at the station in Milan and their arrival at the concert venue the following afternoon, accompanied by Neil Aspinall.

RELEASE HISTORY

This silent footage was included in the Italian video *I Favolosi Beatles*.

71. Concert

Date: 24 June 1965
Time: 4:30 p.m.
Location: Velodromo Vigorelli, Milan
Length: 2:56

The first of two concerts in this sporting arena was less than one-third sold out, and the sparseness of the audience is evident in some amateur footage of the show. It was filmed by one of the support acts, singer Peppino Di Capri, and includes portions of "She's a Woman" and "Baby's in Black." The silent footage was broadcast with a soundtrack of an unrelated live version of "She's a Woman" (from Houston), and has been slowed down and padded out to repeat portions to match the length of the song.

RELEASE HISTORY

This silent color footage circulates on video from a recent broadcast on TG2-TV.

72. Concert

Date: 25 June 1965
Time: 4:30 p.m.
Location: Palazzo dello Sport, Genoa
Length: 0:59

The Beatles left Milan this morning and were driven to Genoa for another pair of concerts. About a minute of silent color 8 mm film exists from the afternoon show, apparently shot from the audience by one Mauro Casagrande. Among the songs captured are bits of "A Hard Day's Night" and "Everybody's Trying to Be My Baby."

RELEASE HISTORY

This silent color footage circulates from a latter-day broadcast on Italian TV.

73. Interview

Date: 26–27 June 1965
Location: Parco dei Principi Hotel, Rome (?)
Interviewer: Carmela Anna Fortunata (?)
Length: 2:05

This Italian interview sounds as if it may have been taped following a press conference (whether in Milan, Genoa, or Rome is difficult to ascertain, although it initially traveled with a recording of a Rome concert). John talks about their hairstyle being a gimmick, Paul (misidentified by the narrator as John) claims to have Ringo's autograph "mounted on the wall in my toilet," and Ringo (misidentified as George) says he loves to hear the fans screaming.

RELEASE HISTORY

1980: This interview first appeared, in mediocre sound, on the bootleg EP *Live in Italy.* It was officially released (slightly truncated) on the LP *The Beatles Talk Downunder (And All Over), Volume 2,* copied on CD as *Inside Interviews: Talk Downunder: Sydney to Seattle.*

74. Concert

Date: 27 June 1965
Time: 4:30 p.m.
Location: Teatro Adriano, Rome

[A.] **Twist and Shout** (1:06)
[B.] **She's a Woman** (2:39)
[C.] **intro** (0:32)
[D.] **I'm a Loser** (2:18)
[E.] **intro** (0:36)
[F.] **Can't Buy Me Love** (1:59)
[G.] **intro** (0:26)
[H.] **Baby's in Black** (2:02)
[I.] **intro** (0:36)
[J.] **I Wanna Be Your Man** (1:59)
[K.] **outro** (0:15)
[L.] **intro** (0:20)
[M.] **A Hard Day's Night** (2:20)
[N.] **intro** (0:32)
[O.] **Everybody's Trying to Be My Baby** (2:09)
[P.] **intro** (0:22)

[Q.] Rock and Roll Music (1:55)
[R.] intro (0:33)
[S.] I Feel Fine (2:10)
[T.] intro (0:28)
[U.] Ticket to Ride (2:56)
[V.] intro (0:41)
[W.] Long Tall Sally (0:38)

Flying to Rome directly after the second Genoa concert, the Beatles enjoyed a day off on the twenty-sixth before performing for two consecutive days at Rome's Teatro Adriano. The demand for tickets hardly warranted four shows (two each night), which meant performing to half-empty houses most of the time.

A fair-quality audience recording circulates, reportedly from the first of the four shows (although there's nothing on the tape to identify it as Rome, let alone a matinee performance). The beginning of "Twist and Shout" and last half of "Long Tall Sally" are both missing. Paul makes halfhearted attempts to interact with the audience in Italian, mostly limited to a *ciao* and several *grazzi*'s. John introduces "A Hard Day's Night" as coming from the film *Tutti Per Uno,* the movie's Italian title. Prior to "Ticket to Ride," George helpfully points out that "the intro may be a little bit out of tune, but I hope you don't mind."

NOTE

In his December 1970 interview for *Rolling Stone,* John was asked about live Beatles albums and mentioned the Hollywood Bowl and Shea recordings, then added: "There's one in Italy apparently that somebody recorded there." This hazy offhanded comment led collectors on a search for the mysterious concert recording, which many believed could be found on an LP titled *The Beatles in Italy.* Such an LP was in fact released in mid-1965 in Italy to coincide with their concerts but featured no live performances; the songs didn't even match their set list, instead being a compilation of non-LP tracks (the *Long Tall Sally* EP and both sides of the "From Me to You," "I Want to Hold Your Hand," "I Feel Fine," and "Ticket to Ride" singles).

RELEASE HISTORY

1985: This concert first appeared in fair quality on the vinyl bootleg *Arrivano I* «Capelloni». A very clean copy of this source was used on the Bulldog CD *Beatles in Italy 1965,* but it's still taken from either an LP or the LP's master tape, as evidenced by the side break separating **K** and **L**. The entire show runs nearly a half step too fast on both sources.

75. Concert

Date: 27 June 1965
Time: 9:30 p.m.
Location: Teatro Adriano, Rome

[A.] intro (0:27)
[B.] Twist and Shout (1:16)
[C.] She's a Woman (2:41)
[D.] intro (0:36)
[E.] I'm a Loser (0:35)

This in-line recording is definitely from one of the late shows, as Paul greets the audience with "Evening, all," but we'll have to take the word of bootleggers that it comes from the twenty-seventh. After an enthusiastic introduction by the MC and a young helper, George decides to test the mic with a *Help!* reference, shouting "Kaili!" John interjects a bit of nonsense babbling during the pause in the opening bars of "I'm a Loser."

Three minutes and thirty-eight seconds of silent, super 8 mm footage also circulates from the June 27 concerts, including clips of "Twist and Shout," "She's a Woman," "I'm a Loser," "Baby's in Black," "I Wanna Be Your Man," "Everybody's Trying to Be My Baby," and "Ticket to Ride."

RELEASE HISTORY

1980: A good-quality tape of **B–E** (with the first 15 seconds of **B** missing) was included on the bootleg EP *Live in Italy,* misidentified as coming from one of the Milan concerts. This source was copied on the bootleg CD *Beatles in Italy 1965.*

1995: The Italian video *I Favolosi Beatles* included excellent-quality versions of **A,** the first 10 seconds of **B,** the end of **D,** and the beginning of **E.**

2000: The CD-R *The A.M. Tape* reassembled this concert from various sources, including the EP and video, plus an excellent copy of most of **B** from a 1997 radio broadcast. Unfortunately, it substitutes a version of **C** that was the soundtrack of a TV broadcast of the silent Milan footage (see the June 24 entry), but the song is from neither Milan nor Rome. (It's from the evening show in Houston.) The silent 8 mm footage from Rome circulates on video.

76. Newsreel footage

Date: 1 July 1965
Time: afternoon
Location: Airport and Hotel Phoenix, Madrid
Length: 2:31

Leaving Nice around 3:45 p.m., the Beatles flew to Madrid for their first Spanish concerts, both of which would be held in bullrings. Their arrival at Madrid Airport was captured from several angles and is easily distinguished by John's white coat and checkered cap. In addition to the standard "wave from the steps of the plane" shots, the footage includes the entourage walking through the terminal, driving off in a limo, and attending a press reception (Paul holds a rose in his teeth), probably at their hotel.

RELEASE HISTORY

This silent footage is available on video from a few different sources, notably a 1995 TV special, *Que Vienen Los Beatles.*

77. Newsreel footage

Date: 2 July 1965
Location: Hotel Phoenix, Madrid
Length: 0:59

On the second day of their stay at the Hotel Phoenix, the Beatles attended another reception that was also captured on film. Each Beatle autographs a cask of sherry, which is then ceremoniously poured into glasses, first clumsily by John and then by a professional, and sampled by all. The group also poses for photos with flamenco dancers (see following entry).

RELEASE HISTORY

This silent footage is available on video from a few different sources, notably a 1995 TV special, *Que Vienen Los Beatles.*

78. Radio interview

Date: 2 July 1965
Location: Hotel Phoenix, Madrid
Interviewer: Graham Webb
Broadcast: Radio Caroline
Length: 2:31

Since flamenco music is being performed in the background (and gets a round of applause), this interview with Graham Webb for pirate radio was probably recorded during the sherry-drinking session described previously.

The conversation revolves around the MBE situation, particularly the negative reaction of some previous recipients who returned their medals to the palace in disgust. John bluntly points out that most of them were sent back by military men, and he feels that making people happy is more worthy of recognition than "killing people." George is quick to note a heavily honored Australian fellow who stuck up for them, and John reckons the British public is split fifty-fifty on the matter. Webb tries to determine their future plans, a futile task as most interviewers had already discovered. Ringo hopes to move into films "as a camera," Paul gives his usual nonresponse of "I've never made plans," and the full extent of George's itinerary is to "have a wash and a shave and go to the show."

RELEASE HISTORY

1983: This interview was released on the picture disc EP *Timeless II ½: The Beatles Around the World.* It has been reissued on the CD *Inside Interviews: Talk Downunder: Sydney to Seattle.*

79. Concert

Date: 2 July 1965
Time: 8:30 p.m.
Location: Plaza de Toros de Las Ventas, Madrid
Length: 1:52

A single evening concert was held in Madrid and documented in two separate newsreels (both silent, unfortunately). With John wearing a black gaucho hat, the Beatles are seen performing fragments of "She's a Woman" and "Can't Buy Me Love," among other unidentifiable snippets.

RELEASE HISTORY

This silent footage is available from a few different sources, notably a 1995 TV special, *Que Vienen Los Beatles.*

80. Newsreel footage

Date: 3 July 1965
Time: afternoon
Location: Airport, Barcelona
Length: 1:24

A 2:45 p.m. flight carried the Beatles from Madrid to Barcelona. Newsreel footage includes shots of the group emerging from the Iberia Airlines plane, donning matador hats, and driving off in a car.

RELEASE HISTORY

This silent footage is available from a 1995 TV special, *Que Vienen Los Beatles.*

81. Concert

Date: 3 July 1965
Time: 10:45 p.m.
Location: Plaza de Toros Monumental, Barcelona
Length: 0:58

Camera crews followed the Beatles backstage at the Plaza de Toros to catch John and Neil entering a doorway marked AREO CABALLEROS and Paul giving a brief salute. The group can also be seen entering the arena (John wears his gaucho hat again) and performing bits and pieces of unidentifiable songs; most of the footage actually focuses on the audience.

RELEASE HISTORY

This silent footage is available from a 1995 TV special, *Que Vienen Los Beatles.*

81a. Newsreel footage

Date: 4 July 1965
Location: London Airport
Broadcast: 4 July 1965
ITV
Length: 0:14

Paul drew the short straw and agreed to represent the Beatles at the annual Ivor Novello Awards luncheon. ITV News filmed his acceptance from Sir Billy Butlin of one of the group's five awards for songwriting excellence.

RELEASE HISTORY

This silent footage circulates on video.

82. Amateur footage

Date: 29 July 1965
Location: TVC Studios, London
Length: 1:46

While the Beatles merchandising boom had calmed down by the summer of 1965, one area that remained untapped was Beatle cartoons. King Features Syndicate, a U.S. company, teamed up with TVC Studios in London and other independent animation studios around the world to produce two seasons of a generally dreadful series titled *The Beatles*. Prior to its September 1965 launch, the flesh-and-blood Beatles visited TVC for an awkward photo opportunity. Judging from this color home movie and other photos of the event, they probably enjoyed the free drinks more than the goofy character model sheets pinned to the walls.

RELEASE HISTORY

This silent color footage circulates on video.

83. Newsreel footage

Date: 29 July 1965
Time: evening
Location: London Pavilion
Length: 2:28

The scenes were nearly identical to a year earlier when *Help!* had a royal premiere at the London Pavilion, again attended by Princess Margaret and her husband. ITV News filmed about a minute of the occasion, and AP and Reuters cameras were there as well.

All captured basically the same material: over ten thousand fans cheering in Piccadilly Circus and occasionally being dragged away by police; the arrivals of Richard Lester, George Martin, the Beatles accompanied by Brian, Cynthia, Maureen, and costar Victor Spinetti; the receiving line with Princess Margaret chatting to the Beatles for quite a while.

RELEASE HISTORY

This silent footage circulates on video; the ITV clip was released on the video compilation *The Beatles 1962 to 1970* and the remainder is a bonus on the home video reissue of *Help!*

84. Radio interview

Date: 30 July 1965
Location: Saville Theatre, London
Interviewer: Dibbs Mather
Broadcast: British Information Service
The Beatles
Length: 4:45

For the first and only time in 1965, the Beatles were scheduled to perform on a live TV broadcast August 1. As they rehearsed in the Saville Theatre for that appearance, the group recorded an interview with Dibbs Mather for a BBC Transcription Service disc titled *The Beatles*. The finished product was distributed to U.S. radio stations via the British Information Service, a branch of the British Council.

Amid a running gag about identifying which Beatle is speaking, and discussion of their new film, the conversation touches on some serious topics. Regarding their growing impatience with concert tours, George explains that since they've had to churn out the same thirty minutes of hits each night, their proficiency and flair for improvisation has all but disappeared, while Paul charts the course of their set lists from strictly rock to "fruitier" numbers and back to rock again. Mather points out how clean their public image is, unlike other musicians notorious for driving under the influence or using drugs. Paul disingenuously claims they're "not like that," and John, who had experienced his first LSD trip in recent months, says they haven't been arrested because "we get somebody to drive us." A recording of John reading "The National Health Cow," joined near the end by his bandmates, probably also originates from this program.

RELEASE HISTORY

1972: Portions of this interview were rebroadcast in BBC Radio's documentary *The Beatles Story.*

1998: These same segments, including the "National Health Cow" reading (which is mislabeled as being from the *Today* broadcast of June 16) were bootlegged on *Attack of the Filler Beebs!, Episode Two.*

2000: A slightly more complete version of one of the segments appeared on *The Beatles Broadcast Collection, Trailer 2.* Both this and *Filler Beebs* are needed to obtain a complete recording.

85. TV performance

Date: 1 August 1965
Time: 9:10–10:05 p.m.
Location: ABC Theatre, Blackpool
Hosts: Mike Winters, Bernie Winters
Broadcast: live
ABC
Blackpool Night Out

[A.] I Do Like to Be Beside the Seaside (0:44)
[B.] chat w/Ringo (0:20)
[C.] intro (0:42)
[D.] I Feel Fine (2:07)
[E.] intro (0:26)
[F.] I'm Down (2:08)
[G.] intro (0:20)
[H.] Act Naturally (2:24)
[I.] intro (0:30)
[J.] Ticket to Ride (2:15)
[K.] intro (0:30)
[L.] Yesterday (2:07)
[M.] intro (0:46)
[N.] Help! (2:17)
[O.] outro/closing theme (Can't Buy Me Love) (1:13)

Amazingly, the Beatles hadn't performed live on British TV in over a year, since their July 1964 appearance on *Blackpool Night Out.* They returned to the show this evening for what would be their final non-mimed UK TV performance until "All You Need Is Love" in 1967. Camera rehearsals this afternoon were taped to check on the all-important sound quality, but the recordings were undoubtedly scrapped soon afterward. Their set consisted of both sides of their new single, the two previous single A-sides, and two tracks from their new album. The broadcast ranked number 4 in the ratings for the week, but the Beatles' performance received mixed reviews from the press.

The show opens (**A**) with what is apparently a pretaped teaser (no audience screaming is audible) with the Beatles joining hosts Mike and Bernie Winters in a brief rendition of "I Do Like to Be Beside the Seaside" (this doesn't appear on the circulating video). Later, Ringo appears onstage (**B**) to open the show proper: "Good evening and welcome to *Blackpool Night Out.*" Unlike their two previous appearances in this series, the Beatles declined to take part in a comedy skit, although one had been written for them.

Instead, they interjected a bit of their own humor into the act. Ringo sends up Paul's standard "We're gonna give our drummer a chance to sing now" announcement by introducing himself: "And here he is, all out of key and nervous, singing 'Act Naturally'—Ringo!" Prior to Paul's solo rendition of "Yesterday," George takes the role of a TV presenter for a current UK talent show: "And so, for Paul McCartney of Liverpool, *Opportunity Knocks*!" After the song, John presents Paul with a bouquet of flowers and quips, "Thank you, Ringo, that was wonderful!"

Rather than amplifying his Gibson acoustic, John plays his Rickenbacker for "I Feel Fine" (which lacks the familiar opening feedback); for "I'm Down," he switches to a Vox Continental organ, playing the solo with his elbows. John and George leave the stage for "Yesterday" (Ringo remains at his kit but doesn't play), which has Paul and his guitar joined by a string quartet (probably the house orchestra, not a pretaped backing). Despite having a full day of rehearsal, John manages to mangle the lyrics to "Help!" for the first of numerous times over the course of the month. Ironic, since Paul and George's backing vocals precede John's lead slightly, so they are basically feeding him the words! Over the closing credits (**O**), the Beatles join the Lionel Blair Dancers and the show's hosts and other guests to dance to an instrumental version of "Can't Buy Me Love."

RELEASE HISTORY

1974: The soundtrack to this show (**B–N**) was first bootlegged on the LP *Stockholm,* taped off a TV speaker. It was apparently copied from this source on the CD *Live in the United Kingdom 1962–1965.*

1996: The bootleg CD *Pollwinners go to Blackpool* included the only appearance of **A,** as well as **B–N** and a bit of **O,** all in mediocre quality. The same year, **D** and **I–N** were released in excellent quality on *Anthology 2.* All the songs except "I Feel Fine" appear at least in part in the *Anthology* documentary; **H** is available from this source on the CD-R *Telecasts Three.*

1999: Most of this appearance (**C–N** and most of **O**) appeared on the CD bootleg boxed set *Mythology, Volume 2, taken* from a circulating video. The quality is very good, but noticeably worse than the songs released on *Anthology 2.*

86. Studio session — P, G

Date: 9 August 1965
Location: IBC Studios, London
Producer: John Lennon

[A.] You've Got to Hide Your Love Away (2:09)

At least three of the Beatles met up on this day at IBC Studios in London. The occasion was the recording of "You've Got to Hide Your Love Away" by a Brian Epstein–managed folk group, the Silkie. On hand to lend their assistance were Paul, who played acoustic guitar, George, who played tambourine, and the song's primary composer, John, who stayed in the control room. Ads for the single trumpeted the song as "John Lennon and Paul McCartney produce The Silkie," although it's likely a veteran producer and engineer (perhaps Glyn Johns) were on hand. The Beatle connection helped the single reach the top 10 on the U.S. chart and the top 30 in the UK.

RELEASE HISTORY

1965: This song was released on a single in the UK and the United States, and as an LP title track in the United States only. It's available on the CD compilation *Lennon & McCartney Songbook.*

86a. Newsreel footage

Date: 13 August 1965
Time: noon
Location: London Airport
Length: 0:37

The Beatles set off from London Airport this afternoon for a second North American tour, scaled back considerably from the previous summer. Compared to the exhausting pace of that thirty-two-show marathon, the itinerary was sliced in half, to a mere sixteen concerts in ten cities.

Thirty-seven seconds of silent color footage from their departure appears in the short film *Reflections on Love.* The film, which was shown at Cannes in May 1966, costars Pattie Boyd's sister Jenny and was directed by Joe Massot. George would write the score for Massot's 1968 film *Wonderwall,* and *Reflections of Love* can be seen as a bonus feature on the *Wonderwall* DVD. The Beatles footage, probably shot by Robert Freeman, shows the group waving to fans, posing for press photos, and speeding away in a limo.

RELEASE HISTORY

This silent footage was released on the *Wonderwall* DVD.

87. Newsreel footage

Date: 13 August 1965
Time: 2:30 p.m.
Location: JFK Airport, New York City
Length: 0:52

The Beatles' flight touched down at Kennedy Airport in New York City around 2:30 p.m. local time, and a TV news crew was on hand to cover their arrival as usual.

RELEASE HISTORY

This brief footage circulates among video collectors.

88. Press conference

Date: 13 August 1965
Location: Warwick Hotel, New York City
Broadcast: WABC-AM, New York City
Length: 8:18

A limo trip into Manhattan brought the Beatles to the Warwick Hotel, their headquarters for the next four days. After cleaning up in their suite, they gathered to meet the press, who seemed insatiable as ever. Replacing Derek Taylor as press officer was former Decca employee Tony Barrow, who fielded questions admirably, if not as charmingly as Derek had. The press conference generally follows the usual pattern of inane questions and snappy comebacks; the most famous on this occasion being: "You Beatles have conquered five continents; what do you want to do next?" met instantly by John and Paul's "Conquer six!" There are also questions about Ringo's imminent fatherhood, the MBEs, their new movie, and even the current water shortage in New York City. (George claims they brought their own water.)

RELEASE HISTORY

1982: The bulk of the press conference was released on the LP *Like Dreamers Do,* but there's a bit extra contained on three other sources. The first is 2:09 of newsreel footage traded on video, which also captures their arrival at the hotel. Both the arrival and conference were covered by WABC-AM radio, along with some exclusive interviews (see following entry). Finally, a circulating tape from another radio broadcast has 9 seconds of unique material.

89. Radio interview

Date: 13 August 1965
Time: 7:00–8:00 p.m.
Location: Warwick Hotel, New York City
Interviewer: Bruce Morrow
Broadcast: live
WABC-AM, New York City
Length: 6:35

Following the conference, WABC's "Cousin" Bruce Morrow and his colleague Dan Ingram interviewed each Beatle individually in their thirty-third-floor reception suite. (The Beatles' rooms were actually one floor above.) They also presented the group with "Order of the All-American, 1965" medals, designed by a contest-winning listener as a tongue-in-cheek response to the MBE awards.

Paul reveals that they had been listening to WABC's live coverage from their limousine, and he teases Morrow for prematurely announcing their arrival at the hotel. George says they watched the film *Operation: Crossbow* during the flight overseas, and that he'd like to visit Greenwich Village. Ringo happily accepts best wishes on his six-month wedding anniversary, but stops short of reading the station's name on the back of his medal, fearing that he's being tricked into recording a free promo: " 'Presented to Ringo Starr from the W—' Ohh! I can't say that!"

RELEASE HISTORY

These interviews circulate in good quality from an off-air tape.

90. Radio interview **P, G, R**

Date: 13 August 1965
Time: evening
Location: Warwick Hotel, New York City
Interviewer: Larry Kane
Broadcast: WFUN-AM, Miami
Length: 11:50

Also present at the press reception was their old pal Larry Kane, who recorded interviews with the Beatles for WFUN-AM in Miami. Paul rejects the notion that they were impolite to people in Nassau. Ringo discusses plans for their third film, a Western based on the book *A Talent for Loving,* and complains about rude fans and journalists. George and Kane chat briefly about America, the MBE, and Beatle films.

RELEASE HISTORY

1996: 10:50 of these interviews were released on the promotional CD *The Fab Four On Tour.*

2003: A further minute of material was released on the CD included with the book *Ticket to Ride.*

91. TV performance

Date: 14 August 1965
Time: 8:30 p.m.
Location: CBS Studio 50, New York City
Producer: Bob Precht
Host: Ed Sullivan
Broadcast: 12 September 1965, 8:00–9:00 p.m.
CBS
The Ed Sullivan Show

[A.] **intro** (0:53)
[B.] **I Feel Fine** (2:05)
[C.] **intro** (0:29)
[D.] **I'm Down** (2:09)
[E.] **intro** (0:12)
[F.] **Act Naturally** (2:26)
[G.] **outro** (0:42)
[H.] **intro** (0:05)
[I.] **Ticket to Ride** (2:28)
[J.] **intro** (0:21)
[K.] **Yesterday** (1:58)
[L.] **intro** (0:30)
[M.] **Help!** (2:16)
[N.] **outro** (0:55)

Most of this day was spent back at Studio 50, the site of their *Ed Sullivan Show* triumphs of sixteen months prior. Morning run-throughs for this CBS show were followed by a full dress rehearsal at 2:30 p.m.—since the Miami dress rehearsal from 1964 was videotaped, it's likely this one was too, although if the tape still existed, we probably would have seen it by now. As the show was currently in summer repeats, the Beatles' performance was not aired live, but held back for the season premiere, broadcast September 12. Capitol shrewdly released a single pairing the two songs not yet available in the United States ("Yesterday" and "Act Naturally") on September 14, just in time to achieve maximum promotional value from the broadcast.

For the Beatles' part, they performed the exact same six-song lineup used on *Blackpool Night Out* earlier in the month, right down to repeating Ringo's "nervous" intro to "Act Naturally." The producers of the *Anthology* documentary chose not to include any of this broadcast, although the whole show has circulated in excellent quality among video traders for many years. Presumably it was that overfamiliarity that led them to use the rarer *Blackpool Night Out* versions instead; certainly there is nothing wrong with their performances here, although John bungles the second-verse lyrics to "Help!" again, while Paul scrambles the order of verses in "I'm Down."

RELEASE HISTORY

1973: This performance first appeared on the vinyl bootleg *Peace of Mind* in mediocre quality.

1985: A major upgrade was included on the bootleg LP *The Beatles Conquer America.*

1994: The bootleg CD *The Ultimate Collection, Volume 1: TV Appearances* contained the complete show in excellent quality, taken from the soundtrack of a circulating videotape.

2003: This entire show was released on an excellent-quality DVD, *Ed Sullivan Presents the Beatles.* Sadly, it ended up being the final *Ed Sullivan Show* taped in black and white; if only they'd waited till the end of the tour, perhaps the color equipment would have been up and running!

92. Radio interview

Date: 15 August 1965
Time: 5:00 p.m.
Location: Warwick Hotel, New York City
Interviewer: "Lord" Tim Hudson
Broadcast: San Diego
Length: 26:45

The pinnacle of the Beatles' touring years occurred this evening in a record-setting concert at Shea Stadium, captured for the ages in a splendid TV documentary. First things first, though. Yet another press reception was held at the Warwick Hotel around 5 p.m.; while Larry Kane was a familiar face from last year, there were some newcomers following the tour this time around.

Expatriate British DJ (via Canada and Massachusetts) "Lord" Tim Hudson recorded a number of interviews at the reception for his current station in San Diego. He basically asks the same set of questions to each Beatle (even asking some twice after circulating around the room for a second go-round!): How was their send-off from London; how is the police protection; what did Princess Margaret think of their film at the premiere; are they becoming more conservative in their dress? He concludes by asking each Beatle to sign off with greetings to the fans in San Diego (although he doesn't get any from John, who has to run off and prepare for the Shea concert).

RELEASE HISTORY

These interviews are circulating on tape thanks to their rebroadcast in a 1980 special, *Beyond the Beatle Dream.*

92a. Radio interview P

Date: 15 August 1965
Time: 5:00 p.m.
Location: Warwick Hotel, New York City
Interviewer: Larry Kane
Broadcast: WFUN-AM, Miami
Length: 1:35

During this interview, Larry Kane allowed Paul to refute a couple more rumors: that he was newly engaged to Jane Asher (repeated yet again in a recent news report), and that the group had snubbed Sammy Davis Jr. the night of their arrival in New York. Sammy had actually showed up at the Warwick just as they were going to bed, and Paul cleared up the misunderstanding with him on the phone the next evening.

RELEASE HISTORY

2003: This interview was released on the CD included with the book *Ticket to Ride.*

93. Concert/Documentary footage

Date: 15 August 1965
Time: 9:16 p.m.
Location: Shea Stadium, New York City
Broadcast: 1 March 1966, 8:00–8:50 p.m.
BBC1
The Beatles at Shea Stadium

[A.] **intro** (2:29)
[B.] **Twist and Shout** (1:19)
[C.] **intro** (0:02)
[D.] **She's a Woman** (2:46)
[E.] **intro** (0:31)
[F.] **I Feel Fine** (2:07)
[G.] **intro** (0:37)
[H.] **Dizzy Miss Lizzy** (2:51)
[I.] **intro** (0:32)
[J.] **Ticket to Ride** (2:16)
[K.] **intro** (0:25)
[L.] **Everybody's Trying to Be My Baby** (2:19)
[M.] **intro** (0:47)
[N.] **Can't Buy Me Love** (2:06)
[O.] **intro** (0:36)
[P.] **Baby's in Black** (2:09)
[Q.] **intro** (0:37)
[R.] **Act Naturally** (2:30)
[S.] **intro** (0:38)

[T.] A Hard Day's Night (2:26)
[U.] intro (0:52)
[V.] Help! (2:18)
[W.] intro (1:01)
[X.] I'm Down (2:09)
[Y.] outro (0:50)

Literally and symbolically the zenith of the Beatles' concert career, their 1965 Shea Stadium performance was deemed important enough to be covered by twelve cameras for a TV documentary. The joint NEMS-*Ed Sullivan*-Subafilms production, titled *The Beatles at Shea Stadium,* was filmed over the course of this evening, following the group's helicopter flight into Queens and dressing room tune-ups, interspersed with footage of the opening acts and Murray the K's stage antics.

After Ed Sullivan's stage introduction, the Beatles take the stage to a deafening roar from the assembled 55,600 and perform a twelve-song set (chosen backstage just before going on!), ten of which made it into the film, although all were later subjected to varying amounts of studio sweetening (see the January 5, 1966, entry). Neither "She's a Woman" nor "Everybody's Trying to Be My Baby" made the final cut, but both were included in the film's first print, delivered to NEMS on November 5, 1965. Apple must still retain a copy of this print, as evidenced by their release of the latter song (**L**) in 1996.

In addition to the studio sweetening, the standard record release of "Act Naturally" was dubbed over Ringo's concert performance. Most of the song "A Hard Day's Night" is obscured by Beatle and Brian Epstein interviews, more of which appear throughout the film. These were conducted by Larry Kane, and they include chats from the 1964 tour as well as from New York, Atlanta, San Diego, and probably other cities on the 1965 tour (see later entry for details).

In 2006, the raw audio reels from the Shea filming were auctioned, and a year later, the entire concert appeared on bootlegs. These tapes include all the opening acts (King Curtis, Cannibal and the Headhunters, Brenda Holloway, and Sounds Incorporated), as well as time-filling banter from WABC disc jockeys, who lead the crowd in singing several radio jingles. The Beatles' full set (**A–Y**) reveals the technical flaws that made most of the songs unusable, such as poor sound balance and heavy distortion on the vocals. Ringo's woefully off-key entrance to "Act Naturally" doesn't help matters, either. (And Paul's harmony vocal is inaudible.)

RELEASE HISTORY

Film prints of the *Beatles at Shea Stadium* documentary have been circulating for over thirty years, and good copies are now easily obtained on video, although none look as pristine as that restored for use in *Anthology.* This restoration has reportedly been sitting in Apple's vault since the early 1990s, awaiting release. Reports that an original, unsweetened stereo soundtrack exists to accompany this release seem unlikely, given the release of one song in mono on *Anthology 2.* See the January 5, 1966, entry for further details on the various bootlegs containing the overdubbed soundtrack.

1996: **L** was released on the CD *Anthology 2.* The same year, about a minute of **D** was released on the soundtrack of the *Anthology* VHS, buried under dialogue.

2007: The entire concert (**A–Y**) was bootlegged in very good quality on the CD *The Beatles and the Great Concert at Shea!*

94. Press conference

Date: 17 August 1965
Time: afternoon
Location: Maple Leaf Gardens, Toronto
Length: 18:49

The tour began in earnest this morning as the Beatles flew from New York to Toronto for their only Canadian appearance of the year. Between shows in Toronto, the Beatles held a press conference backstage, and they must have been disappointed with the tone of the questions. Such nongroundbreaking topics as marriage, fans, money, and clothing are covered, with the low point probably being "What kind of shampoo do you boys use?" Still, there are some moments of interest—a well-connected Canadian fan asks Paul whether opportunity knocked on his *Blackpool Night Out* appearance, which causes him to laugh and say nobody would get that reference. A female journalist complains that her tape recorder isn't working and insists on getting a private interview, since she drove thirty miles to get there and waited ninety minutes backstage. Paul, unmoved, mocks her mercilessly: "Thirty miles, the lady drove thirty miles! Okay, give her a big hand!" Near the end, a brazen entrepreneur tries to get their endorsements for some automobile tape decks but is rebuffed.

RELEASE HISTORY

1986: A nearly complete audio recording was released on the LP *Things We Said Today,* later reissued on CD. The circulating tape source has an extra 30 seconds or so at the beginning. In addition, about seven minutes of this conference is traded on video from a broadcast on WXON, channel 20, in Detroit—this comes from newsreel footage with the proceedings in slightly scrambled order.

95. Concert

Date: 17 August 1965
Location: Maple Leaf Gardens, Toronto
Length: 2:52

Just under three minutes of silent film exists from one of the Beatles' two concerts at Maple Leaf Gardens (shot from the audience).

RELEASE HISTORY

This footage circulates among video collectors.

96. Press conference

Date: 18 August 1965
Location: Atlanta
Length: 10:20

From the Great White North to the Deep South, and their one and only concert in Atlanta, where the usual press conference was conducted before the show. The first half of this ten-minute recording largely consists of photo-taking and Tony Barrow's instructions, but before long the Jane Asher and MBE questions begin. Asked if he is proud to have a nightclub (Arthur's) named after his hair, George quips, "I was until I saw the nightclub." Asked to name some favorite American artists, they list Otis Redding, James Brown, Nina Simone, and Chuck Jackson, but say that Elvis Presley has "gone a bit middle-aged."

RELEASE HISTORY

1995: This incomplete recording was bootlegged on *Beatles over Atlanta & Shea Stadium.* About 20 seconds of press conference footage also circulates, and a further 3 minutes reportedly exists.

97. Radio interview — J, G

Date: 18 August 1965
Location: Atlanta
Interviewer: Jerry G. Bishop
Broadcast: WKYC-AM, Cleveland
Length: 7:09

A couple of Jerry G. Bishop's interviews can be traced to this date, probably taped in their hotel suite. George talks about what he's looking forward to in their Los Angeles getaway (privacy and not having to eat hotel food), and argues with Bishop about whether the Beatles should go out of their way to rescue the faltering Cavern Club. Bishop proposes an annual benefit concert, but George feels they've already done more than their share to promote the club, and that its financial problems are due to poor management. John also chats briefly about the current state of pop music, dismissing the current folk-rock rage as a passing phase, and saying pop music has enough variations to last "another five or six years."

RELEASE HISTORY

1982: A portion of the interview with John was released on the LP *The Beatles Talk with Jerry G.*

1983: George's interview and the remainder of John's were included on the LP *The Beatles Talk with Jerry G., Volume 2.*

98. Radio interview

Date: 18 August 1965
Location: Atlanta Stadium
Interviewer: Larry Kane
Broadcast: WFUN-AM, Miami
Length: 2:36

Larry Kane caught up with John backstage at Atlanta Stadium this evening for a brief chat, discussing the differences between baseball and rounders, the problems of magazines printing rumors, and the success of the Shea concert.

RELEASE HISTORY

1996: This interview was released on the promotional CD *The Fab Four On Tour.*

99. Concert

Date: 18 August 1965
Time: 8:15 p.m.
Location: Atlanta Stadium

[A.] **intro** (3:05)
[B.] **Twist and Shout** (1:20)
[C.] **She's a Woman** (2:44)
[D.] **intro** (0:33)
[E.] **I Feel Fine** (2:06)
[F.] **intro** (0:29)
[G.] **Dizzy Miss Lizzy** (1:20)
[H.] **intro** (0:31)
[I.] **Ticket to Ride** (2:09)
[J.] **intro** (0:23)
[K.] **Everybody's Trying to Be My Baby** (2:21)
[L.] **intro** (0:28)
[M.] **Can't Buy Me Love** (2:07)
[N.] **intro** (0:23)
[O.] **Baby's in Black** (2:17)
[P.] **intro** (0:30)
[Q.] **I Wanna Be Your Man** (2:04)
[R.] **outro** (0:36)
[S.] **intro** (0:20)
[T.] **Help!** (2:17)
[U.] **intro** (0:47)
[V.] **I'm Down** (2:08)
[W.] **outro** (0:09)

The Atlanta concert was apparently taped by WQXI, the local radio station promoting the show; their DJ Paul Drew had interviewed the Beatles before (see the April 27, 1964, entry) and would introduce them onstage. The circulating tape is missing a bit of "Dizzy Miss Lizzy" and all of "A Hard Day's Night," but illustrates Atlanta Stadium's outstanding sound system. Only John's rhythm guitar is buried, but the guitars in general have a crisp and clean tone, the drums and bass are audible, and the vocals are upfront. Paul comments on this in his introduction to "I Feel Fine" ("Ooh, it's loud, isn't it? Eh? Great!"), as does John before "Dizzy Miss Lizzy": "Oh, it's great, you can hear it!"

Paul tries to elicit audience participation in "Can't Buy Me Love": "If you all feel like clapping your hands, well do so in this one. I've been saying this for about three days, and nobody ever claps 'em, but don't worry." He introduces the song as "Can't Buy Me, Love," matched by John's "Baby's in Black—pool." Due to the tepid reaction to "Act Naturally" at Shea (it hadn't been released in the United States yet), Ringo's spotlight number is now "I Wanna Be Your Man," brought to us "at great expense."

Paul breaks a bass string during the song, causing John to stall for time while Paul switches to his backup '61 Hofner: "I can't think of anything to say, so why don't you just hum and talk to yourselves for a bit." Speaking of instrumental troubles, John's elbow-playing organ antics had damaged the Vox Continental organ during "I'm Down" in Toronto, but luckily an Atlanta Vox dealer was able to deliver a new keyboard in time for this show.

RELEASE HISTORY

1995: A very good-quality tape of most of this concert (missing **F** and **G**) surfaced on the bootleg CD *Beatles over Atlanta & Shea Stadium,* running too fast and suffering from distortion. Masterdisc speed-corrected and cleaned up the tape for its CD *Atlanta '65;* this source was copied on Vigotone's CD *Atlanta * Munich * Seattle.*

1999: **F** and **G** appeared on the CD-R compilation *Vinyl to the Core,* taken from a CD-R that included the beginnings and endings of each song (thus **G** is incomplete) except "A Hard Day's Night." The source tape was reportedly used during production of the 1982 radio documentary *The Days of Their Lives.*

99a. Press conference

Date: 19 August 1965
Time: afternoon
Location: Sheraton-Lincoln Hotel, Houston
Length: 1:55

The Beatles' 2 a.m. arrival at Houston Airport was especially terrifying as spectators poured onto the runway and surrounded the plane, effectively holding the passengers hostage. There was no way to start the engines and taxi to the gate without the propellers shredding several fans. The Beatles ended up escaping from the rear emergency exit into a van after the plane was slowly towed across the tarmac.

The Houston press conference was held at the group's hotel, prior to their first performance. Footage of the event shows the Beatles seated at a long table in front of two huge banners reading SHERATON-LINCOLN (the hotel) and KILT (the radio station sponsoring their concerts); the latter falls off the wall at one point, startling Ringo. Brian Epstein stands behind them, watching the proceedings.

Most of the footage is silent, but in the brief portion with sound, John can be heard singing the praises of Atlanta Stadium's PA system.

RELEASE HISTORY

This footage circulates on video among collectors.

100. Concert

Date: 19 August 1965
Time: afternoon
Location: Sam Houston Coliseum, Houston

[A.] **intro** (3:21)
[B.] **Twist and Shout** (1:23)
[C.] **intro** (0:01)
[D.] **She's a Woman** (2:52)
[E.] **intro** (0:39)
[F.] **I Feel Fine** (2:12)
[G.] **intro** (0:31)
[H.] **Dizzy Miss Lizzy** (3:05)
[I.] **intro** (0:32)
[J.] **Ticket to Ride** (2:20)
[K.] **intro** (0:29)
[L.] **Everybody's Trying to Be My Baby** (2:24)
[M.] **intro** (0:34)
[N.] **Can't Buy Me Love** (2:10)
[O.] **intro** (0:26)
[P.] **Baby's in Black** (2:22)
[Q.] **intro** (0:54)
[R.] **I Wanna Be Your Man** (2:09)
[S.] **intro** (0:35)
[T.] **A Hard Day's Night** (2:35)
[U.] **intro** (1:03)
[V.] **Help!** (2:23)
[W.] **intro** (0:49)
[X.] **I'm Down** (2:12)
[Y.] **outro** (0:40)

Two concerts were held in sweltering heat at Sam Houston Coliseum, and very good tapes of both exist, possibly recorded by local radio station KILT, which was sponsoring the show. Their DJ Russ "Weird Beard" Knight can be heard introducing both sets as well as plugging a local premiere of *Help!*

From the opening song, it's clear that John's throat is taking a pounding, but he croaks his way through and is generally fine when not singing falsetto. He introduces "Dizzy Miss Lizzy" as being from an album "called Beatles 5 or 65 or 98 or something," and "A Hard Day's Night" as being "our last but one single but one single but one single but one single." While introducing "I Wanna Be Your Man," Paul has to inform Ringo how to switch on his vocal microphone, but he remains fairly inaudible anyway, as does most of the drum kit apart from the cymbals.

Paul tells the enthusiastic crowd to join in with "Can't Buy Me Love," "if you can get yourselves disentangled." The chaos becomes too dangerous, and Knight comes onstage after "A Hard Day's Night" with a warning from the "Houston Security Beatle Division": People in the front rows are getting crushed, and if everyone doesn't move back, the show will be cut short. John's response to the interruption is a nonchalant: "Oh, thank you very much, that was wunnerful."

RELEASE HISTORY

1978: This concert was bootlegged in very good quality on the LP *Live from the Sam Houston Colosseum.*

1993: The concert appeared from tape source on the bootleg CD *The Ultimate Live Collection, Volume 1.*

101. Concert

Date: 19 August 1965
Time: 8:00 p.m.
Location: Sam Houston Coliseum, Houston

[A.] **intro** (4:27)
[B.] **Twist and Shout** (1:22)
[C.] **intro** (0:02)
[D.] **She's a Woman** (2:46)
[E.] **intro** (0:27)
[F.] **I Feel Fine** (2:08)
[G.] **intro** (0:23)
[H.] **Dizzy Miss Lizzy** (3:01)
[I.] **intro** (0:25)
[J.] **Ticket to Ride** (2:16)
[K.] **intro** (0:23)
[L.] **Everybody's Trying to Be My Baby** (2:02)
[M.] **intro** (0:23)
[N.] **Can't Buy Me Love** (2:08)
[O.] **intro** (0:23)
[P.] **Baby's in Black** (2:10)
[Q.] **intro** (0:33)
[R.] **I Wanna Be Your Man** (2:05)
[S.] **intro** (0:33)
[T.] **A Hard Day's Night** (2:32)
[U.] **intro** (0:34)
[V.] **Help!** (2:17)
[W.] **intro** (0:45)
[X.] **I'm Down** (2:08)
[Y.] **outro** (0:49)

In his introduction to the second Houston concert, Russ Knight implores the audience to stay seated and has everyone take a deep breath to calm them down "before we all do our number and faint." The caution worked, as no interruption for crowd control would be necessary.

While the sound mix is slightly improved from the matinee show, John's voice is even rougher, deteriorating entirely on "my baby don't care" and so raspy during "Twist and Shout" that Paul and George crack up laughing at him. Paul introduces Ringo as "somebody who doesn't sing often, drink much, et cetera," and unfortunately Ringo's vocal mic goes dead for the last half of "I Wanna Be Your Man." The rest of the show goes as normal, although for some reason, they play only half of the second guitar solo in "Everybody's Trying to Be My Baby."

A fuzzy 8 mm color home movie (lasting 3:49) circulates from one of the two Houston shows, as does a few seconds of black-and-white TV news footage from a 1985 "twentieth anniversary" broadcast.

RELEASE HISTORY

1978: This concert was bootlegged in very good quality on the LP *Live from the Sam Houston Colosseum.*

1993: The concert appeared from tape source on the bootleg CD *The Ultimate Live Collection, Volume 1.* The show's opening acts can be heard on the CD *The Playing Beatles 2.* The silent home movies and TV report both circulate on video.

102. Radio interview

Date: 15–20 August 1965
Location: New York City, Toronto, Atlanta, Houston, and Chicago
Interviewer: Brian Matthew
Broadcast: 30 August 1965, 10:00–10:45 a.m.
BBC Light Programme
The Beatles Abroad
Length: 15:49

Arriving from England on August 15 was Brian Matthew, who would cover the first week of the tour for BBC Radio, filing reports for various news shows and an eventual documentary, *The Beatles Abroad.* A tape of the original off-air broadcast and some alternate material, from a much cleaner-sounding BBC Transcription disc, both exist. According to Kevin Howlett's book *The Beatles at the BBC,* the latter was a "speech-only version" with some new material added but some omitted (including topical references such as Ringo's wife being pregnant); thus both sources are needed to obtain all the interviews.

Among the clips that obviously originate from August 15 are Matthew discussing customs officers with George, and Paul trying not to sound nervous backstage before the Shea concert. August 16 was a day of recuperation at the Warwick, with Brian Matthew capturing the Beatles' reactions to the Shea concert. John explains a slogan on one of the banners hung out at Shea, and he describes his rather carefree organ performance during "I'm Down." George talks about their journey from helicopter to Wells Fargo armored van and into the stadium, as well as the freedom they now have to walk around in Carnaby Street and not feel out of place now that long hair and mod fashions were catching on. He also jokingly considers hiring Keith Richard to tune his guitars for him (Keith and Mick Jagger had attended the concert). The rest of Matthew's interviews for these shows are difficult to date with any certainty.

RELEASE HISTORY

1999: The off-air source tape first appeared in the bootleg CD boxed set *Mythology, Volume 2.*

2000: After appearing in part in radio documentaries such as *The Beatles Story* and *The Beeb's Lost Beatles Tapes,* the Transcription disc source was included in most complete form on the CD boot *The Beatles Broadcast Collection, Trailer 2.*

103. Concert

Date: 20 August 1965
Time: 3:00 p.m.
Location: Comiskey Park, Chicago
Length: 0:15

After leaving Houston, the Beatles made a return visit to Chicago, this time for two concerts at Comiskey Park. Just under a minute of the afternoon concert was filmed by Associated Press newsreel cameras.

RELEASE HISTORY

A bit of this silent footage was included in the documentary *The Compleat Beatles.*

104. Press conference

Date: 20 August 1965
Location: Comiskey Park, Chicago
Length: 1:51

A couple of minutes of footage circulates from the Chicago press conference. The questions cover such groundbreaking topics as lack of privacy, fans screaming, and hair length.

RELEASE HISTORY

These brief clips circulate on video; the complete footage reportedly lasts ten minutes.

105. Radio interviews

Date: 20 August 1965
Time: evening
Location: Comiskey Park, Chicago
Interviewer: Larry Kane
Broadcast: WFUN-AM, Miami
Length: 15:46

In their basement dressing room between shows at Comiskey, Larry Kane was able to record separate interviews with each Beatle; after this date, he would leave the entourage for a week, joining up again in San Diego. John, whose voice is totally shot at this point, growls his way through a conversation about playing outdoor arenas and Cynthia's reaction to their stage act (she always chides John about making goofy faces).

Ringo says he prefers indoor concerts, where there is at least some semblance of contact with the audience, and complains that baseball is a bit slow-paced. Kane commends the Beatles' recording of "Act Naturally" (not yet released by Capitol), and Ringo expresses surprise that imported copies are getting requested airplay in America.

Speaking with George, Kane gives a backhanded compliment to their performance of "Help!" at the *Ed Sullivan* taping the previous week, seeming amazed that their live arrangement measured up to the studio version. George explains that they try to stick to the basics in the studio, so that songs can be duplicated on stage, without "any of this overdubbing or adding orchestras." By early the next year, this approach would be turned on its head. George also talks a bit about his own songwriting, and how it's been developing so slowly because he has trouble coming up with lyrics, and because he's lazy.

Finally, Paul recounts his father's opposition to his choosing rock music as a career, and he shares some of his prejudices about Americans, based largely on tourists he'd seen in Europe. Kane tries to elicit some serious commentary about President Kennedy's assassination, but Paul's thoughtful answer is ruined when a girl in the background calls John a "tool" and he exclaims in astonishment, "Does that mean the same thing over here? I'm a tool, man! This girl just called me a tool!"

RELEASE HISTORY

1996: These interviews were released on the promotional CD *The Fab Four On Tour.*

106. Newsreel footage

Date: 21 August 1965
Time: 4:15 p.m.
Location: Minneapolis Airport
Length: 0:40

Fifteen minutes of Beatles-related newsreel footage circulate from Minneapolis, including 40 seconds of the airport arrival and 9 minutes of the press conference (see following entry). As the group deplanes, all but George wearing sunglasses, zealous fans run up to them but are intercepted in the nick of time. The rest of the footage, filmed a couple of days later at a local police station, is informally known as "Jerk with a Badge." It consists of an interview with inspector Donald R. Dwyer, who complains about having to enforce a midnight curfew and remove teenage girls from the Beatles' fifth-floor suite, particularly Paul's room.

RELEASE HISTORY

Most of this footage was released on the home video *Fun with the Fab Four,* although it circulates in more complete form. The soundtrack to the "Jerk with a Badge" interview appeared with that title on the bootleg EP *Visit to Minneapolis,* along with some of the press conference.

107. Press conference

Date: 21 August 1965
Location: Metropolitan Stadium, Minneapolis
Broadcast: WDGY-AM, Minneapolis
Length: 26:22

A press conference was held backstage before the show in Minneapolis, and a twenty-six-minute recording circulates of WDGY-AM's live coverage of the event. Rather than have Tony Barrow solicit questions and repeat them over the PA, the WDGY microphone is amplified and passed around among the reporters in the small room. In addition, John Ravenscroft, a representative from KOMA, their sister station in Oklahoma City, is present. Being from Liverpool, he is interviewed briefly, but more interesting is the fact that he would go on to fame on BBC Radio as John Peel, interviewing various Beatles and helping to launch numerous musical careers in the 1970s. When the conference begins, he tries to wow the group with his Merseyside connection, announcing that he learned from Paul's aunt that a school is being built near his house. Paul, unimpressed, simply mumbles that he likes schools.

Some reporters seem ill-prepared, repeatedly asking questions about their long hair (which solicit moans of disgust), but others bring up music-related topics for a change. Reminded that their Capitol contract will expire in a year, someone asks if they would start their own record label, but John presciently observes, "It's too much trouble." They all rave about the Bob Dylan concert they had attended in London in May (and at one point John sings a bit of the just-released "Like a Rolling Stone"). Paul praises Brian Wilson's songwriting, with George singling out their new record ("California Girls"). John says he "wouldn't touch a Vox guitar" although they do use Vox amplifiers. John does, however, drool over a brand-new twelve-string Rickenbacker guitar presented to George at the end of the conference, remarking, "That's the best thing we've ever got! Where's mine?"

RELEASE HISTORY

Excerpts of this conference were captured by newsreel cameras (the footage circulates on video) and subsequently pressed onto numerous legitimate and bootleg LPs. The WDGY audio tape contains the complete proceedings.

108. Concert

Date: 21 August 1965
Time: 8:00 p.m.
Location: Metropolitan Stadium, Minneapolis

[A.] **She's a Woman** (2:22)
[B.] **intro** (0:37)
[C.] **I Feel Fine** (2:06)
[D.] **intro** (0:28)
[E.] **Dizzy Miss Lizzy** (2:57)
[F.] **intro** (0:35)
[G.] **Ticket to Ride** (2:10)
[H.] **intro** (0:17)
[I.] **Everybody's Trying to Be My Baby** (2:18)
[J.] **intro** (0:42)
[K.] **Can't Buy Me Love** (2:04)
[L.] **intro** (0:44)
[M.] **Baby's in Black** (2:13)
[N.] **intro** (0:31)
[O.] **I Wanna Be Your Man** (2:02)
[P.] **intro** (0:41)
[Q.] **A Hard Day's Night** (2:26)
[R.] **intro** (0:35)
[S.] **Help!** (2:15)
[T.] **intro** (1:05)
[U.] **I'm Down** (1:40)

In 1979, Melvin Records released a bootleg EP titled *Visit to Minneapolis,* which claimed to contain three songs from the Beatles' 1965 Minneapolis concert. Closer inspection proved them to be excerpts of a Houston performance, but the real thing finally surfaced twenty-three years later.

Unfortunately, it turned out to be an audience tape recorded from far back in the stadium, with only the introductions, vocals, and booming bass not drowned out by the screams and chattering of the crowd. It's also incomplete, with glitches in "She's a Woman," "Dizzy Miss Lizzy," "Ticket to Ride," and the ending of "I'm Down" cut short. Due to John's sore throat, "Twist and Shout" wasn't performed that evening.

Still, it's better than nothing, and while the performances are difficult to judge (during "Help!" John blanks on the lyric "I know that I just need you like" yet again), the stage patter is entertaining as ever. According to Paul, "I Feel Fine" was "our last but two record release here in good ol' Kinneapolis," while John dedicates "Baby's in Black" to a helicopter that is buzzing the stadium. During "I'm Down," a voice near the tape recorder pleads, "Somebody get out there and do something," but it's not clear whether this is an attempt to restrain or incite a rush to the stage.

RELEASE HISTORY

2002: This fair-quality concert recording surfaced as a series of mp3 files on the Internet that were soon compiled on CD-Rs such as *Minneapolis 21.8.65* and *Minneapolis, 8-21-1965, Detroit 8-13-1966.*

109. Press conference

Date: 22 August 1965
Location: Portland Airport
Length: 0:19

A pair of shows at Memorial Coliseum in Portland, Oregon, along with a visit from Beach Boys Mike Love and Carl Wilson, occupied the Beatles' day. A few seconds of their airport press conference (Paul denying Communist leanings) exist, sourced from a local TV news segment in 1985.

RELEASE HISTORY

This brief footage circulates on video among collectors.

110. Radio interview J, G

Date: 22 August 1965
Location: unknown hotel, Portland
Interviewer: Jerry G. Bishop
Broadcast: WKYC-AM, Cleveland
Length: 2:48

A couple of Jerry Bishop's interviews obviously originate from this date: John complains about fans being told not to scream in Minneapolis the previous day and explains why his throat troubles are making it impossible to sing falsetto in songs like "Help!" and "Ticket to Ride." George lists some of the songs that feature his twelve-string guitar work.

RELEASE HISTORY

1983: These interviews were released on the LP *The Beatles Talk with Jerry G., Volume 2.*

111. Newsreel footage

Date: 23 August 1965
Time: 3:00 a.m.
Location: Los Angeles International Airport
Length: 0:13

Five days of fun in the sun at a private estate in Hollywood—no wonder the Beatles were looking forward to this part of the tour! Of course, the fans circling overhead in rented helicopters and omnipresent journalists made it difficult to relax entirely, but over the course of the week, they managed to hook up with old pal Derek Taylor, hang out with the Byrds and attend one of their recording sessions, view several recent movies, take their first voluntary LSD trip, and meet Elvis Presley. The details of the week's events are best retold in the *Anthology* book, but available recordings give us several glimpses, beginning with a short newsreel clip of their 3 a.m. arrival at Los Angeles International Airport.

RELEASE HISTORY

This footage circulates among video collectors.

112. Newsreel footage

Date: 24 August 1965
Time: afternoon
Location: Los Angeles
Broadcast: KABC-TV, Los Angeles
Length: 3:19

As they had the previous year, the Beatles consented to attend another star-studded Hollywood party, once again thrown by Capitol Records' president, Alan Livingston. Five minutes of raw footage circulates featuring a KABC-TV reporter covering the celebrity arrivals. Eddie Fisher, Rock Hudson, Jack Benny, Edward G. Robinson, and Groucho Marx all stop for brief chats, but when the Beatles exit their limo, with Neil and Mal leading the way, there is only time for a female fan to ask Paul if he's enjoying his rest ("Yes, thank you!") before they disappear behind the front gates.

RELEASE HISTORY

Excerpts of this footage were released on *Fun with the Fab Four,* but a more complete version is traded on video.

113. Radio interview

Date: 13–24 August 1965
Interviewer: Jerry G. Bishop
Broadcast: WKYC-AM, Cleveland
Length: 13:20

On August 25, Jerry G. Bishop assembled several "reports from Los Angeles"—mostly interview snippets with new intros and outros but also a couple of longer recordings. These help to narrow down the dates for several of the interviews on the *Beatles Talk with Jerry G.* picture disc releases. The raw tape contains some material not on the commercial LPs, and vice-versa, but the following at least were recorded between August 13 and August 24.

One interview is easily identifiable by Paul's constant gum-chewing. In it, he confesses to some childhood delinquency: exposing his pet mice to sunstroke and, more shockingly, bludgeoning another child with "a big bar" at the age of five. The latter he blames on his surroundings in the rough Speke district, and the former is redeemed by his nursing the rodents back to health. The punch line? "Then I drowned 'em." Paul also begins to rhapsodize about the joys of capitalism, only to be reminded by Bishop of his song "Can't Buy Me Love"—oops!

John is heard dissing an unknown song (probably "Eve of Destruction," which Bishop asks Ringo about in another interview), calling the lyrics "soft, y'know, concocted." Ringo, meanwhile, chats about superstitions, his newly purchased house in Surrey, and insists adamantly that he has no plans to open a nightclub, despite what George had told Bishop back in Atlanta. ("Ringo's opening a place . . . it'll be open probably about November.")

George's interview, the longest continual recording from this tape, was plundered for several segments on the LPs. He begins by praising the Byrds, but complaining that they need more original compositions up to the standard of their Bob Dylan covers. This is a bold statement from the author of only four songs to date, but George is quick to point out how hard it is for him to write a good lyric, claiming that the melody for "I Need You" was completed in twenty minutes, but it took him a few days to write the words. George then explains how the skiffle boom made him and many other British teens purchase guitars, and he realizes that the Beatle boom has probably inspired an equal number of budding musicians.

Finally, Bishop gives each Beatle a sort of psychological test by asking them to answer the question "Who are you?" Paul stumbles through an uninspired job description, while Ringo talks about being two people—the private "Ritchie" and the public "Beatle Ringo." John simply says he's "Nervin G. Knockers," and George claims to be Dave Clark!

Interestingly, Bishop signs off at the tape's end with "for Brian Matthew on *Top of the Pops*"—according to *The Complete Beatles Chronicle* by Mark Lewisohn, after Matthew's return to London on the twentieth, U.S. broadcaster Jay Peeples filed reports in his stead. I'm not sure whether Peeples is a pseudonym for Bishop, or whether he supplemented or took over for Bishop.

RELEASE HISTORY

1982: Portions of these interview were released on the LP *The Beatles Talk with Jerry G.* The full tape of "reports" circulates in excellent quality among collectors.

114. Press conference

Date: 28 August 1965
Location: Balboa Stadium, San Diego
Length: 8:31

A chartered bus took the Beatles on a short ride south to San Diego this morning for a concert at Balboa Stadium, returning them to Los Angeles after the show. An eight-minute recording of the press conference at the stadium is circulating on the same tape as Jerry Bishop's raw reports, so it was probably captured by his microphone.

During the conference, a lesser-known banning and burning of Beatles records, in Jakarta, Indonesia, is discussed; along those lines, when asked if their music is morally degrading the youth of the world, Paul replies, "If they want Tchaikovsky, they can have it." In a lighter vein, they all claim to be fans of the TV show *The Man from U.N.C.L.E.,* and John quips, "We're not disinterested in politics, it's just politicians are disinteresting."

RELEASE HISTORY

This press conference circulates in very good quality among collectors.

115. Radio interview

Date: 28 August 1965
Location: Balboa Stadium, San Diego
Interviewer: Jerry G. Bishop
Broadcast: WKYC-AM, Cleveland
Length: 12:53

After the press conference, Bishop caught up on the past week's events and recorded interviews with all four Beatles. George is heard giving a thumbs-down to a movie they had seen (probably *Cat Ballou,* based on his comments in the *Anthology* book), but says it's too hard to give an objective review of *Help!* John has no problem doing so, frankly stating that the film gets worse as it goes along, and praising the performances of their costars. He also talks about walking out on *Cat Ballou,* but says he enjoyed *What's New Pussycat,* particularly the acting of Peter Sellers. After reminiscing about art school and saying his memory is too short to write an autobiography, John relates the previous night's Elvis-Beatles meeting. Bishop asks if he jammed with Elvis, and John doesn't quite answer, beyond saying Elvis played a bass guitar while watching TV.

When asked the same question, however, Ringo is clear on the matter: "The boys played guitar, I don't play, though. I played pool with three of his friends." Since Beatles roadie and noted Elvis fan Mal Evans is nearby, Ringo "interviews" him, and Mal declares that he was duly impressed by the King. Paul also says Elvis lived up to his expectations in the flesh, but admits that not only do they think his recording career is in the dumps ("I don't like the new stuff half as much"), but that they said as much to his face! Not surprisingly, when Bishop proposes a "Beatles-Elvis album," both John and Paul immediately reject the idea.

RELEASE HISTORY

1983: These interviews were released on the LP *The Beatles Talk with Jerry G., Volume 2.*

115a. Radio interview

Date: 28 August 1965
Location: Balboa Stadium, San Diego
Interviewer: Larry Kane
Broadcast: WFUN-AM, Miami
Length: 4:33

Larry Kane also elicited the Beatles' reactions to their summit with Elvis Presley. George says they were each given a box of early Elvis LPs as a souvenir of their meeting, and he further confirms the impromptu jam session: "We were playing electric guitars." John and Ringo both admit that everyone present was nervous until the ice was broken. Paul sums up the meeting as "a good laugh, a few drinks, rocking and rolling, playing the instruments, and a bit of billiards, a bit of roulette."

RELEASE HISTORY

2003: These interviews were released on the CD included with the book *Ticket to Ride.*

116. Concert

Date: 28 August 1965
Time: 8:00 p.m.
Location: Balboa Stadium, San Diego
Broadcast: KGTV-TV, San Diego
Length: 0:24

KGTV cameraman Lee Louis filmed portions of the day's events in San Diego, including fans and the bus outside the stadium, the press conference (see earlier entry), and the sole concert at Balboa Stadium that night.

RELEASE HISTORY

An excerpt of this silent footage was made available on the Internet.

117. Press conference

Date: 29 August 1965
Location: Capitol Records Tower, Los Angeles
Length: 36:22

Back in Los Angeles, another press conference was held, this time at the Capitol Records Tower, with the Beatles seated on stools in front of a huge *Help!* banner.

After talking about fans trying to get onstage in San Diego, John says security has been good everywhere except Houston. The funniest moment occurs when KRLA deejay Dave Hull tries to ask John and Paul a question about Bob Dylan, and George laconically reminds Hull that even he and Ringo, "the nonmusical members of the group," are Dylan fans. Nor are they shy about criticizing Capitol's butchered versions of their British LPs while sitting in the company's headquarters—with the president of the company standing right there! (John: "We plan it." Ringo: "And they wreck it.") They do have kind words for the Byrds and Lovin' Spoonful, however, and spend a few moments teasing Curt Gunther, a photographer who had accompanied them on the 1964 tour.

At one point, someone asks about a doctor in San Francisco ("Doctor of what?" John wonders) who accused the Beatles of being Communist stooges. Apparently whoever asked it didn't have their camera rolling, as the exact same question is asked again during the TV portion of the conference, which follows the general questioning. To wrap things up, a pair of fans present the group with piñatas and then Capitol's distribution chief, Stanley Gortikov (which John corrupts to "Rimsky-Kortikov") introduces Capitol president Alan Livingston. Livingston presents them with gold records for Capitol's *Help!* soundtrack album, which they had just finished slagging.

RELEASE HISTORY

Over a half hour of this press conference is available to collectors in various places. Thirteen minutes of newsreel footage circulates on video, a long audio recording is on the bootleg CD *The Complete Hollywood Bowl,* another recording was released on *Things We Said Today* (the CD of which has extra material compared to the LP), and yet another variation, this time in stereo, was released on the CD *Beatles Tapes, Volume 5: The 1965* Help! *Tour.* Although these sources all overlap somewhat, they each contain unique portions.

118. TV interview

Date: 29 August 1965
Location: Capitol Records Tower, Los Angeles
Length: 1:39

During the TV portion of the press conference above, one can hear a (presumably local) TV crew filming individual interviews with each Beatle. The questions cover simple topics such as "What do you like about America?," but what makes it interesting is that the footage of these interviews has turned up on video with an unusual twist. In between the Beatles' answers are reverse-angle shots of a female reporter supposedly asking the questions. But it's clear that these shots were staged later with four stand-ins (wearing ridiculous-looking Beatle wigs) seated on stools facing away from the camera.

RELEASE HISTORY

This footage was released on the home video compilation *Fun with the Fab Four.* The unaltered footage also circulates, without the phony reverse shots.

119. Concert

Date: 29 August 1965
Time: evening
Location: Hollywood Bowl, Los Angeles
Producer: Engeman

[A.] **intro** (1:03)
[B.] **Twist and Shout** (1:24)
[C.] **She's a Woman** (2:48)
[D.] **intro** (0:26)
[E.] **I Feel Fine** (2:10)
[F.] **intro** (0:29)
[G.] **Dizzy Miss Lizzy** (3:03)
[H.] **intro** (0:39)
[I.] **Ticket to Ride** (2:20)
[J.] **intro** (0:20)
[K.] **Everybody's Trying to Be My Baby** (2:22)
[L.] **intro** (0:37)
[M.] **Can't Buy Me Love** (2:10)
[N.] **intro** (0:51)
[O.] **Baby's in Black** (2:17)
[P.] **intro** (0:31)
[Q.] **I Wanna Be Your Man** (2:06)
[R.] **intro** (0:58)
[S.] **A Hard Day's Night** (2:27)
[T.] **intro** (0:59)
[U.] **Help!** (2:19)
[V.] **intro** (0:48)
[W.] **I'm Down** (2:14)
[X.] **outro** (0:27)

As they had the previous year, Capitol Records decided to record the Beatles' 1965 Hollywood Bowl performance for possible release. Three-track tape was used again, with vocals on one track, drums and bass on a second, and guitars (and organ) on the third. Although the group was unsatisfied with the results of the previous year's recording, this time Capitol had two chances to get it right.

This was lucky because on the first night someone unplugged the lead connecting Paul and George's vocal microphone to the recording equipment. The result is that only John's vocals and introductions are audible during the first three numbers. Toward the end of his introduction for "Dizzy Miss Lizzy," John's mic suddenly goes quiet, which indicates that the engineers are trying to locate the problem.

By the time the song ends, all the mics have been restored, but the technical problems continue. Paul's bass amplifier keeps malfunctioning, causing John to stall prior to "Baby's in Black." "I hope you can hear me. I'd be awfully disappointed if you couldn't," he tells the audience emotionlessly. During "I Wanna Be Your Man," Ringo's vocal comes through loud and clear but the backing vocals are nowhere to be heard. After "A Hard Day's Night," Mal has to come out and tend to Paul's amp; to kill time, John whistles and barks, and Ringo plays a short drum flurry.

The Beatles' performance is decent if a bit rote; John continues to botch the lyrics to the second verse of "Help!" The joke introductions continue, as George calls "Everybody's Trying to Be My Baby" "a track off our Beatles '93 album." (There is a glitch in the middle of this song that sounds like a kink in the tape.) To join in with "Can't Buy Me Love," Paul urges the crowd to do anything "except swim" (a large pond separated the stage from the seating).

RELEASE HISTORY

1977: The LP *The Beatles at the Hollywood Bowl* included the following portions of this show in excellent stereo: the last half of **G,** all of **H** and **I,** most of **R,** and all of **U.**

1996: Most of **N** was released on the CD single "Real Love," as an introduction for the August 30 performance of "Baby's in Black."

1997: The entire concert (**A–X**) appeared in excellent-quality stereo on the bootleg CD *The Complete Hollywood Bowl Concerts 1964–65.*

120. Newsreel footage

Date: 30 August 1965
Time: evening
Location: Hollywood Bowl, Los Angeles
Length: 3:31

This newsreel footage begins with the camera crew trying to sweet-talk their way into the venue and catching a few words from Paul as he arrives for the concert. Evidently the sweet-talking paid off, as various portions of the two opening songs were also filmed, albeit from the very back of the venue.

In addition, three minutes of color Hollywood Bowl home movies exist, but as they're silent, it's difficult to tell which night they are from; they seem to contain Paul's "clap your hands" intro to "Can't Buy Me Love" as well as a bit of "Baby's in Black."

RELEASE HISTORY

This footage circulates on video among collectors.

121. Concert

Date: 30 August 1965
Time: evening
Location: Hollywood Bowl, Los Angeles
Producer: Voyle Gilmore

[A.] **intro** (1:09)
[B.] **Twist and Shout** (1:23)
[C.] **She's a Woman** (2:48)
[D.] **intro** (0:22)
[E.] **I Feel Fine** (2:11)
[F.] **intro** (0:32)
[G.] **Dizzy Miss Lizzy** (3:05)
[H.] **intro** (0:31)
[I.] **Ticket to Ride** (2:19)
[J.] **intro** (0:54)
[K.] **Everybody's Trying to Be My Baby** (2:20)
[L.] **intro** (0:34)
[M.] **Can't Buy Me Love** (2:09)
[N.] **intro** (0:29)
[O.] **Baby's in Black** (2:16)
[P.] **intro** (0:33)
[Q.] **I Wanna Be Your Man** (2:07)
[R.] **intro** (0:39)
[S.] **A Hard Day's Night** (2:33)
[T.] **intro** (0:36)
[U.] **Help!** (2:17)
[V.] **intro** (0:51)
[W.] **I'm Down** (2:12)
[X.] **outro** (1:13)

Things went more smoothly on the second night from Capitol's point of view, with only the backing vocals to "I Wanna Be Your Man" going mysteriously unrecorded again. Amplifier problems continue, but George stalls nicely: "We'd like to present John Lennon doing a leap dive from two thousand foot."

As the tour is winding down, the Beatles seem more intent on amusing one another with various asides than communicating with the audience: "You're waving again, Paul! I've warned you about that waving!"; "What a wonderful effort, hey campers?"; "Thank you, Paul, it's great working with you." The performance is musically impeccable apart from a timing issue that throws "I'm Down" out of whack. Lyrically, John runs into the curse of "Help!" yet again during the problematic second verse, and a line from "Ticket to Ride" is rendered "she ought to think rice by me."

Unlike in 1964, Capitol didn't even bother to remix either of the 1965 concerts at the time, and they remained unheard until May 1971, when the three-track masters were sent to Abbey Road. Apple declined to do anything with them, but when the Beatles' EMI contract expired in 1976, the tapes were pulled from the shelf that August and given rough stereo remixes. This may be the source of the unique edit of the August 30 concert used on Yellow Dog's 1993 CD *Hollywood Bowl Complete.*

On January 18, 1977, George Martin took the tapes of both shows to his AIR London studios, transferring them to twenty-four-track tape. Editing and stereo mixing were completed by the twenty-third, with EQ'd safety copies prepared February 16, and a copy made for Capitol on March 22. In June, the album *The Beatles at the Hollywood Bowl* was released, containing excerpts from the 1964 and both 1965 shows. (The sleeve notes inaccurately claim that nothing from the August 29, 1965, concert is used.)

RELEASE HISTORY

1966: **B** was overdubbed on the soundtrack of the TV documentary *The Beatles at Shea Stadium;* it appears from this source on the bootleg CD *Shea!/Candlestick.*

1977: The LP *The Beatles at the Hollywood Bowl* included the following portions of this show in excellent stereo: part of **A**; all of **B, C,** and **F**; the first half of **G**; all of **M, S,** and **T.**

1979: A good-quality but incomplete copy of **W** appeared on the bootleg LP *The Beatles vs. Don Ho,* taken from a radio broadcast with narration.

1993: The bootleg CD *State Fair to Hollywood* included a mono copy of this concert in very good quality, reportedly taken from a radio broadcast. **A, T, V,** and **W** are all slightly incomplete on this issue, which runs a half step too slow throughout. The same year, an excellent-quality stereo copy of the concert appeared on the bootleg CD *Hollywood Bowl Complete,* but many of the introductions (**A, F, J, N, P, R, T,** and **V**) are incomplete.

1996: **O** was released on the CD single "Real Love."

1997: The entire concert (**A–X**), presumably complete at last, appeared in excellent-quality stereo on the bootleg CD *The Complete Hollywood Bowl Concerts 1964–65.* This version has a tape stretch during **E** that is missing from previous releases.

122. Amateur footage

Date: 23–30 August 1965
Location: Los Angeles

A few silent color 8 mm home movies survive from the Beatles' Hollywood stay, mostly filmed poolside, including a shot of Paul wearing sunglasses, grabbing a stack of dollar bills, and grinning wildly.

RELEASE HISTORY

This footage first turned up in the promo for "My Brave Face" and more of it can be seen during the "Yellow Submarine" sequence in the *Anthology* home video documentary.

123. TV footage

Date: 31 August 1965
Time: 1:08 p.m.
Location: Pan American Air Base, San Francisco
Broadcast: KGO-TV, San Francisco
Length: 1:33

The tour wound up where the previous one had started, in San Francisco, with two tumultuous concerts at the Cow Palace. Local media coverage was heavy, and a few primary sources circulate.

The first is a cluster of film clips that probably comes from KGO-TV's archives. It begins with their arrival just after 1 p.m. at the airport (John can be heard singing "San Francisco Bay Blues" as the crew follows them across the tarmac) and continues at the Cow Palace.

RELEASE HISTORY

1996: The audio of this interview (slightly incomplete) was released on *Fab Four CD & Book Set.* The video circulates from the semiofficial release *Live in San Francisco.*

124. Concert

Date: 31 August 1965
Time: 2:00 p.m.
Location: Cow Palace, San Francisco
Broadcast: KGO-TV, San Francisco

[A.] **Twist and Shout** (1:15)
[B.] **She's a Woman** (0:54)
[C.] **intro to Dizzy Miss Lizzy** (0:13)
[D.] **Can't Buy Me Love** (0:05)
[E.] **Baby's in Black** (0:14)
[F.] **I Wanna Be Your Man** (0:20)
[G.] **A Hard Day's Night** (0:35)

Footage of the afternoon concert was captured by KGO-TV. During this show, fans overwhelmed the police force and charged the stage, a bit of which can be seen in the film (a girl is lifted off the stage).

The finished edit of KGO's footage includes portions of **A, F,** and **G,** but it's followed by a jumble of offcuts from the concert, arrival, and press conference. This includes three further fragments of "Twist and Shout" (the intro, opening verse, and final chord), which could be edited to make a nearly complete composite, as well as John's intro to "Dizzy Miss Lizzy" ("We'd like to do a song from an album track . . . LP"), another piece of "I Wanna Be Your Man," and the other incomplete songs listed above.

RELEASE HISTORY

2001: These fair-quality song fragments were included on the CD-R *Blackpool Night Out '64—Upgraded,* taken from the soundtrack of a newsreel and its offcuts, which also circulate on video.

125. Press conference

Date: 31 August 1965
Location: Cow Palace, San Francisco
Broadcast: KGO-TV, San Francisco
Length: 6:09

KGO also filmed a few minutes of the press conference, held on the Cow Palace stage between shows. Not surprisingly, many of the questions focus on the just-concluded melee; asked how the San Francisco police security compared to other cities, Ringo jokes, "What police?" John says their closest scrapes so far came in New Zealand and Houston, and someone wonders whether they are dreading the upcoming evening concert.

RELEASE HISTORY

1996: The audio of this interview (slightly incomplete) was released on *Fab Four CD & Book Set.* The video circulates from the semiofficial release *Live in San Francisco,* plus an alternate source (from a different camera, not KGO's) with some unique footage. KGO's portions are on the CD-R *Blackpool Night Out '64—Upgraded.*

126. Radio interview **J, R**

Date: 31 August 1965
Location: Cow Palace, San Francisco
Interviewer: Jerry G. Bishop
Broadcast: WKYC-AM, Cleveland
Length: 4:15

Jerry G. Bishop taped John's and Ringo's reactions backstage before the final Cow Palace show; Ringo admits he was scared even though he was up on a riser and surrounded by wire. John seems more disgusted with the way certain people in the crowd behaved, singling out a boy who grabbed his hat and dove back into the crowd feet-first. Another annoyance was caused by fans in the front row trying to reel John and Paul in by pulling the microphone leads, causing the mic to smack John in the face and disrupt his rendition of "Baby's in Black."

RELEASE HISTORY

1982: Portions of these interviews were released on the LP *The Beatles Talk with Jerry G.*

1983: The remaining segments were included on the LP *The Beatles Talk With Jerry G., Volume 2.*

127. Concert

Date: 31 August 1965
Time: evening
Location: Cow Palace, San Francisco
Broadcast: KEWB-AM, San Francisco

[A.] intro (1:25)
[B.] Twist and Shout (1:21)
[C.] intro (0:02)
[D.] She's a Woman (2:03)

There is also a lengthy off-air recording from KEWB-AM radio in circulation; this poor-quality tape mostly consists of DJs and reporters filling time prior to the first concert and includes some music from the opening acts. The tape then jumps ahead to the evening show for live coverage of the Beatles' set, including their first two songs.

RELEASE HISTORY

2001: These poor-quality concert recordings (**A–D**) were included on the CD-R compilation *Live: Make as Much Noise as You Like!*, and the entire KEWB radio tape circulates among traders.

128. Radio interviews — P, G, R

Date: 31 August 1965
Location: Cow Palace, San Francisco
Interviewer: Jim Stagg
Broadcast: WCFL-AM, Chicago
Length: 1:55

Jim Stagg had covered the entire 1964 Beatles tour for Cleveland's KYW radio. By 1965, he was working in Chicago, and he managed to catch up with them by tour's end for some brief interviews. These mostly consist of record introductions for Stagg's show: Paul tells people to listen for the Beatles "playing their cellos, violas, and violins" on "Yesterday"; Ringo says his version of "Act Naturally" pales next to Buck Owens's; George has trouble recalling the name of his own song "You Like Me Too Much." Singers Johnny Cash and Joan Baez were visiting the group backstage, so Paul teases Joan by thanking "all the people who came to our concerts, and all the people who don't go to hers."

RELEASE HISTORY

These interviews circulate in excellent quality among collectors.

129. Radio interview

Date: 13 August–1 September 1965
Location: various
Interviewer: Larry Kane
Broadcast: 1 March 1966, 8:00–8:50 p.m.
BBC1
The Beatles at Shea Stadium
Length: 7:49

In a minor coup, Larry Kane was chosen to provide interviews for the soundtrack of the film documenting the Beatles' Shea Stadium concert. Having traveled on both the 1964 and 1965 North American tours, he had plenty of material to offer to NEMS. Most of the interviews are heard over footage of the group preparing for the show, in between other acts; further excerpts (including a chat with Brian Epstein) are heard over their performance of "A Hard Day's Night."

Interspersed among previously examined recordings (from 1964, and August 13 and August 19, 1965) is some material unavailable elsewhere (some of which admittedly may stem from the 1964 tour). The group gives their reactions to playing for such a huge crowd, with George saying it tops even the Hollywood Bowl performance of the previous year. They discuss security, press reactions, gifts from fans, and praise the skyscrapers of New York City. Paul admits he had a poor impression of Americans before he came to the United States and started to meet them. In a clip apparently taped in San Diego August 28, George talks about looking forward to that night's show after a five-day rest.

RELEASE HISTORY

The Beatles at Shea Stadium soundtrack has been released on dozens of bootlegs over the years; the earliest titles on vinyl included *Shea, the Good Old Days* and the misleading *Last Live Show*. The best CD source is probably *Shea!/Candlestick Park*.

130. Radio interview

Date: 13 August–1 September 1965
Location: various
Interviewer: Jerry G. Bishop
Broadcast: WKYC-AM, Cleveland
Length: 41:44

There is little documentation to date the various interviews conducted by Jerry G. Bishop, leaving us to listen for internal clues. Those interviews that couldn't be identified (other than by year) fall under this entry. The majority stem from Bishop's first LP, released in 1982, which in turn is based on an LP he compiled in the fall of 1965.

The proposed LP combined interviews from the tour with extracts of Beatles songs, something that was possible because Capitol considered releasing the album as a follow-up to their 1964 package, *The Beatles Story.* A mono acetate of the LP, titled *Beatle Tour,* was prepared by Capitol on September 26, 1966, by which time many of the references in the disc's narration were out of date. A copy of the acetate circulates among collectors, but it offers no new material beyond what was eventually released in 1982 (minus the Beatle performances and plus new narration and an extra "farewell" recording from 1966).

In general, these conversations are a cut above the usual Beatle interviews, with each group member candidly discussing their childhood, musical development, and their thoughts on wealth, family, and protest singers. Bishop's second LP, released in 1983, also contains a couple of segments that can be traced to 1965. In one, Paul reveals that "What You're Doing" and "Every Little Thing" were written on the previous tour, and John admits that most of their early compositions were Buddy Holly rip-offs. In the other, George discusses plans to film *A Talent for Loving,* praising the book's historical accuracy.

RELEASE HISTORY

1982: The majority of these interviews were released on the LP *The Beatles Talk with Jerry G.*

1983: Further segments were included on the LP *The Beatles Talk with Jerry G., Volume 2.*

131. Radio interview

Date: 1 September 1965
Location: San Francisco
Interviewer: Jerry G. Bishop
Broadcast: WKYC-AM, Cleveland
Length: 0:51

After their two final frenzied concerts at San Francisco's Cow Palace on August 31, the Beatles spent the night recuperating in a Palo Alto hotel, checking out this afternoon for their return flight to England. Before departing, they recorded some farewell messages for Jerry G. Bishop, who had traveled with them on most of the tour. John says they'll be back again in 1966 "if you still want us," and Paul invites Jerry to join them the next time around. A farewell statement from George confirms that plans for another U.S. tour were "almost definite."

RELEASE HISTORY

1982: These brief interviews were released on the LP *The Beatles Talk with Jerry G.,* where they are followed by a recording of a "farewell picture" being taken, but that portion of the tape dates from August 14, 1966.

132. Newsreel footage

Date: 2 September 1965
Time: 5:00 a.m.
Location: London Airport
Length: 2:02

The long flight from the West Coast meant that the Beatles didn't arrive back in London until early this morning. Pathé cameras captured the event for a newsreel titled *Guess Who!* The short black-and-white clip shows the group and Brian Epstein stepping from a bus onto the tarmac and waving to fans prior to being whisked away in a limousine.

RELEASE HISTORY

The 1:16 Pathé newsreel circulates among collectors on video, as do 46 seconds of similar footage shot by Reuters.

133. Press conference R

Date: 14 September 1965
Location: Queen Charlotte Hospital, London
Broadcast: 14 September 1965
ITV
Length: 0:35

The second Beatle to marry also became the second Beatle daddy when Ringo's wife, Maureen, gave birth to Zak Starkey on September 13. The following day, cameras and reporters were present at the Queen Charlotte Hospital as Ringo returned to visit his newborn son. During this brief press conference, Ringo describes Zak's appearance (plenty of hair, and a Starkey nose) to the hungry journalists, as the Beatle baby isn't available to pose for photos yet.

RELEASE HISTORY

1996: An audio recording of this press conference was released on *Fab Four CD & Book Set.* The clip also circulates on video.

134. Interview R

Date: 14 September 1965
Location: Queen Charlotte Hospital, London
Broadcast: 14 September 1965
BBC TV
Length: 1:17

In this BBC News interview, Ringo explains that he had picked out the name Zak well in advance, and that it means "scholar" in Czechoslovakian. In hindsight, it's amusing to hear Ringo insist he doesn't care what Zak grows up to be, even a musician, as long as he doesn't take up the drums! Of course, Zak would go on to drum in his own group, tour with the Who, and play alongside his father on many All-Starr shows.

RELEASE HISTORY

1996: An audio recording of this interview was released on *Fab Four CD & Book Set.* The clip also circulates on video.

135. Newsreel footage R

Date: 22 September 1965
Location: Queen Charlotte Hospital, London
Length: 2:33

Maureen and child were discharged from Queen Charlotte's this day, allowing the world its first glimpse of young Zak. The happy family posed proudly for photos in the hospital doorway, with a nurse cradling the infant. Few fans were present, mostly journalists, as the Starkeys drove home in a Rolls, their newly hired private nurse in tow.

RELEASE HISTORY

Fifty-seven seconds of footage was used in a Pathé newsreel, *Ringo's All Right, Zak,* which circulates on video along with another 1:36 of silent offcuts.

136. Home demo P

Date: ca. September 1965
Location: 57 Wimpole Street, London (?)

[A.] We Can Work It Out (0:41)
[B.] Michelle (0:57)

According to recent accounts by Paul, he and John were still very much a songwriting team at this stage. Most of the *Rubber Soul* compositions were started by one or the other of them and finished off together at John's house in Weybridge, but occasionally they would put down ideas on tape (each had a modest "home studio" by now). One such tape has survived the years and apparently began life as a reel Paul gave to John containing home demos of uncompleted songs. Unfortunately, John recorded over some of it, so we'll never know the original contents, but portions of two demos remain intact.

The tape begins with Paul performing "We Can Work It Out" accompanied by his acoustic guitar, in the key of C. The first verse, chorus, and second verse are identical in content to the final version, and presumably the demo continued without a finished bridge, since that was John's eventual contribution to the song. It's hard to say, since at that point John began to tape some goonish "comedy" over Paul's demo, acting as a compere and reading a Beatrix Potter tale in an exaggerated echo-laden voice while sappy prerecorded music played in the background.

This apparently cut into the beginning of the next song on the tape as well, which was Paul's electric guitar demo for "Michelle." At this point, no words had been written and he merely strummed the same chord pattern he'd had for years (also in C), with a fumbling attempt at a middle eight before concluding with the verse again. A visit from Ivan and Jan Vaughan later inspired Paul to come up with the finished lyrics, and John contributed the middle eight after hearing a Nina Simone cover of "I Put a Spell on You."

RELEASE HISTORY

1988: After being broadcast on episode 88-49 of *The Lost Lennon Tapes* radio series, **A** was bootlegged on the 1991 LP *Nothing But Aging.* This was copied in 1993 on the CD *Arrive Without Aging.*

1994: Both **A** and **B** were bootlegged from a tape source on the *Revolution,* although as with all the material on this Lennon home cassette, they run too fast, rendering the music almost a half step too high in pitch. The extraneous Beatrix Potter material also made its first appearance on this CD.

137. Studio session

Date: 12 October 1965
Time: 2:30–11:30 p.m.
Location: EMI Studio 2
Producer: George Martin

[A.] Run for Your Life—take 1 announcement and chat (stereo) (0:14)
[B.] studio chat (stereo) (0:25)
[C.] Run for Your Life—take 5 (mono) (1:23)
[D.] Norwegian Wood (This Bird Has Flown)—take 1 (stereo) (2:10)

[E.] Run for Your Life—RM1 (2:19)
Mixed: 9 November 1965

[F.] Run for Your Life—RS1 (2:18)
Mixed: 10 November 1965

[G.] Run for Your Life—RS from take 5 (#1) (2:17)
[H.] Run for Your Life—RS from take 5 (#2) (1:33)
[I.] Norwegian Wood (This Bird Has Flown)—RS from take 1 (1:59)

Recording sessions for *Rubber Soul* began this afternoon at Abbey Road with two new songs chiefly composed by John. The first, "Run for Your Life," would end up being the LP's closer; **A** consists of engineer Norman Smith's announcement of "take one" and a few seconds of studio chat from later in the session. This chat seems to link up with some other dialogue (**B**), which has John mentioning his "Jumbo Gibson" acoustic, and a silly exchange with Paul. ("Okay, boys?" "Okay, Johnny!")

At some point in the "Run for Your Life" session, after most of the instruments had been laid down but during his first attempts at adding a lead vocal, John pulled out the demo reel Paul had sent him and taped the work in progress (**C**) from the studio monitors. The original tape begins with a few seconds of rhythm track busking, followed by Norman Smith's take 5 announcement, and carries on through the third verse, before ending abruptly. (Perhaps John erased the end of it with something else; perhaps he just shut off the recorder.)

The finished take of "Run for Your Life" includes a backing track of bass, drums, and acoustic and electric guitars, with overdubs of tambourine, a lead guitar, a double-tracked lead vocal from John, and backing vocals from Paul and George. The released mono mix (**E**) lasts a couple of notes longer at the fade-out than its stereo counterpart (**F**); George Martin's 1987 stereo remix (**G**) is even shorter, and removes a thumping noise during the guitar solo.

With one song in the can, they tackled what was then known as "This Bird Has Flown," spending over four hours perfecting a single take that was later discarded in favor of a remake. Take 1 is nearly identical lyrically to the version eventually released as "Norwegian Wood" (the lines "biding my time" and "drinking her wine" are swapped), but it is the unique arrangement that makes this one of their more interesting outtakes.

The backing has John playing his acoustic guitar in the key of D on one track, joined by Paul's bass and Ringo on percussion (just his bass drum and cymbal) on a second, and John's first lead vocal plus Paul's harmony and George's sitar on a third. For the fourth track overdub, John added a second lead vocal, George another sitar line, Paul maracas, and Ringo finger cymbals. In this version, the sitar solo is half its final length, and George plays answering phrases after each line of lyric in the middle eights.

The raw studio tape (**D**) begins with a "take one" announcement, chat, and count-in, and ends with a snippet of John and George complaining about how hard it was to play! An alternate stereo mix prepared by John Barrett (**I**) separates the two vocal tracks slightly.

RELEASE HISTORY

1965: **E** and **F** were included on mono and stereo pressings of the *Rubber Soul* LP.

1983: The multimedia presentation *The Beatles at Abbey Road* included **B** and a portion of **I.** These both appear in excellent quality on the soundboard tape booted on *Abbey Road Video Show,* but the first part of **B** is missing. Most of the missing dialogue was broadcast in 1984 on Westwood One's *Sgt. Pepper's Lonely Hearts Club Band: A History of the Beatle Years 1962–1970* radio special.

1987: **G,** a new digital remix created by George Martin, was released on the *Rubber Soul* CD.

1988: The vinyl bootleg *Ultra Rare Trax, Volume 5 & 6* included an excellent copy of **I.** This includes the complete song but none of the surrounding studio chat.

1989: A slightly incomplete copy of **C** was aired on episode 89-41 of *The Lost Lennon Tapes.* It was later bootlegged on the vinyl *The Lost Lennon Tapes, Volume 21* and the CD *Arrive Without Aging.*

1992: The bootleg *Hodge Podge* included a murky recording of **D,** which gave us the debut of the studio chat preceding and following the song, as well as 2 seconds of a rehearsal take at the end, which had apparently been erased by take 1 proper. Sadly the song itself, which had an alternate stereo mix, was very incomplete on this release!

1994: **A** was included on the boxed set *The Ultimate Collection, Volume 3: Studio Sessions, 1965–66* in excellent quality.

1996: The only unedited version of **C** was included on an obscure CD-R compilation, *Entomology.* This included the rhythm track busking intro for the first time; a subsequent release on the more common *From Me to You* bootleg includes this busking but omits the original third verse by splicing together a fake looped ending. Geoff Emerick's mix of **D** also saw official release this year on *Anthology 2.*

1999: An excellent-quality copy of the raw studio take of **D** was included on *Turn Me On Dead Man: The John Barrett Tapes,* and similar releases. This is missing the very end of the studio chat and the 2-second rehearsal take—for those, you need the slightly inferior-sounding copy on *More Masters.* The same year, **I** appeared on the bootleg CD *Another Sessions . . . Plus* in excellent quality.

2003: **H** and a portion of **D** were released on the soundtrack of the *Anthology* DVD.

2004: **B** was booted complete and in excellent quality on the CD *A Day in the Life.*

138. Studio session

Date: 13 October 1965
Time: 7:00 p.m.–12:15 a.m.
Location: EMI Studio 2
Producer: George Martin

[A.] Drive My Car—RM1 (2:26)
Mixed: 25 October 1965

[B.] Drive My Car—RS1 (2:26)
Mixed: 26 October 1965

[C.] Drive My Car—RS from take 4 (#1) (2:26)
[D.] Drive My Car—RS from take 4 (#2) (0:16)
[E.] Drive My Car/The Word/What You're Doing—RS (1:54)

Day two of the sessions was exclusively dedicated to recording "Drive My Car," a new Paul composition (with help from John) that would serve as a great opening track to the LP. After three breakdowns/false starts, they completed a backing track of Paul on bass, Ringo on drums, John on tambourine, and George playing an electric guitar line "stolen from Otis Redding's 'Respect,' " as he later put it. Overdubs include piano, cowbell, double-tracked lead and backing vocals, and Paul's lead guitar for the intro, solo, and coda. With no afternoon session this day, the song wasn't completed until after midnight—a first for the Beatles and the precedent for many studio dates to come that lasted into the wee hours.

The mono mix of "Drive My Car" has the track with piano and cowbell mixed relatively lower than on its stereo counterpart (**B**), although it is brought way up for each piano lick during the choruses. For whatever reason, most of George Martin's original stereo mixes during this period (October–November 1965) are very empty in the middle, with all tracks panned to extreme left or right, a technique not used since the days of twin-track recording in early 1963 and thankfully abandoned beginning in 1966. Martin took the opportunity to rectify the situation somewhat in 1987 when remixing *Rubber Soul* for CD, and his remix of "Drive My Car" (**C**) has the vocals panned slightly toward the center, with a touch of reverb added. The *Love* mashup is a tour-de-force incorporating not only the similarly paced "The Word" and "What You're Doing," but the horns from "Savoy Truffle" and the guitar solo from "Taxman."

RELEASE HISTORY

1965: **A** and **B** were included on mono and stereo pressings of the *Rubber Soul* LP in the UK. **A** is also included on the CD-EP *Nowhere Man.*

1987: **C,** a new digital remix created by George Martin, was released on the *Rubber Soul* CD.

2003: **D** was released on the soundtrack of the *Anthology* DVD.

2006: **E** was released on the *Love* CD.

139. Studio session

Date: 16 October 1965
Time: 2:30 p.m.–midnight
Location: EMI Studio 2
Producer: George Martin

[A.] Day Tripper—take 1 (stereo) (2:28)
[B.] Day Tripper—takes 2–3 (stereo) (3:49)
[C.] Day Tripper—monitor mix of take 3 (mono) (2:48)

[D.] Day Tripper—RS1 (2:47)
Mixed: 26 October 1965

[E.] Day Tripper—RM3 (2:49)
Mixed: 29 October 1965

[F.] Day Tripper—RS2 (2:47)
Mixed: 10 November 1966

[G.] Day Tripper—RS from take 3 (2:34)

After a two-day break, the Beatles returned to Abbey Road for a Saturday session and were able to complete "Day Tripper," one side of their next single. We are lucky enough to have all three takes available for study. Each has the standard lineup of drums and bass on one track and two guitars on a second. With Ringo's exhortation, "Let's really rock it this time," the first attempt at a rhythm track (**A**) makes it as far as the "rave-up" section, before someone whistles them to a halt. George is then heard relaying some instructions to Mal Evans. Paul asks the control room if they can do another take right away, and George Martin replies in the affirmative, but the recorder is shut off briefly, allowing us to hear a burst of a taped-over rehearsal take.

As it switches on again (**B**), Paul is impatiently telling someone to put their tea down so another take can begin, while George is still discussing guitar settings with Mal. Take 2 lasts only a couple of bars into the first verse when John switches chords from E to A too early. The third take was "best," and double-tracked vocals from John and Paul, a second lead guitar, and tambourine were added to complete the song. A monitor mix of take 3 (**C**), taken from John's work tape, offers no new material beyond **B,** but has the backing vocals during the guitar solo mixed softer than elsewhere.

Before going home that night, the Beatles also started work on a George Harrison composition, "If I Needed Someone," laying down a backing track of bass, drums, rhythm guitar, and twelve-string electric guitar in one take.

Two stereo mixes of "Day Tripper" were created: The 1965 mix (**D**) has the second lead guitar track kick in a few seconds late. A second stereo mix done in 1966 for the UK (**F**) has more echo on the vocals than the 1965 mix, and has both lead guitar tracks playing from the start. It's also the only mix to conceal a misplaced "Yeah" from John at the start of the coda. The original mono mix (**E**) lasts a bit longer than either stereo mix. A rare engineering glitch occurred when a second or two of the guitar/tambourine track was erased, just after the solo. This blooper can be heard on the aforementioned raw studio tape as well as all originally released mixes, although it has been "corrected" for the greatest hits compilation, *1,* by splicing in a bit of sound from elsewhere in the song. This version is otherwise identical to the 1966 UK stereo mix.

RELEASE HISTORY

1965: **E** was released worldwide on a single and was later released on a CD single.

1966: Capitol released **D** on stereo copies of the *"Yesterday" . . . and Today* LP in the United States. **F** was released in the UK on *A Collection of Beatles Oldies;* this mix is also contained on the *Past Masters, Volume 2* and *The Beatles 1962–1966* CD collections.

1984: Part of **B** (take 3 only) appeared from the raw studio tape (with a unique stereo mix) in Westwood One's *Sgt. Pepper's Lonely Hearts Club Band: A History of the Beatle Years 1962–1970* radio special.

1988: An excellent copy of **B** from tape source (missing most of the studio chat) was bootlegged on *Ultra Rare Trax, Volume 2.* Later that year, **A** and **B** appeared complete, but at the wrong speed on the vinyl boot *Ultra Rare Trax, Volume 3 & 4.*

1994: **A** and **B** were included on *The Ultimate Collection, Volume 3: Studio Sessions, 1965–66* in excellent quality but still running too slow.

2002: **C** appeared in very good quality on the CD-R *As It Happened, Baby!*

2003: **G** was released on the soundtrack of the *Anthology* DVD.

140. Studio session

Date: 18 October 1965
Time: 2:30–5:45 p.m.
Location: EMI Studio 2
Producer: George Martin

[A.] In My Life—monitor mix of take 3 (mono) (1:04)

[B.] If I Needed Someone—RM1 (2:19)
Mixed: 25 October 1965

[C.] If I Needed Someone—RS1 (2:19)
Mixed: 26 October 1965

[D.] If I Needed Someone—RS from take 1 (2:19)

This brief Monday afternoon session began with the final overdubs for "If I Needed Someone." George added a double-tracked lead vocal and John and Paul filled out the three-part harmony; George's lead guitar and Ringo's tambourine apparently shared the remaining track, since the tambourine migrates to the right channel for the guitar's appearances during the solo and coda. The mono and stereo mixes (**B** and **C**) have no major differences, while the CD remix (**D**) has one of the vocal tracks panned slightly to the center.

The rest of the session saw the Beatles bring "In My Life" to near completion in three takes. A backing track of guitars, bass, and drums was augmented by tambourine, a double-tracked lead vocal from John, and harmony vocal from Paul. To fill the instrumental verse, John decided against the standard guitar solo and instructed George Martin to fashion some kind of keyboard solo. Martin's first attempt, using a Hammond organ, was apparently recorded at the end of this session, as a monitor mix of that version (**A**) appears on John's personal reel. This begins just prior to the solo and runs through the end of the song, but it's not clear whether this is another victim of John's erase head or whether he was only interested in capturing the last half of the song for reference purposes.

RELEASE HISTORY

1965: **B** and **C** were included on mono and stereo pressings of the *Rubber Soul* LP in the UK.

1987: **D,** a new digital remix created by George Martin, was released on the *Rubber Soul* CD.

1996: **A** was included on an obscure homemade CD-R compilation, *Entomology.* This source was copied on the bootleg *From Me to You.*

140a. Studio session

Date: 19 October 1965
Location: Marquee Studio, London
Producer: Tony Barrow

[A.] unused Christmas messages (1:32)
[B.] unused Christmas messages (11:57)

As usual, Tony Barrow was in charge of rounding up the Beatles to record the annual Christmas greeting message for their Official Fan Club. The first attempt took place this day at London's Marquee Studio and produced at least a half hour of material, none of it suitable for the disc.

Two separate reels from this session have been auctioned recently, and samples of each were made available via the Internet. A short downloadable file (**A**) consisting of seven snippets features John complaining about Barrow's hackneyed script, plus piano and vocal renditions of "The Twelve Days of Christmas" and "Silent Night" (sung as "Bonfire Night").

A much longer excerpt (**B**) was sold as a CD-R titled *The Lost Beatles Message.* However stale the script was, when they tried to improvise skits to various taped sound effects, the Beatles fared no better. Crying infants put Lennon in the mind of slicing babies, while ringing bells lead to a boxing match, with George as the announcer, Paul the referee, and John as a rhyming Cassius Clay. Ringo's only contribution is to sit back and laugh at the others' antics. A calliope rendition of "Dixie" leads to little more than worries about whether they can use a copyrighted song. The recording ends with Paul exclaiming, "We've gotta pull ourselves together."

In the end, the Christmas message would be done from scratch at EMI November 8, but Barrow didn't let the Marquee session go entirely to waste: A bit of it was used in spring 1966 on the *Sound of the Stars* flexi-disc he produced to promote *Disc and Music Echo.*

RELEASE HISTORY

1966: A very tiny bit of this recording was used on the *Sound of the Stars* flexi-disc. The rest has been issued on various CD-R bootlegs.

141. Studio session

Date: 20 October 1965
Time: 2:30–11:45 p.m.
Location: EMI Studio 2
Producer: George Martin

[A.] We Can Work It Out—take 1 (mono) (2:01)

[B.] We Can Work It Out—RM1 (2:14)
Mixed: 28 October 1965

With the addition of John's "fussing and fighting" bridge, "We Can Work It Out" was now compositionally complete and ready for recording. Transposed to the key of D, the song's backing track contained John on acoustic guitar, Paul on bass, George on tambourine, and Ringo at the drums. The session tape (**A**) begins with Paul reminding John that the song switches back to waltz time for the ending, and take 1 goes well until Ringo forgets about the meter change, staying in 4/4 for the second bridge. They stop playing, and Norman Smith encourages them from the control booth: "It was great up to that bit!"

The second take went smoothly, and track 2 of the tape was filled with an overdub of harmonium (during the chorus and bridges); Paul and John's vocals went onto track 3, with the fourth track being left empty for the time being. A rough mix of the song as it stood (**B**) was made October 28, and it's either that mix or a monitor mix done this day that ended up on John's personal reel.

RELEASE HISTORY

1988: An excellent copy of **A** appeared on the vinyl boot *Ultra Rare Trax, Volume 3 & 4.* Since it's only a one-track recording at this point, subsequent CD releases such as *Unsurpassed Masters, Volume 2* mixed this take into fake "duophonic" stereo.

1992: After being broadcast on *The Lost Lennon Tapes* radio series, **B** was bootlegged on the LP *Arrive without Travelling.* This was copied onto the CD boot *Arrive Without Aging.*

1994: **B** appeared from tape source, but with the count-in slightly clipped, on the CD *Revolution.* The same year, **A** was bootlegged from a slow but excellent tape source on *The Ultimate Collection, Volume 3: Studio Sessions, 1965–66,* with the sole track mixed to the left.

142. Studio session

Date: 21 October 1965
Time: 2:30–7:00 p.m.
Location: EMI Studio 2
Producer: George Martin

[A.] Norwegian Wood (This Bird Has Flown)—take 2 (stereo) (2:27)
[B.] Norwegian Wood (This Bird Has Flown)—take 4 (stereo) (2:34)

[C.] Norwegian Wood (This Bird Has Flown)—RM1 (2:02)
Mixed: 25 October 1965

[D.] Norwegian Wood (This Bird Has Flown)—RS1 (2:02)
Mixed: 26 October 1965

[E.] Norwegian Wood (This Bird Has Flown)—RS from take 4 (2:02)

Having rejected the finished recording from nine days earlier, the Beatles returned to "This Bird Has Flown," with a new arrangement for the second take (**A**). This time the song began with the bridge melody played on double-tracked sitar before continuing with the usual intro and first verse. John and Paul added vocals to the acoustic guitar, bass, and drum backing, but they still weren't happy with the result.

Take 3 is not available, but Mark Lewisohn indicates that it consisted of two acoustic guitars, bass, and vocals, and was now being announced as "Norwegian Wood." The fourth and final take was played in the key of E, with a backing of Paul's bass and George's twelve-string acoustic on track 1, and John's capoed acoustic guitar and his and Paul's vocals on track 3. On track 2, George added his sitar part, and track 4 had added bass drum and tambourine for the last half of the song. The raw tape of take 4 (**B**) begins with John's multiple aborted attempts to play the opening bars and ends with his triumphant cry of "I showed ya!"

With John now satisfied, the song was mixed for inclusion on *Rubber Soul,* where it bore the full title "Norwegian Wood (This Bird Has Flown)." The mono mix (**C**) includes a cough from John, and George's "Sounds good!" comment after his sitar solo; these were mixed out for the stereo mixes on both LP (**D**) and CD (**E**). The evening concluded with two takes of another Lennon tune, "Nowhere Man," with the rhythm on track 1 and main vocals on track 3. They would attempt the song anew the following day.

RELEASE HISTORY

1965: **C** and **D** were included on mono and stereo pressings of the *Rubber Soul* LP.

1987: **E,** a new digital remix created by George Martin, was released on the *Rubber Soul* CD.

1988: An excellent tape of **B** was bootlegged on *Ultra Rare Trax, Volume 2.*

1992: A fair-quality tape of **A** and the very beginning of **B** was bootlegged on the vinyl *Arrive Without Travelling* and the CD *Hodge Podge.*

1999: A vastly improved copy of **A** appeared on bootlegs such as *Turn Me On Dead Man: The John Barrett Tapes.* The version of **B** included on *More Masters* is in slightly inferior quality than elsewhere, but includes a unique stray sitar note at the end of the tape.

143. Studio session

Date: 22 October 1965
Time: 10:30–11:30 a.m.
Location: EMI Studio 2
Producer: George Martin

[A.] In My Life—RM1 (2:23)
Mixed: 25 October 1965

[B.] In My Life—RS1 (2:22)
Mixed: 26 October 1965

[C.] In My Life—RS from take 3 (#1) (2:23)
[D.] In My Life—RS from take 3 (#2) (2:24)

In an hour-long morning session, George Martin applied the finishing touch to "In My Life," erasing his previous organ solo and replacing it with a lovely piano solo, laid down with the tape rolling at half speed. The song was added to the *Rubber Soul* lineup, with the mono and stereo mixes (**A** and **B**) sounding similar, and the CD remix (**C**) adding a splash of reverb to the lead vocal, pulled toward the center of the stereo image.

RELEASE HISTORY

1965: **A** and **B** were included on mono and stereo pressings of the *Rubber Soul* LP.

1987: **C,** a new digital remix created by George Martin, was released on the *Rubber Soul* CD.

2003: **D** was released on the soundtrack of the *Anthology* DVD.

144. Studio session

Date: 22 October 1965
Time: 2:30–11:30 p.m.
Location: EMI Studio 2
Producer: George Martin

[A.] Nowhere Man—RM1 (2:40)
Mixed: 25 October 1965

[B.] Nowhere Man—RS1 (2:40)
Mixed: 26 October 1965

[C.] Nowhere Man—RS from take 4 (#1) (2:41)
[D.] Nowhere Man—RS from take 4 (#2) (2:39)

When the Beatles showed up in the afternoon, they concentrated on remaking "Nowhere Man." The middle of three further backing track takes (acoustic guitar, bass, and drums) was chosen as best, and to this were added the lustrous three-part harmonies from John, Paul, and George, as well as John and George playing identical melodies on their Fender Stratocasters, giving the lead guitar a live/double-tracked feel.

The original mono and stereo mixes (**A** and **B**) ended up on *Rubber Soul,* but there have been two stereo remixes that change the picture somewhat. On the 1965 stereo LP (**B**), the rhythm and most of the lead guitar are at left, with all vocals and the guitar solo at right, and the middle vacant. The 1987 CD mix (**C**) has the rhythm track pulled from left to left-center and one of the vocal tracks placed in right-center rather than extreme right. The 1999 remix, for the reissue of the film *Yellow Submarine* (**D**), has one vocal track at left, the rhythm track centered, and the other two tracks (vocal 2 and all lead guitar) at far right.

RELEASE HISTORY

1965: **A** and **B** were included on mono and stereo pressings of the *Rubber Soul* LP in the UK. **A** is also included on the CD-EP *Nowhere Man.*

1987: **C,** a new digital remix created by George Martin, was released on the *Rubber Soul* CD.

1999: **D** was included on Apple's Yellow Submarine *Songtrack.* A portion of it (or a nearly identical remix) appears on the soundtrack of the *Anthology* DVD.

145. Studio session

Date: 24 October 1965
Time: 2:30–11:00 p.m.
Location: EMI Studio 2
Producer: George Martin

[A.] I'm Looking Through You—take 1 (stereo) (3:12)

[B.] I'm Looking Through You—RS from take 1 (#1) (0:52)
[C.] I'm Looking Through You—RS from take 1 (#2) (2:52)

Following in the footsteps of "Norwegian Wood" and "Nowhere Man," the Beatles spent this entire session perfecting Paul's "I'm Looking Through You," only to discard the finished product in favor of a new arrangement the following month. At this stage, the song's middle eight hadn't been written yet, with a pair of raucous guitar solos instead. The first part of the session was mainly spent learning and rehearsing the song, concluding with a single take of the backing: bass and drums on one track, and acoustic guitar and percussion (bongo and what sounds like woodblocks) on a second. To this were added Paul's first vocal and George's electric guitar on a third track, and Paul's second vocal, John's harmony, organ, and maracas on a fourth.

The raw studio tape (**A**), including the take announcement and Paul's count-in, allows us to hear the song stumble to a halt past the point where it would normally fade out. An alternate stereo mix of this take (**B**) was prepared for the multimedia show *The Beatles at Abbey Road,* with Paul's lead vocal split between the center and right channels. A year or so later, take 1 of "I'm Looking Through You" was scheduled for inclusion on the aborted *Sessions* LP. For this purpose, Geoff Emerick prepared a new mix (**C**), ostensibly in true stereo, but with everything centered apart from the percussion track, which was sent to both channels via Artificial Double Tracking. Unfortunately, this was the mix chosen for commercial release on *Anthology 2.*

RELEASE HISTORY

1983: The multimedia presentation *The Beatles at Abbey Road* included **B.** It can be heard from tape source on the bootleg CD *Abbey Road Video Show.*

1985: The Emerick mix (**C**) created for *Sessions* began to appear on vinyl bootlegs; it can be heard (with some tape damage) on Spank's CD of that title.

1988: The bootleg CD *Ultra Rare Trax, Volume 1* included an excellent tape copy of **A.**

1996: **C** was officially released on *Anthology 2.*

146. Newsreel footage

Date: 26 October 1965
Time: 10:00 a.m.
Location: Buckingham Palace, London
Length: 1:13

This date had long been cleared from the Beatles' schedule to allow them the honor of personally receiving MBE awards from Queen Elizabeth in a ceremony at Buckingham Palace. The world's press showed up as well, and cameras captured the storming of the gates by hundreds of fans, as well as the band's arrival and departure by limousine.

RELEASE HISTORY

A Pathé newsreel of the event titled *Beatles at Palace* circulates on video, and some U.S. news footage of the event (from ABC) appears in the *Anthology* home video.

147. Press conference

Date: 26 October 1965
Time: noon
Location: Saville Theatre, London
Length: 2:18

After displaying their new medals, the Fabs held a press conference at the Saville Theatre in London, also captured in still and moving pictures. An audio account of the general questioning that exists may originate in a BBC Home Service news report for *The World at One* broadcast this day. After describing the protocol of the ceremony and recounting having to sign autographs to their fellow recipients, they give a play-by-play of their brief encounter with Her Majesty.

RELEASE HISTORY

1972: Some of this recording was broadcast in the BBC Radio documentary *The Beatles Story.* It appears from that source on the CD *Inside Interviews: Beatlemania.* There is also some news footage with extra material circulating on video.

148. Interview

Date: 26 October 1965
Time: afternoon
Location: Saville Theatre, London
Interviewer: Robert Dougal (?)
Length: 1:19

The Fabs recount meeting the queen for a Reuters newsreel. For those who are interested, the regal conversation went approximately as follows:

The queen: It is my pleasure to give you this award.
George: Thank you, ma'am.
The queen: Have you been working hard?
John: No, we've been having a holiday.
The queen: How long have you been together?
Paul: Many years.
Ringo: (singing) "We've been together now for forty years!"
The queen: (after a confused pause) Did you start it all?
Ringo: No, they did, I was the last to join. I'm the little fella.

RELEASE HISTORY

This clip circulates among collectors as part of a Japanese TV documentary; a bit of it is also seen in the *Anthology* home video.

149. Interview

Date: 26 October 1965
Time: afternoon
Location: Saville Theatre, London
Broadcast: 26 October 1965
ITV
Length: 0:39

Another reenactment of the majestic meeting for ITV News; the anecdote is getting quite dry by this point.

RELEASE HISTORY

1996: This newsreel clip appears on *Rare Photos & Interview CD, Volume 3* and also circulates on video.

150. Radio interview J

Date: 26 October 1965
Time: afternoon
Location: Saville Theatre, London
Length: 1:56

John also granted an interview for French radio, recounting the royal reception yet again and speculating whether Prince Charles is a Beatles fan.

RELEASE HISTORY

1986: This interview was included on the vinyl bootleg *A Paris*. It was copied from this source on the CD-R *City of Light*.

151. Studio session

Date: 29 October 1965
Time: 2:00–4:00 p.m.
Location: EMI Studio 2
Producer: George Martin

[A.] We Can Work It Out—take 2 (stereo) (2:24)

[B.] We Can Work It Out—RM3 (2:12)
Mixed: 29 October 1965

[C.] We Can Work It Out—RS1 (2:11)
Mixed: 10 November 1965

[D.] We Can Work It Out—RS2 (2:13)
Mixed: 10 November 1966

[E.] We Can Work It Out—RS from take 2 (2:10)

The three previous studio dates for *Rubber Soul* had been mixing sessions only. At the last of these, a rough mix of "We Can Work It Out" convinced the group that something was missing, so they spent a couple of hours this afternoon filling track 4 of the tape with more harmonium (during the verses only) and a second lead vocal from Paul. The session tape of take 2 (**A**), incorporating these additions, includes Paul's count-in and continues past the end of the song.

With the song complete, mono mixes of this and "Day Tripper" were made at the end of the session. They had already settled upon these two songs as their next single, with both designated as A-sides so as not to slight either one. Along with the single mixes, alternate mono mixes were made of both songs to be used for lip-sync playback during videotaping of a TV special, *The Music of Lennon & McCartney,* the following week. The released mono mix (**B**) has some strange fluctuations in volume. As with "Day Tripper," two stereo mixes of this song were prepared: a 1965 mix for the United States (**C**) and a 1966 mix for the UK (**D**). The chorus/bridge harmonium (track 2 of the tape) is placed in the center on the U.S. mix and to the right on the UK mix; otherwise, they are basically identical.

RELEASE HISTORY

1965: **B** was released worldwide on a single, and was later released on a CD single.

1966: Capitol released **C** on stereo copies of the *"Yesterday" . . . and Today* LP in the United States. **D** was released in the UK on *A Collection of Beatles Oldies;* this mix is also contained on the *Past Masters, Volume 2* and *The Beatles 1962–1966* CD collections.

1984: Most of **A** appeared from the raw studio tape (with a unique stereo mix) in Westwood One's *Sgt. Pepper's Lonely Hearts Club Band: A History of the Beatle Years 1962–1970* radio special. This source was copied on the CD *Ultra Rare Trax, Volume 2* and faded early to omit the narration.

1994: After various appearances on vinyl and CD bootlegs, **A** was included in best quality yet on *The Ultimate Collection, Volume 3: Studio Sessions, 1965–66,* albeit running too slow.

2003: **E** was released on the soundtrack of the *Anthology* DVD.

152. TV performance

Date: 1-2 November 1965
Location: Studio 6, Granada TV Centre, London
Producer: Johnny Hamp
Broadcast: 16 December 1965, 9:40–10:35 p.m.
Granada TV
The Music of Lennon & McCartney

[A.] **intro—Peter and Gordon** (1:39)
[B.] **intro—Fritz Spiegl's Ensemble** (0:14)
[C.] **Day Tripper** (3:00)
[D.] **Yesterday** (0:28)
[E.] **intro—Antonio Vargas** (0:59)
[F.] **intro—Dick Rivers** (0:17)
[G.] **intro—Cilla Black** (0:20)
[H.] **intro—Henry Mancini** (0:12)
[I.] **intro—Esther Phillips** (0:15)
[J.] **intro—Peter Sellers** (0:06)
[K.] **We Can Work It Out** (2:20)

A semisuccessful attempt to spotlight John and Paul's songwriting abilities, this TV special consisted of various performers lip-syncing Lennon/McCartney songs, both those written especially for the artists and those covered out of admiration. It's not clear what material was videotaped on which day, but over the course of both days, John and Paul stayed through rehearsals and shooting to introduce many of the acts. George and Ringo also joined them on one of these days to run through both sides of their upcoming single for the cameras. The set was minimalistic, consisting of a huge network of scaffolding, steps, and ladders that the singers all performed on, under, and around.

Part one of the show opens with George Martin conducting his orchestra in a medley that concludes with a shot of a hi-hat cymbal being tapped by two drumsticks, held by John and Paul. Their scripted banter is delivered awkwardly and it's clear neither are very comfortable with the whole idea of the show, let alone the corny manner in which they are participating. They walk past various devices (Victrola, transistor radio, reel-to-reel) ostensibly playing cover versions by artists who couldn't make it, and then introduce Peter and Gordon's rendition of "World Without Love." Lulu is next with "I Saw Him Standing There" (expressly recorded so it could be performed in this show) and then Alan Haven and Peter Crombie duet on a jazz instrumental of "A Hard Day's Night." John and Paul reappear to introduce Fritz Speigl's string ensemble playing a Beatle medley in a ridiculous scene, with the musicians dressed in powdered wigs and an audience of "mod" ladies with blond wigs, sunglasses, and miniskirts. This cuts to a whole line of similarly "gear" go-go dancers, who lead us into the Beatles' performance of "Day Tripper," with the group standing under the scaffolding and playing their usual instruments.

Part two of the show opens with Paul under a spotlight with an acoustic guitar, miming the first verse of "Yesterday" as the camera pulls back. On the word "suddenly," Marianne Faithfull suddenly appears to finish the song. John and Paul then wander around the set discussing foreign language versions of their songs, and along the way, we see Antonio Vargas' flamenco-style "She Loves You" and Dick Rivers' "Ces Mots Qu'on Oublie Un Jour" (aka "Things We Said Today"). A pair of NEMS artists follow, with Billy J Kramer singing "Bad to Me," and Cilla Black joking with John and Paul before performing "It's for You."

The third and final segment begins with the George Martin Orchestra's "Ringo's Theme (This Boy)," again illustrated with a team of dancers. Paul introduces Henry Mancini's solo piano rendition of "If I Fell," and then we get the only moment of sincerity as John enthuses (with obvious admiration) about Esther Phillips, who sings "And I Love Him." Peter Sellers wraps the tributes up with a mock-Shakespearean recitation of "A Hard Day's Night," videotaped earlier in a London studio. The final number is "We Can Work It Out," again performed under the scaffolding, with John now playing an organ borrowed from the set of a Granada soap opera, *Coronation Street.* During the waltz-tempo bars in the bridge, Ringo mimes the drum fills on his head!

In addition to the spoken and musical segments listed above, all four Beatles can be seen standing around the organ in a 4-second clip during the credits, and John and Paul alone appear to congratulate Cilla Black at the end of her number. The entire special runs forty-four minutes.

RELEASE HISTORY

The complete program circulates in very good quality on video, thanks to a rebroadcast on December 30, 1985. None of the spoken bits seem to have been bootlegged anywhere.

153. Studio session

Date: 3 November 1965
Time: 2:30–11:30 p.m.
Location: EMI Studio 2
Producer: George Martin

[A.] Michelle—RM1 (2:42)
[B.] Michelle—RS1 (2:40)
Mixed: 9 November 1965

[C.] Michelle—RM2 (2:34)
Mixed: 15 November 1965

[D.] Michelle—RS from take 2 (2:39)

Sessions continued at Abbey Road, with this day's work devoted to recording "Michelle." The first four hours or so were spent learning, arranging, and rehearsing the song, and then a single take was committed to tape. Drums, acoustic guitar, and bass were supplemented by a lead vocal from Paul (single-tracked for one of the few times on the album). To this, George added some electric guitar over the solo and coda; although this apparently caused a bit of offense as George Martin directed him exactly what melody to play, the result was lovely. This filled up all four tracks of the tape, so to make room a tape reduction was done that combined two of the existing tracks onto a single track of a new reel. For the remainder of the evening, the smooth backing vocals and some additional acoustic guitar were overdubbed onto the newly freed fourth track of the tape.

"Michelle" has been released in four discrete mixes, each differing in length, on various copies of *Rubber Soul*. The mono mix released in the UK (**C**) is the shortest, while the 1987 stereo remix (**D**) is about 5 seconds longer. The original stereo LP mix (**B**) is four guitar notes longer than the CD, and the longest of all is the U.S. mono mix (**A**), which allows five further notes to be heard before fading out. This mix also has a slightly louder drum sound than its UK counterpart, but the easiest way to tell them apart is the discrepancy in timing.

RELEASE HISTORY

1965: **A** and **C** were included on mono pressings of the *Rubber Soul* LP in the United States and UK, respectively, while **B** appeared on stereo pressings worldwide. **C** is also included on the CD-EP *Nowhere Man*.

1987: **D,** a new digital remix created by George Martin, was released on the *Rubber Soul* CD.

154. Studio session

Date: 4 November 1965
Time: 11:00 p.m.–3:30 a.m.
Location: EMI Studio 2
Producer: George Martin

[A.] 12-Bar Original—takes 1–2 (stereo) (7:22)
[B.] 12-Bar Original—rehearsal take (stereo) (1:50)
[C.] 12-Bar Original—edit of take 2 (stereo) (2:53)

[D.] What Goes On—RM1 (2:45)
[E.] What Goes On—RS1 (2:45)
Mixed: 9 November 1965

[F.] 12-Bar Original—RM1 (6:41)
Mixed: 30 November 1965

[G.] What Goes On—RS from take 1 (2:46)

Although time was running out and the album was only half complete, the Beatles were apparently running low on new compositions to record. The usual dilemma of finding a song for Ringo to sing was solved by recasting a vintage Lennon/McCartney throwaway in a rockabilly vein suited to the drummer's recent vocal spotlights. "What Goes On" had been on a short list of contenders for their third single, and with the lyrics revised (Ringo added "about five words" which was enough to net him a cocomposing credit), they recorded it nearly three years later for inclusion on *Rubber Soul.*

The song was simple enough to be recorded swiftly at the start of this late-night session. A single take of the standard Beatles lineup (lead and rhythm guitar on one track, bass and drums on a second) had overdubs of Ringo's lead vocal on a third track, and harmonies from John and Paul plus more guitar from George on the fourth. The original stereo mix (**E**) has slightly wider channel separation than the CD remix (**G**), while the sole mono mix (**D**) is missing a bit of George's guitar work at the end of the song. This doesn't appear to be a neglected overdub, but rather the result of fading that track of the tape early for some reason.

Studio 2 had been booked until 3 a.m., and with a copious amount of time on the clock but no other material at hand, the Beatles decided to lay down some rubber soul of their own. Announced on the tape by engineer Norman Smith as "12-Bar Original," this Memphis-style instrumental was anything but, and seems to be an attempt to simulate any number of Booker T and the MG's recordings. Paul does a decent job with his walking bass line, and Ringo is rock-solid as ever, but John's rhythm guitar work is a bit clumsy, and George's lead guitar very far from inspired. Worst of all is George Martin's embarrassing attempt to get funky, floundering about on the harmonium.

Needless to say, the finished product did not see release at the time, but a recording of the session is available for us to study. The tape begins (**A**) with Paul's reminder to keep a steady tempo, but the first take is botched after only five bars when John forgets to change to the A chord. The second take carries on for six and a half minutes before they mercifully bring it to an end. Following this, nearly two minutes of a rehearsal take (**B**) can be heard (largely erased by the proper takes); knowing that they actually practiced this beforehand makes their final attempt somehow sadder.

In any case, a few days after the album had been mastered, a single mono mix of take 2 (**F**) was created so that each Beatle could have a souvenir acetate of their experiment for their private listening pleasure. One such acetate, dated December 13, 1965, was auctioned at Sotheby's April 7, 1988, for £1,300; a copy appeared on bootleg within months. A severely edited version of "12-Bar Original" (**C**) was released on *Anthology 2* in a strange stereo mix—the bass and drums are centered and the guitar tracks seem to swap places from left to right at various edit points.

RELEASE HISTORY

1965: **D** and **E** were included on mono and stereo pressings of the *Rubber Soul* LP in the UK.

1987: **G,** a new digital remix created by George Martin, was released on the *Rubber Soul* CD.

1988: An excerpt of **F,** from an acetate sold at auction, appeared on the vinyl bootleg *Ultra Rare Trax, Volume 3 & 4.*

1989: The full acetate of **F** was bootlegged on *Unsurpassed Masters, Volume 2,* although the ending fades a bit too quickly, omitting a final cymbal crash. The 1991 bootleg *Acetates* has the ending intact.

1992: A tape containing **A** and **B** was issued on the vinyl boot *Arrive Without Travelling,* as well as the CD *Arrive Without Aging.* Unfortunately this tape is fair quality, runs too fast, and has several dropouts and a small portion missing.

1996: **C** was officially released on *Anthology 2.*

1999: An excellent stereo but slightly incomplete recording of **A** (missing only a final harmonium riff) was included on *Turn Me On Dead Man: The John Barrett Tapes.* In addition, **F** made its debut from a tape source on *Another Sessions . . . Plus.*

155. Studio session

Date: 8 November 1965
Time: 9:00 p.m.–3:00 a.m.
Location: EMI Studio 2
Producer: George Martin

[A.] Beatle Speech—take 1 (mono) (18:55)

[B.] The Beatles' Third Christmas Record—RM1 (6:21)
[C.] Think for Yourself—RM1 (2:16)
[D.] Think for Yourself—RS1 (2:16)
Mixed: 9 November 1965
[E.] Think for Yourself—RS from take 1 (#1) (2:16)
[F.] Think for Yourself—RS from take 1 (#2) (2:16)
[G.] Think for Yourself—RS from take 1 (#3) (1:39)

The backing for George's second contribution to the album, initially titled "Won't Be There with You," was recorded this evening in a single take of bass, drums, and two electric guitars, all occupying a single track. Also on the agenda was the taping of a special message for Christmas to be sent to fan club members. The previous two years had seen them read from prepared scripts, although they hardly stuck to them verbatim. This year they elected to wing it, and to that end, a mono tape machine was set up to capture their conversation between vocal overdub attempts for George's song, in the hopes that some usable ad-libs would be captured.

Almost twenty minutes of this half-hour reel (**A**) has been bootlegged; in the end, none of this dialogue was used for the Christmas message, but a few seconds of looped three-part harmony ended up as part of the *Yellow Submarine* film soundtrack, and more recently, Paul incorporated several extracts from this reel in his *Liverpool Sound Collage.*

One really needs to hear the inflections, accents, and interaction among John, Paul, George, and George Martin (Ringo was probably off playing cards with Mal), so I won't try to transcribe the jokes here. Along the way, references are made to *Juke Box Jury,* Cynthia Lennon, TV deodorant jingles, "Yesterday," Rocky Marciano, the Supermarionation series *Supercar* and *Stingray,* uptight thespians, Frankie Howerd, "Do You Want to Know a Secret," Woody Woodpecker, and Humphrey Bogart. Amid all the banter and tomfoolery, we do get some insight into their studio techniques of the time.

As the tape begins, George is recording his first vocal track, backed by John and Paul, for the song's opening verse. John is having trouble hitting the right notes, and runs through his part several times with George's assistance. George Martin offers to play back their most recent attempt, after which John apologizes for his lack of success. The next take proves ineffective, but the following pass nails down the first verse. Two tries later, they have the second verse completed. The final verse proves especially frustrating, and after three failed attempts, John asks for a quick a cappella rehearsal before they try again (this is the snippet that appears in *Yellow Submarine*).

The rehearsal pays off, and it looks as though the third verse is in the can. George Martin requests George and Paul to redo the final choruses, however, and after their first pass, Martin is heard trying to cue up the right spot in the tape. Unfortunately, he picks the wrong place and on their next try, erases the third verse they had worked so hard on! John is summoned from the lavatory and after a few more attempts (now John knows his part, but Paul makes a flub), the first vocal track is completed. George Martin comes down from the control booth and they all listen to a playback of the work so far. As it's satisfactory, they set up to double-track their singing, standing near a speaker to allow them to hear the first vocal track as they do so. This is where the "Beatle Speech" recording ends, but maracas and tambourine were shaken as they sang on the tape's third track, and the remaining track was filled with a fuzz-tone bass and electric piano overdub.

The song was released as "Think for Yourself" on *Rubber Soul,* and there are no major differences among the mono and stereo LP and stereo CD mixes. However, the song was remixed for inclusion on Yellow Submarine *Songtrack;* this mix (**F**) has the rhythm track and George's solo vocal lines centered and the second vocal track mixed right-of-center, with the rest of the vocals remaining far left and the fuzz bass and piano at far right.

With that task complete, all four Beatles "gathered 'round the Christmas microphone" to record the fan club message (**B**), which was completed by editing together three takes of speech. Accompanying themselves with acoustic guitar and tambourine, the lads warble off-key renditions of "Yesterday," "It's the Same Old Song," and other improvised ditties, while parodying the platitudes of earlier messages and thanking the fans for sending gifts and cards. The most remarkable moment is a sneered mock–protest song version of "Auld Lang Syne," parodying "Eve of Destruction" with references to Vietnam and "bodies floating in the river Jordan."

RELEASE HISTORY

1965: **C** and **D** were included on mono and stereo pressings of the *Rubber Soul* LP. **B** was released on a flexi-disc, titled *The Beatles' Third Christmas Record,* mailed out to fan club members on December 17. It's available on the bootleg CD *The Ultimate Beatles Christmas Collection.*

1987: **E,** a new digital remix created by George Martin, was released on the *Rubber Soul* CD.

1991: The first 15:38 of **A** was bootlegged on *Unsurpassed Masters, Volume 7.*

1994: The final 5:04 of **A** appeared on *The Ultimate Collection, Volume 1: Miscellaneous Tracks;* the beginning of this excerpt overlapped with the previously available portion.

1999: **F** was included on Apple's Yellow Submarine *Songtrack.*

2000: Bits and pieces of **A** were officially released on *Liverpool Sound Collage.*

2003: **G** was released on the soundtrack of the *Anthology* DVD.

156. Studio session

Date: 10 November 1965
Time: 9:00 p.m.–4:00 a.m.
Location: EMI Studio 2
Producer: George Martin

[A.] The Word—RM1 (2:42)
[B.] The Word—RS1 (2:43)
Mixed: 11 November 1965

[C.] The Word—RS2 (2:41)
Mixed: 15 November 1965

[D.] The Word—RS from take 3 (#1) (2:41)
[E.] The Word—RS from take 3 (#2) (1:02)

The penultimate session for *Rubber Soul* lasted until 4 a.m., and was largely spent recording John and Paul's latest creation, "The Word," in three takes. The backing track consisted of rhythm guitar, drums, and Paul on piano. To this was added John's lead vocal, harmonizing with Paul and George, on two further tracks (one of which adds harmonium). For the final track, George played lead guitar, Ringo or John maracas, and Paul bass (Paul was quickly learning that adding bass as an overdub allowed for clearer sound as well as more creative lines). In addition, some falsetto backing vocals were overdubbed near the end of the song.

The stereo and mono mixes released in the UK and the 1987 CD remix all sound similar, but the mix released on U.S. stereo copies of *Rubber Soul* (**B**) has several differences. It's the only mix where John's lead vocal is double-tracked on the song's bridges, and two of the four tracks have swapped stereo channels compared to the UK mix. (Although the track with bass and maracas oddly migrates back to the other channel at the very end, making it likely this was really a rough mix never intended for release.)

As dawn approached, they tackled Paul's "I'm Looking Through You" yet again. Finished versions from both October 24 and November 6 had proved to be insufficient, but the third time was a charm. This arrangement incorporated a newly written middle eight section and was performed in the key of A-flat (probably played in G with a capo on the guitar's first fret). They got as far as perfecting a single rhythm take (acoustic guitar and drums on one track, bass and tambourine on a second) before calling it a hard night's day.

RELEASE HISTORY

1965: **B** and **C** were included on stereo pressings of the *Rubber Soul* LP in the United States and UK respectively, while **A** appeared on stereo pressings worldwide.

1987: **D,** a new digital remix created by George Martin, was released on the *Rubber Soul* CD.

2003: **E** was released on the soundtrack of the *Anthology* DVD.

157. Studio session

Date: 11 November 1965
Time: 6:00 p.m.–7:00 a.m.
Location: EMI Studio 2
Producer: George Martin

[A.] I'm Looking Through You—take 4 (stereo) (2:47)

[B.] I'm Looking Through You—RM1 (2:27)
[C.] You Won't See Me—RM1 (3:21)
[D.] Girl—RM1 (2:28)
[E.] Wait—RM2 (2:11)
[F.] Wait—RS1 (2:11)
[G.] I'm Looking Through You—RS1 (2:23)
[H.] You Won't See Me—RS1 (3:19)
[I.] Girl—RS1 (2:28)
Mixed: 15 November 1965

[J.] I'm Looking Through You—unedited RS1 (2:27)
[K.] You Won't See Me—RS from take 2 (3:18)
[L.] Girl—RS from take 2 (2:28)
[M.] I'm Looking Through You—RS from take 4 (#2) (2:24)
[N.] Wait—RS from take 4 (2:11)
[O.] I'm Looking Through You—RS from take 4 (#2) (0:57)

Sink-or-swim time. Arriving just after dinner, the group sequestered themselves at EMI studios until 7 the following morning, setting a new record and returning to the studio pace of two years prior. John and Paul each arrived with a new song to contribute, and Paul's "You Won't See Me" was recorded first. By the second take, the song had a musical backing of John's piano, Paul's bass, George's electric guitar, Ringo's drums/tambourine (it sounds as though he plays the tambourine as part of his kit), and Hammond organ. As the latter merely consisted of a single A note held over the entire final verse, the part was played by the Beatles' roadie, jokingly credited as "Mal 'Organ' Evans" on the album cover! The remaining three tracks of the tape were apparently reserved for vocals—one for Paul to sing solo lead, one for him to double-track his lead, accompanied by John and George on harmony, and a third for further backing vocals. The stereo LP mix (**H**) has everything mixed far left or right, while the CD remix (**K**) has Paul's solo vocal track (and what sounds like some hi-hat cymbal) mixed toward the center. The solitary mono mix (**C**) has a longer fade-out than the other two variations.

John's new composition, "Girl," also required a mere two takes to complete. The backing consists of bass, drums, acoustic rhythm guitar, and some two-step Mediterranean-style acoustic guitar and cymbal for the end of the song. John also recorded a lead vocal, double-tracked only on the middle eight and chorus and with plenty of heavy breathing. Paul and George sang double-tracked harmonies, and a further lead acoustic guitar part was added. All three released mixes (stereo LP and CD and mono LP) sound similar, although the CD (**L**) has a touch more echo.

With their supply of material exhausted, the Beatles resorted to a first—taking a rejected recording from an earlier album and dusting it off for inclusion on *Rubber Soul.* The master tape of "Wait" was pulled off the shelf from June, and a second guitar part, a second vocal from Paul, maracas, and tambourine were all added to make the song a bit more presentable. The stereo CD mix (**N**) has the original vocal track centered, rather than in the right channel; otherwise, it sounds similar to the stereo and mono LP mixes.

The finish line now in sight, Paul finally completed "I'm Looking Through You" to his satisfaction, adding a lead vocal supported by harmony from John, some Hollyesque flesh-slapping percussion, and some bursts of George's electric guitar and Hammond organ played by Ringo. This left George Harrison as about the only person not to have contributed a keyboard part to these sessions! On the final track of the tape, Paul double-tracked his vocal and Ringo was given the chance to fill in a couple of the organ blasts he had missed on the previous attempt.

The raw studio tape of this take (**A**) begins with Norman Smith's take announcement and some chat between Paul and Ringo (both from the previous night's session) and allows us to hear the entire take with all overdubs. This tape includes two quick false starts on acoustic guitar and the song's full ending, past where it would fade out on release. For some reason, the U.S. stereo LP (**J**) also contains these false starts, even though no alternate mix was created for Capitol; evidently the false starts were pruned when the stereo LP master reel was banded in the UK. The mono mix (**B**) contains a longer fade than any other released version, and the stereo CD remix (**M**) has the second vocal/organ track mixed slightly toward the center.

And with that, the Beatles' work on their sixth album was done; a final session four days later was for remixing only, and *Rubber Soul* went on sale a mere eighteen days after that. By Christmas, it was topping the charts in both America and Great Britain.

RELEASE HISTORY

1965: **B–E** were released on all mono pressings of the *Rubber Soul* LP. **F–I** were contained on stereo pressings, although in the United States, **J** was substituted for **G.**

1987: **K–N,** new digital remixes created by George Martin, were released on the *Rubber Soul* CD.

1999: A near-excellent copy of **A** turned up among the John Barrett tapes and was bootlegged on *Another Sessions . . . Plus.* The bootleg *Mythology, Volume 2* claims to have this recording, but merely splices the opening chat from **A** to a copy of **J.**

2003: **O** was released on the soundtrack of the *Anthology* DVD.

158. Promo clips

Date: 23 November 1965
Time: afternoon–evening
Location: Twickenham Film Studios, London
Director: Joe McGrath
Broadcast: various

- **[A.] Day Tripper—second version** (2:42)
- **[B.] We Can Work It Out—first version** (2:09)
- **[C.] We Can Work It Out—second version** (2:10)
- **[D.] We Can Work It Out—third version** (2:08)
- **[E.] Day Tripper—third version** (2:39)
- **[F.] Help!** (2:13)
- **[G.] Ticket to Ride** (2:53)
- **[H.] I Feel Fine—first version** (2:13)
- **[I.] I Feel Fine—second version** (2:19)

A long day of work at Stage Three of Twickenham Studios, concluding in the small hours of the twenty-fourth, but to good effect. Having abandoned the idea of promoting their records with unique radio performances, leaving the BBC to rely on playing records, the Beatles now put a halt to the practice of doing the rounds of TV shows. Instead the shows would come to them and bargain for the right to air promotional clips (on black-and-white videotape in this case), created by the independent InterTel VTR company, and owned by NEMS Enterprises. In that sense, these were forerunners of the music video era, but the actual clips themselves differed little from the standard performances seen on shows like *Ready, Steady, Go!,* containing no storylines or unrelated images. These are all straightforward "stand on a decorated set and play to the camera" lip-synced renditions.

The proceedings begin with two versions of a clip for "Day Tripper," only the second of which (**A**) is circulating. The group is dressed in black turtleneck sweaters (Paul wears a dark shirt) and jackets, and stand on platforms in front of some shiny pillars. Paul plays his Hofner bass, John a Rickenbacker guitar, and George a brand-new Gibson. During the break that follows the solo, Ringo "marches" in place at his drum kit. At the end of the song, a curtain of tinsel is pulled across the camera lens.

John switches to organ for the next song, "We Can Work It Out," with Paul standing behind him. The first two versions are similar, with George standing near Ringo's drum riser and sitting on the edge of it halfway through each time. Ringo again plays the waltz-time fills on his head, and John attempts to crack Paul up with some comical organ playing. The second version (**C**) can be identified by John's grinning at the camera and whistling during the first verse.

The set is then changed, replacing the pillars with the tinsel curtain and a giant cutout of a French New Year's greeting card; the Beatles also don their Shea Stadium military-style jackets at this point, and Paul sports a black turtleneck. Version 3 (**D**) of "We Can Work It Out" opens with a still photo of John holding up a sunflower, and features George seated the entire time. Starting with the third verse, John goes all out to distract Paul and succeeds in breaking him up completely. John smirks, raises his eyebrows, gives a quick thumbs-up, ends the song with some dainty organ flourishes, and finally puts his left foot up on the keyboard, spreads his arms wide, and bows slightly.

Wearing the same outfits, they have another stab at "Day Tripper" (**E**), this time standing amid giant cutouts representing travel. John and Paul stand behind an airplane, and George and Ringo peer through the windows of a train. Paul slips up on the line "she's a big teaser," miming "tried to please her" instead and laughing at his error. With no kit to sit behind, Ringo shakes a tambourine for the first verse, and plays air drums with his sticks for the second. During the solo, he grabs a saw and begins cutting up the scenery, holds out the tambourine for a single fill, and then goes back to the sticks, only to brandish the saw some more at the song's end.

With several clips for their new single now completed, they turn to the recent past. In anticipation of *Top of the Pops'* year-end review of the hits of 1965, clips are taped for their three previous singles exclusively for that show, broadcast December 25 on BBC1 from 10:35–11:50 p.m. "Help!" (**F**) is performed first, with the foursome seated on a bench holding their guitars, Ringo holding an umbrella. They have ditched the Shea jackets, and George has swapped his black turtleneck for a beige one. During each chorus, they bounce up and down, and fake snow begins to fall during the final verse, startling George and getting in Paul's mouth as he sings.

For "Ticket to Ride" (**G**), Ringo is back at his kit and the other three sit in director's chairs; the backdrop consists of huge blow-up replicas of train tickets. (Get it?) Paul and Ringo both wear heavy coats, and the drummer employs some Keith Moon–style "I'm obviously not playing live" strokes. Even funnier is John's inability to remember which lines end in "yeah"—for the second verse, he leaves his mouth open just in case, then blinks in surprise when none is forthcoming from the playback. On the third verse, he misses the cue entirely, so a second or two after it's heard, he gives an emphatic "yeah" to make up for it.

Finally, "I Feel Fine" (**H**) is performed on a sparse set sprinkled with exercise equipment. John, Paul, and George (only John still has his jacket on) walk on with guitars, with George singing into a punching bag and lapsing into gibberish when the camera catches him singing the wrong verse. Halfway through, Ringo joins them and pedals a stationary cycle. Either before or after this final performance, the group gathers on this set and tucks in to a pile of fish and chips, seemingly unaware that the cameras are rolling; when the playback of "I Feel Fine" begins, only John makes a real attempt to sing along while stuffing his face. It's not clear what the intent of this clip (**I**) was, other than to waste tape; in any case, it wasn't included in the reel NEMS made available to interested TV companies.

It's unknown which versions of "Day Tripper" and "We Can Work It Out" were screened on which shows, but both songs appeared on *Top of the Pops* and *Thank Your Lucky Stars* in the UK, as well as in America on NBCs *Hullabaloo* (including **E**), January 3, 1966, from 7:30–8:00 p.m. One version of "We Can Work It Out" (**D**) was aired on Germany's *Beat Club* (February 12 or March 26, 1966). The *Anthology* documentary includes heavily edited excerpts from most of these promos (excluding **F, H,** and **I**).

RELEASE HISTORY

A video reel containing **A–H** complete with opening slates has been circulating for many years and is now traded in excellent quality (better than the excerpts used in *Anthology,* in fact). The elusive fish and chips promo (**I**) finally surfaced around 1997 from a decent film print, not the original 2-inch video (which may no longer exist). In addition, Apple distributed versions of **F** and **G** in 1993 to promote the CD release of *The Beatles 1962–1966,* but these are marred by a red border framing the picture.

159. Radio interview

Date: 29 November 1965
Time: 2:15–2:45 p.m.
Location: Studio 1, Aeolian Hall, London
Host: Brian Matthew
Broadcast: 25 December 1965, 10:00–11:30 a.m.
BBC Light Programme
Saturday Club #377
Length: 7:23

Not only were exclusive TV performances now out of the question, but the Beatles' days of plugging records with exclusive BBC Radio music sessions had become a thing of the past. They did agree to convene at BBC's Aeolian Hall studios this afternoon and chat with Brian Matthew about nothing in particular for the Christmas Day broadcast of *Saturday Club.* Even at this late date, the Beeb did not preserve master tapes of most programs, so it was a lucky find when the raw session tape for this appearance turned up on a 10-inch reel in the Transcription Department's tape library. This discovery was made during research for the 1988 radio series *The Beeb's Lost Beatles Tapes,* in which just over five minutes of this half-hour tape was aired.

It begins with John, Paul, and Ringo making several attempts to introduce the show, with Ringo repeatedly missing his cue; at the end of this, the three sing an a cappella version of the *Saturday Club* theme song. As Paul croons "Maria" in a heavy Scouse accent, George joins his bandmates to chat with Matthew, although they can't begin until the producer tells the Searchers (probably rehearsing for a musical appearance of their own) to keep the noise down in the background. Discussion of Christmas activities follows, with Matthew explaining away the "no live Beatle music" policy by insisting they take the holiday off, and introducing the record of "We Can Work It Out."

Later in the show, Brian's rendition of a Stanley Holloway monologue, "Brahn Boots," would be heard, and to complement this, each Beatle gives a *Juke Box Jury*–style hit-or-miss assessment of Matthew's performance. This is followed by the playing of "Drive My Car," and the broadcast portion ends with each Beatle saying farewell. The recording concludes with 46 seconds of silliness from the raw studio tape, as John learns that his praise of the Searchers' number won't make sense, for despite their presence in the studio, the group won't appear on the same program as the Beatles. Brian then mistakes Paul's imitation of a typical female Cavern fan for an impression of Terry Doran!

RELEASE HISTORY

1988: 5:25 of these interviews were broadcast in the December 24 episode of BBC Radio's *The Beeb's Lost Beatles Tapes.*

2003: The complete recording was bootlegged on the CD boxed set *The Beatles at the Beeb,* although Kevin Howlett's book *The Beatles at the BBC* describes a bit more of the tape's contents.

160. Radio interview **G**

Date: 30 November 1965
Time: 4:30 p.m.
Location: NEMS Enterprises, London
Interviewer: Brian Matthew
Broadcast: *Pop Profile*
Length: 5:26

Brian Matthew, a clear favorite of the group, was chosen to conduct individual interviews with each Beatle for a BBC Radio series called *Pop Profile,* and he chatted with both George and John on this afternoon at Brian Epstein's NEMS headquarters in London. The shows were not for domestic broadcast in England, but were pressed onto 7-inch 33⅓ rpm Transcription discs and sent to various overseas markets in March 1966. Copies of all four Beatles' discs survive (Paul's and Ringo's would be taped in May 1966), and excerpts were included in *The Beeb's Lost Beatles Tapes.*

George is up first, and he admits to having been a slacker in school, having an interest only in art class, thanks to an encouraging teacher. He quite candidly explains why he's known as the quiet Beatle: He's fed up with responding to "stupid questions" that aren't "worth answering." After praising folk artists such as Bob Dylan, Donovan, Pete Seeger, and Jack Elliott, he recounts having thrown away a lot of his own songwriting attempts because he felt they weren't up to par with the Lennon/McCartney material. Expressing some ambivalence about having children, George nonetheless enjoys being settled down in his own home and having more free time to devote to learning music. He quite rightly recognizes that the less rushed the Beatles are, the more their work is improving.

RELEASE HISTORY

1972: 1:34 of this interview was included in the BBC Radio documentary *The Beatles Story.*

1988: The remainder of this interview was broadcast in the December 31 episode of BBC Radio's *The Beeb's Lost Beatles Tapes.* This source was copied on the bootleg *The Beatles Broadcast Collection, Trailer 2.*

161. Radio interview **J**

Date: 30 November 1965
Time: 5:00 p.m.
Location: NEMS Enterprises, London
Interviewer: Brian Matthew
Broadcast: *Pop Profile*
Length: 4:49

John, still a few years from being the articulate pontificator on current affairs he would become, stumbles through a defense of his own value system. In truth, this was his self-described "fat Elvis" period when he was rather lazy and complacent, and he has a hard time sounding passionate about his beliefs. He does seem to have put some thought into his son Julian's educational future, and explains the pitfalls of both public and private schools. John also laments that he is turning out like most parents, wanting to see his son follow in his own (musical) footsteps.

RELEASE HISTORY

1988: This interview was broadcast in the December 3 episode of BBC Radio's *The Beeb's Lost Beatles Tapes.* All broadcast material is included on the bootleg *The Beatles Broadcast Collection, Trailer* 2, although Kevin Howlett's book *The Beatles at the BBC* describes a bit more of the disc's contents.

. . . TO BE CONTINUED . . .

IN

THAT MAGIC FEELING

The Beatles' Recorded Legacy

Volume Two: 1966–1970

APPENDIX:
MASTER NEWSREEL LIST FOR THE YEARS 1963–1965

When it came to newsreel and TV news footage, I opted only to give entries to items I was actually able to view (or could verify were circulating). However, there is obviously a lot more film of the Beatles out there waiting to be plundered for use in future documentaries. To assist you in identifying which events were filmed, and by which company, here is an index compiled by scouring the written databases for the archives of the Associated Press (AP), the British Broadcasting Corporation (BBC), Independent Television News (ITN), the National Broadcasting Company (NBC), British Pathé (PATHE), and Reuters Newsagency (REU).

I wasn't able to gain access to ABC's or CBS's archives, and have omitted some minor companies (Universal, Movietone) who infrequently covered the Beatles, as well as most non-UK or non-U.S. sources. Also note that Reuters tended to supply footage to ITN and NBC, while the BBC relied on AP, so overlapping clips may reside in more than one archive. When possible, I've given the approximate length of the footage as noted in the database (compare the timings to individual entries to see how much is circulating); "C" indicates color footage.

1963:

Sept 10	Variety Club luncheon	PATHE (1:00)
Oct 13	Interview at London Palladium	ITN (0:49)
	Leaving London Palladium	ITN (0:36)
Oct 16	Interview at Playhouse Theatre	ITN (0:57)
Oct 23	London Airport departure for Sweden	ITN (0:13)
Oct 31	London Airport return from Sweden	AP (1:04), ITN (0:45)
Nov 4	Royal Variety Performance	AP, ITN (1:16), REU (2:06)
Nov 9	Fans queue for tickets at Lewisham Odeon	REU (2:32)
Nov 15	Fans queue for tickets at Southend Odeon	AP (0:46)
Nov 16	Concert in Bournemouth	NBC
Nov 20	Concert at Manchester ABC	PATHE (C/6:21)
Nov 26	Interview at Cambridge Regal	REU (4:10)
Dec 7	Filming *It's the Beatles*	REU (3:24)
Dec 9	Beatles in police van outside Southend Odeon	ITN (0:29)
Dec 20	"Christmas Show" rehearsals	ITN (0:48)

1964:

Jan 14	John, Paul, and George leave for Paris	BBC (0:26), ITN (0:16)
	John, Paul, and George arrive in Paris	ITN (0:28)
Jan 15	John, Paul, and George stroll down Champs-Élysées	BBC (0:24), REU (0:52)
Jan 16	Concert at Paris Olympia	ITN (1:11), REU (1:22)
Feb 5	London Airport return from Paris	AP (0:49), ITN (2:40), REU (0:54)
Feb 7	London Airport departure for United States	ITN (0:51), PATHE (1:19), REU (0:49)
	Fans at Kennedy Airport	AP (1:19)
	Beatles arrive at Kennedy Airport	AP (1:53), NBC, PATHE (1:40)
	Fans outside Plaza Hotel	AP (1:16)
Feb 8	John, Paul, and Ringo in Central Park	NBC (1:17)
Feb 9	*Ed Sullivan Show* marquee	AP (0:56)
Feb 10	Beatles press conferences at Plaza	AP (1:55), BBC (0:22)
Feb 11	Union Station arrival in Washington, D.C.	AP (2:40), PATHE (2:05), REU (0:51)
	Concert at D.C. Coliseum; British Embassy ball	REU (2:48)
Feb 12	Fans at Penn Station; Beatles arrive at the Plaza	AP (1:55)
	Beatles arrive at the Plaza	REU (1:37)
	Fans outside Carnegie Hall	AP (1:20)
	Beatles arrive at Carnegie Hall	AP (3:36)
Feb 16	Interview with Ringo's parents	ITN (0:56)
Feb 22	London Airport return from United States	AP (0:49), BBC (0:35), ITN (7:07), PATHE (5:41), REU (2:23)
	London Airport interview	REU (1:49)
Feb 23	Arrival at Teddington Studio	ITN (1:18)
Feb 25	George's twenty-first birthday	ITN (0:54)
Mar 2	Filming *A Hard Day's Night* on train	BBC (0:43), ITN (0:27), REU (1:25)
Mar 19	Beatles receive Variety Club awards	AP (1:29), BBC (0:18), ITN (1:19), PATHE (4:16), REU (0:51)
Mar 20	Arrival, rehearsal for *Ready, Steady, Go!*	ITN (1:13)

Mar 23	Beatles receive Carl-Alan awards	PATHE
Apr 20	George and Ringo's flat burgled	ITN (0:15)
Apr 22	Beatles at Australia House	REU (2:21)
Apr 23	John at Foyle's luncheon	BBC (0:48), ITN (0:46)
Apr 26	*NME* Poll Winners' Concert	PATHE
Jun 3	Jimmy Nicol rehearses with Beatles	ITN (0:34)
Jun 4	London Airport departure for Denmark	BBC (0:18)
	Departure for and arrival in Copenhagen	ITN (1:05)
	Beatles arrive in Copenhagen	REU (1:19)
	Concert at Copenhagen KB Hallen	ITN (1:00)
Jun 5	Beatles arrive in Amsterdam	AP (1:02), BBC, REU (1:11)
Jun 6	Amsterdam canal voyage	AP (1:15), REU (0:55)
	Canal voyage, concert in Blokker	PATHE (4:06), REU (5:20)
Jun 7	Beatles change planes at London Airport	ITN (0:52), PATHE, REU (1:21)
	Beatles change planes in Beirut	REU (2:40)
Jun 8	Beatles arrive in Hong Kong	REU (1:23)
Jun 11	Beatles arrive in Sydney	AP (1:13), PATHE, REU (1:37)
	Ringo leaves hospital in London	BBC (0:21)
Jun 12	Ringo leaves London for Australia	BBC (1:01), ITN (0:56), REU (0:59)
	Beatles arrive in Adelaide	REU (1:48)
Jun 13	Ringo changes planes in San Francisco	AP (5:20)
Jun 14	Ringo arrives in Sydney	PATHE
	Beatles arrive in Melbourne	BBC (2:43), REU (2:48 + 2:01)
Jun 16	Beatles at Melbourne Town Hall balcony	REU (1:12)
Jun 18	Beatles arrive in Sydney	PATHE
	Concert at Sydney Stadium	PATHE
Jun 21	Beatles arrive in New Zealand	PATHE, REU (1:08)
Jun 29	Beatles arrive in Brisbane	PATHE
Jul 2	London Airport return from Australia	AP (1:00), BBC (1:57)
Jul 6	*A Hard Day's Night* premiere	AP (1:03), ITN (0:29), REU (1:52)
Jul 7	Ringo's birthday at Lime Grove Studio	BBC (0:13)
Jul 10	Liverpool homecoming	AP (0:52), BBC (1:07), ITN (1:13), REU (1:07)
Jul 12	Beatles at Brighton Hippodrome	ITN (0:36)
Jul 19	Rehearsing *Blackpool Night Out*	ITN (0:42)
Jul 28	Beatles arrive in Stockholm	AP (0:44)
Jul 30	London Airport return from Sweden	BBC (0:16)
Aug 18	London Airport departure for United States	ITN (0:40)
	Los Angeles press conference	NBC
	Beatles arrive in San Francisco	AP (1:06), NBC (1:52)
Aug 19	Concert at San Francisco Cow Palace	REU (1:28)
Aug 20	Beatles arrive in Las Vegas	AP
	Concert at Las Vegas Convention Center	REU (1:33)
Aug 21	Beatles arrive in Seattle	AP (1:13)
Aug 23	Concert at Hollywood Bowl	AP (2:49), BBC (0:35)
Aug 28	New York City press conference	BBC (0:45), REU (20:08)
Sept 3	Concert at Indiana State Fair	AP (5:20)
Sept 4	Beatles arrive in Milwaukee	AP (1:07)
Sept 5	Chicago arrival, press conference	NBC
Sept 15	Brian Epstein interview in Cleveland	NBC
Sept 21	Leaving Kennedy Airport for London	AP (2:12)
	London Airport return from United States	AP (0:48), ITN (1:06), REU (1:16)
Oct 1	Beatle bedsheets sold in Chicago	AP (1:21)
Dec 1	Ringo arrives at hospital for tonsillectomy	BBC (0:14), ITN (1:18), REU (0:49)
Dec 10	Ringo leaves hospital	BBC (0:22), ITN (0:48), PATHE (1:26), REU (0:39)

1965:

Jan 28	John skis in St. Moritz	ITN (0:32)
Feb 11	Ringo marries Maureen Cox	BBC (0:46)
Feb 12	Ringo and Maureen honeymoon press conference	AP (1:18), BBC (2:27), ITN (2:42), REU (1:22)
Feb 22	London Airport departure for Bahamas	ITN (0:38), REU (0:49)
	Beatles arrive in Nassau	AP
Mar 11	London Airport return from Bahamas	AP (0:52), BBC (0:26), ITN (1:23), REU (1:36)
Mar 13	London Airport departure for Austria	ITN
	Beatles arrive in Salzburg	AP (0:41)
Apr 6	Receiving award from Radio Caroline	PATHE (0:47)
Apr 12	Filming *Help!* at Twickenham	ITN (0:15)
May 3	Filming *Help!* at Salisbury Plain	AP (1:31), BBC (0:26), ITN (0:30), REU (1:05)
Jun 11	Paul and Jane return from Portugal	REU (1:02)

Jun 12	MBE interviews at Twickenham	AP (0:46), BBC (1:10), ITN (2:02), REU (2:49)
Jul 2	Press conference, concert in Madrid	REU (1:42)
Jul 4	London Airport return from Spain	BBC (0:34), ITN (0:50)
Jul 13	Paul accepts Ivor Novello Award	ITN (0:14)
Jul 29	*Help!* premiere	AP (5:20), BBC (1:10), ITN (1:02), REU (2:43)
Aug 13	London Airport departure for United States	BBC (0:30)
	Beatles arrive in New York City	AP (1:02), REU (1:30)
	New York City press conference	AP (1:30)
Aug 15	Concert at Shea Stadium	BBC (1:20)
Aug 17	Beatles arrive in Toronto	REU (1:26)
Aug 18	Atlanta press conference	REU
Aug 20	Arrival, press conference in Chicago	NBC
	Concert at Comiskey Park, Chicago	AP (0:56)
Aug 29	Arrival at Hollywood Bowl	REU (0:48)
Sept 2	London Airport return from United States	PATHE (1:16), REU (1:06)
Sept 14	Ringo press conference about Zak	AP (1:32), BBC (1:30), ITN (0:35), PATHE
Sept 22	Maureen & Zak leave hospital	PATHE (0:57)
Oct 26	Beatles receive MBEs at Buckingham Palace	AP (1:18), BBC (1:20), PATHE (1:13), REU (2:03)
	MBE press conference at Saville Theatre	BBC (1:42), REU (0:55)
	Palace and press conference footage	ITN (1:35)

GLOSSARY

Acetate: a disc (metal coated with vinyl) pressed for demonstration purposes in a very limited number of copies

Backing track: the first layer of a recording to be taped (usually just instruments, perhaps with a guide vocal)

Beeb: short for the BBC (British Broadcasting Corporation)

Breakdown: a performance of a song that doesn't make it to the end for whatever reason

CD-R: a (recordable) compact disc

Demo: a rough recording used to demonstrate a song to another artist or to an arranger or a producer

Double-tracking: recording the same vocal or instrumental performance on two separate tracks of the tape to give a fuller, but not identical, sound

Duophonic: Capitol Records' method of giving a mono recording "fake" stereo sound (see Rechanneling)

EP: a 7-inch 45 RPM extended-play record, usually with two songs per side

EQ: equalization; manipulation of sonic frequencies to achieve a certain sound (heavy bass, bright treble, warm midrange)

Fabs: another collective moniker for the Beatles (short for Fab Four)

LP: a 12-inch 33 RPM long-playing record album

Macca: nickname for Paul McCartney

Mix: to combine various tracks of a tape (usually 2, 4, or 8 in the Beatles' case) down to a two-channel (for stereo) or one-channel (for mono) recording

Monitor mix: a rough external recording for reference purposes, made by pointing a microphone at the studio speakers during playback

OOPS: acronym for Out of Phase Stereo; a method of isolating the material in a stereo recording that is not common to both channels (anything not in the middle)

Outfake: a recording that is not what it seems, usually passing off a song as something new by manipulating the sound

Outtake: a performance of a song (or scene in a film) not used in creating the final product

Overdub: to add new sound to an existing tape

RM, RS: remix from multitrack tape to mono or stereo

Rechanneling: a method of producing pseudostereo from a mono source by reducing bass frequencies in one channel and treble in the other

Reduction: a method of combining many tracks on one tape to a lesser number of tracks on a second tape, freeing space for further overdubs

Rhythm track: see Backing track

Rough mix: a mix for reference purposes, or to provide the artist with a quick unpolished copy of their work

Track: A segment (usually a complete song) of an album. Also, a division of magnetic recording tape into discrete, simultaneously recordable segments (twin-track, four-track, eight-track, and so on)

SELECTED BIBLIOGRAPHY

THE HOLY TRINITY:

The Beatles Anthology by the Beatles
The Beatles: Recording Sessions by Mark Lewisohn
The Complete Beatles Chronicle by Mark Lewisohn

GENERAL INFORMATION/BIOGRAPHIES:

The Beatles by Hunter Davies
The Beatles at the BBC by Kevin Howlett
The Beatles Forever by Nicholas Schaffner
Beatles Gear by Andy Babiuk
How They Became the Beatles by Gareth L. Pawlowski
John Lennon in My Life by Pete Shotton and Nicholas Schaffner
Lennon by Ray Coleman
The Man Who Made the Beatles: An Intimate Biography of Brian Epstein by Ray Coleman
McCartney by Chris Salewicz
Paul McCartney: Many Years from Now by Barry Miles
Shout!: The True Story of the Beatles by Philip Norman
Yesterday: My Life with the Beatles by Alistair Taylor

DISCOGRAPHICAL DETAILS:

All Together Now by Harry Castleman and Walter J. Podrazik
The Beatles: An Illustrated Record by Roy Carr and Tony Tyler
The Beatles—From Cavern to Star-Club by Hans Olof Gottfridsson
The Beatles Price Guide for American Records by Perry Cox and Joe Lindsay
The Beatles' Story on Capitol Records by Bruce Spizer
The Beatles: The Ultimate Recording Guide by Allen J. Wiener
Beatles Undercover by Kristofer Engelhardt
Do You Want to Know a Secret? by L.R.E. King
Every Little Thing by William McCoy and Mitchell McGeary
Fixing a Hole by L.R.E. King
The 910's Guide to the Beatles' Outtakes by Doug Sulpy
Not for Sale by Belmo

MUSICAL ANALYSIS:

A Day in the Life: The Music and Artistry of the Beatles by Mark Hertsgaard
The Art & Music of John Lennon by John Robertson
The Beatles as Musicians: The Quarry Men Through Rubber Soul by Walter Everett
Tell Me Why: A Beatles Commentary by Tim Riley

FILMS/PHOTOGRAPHS:

Beatles at the Movies by Roy Carr
The Beatles Files by Andy Davis
The Beatles in Richard Lester's A Hard Day's Night, edited by J. Philip Di Franco
Richard Lester and the Beatles by Andrew Yule
With the Beatles: The Historic Photographs of Dezo Hoffmann, edited by Pearce Marchbank

QUOTES:

A Hard Day's Write by Steve Turner
Beatles in Their Own Words, edited by Barry Miles
Beatlesongs by William J. Dowlding
John Lennon in His Own Words, edited by Barry Miles
Paul McCartney in His Own Words by Paul Gambaccini

TIMELINES:

The Beatles: A Day in the Life by Tom Schultheiss
The Beatles: A Diary by Barry Miles
The Beatles: An Illustrated Diary by Har V. Fulpen
The Beatles London by Piet Schreuders, Mark Lewisohn, and Adam Smith
The Beatles: 25 Years in the Life by Mark Lewisohn

TOURS:

The Beatles Down Under by Glenn A. Baker
The Beatles Live! by Mark Lewisohn
Beatles '64: A Hard Day's Night in America by A.J.S. Rayl, photographs by Curt Gunther
Love Me Do: The Beatles' Progress by Michael Braun

PERIODICALS:

Beatlefan
Beatles Book Monthly
Beatlology
Belmo's Beatleg News
Goldmine
Good Day Sunshine
Illegal Beatles
Mersey Beat
Mojo
Musician
New Musical Express
910
Rolling Stone
Strawberry Fields Forever

DISCOGRAPHY

1 (CD: Apple/Capitol CDP 7243 5 9325 2 8)
1965 Talk Album—Ed Rudy with New U.S. Tour (LP: Radio Pulsebeat News L-1001/1002)
1989 Beatleg News Christmas Record (bootleg EP: WS01-A/B)
300,000 Beatle Fans Can't Be Wrong (bootleg CD: Quarter Apple PCS 7290/7291)
300,000 Beatle Fans Can't Be Wrong (bootleg LP: B1+B2; CD: Living Legend LLRCD 031)

Abbey Road Tape, Volume 1 (CD-R: Unicorn UC-082)
Abbey Road Video Show (bootleg CD: Strawberry STR 020)
ABC Manchester (bootleg LP: Wizardo WRMB 361)
Acetates (bootleg CD: Yellow Dog YD 009)
Ain't She Sweet (EP: Polydor 21965)
Airtime (bootleg LP: L-7198-Subway MX-4729)
Alf Together Now (bootleg CD: Spank SP-148)
All Our Loving (CD: One Way OW 10840)
All the Best from Australia (bootleg CD: Boxtop BT 9607)
"American Bandstand" Salutes the Beatles (CD-R)
The A.M. Tape (CD-R: No Label Records NLR 0001)
Another Sessions . . . Plus (bootleg CD: Vigotone VT-180)
Anthology 1 (CD: Apple CDP 7243 8 34445 2 6)
Anthology 2 (CD: Apple CDP 7243 8 34448 2 3)
Anthology Plus (bootleg CD: Invasion Unlimited 9750-2)
Anthropology (CD-R: Silent Sea SS005)
A Paris (bootleg LP: Neon 2CO06-1956)
April to August 1963 (CD-R: Lazy Tortoise)
Arrivano I «Capelloni» (bootleg LP: Clean Sound CS 1008)
Arrive Without Aging (bootleg CD: Vigotone VT-6869)
Arrive Without Travelling (bootleg LP: Vigotone VIGO 69)
Artifacts (bootleg CD: Big Music BIG BX 006)
As It Happened, Baby! (CD-R: RAR/Darthdisc)
*Atlanta*Munich*Seattle* (bootleg CD: Spank SP 145)
Attack of the Filler Beebs!, Episode 1 (CD-R: Silent Sea Productions SS001)
Attack of the Filler Beebs!, Episode 2 (CD-R: Silent Sea Productions SS002)
Australian Tour 1964 (bootleg CD: Yellow Dog YD 070/071)

"Baby It's You" (CD single: Apple R 6406)
Back-Track (bootleg CD: BT 6267 2)
Baggy Sweegin' U.S.A.! (CD-R: JFC-001)
The Beatles (CD-EP: Capitol C2-15867)
The Beatles & Murray the K: As It Happened (EP: BRS-½)
Beatles VI (LP: Capitol T-2358)
Beatles '65 (LP: Capitol T-2228)
The Beatles 1962–1966 (LP: Apple PCSP 717)
The Beatles 1962–1966 (CD: Apple CDP 7 97036 2 2)
The Beatles American Tour with Ed Rudy (LP: Radio Pulsebeat News Documentary No. 2)
The Beatles and the Great Concert at Shea! (bootleg CD: His Master's Choice HMC 001)
The Beatles at the BBC—Parts 1 & 2 (CD-R: Unicorn UC-077/8)
The Beatles at the Beeb (bootleg CD: Yellow Dog BTR-001-012)
The Beatles at the Beeb—TV (bootleg CD: Panda BBCBCD 1454)
The Beatles at the Beeb, Volumes 1–13 (bootleg LP: Beeb Transcription BB 2172-2184/S)
The Beatles at the Beeb w/Pete Best (bootleg LP: Drexel BEEB 6263)
The Beatles at the Hollywood Bowl (LP: Capitol SMAS-11638)
Beatles Bop—Hamburg Days (CD: Bear Family BCD 16583 BH)
The Beatles Broadcast Collection, Trailer 1 (bootleg CD: Yellow Dog YD 074/075)
The Beatles Broadcast Collection, Trailer 2 (bootleg CD: Yellow Dog YD 076/077)
The Beatles Complete—January 1 to September 5, 1962 (CD-R: Silent Sea)
The Beatles Complete—July 6, 1957, to April–May 1960 (part 1) (CD-R: Silent Sea)
The Beatles Complete—September 11 to December 21, 1962 (CD-R: Silent Sea)
The Beatles Conquer America (bootleg LP: NEMS SHU 6465)
Beatles for Sale (LP: Parlophone PCS 3062)
Beatles for Sale (CD: Parlophone CDP 7 46438 2)
The Beatles Greatest (LP: Odeon SMO 83 991)
Beatles in Italy 1965 (bootleg CD: Bulldog BGCD 006)
The Beatles in Montreal (bootleg CD: Secret Garden Records 45-R 0420)
The Beatles Introduce New Songs (EP: Capitol PRO-2720/1)
The Beatles' Million Sellers (CD-EP: Capitol C2-15862)
Beatles Over Atlanta & Shea Stadium (CD-R)
A Beatles Press Conference (Cassette: Beatles Interview)
The Beatles' Second Album (LP: Capitol T-2080 and ST-2080)
The Beatles' Second Open-End Interview (7-inch 33⅓ RPM single: Capitol Compact 33 PRO 2598/2599)
The Beatles' Story (LP: Capitol STBO 2222)
The Beatles Talk Downunder (LP: Raven RVLP 1002)
The Beatles Talk Downunder (And All Over), Volume 2 (LP: Raven RVLP 1013)
The Beatles Talk with Jerry G. (LP: Backstage BSR-1165)
The Beatles Talk with Jerry G., Volume 2 (LP: Backstage BSR-1175)
Beatles Tapes: The Beatles in the Northwest (CD: Jerden JRCD 7006)
Beatles Tapes, Volume 2: Early Beatlemania 1963–1964 (CD: Jerden JRCD 7028)
Beatles Tapes, Volume 3: The 1964 World Tour (CD: Jerden JRCD 7041)
Beatles Tapes, Volume 4: Hong Kong '64 (CD: Jerden JRCD 7042)
Beatles Tapes, Volume 5: The 1965 Help! Tour (CD: Jerden JRCD 7065)
The Beatles vs. Don Ho (bootleg LP: Melvin MM08)
Beatle Talk (LP: Great Northwest Music Co. GNW-4007)
Beautiful Dreamer (bootleg LP: NEM 61842)
The Best of Billy J Kramer & the Dakotas (CD: Imperial CDP-7-96055-2)

Blackpool Night Out '64—Upgraded (CD-R: Unicorn UC-088)
The Braun-Kirchherr Tapes (CD-R: BATZ 0197-0198)
Broadcasts (bootleg LP: Circuit LK 4450)
By Royal Command (bootleg EP: Deccagone 1108)

Can You Hear Me? (CD-R: JFC-006)
The Carroll James Interview (EP: Carroll James CJEP 3301)
The Cavern Tapes Circa 1962 (bootleg CD: CT62-2)
Cilla 1963–1973, the Abbey Road Decade (CD: Zonophone 7243 8 57053 2 8)
City of Light (CD-R: Darthdisc DD 007/8)
A Collection of Beatles Oldies (LP: Parlophone PMC 7016)
The Complete BBC Sessions (bootleg CD: Great Dane GDR-9326/9)
The Complete BBC Sessions—Upgrade (CD-R: Purple Chick PC-31)
The Complete BBC Sessions—Upgraded for 2004 (CD-R: Purple Chick PC-71-80)
The Complete Christmas Collection (bootleg CD: Yellow Dog YD 031)
Complete Controlroom Monitor Mixes, Volume 1 (bootleg CD: Yellow Dog YD 083/84)
Complete Controlroom Monitor Mixes, Volume 2 (bootleg CD: Yellow Dog YD 085/86)
The Complete Hollywood Bowl Concerts (bootleg CD: Midnight Beat MBCD 108/109)

Danmark & Nederland June 1964 (bootleg CD: Why Not WN 3002)
A Day in the Life (bootleg CD: Yellow Dog YD 2001)
The Day the Beatles Came to Town (CD-R)
"Day Tripper" (CD single: Parlophone CD-R 5389)
De Bietels Tussen De Bollen (LP: Beatles Unlimited, BU 1-1984)
The Decca Tapes (bootleg LP: Circuit LK 4438)
December 1963 (bootleg LP: ODD FOUR)
Deflating the Mythology (CD-R)
Die Beatles In Deutschland 1966! (bootleg CD: Invasion Unlimited IU 9647-1)
Dig It! (bootleg LP: NEMS FAB-1234)
Directly from Santa Claus (bootleg LP: SC 007)
District of Columbia (bootleg LP: CBM 1100)
Doll's House (bootleg LP: Maidenhead MHR JET 909-1)

East Coast Invasion (CD: One Way OW 10841)
Ed's Really Big Beatles Blasts (bootleg LP: Melvin MM05)
Et Maintenant Une Chanson (New Version) (CD-R: NLR9806)

Fab Four CD & Book Set (CD: Mastertone 8016)
The Fab Four On Tour (CD: Dynamic Images)
File Under: Beatles (bootleg LP: Gnat GN70075-1)
Free as a Bird (bootleg CD: FAB 1)
"Free as a Bird" (CD single: Apple C2 7243 8 58497 2 5)
From Britain . . . with Beat! (CD: One Way OW 10842)
From Me to You (bootleg CD: Roaring Mouse DPRO-79971)
From Us to You—A Parlophone Rehearsal Session (bootleg LP: LMW-281F)
Fuck! (bootleg LP: Sapcor 33)

The Garage Tapes (bootleg CD: Kremo Music Productions SELCD18)
The Golden Beatles (CD: Overseas 30CP-56)
The Great American Tour 1965 Live Beatlemania Concert (LP: Lloyd's ER MC LL-1007/8)
Great to Have You with Us (bootleg LP: MHR-JET-909-3)

Hamburg Twist (EP: PRE 240003)
Happy Birthday (bootleg LP: Wizardo 345)
A Hard Day's Night (LP: Parlophone PCS 3058)
A Hard Day's Night (LP: United Artists UAL 6366)
A Hard Day's Night (CD: Parlophone CDP 7 46437 2)
Have You Heard the Word (bootleg LP: CBM 3620)
Hear the Beatles Tell All (LP: Vee Jay VJ PRO-202)
Help! (LP: Parlophone PMC 1255 + PCS 3071)
Help! (CD: Parlophone CDP 7 46439 2)
"Help!" (CD single: Parlophone CDR 5305)
Help! Original Mix (bootleg CD: Masterfraction MFCD 012/013)
Help! Sessions (bootleg CD: B4 Records FF001)
Here We Go (bootleg CD: Great Dane GDRCD 9326/10)
Here, There, and Everywhere (CD: One Way OW 10843)
Hey Jude (LP: Apple SW 385)
Historic Interviews, Volume 2 (cassette)
The History of Syracuse Music, Volumes 12/13 (LP: Blue Wave 105)
Hodge Podge (bootleg CD: Black Dog BD 001)
Hold Me Tight (bootleg CD: Condor 1990)
Hollywood Bowl Complete (bootleg CD: Yellow Dog YD 034)

"I Feel Fine" (single: Capitol 5327)
"I Feel Fine" (CD single: Parlophone CDR 5200)
I'm a Loser (bootleg CD: Nanao Records NR-001)
In Case You Don't Know . . . (bootleg CD: Spank SP-110)
Inside Interviews: Beatlemania (CD: Laserlight 12 678)
Inside Interviews: Talk Downunder: Australia Beatlemania (CD: Laserlight 12 679)
Inside Interviews: Talk Downunder: Sydney to Seattle (CD: Laserlight 12 680)
It's All in the Mind Y'Know (bootleg CD: Beat CD 017)
"I Want to Hold Your Hand" (CD single: Parlophone CDR 5084)

Jellybeans Hailing in Dreamlike Noise (bootleg CD: Whoopy Cat WKP-0036)
Jimmy Nicol and the Beatles (bootleg CD: Desperado Records DP1)
John, Paul, George and Jimmy (bootleg LP: Wizardo WRMB 501)
John, Paul, George & Ringo, Through the Years (bootleg CD: Fab Four Rarities FFR9112)

A Knight's Hard Day (bootleg LP: Sapcor 31)

Lennon & McCartney Songbook (CD: Connoisseur Collection VSOP CD 150)
Les Beatles (10-inch LP: Polydor 4900)
Let's Do the Twist, Hully Gully, Slop, Surf, Locomotion, Monkey (LP: Polydor SLPHM 237622)
Like Dreamers Do (LP: Backstage BSR-1111)
Live at the BBC (CD: Apple PCSP 726)

Live! at the Star-Club in Hamburg, Germany, 1962 (CD: Lingasong LING 95)
Live Concert at Whiskey Flats (bootleg LP: Whiskey Records 510)
Live from the Sam Houston Colosseum (bootleg LP: Audifon BVP006)
Live in Europe & US TV Casts (bootleg LP: CBM 3571)
Live in Italy (bootleg EP: ITA-128)
Live in Melbourne 1964 and Paris 1965 (bootleg CD: Pyramid RFT CD 001)
Live in Melbourne, Australia 7/16/64 (bootleg LP: Instant Analysis MB 1034)
Live in Paris 1964 and in San Francisco 1966 (bootleg CD: Pyramid RFT CD 002)
Live in Paris 1965 (bootleg CD: Swingin' Pig TSP-CD-008)
Live in the United Kingdom 62–65 (bootleg CD: Bulldog BGCD 11112)
Live: Make as Much Noise as You Like! (CD-R: FLO 006)
Live Paris Olympia, January 1964 (bootleg LP: CBM 3688)
Liverpool May 1960 (bootleg LP: Indra M5-6001)
Liverpool Sound Collage (CD: Hydra LSC01)
London Palladium (bootleg LP: CBM 3687)
Long Tall Sally (CD-EP: Capitol C2-15857)
Lost and Found (bootleg CD: Quarter Apple PCS 7287)
Love (CD: Capitol 0946 3 79810 2 3)
LS Bumblebee (bootleg LP: CBM 3626)
The Lost Paris Tapes (bootleg CD: Dr. Pataphysical DP 027)

Mach Shau! (bootleg LP: Savage SC 12620/L-20819)
March 5, 1963, plus the Decca Tape (bootleg CD: Vigotone VT-123)
Mary Jane (bootleg LP: TMOQ MJ 543)
Maybe You Can Drive My Car (bootleg CD: YD-Orange 019)
Meet the Beeb (bootleg LP: Beeb Transcription BB 2190/9)
Message to Australia (bootleg CD: Yellow Dog YD 2004)
Mister Twist (EP: Polydor 21914)
More Masters (bootleg CD: Roaring Mouse DPRO-7997 4/5/6)
Moviemania! (CD: One Way OW 10844)
Music City/KFWBeatles (single: Capitol Custom RB-2637/2638)
My Bonnie (LP: Polydor SLPHM 237112)
Mythology, Volume 1 (bootleg CD: Strawberry 008-010)
Mythology, Volume 2 (bootleg CD: Strawberry 011-014)

New York Radio 1964–1969 (CD-R)
The NME *Pollwinners' Concert 1965* (bootleg CD: Vigotone VT-166/7)
Northwest Nights (CD-R: Darthdisc DD 001/2)
Not a Second Time (CD: One Way OW 10845)
Not for Sale (bootleg LP: NEMS MOP 910)
Not for Sale (bootleg CD: Condor 1986)
Not Guilty (bootleg LP: NEMS EHMV MCS 6469)
Nothing but Aging (bootleg LP: Vigotone VT-LP-68)
Nowhere Man (CD-EP: Capitol C2-15864)

Official IBBB Interview (7-inch 33⅓ RPM single: IBBB-45629)
Open-End Interview: A Hard Day's Night (7-inch picture disc: Cicadelic/BIOdisc 001)
Open-End Interview with the Beatles (7-inch 33⅓ RPM single: Capitol Compact 33 PRO 2548/2549)
The Original Decca Tapes & Cavern Club Rehearsals 1962 (bootleg CD: Yellow Dog YD 011)
Outtakes 1 (bootleg LP: TMOQ 71048)
Outtakes 2 (bootleg LP: TMOQ 71049)

Paris Sports Palais (bootleg LP: CBM LPPA 77)
Past Masters, Volume 1 (CD: Parlophone CDP 7 90043 2)
Past Masters, Volume 2 (CD: Parlophone CDP 7 90044 2)
Peace of Mind (bootleg LP: CBM 3670)
The Playing Beatles 2 (bootleg CD: Great Dane GDRCD 9304/A-B)
Please Please Me (LP: Parlophone PCS 3042)
Please Please Me (CD: Parlophone CDP 7 46435 2)
Pollwinners go to Blackpool (bootleg CD: M-Beat Music MBCD 001)
Puttin' On the Style (bootleg CD: Black Dog BD 009)

The Quarrymen at Home (bootleg LP: Blackshop BS 007)

Radio Sessions 1962–65 (bootleg CD: Masterfraction MFCD 006/007)
Rare Beatles (bootleg LP: CBM 5030)
Rare Photos & Interview CD, Volume 1 (CD: MasterTone Multimedia Ltd. JG 001-2)
Rare Photos & Interview CD, Volume 2 (CD: MasterTone Multimedia Ltd. JG 002-2)
Rare Photos & Interview CD, Volume 3 (CD: MasterTone Multimedia Ltd. JG 003-2)
Rarities (LP: Capitol SHAL-12060)
"Real Love" (CD single: Apple C2 7243 8 58544 2 2)
Recovered Tracks (bootleg LP: Bornoby Records FF-9)
Re-introducing the Beatles (bootleg LP: Sapcor 28)
"Remember, We Don't Like Them, We Love Them" (single: IBBB-ZTSC-94736)
Revolution (bootleg CD: Vigotone VT-116)
Road Runner (bootleg CD: RA-001)
Rock 'N' Roll Music (LP: Capitol SKBO 11537)
Rory Storm & the Hurricanes: The Complete Works (CD: Street RS01)
Rough Notes (bootleg LP: POD L2408)
'Round the World (CD: One Way OW 10846)
Rubber Soul (LP: Capitol T-2442 + ST-2442)
Rubber Soul (LP: Parlophone PMC 1267 + PCS 3075)
Rubber Soul (CD: Parlophone CDP 7 46440 2)
Ruling Queen Elizabeth II . . . the Beatles Live in the United Kingdom 1962–1965 (bootleg CD: Bulldog BGCP 90512)

Seattle Press Conference (7-inch single: Topaz T-1353)
Sessions (bootleg CD: Spank SP-103)
The Seven Years of Christmas (bootleg CD: Yellow Dog YD 082)
Shea!/Candlestick Park (bootleg CD: Spank SP-109)
Soldier of Love (bootleg LP: Contra Band TB-1022)
Something New (LP: Capitol T-2108 + ST-2108)
Stars of '63 (bootleg CD: Swingin' Pig TSP-CD-005)
State Fair to Hollywood (bootleg CD: Great Dane GDRCD 9315)
The Stereo Walk (bootleg LP: B4)
Stockholm (bootleg LP: CBM ST 1040-4179)
Strong Before Our Birth (CD-R: Purple Chick PC-68)
Studio Collection (CD-R: Unicorn UC-076)
Studio Sessions (CD-R: Tobe Milo TMCD-4Q30)

Sweden 1963 (bootleg LP: CBM 3795)
Swedish Fan Club Tape (CD-R: Unicorn UC-085)

Telecasts One (CD-R: Silent Sea SS 019)
Telecasts Two (CD-R: Silent Sea SS 020)
Telecasts Three (CD-R: Silent Sea SS 021)
Television Out-takes (bootleg EP: Tobe Milo 4Q 3/4)
That'll Be the Day: The Music That Inspired the Beatles (bootleg LP: King Horn B0-1958)
Things We Said Today (CD: One Way OW 10847)
"Ticket to Ride" (CD single: Parlophone CDR 5200)
Timeless II (CD: Overseas 30CP-76)
Timeless II½ (7-inch picture disc: Silhouette SM 1451)
Tour Years 63–66 (bootleg LP: Honeysuckle ENG 4001)
"A Trip to Miami" (single)
Turn Me On Dead Man: The John Barrett Tapes (bootleg CD: Vigotone VT-178/179)

The Ultimate Beatles' Christmas Collection (bootleg CD: Vigotone VT-172/173)
The Ultimate Collection, Volume 1: The Early Years, 1962 (bootleg CD: Yellow Dog YDB 101)
The Ultimate Collection, Volume 1: TV Appearances (bootleg CD: Yellow Dog YDB 102)
The Ultimate Collection, Volume 1: Miscellaneous Tracks (bootleg CD: Yellow Dog YDB 103)
The Ultimate Collection, Volume 2: Live, Live, Live (bootleg CD: Yellow Dog YDB 201)
The Ultimate Collection, Volume 2: Studio Sessions, February 11, 1963 (bootleg CD: Yellow Dog YDB 202)
The Ultimate Collection, Volume 2: Studio Sessions, March 5 and . . . (bootleg CD: Yellow Dog YDB 203)
The Ultimate Collection, Volume 3: The Radio Years at the Beeb (bootleg CD: Yellow Dog YDB 301)
The Ultimate Collection, Volume 3: Studio Sessions, 1964 (bootleg CD: Yellow Dog YDB 302)
The Ultimate Collection, Volume 3: Studio Sessions, 1965–66 (bootleg CD: Yellow Dog YDB 303)
The Ultimate Live Collection, Volume 1 (bootleg CD: Yellow Dog YD 038/39)
Ultimate Live Masters (bootleg CD: Secret Trax ST 200020)
The Ultimate Radio Bootleg, Volume 3 (LP: Mercury MK2-2-121)
Ultra Rare Trax, Volume 1 (bootleg CD: The Swingin' Pig TSP CD-001)
Ultra Rare Trax, Volume 2 (bootleg CD: The Swingin' Pig TSP CD-002)
Ultra Rare Trax, Volume 3 (bootleg CD: The Swingin' Pig TSP CD-025)
Ultra Rare Trax, Volume 3 & 4 (bootleg LP: The Swingin' Pig TR 2190 S)
United Artists Presents A Hard Day's Night (LP: United Artists SP-2359/60)
Unsurpassed Masters, Volume 1 (bootleg CD: Yellow Dog YD 001)
Unsurpassed Masters, Volume 2 (bootleg CD: Yellow Dog YD 002)
Unsurpassed Masters, Volume 6 (bootleg CD: Yellow Dog YD 012)
Unsurpassed Masters, Volume 7 (bootleg CD: Yellow Dog YD 013)

Vancouver 1964 (bootleg LP: Trademark Of Quality TMOQ 72012)
Video 1 (CD-R: RAR007)
Vinyl to the Core (CD-R)
Visit to Minneapolis (bootleg EP: Melvin MMEP001A)
The VJ Story (bootleg CD: Beat 014)

We'd Like to Carry On (CD-R: JFC-005)
West Coast Invasion (CD: One Way OW 10848)
Wildcat! (bootleg CD: Madman 13-14)
With the Beatles (LP: Parlophone PCS 3045)
With the Beatles (CD: Parlophone CDP 46436 2)
Wonderful Picture of You (bootleg LP: Circle SKI 5430)

Ya Ya (EP: Polydor EPH 21485)
Yeah Yeah Yeah—The Beatles in the U.S.A. (EP: WQ 1096)
Yellow Matter Custard (bootleg LP: CBM 204)
Yellow Submarine *Songtrack* (CD: Apple CDP 7243 5 21481 2 7)
Yesterday (CD-EP: Capitol C2-15863)
"Yesterday" . . . and Today (LP: Capitol T-2553 + ST-2553)
Youngblood (bootleg LP: Audifon BVP 005)

SONG, SHOW, AND FILM TITLE INDEX

ABOUT THE AUTHOR

John C. Winn was born in Berkeley, California, nine months after the final Beatles recording session. He was bitten by the Beatle bug at an early age and has been collecting, researching, and enjoying their recordings for most of his life. He has written six books about their career, as well as numerous magazine articles and columns. John currently lives in Vermont, surrounded by thousands of Beatles CDs, DVDs, books, tapes, and vinyl. His favorite album is *Revolver.*